Social

Inequality

LOUIS KRIESBERG

Syracuse University

PRENTICE-HALL, INC.

Englewood Cliffs, New Jersey 07632

Library of Congress Cataloging in Publication Data

KRIESBERG, LOUIS.
    Social inequality

    Incudes bibliographies and index.
       1. Equality.   2. Social classes.   Social
status.   4. Social values.   5. Power (Social
sciences).   I. Title.
HM136.K76   301.44   78-25785
ISBN 0-13-815860-6

Printed in the United States of America

10   9   8   7   6   5   4   3   2   1

*Editorial/production supervision and
   interior design by Barbara L. Christenberry
Cover design by Jerry Pfeifer
Manufacturing buyer: Nancy J. Myers*

PRENTICE-HALL INTERNATIONAL, INC., *London*
PRENTICE-HALL OF AUSTRALIA PTY. LIMITED, *Sydney*
PRENTICE-HALL OF CANADA, LTD., *Toronto*
PRENTICE-HALL OF INDIA PRIVATE LIMITED, *New Delhi*
PRENTICE-HALL OF JAPAN, INC., *Tokyo*
PRENTICE-HALL OF SOUTHEAST ASIA PTE. LTD., *Singapore*
WHITEHALL BOOKS LIMITED, *Wellington, New Zealand*

ACKNOWLEDGMENTS

For the data presented in the tables of this book, I am indebted to several sources. Some of the tables are derived from United States Government publications and are in the public domain; others were prepared by me from data collected by the National Opinion Research Center in one of its national General Social Surveys or from data gathered by Charles L. Taylor and Michael C. Hudson, as described in the *World Handbook of Political and Social Indicators* (Ann Arbor, Mich.: Inter-University Consortium for Political Research, 1971). I am grateful for the use of these data. In addition, I wish to acknowledge the sources for the following specific tables and figures.

Table 2.3: From Robert W. Hodge, Paul M. Siegel, and Peter H. Rossi, "Occupational Prestige in the United States," *American Journal of Sociology* 70, Nov. 1964, 286-302. Reprinted by permission of the University of Chicago Press.

Table 2.4: From Albert J. Reiss, Jr., *Occupations and Social Status,* Tables VII-3 and B-1. Copyright ©1972 by The Free Press, a Division of the Macmillan Company. Reprinted with permission of Macmillan Publishing Co., Inc.

Table 2.6: From James D. Smith and James N. Morgan, "Dynamics of Income Distribution," *American Economic Review,* May 1970, Table 1, p. 287. Used by permission of the American Economic Association.

Table 3.1: From Oscar Oranti, *Poverty Amid Affluence,* Table A, p. 158. Copyright © 1966 by The Twentieth Century Fund, Inc., New York.

Table 3.4: From Selma Goldsmith, "Changes in the Sizes of Distribution of Income," *American Economic Review,* May 1957, Table 4. Used by permission of the American Economic Association.

Table 3.5: From Edward C. Budd (Ed.), *Inequality and Poverty.* Table 1 in "An Introduction of the Current Issue of Public Policy" (New York: W. W. Norton & Company, Inc., 1967). Used by permission of W. W. Norton & Company, Inc.

Table 3.7: From Robert J. Lampman, *The Share of Top Wealth-Holders in National Wealth, 1922-1956* (Princeton, N.J.: Princeton University Press, 1962), Tables 93 and 94. Used by permission of the National Bureau of Economic Research.

Table 3.9: From W. Lloyd Warner and James C. Abegglen, *Occupational Mobility in American Business and Industry, 1938-1952.* (Minneapolis: University of Minnesota Press, 1955). Used by permission of the University of Minnesota Press.

Table 4.1: From I. B. Kravis, Z. Kenessey, A. Heston, and R. Summers, *A System of International Comparisons of Product and Purchasing Power,* Tables 1.1 and 1.3. Published 1975 for The World Bank by The Johns Hopkins University Press.

Tables 4.2 and 4.3: From United Nations Department of Economic and Social Affairs, *Statistical Yearbook, 1973,* Tables 137, 182, and 19. Copyright, United Nations 1973. Reproduced by permission.

Table 4.4: From *Production Yearbook, 1973,* Tables 136 and 137. Copyright Food and Agriculture Organization of the United Nations. Used by permission.

Table 4.5: From Felix Paukert, "Income Distribution at the Different Levels of Development," *International Labour Review* (Geneva), Vol. 108, Nos. 2-3, August-September 1973, Table 6, pp. 114-115. Copyright International Labour Organisation 1973. Reprinted by permission.

Table 4.6: From the *Year Book of Labour Statistics 1974,* Table 2, p. 46. Copyright © International Labour Organisation, Geneva, 1974. Reprinted by permission.

Table 4.7: From Marshall Singer, *Weak States in a World of Power,* Table 6.2. Copyright ©1972 by The Free Press, a Division of the Macmillan Company. Reprinted with permission of Macmillan Publishing Co., Inc.

Table 5.4 and Figure 5.1: From Peter M. Blau and Otis D. Duncan, *American Occupational Structure,* Table 2.4 and path diagram, p. 170. (New York: John Wiley, 1967). Used by permission of Peter M. Blau.

Footnote 3, Chapter 6, path model: From Z. Safar, "The Measurement of Mobility in the Czecho-Slovak Socialist Society," *Quality and Quantity: European Journal of Methodology* 5 (1971), 193. By permission of Societa Editrice and Elservier Scientific Publishing Co.

Contents

v

Preface

The study of social inequality is particularly exciting now. Spirited controversies about policy and theoretical issues abound. New information is appearing as a result of new research methods and the study of previously neglected topics. I wrote this book to help make the current work accessible by presenting it in an illuminating context. New empirical studies and fundamental theoretical issues are related to each other in a comprehensive and systematic manner that has relevance for social policy.

This book is comparative and global in orientation. Inequality in economically developing and developed countries and in societies with market and with centrally planned economies are compared. I also consider the world as a stratified system. Nations vary in their dependence and subordination to each other, and that significantly affects inequality within countries. Stratification within the United States, nevertheless, is the focus of most attention, and changes in specific aspects of inequality are closely examined.

This book provides considerable empirically based information about variations in inequality. Such information is an important contribution of sociological research. I have presented material from older studies as well as the most recent for two reasons: first, to indicate how methods and ideas change with consequent changes in the facts of stratification, and second, to aid in comprehending current work, since researchers often are reacting to previous research. I have also prepared new analyses in order to better illustrate and test certain ideas.

Inequality in class, status, and power are fully described. Variations over time in the United States and among the countries of the world are systematically examined. Then we consider how relative class, status, or power standing are related to each other.

I take theory seriously in this book. Several theoretical orientations accounting for inequality in class, status, and power are separately presented and their similarities and differences examined. They are then applied to the data presented. This makes it possible to assess the adequacy of different theoretical orientations and to develop a comprehensive explanation of several aspects of inequality.

That is why this book is organized differently than other books about inequality. The examination of theories follows, rather than precedes, a description of variations in inequality. Of course, descriptive facts cannot be understood aside from theory; but theory cannot be understood without knowledge about the phenomena the theorists are trying to explain. Concepts, data, and theory are intertwined. The advantage of paying attention to variations in inequality before trying to explain them is that it is easier to assess alternative theoretical orientations. In this way, the theories are not presented and then forgotten. If the reader wishes to keep in mind alternative approaches as the evidence about inequality is reviewed, it is possible to read Chapter 11 before Chapter 3.

The attention to policy implications stems from my concern about the extent of social inequality and the controversies regarding efforts to modify it. As I discuss in the concluding chapter, there are many contradictory forces affecting the future degree of social inequality. Antagonisms among people are likely to increase, especially if the rate of economic expansion slows in the face of environmental constraints. The emerging tensions are indicated by the rising demands from third world countries for a larger share of the world's resources, and within developed countries by cries to reduce taxes, concerns about the costs of welfare programs, and fears of destroying work incentives by programs aimed at reducing poverty and inequality. We need to have good information about the extent of inequality, its consequences, and the forces which tend to increase and decrease it in order to choose policy alternatives wisely.

I have tried to present the evidence and the theories in an objective and balanced manner. But social inequality engages our moral concerns and it is advisable that I share my own preferences, since they undoubtedly affected what I chose to emphasize. This may also help the reader recognize her or his preferences, and thus read the book with increased awareness of its implications.

I am dismayed by the immense degree of class, status, and power inequalities in the world. I do not think these are just or reflect a sound moral judgment on the relative worthiness of individuals, families, or peoples. I am convinced that reducing the greatly unequal distribution of material privileges, social respect, and power over others will enhance the lives of everyone. Human capabilities are wasted when some people have much less power, privilege, and prestige than others. There are psychic costs to those ranked high as well as low; large hierarchical differences are sustained at least in part by oppression and manipulation—and that hurts us all. I believe in working to selectively reduce inequality, acknowledging that all aspects of inequality cannot be simultaneously reduced. I recognize, also, that there are costs to increasing equality and those costs are not evenly borne.

This book provides material relevant to assessing what modifications in inequality can be made and what some of the implications of those efforts would be. I hope that the information, ideas, and ways of thinking about issues presented in this book will help the reader understand better the opportunities to change or sustain the present degree of inequalities in the world.

ACKNOWLEDGMENTS

I wish to express my appreciation to those persons who read drafts of one or more chapters of the book, Mark Abrahamson, J. David Edelstein, Norval Glenn, Irving Kriesberg, Carol Kronus, Warren O. Hagstrom, Neil Smelser, and Dale Tussing. I have not always taken their advice; but the book is much improved by the suggestions I did follow. In addition, the work has benefitted from the questions and comments by students in my graduate and undergraduate social stratification courses and from conversations with many colleagues, Lois A. Kriesberg, Jean Langlie, William Pooler, Allan Mazur, Ephraim Mizruchi, Manfred Stanley, and Vincent Tinto. I appreciate the cheerful and conscientious typing and retyping of the manuscript by Susan Philips, Nancy Klein, and Kathleen Conway. I wish to acknowledge the support and assistance of many people at Prentice-Hall, Edward H. Stanford, Barbara Christenberry, Louise Hockett, and Pat Cahalan. The indexes were prepared by Md. Nazrul Islam.

PART I

Introduction

chapter 1

Questions and Moral Dilemmas

What though on hamely fare we dine,
Wear hoddengray, an' a' that;
Gie fools their silks, and knaves their wine,
A man's a man for a' that.
For a' that, an' a' that,
Their tinsel show, an' a' that;
The honest man, tho' e'er sae poor,
Is king o' men for a' that.   *Robert Burns*

All humans, in some ways, are alike and equal: We are all mortal; we have similar experiences of grief and joy, love and loneliness; we all seek and expect some degree of recognition and respect. But there are differences and inequalities among people as well; for example, not everyone receives the same deferential treatment from others. Inequalities also are evident in the goods we possess, the material conditions under which we live, and the power we have over others. This book begins by examining such social inequalities and their implications for people's lives. We then move on to discuss how variations in inequalities come about, persist, and change.

Social inequality can be discussed more meaningfully if we understand the roles that people occupy. Roles help to determine the extent of our control over others, how much deference we receive; and the amount of wealth, information, and other resources we possess. A *role* is a set of expectations and behavior associated with a position. For example, David Rockefeller is rich. He is rich partly because his position as president of the Chase Manhattan Bank commands a large salary and brings him into contact with people who share helpful information for investments. In addition, David Rockefeller is the grandson of John D. Rockefeller, who amassed a large fortune. His several roles are embedded in a set of rules and expectations about private ownership or wealth, family relations, inheritance, and jobs; they help to explain how come David Rockefeller is rich.

MEANINGS OF SOCIAL INEQUALITY

Even the most casual observation and reflection will demonstrate that people are not regarded equally, do not act equally, and do not have the same access to desired possessions. In order to describe and explain social inequalities, however, there must be a clear understanding of what is meant by social inequality and how it varies. The general agreement that people are not equal breaks down when we try to specify who and what are unequal and the extent to which they are unequal. Therefore, we must define terms like *social inequality* and *social stratification* before proceeding.

Inequality refers to a hierarchy in which some persons, groups, or positions are regarded as having more desirables than some other persons, groups, or positions. Inequality also implies superiority and inferiority. Ranking within the hierarchy may be determined by those who are ranked or by an outside observer or analyst. For example, a particular group of people may agree about what constitutes a good life-style, and rank high those who exemplify that standard,

4

and rank low those who deviate from it. Or an observer-analyst may decide that ownership of wealth is an important class criterion and that those who own much wealth are above those who do not.

Social has two meanings in the term *social inequality*. It refers to the idea that rank depends on the relationship of people in a hierarchy. For example, the position of president of the United States is powerful because many people entrust the incumbent of that office with tremendous authority. Similarly, a wealthy person is acknowledged by others as having control over certain material resources. The second meaning of *social* is that inequality is a relative matter; it can be seen not by looking at a single unit, but by comparing one unit with another. A group of persons have high incomes only in comparison with others who have low incomes; moreover, what is high and low differs over time and among societies.

In this book social stratification is distinguished from social inequality. *Social stratification* refers to the persistent pattern or system of inequality based on rules and structures. Although we will use the term primarily to discuss institutionalized inequalities, social stratification has other meanings as well. It may connote, for example, the existence of social strata, distinctive categories of people or positions that are ranked. The term also may refer to the allocation process—particularly as it occurs between generations—that places people in occupational and other positions. These matters will be discussed in Chapters 5 and 6 and 11-13.

The concept social stratification helps explain continuing inequality, an inequality that is maintained by norms and structures supported by groups that benefit from the prevailing system of inequality. This explanation, however, does not account for variations in inequality. They may derive from normative and cultural differences, economic conditions, personality characteristics of dominant persons, or many other factors. These and other reasons for inequality are discussed in Chapters 10-13.

Social inequality exists on many levels, from small, intimate groups to formal organizations and communities. Our concern, however, is with inequalities found within and between larger social systems such as countries and national cultures.

MORAL AND VALUE DILEMMAS

Our interest in social inequality is not only intellectual and scholarly. As social beings we respond emotionally to the subject. We care about social justice, the extent of inequality, and our own social ranking. We also place importance on such social values as personal freedom, communal solidarity, and material well-being. These concerns help shape and direct our questions about social inequality. However, there are innumerable questions and data regarding social inequality, and we must be selective. One basis for selecting questions and therefore, relevant data is moral relevance. Because our moral and value concerns help guide our inquiries, it is important that we acknowledge them so as to avoid forming biased questions. We should also pay attention to the values and standards of others, even when they differ from our own because that increases our awareness of our own. Recognizing value dilemmas can also make us more sensitive to the issues involves in the study of inequality and help us to examine the issues objectively. If we are interested in social action, we can combine objective findings with our personal feelings about social inequality to act more effectively.

Dilemmas Concerning Inequality

Social equality is a widely shared value. By virtue of our humanness, we are all equally worthy of respect and the opportunity for self-realization. An emphasis on that value seems to be deepening and widening in the contemporary world (Beteille 1969; Parsons 1970; Gans 1974). While the desirability of human equality is generally acknowledged, in certain circumstances its primacy or importance may be denied. This evaluation is based on having other values and the belief that the attainment of all values is not possible. The moral and value dilemmas created by such multiple values and beliefs will be discussed in the next section of this chapter.

Moral disagreements and dilemmas about equality also arise because equality itself has many dimensions and aspects. People differ about how much equality is desirable regarding even a single dimension of equality. Thus, some people desire, urge, and strive for total equality in power or wealth. Some revolutionaries, for example, believe that all power differences should be abolished.

> The revolutionary group must clearly see that its goal is not the "seizure of power," but the dissolution of power—indeed, that the entire problem of power, of control from below and control from above, can be solved only if there is no above or below (Bookchin 1971, p. 358).

Other people feel that differences in power or wealth are acceptable, that some persons deserve more than others. Even they may reject *great* differences in inequality or decry a condition when some people are below a minimal level of material well-being or civil rights. People may argue for reducing but not ending inequality in a given dimension, believing that it cannot be ended. As Gandhi said in 1927: "My ideal is equal distribution, but so far as I can see, it is not to be realized. I therefore work for equitable distribution" (Gandhi 1958, p. 118). What we believe is attainable, then, affects our value preferences.

Since every dimension of inequality can vary in several ways, the relationship among those ways may be the source of dilemmas. Thus, class inequality can vary in distribution and in mobility or, in other words, between the degree of equality of outcome and the degree of equality of opportunity. We may favor both kinds of equality and this may or may not be the source of a moral dilemma, depending on how we think those aspects of equality are related. Suppose one favors both equality of outcome and of opportunity and believes that insofar as people live in similar class circumstances, the opportunities for mobility will be relatively equal; then there need not be any dilemma. But suppose one believes that large class differences are necessary to motivate people to work hard and competively and that such motivation is necessary to produce equality of opportunity, then there would be a dilemma because maximizing both conditions would seem to be incompatible.

It is also possible to imagine how individual equality of opportunity might result in creating large differences in outcome among different strata. Michael Young (1961) in his report on a hypothetical meritocracy, describes what a society would be like if there were equal opportunity based strictly on merit. His description suggests how lower strata would become bereft of able leaders, and how their members then would be less capable of organizing and defending their own interests. Furthermore, since everyone would know that the persons in superordinate positions had been selected because of merit, their authority and claims for prestige and rewards would be readily acknowledged. The social distance between strata consequently would become greater than it would be otherwise.

People are unequal along many dimensions and we desire to be ranked highly in each, but we may differ in our emphasis upon one or another dimension. Some people value power or status particularly highly. In the United States, many people are very concerned with interpersonal social equality and this can compensate for low power or class rankings. Consequently, social equality in interpersonal relations tends to soothe class antagonisms. For example, people often seem willing to accept power inferiority if superiors treat them as equally human. Subordinates not allowing superiors to "put on airs" is an expression of this attitude. The American insistence on social equality, however, has been a source of irritation to the gentility of other countries. Frances Trollope, for example, discussed the "servant peoblem" during her visit to the United States in the 1820s:

> The greatest difficulty in organizing a family establishment in Ohio is getting servants, or, as it is there called, "getting help," for it is more than petty treason to the Republic, to call a free citizen a *servant* (Trollope 1949, p. 52).

Favoring or promoting one dimension of equality sometimes may be viewed as incompatible with favoring another. Such contradictions are based on beliefs about the empirical relations among the various dimensions of inequality. For example, favoring equality in power may seem to be consistent with favoring equality in wealth. But this assumption may prove to be inaccurate, depending on the circumstances and the beliefs that people have about them. During some periods of history, great power differences have been valued as a means to reduce class differences. For example, state power has been used by revolutionary leaders to abolish a wealthy class of landowners. As Mao Tse-tung said in 1949:

> Our present task is to strengthen the people's state apparatus—mainly the people's army, the people's police and the people's courts—in order to consolidate national defense and protect the people's interests. Given this condition, China can develop steadily, under the leadership of the working class and the Communist Party, from an agricultural into an industrial country and from a new-democratic into a socialist and communist society, can abolish classes and realize the Great Harmony. The state apparatus, including the army, the police and the courts, is the instrument by which one class oppresses another. It is an instrument for the oppression of antagonistic classes; it is violence and not "benevolence. . . ." We definitely do not apply a policy of benevolence to the reactionaries and towards the reactionary activities of the reactionary classes (Mao 1971, p. 380).

Other persons, of course, may question Mao's beliefs about the empirical relationship between state power and the ending of class differences, or the relative importance of valuing power differences over class differences.

The particular dilemmas created by balancing between equality of power and equality of economic wealth depend in part on the social system within which the balancing occurs. In contemporary American society, the dilemma usually is seen as having to choose between liberty and equality. Should people be free to do as they wish within the limits of a private-ownership market system even if this freedom creates inequality in material well-being? Or should individual rights of acquisition, especially of the means of production, be limited in order to maintain more equality of income and wealth; The answers to such questions are affected by our beliefs about the empirical relationship between economic inequality and the freedom to dispose of privately owned (state-guaranteed) property.

Hayek, for example, has argued that socialists destroy freedom in trying to achieve more equality through planning and public ownership.

> It is only because the control of the means of production is divided among many people acting independently that nobody has complete control over us, that we as individuals can decide what to do with ourselves. If all the means of production were vested in a single hand, whether it be nominally that of "society" as a whole or that of a dictator, whoever exercises this control has complete power over us (Hayek 1944, p. 104).

The autonomy of persons in disposing material goods is itself an aspect of equality, and freedom from control by others is a kind of power. According to Hayek's reasoning, then, equality of political power is consistent with large class inequalities.

Dilemmas Concerning Equality and Other Values

Equality may be valued as an end in itself—an embodiment of a fundamental good. Or equality may be valued as a means to some other, even higher end; for example, as a means by which the skills and resources of all humans can be maximized. In either case, we are aware of other important values: wealth, material production, truth, creativity, justice, and salvation. These values may or may not seem campatible with equality. Whether they appear consistent with equality depends on our conception of each and on our beliefs about their factual relationships.

Consider the value of material well-being, which is widely desired in the contemporary world. People generally want good food, clothing, and housing, not only for themselves but also for those they love. People may agree to, or even argue for the necessity of, a few persons having great power, status, or wealth in order to enhance their own material well-being. It might be asserted, therefore, that wealth must be concentrated; rich people make investments, and the capital accumulation that is produced forms the basis for economic activity and increased gains. The amassing of such wealth in private hands or in the hands of state leaders means large economic and/or political inequalities. Without such concentration, the masses would be condemned to small-scale production involving relatively little division of labor. There certainly would not be an advanced or highly productive technology.

Some people argue further that relatively few persons are able to effectively organize the necessary human and nonhuman resources to build a successful enterprise. Such entrepreneurial and managerial skills, they believe, should be rewarded on the basis of justice and as an incentive. As Sumner said of a business founder and his workers:

> He and they together formed a great system of factories, stores, transportation, under his guidance and judgment. It was for the benefit of all; but he contributed to it what no one else was able to contribute—the one guiding mind which made the whole thing possible. In no sense whatever does a man who accumulates a fortune by legitimate industry exploit his employees, or make his capital "out of" anybody else. The wealth which he wins would not be but for him (Sumner 1883, p. 47).

Inequality also can provide an incentive to the lower-ranking persons. It may be argued that the threat of poverty or degradation or physical punishment is necessary to keep everyone working, and that without such inducements the material well-being of all would suffer.

According to other arguments, however, inequality retards rather than enhances material well-being. It can be argued that for economic development to occur, people must feel that they have a collective stake in the process. They will be more willing to make the sacrifices necessary for investments and future production if they feel that the sacrifices will be shared equally. In addition.

9

rewarding everyone with status, autonomy, and a decent standard of living creates an incentive for diligence and effort. Even technologically advanced societies achieve increased material benefits for all if everyone receives a relatively equal income, since having a majority of people with substantial incomes, provides a large market for the consumption of goods produced. Maintaining full production in a market economy requires continued and growing effective demand. These and other assertions argue that equality helps all members of the social system achieve material well-being.

In addition to equality and material well-being, many of us value truth and creativity. We value intellectual and aesthetic achievements, both for the pleasure they give and for the knowledge and control over nature they provide. Indeed, people may be willing to accept lower status, power, or income in order to attain those goals. The argument for the necessity of such an exchange states that since some people are more capable than others of being creative or discovering new information, they should be given all the necessary resources and rewards to make these contributions. This condition requires the subordination, deference, and material sacrifice of others. It is further asserted that the advancement of science or art is necessarily a product of the elite, because the masses are unable to make important contributions to it.

It also may be argued, however, that equality is not inconsistent with creativity and truth. The capacity for significant creativity is undoubtedly much more widespread than has been realized in any social system. If nearly everyone has the supporting resources and expectations to make significant achievements, many more people will be creative than if support is given to only a few. Furthermore, to attain truth, we need many ideas and a way for discarding falsehoods; for this the discovery of error is critical. If many people pay attention to new ideas and their criticisms are noticed, fewer errors will survive. Depending upon the aspects of equality considered and the beliefs one has about the relationship between social inequality and creativity and truth, therefore, valuing equality and truth may be seen as consistent or inconsistent.

Finally, we will consider dilemmas arising from desiring justice or equity. Many people feel that equality is not fair, and that people should be rewarded on the basis of intention, effort, or achievement. Some standards of fairness dictate that people should *not* be equally rewarded (Nozick 1974). According to this belief, persons who work hard or who have good moral character should receive more than persons who do not exert themselves or who are of poor moral character. Another view is that persons who contribute more than others, regardless of effort, should be rewarded more. On the other hand, as we have noted earlier, some people regard equality itself as the fairest distribution of reward because it acknowledges the essential worthiness of every human being.

In recent years philosophers and social scientists have sought to understand the nature of justice and its relationship to equality. Rawls (1971) has stimulated a great deal of thought and discussion by proposing a theory of justice. A just social order, he argues, is based on two principles. In their simplest form they are:

First: Each person is to have an equal right to the most extensive basic liberty compatible with a similar liberty for others.

Second: Social and economic inequalities are to be arranged so that they are both (a) reasonably expected to be to everyone's advantage, and (b) attached to positions and offices open to all (p. 60).

The first principle suggests that justice requires the equality of certain minimal conditions or rights for all persons, particularly with regard to civil rights (Margolis 1977). The second principle states that inequalities in social and economic conditions can be just if everyone gains by them and if they exist in positions to which everyone has equal access. Coleman (1974) has pointed out the bureaucratic and impersonal nature of this concept of justice. He also has shown that in developing his theory, Rawls suggests a view of individuals making a social contract with a single corporate entity: the society or state. Coleman argues that in reality we belong to many corporate entities such as businesses, families, schools and ethnic groups and we can be thought to be making contracts with each of them.

It becomes clear that considerations of inequality are deeply intertwined with moral questions. How much inequality is good? How important is equality as compared with other values? Which aspects of equality are especially valuable? Although these questions will not be discussed in detail in this book, the reader should keep them in mind, because they will help indicate the significance of the empirical evidence reviewed. As the discussion has demonstrated, our personal choices regarding the value and importance of equality are related to our factual beliefs about the relationship between equality and other values we hold.

QUESTIONS ABOUT INEQUALITY

Three questions form the organizing structure of this book. How much does inequality vary? How do variations in inequality affect people's lives? How can variations in inequality be explained? Before reviewing the answers given by sociologists and other social scientists, which we do in the remainder of the book, it will be useful to consider several kinds of ideological answers. This will place the sociological answers in the context of public controversy and make the practical implications of the sociological disputes more evident. Ideologies interweave beliefs about social inequality and preferences about it and on that basis hold out goals and ways to reach them. Reformers, revolutionaries, and defenders of the status quo all have ideas about the extent of inequality, the consequences of varying degrees of inequality, and explanations for the way it is and how it might be altered. Among the many ideologies which have been formulated, such as anarchism, communism, fascism, and liberalism, we will examine three general ideological orientations: conservative, radical, and liberal.

A conservative orientation usually includes the belief that inequality is a natural and inevitable phenomenon. Aristotle, in *Politics*, expressed this idea when he wrote:

> That some should rule and others be ruled is a thing not only necessary, but expedient; from the hour of birth, some are marked for subjection, others for rule. . . .The male is by nature superior, and female, inferior; and the one rules, and the other is ruled; this principle, of necessity, extends to all humanity . . . some men are by nature free, and others slaves, and for these latter slavery is both expedient and right (Aristotle 1947, pp. 559-61).

Conservatives also generally support existing inequalities. To seek a return to an earlier, more unequal condition would be a reactionary orientation.

Liberals tend to favor modifying and reforming inequalities, particularly inherited ones. They emphasize individual liberty, especially political freedom. To establish a free government, Jefferson, for example, thought that the foundations of an inherited aristocracy must be broken:

> To annul this privilege, and instead of an aristocracy of wealth, of more harm and danger, than benefit, to society, to make an opening for the aristocracy of virtue and talent, which nature has wisely provided for the direction of the interests of society, and scattered with equal hand through all its conditions, was deemed essential to a well ordered republic (Padover 1952, p. 39).

Radicals generally seek fundamental reductions in the degree of inequality. One type of radical thought was developed by Karl Marx, who viewed capitalism as a system with inherent antagonistic inequalities. Marx believed that after a transition from capitalism and the first phase of communist society, a new society would emerge:

> In a higher phase of communist society, after the enslaving subordination of the individual to the division of labour, and therewith also the antithesis between mental and physical labour, has vanished; after labour has become not only a means of life but life's prime want; after the productive forces have also increased with the all-round development of the individual, and all the springs of cooperative wealth flow more abundantly—only then can the narrow horizon of bourgeois right be crossed in its entirety and society inscribe on its banner: From each according to his ability, to each according to his needs! (Tucker 1972, p. 388).

The possibility of a new age in which exploitation and material and cultural impoverishment are abolished is envisaged by many radicals.

Proponents of differing ideological orientations also vary in their approach to the three organizing questions mentioned above. We will note some of these variations as we discuss the questions and give an overview of the issues which will be examined in answering the questions in later chapters.

To answer the first organizing question, "How much does inequality vary?" it is necessary to specify the units that are unequal and the dimensions and degrees of inequality. Chapter 2 discusses the units which are unequally ranked: individuals, roles, families, and social systems. Chapter 2 also distinguishes among class or economic inequalities, status or prestige inequalities and power inequalities. How each dimension can vary in range, distribution, and mobility is also examined. Chapters 3-7 describe the actual variations in class, status, and power inequalities in the United States and other social systems. The examination of these variations closely follow the empirical evidence. To sensitize the reader to implications of the concepts and findings, the conservative, liberal, and radical orientations toward variations in inequality will be briefly noted here.

Conservatives tend to see the stratified units as persons or perhaps families but not as classes, positions, or roles. Inequality, they believe, is natural, reflecting the inherent differences among persons. Conservatives tend to assume that whatever the degree of inequality, it is not too great, and that, in any case, it is inevitable and bound to continue. They stress status inequality rather than class and power differences.

Liberals also tend to see individuals as the units that are unequal, but some emphasize that positions rather than the incumbents are rewarded. Although they generally consider the existing inequality to be excessive and favor reducing it, liberals do not believe that inequality can be totally abolished. They are more concerned with equality of opportunity or mobility than with equality of outcome or minimizing the unequal distribution of prestige, power, or material conditions.

Radicals usually emphasize large groups—social classes or ethnic communities—as the units of inequality. They seek an end to inequality between such large categories of people, and envisage the possibility of ending or drastically reducing many other forms of inequality as well. Radicals are often more concerned with class and status inequalities than with power inequality.

The second major question in this book pertains to the consequences of inequality. Chapter 9 examines the effects of inequality on individuals, and reviews sociological research findings on the correlation between behavior and attitudes and socioeconomic rank. In Chapter 10 we will consider possible collective reactions to inequality, such as protests and rebellion by lower-ranked groups.

These topics also receive different ideological treatments. Conservatives emphasize individual adjustments and accommodations to inequality as a means for successfully fitting into the stratification system. Collective reactions are not given attention, except as unusual disruptions. Liberals focus on the consequences of having less than some minimal standards, and thus tend to be concerned with poverty and violations of civil liberties. While collective reactions channeled through established institutions, such as legitimate political systems, are given a great deal of attention, those outside institutionalized channels are generally decried or ignored. Radicals, on the other hand, are interested in the consequences of inequality for persons at the highest strata levels and emphasize the relationship between strata. This relationship is often viewed as one in which high-ranking persons exploit and manipulate those in the lower strata. Collective reactions are often stressed, particularly ones that break conventions. These reactions are sometimes viewed as the fundamental ways in which stratification systems are altered.

The third major matter pursued in this book is to *explain* variations in inequality. Chapter 11 looks at explanations for varying inequalities in material well-being, status, and power. In accounting for inequalities in these dimensions, we will concentrate on five major sociological approaches, each of which emphasizes different factors and processes.

Two approaches entail functional explanations of inequality. One approach stresses status inequality and the values and norms of the society (Parsons 1970). Proponents contend that some societies have cultures whose values foster great inequality and little mobility; other societies stress values that tend to narrow the range between the top and the bottom of the stratification scale and also promote equality of opportunity. Another view of this approach is that society members differ in their actualization of cultural values, which necessarily results in their being evaluated unequally. This approach also emphasizes the interdependence of the institutions making up a social system and hence the mutual dependence of the stratification subsystem with other subsystems in the society.

The other functional approach emphasizes the motivational requirement of a society (Davis and Moore 1945). Theorists taking this approach argue that people need to be rewarded with prestige and material benefits in order to be motivated to prepare for and work hard in important positions. Rewards differ according to the functional importance of the positions and the scarcity of people who can fill them. Consequently, societies with a high degree of specialization will tend to have an elaborate reward system and relatively great inequality.

The third and fourth approaches stress conflict among contending groups. In one approach, developed by Karl Marx (Tucker 1972), the differences between the owners of the factories and other means of production and the employees is the basis for classes and class conflict. The emphasis of Marxists is on objective material conditions, the reality external to consciousness but which underlies consciousness. Another conflict approach stresses divisions based on coercive strength (Collins 1975). Groups differ in the resources they can organize for coercion to gain power; groups with power then use it to gain economic goods and services. Prestige follows.

The focus of the fifth approach is on objective demographic and technological factors such as population size, fertility, and methods of production (Blau 1977). In this view the form and level of technology of production set limits to the degree of inequality. For example, in a society with a primitive technology people depend on hunting animals and gathering wild plants, the population is small, and there is no economic surplus and little material inequality. And an advanced industrial society must have a high level of technical skills, which means minimal social and economic conditions, for most people must be at a high level, and there must be relatively open competition for superior positions. (See, for example, Kerr et al. 1964.) The large population that can be supported by highly developed technologies also makes possible considerable specialization and hence requires elaboration of coordination; this fosters inequality.

In Chapters 12 and 13 these approaches will be applied and compared in order to explain the variations in inequality described in earlier chapters. The applications will also enable us to assess the relative adequacy of those approaches. Sociologists often combine those theoretical orientations, but with very different emphases.

Explanations of varying inequalities also are contained in the ideologies that we have been discussing. These explanations typically involve diagnosing what is wrong and prescribing corrective action. This procedure generally entails placing blame for the condemned inequality.

Conservatives usually defend existing inequalities rather than condemn them. They emphasize the way in which the existing inequality helps to maintain the society as a whole—for example, by motivating people to do what needs to be done and by discouraging them from doing what should not be done. Another conservative argument in defense of inequality is based on the observation that people and even classes are interdependent. Soviet writers, for example, use this argument to justify stratification in the Soviet Union, claiming that inequality at the present stage of socialism there is consistent with cooperation between "nonantagonistic" classes (Ossowski 1963). There also are conservatives who cite differences in human ability as the reason for inequality; some people, they say, are smarter and harder working than others, and they therefore get more of what people generally want. According to this argument, people who are poor, powerless, and of low status are to blame for their condition. As Banfield contends in describing the problems, like poverty, of the lower class: "At bottom [it is] a single problem: the existence of an outlook and style of life which is radically present-oriented and therefore attaches no value to work, sacrifice, self-improvement, or service to family, friends, or community" (Banfield 1970, p. 211).

Liberals offer a wide range of reasons for inequality. Some blame an open, competitive marketplace in which some persons do better than others, due to differences in training, talent, and motivation. Some liberals account for inequality in terms of the society's rules, which preserve the ranking of some groups at the expense of others; but the rules are established by the members of the society and therefore are reformable by them. And when inequality is greater than they feel it should be, liberals spread the responsibility widely among various groups and argue that it rests partly on misunderstandings. They reason that if there were greater understanding among different groups and a recognition of common interests, inequalities might be reduced through compromise and general agreement. Efforts to reduce status differences based on race and ethnicity sometimes exemplify this view.

Radicals generally explain inequality in terms of coercion, fraud, and manipulation by the higher-ranked groups—the rich and the powerful. Other radicals blame the system that places one group above the other. In this view, only a struggle by the person in the lower ranks can force the upper strata to yield their unfairly taken gains. Radicals also stress that material conditions and the historical circumstances determine when and how the stratification system is transformed. For example, André Gorz, reflecting on the French student and worker upheavals of May 1968, concluded:

> Henceforward, we know that advanced capitalist society is vulnerable; that it is rent by contradictions which may explode into revolutionary crises . . . that the essence of a revolutionary organization is to be ready for revolution. . . . The other eventuality is that of a long process, which must be utilized for political preparation in depth, and for actions of partial rupture, spaced out in time. This preparation and these actions include the constant repetition, by active minorities . . . of insurrectionary acts of a symbolic and exemplary kind (Gorz 1971, pp. 341-42).

Gorz's statement also indicates the important role of a vanguard revolutionary party in radical ideology.

In keeping with the nonideological nature of this book, questions and answers regarding social inequality have been formulated without reference to personal values and specific programs of action. Variations in inequality, their consequences, and their explanations will be discussed factually, for it is hoped that such a presentation will facilitate rational and effective actions by those who seek greater justice.

REFERENCES

ARISTOTLE. 1947. Politics, Book I, Chapter 5. In Richard McKeon (Ed.), *Introduction to Aristotle.* New York: The Modern Library.
BANFIELD, EDWARD C. 1970. *The Unheavenly City.* Boston: Little, Brown and Company.
BETEILLE, ANDRE. 1969. "The Decline of Society Inequality," Pp. 362-380. in Andre Beteille (Ed.), *Social Inequality.* Baltimore: Penguin Books.
BLAU, PETER M. 1964. *Exchange and Power in Social Life.* New York: John Wiley.
BLAU, PETER M. 1977. *Inequality and Heterogeneity.* New York: The Free Press.
BOOKCHIN, MURRAY. 1971. "Post-Scarcity Anarchy." In Arthur Lothstein (Ed.), *All We Are Saying. . . .* New York: Capricorn Books. (Originally published in *Anarchos,* Spring 1969).

COLEMAN, JAMES S. 1971. "Review Essay: Inequality, Sociology, and Moral Philosophy," *American Journal of Sociology* 80 (November):739-764.

DAVIS, KINGSLEY and WILBERT MOORE. "Some Principles of Stratification," *American Sociological Review* 10 (April, 1945) 242-249.

GANDHI, MAHATMA. 1958. *All Men Are Brothers* (Krishna Kripalani, Ed.). Paris: United Nations Educational, Scientific and Cultural Organization, World Without War Publications.

GANS, HERBERT J. 1974. *More Equality*. New York: Vintage Books.

GORZ, ANDRE. 1971. "The Way Forward." Pp. 320-342. in Arthur Lothstein (Ed.), *All We Are Saying. . . .* New York: Capricorn Books. (Originally published in 1968).

HAYEK, FRIEDRICH A. 1944. *The Road to Serfdom*. Chicago: University of Chicago Press.

KERR, C., J. T. DUNLOP, F. HARBISON and C. A. MYERS. 1964. *Industrialism and Industrial Man*. New York: Oxford University Press. (Originally published in 1960.)

MAO TSE-TUNG. 1971. "On the People's Democratic Dictatorship." In *Selected Readings from the Works of Mao Tsetung*. Peking: Foreign Language Press. (Originally published June 30, 1949.)

MARGOLIS, JOSEPH. 1977. "Political Equality and Political Justice," *Social Research* 44 (Summer):308-329.

NOZICK, ROBERT. 1974. *Anarchy, State, and Utopia*. New York: Basic Books.

OSSOWSKI, STANISLAW. 1963. *Class Structure and Social Consciousness*. New York: Free Press.

PADOVER, SAUL K. 1952. *Jefferson*. New York: New American Library.

PARSONS, TALCOTT. 1970. "Equality and Inequality in Modern Society, or Social Stratification Revisited." Pp. 13-72 in Edward O. Lauman (Ed.), *Social Stratification*. Indianapolis: Bobbs-Merill.

RAWLS, JOHN. 1971. *A Theory of Justice*. Cambridge, Mass.: Harvard University Press.

SUMNER, WILLIAM GRAHAM. 1883. *What Social Classes Owe Each Other*. New York: Harper.

TROLLOPE, FRANCES. 1949. *Domestic Manners of the Americans*. New York: Alfred A. Knopf. (Originally published in 1832.)

TUCKER, ROBERT C. 1972. *The Marx-Engels Reader*. New York: W. W. Norton. (*The German Ideology* was written in 1845-46 and originally published in 1932.)

YOUNG, MICHAEL. 1961. *The Rise of the Meritocracy: 1870-2033*. Baltimore: Penguin Books. (Originally published in 1958.)

chapter 2

Dimensions and Degrees

Better is he that is lightly esteemed,
and hath a servant,
Than he that playeth the man of rank
and lacketh bread.   *Prov. 12:9*

The concepts of inequality and their appellations have ideological implications and relevance for the moral dilemmas discussed in Chapter 1, as well as being crucial for theoretical reasoning and empirical analysis.

In this chapter, therefore, we will explicitly distinguish the various aspects of inequality—who or what is unequal, in which ways they are unequal, and the extent of their inequality—and select specific kinds of units, dimensions, and degrees for concentrated analysis.

Although people have been concerned with inequality throughout human history, contemporary views all relate in some way to Karl Marx and his work. We are all post-Marxians. A review of Marx's analysis of class and class conflict will therefore serve as a basis for discussing more recent analyses of inequality, even writings by persons who disagree with what he wrote. We will focus on Marx's theory, which should be distinguished from his efforts in leading a social movement and certainly from the policies of "Marxists" who presently lead organizations and governments.

Karl Marx (1818-1883) presented his theory on class and class conflict as scientific and empirical, although contemporary readers may find it "philosophical" due to the fact that many of its arguments are combinations of assertions, defintions, and logic. Nevertheless, Marx based his theory on evidence from the world about him. He tried to account for a fundamental change in the world—the emergence and expansion of capitalism—in a way that would explain previous major changes and predict future ones. Class struggles, he decided, best explain such major historical shifts.

Marx and Friedrich Engels, his collaborator, lived during the early period of rapid industrialization. Workers—men, women, and children—labored twelve hours a day and more in factories separated from their homes. Despite high productivity, however, the workers were impoverished; in many ways their living conditions were becoming worse. Marx and Engels studied this development and tried to explain these changes. They believed that these conditions were an inherent feature of capitalism.

Marx sought to develop a comprehensive theory to explain the major historical changes of the past and the nature of capitalism. His first premise was that "life involves before everything else eating and drinking, a habitation, clothing and many other things. The first historical act is thus the production of the means to satisfy these needs, and production of material life itself" (Tucker 1972, p. 120). The means of production, then, are the basis of human life; they shape the mode of production and the social organization of society. The mode of production is the substructure also for the cultural and intellectual features of a society; the ruling ideas of an epoch are the ideas of the ruling class.

The capitalist society and the bourgeoisie class emerged from feudalism with the development of industry and the growth of a world market that furthered the expansion of capital and large-scale industry. Marx explained this change in the *Communist Manifesto*.

> Modern industry has established the world market, for which the discovery of America paved the way. This market has given an immense development to commerce, to navigation, to communication by land. This development has, in turn, reacted on the extension of industry; and in proportion as industry, commerce, navigation, railways extended, in the same proportion the bourgeoisie developed, increased its capital, and pushed into the background every class handed down from the Middle Ages (Tucker 1972, p. 337).

A major portion of Marx's theoretical work is his analysis of capitalism (Marx 1906). Capital, according to Marx, is accumulated labor; hence, what is produced with it is derived from human labor. Capital increases the productivity of labor; but as long as capital is privately owned, such increases in productivity give only capitalists larger profits. This condition exists because workers need to be paid only enough for their maintenance and replacement, and increased productivity actually lowers the cost of meeting their minimal needs. And while the cost—the labor value of products—declines, the price of a commodity may increase or at least remain the same. The difference between the labor value of a commodity and its selling price, or exchange value, is surplus value, which is taken by the owners of the means of production. This analysis describes the essence of the exploitation of labor under capitalism. On the whole then, the proletariat become poorer and capitalists become richer. Furthermore, because the proletariat do not own or control the product of their labor and because the division of labor is so specialized that they cannot grasp the entire process, they become alienated from their work.

Given these conditions, the workers are drawn together into a single class in opposition to the capitalists or bourgeoisie. The very development of large-scale factories gives more workers the opportunity to communicate with each other. As the proletariat increases and become conscious of their exploited situation and as the capitalists decline in number, the emergence of a new system becomes inevitable. With the formation of two antagonistic classes, the class struggle intensifies and the capitalists are overthrown. The working class now becomes synomonous with society and owns the means of production; classes cease to exist.

For Marx, then, the basic form of inequality under the capitalist system exists in the disparity in wealth: between the owners of the means of production and the proletariat—the propertyless wage slaves. This condition is objective, existing independently of the workers' subjective awareness. The major units of society are the classes themselves. Other kinds of social inequality are minor and derive from this basic class inequality.

Today there are several interpretations and modifications applying Marx's thinking to contemporary world conditions. Once his ideas have become embodied into organizations, they may even be used to justify policies that other interpreters of Marx would see as inconsistent with his views. Some observers believe, for example, that Soviet leaders, under the banner of Marxism-Leninism, use government power to create the economic conditions appropriate to socialism. In Chapter 11 we will examine critiques and defenses of contemporary Marxist approaches.

The following section begins by identifying the describing the units, dimensions, and degrees of inequality. The discussion then focuses on how these elements combine to form different types of stratification systems: feudal, capitalist, and socialist.

UNITS

In studying inequality the distinction between positions and persons is basic. Position refers to a place in a given social structure; particularly significant for stratification are places in occupational structures. Positions are characterized by the set of expectations members of the social structure have about how the position is to be filled—the expectations pertain to the rights and obligations of the position. Person refers to a human acting being who fills several positions at the same time. Sometimes we will use the term persons to refer to individuals and sometimes to individuals aggregated in families or other groupings. Power, prestige, and material resources may be attached to a position, regardless of the incumbent, or to a person, whatever his or her position.

As we shall see, a great deal of sociological research concerns position. We have data on the prestige of occupations and on the salaries and wages accruing to different occupations. We know that offices differ greatly in the authority they give incumbents to command action from others. Sets of positions can be categorized together and regarded as classes. Thus the working class includes a variety of manual occupations and wide variations in wages.

We can learn about the inequality of people by studying the positions they occupy, but it is also important to study inequality among persons directly. One way of studying inequality among persons is to consider each individual as a separate being. Even when this method is employed, however, certain people, such as minors, may be excluded. And since humans do not generally live as isolated beings, it is sometimes necessary to use families or households as the units of study. This method poses another set of conceptual and empirical problems. Should all members of the family or household be added together, or should one member, such as the husband, represent the family?[1]

---

[1] The U.S. Bureau of the Census designates one person in each family as the head. "Women are not classified as heads if their husbands are resident members of the family at the time of the survey" (U.S. Bureau of the Census 1977b, p. 266. The designation of the family head will not be used in the 1980 census.

Finally, persons may be grouped together into collectivities which themselves are ranked. Collectivities such as ethnic groups, countries, communities, or corporations can be considered as units within a larger hierarchical system. Thus, ethnic groups are ranked in status, have more or less power, and have, on the average, higher or lower material conditions. Countries also differ in power, wealth, and prestige; in international stratification, they are the units that are ranked (Lagos 1963; Horowitz 1972). International stratification also refers to class, status, and power inequalities that transcend geographic boundaries and involve such large nongovernmental units as multinational corporations, international trade unions, churches, and ethnic collectivities.

DIMENSIONS

It is possible to rank the various ways in which positions and people differ. The three dimensions of ranking used in this book—class, status, and power—have been selected for several reasons. Not only do they matter to people, but the ranking is relatively clear. For example, there is widespread popular understanding of which class or material conditions are better than others. The hierarchy for status also is generally understood, because according deference is an overt action. And power is clearly ranked because it involves a social relationship of subordination and superordination.

Another reason why these three dimensions are worthy of emphasis is because they tend to be institutionalized in the large-scale social structures that are the focus of our concern. Class differences are embodied and supported by major societal institutions pertaining to property, money, and the division of labor. Status differences often are less institutionalized, but deference patterns are frequently learned and maintained through socialization in families and schools. Power differences clearly are institutionalized and maintained in the political structure of countries and in such organizations as the military.

These dimensions are particularly significant because they affect nearly every aspect of social life. The workings of any aspect of life in large social systems cannot fully be understood without considering the context and basis for action that variations in class, status, and power provide.

Finally, these dimensions have been selected for discussion because a great amount of sociological work has been done regarding each of them. Although this sociological emphasis is largely due to the reasons given above, the emphasis also in part derives from the work of Max Weber (1864-1920), who was strongly affected by the questions and answers that Marx formulated. Basically, Weber expanded Marx's thought and applied it to political, military and religious structures and ideologies (Gerth and Mills 1946, pp. 46-50). In doing so, he contradicted the primacy of Marx's economic materialism of objective conditions of production. His work also reflected his own historical circumstances. He lived in

Germany at a time of unification, industrialization, and urbanization. And while the national government grew, the Junkers—the aristocratic land owners of Prussia—remained a dominant political force, and the rising industrialists sought honorific titles. Class differences were not overriding all other differences; status concerns persisted, and state power and nationalism severed class identities. Max Weber theorized that three major dimensions of inequality could be distinguished: class, status, and power.

Class, Status, and Power

For Weber, *class* refers to people sharing similar living conditions and prospects, which are shaped by their place in the labor or commodity market. It is that shared component of their living conditions which is shaped "exclusively by economic interests in the possession of goods and opportunities for income" (Gerth and Mills 1946, p. 181). Class inequality, then, refers to the differences in people's material conditions and life opportunities resulting from their market situations.

Status refers to that component of people's lives that is determined by a specific, positive or negative, social estimation of honor. Weber writes, "Status honor is normally expressed by the fact that above all else a specific style of life can be expected from all those who wish to belong to the circle" (Gerth and Mills 1946, p. 187). Thus status groups are usually communities, which, according to Weber, are characterized by a feeling among members of belonging to one another; that is, they are contracted to "associations," where individuals calculate their interests.

Weber defines power as "any chance (no matter whereon based) to carry through one's own will, within a social relationship, even against the resistance of others."[2] He discusses this kind of power in terms of "parties," which may represent interests based on class or status or a mixture of both. Power may be legitimate or nonlegitimate. *Legitimate power* exists when subordinates believe that their superordinates have the right to command; Weber refers to this power as authority. Nonlegitimate power is based on force or manipulation by persons with power over those without. The distinction between these two kinds of power is analytic and not readily apparent in everyday life.

The conceptions of class, status, and power in contemporary sociological research differ somewhat from Weber's concepts. This difference reflects theoretical developments and changes in research methods. Weber's research was on a grand historical scale, comparing the rise of capitalism in Europe with conditions in China, India, and the Middle East. Much recent research, however, has focused on inequalities within a city or a country, and often has been based on

---

[2] "One" may be an individual or a collectivity (Weber 1925; Gerth and Mills 1946, p. 180; Walliman et al. 1977).

interviews with a sample of residents. Although each research style has unique advantages, each one also constrains the researchers to use particular kinds of measures as indicators for a concept; but then the concept may be redefined to match the available indicators.

In this book, class, status, and power inequalities will be examined separately and together. These inequalities will be defined in somewhat broader terms than those set forth by Weber in order to apply to a variety of theoretical approaches and to be consistent with contemporary research.

Class inequality refers to differences in the material privileges associated with positions or the material resources possessed or controlled by persons. Typically, these differences are in money income and in ownership or control of property, such as land or factories. So defined, class differences are objective; they exist independently of people's awareness. Furthermore, this conception of class inequality generally assumes a continuous gradient of ranked differences. For example, money income is infinitely divisible and does not in itself have any natural dividing lines that would mark off one stratum from another. Nevertheless, it is often theoretically and empirically useful to distinguish strata and treat one set of people as an aggregate who tend to share similar life experiences. Distinguishing strata is especially relevant in discussing social classes, classes, and class conflict. These terms will be examined after power and status inequalities.

Status inequality refers to differences in prestige or honor accorded to persons or positions. The prestige or honor may be based on shared standards regarding life-style or ancestry, or on symbols or characteristics associated with different positions, for example, uniforms or other special clothing. Status differences are also manifested in the deference one person shows another, that is, in who is according respect and honor to whom. Status ranking, then, depends on shared subjective awareness.

Power inequality refers to differences among people in their ability to impose their will upon others. We will be examining two forms of power: the ability to command obedience from others and the ability to refuse control by others. In the first kind, the policy holder directs others to act, whether this is to organize and mobilize people for a purpose which they all desire or to gain resources at the expense of those who are powerless (Parsons 1969; Mills 1956). The second form of power is the ability to reject commands from others and to be autonomous. In the former case we speak of participation in collective decision making and in the latter of civil rights and civil liberties.

All the kinds of power we will be discussing are based on coercion (Blau 1964). That is, power rests on the ability to punish or threaten to punish those who do not comply. But earlier, we noted that Weber distinguished between legitimate and nonlegitimate power and that legitimate power, or authority, rests on the subordinates' acknowledging the right of others to command or to reject commands. It is true that the authority of a person (based on personal qualities or the office he or she holds) rests on agreement by others.

This means, however, that for any given individual obedience will be supported, and maybe enforced, by the others who accord the power holder the right to exercise authority. A king's power, for example, rests on the acceptance of his legitimacy by ministers and soldiers and if they withdraw that acceptance, the king's power would vanish (Sharp 1975).

In social reality, these three dimensions of inequality are inextricably interrelated. Each person fills several class, power, and status positions and has many characteristics that are variously ranked in terms of class, status, and power. Although a person's or group's level along one of these dimensions often is similar to the ranking on the others, the rankings are never identical. The congruence of persons and positions on different ranking systems contributes to the formation and identification of social strata. Social classes, for example, are commonly understood as categories of persons who share certain objective life circumstances and who have an awareness of themselves as members of a particular social class. Class membership strongly influences their personal interaction; people in the same social class tend to associate with each other.

In studying the way that people in communities structure their lives, social scientists have sometimes used the term *social classes* to refer to strata based on class, power, and especially on status differences. Warner and Lunt (1941), for example, have noted the way that people in communities define classes and associate in terms of social classes. They have reported on how people evaluate occupations, income, life-style income, and other matters to determine who is above them and who is below. Their findings show that people tend to interact socially with others of about the same status; however, people from below generally try to associate with their betters and those above limit their interaction with those below them.

The idea of social classes also is generally understood to involve subjective identification and consciousness; sometimes sociologists stress that members of different classes think of themselves as members of conflict groups (Dahrendorf 1959). In this book references to *social* classes generally will include such subjective references, but classes will refer to aggregations of persons who share an objectively similar material condition, such as annual income.

System Contexts

Social inequality always exists within a *social system*—bounded, inter-related set of roles, structures, or persons. Inequality must be viewed within a system context because rankings are relative; references to "high" or "low," "up" or "down," are meaningful only in the context of a set of persons or positions. A person is rich or poor, for example, compared with some other person. To determine if a person is rich or poor, it is necessary to know with whom that person is being compared. Given the very different qualities of class, status, and power inequalities, each inequality can be most efficiently studied in its own system context.

Class inequalities are best considered within the context of an economic system. The rich and the poor are usually compared within the same economic order. In contemporary societies, as Weber noted, that economic order is the market. Weber also observed that there are many different markets—for example, those dealing in labor, credit, and commodities. Persons can be variously unequal in each market (Wiley 1967). Money is generally the currency used to indicate the degree of inequality in these markets.

Even larger collectivities, such as countries, can be regarded as parts of a broader economic system, but it takes some reflection. Countries—or, more precisely, segments of countries—trade with each other, lend and borrow money for investments, and engage in other economic transactions. The transactors may be governments, agencies, multinational corporations, or small traders. In any case, the result is a larger economic system that may be marked by strong class differences. Some countries are relatively poor and economically dependent on other nations.

In the case of status inequalities, the system is a culture. The members must share values and standards that have been established for evaluating persons and positions. The basic "currency" in a culture is respect given and received. The culture may be shared by members of a small group, a religious or ethnic community, two societies, or an entire civilization.

Power inequality exists within a political order—a system consisting of groups that are organized to assert and resist coercion. They mobilize persons or structures to support them against others and to pursue shared policies. This mobilization occurs within cities and voluntary associations and among political parties and countries. The dominant political order in the contemporary world is the one established by governments. Their claims are pervasive; nearly all the land on earth is divided among governments claiming jurisdiction over territories they control. We will generally examine power inequalities in terms of political orders as defined by governments.

The limits of governmental jurisdiction are ultimately based on coercion. Governments sometimes are defined as groups that monopolize the right to use violence. But, as noted above, the ability to threaten or apply coercion depends on the agreement of at least some subordinates willing to act together to coerce others. To this extent, the power rests on rules and authority. In most countries members usually accept the legitimacy of the state and government. Political orders, however, also include collectivities that do not accord legitimacy to those exercising power, and some collectivities may generally lack agreement about the legitimacy of any common authority. Within some countries, for example, an ethnic group coercively subordinated may reject the legitimacy of the subor- dinators, resulting in a civil war. Countries themselves may be viewed as part of a larger political order or system in which there is considerable power inequality and no shared authority.

I point out the different system context of each dimension to indicate that when we use a single context, such as a country, to consider all the dimensions of inequality, we distort reality to some extent. Given the way information is collected and reported, we are usually forced to use countries as the systems within which we study class and status as well as power inequality. In addition, the country context actually is in many ways paramount.

Relating Dimensions to Units

Class inequality will be viewed mostly in terms of differences in wealth and income. In considering wealth, we must examine whether it is the person or the position which owns it. A major form of wealth is capital, or the means of production. Marx contended that the fundamental class distinction was between the owners of the means of production and the proletariat, who had only their labor to sell; but we are less clear these days about who does and does not own the means of production. This issue has been discussed often in terms of the separation of ownership from control. Berle and Means (1933) and Burnham (1941) have argued that the ownership of the modern corporation is becoming so diffuse that effective control of most corporations does not rest in the hands of any individual or family but in the offices of the corporate managers. Some observers argue, however, that a few families can and do exercise effective control over vast resources; indeed, the diffusion of ownership allows them to control great amounts of capital with the relatively small amount that they themselves own (Gordon 1945; Kolko 1962). Evidence regarding these arguments will be examined in Chapter 3. It is sufficient here to note that when we speak of wealth inequality we may be speaking of personal ownership or of control by positions. The same issue is pertinent to class differences in socialist countries. If the means of production are owned by the people as a whole, major wealth differences and classes, as defined by Marx, cease to exist; but inequality of control over the means of production may nevertheless exist.

The other major measure of class differenes is income, which is usually calculated in terms of annual income for a family or household. The income may be earned by only one or by two or more members. When the whole family or household was a single productive unit and was economically self-sufficient, the income was more readily viewed as a joint product. This is no longer true, and yet individuals generally do not live as separate economic units. Using family income obscures, however, the diverse class situation of its members. Thus, given the present labor market conditions and definition of work, if a husband is employed and the wife is not, she may have no income, even if her husband's is high. This situation becomes apparent when the family unit is broken and the wife becomes poor (Kriesberg 1970). Family or household income is affected by the age and number of household members, but who is to be considered a member at any given time or over what period of time is not always clear.

The attribution of status inequalities to different units is relatively clear.

Many positions have a specific prestige accorded to them. As we shall see in detail in Chapters 5 and 6, there is a generally accepted prestige ranking of the occupations in contemporary societies. When status is attached to the way people live, there is less consensus. However, there probably is widespread agreement on what constitutes an upper-class life-style as opposed to a lower-class one.

Gender and ethnicity present special conceptual problems. The sexes and the various ethnic groups differ in many ways which are not ranked. They are just different. In addition, membership in one or another category may be highly related to power and class differences, aside from any status inequality. Nevertheless, membership in a sex or in an ethnic category often is the basis for evaluation and ranking as higher or lower in status. In this book, we will study gender and ethnic differences primarily as status differences and see how those are related to class and power differences. We will regard those status differences as qualities of the persons and not of positions.

Finally, power inequalities also exist among positions and persons. Offices, for example, vary greatly in power. This power often is separate from the incumbent of a particular office, as illustrated by the difference in power a person has as President of the United States and after he leaves office. Conversely, a person may be powerful apart from the office he or she occupies. In the case of an individual, power may be based on knowledge, skill or another personal quality. Power differences among families, groups, and collectivities may be based on differential control over resources or over offices wielding great power. Such control may create a ruling class, in which some definable collectivity of persons perpetuates themselves in the commanding offices of a society.

DEGREES

Taking any one dimension of inequality, the degree to which positions or persons can be unequal varies in several ways. Three kinds of variation will be examined: range, distribution, and mobility. Sorokin (1959) refers to range and distribution as height and profile; Barber (1959) calls them span and shape. These variations are briefly identified here. A fuller treatment is provided in the chapters concerning each dimension.

Range

The *range* of inequality is the distance between the top and bottom of the dimension of inequality. By measuring range such questions can be answered as how much richer the richest person is than the poorest person within a given economic system. Similar questions can be answered about positions in a political order or in a status system. The discussion of range of inequality focuses on persons. We are concerned especially with minimal amounts of status, power, and material resources, and the proportion of the system members who have less than each minimum.

Class. People living below a minimally sufficient standard are generally considered to be poor. This concept of poverty deals in absolute terms: Families with incomes below a specific amount of money are poor, regardless of their number or the income levels of other families. The U.S. government uses this concept of poverty to calculate the national poverty line. The Social Security Administration calculates the costs of minimal food requirements of families, varying with the number and ages of the family members. This figure is multiplied by three to establish minimal living standards for all consumption requirements. Farm family minimal subsistence expenses are 85 percent of nonfarm costs. These figures are adjusted annually to take into account changes in the cost of living. In 1975, the poverty line for a two-person family was $3,485 and for a four-person family, $5,469. For unrelated persons not in families, the figure was $2,717 (U.S. Bureau of the Census 1977a).

Rainwater (1974) and Ornati (1956) argue that such a subsistence standard is not enough for participation in the society and that a standard of minimal adequacy should be set. At whatever level, the available amount changes over time and from place to place. For example, our contemporary urban society is geared to the telephone and automobile and people without them have great difficulty in functioning (Tussing 1975). For over twenty years, the Gallup poll has been asking Americans "what is the smallest amount of money a family of four needs to get along in the community?" In 1946 Americans estimated that a family of four needed an annual income of $2,226, and by 1969 they estimated it took $6,225 to get along. In constant 1971 dollars, these estimates represent an increase from $4,615 in 1946 to $6,878 in 1969 (Rainwater 1974, pp. 52-53).

Miller and Roby (1970) argue that poverty should be defined in relative rather than only in absolute terms. According to this view, having an income below a minimal subsistence level is a possible way to define poverty, but it would be more socially meaningful to regard people who have incomes substantially less than the prevailing income to be defined as poor. One way to measure this is to calculate the country's median family income (the income level which divides the families of the country into two equal halves) and then consider 50 percent of that median income as the low income line. Thus, the median family income in the United States in 1975 was $13,719 and half of that is $6,859.50, so families with less than that have low income. There is evidence that people generally regard less than half of the median income to be "not enough to get along" (Rainwater 1974, p. 62). Students of poverty often regard less than half of the median income as low income and less than 40 percent of the median as poverty.

Whether measured in absolute or relative terms, poverty refers to less than the minimal amount of resources or goods—in this case, income. Measures of poverty can indicate one degree of inequality, for example, the percentage of the population who are poor. In 1975, using the measure of poverty developed by the Social Security Administration, 9.7 percent of all U.S. families wer poor; 12.3 percent of all persons were poor; 10.9 percent of all persons in families were poor; and 25.1 percent of all unrelated individuals were poor (U.S. Bureau of the Census 1977a, Table 7.17). The relative measure of poverty indicates a much larger percentage of the population as poor. In 1975, 19.7 percent of all families had incomes of less than half the median family income, and 14.1 percent of all families had less than 40 percent of the median family income (U.S. Bureau of the Census 1977b, Table 3).

Status. In discussing the range of status inequalities, minimal status as well as the overall range will again be considered. Since there is no clearly understood and easily calibrated currency to indicate degree of status, it is impossible to measure the height of status inequality. But we can compare social systems that differ greatly in range. In some systems, certain persons or positions are reviled and considered dirty and degraded, while others are revered, respected, and honored. Such gaps can exist in societies where whole groups are treated as pariahs. This relegation of people may or may not be part of a policy of genocide. In other societies, no groups or positions are reviled or regarded with contempt, just as none seem to be given great respect.

Related to the range of status differences is the idea of a minimal amount of status that is regarded as adequate by members of the social system. Individual persons may interpret this amount to be basic human dignity. Tumin and Feldman (1961), for example, report that in Puerto Rico, people share an ideology about *dignidad* ("worthiness"): Everyone is equally entitled to respect. The status accorded to positions also may differ among societies. In one society, for example, the major occupations may be regarded as honorable while in another society those same occupations may be considered ignoble. Thus, within Israeli Kibbutzim, manual farm labor is extolled while in other social systems it is considered degrading drudgery, to be escaped if possible.

Power. Power inequalities also vary in range. This is true for power exercised over others as well as freedom from power asserted by others. In some political orders—for example in totalitarian systems—persons in leading positions have almost total control over the actions of the collectivity as a whole and obtain obedience from others about a wide scope of matters. In other societies, none of the positions give persons a great amount of control over others. Similarly, societies vary in the degree to which persons have individual and group autonomy. This kind of control refers to defensive and exclusionary power rather than power *over* others. For individuals this power may consist in personal security and privacy; for a collectivity, it may be linguistic or cultural autonomy.[3]

[3] The idea of autonomy as separate from degree of control over others is, of course, an abstraction. In order to have autonomy over personal or group affairs, it is necessary to at least limit the conduct of others. In an interdependent system, this autonomy may require participation in the decision making for the entire system.

The extent of autonomy may be limited, extending only to the most personal and private matters, or it may be extensive and include a wide variety of behavior. As in the case of status, comparing the range in power inequalities over time or among political orders is extremely difficult, because there is no generally accepted measure of power. Nevertheless, some gross comparisons can be made.

Both kinds of power do seem to have levels that people recognize as minimally adequate. For example, voting in elections may be regarded as minimal participation in collective decision making. Or individual civil rights protecting persons from arbitrary arrest and personal harassment may be considered a minimally adequate standard of autonomy. These possibilities will be examined in detail in Chapters 7 and 8. Here it is sufficient to note that political orders differ in the proportion of their members who lack those minimal amounts of power.

Distribution

Two societies may have similar *ranges* of inequality, but the *distributions* of inequality may be quite different. In one society, most people may be near the upper end of the income range and in the other near the lower end. The distribution of status, power, and material resources is another important aspect of inequality. We now turn to consider variations in their distribution.

Class. In considering class inequalities, the focus will be on the distribution of income and wealth. One way to measure income distribution in a social system is to calculate the system's total income and see what percentage of that income is received by different segments of the population. For example, by computing the total income received by families in the United States in 1970, it is possible to determine how much of that income was received by the poorest 5, 10, or 20 percent of families as well as the proportion received by each of the next higher income groups. Income refers to money from all sources: wages, interest, profit, dividends, or other payments. But calculations often do not include income in kind or corporate earnings. Table 2.1 shows that in 1975 the poorest 20 percent of families received 5.4 percent of the total income as compared with 41.1 percent received by the richest 20 percent of families. As can be seen, the distribution of income is much more unequal for unrelated individuals than for families. [4] This difference is due to the fact that a large percentage of unrelated individuals are either very old or very young and tend to have low incomes.

The cumulative percentages of family income are portrayed in Figure 2.1, the curved line depicting the actual distribution of families. The straight diagonal line represents complete equality, wherein each percent of the population receives the same proportion of the total income. The area between the curved line

[4] *Family* refers to a group of two or more persons related by marriage, blood, or adoption and residing in the same household. *Unrelated individuals* refers to persons (not in institutions) not living with any relatives.

TABLE 2.1 Percentage of Aggregate Income Received by Each
Fifth and by the Highest 5 Percent of Families and
Unrelated Individuals, 1975

	Families	*Families and Unrelated Individuals*
Lowest fifth	5.4	3.9
Second fifth	11.8	9.9
Middle fifth	17.6	16.7
Fourth fifth	24.1	24.9
Highest fifth	41.1	44.5
(Highest 5 percent)	(15.5)	(17.0)
	100.0	100.0

Source: U.S. Bureau of the Census, 1977b, Tables 3 and 13.

and the straight diagonal divided by the total area under the diagonal is the Gini
Index (Miller 1971, Appendix B), which is often used as a single summary
measure for the degree of inequality. Although it theoretically varies from 0.0
to 1.0, no society could be close to 1.0 or 0.0. The smaller the index, the less
the inequality. In Figure 2.1, the Gini Index is 0.335.

Whether this figure represents too much or too little inequality depends

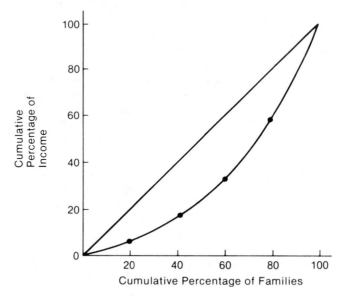

FIGURE 2.1 *Distribution of Family Income, 1975*

Source: U.S. Bureau of the Census, 1977b, Tables 3 and 13.

on one's standards and expectations. For such a number to be meaningful in itself, comparisons must be made of degrees of inequality in different places and at different times. Chapters 3 and 4 undertake this task.

People derive most of their income in the United States from their occupations. Consequently, we need to know about the range and distribution of income associated with occupation roles if we are to understand income inequality among persons. The U.S. census provides some basic information—for example, in 1970, 14 percent of the male civilian labor force were in professional, technical, and similar occupations and the median earnings for this group was $10,735 in 1969. This percent included draftsmen and surveyors, who earned $8,415 as well as aeronautical and astronautical engineers, whose median earnings totaled $14,766 (U.S. Bureau of the Census 1976, Table 589). Seven percent were sales workers with median earnings of $8,451. Fourteen percent were operatives and had median earnings of $6,730.

The median earnings for most occupations represent a wide range of earnings. Jencks et al. (1973, p. 226) have calculated that if income differences were eliminated among occupations but remained unchanged within them, income inequality would be reduced by only one-fifth. However, if income differences among occupations remained the same but were eliminated within them, income inequality would be reduced by about 40 percent.

The annual salary survey made by *New York Magazine* gives some idea of the wide range of earnings among occupations (Allen 1977). In 1976, for example, the salary and bonus of Harold Geneen, chief executive of ITT amounted to $846,398; the salary of a telephone operator at the International Hotel was $6,292. An assistant professor of political science at Yale earned $14,750, whereas an English teacher in a New York high school earned $20,350. While a rewrite man for the Associated Press made $11,700, a *New York Times* reporter and free-lance writer earned $37,000. The salary of *New York Times* columnist and director, James Reston was $54,400. Similar differences in income are evident in the sports, entertainment, and business worlds; indeed, nearly every occupation shows a great range in income.

Inequalities in wealth refer to those in the financial assets, property, and valuables owned by individuals or groups. Wealth is much more unequally distributed than income, and is both a basis for and a result of income inequalities. It is even more difficult to obtain complete and accurate information about wealth than it is about income. The value of many assets may not be reported to reflect current market value. Ownership by minors and spouses or other family members may obscure the concentration of ownership. However, some data on the distribution of wealth in the United States is available.

In 1962, the Federal Reserve Board made a survey of the ownership of all private assets in the United States. Table 2.2 presents data drawn from that study. The findings show that the wealthiest 0.3 percent of the consumer units in the United States owned 22 percent of the country's wealth. This 0.3 percent

TABLE 2.2   Distribution of Wealth by Consumer Units, 1962

Size of Wealth	Number of Households (in millions)	Percentage of Households	Percentage of Wealth
Negative	1.0	1.7	
Zero	4.7	8.1	
$ 1-999	9.0	15.5	
$ 1,000-4,999	10.8	18.6	2.0
$ 5,000-9,999	9.1	15.7	5.0
$ 10,000-24,999	13.3	23.0	18.0
$ 25,000-49,999	6.2	10.7	18.0
$ 50,000-99,999	2.5	4.3	14.0
$100,000-199,999	.7	1.2	8.0
$200,000-499,999	.5	.9	13.0
$500,000 and over	.2	.3	22.0
All units	57.9	100.0	100.0

Source: Projector and Weiss 1966, Tables A16 and A36.

of households were the 200,000 units with assets of $500,000 or more in 1962 dollars. If we add together all consumer units with assets of $25,000 or more, we can see that the wealthiest 17 percent of households owned 75 percent of all private assets. At the other extreme, 10 percent of the households did not have assets that exceeded their debts, and 25 percent of the households possessed less than 1 percent of the total wealth of the country.

Status. Without an easily calibrated standard, such as money, it is difficult to summarize the distribution of status within a social system. The status associated with occupational positions, however, has been studied so extensively that the social rank of occupations is relatively clear. These studies yield prestige scores which provide a fairly precise metric. This makes it easier to study the status of occupational positions than of many other kinds of positions or of kinds of persons. Occupational prestige is also worth examining because occupational status has a great impact upon how people relate to each other, as incumbents of occupational positions, and even how they regard themselves.

There is general but not complete agreement about the relative rankings of occupational positions. Many studies have been done comparing ranking among different kinds of people, and the results have been similar. Furthermore, studies have been made of occupational prestige that provide scores for each occupational position. The results of these studies provides information about the distribution of occupational status in the United States.

The most notable study of occupational prestige was done in 1947 by the National Opinion Research Center (NORC). Respondents throughout the country were asked to rate ninety occupations (Reiss 1961). Each respondent was asked to judge an occupation as having an "excellent," a "good," an "average," a "somewhat below average," or a "poor" standing (or could give a "don't know" rating) when presented with this statement: "For each job mentioned, please pick out the statement that best gives *your own personal opinion* of the *general standing* that such a job has."

The NORC prestige score for each occupation is derived by assigning a numerical value to each rating and averaging the result. Thus, an "excellent" rating was given a value of 100; a "good" rating, 80; an "average" rating, 60; a "somewhat below average" rating, 40; and a "poor" rating, 20. The responses of all the respondents were averaged together to yield the NORC prestige scores. On this basis, if all the respondents rated an occupation as 'average," the NORC prestige score would be 60. The results of the 1947 survey, and its 1963 replication, are presented in Table 2.3. Later sections will examine the changes and continuities in the scores between those two surveys, and at several points in the book these data will be used as sources for analyzing status inequality. Here, we will consider how these data can be used to describe the distribution of occupational status in the United States.

Although respondents were asked to rate ninety occupations, those occupations accounted for less than half the U.S. labor force. Otis Dudley Duncan devised a method of scoring all occupations reported in the census (Reiss 1961). He used information on the education and income of the people in each occupation to construct a socioeconomic index. This index is closely correlated with the NORC prestige scores ($r = 0.91$) and therefore is often used when researchers want to assign an occupational prestige score to a sample of individuals. The calculation of the socioeconomic index for all occupations also makes it possible to determine the distribution of occupational status for persons in the labor force.

In Table 2.4 the U.S. male labor force is distributed in terms of the socioeconomic index. The average index value of about 30 is clearly at the lower end of the 0-99 range. About one-third of the male labor force have scores in the 10-19 stratum. The mode of the population, then, is above the lowest stratum but below the middle of the range, after which the labor force stretches out in declining proportions to the highest statuses.

Power. The difficulties in describing the distribution of power are even greater than in describing status distribution and we are able to make only broad comparisons. Drawing upon the vast literature on different forms of governing and on variations in participation, control, and interests served, we will focus on those topics most pertinent to the central concerns of this book. We will concentrate, here, on relative control over decisions concerning the collectivity as a whole and on the state—the central government claiming sovereignty.

In all countries with sovereign governments, the power to make decisions pertaining to the political order as a whole is vested in certain positions. These positions vary in number from one to many—from an absolute monarch to many

TABLE 2.3 Distributions of Prestige Ratings, United States, 1947 and 1963

Occupation	March, 1947		June, 1963							
	NORC Score	Rank	Excellent[a] (%)	Good (%)	Average (%)	Below Average (%)	Poor (%)	Don't Know[b] (%)	NORC Score	Rank
U.S. Supreme Court Justice	96	1	77	18	4	1	1	1	94	1
Physician	93	2.5	71	25	4	*	*	1	93	2
Nuclear physicist	86	18	70	23	5	1	1	10	92	3.5
Scientist	89	8	68	27	5	*	*	2	92	3.5
Government scientist	88	10.5	64	30	5	*	1	2	91	5.5
State governor	93	2.5	64	30	5	*	1	1	91	5.5
Cabinet member in the Federal Government	92	4.5	61	32	6	1	1	2	90	8
College professor	89	8	59	35	5	*	*	1	90	8
U.S. representative in Congress	89	8	58	33	6	2	*	2	90	8
Chemist	86	18	54	38	8	*	*	3	89	11
Lawyer	86	18	53	38	8	*	*	*	89	11
Diplomat in the U.S. Foreign Service	92	4.5	57	34	7	1	1	3	89	11
Dentist	86	18	47	47	6	*	*	*	88	14
Architect	86	18	47	45	6	*	*	2	88	14
County judge	87	13	50	40	8	1	*	1	88	14
Psychologist	85	22	49	41	8	1	*	6	87	17.5
Minister	87	13	53	33	13	1	1	1	87	17.5
Member of the board of directors of a large corporation	86	18	42	51	6	1	*	1	87	17.5
Mayor of a large city	90	6	46	44	9	1	1	*	87	17.5
Priest	86	18	52	33	12	2	1	6	86	21.5

TABLE 2.3 Distributions of Prestige Ratings, United States, 1947 and 1963 (continued)

Occupation	March, 1947 NORC Score	March, 1947 Rank	June, 1963 Excellent[a] (%)	Good (%)	Average (%)	Below Average (%)	Poor (%)	Don't Know[b] (%)	NORC Score	Rank
Head of a department in a state government	87	13	44	48	6	1	1	1	86	21.5
Civil engineer	84	23	40	52	8	*	*	2	86	21.5
Airline pilot	83	24.5	41	48	11	1	*	1	86	21.5
Banker	88	10.5	39	51	10	1	*	*	85	24.5
Biologist	81	29	38	50	11	*	*	6	85	24.5
Sociologist	82	26.5	35	48	15	1	1	10	83	26
Instructor in public schools	79	34	30	53	16	1	*	*	82	27.5
Captain in the regular army	80	31.5	28	55	16	2	*	1	82	27.5
Accountant for a large business	81	29	27	55	17	1	*	*	81	29.5
Public school teacher	78	36	31	46	22	1	*	*	81	29.5
Owner of a factory that employs about 100 people	82	26.5	28	49	19	2	1	1	80	31.5
Building contractor	79	34	22	56	20	1	*	*	80	31.5
Artist who paints pictures that are exhibited in galleries	83	24.5	28	45	20	5	2	4	78	34.5
Musician in a symphony orchestra	81	29	25	45	25	3	1	3	78	34.5
Author of novels	80	31.5	26	46	22	4	2	5	78	34.5
Economist	79	34	20	53	24	2	1	12	78	34.5
Official of an international labor union	75	40.5	21	53	18	5	3	5	77	37

TABLE 2.3 Distribution of Prestige Ratings, United States, 1947 and 1963 (continued)

	March, 1947		June, 1963							
Occupation	NORC Score	Rank	Excellent[a] (%)	Good (%)	Average (%)	Below Average (%)	Poor (%)	Don't Know[b] (%)	NORC Score	Rank
Railroad engineer	77	37.5	19	47	30	3	1	1	76	39
Electrician	73	45	18	45	34	2	*	*	76	39
County agricultural agent	77	37.5	13	54	30	2	1	4	76	39
Owner-operator of a printing shop	74	42.5	13	51	34	2	*	2	75	41.5
Trained machinist	73	45	15	50	32	4	*	*	75	41.5
Farm owner and operator	76	39	16	45	33	5	*	1	74	44
Undertaker	72	47	16	46	33	3	2	3	74	44
Welfare worker for a city government	73	45	17	44	32	5	2	2	74	44
Newspaper columnist	74	42.5	10	49	38	3	1	1	73	45
Policeman	67	55	16	38	37	6	2	*	72	47
Reporter on a daily newspaper	71	48	7	45	44	3	1	1	71	48
Radio announcer	75	40.5	9	42	44	5	1	1	70	49.5
Bookkeeper	68	51.5	9	40	45	5	1	*	70	49.5
Tenant farmer—one who owns livestock and machinery and manages the farm	68	51.5	11	37	42	8	3	1	69	51.5
Insurance agent	68	51.5	6	40	47	5	2	*	69	51.5
Carpenter	65	58	7	36	49	8	1	*	68	53
Manager of a small store in a city	69	49	3	40	48	7	2	*	67	54.5
A local official of a labor union	62	62	8	36	42	9	5	4	67	54.5

TABLE 2.3 Distributions of Prestige Ratings, United States, 1947 and 1963 (continued)

Occupation	March, 1947 NORC Score	Rank	June, 1963 Excellent[a] (%)	Good (%)	Average (%)	Below Average (%)	Poor (%)	Don't Know[b] (%)	NORC Score	Rank
Traveling concern wholesale concern	68	51.5	4	33	54	7	3	2	66	57
Mail carrier	66	57	7	29	53	10	1	*	66	57
Railroad	67	55	6	33	48	10	3	*	66	57
Plumber	63	59.5	6	29	54	9	2	*	65	59
Automobile repairman	63	59.5	5	25	56	12	2	*	64	60
Playground director	67	55	6	29	46	15	4	3	63	62.5
Barber	59	66	4	25	56	13	2	1	63	62.5
Machine operator in a factory	60	64.5	6	24	51	15	4	1	63	62.5
Owner-operator of a lunch stand	62	62	4	25	57	11	3	1	63	62.5
Corporal in the regular army	60	64.5	6	25	47	15	6	2	62	65.5
Garage mechanic	62	62	4	22	56	15	3	*	62	65.5
Truck driver	54	71	3	18	54	19	5	*	59	67
Fisherman who owns his own boat	58	68	3	19	51	19	8	4	58	68
Clerk in a store	58	68	1	14	56	22	6	*	56	70
Milk route man	54	71	3	12	55	23	7	1	56	70
Streetcar motorman	57	68	3	16	46	27	8	2	56	70
Lumberjack	53	73	2	16	46	29	7	3	55	72.5
Restaurant cook	54	71	4	15	44	26	11	*	55	72.5
Singer in a nightclub	52	74.5	3	16	43	24	14	3	54	74
Filling station attendant	52	74.5	2	11	41	34	11	*	51	75
Dockworker	47	81.5	2	9	43	33	14	3	50	77.5
Railroad section hand	48	79.5	3	10	39	29	18	2	50	77.5
Night watchman	47	81.5	3	10	39	32	17	1	50	77.5
Coal miner	49	77.5	3	13	34	31	19	2	50	77.5

TABLE 2.3 Distributions of Prestige Ratings, United States, 1947 and 1963 (continued)

| | March, 1947 | | June, 1963 | | | | | | | |
	NORC Score	Rank	Excellent[a] (%)	Good (%)	Average (%)	Below Average (%)	Poor (%)	Don't Know[b] (%)	NORC Score	Rank
Occupation										
Restaurant waiter	48	79.5	2	8	42	32	16	*	49	80.5
Taxi driver	49	77.5	2	8	39	31	18	1	49	80.5
Farm hand	50	76	3	12	31	32	22	*	48	83
Janitor	44	85.5	1	9	35	35	19	1	48	83
Bartender	44	85.5	1	7	42	28	21	2	48	83
Clothes presser in a laundry	46	83	2	7	31	38	22	1	45	85
Soda fountain clerk	45	84	*	5	30	44	20	1	44	86
Sharecropper—one who owns no livestock or equipment and does not manage farm	40	87	1	8	26	28	37	2	42	87
Garbage collector	35	88	2	5	21	32	41	1	39	88
Street sweeper	34	89	1	4	17	31	46	1	36	89
Shoe shiner	33	90	*	3	15	30	51	2	34	90
Average	70		22%	32%	29%	11%	6%	2%	71	

*One-half of one percent.
[a] Bases for the 1963 occupational ratings are 651 less "don't know" and not answered for each occupational title.
[b] Base is 651 in all cases.
Source: Hodge, Siegel, and Rossi 1966, Table 1.

TABLE 2.4 Distribution of Socioeconomic Index for U.S. Male
Experienced Labor Force, 1950

Socioeconomic Index	Approximate NORC Score	Number (in millions)	Percentage
0-9	Less than 48	6.3	15.0
10-19	48-58	14.2	33.9
20-29	59-63	4.5	10.8
30-39	64-67	4.8	11.4
40-49	68-70	3.9	9.3
50-59	71-73	2.4	5.6
60-69	74-76	2.8	6.7
70-79	77-81	1.6	3.8
80-89	82-85	1.1	2.5
90-99	86 or more	0.4	1.0
Totals		42.1	100.0

Source: Reiss 1972, Tables VII-3 and B-1.

members of the legislature and executive offices. The number of positions, however, is always smaller than the population as a whole. What is even more crucial in describing the distribution of power is the scope of decision-making authority incumbents of these positions have, their responsiveness and the accountability to which they are subject. Thus, in some countries government decisions may have limited scope; they may not pertain to many spheres of life that are regarded as private or beyond the range of government control. Government officeholders also vary in the degree to which they respond to directives from the entire population or from certain groups within the collectivity.

Such variations can be seen in written rules or constitutions. But there may be vast differences between written law and people's behavior. It is therefore as important to examine how persons fulfill positions as officeholders, voters, subjects, or rulers as it is to know the rights and obligations of the positions.

At present in the United States, power in making collective decisions is vested primarily in the major offices of the federal government: the presidency, Congress, secretaries and staffs of executive departments, and the Supreme Court. The power of these offices is circumscribed by limits on the scope of decisions. The limits are greatest in the realm of personal affairs and family life; invasions of those spheres are usually considered to be illegitimate. There are fewer limits on the right to commit the collectivity as a whole to particular courses of public action. The major constraints on this power is the presumed consensus and especially the concurrence of persons in other major government offices. Important government decisions require coordinating the views of the incumbents of many federal offices. Reaching agreement on U.S. policy sometimes requires more negotiation and more effort than implementing the decision.

The incumbents of these offices are also varyingly accountable and even responsive to nonofficeholders—to voters. In general, elections are inducements for political leaders to pursue policies they think the public prefers. Not everyone in the public, however, is equal in class and status resources useful to officeseekers, for example, to win elections. Consequently, officeholders tend to be more responsive to the preferences of persons with high class and status ranks, such as executives of large corporations, than to preferences of persons with lower ranks, such as retail sales clerks.

How many government offices have autonomous decision-making roles and just how much influence or control various nongovernmental elites have are matters of considerable debate. Alternative views of power distribution in the United States are presented in Figure 2.2. In model A, almost all citizens are throught to have very little power, and only a small group, the incumbents of the commanding positions, have power; there is a unified power elite (Mills 1956). In model B, a vast majority of the people are thought to have little power in making collective decisions, but many groups also have considerable power; they contend with and balance each other and may even veto each other (Rose 1967). In model C, political power is much more equal; nearly all citizens participate significantly in making collective decisions, and few persons have a great deal more power than anyone else.

The distribution of power for persons is also affected by the structures by which people enter and leave positions of political authority. In the United States, as in most modern countries, the political party system is central in this regard. Through the political parties and the factions within each party, the "outs" become the "ins." In addition, parties and factions provide alternative

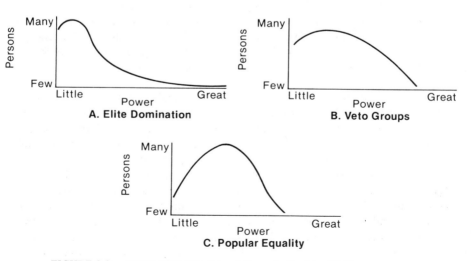

FIGURE 2.2   *Types of Distribution of Power in Decision Making*

policies and a basis for power. An organized group of people is the basis for power. Parties are the most relevant organization for political power. Even when out of office, parties represent the possibility of replacing incumbents; they provide a basis for resistance; and they are a vehicle for communication and cooperation with others. Although political equality is difficult to measure, the existence of more than one effective party, the explicitness of factions within parties, the election procedures and their frequency are indicators of the degree of political equality.

Assessing relative power inequality is formidable when comparing political systems; the ways of exercising influence and control vary considerably, assessments of their effectiveness are doubtful, and there is little agreement about which components of participation are most significant. Another way to measure political equality is to ask people within a political system how much control they believe they have concerning various kinds of collective decisions. For example, in 1959 and 1960, a sample of persons in the United States, Great Britain, Germany, Italy, and Mexico were asked to assume that a law was being considered by their national legislatures and that they thought it unjust or harmful (Almond and Verba 1963, p. 185). They were then asked if they believed they could do something to prevent passage of the law. Seventy-five percent of the Americans thought they could do something about it; 62 percent of the British, 38 percent of the Germans and Mexicans, and 28 percent of the Italians gave the same responses. They were also asked what consideration they thought they would get if they brought a question to a government office. Of the U.S. sample, 48 percent thought they would receive serious consideration, as did 59 percent of the Britons, 53 percent of the Germans, and 35 percent of the Italians; only 14 percent of the Mexicans gave this response. Of course, these indications are influenced by people's personal attitudes as well as by the political system within which they live. But used cautiously, such indicators give some idea of the degree of government responsiveness and popular control (Davis and Coleman 1975). This inference is supported by the finding that in each country, feelings of effectiveness were greater about local regulations than about national regulations, and it is reasonable to believe that such differences reflect reality and not simply personal feelings.

Mobility

The third aspect of inequality to be considered is mobility (Sorokin 1959). Mobility sometimes refers to changes in the ranking of positions or groups of persons within a hierarchy of inequality. Thus, an occupational group may try and even succeed in raising its status by becoming a "profession." Such movements will be referred to as changes in distribution or range of inequality. Mobility will refer to the movement of people along a ranked dimension. This movement may reflect changes in income or wealth from one year to the next or from one generation to the next. Mobility can also refer to persons moving into and out of ranked positions. This movement may occur within a single life career as well as from one generation to the next; thus we can study the extent to which people have the same occupational status throughout their careers or the extent to which their status is the same as that of their parents.

"Equality of opportunity" refers to the likelihood of persons at one level moving to another. Usually it means the probability of children of each rank having the same chance as children in other ranks to enter a higher or lower stratum as adults. Equality of opportunity is analytically distinct from equality of outcome, although empirically they may be related.

Class. To illustrate class mobility, we will examine income changes from one year to the next. Although data are sparse on intergenerational changes some information is becoming available on changes in family income on a longitudinal basis over a year's time (Kriesberg 1970).[5] Table 2.5 presents information on the changes in families' income between 1967 and 1968. The families are categorized in deciles, and for each rank in 1967, the proportion is shown that remained in the same rank or that changed in 1968. Thus, in 1967 families earning less than $1,976 were the poorest 10 percent of families. Of those families, 69 percent were still among the poorest 10 percent in 1968; and 31 percent moved into higher income ranks. Similarly, among the highest income decile, almost 40 percent of families were in lower-ranking deciles a year later. Aside from these top and bottom deciles, with their limits on movement, 60 to 70 percent of the families in each decile moved in one year. These figures indicate considerable movement, but it should be noted that much of it is due to changes in family composition, for example, as children establish families of their own and as parents divorce (Smith and Morgan 1970).

Status. When discussing status mobility, the possibility of no mobility must be considered. Status rank is *ascribed* when it is determined at birth and cannot be altered. Where ethnic or sexual differences are the basis for status ranking, they are usually ascribed, and movement can occur only with great difficulty. Status rankings also may be *achieved.* When mobility is possible—as in movement into different occupational or life-style statuses—the distinction between ascribed and achieved status is important. The distinction should not be regarded as absolute, however, for there are degrees of ascription and achievement in actual status dimensions.

The mixture of ascription and achievement can be seen in intergenerational occupational mobility. The study of mobility usually focuses on the extent to which children inherit occupational status from their parents or differ from their parents in this respect. Studies of intergenerational occupational mobility are usually based on surveys in which a sample of adult men are asked about

[5] The National Opinion Research Center conducts a General Social Survey annually, and respondents in a national sample were asked about current family income and their parent's income. These data will be presented in Chapter 3.

TABLE 2.5 Decile Rank of Families by Total Money Income, 1967-68

Decile Rank, 1967 Income		$2,199	$3,619	$5,069	$6,499	$7,874	$9,399	$10,999	$13,099	$16,859		
		0	1	2	3	4	5	6	7	8	9	Percentage
$ 1,976	0	69.2%	17.7%	4.5%	4.3%	2.7%	.4%	.6%	.4%	.7%	.1%	100.0
$ 3,219	1	19.2	43.9	20.6	8.4	3.5	1.6	1.4	.7			100.0
$ 4,649	2	6.7	22.5	37.2	15.3	8.4	5.2	2.0	2.1	.1	.5	100.0
$ 5,999	3	1.9	5.6	17.8	38.1	21.2	7.4	4.8	1.1	.6	1.5	100.0
$ 7,206	4	1.5	5.7	9.6	19.6	29.7	19.3	7.6	3.9	2.5	.6	100.0
$ 8,602	5	1.4	2.3	3.6	8.1	19.2	34.6	22.4	5.1	1.8	1.6	100.0
$10,175	6	.7	1.3	2.7	3.2	7.8	19.1	34.9	20.3	7.7	2.3	100.0
$11,999	7	.7	.7	.3	.7	4.2	4.9	16.9	40.9	22.6	8.1	100.0
$14,389	8	.7	1.0	2.3	2.0	2.4	3.6	8.6	19.9	43.3	16.1	100.0
	9	.6	1.2	1.9	1.7	2.5	5.1	1.4	4.6	17.5	63.5	100.0

Source: Smith and Morgan 1970, Table 1.

their occupations and those of their fathers. Questions about the father's occupation can refer to different times in the son's or father's life. A question may ask about his father's main occupation or about his father's occupation when the son was at a particular age. The wording of the question reflects different research interests and concerns. Thus, asking about the father's occupational status when the son was entering the labor market or college would indicate an interest in the degree to which family origins limit or channel future occupational achievement. To the degree that the experiences, opportunities, discriminations, and expectations of others determine choices at that stage, occupational status has an ascriptive quality.

Power. Mobility of persons into and out of offices with political authority also can be viewed within a person's career or intergenerationally. In political systems with great power vested in a monarch, there is obviously strong intergenerational continuities in political power. Because royal families and dynasties ascribe power, there is little or no intergenerational or lifetime mobility.

In less ascriptive political systems, power mobility is measured in terms of the turnover rate in elected offices and the degree to which changes are the outcome of regular electoral activities. Research usually has been concerned more with characterizing a political system than with analyzing the mobility of persons or families within it. But insofar as researchers have studied movement into and out of political office by persons, the focus has been on the types of people who hold office—their class origins, current class rank, and status.

CONCLUSIONS

We have looked at several of the many ways in which persons and positions vary in their inequality. It is important to keep this multiplicity in mind. People can be very unequal in some ways and not in others.

Similarly, social systems may be very unequal in one dimension and relatively equal in another and somewhat more equal in one aspect of a dimension than in another. Thus, the data presented in this chapter indicate that wealth is more unequally distributed in the U.S. than is income. Although there are great distances between the positions at the top and the bottom of the power and class dimensions, equality seems greater when we note that most people have more than minimal levels of power and material privileges. We saw that many families change income strata within a year, and it seems reasonable to assume that income mobility is greater than is status mobility.

But the dimensions of inequality and variations within each are not equally important. Keeping in mind their multiplicity, we must also try to understand which ones are most significant—which ones affect the others and have the greatest consequences for society generally. Karl Marx argued that the nature of society was determined primarily by class inequalities. Although this assertion may be true in certain circumstances and at particular times in history, it may not always apply.

One way to think about how these various aspects of inequality fit together and shape each other is to consider different types of stratification systems. Among the major types of stratification systems are the caste, estate, and industrial class systems.

A *caste system*, the traditional form of stratification in India, places great importance on status differences. The highest caste claims religious superiority and avoids contact with the lower castes and with outcastes to avoid defilement. Class and power differences tend to coincide. The range in status, power, and class inequalities is great. There is little mobility, although some subcastes do try to alter their rank within the system and persons are sometimes reduced from their caste level if they deviate from the ritual requirements of their caste. On the whole, caste placement is ascriptive, and marriage is restricted to within the caste. The caste system of India is discussed in more detail in chapter 6.

The *estate system* was prevalent in feudal Europe. Estates were strata with rights and privileges that were more clearly bounded than those in modern industrial societies but less rigid than those in the caste system. Power differences were particularly important and depended on violence or the threat of violence; the nobles were warriors (Bloch 1961). The levels of society were bound together by ties of vassalage. The more powerful lords provided protection and apportioned a certain share of what was produced by others on their land. Power inequalities were highly correlated with class inequalities, and both were highly related to status inequalities. Obligations and rights were diffuse and associated with estate position.

Industrial societies are often characterized as having a *class system*. That is, class inequalities are predominant and are determined by a variety of commodity and labor markets. Class differences underlie power and status inequalities. Even social relations are shaped by class rankings, for example, social interaction between persons in different classes tend to be specific to the transactions involved and do not entail relating with the whole person. There are, however, significant variations in industrial stratification systems, particularly between capitalist and socialist societies. In advanced capitalist countries, such as the United States, class differences are closely related to power inequalities, with the rich having great political power. Status differences are not primary in shaping the society's social structure, although they are important in the formation of the social elite and are fundamental in regard to inequalities related to sex and race. Intergenerational mobility, particularly in class and power dimensions, is not high by the standard of complete equality of opportunity, but it probably is greater in advanced capitalist societies than many other kinds of stratification systems. The range of inequality in class and power is considerable, if measured against an absolute standard of equality, but it probably is less than in some preindustrial societies. Moreover, most members of the societies generally have at least minimal class and power privileges.

In socialist societies, such as the USSR, power inequalities are particularly important. The political party that controls the state dominates and structures class differences, since the economy is centrally planned and is controlled by the government. Class mobility is probably no less, and perhaps more, than in capitalist societies. Power tends to be very unequally distributed, and many people lack certain aspects of minimal political autonomy. Ideological efforts may be directed to reduce the range of status inequality, for example, among occupations or by sex. These efforts may be more successful for individuals than for large groups and collectivities seeking autonomy and status equality.

There are, of course, great variations among contemporary societies characterized as welfare capitalist or state socialist; countries vary in the degree of emphasis placed on welfare and in the degree of economic control exercised by the state. There are also variations in the distribution, mobility, and range of class, power, and status inequalities. These variations are the essence of many contemporary struggles. The chapters that follow examine these variations, their consequences, and their determinants.

REFERENCES

ALLEN, FREDERICK. 1977. "The Sixth Annual Salary Survey," *New York Magazine*, May 9, 42-47.

ALMOND, GABRIEL A. and SIDNEY VERBA. 1963. *The Civic Culture*. Princeton, N.J.: Princeton University Press.

BARBER, BERNARD. 1959. *Social Stratification*, New York: Harcourt, Brace and Company.

BERLE, ADOLF A., JR. and GARDINER MEANS. 1933. *The Modern Corporation and Private Property*. New York: Macmillan.

BLAU, PETER M. 1964. *Exchange and Power in Social Life*. New York: John Wiley.

BLOCH, MARC. 1961. *Feudal Society*. Chicago: University of Chicago Press.

BURNHAM, JAMES. 1941. *The Managerial Revolution*. New York: John Day.

DAHRENDORF, RALF. 1959. *Class and Class Conflict in Industrial Society*. Stanford: Stanford University Press.

DAVIS, CHARLES L. and KENNETH M. COLEMAN. 1975. "Political Symbols, Political Efficacy and Diffuse Support for the Mexican Political System," *Journal of Political and Military Sociology*, 3 (Spring): 27-42.

GERTH, H. H. and C. WRIGHT MILLS (Eds.). 1946. *From Max Weber: Essays in Sociology*. New York: Oxford University Press.

GORDON, ROBERT AARON. 1945. *Business Leadership in the Large Corporation*. Washington, D.C.: The Brookings Institution.

HODGE, R. W., PAUL M. SIEGEL, and PETER H. ROSSI. 1964. "Occupational Prestige in the United States," *American Journal of Sociology* 70 (Nov.), 286-302.

HOROWITZ, IRVING LOUIS. 1972. *Three Worlds of Development*, 2nd Ed. New York: Oxford University Press.

JENCKS, CHRISTOPHER, MARSHALL SMITH, HENRY ACLAND, MARY JO BANE, DAVID COHEN, HERBERT GINTIS, BARBARA HEYNS, and

STEPHAN MICHELSON. 1973. *Inequality: A Reassessment of the Effect of Family and Schooling in America*. New York: Harper & Row.

KOLKO, GABRIEL. 1962. *Wealth and Power in America*. New York: Praeger.

KRIESBERG, LOUIS. 1970. *Mothers in Poverty*. Chicago: Aldine.

LAGOS, GUSTAVE. 1963. *International Stratification and Underdeveloped Countries*. Chapel Hill: The University of North Carolina Press.

MARX, KARL. 1960. *Capital: A Critique of Political Economy*. Chicago: Charles Kerr. (Originally published in 1867.)

MILLER, HERMAN P. 1971. *Rich Man, Poor Man*. New York: Thomas Y. Crowell.

MILLER, S. M. and PAMELA ROBY. 1970. *The Future of Inequality*. New York: Basic Books.

MILLS, C. WRIGHT. 1956. *The Power Elite*. New York: Oxford University Press.

ORNATI, OSCAR. 1956. *Poverty Amid Affluence*. New York: Twentieth Century Fund.

PARSONS, TALCOTT. 1969. *Politics and Social Structure*. New York: Free Press.

PROJECTOR, DOROTHY and GERTRUDE WEISS. 1966. *Survey of Financial Characteristics of Consumers*. Washington D.C.: Federal Reserve System.

RAINWATER, LEE. 1975. *What Money Buys: Inequality and the Social Meaning of Income*. New York: Basic Books.

REISS, ALBERT J., JR. 1961. *Occupations and Social Status*. New York: Free Press.

ROSE, ARNOLD M. 1967. *The Power Structure: Political Process in American Society*. New York: Oxford University Press.

SHARP, GENE. 1973. *The Politics of Nonviolent Action*. Boston: Porter Sargent Publisher.

SMITH, JAMES D. and JAMES W. MORGAN. 1970. "Dynamics of Income Distribution: Poverty and Progress," *American Economic Review*, 60 (May) 286-295.

SOROKIN, PITIRIM A. 1959. *Social and Cultural Mobility*. Glencoe, Illinois: Free Press (Reprint of *Social Mobility* originally published in 1927).

TUCKER, ROBERT C. 1972. *The Marx-Engels Reader*. New York: W. W. Norton. (Reprint of *The German Ideology*, originally published in 1846).

TUMIN, MELVIN M. with ARNOLD FELDMAN. 1961. *Social Class and Social Change in Puerto Rico*. Princeton, N.J.: Princeton University Press.

TUSSING, A. DALE. 1971. *Poverty in a Dual Economy*. New York: St. Martin's Press.

U.S. BUREAU OF THE CENSUS, 1977a. Current Population Reports, P-60, No. 106, "Characteristics of the Population Below the Poverty Level, 1975." Washington, D.C.: Government Printing Office.

U.S. BUREAU OF THE CENSUS. 1977b. Current Population Reports, P - 60 No. 105, "Money Income in 1975 of Families and Persons in the United States." Washington, D.C.: Government Printing Office.

U.S. BUREAU OF THE CENSUS. 1976. *Statistical Abstract of the United States: 1976*. 9th Ed. Washington, D.C.: Government Printing Office.

WALLIMAN, ISIDOR and HOWARD ROSENBAUM, NICHOLAS CH. TATSIS, and GEORGE V. ZITO. 1977. "Misreading Weber: Abuses of the Concept of 'Macht'." Syracuse University: Unpublished Paper.

WARNER, W. LLOYD and PAUL S. LUNT. 1941. *The Social Life of a Modern Community*. New Haven, Conn.: Yale University Press.

WILEY, NORBERT F. 1967. "America's Unique Class Politics: The Interplay of Labor, Credit and Commodities Market," *American Sociological Review* 32 (August): 529-541.

PART II

Variations in Inequality

chapter 3

American Class Variations

We should measure the prosperity of a nation
not by the number of millionaires—but by
the absence of poverty.   *W. E. B. DuBois*

The aspects of class inequality discussed in Chapter 2 can vary in a number of ways. A comparison of the income distribution in the United States over the last thirty years and of the distribution in different social systems will indicate what variations are likely to occur. This information makes it possible to explain or account for inequality. If we know why inequality varies, we can more readily maintain or change it.

Chapter 3 begins by reviewing the available information on variations in the range, distribution, and mobility of class inequality. These variations are examined as they have occurred in U.S. history, particularly in recent decades. Chapter 4 reviews the current situation in other social systems. Although the discussion of variations will touch on such related topics as ideologies, level of economic development, and government actions, no systematic theoretical accounting of variations will be undertaken until Chapters 11 and 12.

The question of whether the United States is getting more or less equal is a topic of continuing debate. Marx predicted that under capitalism the proletariat would become increasingly impoverished or, as some interpreters infer, worse off relative to the capitalists. Some contemporaries contend that while the material standard of living has risen for everyone, the relative income and wealth has remained unchanged. Others claim that the poor have benefited relative to the rest of the society while still others assert that the middle class has gained most. There also are differing views on the rate of mobility and on changes in those rates. These continuing debates indicate that the facts are ambiguous. Due to the limited data, investigators have had to be ingenious in using information to reconstruct relevant and comparable data for past years. Consequently, researchers can easily disagree about the assumptions made in such reconstructions. Furthermore, since people ask different questions, they are bound to disagree about which facts are relevant. We will ask one question at a time and be explicit and precise about the evidence relevant to providing answers.

RANGE

To answer the question, "has the proportion of Americans living in poverty been declining?" it is necessary to clarify what is meant by poverty and to be specific about the time periods being compared. It is inappropriate to define poverty in terms of current standards and use the same standards for the 1770s.

If we so measured poverty in the United States during the revolutionary period, the proportion of poor would be immensely greater than today. Poverty is better considered in terms of the prevailing standard of living in a particular period. A useful, and frequent definition of poverty, then, is that it means lacking a minimal adequate absolute standard of living, judged by the criteria of the time.

Jackson Turner Main (1965) studied the American social structure of the revolutionary period. Using the standards of the time, he concluded that one-fifth of the white men were in the lower class, and that between one-third and two-fifths of all men were in the lower class. The lower class included "Negro slaves, white servants, and landless laborers employed by property owners such as farmers, artisans, and merchants. If defined by income, the lower class characteristically had almost none except that they were given food, clothing, and shelter" (Main 1965, p. 272).

The proportion in poverty probably increased with the commercialization of agriculture and with early industrialization. But specific figures are unavailable prior to 1960, and estimates go back only to the 1930s.

When President Roosevelt spoke in the 1930s of a third of the nation being ill-fed, ill-clothed, and ill-housed, it was about that proportion of the population that was below the minimal standards of the time. When the War on Poverty was launched in the mid-1960s, the proportion of families and unrelated individuals below what was then regarded as minimal was about one-fifth. In 1969, about 15 percent of American families and unrelated individuals had income below the official poverty line set by the government (U.S. Bureau of the Census, 1971). If poverty is measured in terms of minimal adequacy, the results show a general decrease in the proportion of Americans in poverty.

This decline has not been continuous. Ornati (1966) has calculated the proportion of the American households with an income below minimum subsistence, adequacy, and comfort. Using living standards for years between 1929 and 1960, he and his associates estimated what income would be needed to provide the barest necessities of life; minimally adequate food, clothing, and housing; and a proportionate share of available goods and services. As can be seen in Table 3.1, the proportion of households in poverty increased for all three standards during the depression of the 1930s, markedly decreased during World War II, rose again and then again declined with fluctuations. Presumably, full employment, or the lack of it, is closely related to the proportion of poor. The employment factor seems more relevant to such shifts than assuming changes in people's willingness to work.

More recent changes can be studied with the aid of data provided by the U.S. Bureau of the Census and the federal government's definition of poverty. Figure 3.1 shows the proportion of households (families and unrelated individuals) with incomes below the poverty line from 1959 to 1975. As can be seen,

TABLE 3.1   Percent of U.S. Households Below Three Budget Levels,
             by Contemporary Standards, 1929-60

Year	Below Minimum Subsistence Level	Below Minimum Adequacy Level	Below Minimum Comfort Level
1929	26	43	48
1935-36	27	46	64
1941	17	32	48
1944	10	15	45
1947	15	27	39
1950	14	28	41
1951	12	25	37
1952	12	22	36
1953	14	23	39
1954	14	27	44
1955	12	28	43
1956	11	26	44
1957	10	25	40
1958	13	28	41
1959	12	27	37
1960	11	26	40

Note: The marked discontinuity in percentages between 1941 and 1944 and between 1944 and 1947 is due to the combination of the following factors: The table deals with civilian population only; there was a significant change in income distribution during these years; and there was a large upgrading of budget standards between 1944 and 1947, while between 1941 and 1944 budget standards remained relatively unchanged.

Source: Ornati 1966, Table A, p. 158.

there has been a decline in the proportion of poor since 1959, particularly during the years of the War on Poverty, in the latter half of the 1960s.

Between 1929 and now the proportion of Americans below the poverty level has shown a general but not steady decline. This is true when poverty is defined in terms of a minimal standard of living, even if that standard takes into account changes in what is considered necessary for a minimally adequate standard of living. If we take into account payments in kind, such as food stamps, the proportion in poverty would be substantially lower than if we consider only monetary income (Haveman 1977).

If poverty is measured in relative terms, the results are different. Table 3.2 presents the median income and the percentage of families with less than 40 percent of the median family income from 1947 to 1975. As noted in Chapter 2, when people are asked what they need to "get along," the amount they state is about half of the median family income (Rainwater 1973). Clearly, there has not been the same kind of general decline in the proportion of Americans who are *relatively* poor. During these years, between 13 and 15 percent of American families had less than 40 percent of the median family income.

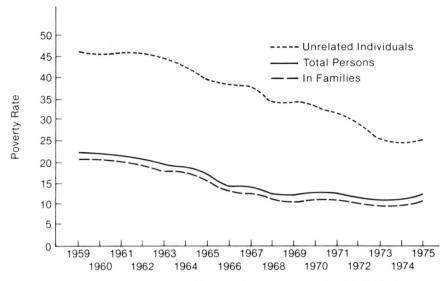

FIGURE 3.1 *Proportion of Persons, Families and Unrelated Individuals below the Poverty Level, 1959-75*

Source: Adapted from U.S. Bureau of the Census, *Current Population Reports*, Series P-60, No. 97 (Washington, D.C.: Government Printing Office, 1977), Table 1, p. 15.

TABLE 3.2 Median Income and Percent of Families below 40 Percent of Median Income, 1947-75

Year	Median Income (in 1975 dollars)	Proportion with Less than 40 Percent of Median Income
1947	7,393	14.6
1951	7,684	18.5
1955	8,881	15.4
1960	10,214	15.4
1963	10,984	14.8
1966	12,491	13.6
1969	13,849	13.4
1972	14,301	14.0
1974	14,082	13.6
1975	13,719	14.1

Source: Based on data in Table 11, U.S. Bureau of the Census, 1977, *Current Population Reports,* Series P-60, No. 105, p. 49.

DISTRIBUTION

To assess the distribution of material goods and services, it is necessary to study the distribution of income and of wealth. Has the middle class been expanding in size relative to the lowest and highest classes? Has the concentration of material benefits among the upper class been increasing or decreasing? Has the poorest class increased its share of national income? There are a variety of studies for different historical periods and a number of methods and concepts that examine such questions.

Income

Since changes in wage differences can be traced back further in time than changes in the distribution of personal income, and since wages are a primary source of income, we will examine wage trends before changes in income distribution. Personal income includes nonwage sources and is relevant for persons not in the labor force.

Main's (1965) study of revolutionary America provides a rough description of the proportion of workers at different economic levels. The lower class, he concluded, consisted of the one-third to two-fifths of the male labor force with little or no income. They were provided food, clothing, and shelter by their masters or employers. This lower class included Negro slaves, white servants, and landless laborers.

The middle class consisted of small property holders who were usually self-employed. This largest and most important segment of American revolutionary society included probably 70 percent of the whites and was made up of several occupational groups (Main 1965, p. 273). The largest group was the small farmers, comprising 40 percent of the whites and one-third of the whole population. The next largest group was the artisans. Also included in this middle class were those in the professions, except lawyers, who usually had incomes above the middle-class level, and teachers, who often ranked economically below skilled workers. Roughly 10 percent of the white population comprised the upper class. This class included large landowners, some ministers and doctors, most lawyers, a few artisans, and perhaps half of the merchants (those who earned enough to be in the upper class).

Main examined changes in the relative sizes of these social classes prior to the American Revolution. He concluded that there was a trend toward increasing inequality, which the American Revolution temporarily reversed. This war, like later ones, was associated with greater class equality.

Lindert and Williamson (1976) reviewed many studies and data on wage differences in the nineteenth and twentieth centuries. They concluded that the pay differences between skilled and unskilled workers increased greatly between 1820 and 1860; teachers, too, earned increasing amounts relative to unskilled

58

workers. Income gaps narrowed a little during the Civil War and then returned to prewar levels by about 1873. Pay differentials tended to converge until around 1896, when they widened considerably. Inequality peaked in 1916 and 1929. Then, between 1929 and 1951, pay differential converged slightly, with the lowest paid groups gaining the most. There since has been a small drift toward greater inequality. Higher paid professionals, notably physicians, and nonfarm managerial workers fared relatively well.

Miller (1966) conducted a detailed analysis of income distribution and wage differentials between 1939 and 1960 and reached the same conclusion. He found that from 1939 to 1950, men in lower-paid jobs made relatively greater gains in wages than those in higher-paid jobs; that is, the differentials decreased. But in the next decade, 1950-60, the greatest relative gains were made by the higher-paid workers, thus increasing the wage differentials. Detailed findings of Miller's study are presented in Table 3.3.

The earliest reliable data on the distribution of personal income dates from 1913.[1] The National Bureau of Economic Research conducted several studies of income distribution in the United States from 1913 to 1921. The estimates in these studies were based on incomes received, as recorded in tax returns and reports on wages and salaries; and on production figures, as reported in statistics on, for example, coal mined or materials manufactured. Mitchel et al. (1921, p. 116), found that the highest 5 percent of income receivers had about 33 percent of the national income from 1913 to 1916; they received 29 percent in 1917, 26 percent in 1918, and 24 percent in 1919 (when this data series ended). King (1930, pp. 174-77), also reports that during World War I the share of national income received by the highest income brackets declined; later years indicated that the share increased after the war from 1920 to 1926 (when the data series ended).

Kuznets used income tax returns to calculate the proportion of the national income received by the highest 1 and 5 percents of income recipients from 1913 to 1948. The resulting estimates are, in his words, "crude approximations" (Kuznets 1966, p. 206). Using tax returns for such a study is subject to error due to omissions in reporting income for tax purposes; reducing personal tax returns to units comparable to the population (such as families or individuals); and assessing the total population income. Taking these difficulties into

---

[1] Data were prepared for the years 1910-37 by the National Industrial Conference Board. These data were reported in the U.S. Census Bureau's *Historical Statistics of the United States, 1789-1945*; but they were judged too inaccurate and were not included in the later edition, *Historical Statistics of the United States: Colonial Times to 1957* (Miller 1971, p. 51.) Other students of inequality continue to use the data (Kolko 1962, p. 14.) The data indicate that the percentage of the national income received by the highest 10 percent of income recipients increased during the 1920s and decreased during the depression. It is noteworthy that the percentage received by the lowest income recipients decreased during the 1920s and 1930s. The constancy in the proportions may be even more significant. The upper 20 percent of the income recipients generally received about half of the aggregate national income.

TABLE 3.3   Increase in Wages or Salaries of All Male Workers by Major Occupations, 1939-50 and 1950-60

| | *Percent Increase* | |
Occupation	1939-50	1950-60
Professional, Technical, and Similar Workers	114	64
Managers, Officials, and Proprietors (Except Farm)	95	65
Clerical and Similar Workers	111	60
Sales Workers	147	51
Craftsmen, Foremen, and Similar Workers	160	60
Operative and Similar Workers	172	56
Service Workers (Except Private Household)	176	37
Farm Laborers and Foremen	219	− 9
Laborers (Except Farm and Mine)	175	38

Source: Miller 1966, Table III-6, pp. 82-83.

account, Kuznets's calculations indicate that the proportion of total income received by the highest income brackets has declined since 1913. The top 5 percent of the population received about 25 percent of the total income until the beginning of the depression; the figure dropped to 17 percent during World War II and since then has been stable. Estimates for income shares after federal income taxes yield a larger decline—from about 24 to about 14 percent (Kuznets 1966, Table 4.5, p. 211).

Kuznets's estimates have been labeled inaccurate and the decline questioned (Kolko 1962; Perlo 1954; and Goldsmith 1957). Some claim that the inaccuracy is due to the increase in income tax evasion, legal and illegal, particularly among the wealthy. Others say that Kuznets's figures do not take into account the expansion of nonmonetary income, which has benefited the top income receivers. The expense account for example, is a substantial factor in the standard of living of upper management. Dining out, traveling, and the use of houses, country clubs, and automobiles make significant differences in the way of life.

There are also many forms of indirect payment. Large corporations may give executives "stock options," which enables these employees to purchase stock below market value. Purchasing corporation stock gives them an investment in the company; it can also be an important source of income and wealth. In 1971, for example, the Times Mirror Company set aside 115,000 shares of common stock for purchase by top executives for "not less than 10 cents a share," and some officials purchased 5,000 shares at that minimum amount when they were being sold in the market at $47.00 to $57.25 a share (*Business Week* 1972a, p. 55).

Loans at little or no interest is another way in which certain positions give individuals access to important sources of income. Xerox, for example, made some stock available at 50 percent of the market value and loaned the purchase price at a 4 percent interest rate. In addition, income from purchasing bonds or from buying and selling capital is generally taxed much less than income from wages or salaries. Although high-income receivers may increasingly obtain non-monetary income, the opposite is true for low-income receivers. Nonmonetary income probably has declined for lower-income people as a result of the decrease in food raised for home consumption and in processing food and making clothes at home.

In studying income distribution, the total income to be apportioned may present difficulties. Goldsmith points to the difference between national income and personal income.

> National income includes and personal income excludes elements of production not paid out to persons—undistributed corporate profits, the corporate inventory valuation adjustment, taxes on corporate profits, and contributions for social insurance—whereas the reverse is the case for elements of income received by persons not accruing in production—transfer payments and government interest (Goldsmith 1957, p. 129).

It can be argued that national income should be the total amount to be divided among income receivers in the society. In this definition, corporation profits not distributed in dividends would be allocated in the same ratio as the stockholdings.

In addition to defining total income, an appropriate income-receiver unit must be selected. Researchers have to decide whether to use all persons, adult individuals, families, households, or some other unit for their studies. Kuznets, in his study based on income tax returns, calculated the income per tax return and the population represented by the tax returns for each income class. He then determined the per-capita income for members of each income class. It has been argued that consumer units or households are more appropriate units than personal tax returns, since people's class standings are determined by membership in such groups.

Efforts have been made to recalculate the data of Kuznets and others to take into account these and other criticisms. One such study was made by Goldsmith (1957), who calculated the percentage of the total personal and national incomes received by the top 5 percent of consumer units. Some of these findings are presented in Table 3.4. As can be seen, the share of income received by these units declined from 1929 to 1939 and from 1939 to 1955. The magnitude of the decline varies depending on which definitions of income are used.

Budd (1967) has compiled data for the period from 1929 to 1962 referring to families and to personal income; he included nonmonetary income such as wages in kind. Table 3.5 shows a general level of inequality similar to the level reported above. Once again there was a slight shift toward less inequality during

TABLE 3.4 Percentage Share of Top 5 Percent of Consumer Units in Using Various Definitions of Family Personal Income

	1929	1939	1950-55 Average	Percent Decrease*	
				1929-to 1950-55	1939 to 1950-55
Family Personal Income (before Income Taxes)	30.0	25.8	20.7	31	20
Family Personal Income after Federal Individual Income Tax Liability	29.5	24.8	18.5	37	25
Family Personal Income Plus Undistributed Corporate Profits	32	28	26	20	7
Undistributed Corporate Profits, Corporate Income Taxes, and Inventory Valuation Adjustment	33	27	25	22	6

*Based on unrounded figures.

Source: Goldsmith 1957, Table 4, p. 517.

TABLE 3.5 Percentage Share of Family Personal Income[a] by Quintiles and Top 5 Percent of Consumer Units[b] Selected Years, 1929-62

Quintiles	1929	1935-36	1941	1944	1947	1950	1951	1954	1956	1959	1962
Lowest	3.5	4.1	4.1	4.9	5.0	4.8	5.0	4.8	4.8	4.6	4.6
Second	9.0	9.2	9.5	10.9	11.0	10.9	11.3	11.1	11.3	10.9	10.9
Third	13.8	14.1	15.3	16.2	16.0	16.1	16.5	16.4	16.3	16.3	16.3
Fourth	19.3	20.9	22.3	22.2	22.0	22.1	22.3	22.5	22.3	22.6	22.7
Highest	54.4	51.7	48.8	45.8	46.0	46.1	44.9	45.2	45.3	45.3	45.5
Total	100.0	100.0	100.0	100.0	100.0	100.0	100.0	100.0	100.0	100.0	100.0
Top 5 Percent	30.0	26.5	24.0	20.7	29.9	21.4	20.7	20.3	20.2	20.2	19.6
Gini Concentration Ratio	.49	.47	.44	.39	.40	.40		.39	.39		.40

[a] Family personal income includes wages and salary receipts (net of social insurance contributions), other labor income, proprietors' and rental income, dividends, personal interest income, and transfer payments. In addition to monetary income flows, it includes certain nonmonetary or imputed income such as wages in kind, the value of food and fuel produced and consumed on farms, net imputed rental of owner-occupied home, and imputed interest. Personal income differs from national income in that it excludes corporate profits taxes, corporate savings (inclusive of inventory valuation adjustment), and social security contributions of employers and employees, and includes transfer payments (mostly governmental) and interest on consumer and government debt.

[b] Consumer units include farm operator and nonfarm families and unattached individuals. A family is defined as a group of two or more persons related by blood, marriage, or adoption, and residing together.

Source: Budd 1967, Table 1, p. xiii.

63

the 1930s depression and there was also a decline in inequality during World War II similar to the one that occurred during World War I. Since World War II, the inequality of personal-income distribution appears to have been unchanged.

All these data refer to income before taxes. The federal income tax is supposed to be progressive, with higher income recipients paying higher taxes. Actually, the tax is not very progressive; the income distribution before and after taxes is similar. In 1962, for example, the poorest fifth received 4.6 percent of the national income before taxes and 4.9 percent after taxes. The richest 5 percent received 19.6 percent before taxes and 17.7 percent after taxes (Budd 1967, pp. xii and xvi).

The U.S. Bureau of the Census provides current information on income distribution. Table 3.6 shows the income received by families and unrelated individuals from 1947 to 1975. Income in this table refers to money wages or salary, net income from self-employment, dividends, interest, social security, public assistance, and pensions. It does not include money received from the sale of property such as stocks, or nonmonetary or imputed income, included in Table 3.5.

The data in Table 3.6 indicate a slight decrease in inequality among families and unrelated individuals between 1947 and the end of the 1960s, and a slight increase in inequality since then. This trend is shown by the variation in the proportion of aggregate income received by the lowest and the highest quintiles and by the changes in that income of the top 5 percent. The overall inequality can be summarized by the Gini ratio, described in Chapter 2. The Gini ratios for 1947, 1959, 1966, and 1975 are: .418, .409, .399, and .411, respectively. On the whole, there is great stability in income inequality since the end of World War II.

Comparisons over time are difficult to make because the units of analysis themselves may change. The composition of families, for example, may change over time. Higher absolute levels of income and social security assistance for elderly persons combined with the desire of older people to maintain their own households has resulted in a smaller proportion of older people living with their children. Kuznets (1962) believes this change is responsible for higher measured inequality, reasoning that older people tend to have a greater variability in income and many of them have very low incomes. If they were living with their children, those low-income units would be averaged into more prosperous family incomes. Empirical analysis, however, does not support this reasoning. Miller carefully examined the degree of income inequality for different demographic categories of people, and concluded: "Stability in the overall income curve reflects in large measure stability in the component distributions" (Miller 1966, p. 20).

In summary, income distribution in the United States is not becoming more unequal; it was even more unequal in the past than it is now. The shift toward less inequality that occurred during the 1930s and World War II has stabilized since then and may have even decreased slightly. If only money

TABLE 3.6   Share of Aggregate Income Received by Each Fifth
and Top 5 Percent of Families and Unrelated
Individuals, 1947-75

Year	Percentage of Aggregate Income					
	Lowest Fifth	Second Fifth	Middle Fifth	Fourth Fifth	Highest Fifth	Top 5 Percent
1947	3.5	10.6	16.8	23.6	45.5	18.7
1948	3.5	10.8	17.2	23.9	44.7	18.1
1949	3.2	10.5	17.2	24.2	44.9	17.9
1950	3.1	10.6	17.3	24.1	44.9	18.2
1951	3.5	11.2	17.6	24.1	43.6	17.5
1952	3.5	10.9	17.3	24.1	44.3	18.4
1953	3.2	10.8	17.6	24.5	43.8	17.3
1954	3.1	10.4	17.5	24.7	44.4	17.5
1955	3.3	10.6	17.6	24.6	43.9	17.5
1956	3.4	10.8	17.7	24.5	43.5	17.2
1957	3.4	10.9	18.0	24.7	42.9	16.5
1958	3.3	10.8	17.9	24.8	43.3	16.5
1959	3.2	10.6	17.7	24.7	43.9	17.1
1960	3.2	10.6	17.6	24.7	44.0	17.0
1961	3.1	10.2	17.2	24.6	44.9	17.7
1962	3.4	10.4	17.5	24.8	43.9	16.8
1963	3.4	10.4	17.5	24.8	43.9	16.9
1964	3.4	10.4	17.3	24.8	44.1	17.2
1965	3.6	10.6	17.5	24.8	43.6	16.6
1966	3.8	10.7	17.5	24.7	43.4	16.7
1967	3.6	10.6	17.5	24.8	43.4	16.5
1968	3.8	10.7	17.4	24.7	43.5	16.8
1969	3.7	10.5	17.4	24.7	43.7	16.8
1970	3.6	10.3	17.2	24.7	44.1	16.9
1971	3.7	10.2	17.1	24.7	44.3	17.0
1972	3.7	10.0	16.9	24.7	44.8	17.4
1973	3.8	10.0	16.9	24.8	44.5	17.0
1974	3.9	10.1	16.8	24.7	44.4	16.9
1975	3.9	9.9	16.7	24.4	44.5	17.0

Source: U.S. Bureau of the Census 1977, Table 13, p. 57.

income is considered, it definitely has decreased. Whether the emphasis is on
the persistence of or change in inequality depends on how inequality is evaluated, on beliefs about the possibility of change, and on the time perspective
taken.

Wealth

The discussion of wealth begins with changes in personal wealth inequalities and then moves on to examine corporate wealth inequalities.

Personal wealth. Wealth inequalities are closely related to persisting income inequalities, particularly among people with the highest incomes. A survey conducted by the Board of Governors of the Federal Reserve System (Projector and Weiss 1966) found that in 1962, of the consumer units with incomes under $3,000, only 16 percent had some inherited assets. Of those with incomes of $100,000 or more, 66 percent had some inherited assets, and for 57 percent of the units, the inherited portion of total assets was substantial (Projector and Weiss 1966, Table A32, p. 148).

As pointed out in chapter 2, personal wealth is very unequally distributed in the United States. Although evidence of past inequalities is scarce, some exists. Blumin (1969), citing tax-assessment data for Boston, indicates an increase in wealth inequality between 1820, 1830, and 1845. (Schutz coefficients of inequality, similar to Gini ratios, were .537, .637, and .694, respectively.) Soltow (1975) analyzed 1860 U.S. census data; these records include wealth declarations and other information for every free individual. He studied only urban men, in order to make his findings more comparable to the current male population than would be the case if he used the total population of 1860. Soltow found that among urban males, the wealthiest .1 percent of the adult males had 15 percent of the wealth and .88 percent had 43 percent, whereas 50 percent were propertyless. The Gini ratio was extremely high: .924 for the ten urban counties in the sample.

Lampman (1962) used estate tax returns to estimate the proportion of the country's wealth owned by the richest people. Using mortality rates adjusted to the favorable life expectancy of the wealthy, he computed how many persons were alive with the same estate size for each person who had died in a given year.[2] Using this method, he was able to estimate the share of personal wealth held by the richest people from 1922 to 1956. Some of his findings are presented in Table 3.7. Although the magnitude of concentration is greater than for income, shifts in the degree of concentration are similar. In 1922 the wealthiest 1 percent of adults had almost one-third of the personal wealth; their share increased to 36 percent during the 1920s and then decreased during the 1930s and 1940s. Since then it has risen to about 25 percent and stabilized. In 1970 it is estimated that 1 percent of the population continues to own about 25 percent of the country's wealth (*Business Week* 1972b).

The small decline in the degree of wealth concentration between the 1920s and the present does not apply to all kinds of wealth. Although ownership of

[2] This technique is called the "estate-multiplier method." Lampman gives a hypothetical example to illustrate the method.

Suppose that out of a population of 1,000 men aged 40 to 50, two men died in one year with estates of $100,000 or more. Suppose, further, it is known that 5 percent of all the 1,000 men 40 to 50 died in that year. Then it may be assumed that the two men who died with $100,000 were 5 percent of all the living men in the group with $100,000. Hence, to estimate the number of living men with $100,000, we should multiply two by twenty (the inverse of 5 percent) to get the answer of 40 living men with $100,000 or more (Lampman 1962, p. 14).

TABLE 3.7   Percent of Wealth Held by the Most
             Wealthy, 1922-56

Year	Top 1 Percent of Adults	Top 5 Percent of Population
1922	31.6	29.8
1929	36.3	32.4
1933	28.3	25.2
1939	30.6	28.0
1945	23.3	20.9
1949	20.8	19.3
1953	24.3	22.7
1954	24.0	22.5
1956	26.0	25.0

Source: Lampman 1962, Tables 93 and 94, pp. 202 and 204.

real estate, insurance, and government bonds is less concentrated now, there has not been a similar decline in corporate ownership. In 1922, the richest 1 percent of adults owned about 60 percent of the corporate stock. The proportion increased during the 1920s and 1930s; it fell between 1939 and 1945, but has risen since and in 1953, with the top 1 percent of adults now holding about 75 percent of the corporate shares (Lampman 1962, Table 97, p. 209.)

Later data are available from the *Survey of Financial Characteristics of Consumers*, conducted by the Board of Governors of the Federal Reserve System. In 1962 a sample of households in the United States were questioned about their property, assets, and liabilities. It was found that the wealthiest .34 percent of all household units (those with $500,000 or more) held 41 percent of all public stock (Projector and Weiss 1966). Households with $200,000 to $499,999 constituted .86 percent of all units and held 24 percent of the public stock. In short, the wealthiest 1.2 percent of the households held 65 percent of the country's stock. The categories and units of the survey are not strictly comparable with those Lampman used, and it is therefore difficult to determine whether there has been any lessening of concentrated ownership of corporate shares.

The *Survey of Financial Characteristics of Consumers* does provide information about the wealth of all households. A summary of the distribution of wealth was presented in Table 2.3. The wealthiest 1.2 percent of the households had about 35 percent of all personal wealth, whereas 60 percent of the least wealthy households held only 7 percent of the country's wealth. The Gini ratio is about .75.

The concentration of wealth among individuals and families is extremely great in the United States, and probably was even greater fifty years ago. The evidence of some lessening concentration during the last fifty years does not indicate any decrease in the concentration of ownership in the means of production. There may be more equal sharing of wealth used in personal consumption.

Corporate wealth. Although wealth is generally viewed in terms of personal ownership, collective ownership by corporations is of immense importance in understanding the current distribution of wealth in the United States. Wealth, in the form of industrial capital and natural resources, is largely owned by corporations. Corporate ownership raises important issues concerning wealth concentration in addition to those considered above. Corporations can act as single units, thereby increasing the concentration of effective wealth. Thus a single corporation may own enough shares in other corporations to control them without owning them entirely; the single corporation would then control much more resources than it owns. Similarly, a person or family may own a dominant share of a corporation and thus have control over the wealth of other corporations. On the other hand, many small shareholders exchange their wealth for some dividend income, but those who control the corporation, in effect, control that wealth.

This discussion also raises the question of who controls a corporation. That is, to what extent do individuals or families control corporations when they own 5 or 10 percent of the shares? To what extent do the occupants of particular positions control wealth, aside from the share of ownership those incumbents may have? In other words, have contemporary corporations become so diffuse in ownership that nobody owns them sufficiently to control them, and have the managers, without owning them, gained effective control?

These and other related questions must be considered one at a time. One way to examine the ownership of resources and factories is to consider how the labor force is distributed. For example, the number of people who are self-employed and who are employed by others can be calculated. In a capitalist economy, declining proportions of men and women who are self-employed indicates that ownership of the means of production is becoming more concentrated.

Changes in technology and organization underlie changes in occupational distribution and self-employment. Increased productivity of farms and factories has been accompanied by an expansion of service occupations. White-collar occupations have proliferated and expanded. This growth has been especially great in what is sometimes called the "new middle class." Traditionally, the middle class has referred to self-employed professionals, business people, and farmers. But there has been a dramatic increase in office workers, salespeople, salaried professionals, and managers. In *White Collar* (1953), C. Wright Mills characterizes the change as follows:

> Negatively, the transformation of the middle class is a shift from property to non-property; positively, it is a shift from property to a new axis of stratification, occupation. The nature and well being of the old middle class can best be sought in the condition of entreprenurial property; of the new middle class, in the economics and sociology of occupations. The numerical decline of the older, independent sectors of the middle class is an incident in the centralization of property; the numerical rise of the

newer salaried employees is due to the industrial mechanics by which the occupations composing the new middle class have arisen (Mills 1953, p. 65).

The transformation has occurred as a result of several shifts. First, there has been a great decrease in the proportion of agricultural workers. In addition, production in small artisan shops has been superseded by large-scale manufacturing. Finally, the one-person or family retail establishment has declined with the advent of chain stores and large corporate retailing establishments.[3]

The relationship of these shifts to changes in the proportion of self-employed can be seen by looking at the proportion of self-employed in various industries. In 1973 in the United States, only 8 percent of the economically active population was self-employed and another 1 percent were family workers; 91 percent were salaried employers or wage earners (International Labor Organization, 1974). In the agriculture, hunting, forestry, and fishing industries, 39 percent were employed by others, and the rest were either self-employed or family workers. But only a small proportion of the labor force—4 percent—was in those industries. Back in 1820, about 72 percent of the gainfully employed were in agriculture alone; by 1870 the proportion had fallen to 53 percent and by 1930 to 21 percent (U.S. Bureau of the Census 1960 and 1973). The proportion of persons working in manufacturing has expanded, and manufacturing itself has become an increasingly large-scale operation. In 1973, 25 percent of the U.S. labor force was engaged in manufacturing, and 99 percent of persons in manufacturing were salary or wage earners. Even in the wholesale and retail trade, restaurant, and hotel industries, 89 percent were employed by others outside the family.

Nearly everyone in the United States is employed by someone. The magnitude of the proportion of the labor force employed by others suggests collective or corporate ownership not only of the means of industrial production but also of the distribution of goods to consumers and the provision of services such as education. It is important, therefore, to examine the distribution of ownership and control of those large organizations. Of particular interest is the concentration of ownership in industry. The magnitude and resources of industrial production are such that if industry ownership and control is concentrated, there is not only great economic inequality but also inequalities of power and status.

One way to assess the concentration of capital on which employment is based is to study the concentration of corporate wealth. Our focus is on manufacturing because of its pivotal role in the economy and because considerable analysis has been done on the subject. Of all manufacturing assets in the United States, 98 percent are owned by corporations (Mueller 1964). To

---

[3]Some of the decline in self-employment may be more apparent than real. Some small business operators and even professionals incorporate themselves. They then become salaried employees (in corporations they solely own). This situation has tax and liability advantages.

measure such concentration, it is necessary to determine the percentage of total corporate manufacturing assets, net capital assets, or profits owned by the largest one hundred or two hundred corporations. Thus, in 1962, the one hundred largest manufacturing corporations owned 46.8 percent of the total corporate manufacturing assets. They owned 55.1 percent of net capital assets, and around 57.6 percent of net profits (Mueller 1964). The five largest corporations alone had 20 percent of the total net profits of all corporations.

By almost any standard, this level of concentration is high. Unlike the findings of declining income inequalities and the proportion below minimal income levels, there has been increasing concentration of ownership of manufacturing industries. Mueller (1964) calculated that in 1950, the 100 largest corporations had 40.2 percent of the total corporate assets, compared with 45.7 percent in 1962. Using other data, he concluded that between 1947 and 1962 the share of all manufacturing assets held by the 113 largest corporations increased about 25 percent.

Examination over a longer time period also reveals increasing corporate concentration. Means (1964) calculated the degree of corporate concentration for 1962 using the same methods Berle and he (1933) used in 1929. In 1929, the one hundred largest corporations legally controlled 44 percent of the nation's total net capital assets. By 1962, this proportion had risen to 58 percent of the net capital assets of all manufacturing corporations.

Students of corporate concentration arrive at somewhat different numbers in these matters because many judgments have to be made in such calculations. This variation reflects the ambiguity and the complexity surrounding corporate wealth. One important issue is the extent to which one corporation controls another. Generally, corporations consolidate in their published reports only those subsidiaries in which they have 95 to 100 percent of the voting stock. The stocks they own in other corporations, even when these shares give them legal control, are reported as "investment in subsidiaries," for example, thus understating the assets that they legally control. Means's (1964) attempt to isolate each corporation with more than 50 percent of its stock owned by one of the large corporations and to consolidate its assets with those of its parent corporation is why his figures indicate more concentration than do Mueller's, cited earlier.

Corporate ownership. The question of who owns the corporations is concerned with inequalities in personal wealth. The concentration of corporate wealth underscores the significance of personal wealth inequalities. As noted earlier in this chapter, the concentration of ownership of corporate stock is even greater than the concentration of all kinds of wealth combined. In 1962, .3 percent of the country's households had 22 percent of the nation's wealth and 41 percent of the public stock (Projector and Weiss 1966).

Some observers argue that ownership of stock has become so widely distributed that individuals or families rarely control corporations anymore. It is true that stock ownership has become more widespread. In 1951, only

9 percent of the nation's households owned stocks (including mutual funds). This proportion rose to 20 percent in 1963 and to 26 percent in 1970 (Katona, Mandell, Schmiedeskamp 1971, Table 6-1, p. 98). Since then, there has been a decline in the number of shareholders, due to sagging stock prices and inflation (*New York Times*, 10 December 1975, p. 1).

If the owners of the corporate stock do not control the corporation, who does? According to some observers, the managers have control. As Berle phrases it:

> When an individual invests capital in the large corporation, he grants to the corporate management all power to use that capital to create, produce and develop, and he abandons all control over the product. He keeps a modified right to receive a portion of the profits, usually in the form of money, and a highly enhanced right to sell his participation for cash. . . . 1,100,000 shareholders could not possibly run American Telephone and Telegraph Company. . . . No large enterprise could possibly go forward except under a unified and concentrated system of organization and command (Berle 1954, pp. 30-32).

Even if some shareholders wanted to exercise control, management could thwart them. It is management that appoints the proxy committee and solicits proxy votes from shareholders. With such proxys, management need not own shares to have effective voting power. Even when stockholders vote on specific issues by mail, management authority can be quite convincing to satisfied shareholders, and the stockholders tend to support management recommendations.

Others have contended that corporations are dominated by particular families or controlled by outside investors such as banks (which, in turn, are dominated by particular persons). In this view, control is becoming more concentrated, not passing from the hands of the owners. Sweezy said, in his description of the situation, that "the great majority of owners are stripped of control in favor of a small minority of owners" (Sweezy 1956, p. 262).

The facts relevant to assessing the validity of these and similar assertions are difficult to uncover. Ownership may be diffused through an extended family and not be readily attributable to any person or small family. Another difficulty in tracing the connections is the practice of "pyramiding." In this system, someone owns enough shares to control one corporation, and that corporation owns enough shares in a third corporation to control it. The first and third corporations together may own enough shares in a fourth corporation to control it. This process may be extended through several such steps, so that a relatively small investment may be used to gain control over several corporations. Another difficulty in determining corporate control by investors arises from the fact that individuals can own shares and have them held in "street names"—that is, fictitious names—with the real names known only to the stockbroker.

Conceptual ambiguities also confound the issue. For example, to what extent should we treat a friendship group as a single unit? A small group of friends may cooperate to dominate a corporation, with no one person having a controlling share of stock. Other ambiguities relate to the degree to which owners and managers are separable. A controlling share of stock of one corporation may be held by a mutual fund and that control is exercised by the managers of the fund. Bank managers also can be very influential in corporate decisions, not only through bank ownership of corporate shares, but by virtue of loans extended to corporations. Finally, corporate managers themselves may own shares in the corporation that employs them.

The very concept of "control" is ambiguous and thus complicates determining who has corporate control. Do we mean the power to hire and fire managers, to direct day-to-day decisions, or to set major policies? What percentages of shares constitutes control? The ways in which analysts answer these and related questions strongly affects the results of their investigations. Ideological and theoretical biases may significantly affect the way researchers choose to answer (Zeitlin 1974).

It is possible and indeed necessary, however, to examine the available evidence. It is critical to understand the way in which the evidence was collected. The first and most influential study on corporate control was conducted by Berle and Means (1933). They studied the two hundred largest (in gross assets) nonbanking corporations in the United States as of 1930. They examined the concentration of shareholders in each corporation, taking into account possible pyramiding and the issue of nonvoting shares. They distinguished control by private and by majority ownership; minority control (working control by shareholders with more than 20 percent of the shares); and control by legal device (pyramiding, issuing nonvoting stock, and holdings by trusts). If they could not discover control of one of the types above, they concluded that there was management control or joint management-ownership control. Corporations classified under management control had no more than 5 percent of the voting stock owned by one group of shareholders.

Berle and Means estimated that 10.5 percent of the corporations, which had 30 percent of the assets of all corporations, were clearly management controlled; another 22 percent of the corporations, which controlled 14 percent of all assets, were probably management controlled (1933, Table 14, p. 116). Most corporations were still controlled by owners, but the researchers emphasized that the separation of ownership from management was most significant and presumably increasing.

Later studies and reanalyses, however, have found more rather than less frequent ownership control. The Seventy-fifth Congress authorized and directed a select committee, the Temporary National Economic Committee (TNEC), to study economic concentration. The TNEC study concluded that there was a visible center of ownership control in more than two-thirds of the two hundred largest corporations (TNEC 1940, p. 103). Others have argued that by taking into account financial connections and interlocking directorates, centers of control can be found for almost all large corporations (Perlo 1957; Lundberg 1969).

Burch (1972) systematically studied the country's largest (in sales) 300 industrial firms and 150 other kinds of large corporations, using data from newspapers and business magazines as well as from government publications. He set two conditions to classify a corporation as probably family owned: At least 4 or 5 percent of the voting stock had to be held by an individual, family, or group of families; and the family had to be represented on the company's board of directors, generally over an extended perior of time. If there was some, even inconclusive evidence of these conditions, the corporation was considered possibly under family control. If there was no evidence that these conditions were met, the corporation was assumed to be probably management controlled. By these standards, in 1965, 39.5 percent of the largest two hundred firms were *probably* family controlled, 17.5 percent were *possibly* family controlled, and 43 percent were *probably* management controlled. If privately owned firms of the same size were included, the proportion of family-controlled firms would be 40.5 percent. When smaller firms are included, the proportion of family-controlled companies increases.

The proportion of corporations which are regarded as family controlled is partly a matter of definition. But by almost any conception, we must conclude that in many of the largest corporations, ownership is concentrated enough for a small group like a family to dominate policy and control managers (Zeitlin 1974). The ownership of stocks is highly concentrated, despite increases in the proportion of American stockholders.

Thus far, personal wealth and income have been discussed in terms of individuals and separate households. When we examine corporate control it is necessary to consider extended families of parents, children and grandchildren, brothers, sisters and cousins. Family members may have dominant positions in diverse corporations; as a single extended family, the control is greater than what it would be for these persons or their nuclear families alone. Notable examples of such extended families are the duPonts, the Mellons, and the Rockefellers. The duPont family is estimated to have 250 members who have large corporate holdings and 75 to 185 members who form a cohesive group (Lundberg 1969, pp. 165 and 171) The family is able to act in a unified manner through a network of family trusts and holding companies. Although it is difficult to determine the value of the duPont's corporate property or the extent of family control, Lundberg has estimated a minimum of $7.6 billion in 1964 from investments in E. I. duPont de Nemours Company, General Motors Corporation, Christiana Securities Company, and the U.S. Rubber Company (Uniroyal, Inc.).

The Mellon family's corporate wealth is particularly concentrated in the Aluminum Company of America, Gulf Oil Corporation, and Koppers Company. The value of the family's share in those companies in 1964 market prices has been estimated at $4.7 billion (Lundberg 1969, pp. 177-182). The Rockefellers' wealth is about equal to the Mellons', and includes control over such enterprises as the Chase Manhattan Bank, Rockefeller Center, and Rockefeller Foundation holdings. The largest holdings are the Standard Oil Company (of New Jersey, Indiana, and California), the Socony Oil Company (subsidiary of Mobil Oil Corporation), Consolidated Oil and Gas Company, Bethlehem Steel Corporation, and the Atlantic Refining Company (Lundberg 1969, pp. 182-191).

MOBILITY

Discussions of the wealth of extended families introduces us to one kind of class mobility: variations in intergenerational inheritance of wealth. It is possible to study the mobility of persons within their own lifetimes and between generations, taking note of changes in personal income and wealth as well as movement into and out of positions with varying amounts of income or wealth.

Chapter 2 presented information on the changes in family income over one year's time (Table 2.6). We saw a considerable turnover in the income of families even in one year. Other data from the same study (Morgan et al. 1974) show that a large proportion of families rise out of and fall into the lowest income quintile. Over a five-year period, from 1967 to 1971, 35 percent of the American families had incomes within the lowest quintile for at least one year; but only about 9 percent were as poor for all five years.

These changes in family income are in large part attributable to changes in family composition: deaths, divorces, and children entering and leaving the family. In addition, in a society where nearly everyone's income depends on employment, people who become unemployed or leave the labor force are likely to suffer great declines in income, as is generally the case for elderly persons in America. In 1969, 31 percent of the unrelated individuals and families with heads sixty-five years old and over were poor, compared with 11 percent for families and unrelated individuals headed by persons under sixty-five years of age. The life cycle within American society is associated with marked changes in income.

Intergenerational patterns of income mobility are difficult to assess. The variability within the life span itself creates problems in assessment and respondents generally do not know or recall what their parents' income was when they were children living with their parents. We lack precise information about the intergenerational continuance of income or of particular income levels, such as poverty or wealth.

Despite the widespread belief that poverty continues from generation to generation, the evidence to this effect is very sparse (Kriesberg 1970, pp. 167-181). In a few studies of families receiving Aid to Families with Dependent Children (AFDC), the respondents were asked whether their parents had ever received any form of public assistance (Burgess and Price 1963; Greenleigh

Associates 1964; and Podell 1968). The estimates range from 15 to 48 percent, varying with time and place. Comparisons can be made between these figures and the proportion of the parental generation who received any form of public assistance, including during the depression. Estimates show that in 1935, 20 percent of the population received some form of relief, and in some states the proportion was as high as 40 percent (Adams 1940, p. 227; Schlesinger 1959, p. 263). Those proportions were for a given year, but since families moved on and off relief rolls, the proportion who had ever received some form of public assistance was probably much greater. Undoubtedly, currently poor persons are more likely to have grown up in families which were impoverished than are persons who are not now poor. But many poor people do *not* come from impoverished families of origin, and many poor people have nonpoor backgrounds. There is considerable movement into and out of poverty between generations as well as within generations.

What chances do the children of people at different strata have of entering other income levels? A part of the answer is available from a national survey. In 1974, a cross-section of Americans were asked: "Thinking about the time when you were 16 years old compared with American families in general then, would you say your family income was—far below average, below average, average, above average, or far above average?" They were asked a similar question about the current income of their own families. A majority of respondents reported that their current family income was about average, and a majority reported that their parents' incomes were about average. But the proportion reporting below-average incomes was somewhat larger for the parental than for the respondents' generation. As can be seen in Table 3.8, there is only a small relationship between the respondents' income and that of their parents (the rank order correlation, the Kendall Tau C is only 0.13). The low correlation means that there is considerable upward and downward mobility. For example, of the respondents with parental incomes far below average, 8.8 percent reported current incomes above average and 2.0 percent far above average. Of the respondents whose parents' incomes were far above average, 8 percent reported incomes far below average and 16 percent reported incomes below average. Of course, people use different standards of what is above and below average, depending on where they come from and with whom they are comparing themselves, consequently these findings indicate subjective meanings more than objective, external circumstances.

Movement into and out of the small segment of the population that is extremely wealthy is another matter. There have not been systematic studies of the intergenerational mobility of the very rich. The evidence that does exist indicates that the children of the wealthy are generally wealthy themselves, and that wealthy persons usually have wealthy parents (Lundberg 1969; Baltzell 1964; Domhoff 1971). Although there are some "new rich"—persons who have made fortunes in new industries—very often even these people have come from

TABLE 3.8   Current Family Income by Parental Income

Current Income	Parental Income				
	Far Below Average	Below Average	Average	Above Average	Far Above Average
Far Below Average	11.8%	4.7%	2.4%	3.1%	8.0%
Below Average	28.4	29.3	17.4	15.1	16.0
Average	49.0	49.6	62.9	44.8	40.0
Above Average	8.8	15.9	16.4	35.9	12.0
Far Above Average	2.0	0.5	0.8	12.0	24.0
Totals	100.0	100.0	99.9	100.1	100.0
	(102)	(365)	(780)	(192)	(25)

Kendall Tau C = 0.13.

Source: Based upon data from the National Opinion Research Center, 1974 General Survey.

not poor or middle-income levels, but families of substantial means. Pessen (1973) studied the wealthy in New York, Philadelphia, and Brooklyn during the second quarter of the nineteenth century. He found that they, too, usually inherited wealth or married into wealthy families.

Another kind of mobility is the movement of persons into class-related positions. Researchers study, for example, the class origins of people in high occupational positions. Occupations can be ranked and studied as a status hierarchy or in terms of material conditions and economic class. Chapter 4 examines intergenerational occupational mobility as status mobility. Here we will concentrate on the incumbents of the highest business positions. There have been a few studies made of the class origins of American corporate leaders.

Taussig and Joslyn (1932) studied the occupational origins of the leading business persons in 1928. They mailed questionnaires to persons holding positions as major executives, partners, some other high position in businesses large enough to be of more than local significance in their respective fields. Warner and Abegglen (1955) repeated the study for 1952 business leaders making it possible to see whether mobility into top business positions was becoming more or less equal. In 1952, 24 percent of the business leaders had fathers who had been major executives or owners of large businesses, and 28 percent had fathers who had been minor executives or owners of small businesses; the comparable percentages for the 1928 business leaders was 31 and 27.

There seems to have been a small increase in the proportion of business leaders entering from outside of the business strata. To be sure that this rise reflects an increase in equal opportunity, it is necessary to take into account the occupational distribution in the fathers' generation for each set of business leaders. The relevant data are presented in Table 3.9. In 1928, 12 percent of the business leaders' fathers had been farmers, and in 1952 this proportion had fallen to 9 percent. But the proportion of the adult males who were farmers in

TABLE 3.9 Occupational Origins of 1928 and 1952 U.S. Business Leaders Compared with U.S. Adult Males of 1900 and 1920

Occupation	1928 Group		1952 Group	
	Fathers of Business Leaders	Adult Males of 1900	Fathers of Business Leaders	Adult Males of 1920
Manual Workers	11%	45%	15%	47%
Clerk or Sales	5	7	8	10
Business Owner or Executive	58	7	52	11
Professional	13	3	14	4
Farmer	12	38	9	27
Other	1	1	2	1
Total	100	100	100	100

Source: Warner and Abegglen 1955, Table 7, p. 46.

the parental generation also had fallen (from 38 to 27 percent); consequently, the chances of a farmer's son becoming a business leader really had not changed. For sons of business owners or executives, the chance for also entering these businesses had declined slightly. Of course, the absolute magnitude is still high: in 1952, 66 percent of the business leaders had fathers who were business owners or executives or professionals.

Other studies, using historical records, cover a longer span of years (Miller 1952; Keller 1963). These studies also showed a high proportion of business leaders whose fathers were in the business strata. The research also supports the inference that the opportunities for children in the nonbusiness strata to enter the business elite were even less equal in the past.

CONCLUSIONS

This chapter has examined several different kinds of class inequality—range, distribution, and mobility—and has considered each in terms of income and wealth. Although income and wealth generally have been discussed independently, they tend to be correlated; thus, inequality of wealth is a cause and a consequence of income inequality. As will be seen in later chapters, this correlation has implications for the relationship between class inequality and inequalities of power and status. It also has implications for the persistence of all aspects of class inequality.

Although the information on inequality is limited, some general descriptive assessments can be offered. The considerable class inequality that exists in the United States has persisted for the past fifty years—the period in which minimally comparable data exists. These data show a general decline in the proportion of the population in poverty, if measured in terms of an absolute, minimal amount of income. This decline has not been steady, however, the proportion in poverty increased during the depression, decreased during World War II, increased after the war, and then was stable until a small decline began in the 1960s. Poverty measured in relative terms has been stable and has not shown any general decline.

Measured against perfect equality, the distribution of income has been and continues to be very unequal. Income was probably even more unequally distributed before World War II, but it has not materially changed since then. The share of the total income received by the highest 5 percent of income recipients seems to have declined somewhat between 1929 and 1945.

Wealth is much more unequally distributed than income. Personal wealth has probably become more equally distributed in the past fifty years, but wealth in the form of corporate shares has not; concentration in ownership of the means of production has increased, as is reflected in the decline in self-employment.

The degree of inequality in contemporary United States can be usefully assessed in comparison with other countries, as well as in historical perspective. Chapter 4 examines the variability in class inequality in other countries and the world as a whole. This is important in its own right as well as a means to assess inequality in the U.S.

REFERENCES

ADAMS, JAMES TRUSLOW (Ed.). 1940. *Dictionary of American History*. New York: Scribner's.

BALTZELL, E. DIGBY. 1964. *The Protestant Establishment*. New York: Random House.

BERLE, ADOLF A., JR. and GARDINER MEANS. 1933. *The Modern Corporation and Private Property*. New York: Macmillan.

BERLE, ADOLF A., JR. 1954. *The 20th Century Capitalist Revolution*. New York: Harcourt Brace Jovanovich.

BLUMIN, STUART. 1969. "Mobility and Change in Ante-Bellum Philadelphia." In Stephan Thernstrom and Richard Sennett, (Eds.) *19th Century Cities: Essays in the New Urban History*. New Haven: Yale University Press, 165-206.

BUDD, EDWARD C. (Ed.). 1967. "An Introduction to a Current Issue of Public Policy," pp. X-XIX in *Inequality and Poverty*. New York: W. W. Norton.

BURCH, PHILIP H., JR. 1972. *The Managerial Revolution Reassessed*. Lexington, Mass.: Lexington Books.

BURGESS, M. ELAINE and DANIEL O. PRICE. 1963. *An American Dependency Challenge*. Chicago. Ill.: American Public Welfare Association.

BUSINESS WEEK. 1972a. "There's Big Money in the Fringes," (May 60: 55-56.

BUSINESS WEEK. 1972b. "Who Has the Wealth in America?" (August 5): 54-56.

DOMHOFF, G. WILLIAM. 1971. *The Higher Circles*. New York: Vintage Books.

GLENN, NORVAL D. 1974. "Income Inequality in the United States," pp. 391-398. In Joseph Lopreato and Lionel S. Lewis (Eds.), *Social Stratification: A Reader*. New York: Harper & Row.

GOLDSMITH, SELMA F. 1957. "Changes in the Size Distribution of Income," *American Economic Review* 47 (May). 504-518.

GREENLEIGH ASSOCIATES. 1964. *Public Welfare: Poverty-Prevention or Perpetuation*. New York: Greenleigh Associates.

HAVEMAN, ROBERT H. 1977. "Introduction: Poverty and Social Policy in the 1960s and 1970s—An Overview and Some Speculations," Pp 1-19 in R. Haveman (Ed.) A Decade of Federal Antipoverty Programs. New York: Academic Press.

INTERNATIONAL LABOUR ORGANIZATION. 1974. *1974 Yearbook of Labour Statistics*. Geneva: International Labour Organization.

KATONA, GEORGE, LEWIS MANDELL and JAY SCHMIEDESKAMP. 1971. *1970 Survey of Consumer Finance*. Ann Arbor, Mich.: Survey Research Center, The University of Michigan.

KELLER, SUZANNE. 1963. *Beyond the Ruling Class*. New York: Random House.

KING, WILLFORD ISABELL. 1930. *The National Income and Its Purchasing Power*. New York: National Bureau of Economic Research.

KOLKO, GABRIEL. 1963. *Wealth and Power in America*. New York: Praeger.

KRIESBERG, LOUIS. 1970. *Mothers in Poverty*. Chicago: Aldine.

KUZNETS, SIMON. 1962. *Income Distribution and Changes in Consumption*. New York: Institute of Life Insurance.

KUZNETS, SIMON. 1966. *Modern Economic Growth*. New Haven: Yale University Press.

LAMPMAN, ROBERT J. 1962. *The Share of Top Wealth-Holders in National Wealth, 1922-1956*. Princeton, N.J.: Princeton University Press.

LINDERT, PETER H. and JEFFREY WILLIAMSON. 1976. "Three Centuries of American Inequality," pp. 69-123. In Paul Uselding (Ed.), *Research in Economic History*. Greenwich, Conn.: Jai Press.

LUNDBERG, FERDINAND. 1969. *The Rich and the Super-Rich*. New York: Bantam Books.

MAIN, JACKSON TURNER. 1965. *The Social Structure of Revolutionary America*. Princeton, N.J.: Princeton University Press.

MEANS, GARDINER C. 1964. "Economic Concentration," pp. 8-19, in *Hearings Before the Subcommittee on Antitrust and Monopoly of the Committees on the Judiciary* United States Senate, 88th Congress, 2nd Session, pursuant to S. Res. 262. *Part 1: Overall and Conglomerate Aspects*. Washington, D.C.: Government Printing Office.

MILLER, HERMAN P. 1966. *Income Distribution to the United States*, Washington, D.C.: Government Printing Office.

MILLER, HERMAN P. 1971. *Rich Man, Poor Man*. New York: Thomas Y. Crowell.

MILLER, WILLIAM (Ed.). 1952. *Man in Business: Essays in the History of Entrepreneurship*, pp.3-27. Cambridge: Harvard University Press.

MILLS, C. WRIGHT. 1953. *White Collar*. New York: Oxford University Press.

MITCHEL, WESLEY C., WILFORD I. KING, FREDERICK R. MACAULAY, and OSWALD W. KNAUTH. 1921. *Income in the United States: Its Amount and Distribution, 1909-1919*. New York: Harcourt Brace Jovanovich.

MORGAN, JAMES H., KATHERINE DICKINSON, JONATHAN DICKINSON, JACOB BEMUS, and GREGG DUNCAN (Eds.). 1974. *Five Thousand American Families: Patterns of Economic Progress*, Vols. 1 and 2. Ann Arbor: Institute for Social Research.

MUELLER, WILLARD P. 1964. "Recent Changes in Industrial Concentration, and the Current Merger Movement," pp. 111-129 in *Hearings Before the Subcommittee on Antitrust and Monopoly of the Committee on the Judiciary*, United States Senate, 88th Congress, 2nd Session. *Part I: Overall and Conglomerate Aspects.* Washington, D.C.: Government Printing Office.

THE NEW YORK TIMES, December 10, 1975, p. 1.

ORNATI, OSCAR. 1966. *Poverty Amid Affluence.* New York: Twentieth Century Fund.

PERLO, VICTOR. 1954. "Review of Shares of Upper Income Groups in Income and Savings," *Science and Society* 18 (Spring), 168-173.

PERLO, VICTOR. 1957. *The Empire of High Finance.* New York: International Publishers.

PESSEN, EDWARD. 1973. *Riches, Class, and Power Before the Civil War.* Lexington, Mass.: D. C. Heath.

PODELL, LAWRENCE. 1968. *Families on Welfare in New York City*, Preliminary Report No. 5, "Welfare History and Expectancy." New York: The Center for Social Research, The City University of New York.

PROJECTOR, DOROTHY and GERTRUDE WEISS. 1966. *Survey of Financial Characteristics of Consumers.* Washington, D.C.: Board of Governors of Federal Reserve System.

RAINWATER, LEE. 1974. *What Money Buys: Inequality and the Social Meanings of Income.* New York: Basic Books.

SCHLESINGER, ARTHUR, JR. 1959. *The Coming of Roosevelt.* Boston: Houghton Mifflin.

SOLTOW, LEE. 1975. "The Wealth, Income, and Social Class of Men in Large Northern Cities in the United States in 1960," in James D. Smith (Ed.), *The Personal Distribution of Income and Wealth.* New York: National Bureau of Economic Research.

SWEEZY, PAUL M. 1956. *The Theory of Capitalist Development.* New York: Monthly Review Press. Originally published in 1942.

TAUSSIG, F. W. and C. S. JOSLYN. 1932. *American Business Leaders.* New York: Macmillan.

TEMPORARY NATIONAL ECONOMIC COMMITTEE (TNEC). 1940. *The Distribution of Ownership in the 200 Largest Non-Financial Corporations.* Monograph 29. Washington, D.C.: Government Printing Office.

U.S. BUREAU OF THE CENSUS. 1960. *Historical Statistics of the United States, Colonial Times to 1957.* Washington, D.C.: Government Printing Office.

U.S. BUREAU OF THE CENSUS. 1971. *Statistical Abstract of the United States: 1971.* (92nd Edition), Washington, D.C.: Government Printing Office.

U.S. BUREAU OF THE CENSUS. 1973. *Statistical Abstract of the United States: 1973.* (94th Edition). Washington, D.C.: Government Printing Office.

U.S. BUREAU OF THE CENSUS. 1977. *Current Population Reports*, Series P-60, No. 105. "Money Income in 1975 of Families and Persons in the United States." Washington, D.C.: Government Printing Office.

WARNER, W. LLOYD and ABEGGLEN, JAMES C. 1955. *Occupational Mobility in American Business and Industry*. Minneapolis, Minn.: University of Minnesota Press.
ZEITLIN, MAURICE. 1974. "Corporate Ownership and Control: The Large Corporation and the Capitalist Class," *American Journal of Sociology* 79 (March), pp. 1073-1119.

chapter 4

World Class Variations

No man is an island, entire of itself;
every man is a piece of the Continent, a part of the Maine:
If a clod bee washed away by the Sea, Europe is the less,
as well as if a Manor of thy friends or thine owne were;
any man's death diminishes me, because I am involved in Mankinde:
And therefore, never send to know for whom the bell tolls:
It tolls for thee.   *John Donne*

The United States cannot be understood alone because it is not alone; it is part of a much larger system of social relations. Because inequalities in the United States are related to those elsewhere, we must inquire about that larger system. Only by comparing inequalities among different social systems can we develop explanations for differences in inequality. Furthermore, the degree of inequality has social meaning only if we have some basis for comparison. Whether we feel there is much or a little inequality in America is affected by how much inequality we think exists elsewhere in the world. Finally, inequalities in other social systems should be considered because most people live elsewhere.

We will compare class inequalities in the United States with those in other countries and also in noncountry systems by looking at the world as a single social system composed of subsystems that do not necessarily coincide with the political boundaries of a country (such entities as multinational corporations, for example).

COUNTRY COMPARISONS

The extent of poverty and the distribution of income and wealth vary among the countries of the world. Aspects of that variation are explored below.

Range

To what degree do countries vary in the range of material conditions? More specifically, what proportion of the prople in various countries have less than a minimal standard of living? What percentage are poor?

Most of the world's people are poor; certainly they are poor if we define poverty in the monetary terms used in the United States. There still are some people, usually those living in small groups and isolated by culture and geography, who subsist as hunters and gatherers, or as nomads herding animals. Possibly they do not think of themselves as poor. But nearly all the people of the world are part of vast market systems and most are poor not only by American standards but also by their own definitions.

Among the several ethnic or tribal communities in Kenya, for example, many Masai live by their traditional herding of cattle, relatively unaffected by the larger market systems. They construct their dwellings from materials they collect and live largely on the food their cattle provide. But most of Kenya's population is involved in the urban labor market or employed in raising tea,

83

coffee, or other products for sale. They must purchase the goods used for clothing and housing; they must purchase much of their food. Most of them are poor.

Throughout the world, most persons are peasants raising some food for themselves and some products for sale. Urban centers are crowded and surrounded by large squatter villages: places where people construct makeshift shelters and take up residence with few or none of the services usually considered essential for urban living. These squatter villages have many names; in Brazil they are called *favelas*. A resident in one, Carolina Maria de Jesus (1963) wrote about her life there:

> We are poor, and we live on the banks of the river. The river banks are places for garbage and the marginal people. People of the *favelas* are considered marginals. No more do you see buzzards flying the river banks near the trash. The unemployed have taken the buzzards' place.

Because economically underdeveloped countries generally lack adequate data, precise comparable information on the incidence of poverty worldwide is not available. Instead, indirect measures of poverty must be used.

Gross National Product per capita (GNP/cap) is sometimes used to indicate a country's general standard of living. Since we will use information about GNP throughout this book, we should clearly define what it measures: GNP refers to the monetary value of all goods and services annually produced for sale in a country plus an estimate of the value of such government services as police, education, and national defense (Lekachman 1972, p. 6). To compute the GNP per capita, the country's GNP is divided by its population.

The figures for GNP, although widely used, are crude and often inadequate. Special difficulties arise in using GNP to compare living standards among countries. GNP does not include goods and services consumed by the producers themselves, yet in many countries people live primarily on what they produce themselves, not on what they buy in a market. Thus, people in underdeveloped countries can exist on a GNP per capita of $75. Moreover, people in different nations have diverse patterns of spending money and the prices of particular goods and services vary in different countries. Or the very style of providing for basic necessities varies: Japanese housing and furnishings, for example, are simpler than American.

Methods have been devised to make comparisons of GNP figures more accurate. One method corrects for the high cost of economic development, including costs of increased pollution and traffic accidents, for example (Nordhaus and Tobin 1972). Another computes GNP in international dollars rather than official exchange rates, which can be quite different. (GNP figures usually are based on calculations measured in the national currency, then converted to the United States currency at the official exchange rates. Exchange rates do not completely reflect variations in the price structure of different countries.) A combined effort of the Statistical Office of the United Nations, the World Bank, and the International Comparison Unit of the University of Pennsylvania developed a system of international comparisons based upon a world price structure (Kravis et al. 1975). The international prices and the product values are used to develop international dollars and these were used to determine Gross Domestic Product (GDP). GDP is the same as GNP except that income from investment abroad is excluded. In Table 4.1, GDP for the countries used in developing international dollars are shown in both United States and international dollars. Although the rank ordering of the countries is little changed, the magnitude of the difference in per capita GDP is altered greatly. Thus, in United States dollars at exchange rates, the Federal Republic of Germany ranks second among the ten countries studied and has a per capita GDP that is only about 64 percent of that of the United States. But measured in terms of international dollars, it ranks third and has 74.7 percent of the per capita GDP of the United States. India ranks tenth with only 2 percent of the GDP of the United States, measured in United States dollars at the exchange rates; in international dollars it ranks ninth and has a per capita GDP that is about 8 percent of that of the United States.

GNP per capita, calculated at exchange rates, is frequently used to compare the general standard of living in different countries, and despite its many difficulties, we will use it in this way. It does provide a general ranking of the average standard of living of most countries with market economies. It does not provide an indicator of inequality. In some countries, comparatively few very rich persons can raise the per-capita income disproportionately; other countries might attain the same average GNP by a more equal distribution of income.

TABLE 4.1   **Comparisons of Per Capita Gross Domestic Product in U.S. and International Dollars**

Countries	*Per Capita Gross Domestic Product, 1970*			
	In U.S. $ at Exchange Rate		**In International Prices**	
	U.S. $	**U.S.=100**	**I $**	**U.S.=100**
United States	4,801	100.0	4,801	100.0
Germany, Federal Republic of	3,080	64.2	3,585	74.7
France	2,902	60.5	3,599	75.0
United Kingdom	2,143	44.6	2,895	60.3
Japan	2,003	41.7	2,952	61.5
Italy	1,699	35.4	2,198	45.8
Hungary	1,037	21.6	1,935	40.3
Colombia	329	6.9	763	15.9
Kenya	144	3.0	275	5.7
India	98	2.0	342	7.9

Source: Kravis et al. 1975, Tables 1.1, p. 6 and 1.3, p.8.

The kind of data used to examine poverty in the United States is not available for all countries, nor even for all industrially developed countries. In countries with centrally planned economies, such as the Soviet Union, the governments, led by Communist parties, direct the economy and also control the flow of information about living standards. Furthermore, some services are provided outside the monetary market and prices for certain products may be subsidized. Nevertheless, some data about the incidence of poverty are available for the Soviet Union in the 1960s (Lipset and Dobson 1973). Soviet researchers have estimated that a minimal budget for an urban family would be 51.4 rubles per person per month. Family budget studies in Leningrad in 1962 and 1963 indicate that 40 percent of the families had less than that amount. Matthews (1972) infers from figures given by Soviet economist S. P. Figurnov that just over 30 percent of the workers and white collar families in the Soviet Union were poor by Soviet standards. He is defining poverty in terms of a minimally adequate level of living according to contemporary standards. The incidence of poverty, on the basis of these studies, is greater in the Soviet Union than in the United States.

Let's look at how Chandler (1969) compared the incidence of poverty in the United States with that in other developed market economies, particularly those of Western Europe. Chandler relied on a number of indirect measures. In one kind of comparison, he applied the economist Engel's law, which states that as income increases, the proportion spent on necessities decreases. Americans, on the average, spend a smaller proportion of their income on food and a larger proportion of their income on shelter than do Europeans. Yet on the whole, there is a small United States superiority in this regard, in that Americans in the lowest income groups spend a smaller proportion of their income on necessities than Europeans in the lowest income groups. By this indicator, the American poor are not as poor as those in Europe. Other indicators show a greater inequality in income levels in the United States than in some European countries; therefore, we could conclude that relative poverty is higher in the United States than in some other countries. Still other measures— rates of infant mortality, longevity, literacy, illegitimacy, and unemployment— indicate a higher incidence of poverty conditions in the United States than in some other countries. Although no simple finding emerges, it does seem that, despite the generally high standard of living in the United States, a relatively significant proportion of the population does not share in the abundance, but lives in poverty.

If we are to systematically compare the proportion of people living in poverty between economically developed and underdeveloped countries and between countries with market economies and centrally planned economies, we must find more indirect indicators than we have been using thus far. The strategy we will follow is to look for indicators that have an upper human limit, then see how close the country's average comes to that limit. We know that the maximum human life span does not change; therefore, we can reason that the higher the average life expectancy in a country, the greater the number of people with a minimal living standard. By the same token we can use death rates and infant mortality rates to indicate the extent to which people lack a minimal standard of living. Calories consumed per person can also indicate of the proportion of the people who have a minimal standard of living: however rich a person is, there is a limit to how much he or she can eat.

In Tables 4.2, 4.3, and 4.4, we can see how these measures differ among selected countries. Although an immense number of observations could be made about the countries, only a few will be mentioned here; the rest will be left for the reader. First, the countries selected vary considerably by each of the measures. People born in some countries are much more likely to stay alive than those born in other places.

Second, the United States, although having the highest GNP per capita, does not lead in all measures. As can be seen in Table 4.3, a woman's life expectancy is greater in Sweden and France; a man's, in Australia, Canada, France, and the German Democratic Republic, Israel, Italy, Japan, and the United Kingdom. Infant mortality rates are lower in Sweden, Japan, France, and other countries. We can see that high average income does not guarantee that the poor receive adequate food and medical services.

On the whole, however, people in the United States and in the other economically developed countries do have higher life expectancy and lower death rates and infant mortality rates than people in the less economically developed countries. The average life expectancy in some countries is desperately short. It is less than fifty years in many countries; it is thirty-seven years in Nigeria and even less in Chad. The infant mortality rates, too, are frightfully high in many less developed countries. For every 1,000 births in Ghana, 156 children die within a year. Clearly, many people in these countries exist in conditions that are barely life-sustaining.

Admittedly, high infant mortality and short life expectancies do not indicate the incidence of poverty alone. They are also affected by climate, sanitation, health delivery systems, culture, and the population's age distribution. For example, all else being equal, a country with a high proportion of older people will have a higher death rate than a country where a high proportion of the population is young.

Information on food consumption throughout the world further documents that severe poverty is widespread. Even obtaining sufficient calories to sustain human activity is not common in much of the world (de Castro 1967). The United States Department of Agriculture Foreign Economic Administration estimates that 92 percent of the Latin Americans were living on diets which did not supply the minimum recommended caloric intake (Chaney and Ross 1971, p. 49). The United Nations Food and Agriculture Organization gives a daily caloric requirement of 3,200 for a man and 2,300 for a woman (the requirement is a function of body weight, level of activity, and other factors). Assuming 2,750 calories per day as a minimum standard, we can compare the calories

TABLE 4.2 Per Capita National Income and Per Capita Energy Consumption for Selected Countries

Country	Per Capita National Income (In U.S. Dollars)	Per Capita Consumption of Energy, 1972 (In Million Metric Tons of Coal Equivalent)
Algeria	259 (1969)	533
Australia	2919 (1971)	5701
Bolivia	214 (1971)	210
Brazil	422 (1971)	532
Burma	68 (1969)	58
Canada	4231 (1972)	10757
Chad	63 (1963)	20
Chile	515 (1971)	1516
Colombia	426 (1972)	610
Cuba		1168
Czechoslavakia		6844
Egypt	202 (1970)	324
France	3403 (1972)	4153
Germany (Federal Republic of)	3739 (1972)	5396
Ghana	238 (1970)	152
Greece	1327 (1972)	1607
India	88 (1969)	186
Indonesia	112 (1972)	133
Iran	367 (1971)	954
Iraq	278 (1969)	642
Israel	2007 (1972)	2712
Italy	1987 (1972)	2796
Ivory Coast	321 (1971)	309
Jamaica	714 (1972)	1568
Japan	2462 (1972)	3251
Kenya	151 (1972)	165
Lebanon	521 (1970)	889
Mexico	681 (1971)	1318
Morocco	250 (1972)	223
Nigeria	85 (1963)	66
Pakistan	205 (1971)	158
Peru	316 (1971)	622
South Africa	734 (1972)	2770
Sweden	4669 (1972)	5739
Tanzania	106 (1972)	49
United Kingdom	2479 (1972)	5398
United States	4981 (1972)	11611
Yugoslavia		1610

Source: United Nations Department of Economic and Social Affairs, Statistical Yearbook, 1973, Table 137, pp. 347-350 and Table 182, pp. 590-595.

TABLE 4.3 Life Expectancy and Death Rates for Selected Countries

Country	Expectation of Life at Birth			Death Rate (per 1,000)		
	Male	Female	(Year)	Crude	Infant	(Year)
Algeria	51	–	(1965-70)	17	86	(1965-70)
Australia	68	74	(1960-62)	9	17	(1972)
Bolivia	50	50	(1949-51)	19	77	(1965-70)
Brazil	61	–	(1965-70)	10	–	(1965-70)
Burma	48	–	(1965-70)	17	195-300	(1965-70)
Canada	69	75	(1965-67)	7	17	(1972)
Chad	29	35	(1963-64)	25	160	(1965-70)
Chile	60	66	(1969-70)	9	79	(1970)
China (People's Republic of)	50	–	(1965-70)	15	–	(1965-70)
Colombia	44	46	(1950-52)	11	71	(1965-70)
Cuba	67	–	(1965-70)	8	34	(1965-70)
Czechoslovakia	65	73	(1970)	11	21	(1972)
Egypt	52	54	(1960)	13	103	(1971)
France	69	76	(1970)	11	16	(1972)
German Dem. Rep.	69	74	(1967-68)	14	18	(1972)
Germany (Federal Republic of)	67	73	(1968-70)	12	23	(1972)
Ghana	46	–	(1965-70)	18	156	(1965-70)
Greece	67	71	(1960-62)	8	27	(1971)
India	42	41	(1951-60)	17	139	(1965-70)
Indonesia	48	48	(1960)	19	125	(1965-70)
Iran	50	–	(1965-70)	17	–	(1965-70)
Iraq	52	–	(1965-70)	16	20	(1965-70)
Israel	70	73	(1972)	7	21	(1972)

TABLE 4.3   Life Expectancy and Death Rates for Selected Countries (continued)

Country	Expectation of Life at Birth			Death Rate (per 1,000)		
	Male	Female	(Year)	Crude	Infant	(Year)
Italy	68	73	(1964-67)	10	28	(1972)
Ivory	– 41	–	(1965-70)	23	138	(1965-70)
Jamaica	63	67	(1959-61)	7	26	(1972)
Japan	69	74	(1968)	7	12	(1971)
Kenya	47	51	(1969)	18	55	(1965-70)
Lebanon	–	–		5	14	(1965-70)
Mexico	61	64	(1965-70)	9	61	(1965-70)
Morocco	– 51	–	(1965-70)	17	149	(1965-70)
Nigeria	37	37	(1965-66)	25	–	(1965-70)
Pakistan	54	49	(1962)	18	142	(1965-70)
Peru	53	56	(1960-65)	11	73	(1965-70)
Poland	67	74	(1970-72)	8	29	(1972)
South Africa	– 49	–	(1965-70)	17	–	(1965-70)
Sweden	72	77	(1969)	10	11	(1972)
Tanzania	– 40-41	–	(1967)	22	160-165	(1967)
United Kingdom	68	74	(1968-70)	12	18	(1972)
United States	67	75	(1971)	9	19	(1972)
USSR	65	74	(1968-69)	9	24	(1972)
Yugoslavia	65	69	(1968-70)	9	43	(1972)

Source: United Nations Department of Economic and Social Affairs, Statistical Yearbook, 1973, Table 19, pp. 80-85.

TABLE 4.4   Food Consumption Per Capita for Selected Countries

Country	Per Capital Calories (Per Day)	Year	Per Capita Proteins (In Grams)
Algeria	1890	1964-66	55.7
Australia	3160	1963-65	91.5
Bolivia	1760	1964-66	45.8
Brazil	2820	1970	66.8
Burma	2010	1964-66	44.1
Canada	3200	1966-68	95.8
Chad	2240	1964-66	78.4
Chile	2560	1970	65.9
China (People's Republic of)	2050	1964-66	57.2
Colombia	2140	1970	50.0
Cuba	2500	1964-66	62.8
Czechoslavakia	3030	1964-66	83.3
Egypt	2770	1968-69	79.9
France	3270	1969-70	102.6
German Democratic Republic	3040	1964-66	76.4
Germany (Federal Republic of)	3180	1969-70	83.0
Ghana	2070	1966-68	43.0
Greece	2900	1967	98.9
India	1990	1969-70	49.4
Indonesia	1920	1970	42.8
Iran	2030	1964-66	55.2
Iraq	2050	1964-66	57.8
Israel	2990	1969-70	91.5
Italy	3020	1969-70	87.9
Ivory Coast	2430	1964-66	59.1
Jamaica	2260	1964-66	59.1
Japan	2470	1970	76.9
Kenya	2200	1970	68.0
Lebanon	2360	1964-66	69.9
Mexico	2620	1964-66	66.3
Morocco	2130	1964-66	57.7
Nigeria	2290	1970	59.9
Pakistan	2410	1969-70	54.9
Peru	2190	1968	54.6
Poland	3140	1964-66	93.2
South Africa	2730	1964-66	77.0
Sweden	2850	1970-71	80.0
Tanzania	1700	1970	42.5
United Kingdom	3170	1970-71	86.8
United States	3300	1970	98.6
USSR	3180	1964-66	92.2
Yugoslavia	3130	1968	91.6

Source: United Nations Food and Agriculture Organization Production Yearbook, 1973, Table 136, pp. 442-448 and Table 137, pp. 449-455.

available per person in the selected countries listed in Table 4.4. In many of the countries, calories per person are below the minimum standard. Even in countries with a higher than minimum average, some people fall below the minimum. Among the countries listed in the table, the United States has the highest average consumption (New Zealand and Ireland, not listed in the table, exceed even the United States). But in the less economically developed countires, the average falls quite low: 1,990 in India; 1,890 in Algeria, and 2,200 in Kenya. Because actual intake is lower than the nutrients *available* for consumption, which is what is reported in Table 4.4, the situation is actually much worse than the figures indicate.

In addition to the total caloric consumption many specific nutritional needs are vital for life. One such requirement is protein. Although minimal protein requirements vary with body size, quality of protein, and life cycle stage, the recommended dietary allowance is 60 grams of protein a day (Chaney and Ross 1971, p. 100). Again, the data presented in Table 4.4 indicate that in many countries the per capita protein available is below the recommended level. Obviously many if not most people in those countries suffer some protein deficiency.

Distribution

Income and wealth can be distributed more or less equally. People can be equally poor or equally well off. We will review the evidence on variations in the distribution first of income and then of wealth among countries at different levels of economic development and with different economic systems.

Income. Although information about income inequality in different countries is beginning to accumulate, comparisons are difficult and should not be regarded as precise. Nevertheless, large inequalities in money income among countries undoubtedly indicate real differences in the degree of inequality. A basic set of data on personal income in many countries is presented in Table 4.5. It shows the proportion of all personal income received by the lowest 20 percent and by the highest 5 percent of the families or households. We can also see the degree of inequality of the overall distribution, as measured by the Gini ratio. Clearly, a few countries have a more equal distribution of income than the United States; many have a more unequal distribution. In Australia, for example, the poorest 20 percent of the families or households received 6.6 percent of the total personal income of the country; the wealthiest 5 percent received 14.4 percent of the total. The Gini ratio was .30. In the United States, the lowest 20 percent received 5.6 percent of the income and the highest received 14.8 for a Gini ratio of .34.[1] Among the countries in the table, Israel is also more equal

---

[1] This finding is not the same as that reported in Table 3.5. There, we saw higher Gini ratios reported. The difference has to do with the results from the different basis for calculating income. The income data reported in Table 3.5 include imputed nonmonetary income that is not included in the figures reported in Table 4.4.

TABLE 4.5   Indicators of Personal Income Inequality in Selected Countries

Country	Percent of Total Personal Income Received by Percentiles		
	Lowest 20%	Highest 5%	Gini Ratio
Australia (1966-67)	6.6	14.4	.30
Bolivia (1968)	3.5	35.7	.53
Brazil (1960)	3.5	38.4	.54
Burma (1958)	10.0	28.2	.35
Chad (1958)	8.0	23.0	.35
Chile (1968)	5.4	22.6	.44
Colombia (1964)	2.2	40.4	.62
France (1962)	1.9	25.0	.50
Germany, Federal Republic of (1964)	5.3	33.7	.45
Greece (1957)	9.0	23.0	.38
India (1956-57)	8.0	20.0	.33
Iraq (1956)	2.0	34.0	.60
Israel (1957)	6.8	11.2	.30
Italy (1948)	6.1	24.1	.40
Ivory Coast (1959)	8.0	29.0	.43
Jamaica (1958)	2.2	30.2	.56
Japan (1962)	4.7	14.8	.39
Lebanon (1953-60)	3.0	34.0	.55
Mexico (1963)	3.5	28.8	.53
Morocco (1965)	7.1	20.6	.50
Nigeria (1959)	7.0	38.4	.51
Pakistan (1963-64)	6.5	20.0	.37
Peru (1961)	4.0	48.3	.61
South Africa (1965)	1.9	27.0	.56
Sweden (1963)	4.4	17.6	.39
Tanzania (1964)	4.8	42.9	.54
United Kingdom (1964)	5.1	19.0	.38
United States (1969)	5.6	14.8	.34

Source: Paukert 1973, Table 6, pp. 114-115.

than the United States. Although India's Gini ratio is just under the Gini ratio for the United States, the income received by the top 5 percent of the families and households is even greater; the difference lies in the greater share received by the upper 60 percent within the United States.

In many countries, income inequality is much greater than in the United States. In Columbia, for example, the lowest 20 percent of the families and households received only 2 percent of the income; the top 5 percent received 40 percent. In countries where the total income is generally low, this, of course, means that the lowest income receivers are in absolute terms extremely poor. Obviously, there is considerable variation among the countries listed.

Comparisons of income inequality between centrally planned economies and market economies are even more difficult to make than comparisons among market economies. Price structures, the availability of information, and the ways of reporting information differ considerably. In centrally planned economies, such as the Soviet Union, income is almost entirely derived from wages and salaries and transfer payments—that is, money transferred by the government in the form of family allowances and old-age pensions. Because the amount of wage and transfer payments is determined by the government, the level of income inequality largely reflects governmental policy. Even in a centrally planned economy goods and services may be privately produced and privately sold or bartered, either legally or illegally. However, such activities probably do not radically alter the income distribution as determined by wage schedules and transfer payments. In addition, many special benefits are given to a select few, not as direct money payments, but in travel, housing, and other prerequisites. If these could be included in income, they undoubtedly would increase inequalities. Of course, such prerequisites are also often excluded from reported income by business executives in market economies as well.

We can examine some information on income inequality in centrally planned or command economies, if we limit ourselves to persons employed in certain occupations and to income from employment and from transfer payments. Such data are available for the German Democratic Republic (East Germany) (Schnitzer, 1974).

Information on income distribution in East Germany includes data on household income for all workers employed in state enterprises, administrative organs, producer cooperatives, trade organizations, and independently employed professionals. It includes regular wages and bonuses but not special ones. Transfer payments such as family allowances are included; income tax is not taken into account. In 1970, the lowest 20 percent of the households had 10.4 percent of the total household income. The information on the proportion received by the highest 5 percent is not reported. The Gini ratio was calculated to be .19, based upon the five quintiles of households. Clearly, income is more equally distributed in East Germany than among the countries we have discussed thus far.

Other analyses also indicate that income is more equally distributed in centrally planned economies than in market economies (Parkin 1971; Miller and Rein 1975). The *possibility* that government policy can dictate a more equal income distribution does not mean it always does so. In the Soviet Union, policies have at times emphasized equality; at other times, provided income incentives. In the early 1930s, an anti-equalitarian campaign increased the differences in income between low- and high-paid workers; wage differentials were probably greater than in the United States. After the Twentieth Party Congress in 1956, wage inequalities were reduced considerably (Yanowitch 1963). Wage differences now are probably smaller in the USSR than in European market economies (Parkin 1971). However, subsidization for housing and other benefits, which are disproportionally given to those in elite positions in the USSR, are difficult to include in income figures and undoubtedly increase the inequality (Lipset and Dobson 1973).

The changes in the degree of equality in income distribution that apparently have occurred in the Soviet Union are possible because of central planning and state control of wages and salaries. A market economy without private owner-ship can produce income distributions similar to that of a market economy with private ownership. In Yugoslavia, the means of production are collectively owned but the factories and other productive organs are self-managed by the employees themselves to a significant degree. The United Nations Economic Commission for Europe (1967) provides information on the distribution of income of consumer units in Yugoslavia in 1963. They report that the lowest 20 percent of the consumer units received 7.9 percent of the total income and the top 5 percent received 15.2 percent. Additional calculations show the Gini ratio to be .36. Compared to capitalist market economies, Yugoslavia's income is relatively equally distributed, but not appreciably more so than the relatively equalitarian countries such as Australia, Israel, and even the United States.

Wealth. Comparative information on wealth inequalities is even sparser than comparative income data. Comparisons of only a few aspects of wealth are possible at all, and for some of these, for only a few countries. But because variations in wealth are so important, we will examine indirect as well as direct indicators. We will look at the concentration of all forms of wealth, at the ownership of corporations, of land, and at the proportion of the population that is self-employed.

High as concentration of wealth is in the United States, it is exceeded in the United Kingdom. One estimate states that in 1960 1 percent of the British population owned 42 percent of the total personal wealth (Miliband 1969, p. 25). Other estimates are lower, but still show the concentration as greater than in the United States (Atkinson 1975). As we discussed in Chapter 3, 1 percent of the American population is estimated to own about 25 percent of the country's personally possessed wealth. Ownership of corporate shares is also more concentrated in Britain than in the United States. In 1961, 1 percent of the adult population owned 81 percent of the privately owned company shares, compared to 76 percent in the United States in 1953 (Miliband, 1969, p. 26).

In most countries of the world, agriculture is still the dominant sector of work. Class systems in many countries today, as in nearly all the countries in the past, are characterized by the variation in agricultural enterprises and agricul-tural systems. Stinchcombe (1961) has distinguished five major types of agricul-tural enterprises producing goods for a commercial market. His discussion excluded the community-as-enterprise systems of Israel and of Eastern Europe or China. Although many systems are undergoing rapid change and some of them have almost disappeared as a result of revolution or major reform efforts, it is useful to be familiar with the variety.

The five types of agricultural enterprises Stinchcombe distinguishes are: the manorial or hacienda; family-sized tenancy; family smallholding; plantation; and ranch systems. In the manorial or hacienda system, the land is divided into domain land and labor subsistence land, with domain land devoted to production for the market. The subsistence farmers owe work on the lord's or hacienda owner's domain lands. This system was common in Mexico prior to the 1910 revolution and in the Peruvian highlands until reforms began in 1968. It tends to exist in areas with low-cost land and little market in land.

In the family-size tenancy system, small parcels of highly valuable land are worked by families who do not independently own the land. The tenants pay rent on the land, in money or in kind; they may have title to the land, but they pay interest on their continuing debt to others who collect interest on the loans secured by the land. This system is most common in highly labor- and land-intensive agriculture such as rice and cotton. Land-intensive agriculture entails much labor used in a small area with a high yield per acre.

In family smallholding enterprises, a family works the farm, but unlike tenancy, the family owns the land. This is common in the central and northeastern United States as well as in Japan after the land reforms following World War II.

Plantations are worked with either wage or slave labor and are most common in producing labor-intensive crops requiring high capital investment on relatively cheap land, as in rubber or sugar cane crops. Finally, ranches are characterized by large-scale production, usually of labor-extensive crops such as wool or beef, on land of low value. Wage labor typically live in company barracks and eat in company messes.

In a more recent analysis directed at studying agrarian revolutions, Paige (1975) encompasses these types by using two dimensions to characterize forms of export agricultural organization: cultivators and noncultivators, with the cultivators tending to be subordinate to the noncultivators. The two categories vary in their major source of income. Cultivators draw their income predominantly from either land or wages, noncultivators from land or capital. These two dimensions combine into four major kinds of agricultural organizations: (1) hacienda, (2) sharecropping or migratory labor, (3) small holding, and (4) plantation.

Consider first the agricultural organizations in which the noncultivators derive their income from the land they own. Where the noncultivators draw their income from the crops produced on their land and cultivators draw their income from the parcels of land they own, commercial haciendas exist. Where the noncultivators receive their income from the land they own and cultivators from the wages they earn, the agricultural organization is sharecropping (tenancy) or it may involve migratory labor.

Noncultivators can also receive their income from capital: financial or industrial. In one case, "the upper class surrenders control of the direct cultivation to a system of decentralized small farms, while in the other the upper class controls the agricultural enterprise directly, usually through a joint stock corporation" (Paige 1975, p. 14) In the former case, the cultivators' source of income is the land they own and the small-holding farming system results; in the latter case, the cultivators' source of income is wages and this constitutes the plantation system.

Class relations differ among these types of agricultural enterprises. The systems of stratification, in a sense, are bounded by each type. Within most countries, more than one type of agricultural enterprise exists. Data on the concentration of landholdings do not provide sufficient information to properly make all these distinctions. Nevertheless, we do get a rough idea of the concentration of ownership of a basic resource in agricultural production. Information on the proportion of the agricultural labor force that is employed by others also helps indicate the type of agricultural enterprise and the extent to which farmers do not own their own means of production.

Data on inequality of land ownership have been calculated for the *World Handbook of Political and Social Indicators* (Taylor and Hudson, 1971). The authors based their calculations on information from the United Nations Food and Agricultural Organization and other sources. The data refer to landholdings any part of which is used for agriculture; no distinction is made regarding the proportion of the landholding that is not arable or is used only for pasture. Farms are divided into categories according to size; the number of acres and the number of farms in each category are used to calculate the Gini ratios. Both standardized and unstandardized ways of rating size of holdings were used. In the unstandardized version, the categories given by the reporting country were used, although a "big" farm in Australia differs from a "big" farm in Belgium. This has the advantage of reflecting the general intensity of land use; thus, in countries with ranches, large landholdings would be more frequent. In the standardized version, the same sizes were used to classify the farms in all countries. The latter version seems to provide more comparable data, but the meaning of very large holdings in countries with intensive agriculture might well be different from that in a country with less intensive use. In any case, the two measures are highly correlated with each other (Pearson correlation coefficient is .79 for the 29 countries where data exist for both indicators).

The first half of Table 4.6 shows that land holdings are generally very unequal. In Peru, for example, the inequality of landholdings was extremely high before the land reforms begun by the government that took power in 1968. Current information on a comparable basis is not available, but the extent and swiftness of the change is indicated by the proportion of the workers in agriculture who are employed by others. In 1970, it was 12.9 percent, as shown in the last two columns of Table 4.6; in 1961, according to the *International Labour Organization Yearbook*, 31.1 percent were wage workers. The land reform in Mexico, following the revolution in 1910, may not be as striking, but the

TABLE 4.6 Land Inequality and Employment Status in Selected Countries

Country	Land Inequality* Gini Ratios		Employment Status**				Agriculture	
				Total Labor Force				
	Unstandardized	Standardized	Year	% Self-Employed	% Salary or Wage Workers	% Family Workers	% Salary or Wage Workers	Year
Australia	.88	.48	1960	12.5	86.9	.6	36.5	1971
Brazil	.85	–	1960	35.3	54.8	9.9	25.4	1970
Columbia	.86	.84	1960	33.6	58.1	8.3	42.2	1964
Egypt	.67	–	1964	29.4	53.9	16.7	38.2	1966
Germany, Federal Republic of	.67	–	1960	9.4	85.1	5.5	13.8	1972
India	.53	–	1955					–
Indonesia	–	–	–	43.0	33.5	23.5	23.2	1971
Iran	.62	.57	1960	41.3	48.8	9.9	25.3	1966
Iraq	.88	.86	1958					–
Israel[1]	–	–	–	21.7	75.2	3.1	30.5	1973
Italy	.72	–	1969	21.7	73.6	4.7	–	1971
Ivory Coast	–	–	–	80.6	11.3	8.1	5.6	1964
Japan	.47	.15	1960	19.2	64.6	16.2	20.4	1970
Mexico	.69	–	1960	31.3	62.2	6.5	49.0	1970
Pakistan	.65	.44	1960	51.9	17.6	30.5	7.7	1972
Peru	.93	–	1961	45.4	38.8	15.8	12.9	1970
South Africa	.70	–	1960					–
Sweden	.51	.50	1961	7.9	92.1	–	56.3	1973
Tanzania	–	–	–	74.8	9.0	16.2	2.9	1967
United Kingdom	.72	.70	1960	6.6	92.7	0.7	56.9	1966
United States	.71	–	1959	8.0	90.9	1.1	39.1	1973
Yugoslavia[2]	.44	–	1950	24.3	53.1	22.7	7.1	1971

[1] Employers and workers on own account includes producers' cooperatives and communal farms (Kibbutzim).
[2] Salaried employees and wage earners include members of producers' cooperatives.

Sources: *Taylor and Hudson; **International Labour Organization Yearbook 1974, Table 2, pp. 54-139.

hacienda system had been very pervasive and the information in Table 4.6 does indicate greater agricultural equality in Mexico than in the other Latin American countries in the table. Interestingly, in many predominantly agricultural countries, most people are self-employed as farmers. Consider Tanzania, Pakistan, and the Ivory Coast in Table 4.6. Even the landholdings are more equal than in some economically developed countries, such as the United States. Among the developed countries, the apparent equality in Japanese agriculture indicates the extent of the land reform that occurred under the American military occupation following World War II.

Countries that are unequal in personal income distribution also tend to be unequal in land ownership.[2] This is more likely to be true in largely agricultural economies than in industrial ones.

The dependence of much of the world's population on agriculture also means that many people in less industrialized countries continue to own their own means of production. Despite the concentration of land ownership, many peasants and small subsistence farmers do own a piece of land. In an industrialized country, such as the United States, nearly everyone is employed, but in less industrialized countries self-employment is much more common, as is shown in the second half of Table 4.6.

Small farm holdings, although worked by the owners, may produce crops for export, making the owners dependent on markets they cannot control. They may live precariously and depend on those who can give them credit or who control the distribution of their goods. In many countries, agriculture is conducted in the form of plantations with large numbers of agricultural wage workers. In some countries then, even in economically developing ones, a high proportion of agricultural laborers may be employed by others. In the United States, about 40 percent of the workers in agriculture, forestry, and fishing are employed by others; in Mexico, the percentage is greater, about 50 percent (International Labour Organization 1974, Table 2A). Developing countries have many other industries that do not involve large-scale enterprise and many artisans produce goods independently. Such manufacturing enterprises may consist of a store or stall where furniture, shoes, or other products are made by one person or a family. Thus, while in the United States 99 percent of the workers in the manufacturing industry are employed by others, in Mexico, only 77 percent are.

Inequality of wealth, then, is complex and to compare its variations among

[2] The Gini ratio for personal income inequality is correlated .59 with standardized land inequality among the fifteen countries for which data exist for both indicators. Personal income equality is correlated with unstandardized land inequality .46, among the thirty countries for which data exist for both indicators. These are strong relationships. It is possible that income equality, among market societies, depends on not too unequal land ownership. Or both income and land equality may be determined by the same factors. In any case, the results strengthen the idea that land ownership is an indicator of overall class inequality and the standardized measure is more useful in this regard than the unstandardized one.

different countries is difficult. Industrialization does create great concentration of wealth, especially if we consider ownership of the means of production. It is possible that in poor countries, where the average amount of wealth is relatively small, large proportions of people own the means of producing their own necessities or producing products they can exchange for them. In countries with greater average wealth, however, the personally held wealth, particularly wealth used in consumption, may be somewhat more equally distributed than in poorer countries.

The difficulties of comparing wealth inequalities are even greater if we include centrally planned countries with extensive public, state, or collective ownership. Does it make sense to speak of wealth inequality in countries with very little private ownership? If the "people" own the means of production, wealth is presumably equally distributed. But is it? The earlier discussion of the managerial revolution should help us here. Ownership of property can be separate from control. Let us consider some possible arrangements in different countries.

In the Soviet Union and in East European countries with Communist party governments, the people collectively own the means of production and the government manages the enterprises. In Israel, the members of a Kibbutz (collective farm) own and manage it. In many countries, various degrees of worker-control or worker-management exist. In Yugoslavia, for example, a great deal of control is vested in the workers of an enterprise; they can help choose and dismiss the directors of the plants and through their representatives help determine the full range of managerial decisions. Even in countries with private ownership, workers may directly and indirectly participate in managerial control. Thus, in West Germany the laws of codetermination require representation of the workers in the board of directors of large companies. Even without worker management, the public exercises some control over private capital. In the United States, for example, government regulatory agencies limit business decisions so that they do not harm, in specified ways, the public's interest.

In comparing wealth inequality, then, we must consider not only who owns wealth but who controls its use. We must examine the actual operations as well as the formal rules. The decisive questions about inequality of wealth vary among different kinds of economies. In the centrally planned economies, questions about popular control of government policies and questions about whose interest the government policies serve are crucial. In systems with worker management or worker participation in management, the decisive question is to what extent workers actually make the decisions; do they, or the managers, or the state have effective control of the enterprise? Although the evidence is not clear, it seems that, on the whole, workers have effective influence on many policies directly affecting their day-to-day work activities. Policies having to do with investments and marketing are generally under the direction of the managers and they operate within tax, market, and other conditions influenced or determined by the government.

In countries with private ownership of wealth, government policies on money supply, prices, taxes, and more specific business regulations all exercise some effect on the way that wealth is used. The greater the government control, the more important it is to know who controls the government in order to understand who actually controls wealth. In this regard, the distinction between private and collective ownership is not a sharp one and many of the same issues exist in both kinds of economies. The distinction between class and power dimensions of inequality is also revealed to be a difficult one to make in describing the empirical reality. The distinctions are useful analytically, but the real world is not so neatly divided.

Comparisons of class inequality in different countries are always difficult and sometimes impossible; since there is a lack of comparable data. So little information is available about mobility into and out of class positions that we are omitting a comparative discussion. We will consider intergenerational mobility of occupational status in the next two chapters. Comparisons are also difficult because the meaning of many concepts alter when they are examined in different contexts, as we saw in the case of wealth inequality. Thinking about such problems, however, at least helps us to understand inequality within each country or economic system.

GLOBAL INEQUALITIES

In many ways, countries are arbitrary and inappropriate systems within which to analyze class inequalities. Class differences are best examined within a bounded market or economic system. For some purposes, segments of a country may be a more appropriate system within which to study class inequality. For example, Paige (1975), in his study of agrarian revolutions, examined agricultural export sectors within developing countries. He selected the major producing regions for a given export crop within a given country—for example, the coffee-producing highlands of Kenya. Each sector was categorized according to the dominant type of agricultural organization. As defined by this method, the world has many more economies than countries.

In this book we will not discuss subnational economies, but we will pay attention to markets and class systems that incorporate, transcend, and cut across countries. In many senses, there are no national economies, only a world economy (Wallerstein 1974; Chirot 1977; Rubinson 1976). Goods are traded on a global basis, and capital owned by people in one country is invested in another. Laborers, craftsmen, and professionals move from one country to another to work for a few months, a few years, or the rest of their lives. The opportunities of owners of capital, of industrial employees, and of professionals are affected by their place in the world economy.

We know this is so. But how do we comprehend and analyze a world system that binds everyone together into one vast, interrelated network? We can do so only piece by piece. This book will examine separately different aspects of the total world economy. We have already looked at countries as independent systems. This section will first consider countries as units making up the world economy and examine them as if they were ranked units. We will then discuss units that transcend national boundaries, as do multinational corporations.

Inequality Among Countries

We begin our description of international stratification by looking at the relative income, wealth, or material resources of whole countries. Given the ambiguities of comparing GNP, we will use energy consumption. Information about energy consumption is available for centrally planned as well as market economies and is published in the *United Nations Statistical Yearbook.* The total amount of energy consumed in a country is an indicator of the aggregate material resources available to that society. We can leave aside questioning whether higher energy consumption per capita necessarily means a higher living standard (Mazur and Rosa, 1974). A country with a large proportion of the world's energy consumption is in a position to economically dominate other countries.

Given the great range in economic development and in population size among the countries of the world, the gross amount of energy consumed in different countries varies widely. The United States in 1972 used almost two and one-half billion metric tons of coal equivalence in energy—one-third of the total world's energy consumption. The United States clearly has the largest mass of economic wealth. The Soviet Union consumes 15.92 percent of the world's energy; West Germany, 4.49 percent; India, 1.37 percent; and Kenya, 0.03 percent.

Ranking countries by total energy used or per capita energy usage or by some other measure of wealth or income does not tell us all we need to understand international stratification. We must know *how* the countries (or their governments and peoples) interact and are related to each other. Furthermore, we need to ascertain to what extent that relationship is hierarchical—does it or does it not involve domination, dependency, or subordination? Some writers have discussed such relations in terms of economic, political, or cultural imperialism (Lenin 1933; Lichtheim 1971).

In this work, we want to examine inequality between countries, with particular attention to the hierarchical quality of that inequality. We must consider those aspects of material relations that involve some degree of superordination and subordination. In spite of the obvious difficulties in doing this, it is extremely important that we do so. Not only would that tell us a great deal about the structure of the world, but it would help to *explain* inequalities within each country. One difficulty is that "countries" do not interact or have relations. "Countries" is a shorthand term used to refer to collections of persons or government officials acting in the name of their countries. We might better refer to governments or ministries, to corporations or traders, to buyers and sellers. But because information is generally not available in this fashion, we are forced to use data aggregated in terms of countries. But talking about the inequality of countries is a gross simplification. When we discuss how the relations between countries affects inequality within each, this will become clearer and will also be one way to modify the gross simplifications.

In this chapter we focus on material or economic inequality between countries; aid, trade, and investment will be discussed in ways that indicate possible domination and dependency between countries.

Trade. Presumably, trade in any product is mutually beneficial to the trading partners; otherwise they would not carry on the exchange. Yet, one side may be able to exact better terms; one partner to the exchange may have more of a monopoly on the products it is offering for sale than the other does. Or one partner may have many potential customers who will bargain against each other. The side with the stronger bargaining position, then, is dominant in the exchange.

A common indication of overall trade dependency between countries is the relative importance of trade to the trading partners. A related indicator is the importance of trade to a country's Gross Domestic Product (GDP). Thus, we can consider the dollar value of country X's trade with country Z relative to X's total GDP. If the proportion were very high, country X would be considered dependent upon country Z. Presumably, policies followed by country Z would have great impact upon country X; therefore, country X would be more accommodative. If X has no other important trading partner, that dependence would be still greater.

The immense differences in Gross Domestic Product among the countries of the world cause many asymmetrical relations. One large country may be a major trading partner for many smaller countries, but that trade may constitute only a small proportion of the large country's GDP. This is most obviously the case with the United States; it has a very large GDP and a vast domestic market and foreign trade makes up a very small proportion of its GDP. In general, the industrially developed countries do most of their trading with each other; but in none of them does foreign trade make up a large proportion of its GDP. On the other hand, less economically developed countries tend to have asymmetrical trading relations with the developed countries. Again, this does not, in itself, mean that every exchange or even the bulk of the trading exchanges are exploitive or disadvantageous to the trader from the less developed country. But the country as a whole, and probably the government of the country, is more dependent on the trade: there is an asymmetrical relationship.

Table 4.7 shows the relative magnitude of trade between the major economic powers and many other countries (Singer 1972, Table 6.2). The major power is listed with selected countries that have had some historical association with it; the countries are ranked in terms of their trade relative to their GDP.

Thus, the total foreign trade of Honduras with the United States is equal to 26 percent of Honduras' GDP—very large relative to its GDP. The relative importance of foreign trade for the United States is tiny. Some countries have even larger ratios of trade to GDP with other powers: Gambia with the United Kingdom and the Congo (now Zaire) with France.

Foreign aid. Aid would seem to be a clearer indicator of dependency. The recipient is dependent on the provider of the technical assistance, the loans, or the outright grants of money. Actually, however, loans and other forms of assistance are usually given with reservations—possibly to purchase goods from the country giving aid. The loan or grant, then, is likely to be returned to the grantor country to purchase goods, thus generating employment and taxes. In any case, such assistance helps establish ties that bind the economy of the recipient country to the grantor. Although foreign aid is generally small relative to the GNP of the recipient country, it can be very high (Singer 1972). For example, French aid to the Congo (now Zaire) in 1966 totaled about 40 percent of that country's GNP; United States aid to Laos in 1963 was about 31 percent of its GNP. The United States has been by far the largest supplier of foreign aid since World War II. After the war, much of the aid went to help the economies of non-Communist Europe. Aid to the less developed countries has since become greater, but it has largely taken the form of loans rather than grants and has been given in large measure to military allies located near to Communist powers (Magdoff 1969). The Soviet Union, France, the United Kingdom, Germany, Japan, and the People's Republic of China are also important generators of aid, each to its own set of countries. Aid is granted to countries with historical ties, such as former colonies, or to allies in the Cold War. Only India has received major amounts of aid from both the United States and the Soviet Union at the same time.

Foreign investment. The third form of international stratification to be considered is investment. Generally, this refers to the extent to which companies from one country own factories, farms, or other capital in other countries. Again, the United States is clearly the dominant power. The absolute magnitude of United States capital assets abroad is immense. In 1970, direct long-term investments by private United States companies in other countries was over $78 billion (U.S. Bureau of the Census 1973, Table 1276). In addition, there are private direct investments in foreign portfolios and short-term investments, as well as Government long-term credits and liquid assets. The total United States assets abroad were $166.9 billion in 1970. This compares with a total Gross Domestic Product of the world's market economies of $2,491.6 billion; the total among the developing market economies was $391.6 billion (United Nations Department of Economic and Social Affairs, 1974).

Most the the United States direct investments are in Canada and other countries with developed market economies. In fact, two-thirds of the private long-term investments in 1970 were in the developed market economies. But the

TABLE 4.7 Trade of Selected Countries with Major Powers as a Percent of Gross Domestic Product, 1967 (Grouped by Historical Association and Ranked Within Group)

Country	Percent of GDP Accounted for by Total Trade with:								Approximate Percent of GDP Accounted for by Trade with All Major Powers
	USA	UK	EEC[1]	France	Soviet Bloc[2]	USSR	Japan	Inter-Regional	
United States and Associated States									
USA	0	0	1	0	0	0	1	2	4
Honduras	26	1	12	0	0	0	2	12	53
Panama	21	1	3	0	0	0	2	7	34
Bolivia	19	12	6	0	0	0	3	5	45
Peru	13	1	8	1	0	0	3	3	28
Mexico	8	0	2	1	0	0	1	1	12
Colombia	8	1	3	0	0	0	0	1	13
United Kingdom and Associated States									
United Kingdom	4	0	6	1	1	1	1	7	19
Gambia	3	53	28	0	ND	ND	9	2	95
Ireland	5	38	8	2	1	0	1	3	56
Kenya	4	16	11	1	1	0	2	3	37
Jamaica	22	13	3	1	0	0	1	10	49
South Africa	6	12	9	1	0	0	4	5	36
Iran	4	8	10	2	2	1	9	2	35
Israel	7	8	8	1	1	0	0	0	21
Australia	5	5	4	1	0	0	4	1	19
Canada	26	3	2	0	0	0	2	1	34
India	3	1	1	0	1	1	1	1	8

TABLE 4.7 Trade of Selected Countries with Major Powers as a Percent of Gross Domestic Product, 1967 (Grouped by Historical Association and Ranked Within Group) (continued)

Country	Percent of GDP Accounted for by Total Trade with:								Approximate Percent of GDP Accounted for by Trade with All Major Powers
	USA	UK	EEC[1]	France	Soviet Bloc[2]	USSR	Japan	Inter-Regional	
France and Associated States									
France	2	1	10	0	1	0	0	3	17
Congo (now Zaire)	4	8	75	42	3	1	1	5	96
Algeria	1	1	36	29	ND	ND	0	1	39
Ivory Coast	5	1	34	23	0	0	1	3	44
Chad	2	1	18	13	1	ND	1	3	26
Lebanon	8	6	25	7	4	1	2	17	62
Soviet Union and Associated States									
USSR	0	0	1	0	3	0	0	3	4
Bulgaria	0	0	3	1	29	20	0	29	32
Germany (East)	0	0	3	0	21	12	0	21	24
Czechoslovakia	0	1	3	0	20	10	0	20	24
Japan and Associated States									
Japan	6	1	1	0	1	1	0	4	13
Korea (South)	14	0	2	1	0	0	16	5	37
China (Taiwan)	12	0	3	0	0	0	13	9	37
Thailand	6	2	6	1	0	0	12	9	35

[1] Trade with the European Economic Community (EEC) includes trade with France. Percentages were calculated by combining the trade figures of each country with Belgium-Luxembourg, Netherlands, West Germany, Italy, and France and dividing the total by the estimated Gross Domestic Product of the country concerned.

[2] Trade with the Soviet Block includes trade with the Soviet Union but excludes trade with China.

Source: Singer 1972, Table 6.2.

relative magnitude of United States investments for a developed and a developing country usually is quite different. Private United States direct investments constitute 1.8 percent of France's GDP; 0.8 percent of Japan's; 6.7 percent of England's. In Peru they are 15 percent, in Columbia, 12 percent, and in Venezuela, 25 percent.

International stratification or class inequalities among countries are measured in many other ways as well. We can look at payments of interest on loans or of money for licenses and consider the role of foreign nationals in management. We can examine the extent to which workers in one country are dependent on employment in other countries—an important matter for workers from Mexico, Spain, Italy, and many other countries.

System of inequality. Asymmetry in trade, aid, investment, and other economic relations are generally related so that the economy of one country is dependent in many ways upon the economy of another. We will discuss some patterns of international stratification now and examine them further in later chapters, particularly Chapters 8 and 11.

Travis (1975) has calculated several indicators to assess the scope and intensity of economic dependency. A country, let it be called Z, is considered economically dependent on another country, X, insofar as the following conditions are present: (1) Z uses X's monetary system; (2) X's technical aid to Z exceeds 20 percent of Z's total technical aid and 5 percent of its GDP; (3) Z's total trade with X exceeds 20 percent of its total trade and 10 percent of its GDP; and (4) similar indicators are made separately for imports and exports. Travis examined the economic dependency of the world's countries on each of nine countries: United States, Great Britain, France, the Soviet Union, Japan, Italy, Germany, Belgium, and South Africa. Using eight indicators for the scope of economic dependency, he found the United States to have by far the most dependents. Great Britain is next; it has almost as many countries dependent in total trade, but has many fewer aid and investment dependents. Third is France; its dependents are mostly of the French community. The Soviet Union is fourth; its trade dependents are Afganistan and all Communist countries except China, Poland, and Rumania. The other countries have few economic dependents.

Intensity of economic dependency was measured by twelve indicators. The results are different and more unexpected. The United States no longer ranks first in the intensity of its economic relations. South Africa has the most intensive economic relations with its dependents. The countries most tied to it are Botswana, Swaziland, and Lesotho; they send 49 percent, 16 percent, and 16 percent of their labor force to work in South Africa; they use the South African currency and the South African Central Bank as their national banks. France also has deep economic dependence relations, dominating the trade of the countries economically dependent upon it. The Soviet Union has two forms of economic dependence with two largely distinct sets of countries: It has intense dependence relations with its Communist trade partners; in Eastern Europe this is institutionalized in the economic association, Council of Mutual Economic Assistance, generally known as COMECON. The Soviet Union also has intense aid relationships with the less developed Communist and non-Communist states. The United Kingdom still has intense trade relations, largely in the receipt of exports from other countries. The United States ranks next, followed by Belgium, Italy, Japan, and the Federal Republic of Germany.

Clearly the United States is the dominant economic power; the scope of its dependence exceeds all other countries. But the intensity of many countries' dependence on countries such as South Africa, France, and the Soviet Union, reduces the overall economic rank of the United States from what it would be if we considered only the overall magnitude of the United States trade, aid, and investments.

World class stratification entails more than the ranking of individual countries. Rather, it is more adequately viewed as a system of relations among groups of countries. One division which has been considered fundamental to international stratification is between the economically developed countries and the underdeveloped or developing countries (Lagos, 1963). This distinction has been elaborated further to distinguish three worlds of development: the developed capitalist economies, the Soviet-led countries, and the third world of underdeveloped capitalist economies (Horowitz, 1972). This distinction includes ideological and power differences as well as class inequalities to characterize the world stratification system.

Many contemporary observers, using the concepts of economic dominance and dependency, view the international stratification system as one characterized by a dominant core with a dependent periphery (Wallerstein, 1974; Chirot, 1977). In this view, the economies which developed manufacturing and trade in forming the capitalist world system were able to impose their dominance and keep other economies dependent and hence underdeveloped. The major core societies in the first part of the twentieth century were Great Britain, the United States, France, and Germany. Other societies, such as Italy, Russia, and Japan, were semi-peripheral seeking to become core societies; most of the world was and is largely peripheral.

At present, however, the world system cannot be neatly divided between core, semi-periphery, and periphery. The core is enlarged considerably by the inclusion of former peripheral societies such as Canada, Australia, Italy, and Japan. The communist societies in some ways are outside of the capitalist world market system, but not entirely.

Even many of the peripheral societies are ruled by governments seeking, with some success, to gain increased control over the economies of their countries and thus reduce their dependence. Despite the confusion about the current world economic system, it is important and useful to keep this perspective in mind as one component of inequalities on a world scale. Status and power inequalities are mixed together with these class inequalities as we shall see in Chapters 6 and 8.

Transcountry Inequalities

People have class relationships that cut across territorial states. Countries are not the sole units that interact in a market relationship. People work and employ others to work within class systems that, although part of a national economy, are in another sense always part of the world economic system as well. Working conditions in one country somewhat affect workers in the same industry throughout the world.

Trade and investment are not carried on between countries except in an abstract and aggregate sense; rather such exchanges usually take place between companies. Some people in several countries are deeply affected in these exchanges; others are hardly touched. Partly because of this varying involvement, as we shall see later, foreign trade and investment activities profoundly affect class inequalities within a country and help shape class inequalities among the world's people as a whole.

We approach this complex matter by examining the organizations to which persons in different class positions belong and within which they have class relations. We will include multinational corporations (MNC) and international nongovernmental organizations (INGOs) of business and labor. International nongovernmental organizations are an increasingly significant part of the world social system (Skjelsback 1972). They are nonprofit associations, usually federations of national associations. Three-fourths of these organizations have persons or national associations that are members in their capacity as incumbents of occupational roles (Kriesberg 1976) A little over half of these occupationally related INGOs involve professional roles, such as various medical specialties.

Multinational corporations. The significance of the world economy as the important system within which class relations should be studied has been made dramatically clear by the rapid growth of multinational corporations (Modelski 1972; Vernon 1971; Kindleberger 1970). A corporation can be multinational in any one of three ways: (1) it could draw its managers and workers from several different countries; (2) it could be owned by investors from several countries; or (3) it could have factories or other direct investments in many countries. Few corporations are multinational in the first two ways. Typically, ownership and higher management are from one country and investments are held in several countries. Having such investments may be enough to define a corporation as a MNC. Those foreign investments may be a large or small percentage of the corporation's total assets and even a minimal proportion may be used to define a MNC. Generally multinational corporations are defined as a number of business establishments in different countries bound by common ownership or control and being responsible to a common management strategy (Feld 1972,

p. 23). Observers use different definitions of MNC and therefore arrive at varying estimates of their overall magnitude and growth. Which definitions are appropriate depend on the questions being asked.

MNCs have grown in number and size as national corporations have expanded their foreign investments. One reason for foreign investment is to "get behind other countries' tariff walls": a subsidiary operating in another country does not have to pay customs duty on the products it makes and sells within that country. Such foreign investments may take the form of building new factories or other production units or of buying and taking over existing foreign companies. Another reason for foreign investment is to ensure access to resources that will be used and sold in the country of the parent company or in third countries. Still a third reason is to carry on a larger and more efficient scale of operations than is possible within a single country.

Lower labor costs in other countries also attract foreign investment. Just as new plants in the United States were established in the southern states to avoid higher wage rates and trade unions, so foreign investments may be made to avoid more costly working conditions. This can result in the loss of jobs or depressed wages in the regions of the country or the world from which the capital is flowing.

MNCs have long existed, but recently they have increased greatly in scope and magnitude. One indication of the vast role that MNCs play in the world economy is their size. General Motors has production facilities in twenty-four countries; in 1967, 15 percent of its total assets were in foreign countries, excluding Canada (Rose 1968). General Motors is comparable in size to many countries. If countries and corporations were ranked together, using a country's GNP and a corporation's gross annual sales, General Motors would rank 23rd, between Argentina and Switzerland. General Motors' total sales in 1969 were $24.3 billion (Brown 1972, Table D). Standard Oil of New Jersey has production facilities in 45 countries, 56 percent of its assets are abroad, and 52 percent of its net income is from abroad (Rose 1968). Its total sales in 1970 were $16.55 billion; this compares to a GNP of $17.50 billion for South Africa and $15.77 billion for Denmark (Brown 1972).

It has been estimated that in the late 1960s, goods produced through international investments totaled over $400 billion (Feld 1972). That would constitute over 15 percent of the total gross domestic product of all the market economies (non-Communist) of the world. A few corporations are so immense that they produce a large proportion of the world's goods.

The very largest MNCs are predominently based in the United States. Among the twenty largest industrial corporations in 1968, all except one (Royal Dutch/Shell), were affiliated with the United States. In 1970, Volkswagen, Philips, British Petroleum, and Nippon Steel had entered the top twenty, displacing four American corporations (Feld 1972, p. 34). Overall, the United States foreign investment still is predominant; it is estimated that in the mid-sixties, about 60 percent of the book value of the world's direct foreign investments was held by American companies (Modelski 1972).

Concentration of production by MNCs, even on a global scale, is considerable. In some commodity markets multinationals play a more dominant role than in others. For example, MNCs are much more significant in oil, chemicals, and electronics than in steel. In the steel industry a few companies produce significant proportions of the world production of steel, but this is true of companies producing and marketing steel within single countries, as in the United States. MNCs have played a particularly large role in the oil industry (Jacoby 1974). A few large MNCs produce most of the foreign oil (outside the United States, Canada, and the Communist countries). In 1953, the seven largest producers were: Standard Oil of New Jersey (now Exxon), Royal Dutch/ Shell, British Petroleum, Gulf, Texaco, Standard Oil of California, and Mobil. They produced 87 percent of all foreign oil; Exxon alone produced 25 percent. By 1972, new producers (especially government-owned ones) entered the market and the share of the foreign oil produced by these seven companies declined to 71 percent; Exxon's share fell to 15 percent. The world oil revolution of 1973-74 produced dramatic changes with the nationalization of dominant shares in the producing subsidiaries of many multinationals. Petronin, the national oil company of Saudi Arabia, NIOC of Iran, and KNPC, the government-owned oil company of Kuwait, became three of the world's seven largest oil producers (Jacoby 1974, p. 190). The governments forming the Organization of Petroleum Exporting Countries (OPEC) took over much of the pricing control previously exercised by the cartel the major multinational oil companies had formed (Sampson 1975). But the MNCs have been able to pass on the price increases to the consumer and their profits have not been adversely affected.

This radical transformation of the world's oil economy as well as efforts by national governments to impose restrictions on the actions of multinationals indicate some of the limits on MNCs as autonomous actors in the world. Yet, their ability to raise and transfer funds from one part of the world to another and their vast size indicate they are not simply instruments of one or another government.

International nongovernmental business organizations. In a sense, each multinational corporation constitutes a class system. Some people own the capital and many are employed as workers, supervisors, and managers. In another sense, the MNCs are part of a world class system in which workers and other employees confront or are dominated by the owners of the means of production and their agents. If we take this wider view, we can see major class categories on a global basis and organizations based upon people being in different categories.

One form of owner organization is the international cartel. Cartels are associations of independent business organizations in an industrial field who organize to control the market. They may agree to set prices for their goods and to control production in order to maintain the set price. They may agree to divide the market to avoid competing against one another. Such cartels have usually operated with the support of their home governments (Myrdal 1956, p. 47). Within many commodity markets, then, purchasers are at a disadvantage. Cartels have been particularly successful in heavy industries such as mining, chemicals, fuels, and transportation. They also are important in the control of products such as drugs, rubber, quinine, and optical instruments. They have not been as successful for producers of primary commodities. Because of this, governments and peoples in developing countries believe they are forced to pay high prices and yet have been unable to forge cartels of their own to control the prices of the primary commodities they produce.

Some international organizations include cartel activities among their other operations. For example, the International Air Transport Association (IATA) founded in 1945 (as successor to the International Air Traffic Association founded in 1919), operated with a staff of three hundred persons and a budget of over $3 million in 1972 (Tew 1972). Membership is open to air transport enterprises operating a scheduled air service authorized by a country eligible for membership in the international governmental organization, the International Civil Aviation Organization. The IATA is officially designated, by those governments, to consider fares and rates and to concern itself with technical and legal problems, reconciling different national codes, and coordinating interline timetables and connections (Marx 1953, p. 281).

In addition to international nongovernmental business organizations within particular industries or concerned with particular commodities, some international nongovernmental organizations represent more general interests of business owners and managers. The International Chamber of Commerce is one such important organization. It was founded in 1920 and in 1972 had members (national committees) from forty-three countries, a paid staff of fifty, and a budget of $680,000 (Tew 1972). Many of its activities are conducted through committees of experts drawn from the members. Its major activities have been directed toward the facilitiation and development of international trade (Ridgeway 1938).

International governmental and nongovernmental organizations form a complex web of relationships. For example, the International Organization of Employers was founded in 1919, the same year as the founding of the International Labor Organization (ILO). While the ILO consists of representatives from governments, workers, and managers, one of the major activities of the International Organization of Employers is to help present employer views before the ILO and before the Economic and Social Council of the United Nations.

International nongovernmental worker organizations. Transnational class relations are also manifest in international trade union organizations. Trade unions function beyond the territorial states in three major ways. First, some national trade unions themselves conduct extensive foreign activities. Second, national trade unions federate together to formulate common policies and to assist each other. Third, national trade unions in a particular industry sometimes band together in international trade secretariats to carry on trade union activities on a transcountry basis.

National trade union activity in other countries has been both economic and political-ideological in purpose (Harrod 1972). For example, the American Federation of Labor-Congress of Industrial Organizations (AFL-CIO) overseas activity has been directed in part against Communist party trade union activity and in part toward helping workers in other countries organize and attain improved wages and working conditions (Windmuller 1954; Cox 1972).

There are three major international federations of trade unions (Feld 1972; Windmuller 1969). The International Confederation of Free Trade Unions (ICFTU) has members from nearly one hundred countries; the major British trade unions and the German Federation of Trade Unions belong to the ICFTU. The World Federation of Trade Unions (WFTU) is dominated by Communist-led trade unions. Although far fewer countries are represented, the number of workers represented is greater than in the ICFTU because trade union membership is much more extensive in Communist countries. Major union federations from non-Communist countries are also represented in the WFTU, including the French Confederation of Labor (CGT). The third international federation is the World Confederation of Labor (WCL), formerly the International Federation of Christian Trade Unions. The WCL has trade union representation from about seventy-five countries but has the smallest number of members represented by the member organizations.

The third form of international trade union organization is the international trade secretariat. Unions in the same field of work combine efforts and resources to improve their working conditions on a global basis. They are particularly strong where they involve international transportation or trade or have a long history of international cooperation. One of the most important trade secretariats is the International Metalworkers Federation. It was founded in 1873 and is now affiliated with the ICFTU. It has members from fifty countries, totaling over nine million workers.

The previous discussion of the reasons that multinational corporations invest abroad suggests the rationale for multinational trade unions. Workers in high-wage parent countries face job losses when production is moved to low-wage areas. Therefore it is in their interests to help raise wages in other countries. Furthermore, workers in low-wage countries have an inducement to cooperate in raising their wages and can usually do so without the threat of losing their jobs (because investments are frequently made in those countries for other reasons, such as expansion of the market and access to resources). Without union coordination a corporation with plants in several countries can pit one group of workers or unions against another and, by "whipsawing," force one and then the other to settle for lower terms than it otherwise would do. In addition, many multinational corporations are able and willing to pay high wages and this is another inducement for workers to form company-wide multinational trade unions.

Despite all these inducements, multinational trade unionism has lagged (Cox 1972; Günter 1972). This is due both to particular barriers and to particular alternative ways of meeting the problems posed to the workers by the expansion of multinational corporations (Ulman 1975). One major barrier is that unionists are especially concerned about their earnings relative to other workers in their own country. The ranking of occupational earnings is very stable and similar in many countries, but the spread of knowledge about wages in different countries could lessen the tendency of workers to think of their wages only in a national orbit.

In addition, national policy makers often pursue policies of economic growth and equilibrium in the balance of payments—policies that may be counter to multinational trade unionism. Then, too, the diversity of social security and other social welfare programs in different countries makes accurate wage comparisons difficult and interferes with reaching common wage agreements. The European Economic Community is making progress in reducing differences in social security systems among its members. In addition, trade unions themselves differ in ideology and structure and this handicaps coordination among countries.

Alternatives to multinational trade unions also makes their continued growth less likely. Unions in some countries have begun to bargain with their employers to guarantee that the company will not shut down a plant or that it will make future investments to assure jobs for a particular group of union members. Increased worker involvement in industrial management (worker participation or codetermination) is another way in which workers in one country can try to solve their problems with multinational corporations. National trade unions also use their political power to induce their national governments to take domestic and even foreign policy actions to protect their jobs.

These barriers and the alternatives may, at least in the short run, interfere with the emergence of trade unions on an international scale as effective countervailing forces against the multinational corporation. In some instances and in the longer run, however, the development of international worker trade unions can be effective. International trade union efforts toward harmonization of wages and working conditions are matters of continuing and extensive discussion (Weinberg 1975).

CONCLUSIONS

Although our information about inequality is highly limited, some general descriptive assessments can be offered. Considerable variation in all forms of class inequality exists throughout the world. Among contemporary societies, the United States has relative equality in material conditions. Many countries have greater overall inequalities in income and wealth, and larger proportions of the populations lack minimal standards of living. Some countries, however, have greater equality in one or more ways than the United States.

When we considered the world as a single social system, viewing countries as units, we saw that they could be ranked in terms of material conditions and in relative degrees of class dominance and dependency. Generally, the economically developing countries are relatively dependent; the United States has a particularly wide scope of such dependents. But the countries cannot be ranked in a single hierarchy; the Soviet Union and other countries have economic dependents, some tied to them more intensively than the American dependents are to the United States. In addition to countries, we saw that there are interests and organizations that transcend and cut across territorial states. These are manifestations of class differences in markets of world or regional scope. The most dramatic of these manifestations are the multinational corporations.

REFERENCES

ATKINSON, A. B. 1975. "The Distribution of Wealth in Britain in the 1960s—The Estate Duty Method Reexamined." In James D. Smith (Ed.), *The Personal Distribution of Income and Wealth.* New York: National Bureau of Economic Research.

BROWN, LESTER R. 1972. *World Without Borders.* New York: Random House.

CHANDLER, JOHN H. 1969. "Perspectives on Poverty: An International Comparison," *Monthly Labor Review,* 92 (2):55-62.

CHANEY, MARGARET S. and MARGARET L. ROSS. 1971. *Nutrition.* (8th Ed.), Boston: Houghton-Mifflin.

CHIROT, DANIEL. 1977. *Social Change in the Twentieth Century.* New York: Harcourt Brace Jovanovich.

COX, ROBERT W. 1972. "Labor and Transnational Relations." In Robert O. Keohane and Joseph S. Nye, Jr. (Eds.), *Transnational Relations and World Politics.* Cambridge, Mass.: Harvard University Press.

DE CASTRO, JOSUÉ. 1967. *The Black Book of Hunger.* New York: Funk and Wagnall.

DE JESUS, CAROLINA MARIA. 1963. *Child of the Dark.* New York: New American Library.

FELD, WARNER J. 1972. *Nongovernmental Forces and World Politics.* New York: Praeger.

GUNTER, HANS (Ed.). 1972. *Transnational Industrial Relations.* London: Macmillan.

HARROD, JEFFREY. 1972. *Trade Union Foreign Policy.* Garden City. N.Y.: Doubleday.

HOROWITZ, IRVING LOUIS. 1972. *Three Worlds of Development.* (2nd Ed.). New York: Oxford University Press.

INTERNATIONAL LABOUR ORGANIZATION. 1974. *1974 Yearbook of Labour Statistics.* Geneva: International Labour Organization.

JACOBY, NEIL H. 1974. *Multinational Oil: A Study in Industrial Dynamics*. New York: Macmillan.
KINDLEBERGER, CHARLES P. (Ed.). 1970. *The International Corporation: A Symposium*. Cambridge, Mass.: MIT Press.
KRAVIS, I. B., Z. KENESSEY, A. HESTON, and R. SUMMERS. 1975. *A System of International Comparisons of Gross Product and Purchasing Power*. Baltimore: Johns Hopkins University Press.
KRIESBERG, LOUIS. 1976. "Varieties of ISPAS: Their Forms and Activities." Paper presented at the Conference of International Scientific and Professional Associations as Transnational Actors, University of Pennsylvania.
LAGOS, GUSTAVO. 1963. *International Stratification and Underdeveloped Countries*. Chapel Hill: University of North Carolina Press.
LEKACHMAN, ROBERT. 1972. *National Income and the Public Welfare*. New York: Random House.
LENIN, VLADIMER I. 1933. *Imperialism, the Highest Stage of Capitalism*. New York: International Publishers. (Originally published in 1916.)
LICHTHEIM, GEORGE. 1971. *Imperialism*. New York: Praeger.
LIEBENBERG, M., and J. M. FITZWILLIAMS. 1961. "Size Distribution of Personal Income, 1957-60," *Survey of Current Business* (May).
LIPSET, SEYMOUR MARTIN and RICHARD B. DOBSON. 1973. "Social Stratification and Sociology in the Soviet Union," Survey No. 3, 88 (Summer):114-185.
MAGDOFF, HARRY. 1969. *The Age of Imperialism*. New York: Walker.
MATTHEWS, MERVYN. 1972. *Class and Society in the USSR*. New York: Walker.
MARX, DANIEL, JR. 1953. *International Shipping Cartels*. Princeton, N.J.: Princeton University Press.
MAZUR, ALLAN and EUGENE ROSA. 1974. "Energy and Life Style," *Science*, 186 (November 15):607-610.
MILIBAND, RALPH. 1969. *The State in Capitalist Society*. New York: Basic Books.
MILLER, S. M. and MARTIN REIN. 1975. "Can Income Redistribution Work?" *Social Policy* 6 May/June: 3-18.
MODELSKI, GEORGE. 1972. "Multinational Business: A Global Perspective," *International Studies Quarterly* 16 (December):5-30.
MYRDAL GUNNAR. 1956. *An International Economy*. New York: Harper.
NORDHAUS, WILLIAM and JAMES TOBIN. 1972. "Is Growth Obsolete?" Fiftieth Anniversary Colloquium V. National Bureau of Economic Research. New York: Columbia University Press.
PAIGE, JEFFREY M. 1975. *Agrarian Revolution*. New York: Free Press.
PARKIN, FRANK. 1971. *Class Inequality and Political Order*. New York: Praeger.
PAUKERT, FELIX. 1973. "Income Distribution at the Different Levels of Development: A Survey of Evidence," *International Labour Review*, 108 (August-September): 97-125.
RIDGEWAY, GEORGE L. 1938. *Merchants of Peace*. New York: Columbia University Press.
ROSE, SANFORD. 1968. "The Rewarding Strategies of Multinationalism," *Fortune* 78 (September 15):100-105.
RUBINSON, RICHARD. 1976. "The World Economy and the Distribution of Income Within States: A Cross-National Study," *American Sociological Review* 41 (August):638-659.

SAMPSON, ANTHONY. 1975. *The Seven Sisters: The Great Oil Companies and the World They Made*. London: Hodder and Stoughton.
SCHNITZER, MARTIN. 1974. *Income Distribution: A Comparative Study of the United States, Sweden, West Germany, East Germany, the United Kingdom, and Japan*. New York: Praeger.
SINGER, MARSHALL. 1972. *Weak States in a World of Powers*. New York: Free Press.
SKJELSBAEK, KJELL. 1972. "The Growth of International Nongovernmental Organization in the Twentieth Century," in Robert O. Keohane and Joseph S. Nye (Eds.), *Transnational Relations and World Politics*. Cambridge, Mass.: Harvard University Press, pp. 70-92.
STINCHCOMBE, ARTHUR L. 1961. "Agricultural Enterprise and Rural Class Relations," *American Journal of Sociology* 67 (September):165-176.
TAYLOR, CHARLES LEWIS and MICHAEL C. HUDSON. 1971. *World Handbook of Political and Social Indicators II: Section I: Aggregate Data; Section II: Annual Event Data*. Ann Arbor, Mich.: Inter-University Consortium for Political Research.
TEW, E. S. (Ed.). 1972. *Yearbook of International Organizations, 14th (1972-73) Edition*. Brussels, Belgium: Union of International Associations.
TRAVIS, TOM ALLEN. 1975. "Toward a Comparative Study of Imperialism." Paper presented at the Sixteenth Annual Convention of the International Studies Association, Washington, D.C.
ULMAN, LLOYD. 1975. "Multinational Unionism: Incentives, Barriers, and Alternatives," *Industrial Relations*, 14 (February):1-31.
UNITED NATIONS DEPARTMENT OF ECONOMIC AND SOCIAL AFFAIRS. 1974. *Statistical Yearbook, 1973*. New York: United Nations.
UNITED NATIONS ECONOMIC COMMISSION FOR EUROPE. 1967. *Income in Postwar Europe: A Study of Policies, Growth, and Distribution*. Geneva: United Nations.
UNITED NATIONS FOOD AND AGRICULTURE ORGANIZATION. 1973. *Production Yearbook*, Vol. 25. Rome: United Nations.
U.S. BUREAU OF THE CENSUS. 1973. *Statistical Abstract of the United States: 1973*, (94th Ed.). Washington, D.C.: U.S. Government Printing Office.
VERNON, RAYMOND. 1971. *Sovereignty at Bay: The Multinational Spread of U.S. Enterprises*. New York: Basic Books.
WALLERSTEIN, IMMANUEL. 1974. *The Modern World System*. New York: Academic Press.
WEINBERG, NAT. 1975. "The Multinational Corporation and Labor." In Abdul A. Said and Luis R. Simmons (Eds.), *The New Sovereigns*. Englewood Cliffs, N.J.: Prentice-Hall.
WINDMULLER, JOHN P. 1954. *American Labor and the International Labor Movement 1940 to 1953*. Ithaca, N.Y.: Cornell University.
WINDMULLER, JOHN P. 1969. *Labor Internationals: A Survey of Contemporary International Trade Union Organizations*. Ithaca, N.Y.: New York State School of Industrial and Labor Relations, Cornell University.
YANOWITCH, MURRAY. 1963. "The Soviet Income Revolution," *Slavic Review* 22 (December):683-697. Reprinted in Celia S. Heller (Ed.), *Structured Social Inequality*. New York: Macmillan.

chapter 5

American Status Variations

I said something to Mrs. Duncan about being related to the Montgomerys. She said; "Well, that is nothing to be proud of. I wouldn't brag about it!" I said I didn't see why not; my father had always taught me to be proud of the Montgomery blood in my veins. Then she said that the first Montgomery was nothing but a gambler, and that was nothing to be proud of. Well, that isn't true! He wasn't *really* a gambler. . . .*Upper-upper respondent from Deep South (Davis, Gardner, and Gardner 1941, p. 67)*

Important as the material conditions of life are to people, as social beings they care very much about what others think of them; they are pleased when others think well of them, dismayed when others look down on them. This chapter will describe the range and distribution of status in the United States and the extent to which Americans are mobile in status. We will determine how people are ranked in status, how much inequality now exists, and whether we are moving toward or away from greater equality.

For a status hierarchy to exist, people must agree on the standards by which they evaluate each other; they must agree about what constitutes high and low status. Furthermore, people must differ in what they are, what they possess, or what they do, and these differences must be assigned a value. When such a hierarchy is established, people who rank high agree that they are superior and people who rank low agree that they are indeed inferior. In reality, such complete consensus does not exist: people disagree, with greater or lesser conviction, about who has higher status. We should also keep in mind that when people highly value what they equally share—for example, their common humanity or good character—they will value each other equally. In this book, however, we will examine inequalities of prestige and deference based on evaluations of what is not shared.

Individuals have high or low prestige because of the *positions* they occupy or the *families* or collectivities to which they belong. Individuals may be esteemed well or ill, depending upon how well they play their roles, but such esteem is not the same as social status. When we examine status, we are dealing with groups or categories that rate each other as social entities. Because in the United States and in many cultures, how a person earns a living is an important basis for deciding how much respect to show her or him, the *positions* considered are largely occupational ones. When we examine status inequality among *persons*, we will consider families and collectivities. In everyday life, we may rate some families as being of "good stock" and others as disreputable, even when recognizing that individuals within such families may or may not be admirable as human beings. This chapter concentrates on a few categories of persons. In examining families, it focuses on social elites. In examining collectivities, it looks particularly at ethnic and sex categories within cultures and also at countries and cultures within the global system.

When people speak of Americans as being equalitarian, they are often referring to the equality of social relations. Americans think of themselves as being informal, as not "putting on airs" with each other. They think of themselves as neither deferential nor haughty because of differences in family back-ground or offices held. They implicitly compare themselves to Europeans, who supposedly pay much more attention to status differences. Before making such comparisons, we will consider changes over time in the range, distribution, and mobility of status in the United States.

Since status depends on the standards of evaluation of a set of people who agree about those standards, many different status systems can co-exist. This chapter examines four major status systems and the trends in inequality within them: (1) persons in their occupational roles, (2) persons in their life styles, (3) persons in their race and ethnicity, and (4) persons in their gender.

OCCUPATIONAL POSITIONS

Occupational roles are accorded differing amounts of respect and prestige, with the relative prestige of an occupation closely related to income. Learning what somebody does for a living is a common way of placing a person in a stratification system. In addition, people in the same occupation or type of occupation share interests and ways of life that, in turn, contribute to their status ranking. Occupations, then, have a crucial place in determining a person's overall status.

Range

To begin reviewing the extent of inequality in occupational status, we can examine the range between the top and bottom of the prestige hierarchy and also the proportion of roles which have less than minimal respect accorded to them. It was very difficult to discuss the range of class differences even when we could use money as a measuring rod. Because there is no equally reliable metric for measuring status, we can only make rough comparisons and estimates.

In the last chapter we spoke of a minimal standard of living beneath which people were considered to be poor. No similar concept can be found in the status dimension; a clear line cannot be drawn between minimally adequate and inadequate respect. But within some cultures, certain positions may be regarded as lacking minimal respect. By "minimal respect," I refer to shared recognition of the basic worthiness of a person or of the activity associated with a position. The idea is that certain activities or persons are regarded not only as low in respect, but so low as to be considered less than human; hence, less than minimally adequate. No precise line can be drawn, but it will be useful to think about minimal honor, dignity, or respect.

In the United States, nearly all work that others will pay for is considered at least minimally respectable. But some kinds of work are considered dishonor-able and dirty (Hughes 1962). Even those who work at such occupations often regard their work as shameful, although they may defend its usefulness and their worth. For example, one prostitute argues that members of her occupation help protect people:

> I am not ashamed to be a prostitute. Well, you're going to do it anyway so you might as well get paid for it. It's a job. Most countries it's legal all except this backward country we live in. The minute they start picking up prostitutes you hear two or three charges of rape, molesting kids and all of that. What's to be ashamed of? (Talbert 1975, p. 88).

Her defensiveness, nevertheless, indicates her recognition of the prevailing negative evaluation of prostitution as an occupation.

We lack systematic evidence about how attitudes have changed regarding which occupations are beneath respect. Nevertheless, there are reasons to argue that more occupations were considered immoral or dishonorable in America in the nineteenth century than at the present. The gradual increase in secularism has reduced the religious judgments about a variety of activities. Acting and other kinds of entertainment suffered from moral condemnation in the past; they do not in contemporary America. And there was slavery. Slavery entailed a status degradation related to rare and great powerlessness, as we will discuss later. Although slaves were also workers, the status of slave work was below today's minimal standards of human decency. Even at that time, the slave lacked minimal status, whatever recognition an individual slave may have received as a human or as a "good slave."

On the whole, over the last two hundred years of American history, the proportion of positions that are granted less than a minimally adequate amount of respect has probably decreased. As a consequence, the range between positions with high and low status also has probably decreased. On the other hand, certain positions in the United States have taken on extraordinarily high status, perhaps unmatched in the American past. Political offices are accorded a much greater degree of respect than given in earlier periods of American history or given to any other positions, as evidenced by the deference shown to the office of the president of the United States in contemporary times (Trollope 1949, pp. 142-145). The events associated with "Watergate" indicate the extent to which the office had become an imperial one. Even as these events have reduced the esteem given a particular officeholder, they have not destroyed the great respect and awe given to the office. Changes in the range of status suggested above are unmeasured and probably unmeasurable, yet they are of great importance to people and deserve thought.

Distribution

In considering the allocation of prestige among the various major occupations, we have more systematic evidence than for most aspects of status. Over the past fifty years, sociologists and others have been asking samples of

Americans how much prestige they think different occupations have. Major national surveys were conducted by the National Opinion Research Center in 1947 and 1963. The basic findings were briefly discussed in Chapter 2 and presented in Table 2.4. The data now require closer examination.

Consider the 1963 findings. On the whole, most people agree in their general rating of each occupation. For example, 71 percent of the people thought that the general standing of physicians in their community was excellent; an additional 25 percent thought it was good. The consensus is greater among high prestige occupations than among middle and low ones. Some kinds of occupations have a particularly wide spread of evaluations—this is true of the artistic occupations: author, musician, painter. There are even some occupations for which no more than a third of the respondents agree that the occupation is generally regarded to have excellent, good, average, below average, or poor standing. This is true of low ranking occupations—for example, farm hand and coal miner.

Agreement is very high, however, about the average ranking of occupations among persons in different social categories. Albert J. Reiss, Jr. (1961) systematically examined the degree of similarity in the average ratings given by people in different settings. Thus, he compared people in different regions of the United States and found substantial agreement on the relative standing of a majority of the occupational positions rated. The major difference was between the South and the Northeast. Residents of the South gave lower ratings to the science and science-related occupations and higher ratings to minister, captain in the regular army, bookkeeper, railroad conductor and a few others than did residents of the Northeast.

Reiss also examined variations by size of the community of residence, years of education, occupational position, economic level, sex, and age and found some variations in each case. For example, the more years of schooling persons have, the less likely they are to rate craft, operative, and unskilled jobs as excellent or good. As a further example, professional persons are less likely to give high ratings to airline pilot, undertaker, and carpenter. One final example: women place somewhat higher evaluations on the more prestigious occupations that are predominantely female, on artists and musicians, and on religious occupations than do men. Perfect consensus, then, about the rating of occupations in this country does not exist (Hyman 1953), but the general rank ordering of the various occupations is similar among all categories of persons.

The stability of the occupational prestige ratings over the period of time for which comparable data are available is very high. The pioneering study on occupational prestige was done by George S. Counts (1925) and several have been done since. The correlations between the occupational prestige ratings of 1925 and 1963 is 0.93 (Hodge, Siegel, and Rossi 1964), and the correlation between the 1947 and 1963 NORC study results is 0.99. Nevertheless, particular occupations have changed their relative status in the course of time. Comparing the 1947 and 1963 surveys, we see that professions such as physician and civil engineer rose in prestige while cultural or communication-oriented occupations such as musician and radio announcer declined. Scientific occupations and outdoor-oriented occupations increased markedly in prestige. But the largest *increase* was among dead-end occupations like night watchman, janitor, garbage collector, and street sweeper.

The occupational distribution is gradually shifting so that more people have jobs with higher prestige. This can be seen by looking at the distribution of the socio-economic index for the male experienced labor force. In Chapter 2, we discussed this and presented the distribution for 1950 in Table 2.5. Table 5.1 shows the changes since then: In 1950, the proportion of the male labor force in occupations with socio-economic indices of less than 20 (or NORC scores of less than 59) stood at 49 percent; by 1962, it had fallen to 38 percent; by 1973, to 33 percent. The proportion of the labor force in more prestigious occupations increased correspondingly.

Braverman (1974) argues, however, that work itself is becoming increasingly degraded. The routinization and specialization of labor has made workers less and less in command of the work process, in white-collar jobs as well as manual jobs. Braverman points out that the shift from laborer to semi-skilled worker generally has not meant an increase in skills required. For example, a farm laborer or a teamster had and used a wide variety of knowledge; a semi-skilled worker generally operates a machine, a job that takes only a few hours or a few weeks of training.

Braverman's argument is a useful corrective to the idea that there has been a massive upgrading in the work experiences of the labor force. Undoubtedly

TABLE 5.1   Distribution of Socio-Economic Index for the Male Experienced Labor Force 1950, 1962, 1973

Socio-Economic Index	Approximate NORC Score	Percent of Labor Force		
		1950	*1962*	*1973*
0- 9	Less than 48	15.0	10.8	8.5
10-19	48-58	33.9	26.8	24.2
20-29	59-63	10.8	11.0	12.0
30-39	64-67	11.4	10.2	9.8
40-49	68-70	9.3	11.3	10.8
50-59	71-73	5.6	7.0	6.3
60-69	74-76	6.7	9.9	11.4
70-79	77-81	3.8	7.0	9.2
80-89	82-85	2.5	4.6	6.2
90-99	86 or More	1.0	1.4	1.6
Totals		100.0%	100.0%	100.0%

Source: 1950 data from Table 2.5; 1962 and 1973 data provided by Robert M. Hauser from the 1962 and 1973 OCG surveys conducted by the U.S. Bureau of the Census.

some shifts in the occupational distribution suggest a great expansion of positions with higher skill requirements and responsibility when that has not occurred. Yet, many physically arduous tasks have been reduced, some repetitive activities have been eliminated, and the perquisites of white-collar employment have been extended to a larger proportion of the labor force.

However assessed, the occupational structure associated with industrialization has undergone a large-scale transformation. The proportion of the labor force engaged in agriculture has declined massively; people working in manufacturing and most recently in service industries has greatly increased. Along with this the number of persons in manual occupations has declined and the number of those in white-collar employment has increased. These changes in occupational distribution significantly affect intergenerational occupational mobility.

Mobility

Mobility refers to the movement of persons into and out of positions. This section will examine first movement between generations and then movement within generations.

Intergenerational mobility. The changes in occupational status from parent to child have long been a matter of great popular as well as sociological interest. We want to know what the chances are of a child's moving up or slipping down in status. We want to know to what extent those in upper status positions recruit their members from families who are similarly situated. We want to know whether the opportunities for advancement in status are becoming greater or smaller. We also want to know if movement from one stratum is as easily accomplished as movement from a different stratum. In other words, do people of different origins have equal opportunity to move up, move down, or remain at the same level?

Intergenerational social mobility is generally studied by examining changes in occupation between fathers and sons. The basic source of information about such changes are surveys of contemporary individuals. Respondents are asked about their own occupation and that of their fathers and sometimes their mothers. As we noted in Chapter 2, simple as this procedure seems, it has many difficulties. For example, should we compare the occupations of the father and son at the same stage in their career or at the son's present stage and the father's when the son was growing up? Usually, because we want to see how equal the chances are of moving out of different status ranks, we ask for the parent's occupation before the respondent embarked on his or her own career—say, at age sixteen. Notice that we are asking each respondent about one father. In the resulting tables then, every father has one son. In reality, some fathers had no sons; some had several. Those differences have been related to occupational status. Furthermore, since the sons are many different ages, they represent several different historical generations, periods with varying occupational distributions.

Table 5.2 presents data from a recent national survey in which respondents were asked their own occupations and their fathers' occupations when the respondents were about sixteen. Men and women were interviewed, but the information in Table 5.2 is taken only from the male respondents. Part A presents the actual number of sons in each occupational category with fathers in each category. The data make it possible to answer two different kinds of questions: (1) What is the chance of a son's inheriting the same occupational stratum as his father or entering each other stratum? and (2) Among the sons, what proportion of each stratum is filled by offspring of fathers from other strata? The first question asks what is the outflow from each stratum and the second asks what is the inflow.

To answer the first question, we calculated the proportion of sons in each occupational category for fathers in each category (see Part B of Table 5.2). Consider the 34 fathers who were professional, technical, or similar workers: 29 percent of them had sons who were in the same stratum; 41 percent had sons who entered managerial, sales, clerical, and similar occupations. Less than one-third of these sons entered manual occupations and none entered farming occupations. The proportions are about the same for fathers who were managerial, sales, clerical, and similar workers. On the one hand, among craftsmen and similar workers, most had sons who were also manual workers. Among fathers who were operatives, service workers and nonfarm laborers, only 10 percent had sons who became professional, technical, or similar workers and about 40 percent had sons who remained in the same stratum. Sons of fathers in farming occupations generally moved into manual occupations. On the whole, sons tend to enter the same stratum as their fathers, but many move into other strata. The movement is somewhat confined by the manual/nonmanual distinction, with those whose fathers had manual occupations tending to remain in manual occupations.

We can also look at the percentages in the other direction (see Part C of Table 5.2). Consider the ninety five sons who are professional, technical, and similar workers. Only about one in ten of them had fathers in the same occupational stratum. Over one-third had fathers in other white-collar occupations. Over half had fathers who were not in white-collar occupations. The occupational origins of the sons in managerial, sales, clerical, and similar occupations follow the same pattern. Manual workers are largely the sons of manual workers. The chances of a father's son being in a particular occupational category and the chances of a son having a father from a particular occupation are not the same because the occupational distribution among the sons and the fathers are very different. The proportion of sons in farming has declined greatly while the proportion in white-collar, and particularly professional, occupations has increased. Consequently, the chances of a father in a professional or technical occupation having a son in a similar position is high. But few sons in those occupations had fathers who were so employed.

Overall, only a moderate correlation is found between the occupations of

TABLE 5.2 Part A: Occupations of Fathers and Sons

Fathers	*Sons*					
	Professional, Technical, and Similar Workers	Managerial, Sales, Clerical and Similar Workers	Craftsmen and Similar Workers	Operatives, Service and Nonfarm Laborers	Farmers, Farm Managers, and Laborers	Totals
Professional, Technical, and Similar Workers	10	14	6	4	0	34
Managerial, Sales, Clerical and Similar Workers	35	51	18	21	0	125
Craftsmen and Similar Workers	20	28	52	46	0	146
Operatives, Service and Nonfarm Laborers	14	26	40	58	2	140
Farmers, Farm Managers, and Laborers	16	24	31	50	19	140
Totals	95	143	147	179	21	585

TABLE 5.2   Part B: Father's Occupations by Son's Occupational Outcomes (Outflow)

Fathers	*Sons*					
	Professional Technical and Similar Workers	Managerial Sales, Clerical and Similar Workers	Craftsmen and Similar Workers	Operatives, Service and Nonfarm Laborers	Farmers, Farm Managers, and Laborers	Totals % (N)
Professional, Technical, and Similar Workers	29.4	41.2	17.6	11.8	0	100.0% (34)
Managerial, Sales, Clerical and Similar Workers	28.0	40.8	14.4	16.8	0	100.0% (125)
Craftsmen and Similar Workers	13.7	19.2	35.6	31.5	0	100.0% (146)
Operatives, Service Nonfarm Laborers	10.0	18.6	28.6	41.4	1.4	100.0% (140)
Farmers, Farm Managers, and Laborers	11.4	17.1	22.1	35.7	13.6	99.9% (140)

TABLE 5.2   Part C: Sons' Occupations by Fathers' Occupations (Inflow)

Fathers	Sons				
	Professional Technical and Similar Workers	Managerial, Sales, Clerical and Similar Workers	Craftsmen and Similar Workers	Operatives, Service and Nonfarm Laborers	Farmers, Farm Managers, and Laborers
Professional, Technical, and Similar Workers	10.5	9.8	4.1	2.2	0
Managerial, Sales, Clerical and Similar Workers	36.8	35.7	12.2	11.7	0
Craftsmen and Similar Workers	21.1	19.6	35.4	25.7	0
Operatives, Service and Nonfarm Laborers	14.7	18.2	27.2	32.4	9.5
Farmers, Farm Managers, and Laborers	16.8	16.8	21.1	27.9	90.5
Totals %	99.9%	100.1%	100.0%	99.9%	100.0%
(N)	(95)	(143)	(147)	(179)	(21)

Source: National Opinion Research Center, Spring 1974, General Social Survey.

the fathers and the sons. Numbers were assigned to the ranked categories in order to calculate a rank correlation. In this sample, the correlation is .34; the correlation between the fathers' and daughters' occupations is only slightly less; it is .30.

Table 5.3 presents information on the sons' occupational prestige as related to the fathers' occupational prestige. The respondents are the same as in Table 5.2. The occupations have been categorized by their occupational prestige scores, which were developed by asking respondents in a national survey to estimate the social standing of occupations, using a nine-step ladder. The first, fifth, and ninth steps were labeled bottom, middle, and top, respectively. The ratings of all the respondents were combined to yield the prestige scores (Siegel, Rossi, and Hodge 1975). We will sometimes refer to these scores as the Siegel occupational prestige scores to distinguish them from the socio-economic index developed by Duncan and described in Chapter 2.

In Table 5.3, only the outflow percentages are shown. The overall pattern is similar to that seen in Table 5.2: there is considerable occupational inheritance; the movement is greatest between occupations that are closest in prestige and is more apt to be upward than downward. The correlation is .25 between fathers' and sons' and .28 between fathers' and daughters' occupational status. Note that in using the prestige scores, there is no sharp distinction between white-collar and manual occupations, which account for the lesser correlation than found when relating major occupational catetories. Movement, for men anyway, is constrained within either manual or nonmanual occupational categories.

Intra-generational mobility. We must also consider the extent to which people change status in the course of their life career. Do people generally enter and remain on jobs of the same status throughout their career? Do they usually enter low status jobs and move upward in the course of their life? Do they move often? Do they move both upward and downward? Such movements are significant. Even if the difference in status from top to bottom were great, status would have one meaning if people frequently changed positions in their lifetime, another if they remained in fixed positions. In general, in the United States, people move frequently in the course of the work career, and, most typically, this movement is upward. Many persons with white-collar jobs have held manual jobs (Lipset and Bendix, 1960) but few persons regularly move back and forth between a low- and a high-status job.

Blau and Duncan (1967) conducted a large-scale study of the American occupational structure, using the "Occupational Changes in a Generation" (OCG) survey. They used data collected by the United States Bureau of the Census as an adjunct to the monthly "Current Population Survey." In March 1962, about 20,700 men ranging in age from 20 to 64 years were interviewed. Table 5.4, taken from this study, shows the movement from the first job to the respondent's then current occupation. As in intergenerational mobility, although there is considerable stability and movement, the movement is generally to similarly

TABLE 5.3   Sons' Occupational Prestige by Fathers' Occupational Prestige, 1974

Father's Occupational Prestige Score	Sons' Occupational Prestige Score							
	51 or More	46-50	41-45	36-40	31-35	21-30	20 or Less	Totals % (N)
51 or More	32.5	30.0	0.0	17.5	5.0	7.5	7.5	100.0% (40)
46-50	27.4	31.6	5.3	14.7	5.3	10.5	5.3	100.1% (95)
41-45	15.3	15.3	20.2	11.7	14.7	12.3	10.3	99.9% (163)
36-40	17.0	13.6	10.2	23.9	14.8	14.8	5.7	100.0% (88)
31-35	11.0	20.5	6.8	17.8	9.6	23.3	11.0	100.0% (73)
21-30	12.5	25.0	9.7	9.7	9.7	19.4	13.9	99.9% (54)
20 or Less	11.1	7.4	9.3	9.3	20.4	18.5	24.1	100.1% (54)
Totals (N)	(102)	(116)	(64)	(86)	(69)	(87)	(61)	(585)

Source: National Opinion Research Center, Spring 1974, General Social Survey.

ranked occupations and is more upward than downward. More specific patterns are also worth noting. Retail sales is a common first job, but men leave it to become managers, clerical workers, proprietors, and salaried professional workers. In general, men beginning their career in white-collar jobs remain in such occupations. Men who begin as craftsmen generally remain in manual occupations; if they leave, they are most likely to become proprietors. Semiskilled and unskilled men who begin their work career as operatives and laborers often move up within the manual occupations, but generally do not enter white-collar occupations.

Allocation. Recent sociological research has tried to trace the steps leading to a person's occupational position—that is, how occupational origins affect occupational attainments. Thus far, we have considered only the overall degree of correlation between, for example, fathers' and sons' occupational status. But equally significant is how the father's occupational status affects the son's and what else affects the son's occupational status. One issue of particular interest is the extent to which education affects occupational achievements.

Blau and Duncan developed a basic model of the occupational attainment process, using four independent variables: father's occupation, father's education, son's education, and son's first job. They found that the correlation between father's occupation and son's 1962 occupational status was .405; the correlation between father's education and the son's occupational status was .322; the correlation between the son's first job and his occupational status in 1962 was .541.

Father's occupational status and education and son's first job are also correlated with each other. Blau and Duncan wanted to see which factors were particularly related to son's occupational status, taking into account the other variables. To do this, Blau and Duncan arranged the variables in what they regard as a reasonable causal sequence. The resulting model is presented in the form of a *path diagram*. Thus, as can be seen in Figure 5.1, they believe that father's education and occupation come first in the sequence. The curved arrow between them, pointed in both directions, indicates that the causal order between these variables is not relevant. The son's education is regarded as prior to the first job and the first job is regarded as prior to the occupation at the time the son was interviewed. The path coefficients on each arrow indicate the strength of that relationship, taking into account the indirect effects of other independent variables. For example, we noted above that the correlation between father's occupation and son's was .405, but the path diagram indicates that most of that effect is through the influence of the father's occupation on the son's education and first job. Thus, the path coefficient between father's occupation and son's education is .279 (the son's education is also influenced by the father's education) and the son's education is related to his occupation in 1962 by a path coefficient of .394. Father's occupation also influences the son's first job and that influences, in turn, the son's later occupation. The magnitude of the father's

TABLE 5.4   Mobility from First Job to 1962 Occupation, for Males 25 to 64 Years Old; Outflow Percentages

First Job	Respondent's Occupation in March 1962																	
	1	2	3	4	5	6	7	8	9	10	11	12	13	14	15	16	17	Total[a]
Professionals																		
1. Self-Employed	53.5	25.5	1.8	4.7	2.5	1.5	.0	1.5	.7	.0	.7	.0	.0	.0	2.5	.0	.7	100.0
2. Salaried	6.5	54.5	12.3	2.8	5.5	4.9	.4	1.6	2.0	.4	1.2	1.2	1.0	.1	.3	1.0	.1	100.0
3. Managers	1.2	20.4	35.7	4.3	9.1	6.6	2.3	2.3	4.1	2.9	2.1	1.4	1.2	.6	1.2	.6	.4	100.0
4. Salesmen, Other	.6	8.2	24.1	23.7	12.4	5.0	2.8	.6	3.3	1.3	5.4	3.9	2.8	.0	.0	.4	.0	100.0
5. Proprietors	.9	6.8	19.2	6.4	36.3	2.6	2.6	1.7	2.1	.4	4.3	4.3	3.0	.9	2.1	3.8	.2	100.0
6. Clerical	1.6	13.0	17.3	7.3	5.4	17.6	1.8	4.6	4.3	2.6	5.6	4.2	4.4	1.0	1.8	1.2	.2	100.0
7. Salesmen, Retail	2.1	10.0	15.6	7.4	11.6	11.6	5.1	4.5	4.8	2.9	6.1	7.4	3.1	1.1	1.9	1.0	.1	100.0
Craftsmen																		
8. Manufacturing	.9	8.7	7.8	2.5	12.2	4.1	.7	22.5	7.5	4.3	9.1	3.5	3.7	.8	4.0	2.3	.0	100.0
9. Other	.3	9.0	6.6	1.0	10.3	4.1	3.4	10.9	21.3	4.7	7.1	5.5	3.6	1.4	1.7	1.2	.7	100.0
10. Construction	.3	5.6	3.4	1.6	11.1	3.1	.2	8.8	13.2	26.2	5.0	4.3	2.4	1.0	3.1	2.1	.8	100.0
Operatives,																		
11. Manufacturing	.4	6.1	5.3	2.0	7.0	6.2	1.7	13.4	6.7	4.6	18.8	7.6	4.7	3.2	3.5	2.0	.6	100.0
12. Other	.5	5.0	6.1	3.0	8.7	4.3	1.1	7.3	10.8	6.9	9.6	15.0	6.0	1.4	4.3	1.8	1.0	100.0
13. Service	.5	7.1	4.9	1.4	6.2	5.0	1.2	3.4	6.4	6.2	13.3	7.7	19.8	2.5	5.8	.4	.5	100.0
Laborers																		
14. Manufacturing	.3	5.5	3.9	1.5	2.9	6.2	1.2	10.5	5.3	3.9	18.1	8.8	7.3	8.2	6.3	1.6	1.7	100.0
15. Other	.2	5.5	5.4	2.4	6.7	4.1	1.3	6.1	9.6	6.8	10.5	10.8	6.3	2.4	11.5	2.1	.9	100.0
16. Farmers	.2	2.3	2.6	1.8	3.8	3.0	1.2	4.2	5.9	5.4	8.3	5.0	4.6	1.4	3.6	30.0	5.0	100.0
17. Farm Laborers	.2	1.7	2.4	.8	4.7	2.7	1.1	5.3	6.3	5.5	10.4	9.3	5.8	2.8	6.7	19.3	7.0	100.0

[a]Rows as shown do not total 100.0, since men not in the experienced civilian labor force are not shown separately.

Source: Blau and Duncan 1967, Table 2.4.

132

occupation's influence upon the son's occupation, taking into account these indirect effects, is indicated by the path coefficient of .115. In other words, the son's occupational attainment, insofar as it is explained by these variables, is primarily affected by his education and secondarily by his first job. Obviously, the son's occupational attainment is affected by many factors in addition to those measured in this model.

The model indicates that much of a male's occupational attainment is affected by his social origins, but this is mediated by his educational attainment and his first job. Clearly, there is no sharp distinction between ascribed and achieved status in these matters. To a significant degree, the son's occupational attainment is determined by the family into which he is born and is raised, but how that influence is exerted depends in part upon his own activities. Education, measured in years of formal schooling, plays an important role in the occupational attainment process.

Blau and Duncan, given the large size of their sample, were able to compare the relationship among these variables for different age groups. This comparison of one age cohort with another suggests trends in the occupational attainment process over time. They reached the tentative conclusion that the influence of education on ultimate occupational achievement has increased in recent decades.

What accounts for the relationship between educational attainment and occupational status? Jencks and his associates suggest three possible explanations:

1. People with different amounts of education prefer different occupations.
2. Everyone prefers the same occupations, but people who get a lot of education have cognitive skills or noncognitive traits that make them more competent at high-status jobs.

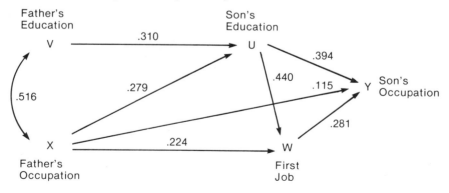

FIGURE 5.1 *Path Coefficients in a Model of the Process of Occupational Attainment*

Source: Adapted from Blau and Duncan (1967, p. 170).

3. Everyone prefers the same occupations, and everyone is more or less equally qualified to work in most occupations, so high-status occupations use arbitrary educational requirements to ration access to desirable jobs (Jencks et al. 1972, p. 181).

Jencks and his associates review and reanalyze data from several studies and conclude that students who do not like school leave earlier and choose occupations that they believe do not require as many years of schooling. Thus, the correlation between educational and occupational preferences at age 17 or 18 are even greater than they turn out to be in actuality. There is much evidence that employers prefer workers with more rather than less education, but it is difficult to determine whether this is because the amount of education indicated a real difference among people relevant to job performance or is simply a way of rationing preferred jobs. Employers need a legitimate device for selecting among applicants; credentials are generally regarded as a fair basis for such selection. Undoubtedly, some, if not most, use of credentials is not determined by the job requirements; rather credentials are used for screening purposes.

Schooling affects occupational status, aside from family background and cognitive skills. Family background and cognitive skills have an important effect on educational attainment but have little direct effect upon occupational status. Jencks and his associates also point out that persons with the same amount of education attain jobs that vary greatly in status. This is due partly to changes in a person's status over his lifetime, partly to character traits such as mental disturbances or high drive to achieve success. But some of the independence between occupational status and educational attainment is probably due to luck —who gets laid off or who gets hired partly depends on what is happening in a given place of employment at a given time. Finally, some of the independence is due to choice—a decision to change from one career for another, as when a person leaves teaching to take up farming.

Trends in mobility. America has long seemed the land of opportunity to its immigrants. They could rise in status as well as in material well being. If they did not fully realize the chances for upward social mobility, their children could. Now we ask, have the chances of lower status people to rise decreased, remained the same, or increased? Has social mobility become blocked with the maturing of the American society?

Community and historical studies of the 1930s and 1940s suggested that opportunities for upward (and downward) mobility were decreasing in America, compared to a more open past. Contributing to such inferences was the fact that some of the communities studied were not growing; achieving upward social mobility meant leaving the community, but persons who left were not included in the study. Actually, even some of the same difficulty in studying social mobility nationwide has occurred. In some years, a million persons have immigrated into the United States and have usually taken low-status jobs; and in other years, many fewer persons have entered. Some immigrants have stayed for

only a few years, then gone to another country. How can researchers define and draw boundaries of a system within which they can assess rates of mobility? Could mobility in Ireland in the 1840s be studied without including the United States? At present, immigration to and from Puerto Rico and Mexico changes with economic circumstances; it is somewhat arbitrary to include or to exclude in a study people who temporarily left the United States when employment opportunities were bad or who re-enter when employment opportunities increase. Nevertheless, this chapter will largely consider the United States as an isolated, tightly bounded social system.

In recent years sociologists and historians have begun to examine old census data, city directories, and tax records to trace the occupational movement of families in particular localities during the nineteenth century and even earlier. The evidence is still incomplete and it is almost impossible to compare the rates of mobility from one study to another and from one setting to another. We can, however, make some assessments of trends from the available evidence.

Sorokin (1959) conducted surveys of occupational mobility in the 1920s and assembled the results of other studies that had been done earlier. His survey included students and the general population in Minneapolis. Sorokin concluded that the trend was toward a *decrease* in the inheritance of occupations from father to son.

Thernstrom (1964) conducted one of the early and most influential historical studies of social mobility in the United States. He studied the occupational and property-owning careers of the sons of several hundred mid-nineteenth century workers in Newburyport, Massachusetts. He found that fewer than 10 percent of the manual workers' sons become nonmanual workers: 26 percent of the sons remained in unskilled ranks, 54 percent had semiskilled occupations, and 13 percent entered skilled occupations. For a variety of reasons, these figures are not exactly comparable to the information provided by the Blau and Duncan survey and others conducted in recent decades. But the evidence suggests more outward flow from manual and unskilled ranks in recent decades than in the mid-nineteenth century. About 20 percent of the sons of laborers in manufacturing industries entered white-collar occupations in 1962 (Blau and Duncan 1967, Table 2.2). Other studies in different cities and other national surveys also indicate that there has been a small trend towards greater upward mobility for sons of workers in the past century (Hauser, Dickinson, Travis, and Koffel, 1975).

In Chapter 3, we reviewed some of the evidence about recruitment into leading business positions. Those studies of the business elite from the late nineteenth century to the present also indicate no decreasing recruitment from the manual occupations. Most business leaders are and were recruited from families in which the fathers themselves had been in business (Miller 1951; Keller 1963).

Intergenerational occupational mobility is very strongly affected by changes in occupational distribution from one generation to another. As we have seen, the decrease in the proportion of low status positions has resulted in a general upward mobility. Intergenerational mobility due to changes in occupational distribution is called structural mobility. Intergenerational mobility due to the exchange of persons, apart from structural mobility, is called circulation mobility. Together, they constitute observed mobility.

Comparing rates of intergenerational mobility in different periods in America is difficult because of the changes in the distribution of occupations over time. Summary measures are affected by the sizes of the different occupational strata in each generation. Researchers have long struggled with this problem and have sought ways to hold constant or standardize changes in occupational distribution so that they might compare the amount of upward and downward mobility between two periods, aside from structural mobility.

One of the early studies to deal with this problem was conducted by Rogoff (1953). She compared intergenerational occupational mobility in Indianapolis in 1910 and 1940. Because marriage license records included information on the groom's occupation and his father's occupation, such comparison could be made. Rogoff used a social distance mobility ratio, which she defined as the "ratio between actual mobility and the amount of mobility we would expect were there no relation between the son's occupational class and the occupational class of his father" (p. 32). She concluded that the overall mobility rate in 1940 was about the same as in 1910, although there were some variations for sons of different occupational origins. Later work has shown that this ratio is affected by the size of the occupational categories and, therefore, by the differences in the occupational structure, casting the findings into doubt. The data have been re-analyzed using methods that better take into account changes in the occupational structure from one time to another (Duncan 1966; Hauser et al. 1975). These results also indicate that there has been no change in the degree of relationship between son's and father's occupations between 1910 and 1940. Tully, Jackson, and Curtis (1970) conducted two surveys in 1969 in Indianapolis and tried to collect data comparable to Rogoff's data. Their findings suggest no change in occupational inheritance between 1967 and 1940, but somewhat greater upward mobility and less downward mobility in 1967 than in 1940.

Hauser, Koffel, Travis and Dickinson (1975), also reanalyzed data from the OCG study conducted by Duncan and Blau. They compared five-year cohorts among the respondents to that survey and also compared the results from four national surveys conducted between 1947 and 1972. They used sophisticated techniques to control for the effects of changing occupational structures. All of these analyses led them to conclude that over the years studied there has been no change in the degree of relationship between son's and father's occupation, other than the change that would reflect changes in the occupational structure. Jencks and his associates (1972, p. 180) reached the same conclusion from their review of available data.

This is an area of extensive research in contemporary sociology and one of increasing sophistication, making some earlier work obsolete. The growing evidence may resolve some controversies, but new ones emerge and some old ones persist. Still, some conclusions may be safely drawn: there is considerable intragenerational occupational mobility, more upward than downward, and more within the white-collar stratum and the manual stratum than between them. Intragenerational occupational mobility is not equal among different strata; it is affected by occupational origins. The correlation between father's and son's occupational status is moderate and the shift is more likely to be upward than downward. Over the last century, the chances of sons from diverse occupational strata to enter occupational strata different from their fathers' has not decreased. Indeed, among lower status occupations it may have increased. Recruitment into elite positions has not become more restricted; if anything, it may be a little more open now than in the past. These trends, however, do not reflect any increase in movement aside from changes in the occupational structure, circulation mobility rates have remained unchanged.

PERSONS

How do people rate others in prestige? What determines the honor and respect people accord to others? Whom do they comfortably associate with as equals? Whom do they strive to interact with and whom do they shun? People may grant prestige to those with power or in elevated positions. But, people also evaluate each other purely by social status. For example, members of a particular status community may judge other people as moral or immoral, as living in an honorable, noble, and high style or in a dishonorable, ignoble, and low style, as having the "right" or "wrong" background in terms of family, race, or ethnicity.

Sociologists have sought to discover to what extent and by what criteria people rank themselves in a status hierarchy. We will review some of the relevant studies, first reviewing research on general social status. Our purpose will be to determine what criteria people use to rate themselves and others. To consider the range in American status and trends in this range, we will refer to studies of persons with very low and very high status. Then we will review research about the entire status distributions, focusing on community studies. Finally, we will consider sociological work on two specific status criteria: race and sex.

General Status

In considering the general, overall evaluation people make of each other, style of life is undoubtedly an important component, yet one about which there may be little consensus: witness the strongly held, divergent attitudes about hippies, highbrows, petty bourgeoise, eggheads, hardhats, and so on. The variety of evaluations indicates the existence of multiple status systems.

Range. In considering the range of the status hierarchy in America, we will refer to studies of groups about which there is presumably considerable consensus. To regard people as having minimal or less than minimal status generally entails a *moral* evaluation of their way of living. Some ways of living may be regarded as immoral and improper. The evaluations may be so harsh that the people thus regarded have less than a minimal amount of status. This may have been and still may be so for the disreputable poor and the vagrants, tramps, and dwellers in Skid Rows (Matza 1966; Wallace 1965). There probably is not and never was complete consensus about the unworthiness of such people. But persons who were thought to refuse to work, who lived in what was regarded as dirt and squalor, or who did not sustain close personal relations with family members have been held in contempt and rejected. Because the proportion of persons in absolute poverty, described in the previous chapter has declined and tolerance for different ways of life has increased, the proportion of the American population who would be regarded as disreputable, as being unworthy of minimal human respect, has probably decreased over the last hundred years.

In order to examine changes between the top and bottom of the status hierarchy, we must consider not only what constitutes minimum status but also the degree of regard and prestige given to those with the highest status. The United States has never had an aristocracy. No set of persons has been regarded as having the right to great respect because of inherited titles. Neither has great deference been shown people because they have a particular way of life. Deference is shown to people who are very rich or powerful, but that can be less a matter of status than acknowledgement of their wealth or power. Certainly, there are circles of families within communities, and within the United States as a whole, who see themselves as a social elite. They have their own clubs, associations, and social gatherings. Some kinds of people are excluded who presumably would like to be included. This clearly indicates a status hierarchy.

G. William Domhoff (1971, 1974) has studied the extent to which there is a ruling social class in the United States. His work has focused on showing that a cohesive national status group exists. The ruling status group, he claims, consists of persons who have many shared social experiences. They have generally gone to certain private preparatory schools such as Choate, Groton, Phillips Exeter and St. Paul's. They are listed in the Social Registers and Blue Books. They belong to exclusive social clubs such as the Century, Philadelphia, Casino, Everglades, Somerset, and Union. They interact with each other in these settings and in private retreats. They have a unique style of life and intermarry within the status group.

Domhoff concedes that no one of these indicators unequivocally distinguishes a person who is in the social elite from one who is not. But taken together such indicators help identify members and indicate the scope of the elite. They also can be used to see to what extent the social elite overlaps with political and business leadership. A high overlap would demonstrate that this social group is indeed a ruling class, an issue we will return to in Chapter 7, when we examine the interrelationships between class, status, and power.

There is no clear evidence that this social elite has become increasingly distant or close to other status ranks during the course of American history. City and regional elites began to become integrated into a national social elite before the turn of the nineteenth century (Baltzell, 1958, p. 385). The result was a white, Anglo-Saxon, Protestant (WASP) establishment with great authority. Around the turn of the century, this group "of Protestant patricians not only held the vast majority of positions in the very heart of the national power; it also set the styles in arts and letters, in the universities, in sports, and in the more popular culture which governs the aspirations and values of the masses. . . . The authority of the Victorian establishment was maintained in spite of a great deal of anarchy and alienation at the lower levels of society as well as radical protest at the top" (Baltzell 1964, pp. 12, 15). The breadth and depth of authority of this social elite has been challenged and become more circumscribed in the course of this century. But, as we shall see in later chapters, it is still considerably influential in the spheres of business and government.

Distribution. We now turn to consider the overall distribution of persons within the American status system. We ask how many different evaluated levels are there and what proportion of the people fit into each? What criteria do people use to set off different status ranks or individuals? We begin to review information relevant to these questions by considering the community studies conducted in the United States from the 1930s to the present.

Studying small towns and communities enables a researcher to grasp the integrated way of life of people and to find out what life is really like for people. Some of these studies have given particular attention to the social inequalities within the community as well as the culture and institutions they shared. This was true of the Lynds' (1929) investigation of Middletown prior to the Depression and when they revisited it during the Depression (1937). Lloyd Warner and his associates particularly concentrated upon "social class" or status systems in their research begun in the early 1930s in Newburyport, a long-established New England town of 17,000 persons (Warner and Lunt 1941, 1942; Warner and Srole, 1945). Researchers associated with those studies and others went on to similarly study communities of the South and Midwest (Davis, Gardner, and Gardner 1941; Warner et al. 1949a and b).

Warner adapted the methods he used for an anthropological study of a preliterate Australian tribe to study, with a team of researchers, an industrial American town. They relied upon informants to tell them what the status system was like and where families were located in the status hierarchy. They began with high-prestige, long-time residents and gradually extended their interviews and observations.

Six "classes" or status levels seemed to exist in Yankee City. The people used various names for these strata, and the names were in part influenced by the strata where people themselves were. The researchers used their own terms, ones that entered popular conversation after their works were published: upper-uppers, lower-uppers, upper-middle, lower-middle, upper-lower, and lower-lower. They were able to locate or place nearly every family within one of these levels, using what they called an Index of Evaluated Participation.

In Yankee City during the depression of the 1930s, the distribution of status groups and the characterization of them may be summarized as follows:

1. *Upper-upper*: 1.4 percent of the town's population. This is the old-family elite; they are wealthy and have been wealthy for more than one generation; they maintain a large house in the best neighborhood.
2. *Lower-upper*: 1.6 percent of the population. Although they may, on the average, be richer than the upper-uppers, their money is newer and they are less polished.
3. *Upper-middle*: 1.2 percent of the population. These moderately success-ful business and professional families are less rich than the lower-uppers; they lack some high education and polish.
4. *Lower-middle*: 28.1 percent. These, the small business people, school teachers, foremen in industry, tend to have morals close to Puritan fundamentalism.
5. *Upper-lower*: 31.6 percent. These are the respectable working people who are orderly and keep their houses clean.
6. *Lower-lower*: 25.2 percent. These are the disreputable, slovenly people.

Warner's community studies and the resulting generalizations were criticized on several grounds and Warner and his associates tried to counter these arguments in the course of their subsequent work (Mills 1942; Pfautz and Duncan 1950). One criticism is that they understated the role of economic and political factors. In defense Warner states that he and his associates began their work believing that the economic structure was the underlying one. They were really studying social status, not class. They were also strongly criticized for the apparently imprecise way they gathered data, the nonrigorous way they handled their data, and the inadequacy of their explanation. In later work, Warner, Meeker, and Eells (1949b) developed an Index of Status Characteristics, based on occupation, education, source of income, and area of residence. This comparatively objective method using relatively accessible information gave results very similar to those attained by the original Warner methods. Hollingshead (1949) developed a similar but more fully reported method of ascertaining status rank. Again, the results were not dissimilar from those of Warner. Hollingshead studied Morris, Illinois, as Warner, but Hollingshead used the name Elmtown and Warner called it Jonesville.

Warner's approach has also been criticized as being inapplicable to studies of status inequalities in the country as a whole or even in urban areas where people know little about each other. It should be recognized that there may not be a country-wide status system. We live in many different kinds of communities and each may have its own status system; this is true of occupational and ethnic communities. Many people also live in small territorial communities such as towns, suburbs, and neighborhoods in which people rate each other according to several different criteria and limit their social interaction in terms of those ratings.

More recent work has sought to discover the extent to which people in urban centers and in the country as a whole think of themselves in class and status terms. Much of this work is about class identification. Respondents are sometimes asked how many classes they think there are; in many surveys they are asked whether they belong to the upper, middle, working, or lower class. This approaches the area of class consciousness, which will be discussed in Chapter 10. Other recent research has focused on the criteria people use to rank each other and the extent to which such rankings affect personal interaction and associations. For example, Laumann (1966) studied white males in Cambridge and Belmont, Massachusetts, to ascertain the social distance maintained between people in different occupations. The men were asked to what extent they agreed or disagreed that they liked to have each of seven kinds of social relations with persons in each of several occupations. The social relations varied from having the person as a son-in-law to having him as a next-door neighbor. Laumann found that occupational prestige was a major determinant of an individual's social distance preferences. Regardless of their own occupational status, people preferred close relations with persons of high rather than low prestige occupations. The people with whom they actually engage in social relations, however, is strongly influenced by similarity in occupational status. People tend to associate with persons in occupations with similar status.

Mobility. We do not have the same kind of systematic evidence about intragenerational and intergenerational status mobility of persons that we have for occupational mobility. The boundaries between status categories cannot be clearly marked nor can one know that the boundaries have not changed over time. It is probably most feasible to assess changes in mobility for those in the very high status category. The emphasis upon family lineage and old money to distinguish the social elite and the tendency to intermarry within the elite gives this category a caste-like quality. Baltzell (1964) traces the history of the American WASP establishment and describes its exclusion of Jews and others who do not share their lineage from social intimacy and full membership.

Before considering ethnic and sex characteristics as aspects of status inequality, we make a few observations about general social status. One issue that sociologists and other analysts of the social scene have long debated is whether status inequalities are continuous or discontinuous. It might be argued that there are clearly demarked social classes or status groups, that the members of each category know who belongs and who does not. On the other hand, it can be argued that these are differences of degree and no sharp demarcation can be drawn to mark off different classes. The empirical studies cited and others, while relevant, do not themselves entirely resolve the issue. First, the studies do not indicate that all the people in a community and certainly not in the country as a whole agree about how many status groups or classes there are. But people do think of themselves as belonging to different social classes. They tend to associate with others in the same social class. We will examine the degree of this class consciousness and its meanings in Chapter 10. At this point, it is sufficient to note that people categorize themselves and others within a ranked hierarchy. That social hierarchy is not purely economic, measured by income or wealth. Manners, lineage, style of life, and other qualities are ranked to provide a status hierarchy. If a single criterion had to be chosen, occupational status or prestige ranking would provide a good indicator of this status hierarchy. This is partly because occupation is associated with education and life styles are acquired to a significant degree, through the experience of schooling.

In the terms used in this book, class differences exist in a continuous sequence when measured in income, but are much more discontinuous when measured as wealth in the form of ownership of the means of production. Many status differences are relatively discontinuous. This is true even when broad categories of life styles are distinguished. Sharp discontinuities in status can exist when racial, ethnic, and sex differences are ranked in a status hierarchy. We will briefly discuss these aspects of status next.

Race and Sex Status

There is a vast literature on racial, ethnic, and sexual inequalities. The ranking of persons in terms of these categories is examined in studies of discrimination, prejudice, social distance, and patterns of social relations. Although it is beyond the scope of this book to review all the relevant literature, the hierarchical ranking of people in terms of racial, national, ethnic, religious, and sexual categories cannot be ignored in a discussion of the American status system. We will examine some of the trends in these status dimensions and do so using concepts that will be useful in later discussions of (1) the relations between class, status, and power, (2) their consequences, and (3) explanations of the inequalities.

Although clear lines cannot be drawn to separate the human species into distinct races, *race* as popularly defined and as we use it here, categorizes individuals. Race has long been used in America to assign people high and low status. The early British settlers brought with them beliefs about the natural inferiority and superiority of different races that became institutionalized with the enslavement of blacks and the expulsion of native Americans from the land (Jordan 1974). In effect, members of these categories were denied minimal status. As slaves, blacks were treated as property, the ultimate in dehumanization and depersonalization (Elkins 1959).

Even in this century, blacks, Indians, and other non-Europeans have been treated as separate and inferior. Consider the category defined as blacks. The social distinction between white and black was a sharp one. And because severe status inequalities were attached to the so-called race difference, had to be defined unequivocally as black, white, or something ι solution that generally followed was to treat each person wi ancestry as black and each person with anything except white ance white. This reinforced the insistence upon marriage within these cat not between them, and especially not between a black man and a whi ᵣ woman (who would then have a "black" child). Blacks could therefore be considered a caste insofar as membership in that category was the most important or master status. Until recently this situation existed, especially in the deep South (Davis, Gardner, and Gardner 1941). A professional man who was black could and would be called a "boy" and expected to respond and react as a "colored boy." In that status system, every black was regarded as of lower status than any white.

Several important and interrelated changes have been occurring in the status differences between blacks and whites in the United States. First, the status distance has generally lessened. The proportion of whites who regard the blacks as inherently inferior has steadily declined (Sheatsley 1966; Schwartz 1967; Campbell 1971). Preferences about keeping social distance, especially in intimate and equalitarian relationships have also declined, as have the actual practices of segregation. Blacks are less invisible as members of the larger American society than they were a generation ago.

Nevertheless, segments of the white population still regard themselves as inherently superior to blacks and probably all whites hold stereotypes and beliefs about blacks that tend to give blacks less status. Certainly there is evidence of continuing discrimination against blacks.

Another change has been the reduction in black or white as master statuses. People recognize other status characteristics, such as life style and occupational prestige, as important and treat persons in terms of those other statuses as well as in terms of perceived race.

A third important change is a decline in consensus about the status difference between blacks and whites. Blacks have probably never generally accepted the inferior status assigned to them by whites. But in the past they have shown a preference for some of the qualities of whites, even physical ones. For example, many blacks highly valued straight hair and light skin. The recent emphasis on black as beautiful indicates a crumbling consensus about race as a status indicator. Nevertheless, race may be associated with power or class rankings, even if status differences are not generally accepted.

When we discuss black-white status inequality, we are in many ways discussing a dichotomy, which makes it difficult to discuss the range and distribution separately. We have not tried to do so. We turn now to discuss mobility. As socially defined in this country, race is completely ascribed and people cannot change their race. Actually there is some "passing"; that is, persons deny their racial category and assume a social role as a member of another race.

Racial status mobility may be studied in another sense. We can examine the degree to which blacks and whites have similar and different patterns of occupational mobility. We can determine whether or not blacks have the same chances as whites for upward occupational mobility. The extent to which different status inequalities are interrelated may indicate discrimination by race or it may indicate that whatever causes one kind of inequality causes another.

When Blau and Duncan (1967) compared the patterns of intergenerational occupational mobility for blacks and whites, they found that in their occupational attainments blacks "are handicapped by having poor parents, less education, and inferior early career experiences than whites. Yet even if these handicaps are statistically controlled by asking, in effect, what the achievement would be if they had had the same origins, the same education, and the same first job as whites, their occupational chances are still consistently inferior to those of whites" (p. 209). Moreover, despite the lower occupational status origins of blacks, they are more likely to be downwardly mobile and less likely to be upwardly mobile than whites.

The differences in mobility patterns between whites and blacks is due to the differences in their occupational origins and destinations. If these differences are held statistically constant, the mobility process for blacks and whites is similar. When Hauser and Featherman (1977, pp. 212-15) adjusted the occupational distributions of whites and blacks so they would be the same, they found that the rates of mobility were the same.

The difference in occupational status between blacks and whites increases with education. Blacks, therefore, have less incentive than whites to acquire an education. Siegel (1965) also found greater differences in income between blacks and whites at higher educational levels than at lower ones. "Blacks are less successful than whites in converting their schooling into employment in better-paying occupations" (Stolzenberg 1975, p. 314).

The final American variation in status inequality that we will review is the inequality associated with gender differences. The differences between males and females in procreation are clear, but other differences that are seen to confer status inferiority or superiority are not as apparent. Throughout the course of American history, women have had less status than men. Despite some variations, women have not received equal respect. Their status has not been extremely low; women have not been dehumanized and denied minimal status. Yet the subjegation of women first to fathers, then to husbands, has caused them to be treated in many ways as objects or property rather than as humans.

Women's status relative to man's has not changed steadily in a single direction (Chafe 1972; Kraditor 1968; O'Neill 1969), partly because the differences in men's and women's status are so multidimensional and varied in different contexts. As co-producers in a family farm or other business, a woman's position may have involved more differences in sex-role behavior in the family than it does today; however, it also ensured more equality of status than in a contemporary middle-income family where the male is the sole provider of income.

Over the last century, the status difference between men and women probably has lessened. The degree to which males believe in the inherent inferiority of women and denigrate "women's work" has probably lessened. Perhaps, too, the sex role is less the master status than it has been. More frequently than in the past, women are not seen exclusively as holding roles traditionally associated with females: mother, wife, sex object for men. There is even some effort, currently associated particularly with the women's liberation movement, to reject the status hierarchy that says that masculine activities and manners are superior, women's inferior. Rather, the position is that feminine qualities are to be valued and that men would be better and more fully human if they shared these qualities. Evidence of the acceptance of this argument can be seen in the contemporary emphasis on expressing feelings, valuing intimate social relations, and spurning hierarchical relations. Insofar as men accept these standards, the relative status difference between men and women is lessened. Insofar as women uphold these standards while men do not, the consensus about status ranking is lessened (Bernard 1978).

For all these changes, considerable discrimination is still found in many spheres of social life. In many situations women are not treated seriously and may even be treated as invisible. Equal opportunities in occupations and equal pay are far from universal and at least partly arise from beliefs and expectations by men that women have lesser ability to do "important" things—defined by men as what men do. Thus, lack of equal opportunity and of equal pay are indirect measures of status, but imperfect ones.

Table 5.5 presents some information on the occupational distribution of men and women and the median income received by each in various occupational categories. Women are more highly represented in clerical occupations than men and are much less likely to be in craft occupations than are men. The proportion of men and women in professions and in sales is about the same, but these categories are very broad and women and men differ greatly in the specific occupations they have within those categories. For example, within the professions, men are vastly more likely to be lawyers and physicians; women are much more likely to be elementary school teachers. These variations in specific occupations account in large part for the differences in median income shown in Table 5.5. For example, women in sales made only 26 percent of what men made, largely because women work primarily in retail sales, while men were sales representatives for manufacturers, were in wholesale, or were insurance representatives. But even in retail sales, women earned much less than men. Among elementary school teachers, women earned only 80 percent of what men earned.

Women's status has not been rising steadily (Chafe 1972). If we measure women's equality in terms of participation in the labor force, education, earn-

TABLE 5.5   Occupational Distribution and Earnings among Men and Women in the Labor Force, 1970

Occupation	Percent Distribution		Median Earning		
	Men	Women	Men	Women	Women's ÷ Men's
Professional, Technical and Similar Workers	14.0	15.3	10,735	6,034	.56
(Accountants)*	(1.1)	(.1)	(10,627)	(5,818)	.55
(Elementary Teachers)	(.5)	(4.4)	(8,013)	(6,439)	.80
Managers and Administrators	11.1	3.5	11,277	5,495	.49
Sales Workers	6.8	7.4	8,451	2,238	.26
(Sales Clerks, Retail Trade)	(1.7)	(5.1)	(5,532)	(2,226)	.40
Clerical and Similar Workers	7.6	34.5	7,265	4,232	.58
Operatives, Except	13.8	14.5	6,730	3,635	.54
Total			7,610	3,649	.48

*Parentheses indicate selected occupations within major types.

Source: U.S. Bureau of the Census 1976, Table No. 589.

ings, and occupational distribution, we can see periods of increased inequality followed by periods of gains in equality; but we also see little change in many indicators of socio-economic status.

Female participation in the labor force has increased greatly: 27 percent of American women were in the labor force in 1940; 46 percent in 1975 (U.S. Bureau of the Census, 1976). Nevertheless, women may continue to earn much less, fill lower-prestige occupations, and have relatively fewer years of education than men. Knudson (1969) has documented a decline in the relative status of women in these areas between 1940 and 1960. For example, women as a percent of the faculties in higher education declined from 27.6 percent in 1940 to 24.5 percent in 1950 and 22 0 percent in 1960. In a longer time perspective, some trend toward increasing equality can be discerned for certain indicators. For example, Ridley and Jaffe (1975) examined the similarity in occupational distribution between men and women from 1900 to 1970. They found a slight tendency toward increasing similarity in each decade except in the 1920s and 1950s. Women's earnings as a proportion of men's however, has not become more equal. Among full-time, year-round workers in 1955, women's median earnings were 64 percent of men's; in 1960 it was 61 percent, in 1965 it was 60 percent, and in 1970 it had fallen to 59 percent (U.S. Bureau of the Census, 1971).

146

Only recently have studies of intergenerational mobility among women been undertaken. Prior to the women's movement, research about inter-generational mobility was limited to studies of fathers and sons. We now have some research on occupational mobility of fathers and daughters compared to fathers and sons and on intergenerational status mobility through marriage by women compared to mobility through occupations by men.

Although the occupational origins of men and women are quite similar, their destinations are not. Thus, more women than men are not in the labor force and the occupational distribution of men and women differ greatly. Consequently, women and men have different intergenerational mobility patterns.

Social researchers have sought to find out how different the patterns of female mobility would be if they held constant the differences in labor forces participation and occupational distribution. This problem is similar to compar-ing occupational mobility in two different historical periods. Tyree and Treas (1974) used national survey data to compare men's and women's intergenera-tional occupational mobility, adjusting the labor force participation rates and occupational distributions so that they would be the same. Tyree and Treas found somewhat more intergenerational mobility among women than men. Mobility patterns for particular occupational origins are also somewhat different. Daughters of professional fathers are more likely than sons to enter white-collar occupations, but daughters whose fathers were managers, officials, or proprietors are less likely to have white-collar jobs. Daughters of farmers are more likely than sons to move into white-collar jobs. Looking at destinations, women are particularly likely to move into lower white-collar work: sales and clerical jobs. Hauser and Featherman (1977), in a more intensive analysis of married women and men, reached the same conclusions.

Tyree and Treas (1974) also compared the mobility of women through marriage and through occupations. They found greater mobility through marriage than through occupations. Chase (1975) used the OCG sample of husbands and wives to compare women's status mobility through marriage and men's through occupational attainments. He used first jobs of the men and first jobs of the wife's husbands and both raw and adjusted methods of assessing intergenerational mobility. He found that women's marriages yielded more upward *and* more downward status mobility than did men's occupational attain-ments.

Women's participation in the labor force and their occupational attain-ment are affected by their mothers' occupational positions. Daughters are more likely to be employed outside the home if their mothers had been so employed than if their mothers were not (Kriesberg 1970:157-162). The mother's occupa-tion is related to the daughter's occupational position, even taking into account the father's occupation (Rosenfeld 1978). Among daughters with mothers who were employed outside the home, mother's occupational position explains more of the variation in daughter's occupational attainment than does the father's occupational position. This supports the idea that an employed mother offers a role model, occupational knowledge and additional financial resources that are more important than the father's occupation alone for the daughter's occupational destination.

The differences in status mobility patterns for men and women are not simply a result of discrimination. They also indicate the way in which men and women's lives are affected by nonoccupational institutions, particularly the family, and also the way in which the occupational system is structured to accommodate men's rather than women's work career and to reinforce conventional family roles. We will discuss aspects of this later in the book. At this point it is important to note that family status is not determined solely by men's occupational role; the women's occupation is important—obviously for female-headed families but also for families with a married couple. People tend to average the status of husband and wife in ranking the family. Yet each individual also has his or her own course of status mobility.

CONCLUSIONS

The literature reviewed indicates that status inequalities exist analytically distinct from class and power inequalities. Although ascription is important to status inequality, status differences are also based on achievement. Ascribed status is exemplified by different evaluations of persons because of their race, sex, or family origins. Achieved status in the United States is accorded in terms of life style of persons and is also attached to positions, such as occupational roles. The trend over the last two hundred years of American history has probably been toward some decline in the proportion of the people with minimal or less than minimal status.

Intergenerational occupational mobility is moderate in the United States. If people change occupational status level, most of them move a short distance rather than a long social distance from their fathers' occupational status, and they are more likely to move upward than downward. Variations in structural mobility do exist over time and by sex and race. No trend toward less or more intergenerational circulation mobility seems to have developed in the United States over the past century. The stability of circulation mobility over time and its homogeneity by sex and race suggests the effects of powerful pervasive factors. In this case, the workings of the family are probably crucial.

REFERENCES

BALTZELL, E. DIGBY. 1958. *Philadelphia Gentlemen*. Glencoe, Ill.: Free Press.
BALTZELL, E. DIGBY. 1964. *The Protestant Establishment*. New York: Random House.

BERNARD, JESSE. 1978. "Models for the Relationship Between the World of Women and the World of Men," in Louis Kriesberg (Ed.), *Research in Social Movements, Conflicts and Change.* Greenwich, Conn.: JAI Press, pp. 291-340.

BLAU, PETER and OTIS DUDLEY DUNCAN. 1967. *American Occupational Structure.* New York: John Wiley.

BRAVERMAN, HARRY. 1974. *Labor and Monopoly Capitalism.* New York: Monthly Review Press.

CAMPBELL, ANGUS. 1971. *White Attitudes Toward Black People.* Ann Arbor, Mich.: Institute for Social Research, University of Michigan.

CHAFE, WILLIAM H. 1972. *The American Woman: Her Changing Social, Economic, and Political Role, 1920-1970.* New York: Oxford University Press.

CHASE, IVAN D. 1975. "A Comparison of Men's and Women's Intergenerational Mobility in the United States," *American Sociological Review*, 40 (August):483-505.

COUNTS, GEORGE S. 1925. "The Social Status of Occupations," *The School Review*, 33 (January):16-27.

DAVIS, ALLISON, BURLEIGH B. GARDNER, and MARY R. GARDNER. 1941. *Deep South: A Social-Anthropological Study of Caste and Class.* Chicago: University of Chicago Press.

DOMHOFF, G. WILLIAM. 1971. *The Higher Circles*, New York: Vintage.

DOMHOFF, G. WILLIAM. 1974. *The Bohemian Grove and Other Retreats*, New York: Harper Colophon Books.

DUNCAN, OTIS DUDLEY. 1966. "Methodological Issues in the Analysis of Social Mobility," in Neil J. Smelser and Seymour Martin Lipset (Eds.), *Social Structure and Mobility in Economic Development.* Chicago: Aldine, pp. 51-97.

ELKINS, STANLEY M. 1959. *Slavery: A Problem in American Institutional and Intellectual Life.* Chicago: University of Chicago Press.

HAUSER, ROBERT W., PETER J. DICKINSON, HARRY P. TRAVIS, and JOHN N. KOFFEL. 1975. "Structural Changes in Occupational Mobility among Men in the United States," *American Sociological Review* 40 (October):585-598.

HAUSER, ROBERT M., JOHN N. KOFFEL, HARRY P. TRAVIS, and PETER J. DICKINSON. 1975. "Temporal Change in Occupational Mobility: Evidence for Men in the United States," *American Sociological Review*, 40 (June):279-97.

HAUSER, ROBERT M. and DAVID L. FEATHERMAN. 1977. *The Process of Stratification.* New York: Academic Press.

HODGE, ROBERT W., PAUL M. SEIGAL and PETER H. ROSSI. 1966. *Occupational Prestige in the United States: 1925-1963,"* in R. Bendix and S. M. Lipset (Eds.), *Class, Status and Power.* New York: Free Press, pp. 322-334.

HOLLINGSHEAD, AUGUST. 1949. *Elmtown's Youth.* New York: John Wiley.

HUGHES, EVERETT C. 1962. "Good People and Dirty Work," *Social Problems*, 10 (Summer):3-11. (Originally given as lecture in 1948).

HYMAN, HERBERT H. 1953. "The values Systems of Different Classes: A Social Psychological Contribution to the Analysis of Stratification," in R. Bendix and S. M. Lipset (Eds.), *Class, Status and Power.* New York: Free Press, pp. 526-42.

JENCKS, CHRISTOPHER and M. SMITH, H. ACLAND, M. J. BANE, D. COHEN, H. GINTIS, B. HEYNS, and S. MICHELSON. 1972. *Inequality:*

A Reassessment of the Effect of Family and Schooling in America. New York: Basic Books.

JORDAN, WINTHROP D. 1974. *The White Man's Burden: Historical Origins of Racism in the United States*. New York: Oxford University Press.

KELLER, SUZANNE. 1963. *Beyond the Ruling Class*. New York: Random House.

KNUDSEN, DEAN D. 1969. "The Declining Status of Women: Popular Myths and the Failure of Functionalist Thought," *Social Forces* 48 (December): 183-193.

KRADITOR, AILEEN. 1968. *Up From the Pedestal*. Chicago: Quadrangle Press.

KRIESBERG, LOUIS. 1970. *Mothers in Poverty*. Chicago: Aldine.

LAUMANN, EDWARD O. 1966. *Prestige and Association in an Urban Community*. Indianapolis: Bobbs-Merrill.

LIPSET, S. M. and R. BENDIX. 1960. *Social Mobility in Industrial Society*. Berkeley: University of California Press.

LYND, ROBERT S. and HELEN MERRELL LYND. 1929. *Middletown*. New York: Harcourt, Brace.

LYND, ROBERT S. and HELEN MERRELL LYND. 1937. *Middletown in Transition*. New York: Harcourt, Brace.

MATZA, DAVID. 1966. "The Disreputable Poor," in R. Bendix and S. M. Lipset (Eds.), *Class, Status, and Power*. New York: Free Press, pp. 289-302.

MILLER, WILLIAM (Ed.). 1952. *Men and Business: Essays in the Historical Role of the Entrepreneur*. Cambridge, Mass.: Harvard University Press.

MILLS, C. WRIGHT. 1942. "Review of the Social Life of a Modern Community," *American Sociological Review* 7 (April):263-71.

O'NEILL, WILLIAM L. 1969. *Everyone Was Brave*. Chicago: Quadrangle.

PFAUTZ, HAROLD W. and OTIS D. DUNCAN. 1950. "A Critical Evaluation of Warner's Work on Community Stratification," *American Sociological Review* 15 (April):205-15.

REISS, ALBERT J., JR. 1961. *Occupations and Social Status*. New York: Free Press.

RIDLEY, J. C. and A. J. JAFFE. 1975. "A Brief Note on Occupational Differentiation by Sex in the United States, 1900 to 1970," *The New York Stratification* 27 (November-December):17-19.

ROGOFF, NATALIE. 1953. *Recent Trends in Occupational Mobility*. Glencoe, Ill.: Free Press.

ROSENFELD, RACHEL. 1978. "Women's Intergenerational Occupational Mobility," *American Sociological Review* (February):36-46.

SCHWARTZ MILDRED. 1967. *Trends in White Attitudes Toward Negroes*. Chicago: National Opinion Research Center.

SHEATSLEY, PAUL B. 1966. "White Attitudes Toward the Negro," *Daedalus* 95 (Winter):217-238.

SIEGEL, PAUL. 1965. "On the Cost of Being a Negro," *Sociological Inquiry* 35 (Winter):41-57.

SIEGEL, PAUL S., PETER H. ROSSI, and ROBERT W. HODGE. 1975. *Social Standings in Occupations*. New York: Seminar Press.

SOROKIN, PITIRIM A. 1959. *Social and Cultural Mobility*, Glencoe, Ill.: Free Press. (Originally published in 1927.)

STOLZENBERG, ROSS M. 1975. "Education, Occupation, and Wage Differences Between White and Black Men," *American Journal of Sociology*, 91 (September):299-323.

TALBERT, CAROL. 1975. *Ethnography of Poor Women*. Unpublished Report, Syracuse, N.Y.: Syracuse University Anthropology Department and Health Studies Program.

THERNSTROM, STEPHEN. 1964. *Poverty and Progress: Social Mobility in a Nineteenth Century City*, Cambridge, Mass.: Harvard University Press.

TROLLOPE, FRANCES. 1949. *Domestic Manners of the Americans*. New York: Knopf. (Originally published in 1832.)

TULLY, J. C., E. F. JACKSON and R. F. CURTIS. 1970. "Trends in Occupational Mobility in Indianapolis," *Social Forces* 49:186-200.

TYREE, ANDREA and JUDITH TREAS. 1974. "The Occupational and Marital Mobility of Women," *American Sociological Review* 39 (June):293-302.

U.S. BUREAU OF THE CENSUS. 1971. Current Population Reports, Series P-60, No. 80, "Income in 1970 of Families and Persons in the United States," Washington, D.C.: Government Printing Office.

U.S. BUREAU OF THE CENSUS. 1976. *Statistical Abstract of the United States: 1976* (96th Edition). Washington, D.C.: Government Printing Office.

WALLACE, SAMUEL E. 1965. *Skid Row as a Way of Life*. Totowa, N.J.: Bedminster Press.

WARNER, W. LLOYD and PAUL S. LUNT. 1941. *The Social Life of a Modern Community*. New Haven: Yale University Press.

WARNER, W. LLOYD and PAUL S. LUNT. 1942. *The Status System of a Modern Community*. New Haven: Yale University Press.

WARNER, W. LLOYD and LEO SROLE. 1945. *The Social System of American Ethnic Groups*. New Haven: Yale University Press.

WARNER, W. LLOYD, in collaboration with W. C. Bailey, A. Cooper, W. Eaton, A. B. Hollingshead, C. McGuire, M. Meeker, B. Neugarten, E. Z. Vogt, Jr., and D. Wray. 1949a. *Democracy in Jonesville*. New York: Harper.

WARNER, LLOYD, MARCIA MEEKER, and KENNETH EELLS. 1949b. *Social Class in America*. Chicago: Science Research Associates.

chapter 6

World
Status Variations

Article 1. All human beings are born free and equal in dignity and rights. They are endowed with reason and conscience and should act toward one another in a spirit of brotherhood.

Article 2. Everyone is entitled to all the rights and freedoms set forth in this Declaration, without distinction of any kind, such as race, colour, sex, language, religion, political or other opinion, national or social origin, poverty, birth or other status. . . . *Universal Declaration of Human Rights Adopted by the General Assembly of the United Nations, 1948*

This chapter compares the extent of status inequalities in different countries of the world. Thus, it provides a basis for assessing whether the status inequality in the United States is relatively high or low and gives information needed to understand the consequences and determinants of status inequality. The final part of the chapter considers status inequalities within systems that transcend and cut across national boundaries, for status inequality depends on shared understanding, understanding that may not correspond to country boundaries.

COMPARISONS AMONG COUNTRIES

Status relations between different racial, cultural, and ethnic groups have long been examined all over the world. More recently, studies have been made of occupational prestige and of the inequality of men and women in different countries. This wealth of material makes it possible to compare the degree of status inequality in different countries.

Status ranking depends upon standards of evaluation. Because such standards vary from culture to culture, comparing status inequality in social systems within differing cultures is very difficult. People in one culture give great importance to lineage in according prestige, those in another to physical prowess. In both cultures, still other standards are added to evaluate the status of persons and positions. Two kinds of comparison of the range and distribution or status between cultures are possible, although very difficult. We can use a single standard of evaluation to compare how persons or positions are ranked *according to that standard* in different cultures. Or, we can take a set of positions or categories of persons and compare how they are ranked *by whatever standards* people in different cultures apply to them. In the first kind of comparison, for example, we might compare the application of the standard that ethnicity be used as a basis for according ascribed status. In the second case, for example, we might select a set of activities, linked together into an occupational role, and compare how that and other occupations are relatively ranked in different societies. Nevertheless, any standard or category of positions is fully meaningful only in its social and cultural context; it is not completely comparable when taken out of its context. Aware of their ultimate incomparability, we will attempt to compare, as best we can, status inequalities in different cultural systems. We should keep in mind that we will make fewer mistakes if we consider only large differences in status rankings; the more precise and small the distinctions we attempt, the more subject to error we are.

Occupational Positions

Everywhere in the world people work. They engage in activities to produce desired goods and services, their activities are grouped together into occupational roles, and those roles are evaluated in terms of status. We will consider the range and distribution of status differences of those positions and mobility into and out of them.

Range. In many cultures, manual labor is considered base and dishonorable. The leisure pursuits of the aristocracy are noble, the vulgar forms of labor repugnant. As Veblen wrote in 1899 in *The Theory of the Leisure Class:*

> During the predatory culture labor comes to be associated in man's habits of thought with weakness and subjection to a master. It is therefore a mark of inferiority, and therefore comes to be accounted unworthy of man in his best estate. By virtue of this tradition, labour is felt to be debasing, and this tradition has never died out (Veblen 1931, p. 36).

This evaluation varies in strength in different cultures. It has been less widely adhered to in the United States than in countries with hereditary aristocracies and masses of poor, subjugated peasants and workers. In some such societies, even persons holding positions where they would benefit by first-hand knowledge and experience in the field or factory shun contact with the masses. For example, architects may avoid visiting the site for new housing or talking with the people who are to live there if the builders or the potential residents are regarded as ignorant laborers. The status difference between manual workers and the occupational elite is very great in such societies.

In some cultures the dominant standards glorify manual labor. The socialist movement, in its many varieties, has espoused the view that manual labor is to be valued, that people who work with their hands are to be honored and respected. The labor Zionist movement, for example, emphasizes the glories of tilling the soil and of building what is needed with one's own hands. In the East European Communist countries, too, the skilled worker is officially given prestige. In the People's Republic of China a variety of efforts are made to give prestige to workers and peasants and to lessen the prestige accorded nonmanual elites. Mao Tse-Tung has sought:

> . . . to wipe out the status distinction between mental work and manual labor, a prominent feature of social inequality inherited from the old society and justified by the Confucian Ideology. . . . The emphasis is . . . on the cultivation of such new values as "respect physical labor," "combine learning with practice," "welcome hardship," etc. "Actors, poets, playwrights and other writers must not be allowed to stay in the city forever," Mao said in 1964. "They should go to farms and factories. Staying in an office they can't produce anything" (Young 1973, p. 53).

The efforts to raise the prestige of manual work to a level above or equal to nonmanual work has probably not been fully effective in these countries. Within the

154

Kibbutzim of Israel, "productive labor," that is, work in the fields and factories, is highly regarded. In the countries of Eastern Europe and in the People's Republic of China, the status gap between nonmanual elites and workers and peasants has undoubtedly been lessened. In many countries, especially those of Western Europe, there probably has also been some decreases in the status gap between, for example, workers and managers. In the recent past, managers expected and received great deference from workers, as exemplified by workers approaching and speaking to managers tentatively and with cap-in-hand.

Distribution Although studies of occupational prestige have been conducted in many countries throughout the world, the results are rarely completely comparable. In some studies a set of occupational titles is presented to a sample of respondents and they are asked about the general standing of each occupation, as was done in the NORC 1947 and 1963 surveys described in Chapter 2. More often the questions are phrased differently. The respondents sometimes are a national sample, but often only persons in urban areas are interviewed and sometimes only students are questioned. If results are to be comparable, then only occupations that exist in the countries being compared can be included. We must either omit occupations that exist in one society and not in another or we use a general term to refer to similar sets of activity in both societies. In the first instance we impose more similarity than actually exists; in the second we distort reality. Thus, the term *farmer* refers to a whole range of roles: members of a collective farm in the USSR, peasants working on a large estate owned by a landlord, families working plots of land they own, working farmers employing wage labor, and so on. Of course, more precision can be given to occupational titles—although this makes the occupations more comparable, it reduces the number of countries that can be compared. In another sense, we wish to compare the relative status of different occupational activities, taking into account the variety of ways in which they are socially organized. An additional difficulty arises from the fact that because certain occupations may not be generally known in some countries, a significant proportion of the people would be unable to rate their prestige.

Some of the opportunities and difficulties offered by comparing occupational prestige ratings in different countries can be indicated by examining the results of a survey conducted in Warsaw, Poland, in 1958. In examining the results we must recognize that a sample of an urban center is not representative of the whole country; it undoubtedly includes a larger proportion of well-educated persons than would be found in a national sample. The results are presented in Table 6.1 and can be compared with the results from the U.S. survey presented in Table 2.4. A sample of 763 Warsaw residents were asked to rate the "social prestige" of a list of occupations (Sarapata and Wesolowski, 1961). Each respondent was asked, "Thinking of their social prestige, how do you rate these occupations: (1) With very great prestige? (2) With great prestige? (3) With average prestige? (4) With low prestige? (5) With very low prestige?"

Several of the occupational titles are not exactly the same in the United

TABLE 6.1 Ranks, Scores, and Distribution of Ratings of Specific Occupations in Relation to Social Prestige (Warsaw, Poland)

Rank	Occupation	Evaluation of Social Prestige (Percentage of Respondents)						Scores[1]
		Very Great	Great	Average	Low	Very Low	Do Not Know	
1	University Professor	79.5	16.7	2.1	0.3	–	1.3	1.22
2	Doctor	61.0	33.2	3.7	0.5	0.4	1.2	1.44
3	Teacher	48.1	33.6	13.9	1.9	0.8	1.7	1.71
4	Mechanical Engineer	33.3	53.1	11.2	0.5	–	1.9	1.78
5	Airplane Pilot	35.6	44.9	15.9	1.3	0.1	2.1	1.83
6	Lawyer, Attorney	34.8	39.7	17.4	4.2	2.0	1.9	1.97
7	Agronomist	25.4	51.4	18.7	1.9	0.3	2.4	1.97
8	Minister of the National Government	38.9	26.8	19.0	8.4	4.9	2.0	2.07
9	Journalist	27.2	39.4	24.0	5.6	1.9	1.9	2.13
10	Skilled Steel-Mill Worker	23.5	39.0	29.9	5.0	0.7	1.9	2.18
11	Priest	32.7	29.0	18.3	7.7	10.5	1.9	2.35
12	Nurse	20.8	32.7	33.2	10.4	1.6	1.3	2.38
13	Machinist	19.5	38.4	34.0	5.8	0.7	1.6	2.51
14	Factory Foreman	7.7	42.1	40.1	7.2	0.8	2.1	2.53
15	Small Farmer	7.3	27.4	43.7	16.1	2.7	2.9	2.53
16	Accountant	7.6	38.8	43.3	6.6	1.2	2.5	2.54
17	Shopkeeper	6.4	21.2	43.6	19.1	7.8	1.9	2.64
18	Tailor With His Own Workshop	7.3	28.2	50.9	10.1	1.7	1.9	2.70
19	Locksmith With Own Workshop	6.8	28.1	49.4	11.2	2.3	2.3	2.73
20	Office Supervisor	5.2	30.9	45.6	12.5	3.5	2.4	2.77
21	Army Officer	8.4	30.0	38.5	15.4	5.8	1.9	2.79
22	Railway Conductor	2.8	13.9	48.3	27.9	4.9	2.1	3.18
23	Policeman	9.4	15.5	32.5	26.7	14.5	1.3	3.21
24	Office Clerk	0.8	9.4	44.6	32.3	10.6	2.3	3.43
25	Typist	1.9	8.1	38.3	32.5	16.2	2.0	3.50
26	Salesclerk	1.2	6.1	39.0	35.6	15.7	2.4	3.59
27	Unskilled Construction Laborer	1.7	4.0	21.1	38.5	32.3	2.4	3.95
28	Cleaning Woman	1.6	5.3	16.9	28.7	45.9	1.6	4.08
29	Unskilled Farm Laborer	1.3	3.6	17.1	30.9	44.6	2.4	4.16

[1] Average of individual scores: 1.00, very great prestige; 2.00, great; 3.00, average; 4.00, low; 5.00, very low.

Source: Sarapata and Wesolowski 1961, Table 7, p. 585.

States and the Warsaw surveys; not only are the samples different but the questions are also worded somewhat differently. Looking only at occupations with identical or almost identical titles, we can see considerable similarity in the overall ranking of occupations in Warsaw and in the United States. Professional occupations tend to be ranked high, unskilled manual workers low. But the variations are interesting. A university professor in Warsaw has more prestige than a college professor in the United States; a teacher has higher prestige in Warsaw than in the United States. A cabinet member in the United States receives a higher prestige rank from his fellow countrymen than does a minister of the Polish national government. An American Army captain has a higher prestige rank in the United States than a Polish Army officer in Warsaw.

Inkeles and Rossi (1956) compared the prestige ratings of occupations in six countries and noted the very high correlations in the rank orderings of the occupations among the six countries. For example, the correlations between prestige ratings in the United States and those in the USSR, Japan, Great Britain, New Zealand, and Germany were all in the nineties.

Inkeles and Rossi also noted discrepancies in the prestige rankings among the six countries. These are presented in Table 6.2. The Soviet sample was drawn from former Soviet citizens who had been in displaced persons camps in Germany, some of whom had recently emigrated to the United States. We do not know how representative a sample they were, but we know that they were taken out of the Soviet Union by the German army for forced labor. Thus, being outside of the USSR did not necessarily indicate that they held anti-Soviet sentiments. Comparisons could only be made for occupations that were studied in each pair of countries being compared. For example, the Buddhist priest in Japan is rated lower than the minister in the United States, United Kingdom, or New Zealand; the farmer is rated lower by Soviet displaced persons than by respondents in the other five countries.

Hodge, Treiman, and Rossi (1966) were able to compare occupational prestige ratings in twenty-four countries in 1966. On the whole, they found very high relationships between the prestige ratings in the United States and in the twenty-three other countries studied. Comparing nonfarm occupations, the average correlation was .91, it ranged from .97 between the United States and New Zealand to .79 between the United States and Poland (Warsaw sample). Among the countries studied the correlations were relatively high with Canada, Turkey, Guam, Norway, and the Philippines; relatively low with the Belgian Congo (now Zaire), India, Sweden, Brazil, and the USSR. Correlations were also higher on the average among white-collar than among blue-collar occupations, which suggests more shared standards about white-collar than blue-collar work.

The similarity in occupational prestige ratings in different countries makes it possible to compare the distribution of positions with varying amounts of prestige in different countries. We know that professional occupations generally have high prestige. The proportion of the labor force in professional occupations varies greatly from country to country. In countries with higher proportions of

TABLE 6.2   Discrepancies[1] in the Rating of Matched Occupations by Pairs of Nations

	Rated Higher in Japan	Rated Higher in United States	Rated Higher in Great Britain	Rated Higher in New Zealand	Rated Higher in USSR
Rated Lower in Japan		Minister, Farmer, Insurance Agent,	Minister, Farmer Insurance Agent	Minister, Farmer, Insurance Agent	Accountant
Rated Lower in United States	Company Director, Labor Leader, Reporter (News), Street Sweeper, Shoe Shiner		Accountant, Chef, Street Sweeper	Accountant, Farmer, Truck Driver, Street Sweeper	Engineer, Worker
Rated Lower in Great Britain	Reporter (News), Street Sweeper	Civil Servant, Truck Driver, Minister Building Contractor, Electrician		Truck Driver	Worker
Rated Lower in New Zealand	Reporter (News), Street Sweeper	Civil Servant, Building Contractor, Bookkeeper, Electrician, Dock Worker	Chef, Bartender		Worker
Rated Lower in USSR	Factory Manager	Scientist, Farmer	Farmer	Farmer	

[1]The authors consistently designated any cited occupation by the title closest and most familiar to Americans. For example, they used *minister* in preference to *Buddhist priest, electrician* rather than *fitter (electrical)*.

Source: Inkeles and Rossi 1956, Table 3, p. 334.

professionals, then, larger proportions of people enjoy higher occupational prestige. This is similarly true of persons in high-level administration and other white-collar positions. Most people, however, are employed in agriculture, in manual industrial employment, or in low-prestige white-collar jobs. The similarity in prestige among those occupations means that the distribution of prestige is not greatly different among countries that differ in industrialization.

Mobility. That the opportunities for intergenerational occupational mobility are more equal in the United States than elsewhere in the world has long seemed self-evident. The reasons why this belief is widely held need examination. Perhaps the belief is based on a tendency for Americans in positions of high status to boast of their low origins, claiming to be "self-made"; on the other hand, Europeans who are in positions of high status tend to deny low origins. The experience of many immigrants entering at the lower occupational levels and having their children assume more prestigeful positions probably contributes to the sense of American uniqueness. But these persons might have experienced the same mobility in Europe. Perhaps, however, the belief is factually correct. The evidence about the actual extent of intergenerational occupational mobility in different countries must be examined.

We will consider evidence about observed mobility before examining circulation mobility. Observed mobility is what people directly experience. As discussed in the previous chapter, it includes structural and circulation mobility. Structural mobility is forced mobility resulting from changes in occupational distribution between fathers' and sons' times. Circulation mobility is exchange mobility; it exists indepedently of such structural changes.

One of the early systematic comparisons of intergenerational occupational mobility was made by Rogoff (1953). She used national surveys conducted in the United States and France. When all occupations were considered, 48.3 percent of the French sons had fathers who were in different occupations than the sons currently filled; among United States sons, 67.5 percent were in different occupations. (If we omit farmers, the mobility in both countries is higher; 59 and 77.1 percent, respectively.) Although mobility, so measured, was higher in the United States than in France, the high rates in both countries was stressed. The inference was made that regardless of historical antecedents, modern industrial society produces a relatively high degree of intergenerational occupational interchange.

During the 1950s national surveys were conducted in more and more countries and by the end of the decade Lipset and Bendix (1959) were able to compare intergenerational occupational mobility in the United States (two surveys), France, Germany (two surveys), Switzerland, Sweden, and Japan. To make the studies more comparable, they considered only three broad occupational categories: farm, manual, and nonmanual.

> The data indicate that a large minority of the sons of the industrial labor force achieve nonmanual positions. In France this group comprises 35

percent of the sons, in Germany 26 to 30 percent, in Switzerland, 44 percent, in Sweden, 29 percent, in Japan, 33 percent, and in the United States, 31 to 35 percent. A smaller percent in each country declines from nonmanual to manual positions, the percentages ranging from a low of 13 percent to a high of 38 percent (Lipset and Bendix 1959, p. 17).

The proportion that moved up from manual to nonmanual strata, among these countries, was regarded as high and similar.

Information about intergenerational occupational mobility in England, Denmark, and Italy were also compared, using occupational prestige categories since the data were so reported. Lipset and Bendix found considerable movement from the low-prestige occupational categories of manual workers, farm workers, and routine nonmanual employees into high-prestige farm ownership and high-level nonmanual positions. In Denmark, 22 percent of the sons with fathers in low-prestige occupations entered high-prestige occupations; this compares to 20 percent in Great Britain and only 8 percent in Italy. They inferred from these studies that intergenerational mobility rates were similar in industrialized societies.

Miller (1975) reasoned that if mobility among several strata were examined, more differences among countries might become evident. He studied more detailed occupational strata and considered upward and downward mobility and occupational inheritance as analytically distinct. Working a little later than Lipset and Bendix, Miller drew on surveys from thirteen countries and city surveys from four other countries.

Since the general trend in industrial societies is toward a higher proportion of the population in nonmanual occupations, Miller suggested that downward mobility might be a better indicator of the openness of the status system than upward mobility. One of the striking findings that emerged from Miller's comparisons is the great extent and variability in downward mobility. In the Netherlands, Puerto Rico, and Great Britain, a little over 40 percent of the sons of nonmanual fathers entered the manual-farmer strata. In France and the United States, the proportion is much less, between 20 and 27 percent, depending upon which of the two surveys conducted in each country is considered.

If we consider relatively large and small proportions of upward and downward mobility, four different combinations are possible: countries with large proportions of both upward and downward mobility; those with small proportions of both; countries with large proportions of upward and small proportions of downward mobility; and those with small proportions of upward and large proportions of downward mobility. Examples can be found for each type. Denmark, Great Britain and Sweden have relatively large rates of both upward and downward mobility. Hungary, Italy, Japan, the Netherlands, and Norway have relatively little downward and great upward mobility. Finland is relatively low in both kinds of mobility.

Miller also examined the mobility in and out of the elite occupations. Elite occupations were defined as professions and high administrative positions. He found that the patterns of mobility into and out of elite positions also varied among the countries studied but the variations were consistent with outflows and inflows across the nonmanual-farmer-manual lines.

These findings demonstrate that integenerational occupational mobility has many different aspects. That mobility is high in one aspect does not necessarily mean that it will also be high in other aspects. The United States, for example, has relatively little downward mobility from the nonmanual stratum but high mobility into that stratum. Its elites are relatively open to sons whose fathers were not in elite positions, but sons whose fathers were in elite positions are more likely to remain in elite occupations themselves in the United States than in other countries.

A new wave of intergenerational occupational mobility studies is presently appearing, in part an outgrowth of sociologists in many countries working together through the International Sociological Association Research Committee on Stratification. Hazelrigg (1974) was able to draw upon some of those studies as well as those used by Miller and thus avoid using studies that were not strictly comparable. Like Miller, he looked at upward and downward mobility as well as occupational inheritance. Some of the findings reported by Hazelrigg are presented in Table 6.3. He found considerable variation in observed mobility rates using three occupational strata: nonmanual, manual, farmer. The countries with the highest mobility rates were Puerto Rico, United States, Yugoslavia, Sweden, and Norway; all showed very large movements from farm to manual work. This was particularly true in Puerto Rico, where 69 percent of the fathers were in farm occupations. Puerto Rico also had relatively little downward mobility due to the same structural factor. Israel has the lowest upward and highest downward mobility of the twelve countries, due to the immigration of persons with nonmanual occupations filling manual and farm occupational roles to form an incipiently industrial society. On the whole, countries with high rates of upward mobility do not have high rates of downward mobility as well.

Hazelrigg also examined the outflow from different strata into the upper nonmanual occupations—those that Miller had labeled *elite*. He found that the sons of *lower* nonmanual or of manual fathers had the best chance of entering *upper* nonmanual stratum in the United States and the poorest chance in West Germany. In the United States, 44 percent of the sons of lower nonmanual fathers entered the upper nonmanual stratum; 22 percent of the sons of manual fathers did. In Germany, the comparable proportions were only 9 percent and 2 percent. Sons of upper nonmanual fathers were most likely to remain in that stratum in Italy, followed by Israel, and least likely to in Puerto Rico and Australia.

To measure circulation mobility, Hazelrigg employed a technique developed by Deming and Stephan (1940).[1] To hold constant structural effects,

---

[1] Earlier studies also attempted to hold structural mobility constant in order to measure exchange mobility alone. The methods used have been shown to be faulty (Duncan 1966). Therefore, I have not discussed those findings, restricting the discussion to observed mobility.

TABLE 6.3 Observed and Circulation Mobility Rates in Twelve Countries

County	Date	Observed Mobility Rates		Circulation Mobility Rates	
		Upward	Downward	Upward	Downward
Australia	1965	.292	.127	.202	.186
France	1964	.278	.118	.162	.148
Hungary*	1949	.241	.053	.112	.108
Israel	1962	.079	.307	.140	.142
Italy	(1963-64)	.289	.081	.143	.137
Japan*	1955	.291	.107	.162	.166
Norway*	1957	.331	.111	.186	.193
Puerto Rico	1954	.412	.099	.167	.168
Sweden*	1950	.376	.092	.202	.191
United States	1962	.409	.077	.191	.175
West Germany*	1955	.255	.118	.172	.175
Yugoslavia	1962	.384	.065	.145	.141

*Data used by Miller in his 1960 study.

Source: Adapted from Hazelrigg 1974, Tables 1, 2, and 5, pp. 474, 476, and 484.

Hazelrigg proportionally adjusted the observed cell frequencies so that the destination distribution of occupations was the same as the origin distribution. The results are presented in the last two columns of Table 6.3. Although the United States still ranks high, Sweden and Australia have even higher rates in circulation mobility. Puerto Rico's high rate of observed mobility turns out to be due largely to structural forces. Hungary, in 1949, had very low circulation and structural mobility.

Hazelrigg and Garnier (1976) were later able to examine the circulation mobility in seventeen countries, with more recent data for Hungary, Japan, Norway, Sweden, and West Germany. Their findings are presented in Table 6.4. They calculated one set of exchange mobility rates as previously described. To make the findings more comparable among the seventeen countries, they also wanted to hold constant the occupational distributions among the countries studied, since varying occupational distributions also affect mobility chances. To hold these differences constant, they adjusted the distributions so that origin and destination frequencies would be identical for *all* countries.

The findings indicate considerable variation among the countries, but show some changes in which countries have relatively large amounts of mobility. When occupational distribution for all countries is held constant, Sweden does not

**TABLE 6.4   Two Measures of Circulatory Mobility
in Seventeen Countries**

County	*Date*	*Circulation Rates*	
		Distribution in Each Country Constant	Distribution in All Countries Constant
Australia	1965	.388	.394
Belgium	1968	.309	.292
Bulgaria	1967	.285	.389
Denmark	1972	.320	.318
Finland	1972	.322	.356
France	1964	.311	.312
Hungary	1963	.277	.337
Italy	1963	.280	.303
Japan	1965	.331	.365
Norway	1972	.422	.415
Philippines	1968	.183	.347
Spain	1968	.256	.298
Sweden	1972	.305	.298
United States	1962	.366	.369
West Germany	1969	.362	.380
West Malaysia	1966	.293	.418
Yugoslavia	1962	.286	.364

Source: Adapted from Hazelrigg and Garnier 1976, Table 1, p. 503.

rank high in mobility. Australia continues to rank relatively high, although it is surpassed by West Malaysia and Norway. Australia is followed by Bulgaria, West Germany, and the United States. Countries with relatively low rates of circulation mobility are Belgium, Spain, Sweden, Italy, and France.

Considerable attention is currently being given to the status attainment *process* in different countries, particularly to the role of education in the allocation of persons to positions. Such studies usually compare two or three countries at a time. Before considering such studies we will note one additional problem in comparing occupational prestige.

Analysts of occupational prestige in different countries usually do not use identical occupational categories. Even when very gross aggregations of occupations are made, they may not be comparable. For example, sales clerks are considered manual workers in Hungary and nonmanual workers in the United States. Similarly, while the International Standard Classification of Occupations (ISCO), developed by the International Labor Organization, considers shop-keepers to be "sales workers," the United States Census classifies them as "managers, officials, and proprietors" (Treiman, 1976). Differences in intergenerational mobility may be obscured or exaggerated when comparing countries using different classifications of occupations.

To properly compare occupational prestige distributions and intergenerational mobility between countries, we must be sure we are using a compatible measuring instrument. Treiman (1976) has constructed such an instrument. He used studies from sixty different places that measured prestige of occupations. From all those studies, he had some information on 509 occupations separately identified within the ISCO scheme. He converted the scores for each occupation into a standard metric, then averaged the scores for each occupation from all the places with available information, thus constructing a Standard International Occupational Prestige Scale. The Standard Scale appears to be as reliable and as valid a measure of occupational prestige throughout the world as there is.

Using the Standard Scale, the average correlation among all the pairs of countries for which comparable data exist is 0.81. The agreement about occupational prestige across countries is high, but not as high as had been supposed, using unstandardized prestige ratings and comparing fewer and more homogeneous countries. Considerable variation in the degree of agreement between pairs of countries exists. For example, the prestige ratings in the U.S. are correlated 0.98 with those of Canada, 0.94 with Great Britain, 0.94 with the Ivory Coast, and 0.93 with Denmark. The correlations are lower among countres as diverse as France (0.70), Poland (0.77), Iraq (0.85), USSR (0.79), Yugoslavia (0.67), and Spain (0.79). They are particularly low with some relatively less economically developed countries such as Zaire (0.54) and New Britain (0.57).

The use of the Standard Scale allows more valid comparisons among countries than would otherwise be possible. It makes it possible to give prestige ratings to many more occupations than is usually done within each country and to compare the average prestige score for all occupations, weighted in terms of the number of incumbents, between countries. Thus, Treiman has calculated that the average prestige score is 39.0 in the United States and 34.6 in India. Although this is certainly different, that it is not even greater may be a surprise. The closeness results because three-fourths of the Indian labor force is in agricultural work, with a Standard Score of 34, while in the United States, about 40 percent of the labor force is in production and related work, with Standard Scores of 33. Therefore, even if larger proportions of American than Indians are in relatively high prestige occupations such as the professions and administration, it only raises the average prestige a few points.

The Standard Scale correlates highly with the Duncan Socio-Economic Index (.86) but the two are not identical. The Standard Scale measures prestige directly; the Socio-Economic Index is based upon the educational and income levels of the persons in each occupation. Using the Standard Scale gives lower correlations of intergenerational occupational inheritance than does using the Duncan Socio-Economic Index. This is due partly to the higher prestige of farmers and the lower prestige of some manual occupations, despite the education and income levels of those workers. One of the major intergenerational occupational movements is from farming to factory employment. Using the Duncan Socio-Economic Index this is likely to be considered upward mobility; using the Standard Scale it would not.

We can now return to studies of intergenerational occupational mobility in different countries. Treiman and Terrell (1975) compared intergenerational occupational mobility using national surveys from the United States in 1962 and Great Britain in 1963. The occupations in the two countries were given prestige ratings using the Standard Scale and therefore can be accurately compared. Treiman and Terrell calculated the correlation between fathers' and sons' occupational status in each country, which does provide an overall measure of the degree of status inheritance. They found that status mobility is somewhat greater in the United States than in Great Britain. The correlation between fathers and sons occupational status was .255 in the United States and .352 in Great Britain. They found, moreover, that the effect of father's status on the son's education and the effect of the son's education upon the son's occupational prestige are about the same in both countries. Despite the differences in the educational system of the United States and Great Britain, their effects upon occupational inheritance are similar. The higher degree of occupational status inheritance in Great Britain reflects the higher direct effects of father's occupational status on the sons in Great Britain than in the United States.

Using the Standard Scale, Treiman (1975) has calculated the correlation between father's and son's occupational prestige for a number of places. The findings are reported in Table 6.5. As can be seen, the correlations are generally very similar, with two exceptions: (1) considering the samples, including sons with farm origins, the United States has relatively more changes between generations than do the other places. (2) Uganda has very high intergenerational mobility; there is little correlation between father's and son's occupational pres-

TABLE 6.5   Correlation Between Father's and Son's Occupational Status in Different Places

Places	Total Sample	Nonfarm Origins
Argentina (Buenos Aires)	0.33	0.44
Australia	0.32	0.37
Chile (Santiago)	0.35	0.36
Great Britain	0.35	0.34
Mexico (Monterrey)	0.35	0.33
Northern Ireland	0.37	0.37
Uganda	0.11	0.15
United States	0.26	0.31

Source: Treiman 1975, Table 3, p. 198.

tige. (The Uganda sample is not a national one but is from one rapidly changing region.) When we consider only those whose fathers were not employed in agriculture, the correlations are generally somewhat higher and the United States is not as unusually low in occupational inheritance.

The correlation between father's and son's occupational prestige is greatly affected by the indices used to measure prestige and the way in which occupations are aggregated. Other studies of international intergenerational occupational inheritance using local prestige scales give different results than those presented in Table 6.4. For example, Broom and Jones (1969) compared prestige mobility in the United States and Australia. They concluded that there is slightly more intergenerational mobility in the United States than in Australia and that more of the mobility is attributable to changes in occupational distribution in the United States than in Australia. This can also be seen in Table 6.3. Jones (1971) used the Australian data to examine the process of occupational attainment and to compare the results with the findings of Blau and Duncan. Jones reports that the correlation between father's and son's occupational prestige, measured somewhat differently in the two countries, is higher in the United States than in Australia. In other words, there is more intergenerational inheritance in the United States than in Australia. These diverse interpretations indicate the degree to which comparisons are strongly affected by the indices and categories that are used to measure occupational prestige.[2]

Safar (1971) studied social differentiation and mobility in the Czechoslovak socialist society. Occupational status was not measured in the same way as in the Blau and Duncan or the Treiman and Terrell studies and therefore cannot be confidently compared. It is interesting, nevertheless, to consider the findings reported on occupational determinants in a society governed by a

---

[2] Jones's analysis focused on the occupational attainment process. He concluded that educational attainment was less important for occupational attainment in Austraila than in the United States.

Communist party. Safar constructed a path model like the one constructed by Duncan and Blau and found that fathers' occupational status was not very related to sons' occupational or educational status. The sons' occupational status was determined largely through education.[3] In other words, the fathers' education was highly related to the sons' education, which in turn was highly related to the sons' occupation.

In summary, these studies on intergenerational occupational mobility indicate a very active research effort and continuing controversy over the means to be used in assessing occupational prestige and mobility. The studies we have reviewed are not always in agreement and we must regard the findings as provisional.

The evidence indicates that the United States has relatively higher rates of observed upward mobility and lower rates of downward mobility than most other countries. Compared to many countries the United States has greater recruitment into elite positions of persons from lower prestige origins. The differences, however, are not very great; intergenerational occupational mobility is found to a significant degree everywhere. Clearly, there is also much occupational status inheritance; this is mediated largely through educational attainment.

The findings regarding circulation mobility are somewhat different. The United States, for example, although still relatively high in intergenerational occupational mobility, is exceeded by West Malaysia, Norway, Australia, and Bulgaria. On the other hand, Belgium, Spain, Sweden, Italy and France have relatively low circulatory mobility.

Persons

Not only are positions ranked in terms of prestige, but people themselves are. This section will consider how people are ranked in terms of their life styles, ethnicity or race, and sex. Of course, it is not that the persons themselves are evaluated, but rather that certain characteristics or qualities of people are given social meaning. It is those characteristics or qualities that are evaluated and ranked. Neither the characteristics nor the people to whom those characteristics

[3] A path model, adapted from Safar (1971), is presented below.

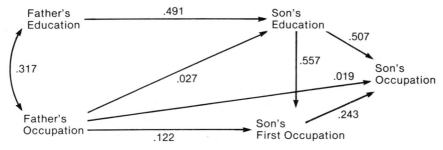

are attributed are inherently superior or inferior. In one time and place, skin color, food preferences, dialect, or another quality will be given symbolic meaning and ranked; in another time or place, they will not be noticed or ranked.

Life Styles. Nearly everything about people can be selected to be ranked. We will consider here some aspects of people's styles of life that are ranked in one or another culture. We begin by discussing a ranking based upon purity versus pollution—a good illustration of such ranking can be found in the caste system of traditional India. The caste system not only ranks status, it determines inequality in income and power as well. At this time, however, we will discuss only the status inequalities among different castes and subcastes in India.

The caste system in India was and is immensely complex (Srinivas 1952). To greatly simplify, it consists of five major divisions or *varnes.* The highest are the *Brahmins,* followed by the *Kahatriyas,* the *Vaishyas* or traders, the *Shudras* or servants and laborers, and at the very bottom, the untouchables. Only the members of the first three *varnas* may study the *Vedas* and perform certain rituals.

The basic unit of the caste system, however, is the *jati.* There are innumerable *jatis.* Each one is endogamous (marrying within the group), usually performs a specific occupation, and possesses a certain amount of cultural and ritual autonomy. According to traditional ideas, each Hindi is born into a particular *jati* because of his or her actions in a previous incarnation; he or she is born into the *jati* he or she deserves. In each of the districts of India there are systems of *jatis.* The *varnas* are at the all-India level, but the *jatis* do not fit neatly into the broad *varna* categories or subcategories.

The ideology or value system by which the *jatis* are ranked involve ideas of purity and pollution and consider certain kinds of activities as polluting. In general, handling or working with human secretions such as excrement or with death and corpses or with animals is polluting. For example, people who work with leather, which is taken from dead cows—themselves holy—are generally impure and of low status. The people who do not do these things and avoid contact with those who do are pure. Purity and impurity help define each other (Dumont 1970). These ideas of purity also determine eating patterns; Brahmins, for example, are usually vegetarians.

Since a person's *jati* is determined by birth, there is no individual mobility. An individual can leave his or her caste only furtively, by "passing." (Rarely, someone who does not adhere to the rules of his or her *jati* may be expelled and suffer a fall in status.) Mobility is most likely to take the form of a *jati* trying to change its standing. Members of a low caste can rise to a higher position by adopting vegetarianism and abstinence from alcohol and by changing their ritual, and taking over, as much as possible, the Brahamic way of life. This process is called "Sanskritization" (Srinivas 1952).

There is often disagreement about the exact hierarchy of *jatis,* even in a given locality and certainly in India as a whole. Ambiguity and lack of consensus are particularly likely among the middle-ranking varnas; the status of the

Brahmins and the untouchables is much more clear-cut. Of course, industrialization and urbanization have further weakened the ritual hierarchy. Gandhi's efforts to raise the status of the untouchables, symbolized by calling them *Harijan* (Children of God), has also improved the very low status ranking of the untouchables.

The status differences in India, because they are associated with caste, are sometimes asserted to be unique to India (Dumont 1970). Yet others argue that the caste system is similar in many ways to the differences between racial and ethnic groups in the United States, South Africa, Ruandi, Japan, and many other places (Berreman 1968). What is particularly striking about the Indian form of caste is its integral relationship to religion and ideas of purity and impurity. Some elements of moral evaluation are to be found in other status rankings—certain ways of living are viewed as proper and others as improper. Probably in every culture, certain activities are regarded as morally superior to others and those evaluations become attached to the person carrying on the activities as well as to the activities themselves. For a more mundane example, compare the status implications of playing tennis versus bowling or going to movies versus going to chamber music concerts in the United States.

We can see the effect of life-style in societies with heredity aristocracies. The way of life of the aristocracy is generally considered superior in status to that of the common people. Moreover, that superiority adheres to the person. The way they speak and carry themselves is considered to be correct and is accorded prestige. George Bernard Shaw's play, *Pygmalion,* illustrates the status differences attributed to persons solely on the basis of their speech, dress, and manners. The play is a satire because it ridicules how dialect, clothing, and manners set people above and below each other. The point is that in actual life, they do.

The United States has often been said to have more status equality than European countries. The informality of manners is part of the denial that some people are better than others; it is an assertion of fundamental human equality. All are expected to recognize this equality, even in the face of large class and power differences. As Weber wrote in 1921:

> The "equality" of status among the American "gentlemen," for instance, is expressed by the fact that outside the subordination determined by the different functions of "business," it would be considered strictly repugnant—wherever the old tradition still prevails—if even the richest "chief," while playing billiards or cards in his club in the evening, would not treat his "clerk" as in every sense his equal in birthright. It would be repugnant if the American "chief" would bestow upon his "clerk" the condescending "benevolence" making a distinction of "position," which the German chief can never dissever from his attitude. (1946 p. 187)

Cultures differ in the range of such status differences, in the distribution of status accorded various life styles, and in an individual's mobility among the status rankings. Some cultures have little status mobility; this is true where racial and ethnic groups are ranked and are regarded as castes. We will discuss racial and ethnic status differences in the next section of this chapter. Cultures also differ in the *range* of status differences. Beliefs in moral or religious superiority and inferiority of people generally entail a great range of status, as we saw in the discussion of caste in India.

What is particularly important in determine the overall distribution of status accorded people because of their life styles is the degree of consensus about the superiority and inferiority of life styles. If differences are merely a matter of personal or group taste, then status inequality cannot be great. Only insofar as there is agreement about what is superior and what is inferior is there a status hierarchy. Systematic evidence on the extent of status differences attached to the way people live is not available.

In some countries the "common" person's manner is glorified, effectively denying prestige to those who claim a "higher" way of living. Consider the manner of dress in revolutionary and socialist countries. In such countries as Israel, People's Republic of China, Cuba, and Tanzania, for example, political leaders demonstrate their "commonness" and their respect for the common people by themselves wearing simple uniforms or open-collared shirts. Speech patterns can also give evidence of this: the vernacular and even "earthy" language is widely used. Informality and the adoption of "common" manners as the proper way of behaving conveys an equality of status among persons. In some of these societies, not only are "common man ways" glorified, but an aristocracy or properly mannered elite is absent or is destroyed.

Ethnic and Racial Groups. Throughout the world, persons identify themselves and are identified by others in terms of ethnicity. Collectivities of persons regard themselves or are regarded by others as a people, a nationality, or a tribe. We will call such collectivities *ethnic groups.* Schermerhorn defines an ethnic group "as a collectivity within a larger society having real or putative common ancestry, memories of a shared historical past, and a cultural focus on one or more symbolic elements defined as the epitome of their peoplehood" (1970, p. 12.) Shibutani and Kwan simply write, "an ethnic group consists of those who conceive of themselves as being alike by virtue of their common ancestry, real or fictitious, and who are so regarded by others" (1965, p. 47).

Ethnic groups are often ranked within a given country. Some have more power and are richer, on the average, then others. Moreover, the differences in social and cultural characteristics attributed to the group are evaluated and ranked. Insofar as the ethnic groups agree about the ranking, it constitutes a status hierarchy: the groups regard each other as superior and inferior. These attitudes are manifested, for example, in stereotypes of each other that convey evaluations. Thus, stereotypes of an ethnic group as stupid, lazy, and selfish show that they have little status. The ranking is also manifested by patterns of discrimination, as when members of one group refuse to associate socially with those of another.

Nearly all countries are ethnically heterogenous. Connor (1972) has estimated that in nearly a third of the contemporary countries of the world the largest ethnic group makes up less than half the country's population. Only about 9 percent of the countries can be considered ethnically homogenous. The heterogeniety arises because people move from one place to another and because state borders are imposed over territories that encompass a variety of pre-existing groups. Europeans, for example, have settled throughout the world; Africans have moved or been moved—particularly to the Western hemisphere; Chinese have settled throughout Asia; Indians have moved to Africa and to many other parts of the world. Moreover, state borders are constantly changing and impose a common political order over peoples who have lived separately in other historical periods. In the Balkans, for example, the boundaries of the Austrian-Hungarian Empire, Greece, Yugoslavia, Czechoslavakia, Serbia, Turkey, and other countries have grown, receded, and sometimes dissolved.

Race is not the same as ethnicity, although the two words overlap in meaning. *Race* refers to several different concepts. Technically it refers to a *population* sharing characteristics known to be genetically transmitted; that is, it refers to a very large number of persons with similar genes who share some genetically inherited characteristics not shared by other populations. Since humans are one species, all share a great deal genetically and clear lines cannot be drawn to separate the human species into distinct races. Very large categories such as Caucasian, Mongoloid, and Negroid are only statistical conveniences.

Popularly, *race* refers to persons who are thought to share a common ancestry and some genetically determined physical characteristics or even psychological and social characteristics. In this book we will use the word *race* in its popular, rather than its technical usage. *Race*, as we will use it, refers to a set of persons *who are believed* to share some genetically determined physical characteristics such as skin color, eye shape, or nose size. Individuals are thus popularly classified into one or another *race* although the term technically refers to populations and each individual has a unique set of genes. So-called race distinctions are often socially clear in a particular place and time, although they differ from one place and time to another. In one circumstance, humans are classified as black or white (in certain epochs in the southern United States); in another they may be classified as white, black, colored, or Asian (South Africa).

To compare the degree of status inequality based on the popular concept of race or ethnicity in different countries requires a common metric, an agreed-on way of measuring status inequality. We do not have such a metric. No such universal measure of the relative ranking of different ethnic groups exists. Moreover, consensus often is not high. Supposedly low-ranking ethnics may not so regard themselves; they may reject that ranking and consider themselves equal or superior to other ethnic groups.

It might be contended that we should compare objective differences in living standards, income, or political power as indicators of status inequality.

Discrimination is presumed to reflect prejudice and status evaluations.[4] But this presents several difficulties. Social conduct is not a direct expression of any individual's or set of individuals' feelings and beliefs (Deutscher 1973). Factors that affect attitudes do not necessarily affect conduct. Conduct is also greatly affected by the constraints and opportunities others provide (Kriesberg 1970). Furthermore, attitudes often reflect and follow conduct, rather than the other way around. Thus, coerced to act a given way, people come to believe that way is right; otherwise, they would think poorly of themselves for having yielded. Or, having acted differently than they would have preferred, they might discover that the actions are pleasant or are rewarded in other ways. These considerations make it difficult to use social conduct, such as social avoidance, as the measure of status ranking.

It is true that ethnic differences are often used in a discriminating manner; power and class inequalities are inextricably interwoven with them. We will examine that in the next chapter. In this chapter we attempt to consider ethnic inequality solely in terms of status. We will not be able to do so entirely since we will refer to some indirect indicators that involve class and power inequalities as well as status inequality.

Countries vary in the inequality of status accorded different ethnic groups. In some places and times, an ethnic group may be deemed to have less then minimal status; its members may be despised and treated as pariahs by the rest of the society or by the dominant ethnic groups. If, as sometimes happens, such differences in status are accompanied by great power differences, the people who are without minimum status may even be subjected to genocidal attempts. Genocide does not occur unless many conditions are present (Dadrian 1974). The dehumanization of the ethnic group is part of the process; the ethnic group must also be physically vulnerable and isolated from possible allies. Violence and the killing of people must also be legitimized and this is facilitated by wars.

The Nazi killing of six million Jews and the Turkish massacre of the Christian Armenians were extreme examples of genocide. Sometimes, a group that has marginal status is expelled and driven from the society where it had lived. For example, "Asians" were driven out of Uganda by Idi Amin.

The attempt to destroy a people or expel them from a society reflects not only the people's low status, but also certain conditions relating to behavior. Such conditions occur as the result of a chain of interaction between the ethnic groups; dehumanization occurs in the course of that interaction. Thus, as a conflict proceeds antagonism grows, and the adversary is regarded as less and less human and therefore subject to increasingly inhumane treatment (Kriesberg 1973).

---

[4] Prejudice refers to a subjective state or attitude; discrimination refers to conduct. People may have prejudices and not act on them in a discriminatory way, perhaps because of laws or social pressure. On the other hand, some people may discriminate, although they have little or no personal prejudice, because such conduct is expected.

Within the range of minimally respected persons in a social system, there are many kinds of distributions of racial and ethnic status inequality. Three dimensions of these distributions are particularly noteworthy. First, the *degree* of status inequality can vary. In some countries the *status* differences of ethnic or racial groups may be relatively small, as in Brazil. Relative status equality may exist because the members of the society view differences among the ethnic and racial groups as minor. Relative status equality can also exist even with socially significant differences in life-style, if pluralism is expected and valued in the society. Then there may be mutual respect among the diverse groups and no consensus about any status hierarchy. Interestingly, the vision of a unitary society that everyone can assimilate into presumes a status hierarchy: new, or minority, or subordinate members of the society are expected to conform and aspire to an established and "correct" way of life.

Second, ethnic or racial status inequality varies to the *extent* that the inequality is institutionalized. Status inequalities can be embodied in laws. In the United States the "Jim Crow" laws in the South segregated Negroes in the use of public transportation, recreational activities, cemeteries, and virtually all aspects of social life. These laws, established after slavery and Reconstruction, developed during the 1890s and the turn of the century and became more rather than less encompassing and detailed (Woodward 1966). In contemporary South Africa detailed, government-sanctioned rules reflect and sustain a status hierarchy.

On the other hand, laws can bar the behavioral expression of status inequalities based on race or ethnicity. Laws may require equal treatment of individuals regardless of race, national origin, or religion. Such laws are increasingly prevalent. Laws may also be written to protect the collective rights of an ethnic or racial group—for instance, the right to their own schools or publications in their own language. This is the case in many countries for at least some ethnic groups in each country. In Canada, French Canadians and English Canadians each have many rights allowing for cultural autonomy.

Even with a very highly developed formal autonomy for different ethnic groups, equality is not assured. In the USSR, where many ethnic groups have their own republic, "Russian culture occupies a favored position among the national cultures, and the Russian people itself is given the honorific title of 'elder brother' in the Soviet family of nations in official pronouncements" (Lipset and Dobson 1973, p. 160).

Finally, the distribution of status inequality varies by the *relative size* of the ethnic and racial groups. A small minority may have little status in a society that is otherwise relatively homogenous ethnically. In Japan this is true of the Burakimin (often called Eta, derogatorily) a distinct and stigmatized hereditary group constitute only 2 percent of the Japanese population (Berreman 1968, p. 9; Devos and Wagatsuma 1966). On the other hand, a small minority may have high status while the large majority is regarded lowly, as in South Africa.

Other societies, racially or ethnically are evenly heterogenous with no single group of overwhelming size. In Kenya the largest ethnic group, the Kikuyu, make up about 20 percent of the population and the next three largest groups, the Luo, Luhya, and Kamba, constitute 14, 13, and 12 percent of the population; there are many smaller ethnic groups (Bienen 1974). Variations in the size of the low-prestige and high-prestige ethnic and racial groups have important consequences for the ways in which the members of the groups act and feel.

Sex. The biological differences between males and females, in every culture, are elaborated into social differences between men and women, and males and females are socialized into masculine and feminine roles. The social differences are evaluated; not only are certain qualities and behaviors deemed more appropriate for one sex or the other, but some are considered more important and better. If men generally do the more significant tasks and have the more valued qualities, then men have superior status. No metric will enable us to measure the relative status of men and women in different parts of the world. Yet, there are many indications that women generally have less status than men.

In industrial societies, parents prefer a child of each sex, but in many agrarian societies they show a pronounced preference for sons (Williamson 1976). In many societies, at least in the past, female infants were more likely to be neglected or left to die than male infants. Analysis of census reports and social surveys sometimes reveal differences in the proportion of males to females, which indicates female infanticide or neglect. For example, a social survey conducted in Peking, China, in 1917 indicates that the female infant mortality rate was nearly 30 percent higher than that of males (Goode 1963, p. 308). The ratio of males to females was also much higher than normal. The sex ratio was greater in each age group and, in fact, increased with age, at least until age 30. Infanticide and neglect were important factors in these differences. In India, the British in 1870 passed legislation to place communities suspected of infanticide under surveillance. Infanticide, nevertheless, persisted. According to the 1911 Indian Census, the shortage of females here and there probably resulted from neglect, which was "due partly to habit and partly to the parents' great solicitude for their sons. The boys are better clothed and when ill are more carefully tended. They are allowed to eat their fill before anything is given to the girl" (cited in Goode 1963, p. 237-238). Table 4.2 shows that in India and Pakistan men had longer life expectancies than women, unlike all other countries for which we have information (cited in Goode 1963, p. 237-238).

The analysis of the available information about current sex ratios and mortality rates in Arab countries does not suggest infanticide, only a failure to register female births—an obvious expression of the lesser value given female children in the Arab world (Goode 1963, p. 123).

In every culture, sex differences are elaborated into gender roles and different sets of activities, ranked in status, are considered appropriate for men and for women. This is revealed partly by the limitations upon women's participation in education, in the labor force, in politics, and even in general social life. Despite these generalities, the status of women in different social systems varies considerably. Because direct measures of the relative status of males and females are not available, we will use indirect ones to illustrate the variations.

In many societies, at present or in the recent past, women are restricted in their movements and in opportunities to mingle with men outside of their family. Under the *purdah* system of India, women were shut away in the back of the house in overcrowded seclusion. In the Arab system, seclusion of women is also marked and social segregation is great. In traditional China, women bound their feet to make them tiny and lovely and, in doing so, became so crippled that their mobility was greatly restricted (Mace and Mace 1959).

Women's access to education compared to men's, can be considered an indicator of the general status of women in a society. To measure this we look at the proportion of women among the students enrolled in various levels of education. If about 50 percent of the students in a given level are women, it is reasonable to argue they have equal access, at least up to that educational level. Data on female enrollment in secondary and higher levels in selected countries are presented in Table 6.6. Several countries have about as many women as men enrolled in secondary schools—that is, schooling beyond the primary grades and prior to college. The secondary level includes vocational education and teacher training. Among the countries with equality are Sweden, Poland, Jamaica, Israel, France, Cuba, and Brazil. On the other hand, some countries have a very small proportion of women enrolled in secondary level schools. For example, in Chad only 11 percent of the students enrolled at the secondary level are women; the proportion is also relatively low in the Ivory Coast, Morocco, India, Pakistan, and Iraq.

When we consider the enrollment at the third level, few countries are equal; in Poland, German Democratic Republic, the Soviet Union, France, and Brazil about fifty percent of the third-level enrolled students are women. But in many more countries, the proportion is small; it is even less than 15 percent in Chad, Morocco, Kenya, and Tanzania.

Participation by women in the labor force is another indicator of the general status of women. Since information on participation in agricultural work is not comparable from one country to another, we will look at the participation of women in nonagricultural work and in white-collar employment. As can be seen in Table 6.7, in the United States and in most countries, about one-third of the persons employed in nonagricultural labor are women. But this varies from over 40 percent in Jamaica, the USSR, Mexico, Ghana, and East Germany to less than 10 percent in Algeria, Iraq, Pakistan, and Tanzania. Except in Iran and Pakistan, women generally make up a large proportion of white-collar workers among the countries for which comparable data are presented in Table 6.7. By these measures, as well as by education, women are not more equal in the United States than in many other countries.

TABLE 6.6   Proportion of Women among Students Enrolled in Secondary and Higher Education for Selected Countries

Country	Proportion Women Students Enrolled	
	Secondary Level	Third Level (College and University)
Algeria	(1975) 34	(1970) 21
Australia	(1974) 49	(1974) 39
Bolivia	(1971) 42	(1965) 26
Brazil	(1972) 52	(1974) 47
Canada	(1974) 49	(1974) 44
Chad	(1973) 11	(1975) 5
Chile	(1976) 54	(1975) 35
Colombia	(1974) 50	(1970) 27
Cuba	(1974) 49	(1974) 36
Czechoslavakia	(1974) 61	(1974) 40
Egypt	(1974) 33	(1974) 29
France	(1970) 51	(1974) 47
German Democratic Republic	—	(1974) 52
Germany (Federal Republic of)	(1975) 51	(1975) 34
Ghana	(1974) 39	(1974) 20
Greece	(1972) 42	(1974) 37
India	(1975) 30	(1974) 25
Indonesia	(1975) 37	(1972) 28
Iran	(1974) 35	(1974) 27
Iraq	(1975) 28	(1974) 29
Israel	(1973) 52	(1974) 46
Italy	(1975) 46	(1974) 39
Ivory Coast	(1974) 24	(1975) 17
Jamaica	(1974) 55	—
Japan	(1975) 49	(1975) 32
Kenya	(1975) 36	(1965) 14
Lebanon	(1972) 43	(1971) 25
Mexico	(1970) 38	(1970) 20
Morocco	(1970) 28	(1974) 10
Nigeria	(1974) 33	(1973) 15
Pakistan	(1974) 28	(1973) 24
Peru	(1970) 43	(1975) 32
Poland	(1975) 55	(1974) 53
Sweden	(1974) 49	(1974) 46
Tanzania	(1975) 31	(1975) 14
United Kingdom	(1973) 49	(1974) 36
United States	—	(1974) 45
USSR	—	(1975) 50
Yugoslavia	(1974) 46	(1974) 41

Source: UNESCO Statistical Yearbook 1976, United Nations Educational, Scientific and Cultural Organization: Tables 45 and 51, pp. 278-336, 346-404.

TABLE 6.7 **Proportion of Women Employed in Nonagricultural and White-Collar Occupations for Selected Countries 1960**

Country	Proportion of Persons in Nonagricultural Employment Who Are Female	Proportion Female White-Collar Workers of All White-Collar Workers
Algeria	3	—
Australia	27	—
Bolivia	37	—
Brazil	26	—
Canada	30	63
Chile	31	53
Colombia	37	37
Cuba	21	50
Czechoslavakia	26	—
Egypt	10	51
France	33	—
German Democratic Republic	41	—
Germany (Federal Republic of)	34	—
Ghana	42	72
Greece	23	47
India	20	29
Indonesia	29	—
Iran	24	22
Iraq	3	—
Italy	24	59
Jamaica	50	48
Japan	33	55
Mexico	43	53
Morocco	16	41
Pakistan	7	27
Peru	30	—
Poland	35	—
Sweden	33	63
Tanzania	8	—
United Kingdom	32	—
United States	33	60
USSR	44	—
Yugoslavia	24	65

Source: Boulding 1969, Appendix 3, pp. 342-346.

The status of women, then, does vary considerably among the countries of the world. Moreover, it has changed very quickly and radically in some countries. For example, in the People's Republic of China, women have moved a long way toward status equality with men from great traditional inferiority (Sidel, 1973). Women participate fully in the labor force; child care is extensive, which increases the mother's mobility for work and other social activities; women generally receive equal or almost equal pay for equal work. Although women are well represented in the professions, they are not well represented in leadership roles. Still, in interpersonal and family roles, traditional patterns persist. Even when men share in housekeeping now, they are still apt to see themselves as "helping" women do women's work.

In short, persons as well as positions are evaluated and ranked in status hierarchies. Life styles, race, ethnicity, and sex are commonly used to accord status. Despite the universality of status hierarchies, countries vary considerably in the range and distribution of status differences. In some countries life styles are regarded as permanent and differ greatly in honor while in other countries such differences are given scant attention. Ethnic and racial inequalities may be institutionalized and sanctioned by governmental authority while in other countries such inequalities are not readily discernable and not overtly sanctioned. Status ranking by sex, generally only indirectly measured, varies considerably from one country to another.

GLOBAL INEQUALITIES

Thus far in this chapter we have considered status inequality within different countries. Now we turn to review how the world as a whole constitutes a system within which countries and transnational entities are ranked in status. For this to occur, the people of the world must share a common value system on which to base the status ranking. In a sense, most humans now share some elements of a world civilization. Talcott Parsons writes of this in terms of the worldwide trend toward modernization: "In particular, the elites of most non-modern societies accept crucial aspects of the values of modernity, especially economic development, education, political independence, and some form of 'democracy.'" (1971, p. 137) We will review some ways in which countries are related within a global status system and then briefly comment on transcountry systems of status ranking.

Status Inequality Among Countries

Most of the people of the world can often do think in terms of a world divided into countries or territorially based states. Numerous studies have explored the perceptions people in different countries have of themselves and of other peoples. For example, in 1948, persons in nine countries were asked to describe people in several countries (Buchanan and Cantril 1953). In that study, Americans were most often described by the British as progressive, conceited, and generous; the English were most frequently described by Americans as intelligent, hard-working, and brave. In each of the nine countries (as in many others). persons were most likely to characterize themselves as peace-loving people. Such stereotypes, while interesting and significant, do not provide a status ranking.

There are no systematic multinational studies of how people in various nations rank countries in status. One study does demonstrate, however, that people can and do rank countries as entities. Shimbori, Ikeda, Ishida, and Kondo (1963) studied the prestige ranking given countries by Japanese students. They found that the students thought there were about three, four, or five "classes" of nations and were able to place each country into one or another class. Further analysis revealed that the economic position of a country was the most important determinant of their ranking.

To examine the status hierarchy of countries, we cannot utilize attitudinal data from many countires, since such data are not available. Indirect indicators of the relative prestige standing of different countries do exist. Thus, we can compare how many students from one country go to a particular other country to study and how many persons in one country read books, view movies, and watch television programs from another country. While such measurements can be interpreted to indicate relative status, or cultural ties, or cultural imperialism, we will use them as indicators of status.

Caplow and Finsterbusch (1968) studied three kinds of interaction between France and the countries with which France most conducted those interactions. They studied foreign trade, exchange of university students, and exchange of printed matter through the mail. Ratios for each kind of interaction were constructed to indicate relative status. Thus, if country A received more students from B than it sent to B, A had more status than B. Caplow and Finsterbusch found that the status order for France and her partners was transitive—that is, the countries could be ordered in a status hierarchy. Switzerland had the highest status, followed by France, Germany, Belgium, United Kingdom, United States, and Italy. They also found a clear trading hierarchy, which differed from the educational exchange hierarchy. The exchange of printed matter by mail also revealed a status hierarchy; again, with a different ordering of countries.

Travis (1975) has constructed several indicators of what he calls "cultural dependence." He measured the extent and degree of the world's dependence on nine countries: the United Kingdom, France, the Soviet Union, the United States, Italy, Belgium, Germany, Japan, and South Africa. As he defines it, "cultural dependence exists where one country's cultural values and norms are deeply affected by and oriented toward the culture of another country without the reverse being true. The extreme of cultural dependence would be where country B apes A's cultures in terms of speaking its language, practicing its religion, imitating its educational system, wearing its dress styles, following its art forms, adopting its values, and in general, viewing A's culture as the quintessence of civilization, all to the derogation and decay of B's indigenous form of culture." (1975, p. 11). He constructed indicators for the scope and intensity of cultural dependence. Thus, for country A's scope, he calculated how many countries had more than 30 percent of its total students studying in country A. To measure intensity, he calculated the average percentage of the other countries' total students studying in A. In other words, scope indicates how many countries have at least a minimal level of dependence upon one of the major countries studied. The measure of the intensity of cultural dependence indicates the magnitude of dependence for countries that are culturally dependent.

The scope of cultural dependence is particularly great for the United Kingdom and the United States; it is almost as high for France. The other countries studied rank very low in the number of countries that are culturally dependent upon each of them. The situation changes when we consider the intensity of cultural dependence. France ranks at the top in this regard; the Soviet Union and Belgium follow. Only then comes the United States and United Kingdom. Italy and Germany are toward the bottom in rank, with Japan and South Africa last. Travis combined all the measures to give an overall ranking for cultural dependence. It is: France, United States, United Kingdom, the Soviet Union, Belgium, Germany, Italy, Japan, and finally, South Africa.

The intensity of other countries' cultural dependence on France is partly a result of France's former colonial policy of assimilation. France sought to inculcate the elites of the former colonies with the French cultural tradition. Although this was not so successful as to maintain them as colonies, these now-independent states use French as the language or as one of the official languages, model their school system on the French, educate most of their college students in France, and in many other ways demonstrate their deference to French culture. The United States' scope is particularly great in number of dependents in student exchange, technical aid, and information flow.

The countries of the world cannot be ranked in a simple, uni-dimensional status hierarchy. But they differ greatly in prestige and the deference people in other parts of the world pay to them. Most commonly, countries are ranked in terms of one generally shared value: material well-being. Highly developed countries where people share the bounties of consumer production are ranked above countries that are less developed. In addition, however, more specific values related to the cultures of particular areas, are the basis for prestige rating. Insofar as these cultures are not shared, we are no longer considering a single status system, but several.

Transcountry Status Inequalities

We conclude by turning to the consideration of status systems that transcend countries or nation-states. Entities greater than national states may themselves be ranked in a status hierarchy and yet may also be viewed as status systems within which persons and groups are rated. Thus, "Western civilization" competes for status with Moslem, Hindi, Chinese, and other civilizations. Insofar as people defer to and model themselves after "Westerners," Western civilization may be viewed as having relatively high status. The pervasiveness of Western fashions, manners, and preferences does indicate a shared status ranking among many people of the world. But many others reject aspects of Western civilization and some political and intellectual leaders foster a return to national cultures.

It should also be recognized that the status ranking within each great culture is not shared by every other culture. Thus, certain styles of behavior and hence certain persons and positions will be awarded high prestige among Moslems but not among Hindus. There are status hierarchies based upon language, ethnicity, religion, and political ideology which transcend and cut across countries. Of course, they do not actually exist independently of countries. When we think of ideological systems, it is often countries or political parties that are the units being ranked.

CONCLUSIONS

We have seen considerable variations in status inequality, even among contemporary societies. The range of occupational status varies, particularly between countires with a traditional noble class that disdains manual work and societies that glorify manual labor and consequently reduce the range in status between laborers and elite occupations. Despite this variation, considerable consensus is found in the prestige *ranking* of occupations among the countries of the world.

We noted the difficulties in comparing intergenerational occupational mobility in different countries and the many different methods that have been applied to meet these difficulties. The results obtained with different methods sometimes do not agree. Consequently, our understanding of the degree of mobility in industrial countries and the uniqueness of America have changed over time. At present, interpreting the findings cautiously, we can see, first, substantial variations in observed mobility among the countries for which we have data. From Hazelrigg's (1974) review of studies in the 1950s and 1960s, the rate of observed upward mobility appears relatively large in the United States and the rate of downward mobility relatively small. But this pattern also occurs in Puerto Rico and Sweden. West Germany, Italy, and Hungary (in 1949) had relatively less mobility, although they, too, have more upward than downward observed mobility. Hazelrigg also studied the flow from other strata into the upper nonmanual stratum; the United States is particularly open to movement from lower nonmanual and manual occupations.

When we control for changes in occupational distribution between generations in order to assess circulation mobility within each country, the results are different. Upward mobility no longer is generally much greater than downward mobility. If we use the same occupational distribution to compare mobility in seventeen countries, the ranking of countries with the highest and lowest rates of circulation mobility is different than that for observed mobility or circulation mobility calculated within each country (Hazelrigg and Garnier 1976). The highest circulation rates are found in West Malaysia, Norway, and Australia; the lowest rates in Belgium, Spain, Sweden, Italy, and France.

Using Treiman's Standard Score, Treiman and Terrell (1975) compared the overall correlation between fathers' and sons' occupational prestige in the United States and Great Britain. They found that the rate of intergenerational mobility was greater in the United States than in Great Britain.

Persons as well as positions are ranked. They may be ranked in terms of style of life and these given moral and religious meaning, as in the caste system in India. The degree to which style of life is morally rated varies greatly from society to society as does the range and distribution of status based upon ethnicity or race. Sex differences are also a basis for status inequality; although women in most social systems have lower status than men, the degree of status inequality varies widely.

Finally, we considered the world as a status system with countires and even larger entities being ranked. There is evidence that people regard some countries and civilizations as having more status than others. But the world is not a single status system and must be viewed as also being divided into several status systems that sometimes contend with each other. Such systems may be based on political ideologies, religions, or great civilizations. Within each are analytically separate status rankings.

REFERENCES

BERREMAN, GERALD D. 1968. "Caste: The Concept of Caste," in D. Sills (Ed.) *International Encyclopedia of the Social Sciences.* New York: Macmillan and Free Press.

BIENEN, HENRY. 1974. *Kenya: The Politics of Participation and Control.* Princeton, N.J.: Princeton University Press.

BOULDING, ELISE MARIE BIORN-HANSEN. 1969. "The Effects of Industrialization on the Participation of Women in Society." Unpublished Ph.D. Dissertation, University of Michigan, Ann Arbor, Mich.

BROOM, LEONARD and F. LANCASTER JONES. 1969. "Father-to-Son Mobility: Australia in Comparative Perspective," *American Journal of Sociology,* 74 (January):333-342.

BUCHANAN, WILLIAM and HADLEY CANTRIL. 1953. *How Nations See Each Other.* Urbana: University of Illinois Press.

CAPLOW, THEODORE AND KURT FINSTERBUSCH. 1968. "France and Other Countries: A Study of International Interaction," *Journal of Conflect Resolution,* 12 (March:1-15.

CONNOR, WALKER. 1972. "Nation-Building or Nation-Destroying?" *World Politics* 24, (April):319-355.

DADRIAN, VAHAKN N. 1974. "The Structural-Functional Components of Genocide: A Victimological Approach to the Armenian Case," in I. Drapkin and E. Viane (Eds.), *Victimology.* Lexington, Mass.: D. C. Heath, pp. 123-136.

DEMING, W. E. and F. F. STEPHAN. 1940. "On a Least Squares Adjustment of a Sample Frequency Table when the Expected Marginal Totals Are Known," *Annals of Mathematical Statistics*, 11 (December):427-444.
DEUTSCHER, IRWIN. 1973. *What We Say/What We do.* Glenview, Ill.: Scott, Foresman.
DeVOS, GEORGE and H. WAGSTSUMA (Eds.). 1966. *Japan's Invisible Race: Caste in Culture and Personality.* Berkeley, Calif.: University of California Press.
DUMONT, LOUIS. 1970. *Homo Hierarchic: The Caste System and Its Implications.* Chicago: University of Chicago Press.
DUNCAN, OTIS DUDLEY. 1966. "Methodological Issues in the Analysis of Social Mobility." Pp. 51-67 in N.J. Smelser and S. M. Lipset (Eds.), *Social Structure and Mobility in Economic Development.* Chicago: Aldine.
GOODE, WILLIAM J. 1963. *World Revolution and Family Patterns.* New York: Free Press.
HAZELRIGG, LAWRENCE E. 1974. "Cross-National Comparisons of Father-to-Son Occupational Mobility," in Joseph Lopreato and Lionel Lewis (Eds.), *Social Stratification: A Reader.* New York: Harper & Row.
HAZELRIGG, LAWRENCE E. and MAURICE A. GARNIER. 1976. "Occupational Mobility in Industrial Societies: A Comparative Analysis of Differential Access to Occupational Ranks in Seventeen Countries," *American Sociological Review* 41 (June):498-511.
HODGE, ROBERT W., DONALD J. TREIMAN, and PETER H. ROSSI. 1966. "A Comparative Study of Occupational Prestige," in Reinhard Bendix and Seymour Martin Lipset (Eds.), *Class, Status and Power,* 2nd Ed. New York: Free Press.
INKELES, ALEX and PETER H. ROSSI. 1956. "National Comparisons of Occupational Prestige," *The American Journal of Sociology,* 61 (January): 329-339.
JONES, F. LANCASTER. 1971. "Occupational Achievement in Australia and the United States: A Comparative Path Analysis," *American Journal of Sociology* 77 (November):527-539.
KRIESBERG, LOUIS. 1970. *Mothers in Poverty: A Study of Fatherless Families.* Chicago: Aldine.
KRIESBERG, LOUIS. 1973. *The Sociology of Social Conflicts.* Englewood Cliffs, N.J.: Prentice Hall.
LIN, NAN and DANIEL YAUGER. 1975. "The Process of Occuaptional Status Achievement: A Preliminary Cross-National Comparison," *American Journal of Sociology* 81 (November):543-562.
LIPSET, SEYMOUR MARTIN and REINHARD BENDIX. 1959. *Social Mobility in Industrial Society.* Berkeley and Los Angeles: University of California Press.
LIPSET, SEYMOUR MARTIN and RICHARD B. DOBSON. 1973. "Social Stratification and Sociology in the Soviet Union," *Survey* No. 3, 88 (Summer:114-185.
MACE, DAVID and VERA MACE. 1959. *Marriage East and West.* Garden City, N.Y.: Doubleday.
MILLER, S. M. 1975. "Comparative Social Mobility," in A. P. M. Coxon and C. L. Jones (Eds.), *Social Mobility.* Hermondsworth, England: Penguin, pp. 79-112. (Originally published in 1960.)
PARSONS, TALCOTT. 1971. *The System of Modern Societies.* Englewood Cliffs, N.J.: Prentice Hall.

ROGOFF, NATALIE. 1953. "Social Stratification in France and the United States," *American Journal of Sociology,* 58 (January):347-357.

SACKS, MICHAEL PAUL. 1976. *Women's Work in Soviet Russia: Continuity in the Midst of Change.* New York: Praeger.

SAFAR, Z. 1971. "The Measurement of Mobility in the Czecho-Slovak Socialist Society," *Quality and Quantity: European Journal of Methodology,* 5: 179-208.

SARAPATA, ADAM and WLEDZIMIERZ WESOLOWSKI. 1961. "The Evaluation of Occupations by Warsaw Inhabitants," *American Journal of Sociology,* 66 (May):581-591.

SCHERMERHORN, R. A. 1970. *Comparative Ethnic Relations.* New York: Random House.

SHIBUTANI, TAMOTSU AND KIEN M. KWAN. 1965. *Ethnic Stratification.* New York: Macmillan.

SHIMBORI, MICHIYA, HIDEA IKEDA, TSUYOSKI ISHIDA, and MOTO KONDO. 1963. "Measuring a Nation's Prestige," *American Journal of Sociology,* 69 (July):63-68.

SIDEL, RUTH. 1973. *Women and Child Care in China.* Baltimore: Penguin.

SRINIVAS, M. N. 1952. *Religion and Society Among the Coorgs of South India.* Oxford: Clarendon Press.

TRAVIS, TOM. 1975. "Toward a Comparative Study of Imperialism." Paper presented at the Sixteenth Annual Convention of the International Studies Association, Washington, D.C.

TREIMAN, DONALD J. 1975. "Problems of Concept and Measurement in the Comparative Study of Occupational Mobility," *Social Science Research* 4:183-230.

TREIMAN, DONALD J. 1976. *Occupational Prestige in Comparative Perspective.* New York: Academic Press.

TREIMAN, DONALD J. and KERMIT TERRELL. 1975. "The Process of Status Attainment in the United States and Great Britain," *American Journal of Sociology,* 81 (November):568-583.

United Nations Educational, Scientific and Cultural Organization. 1976. *UNESCO Statistical Yearbook 1976.* Paris: UNESCO.

VEBLEN, THORSTEIN. 1931. *The Theory of the Leisure Class.* New York: Modern Library (Originally published in 1899.)

WEBER, MAX. 1946. "Class, Status, and Power," in H. M. Gerth and C. Wright Mills (Eds.) *From Max Weber,* New York: Oxford University Press, pp. 180-195. (Originally published in 1921.)

WILLIAMSON, NANCY E. 1976. *Sons or Daughters: A Cross-Cultural Survey of Parental Preferences.* Beverly Hills, Calif.: Sage Publications.

WOODWARD, C. VANN. 1966. *The Strange Career of Jim Crow.* 2nd rev. ed. New York: Oxford University Press.

YOUNG, LUNG-CHANG. 1973. "Mao Tse-Tung and Social Inequality," *Sociological Focus* 6 (Fall):46-58.

chapter 7

American Power Variations and Rank Consistency

It is our duty to be obedient to any governors whom God has established over the places in which we reside.   *John Calvin*

Lack of equal power is often viewed as the fundamental inequality and coercion and violence regarded as the ultimate determinant of status and class inequalities. According to this view, the ownership of property rests on theft and force. Even if we deny such extreme assertions, we must recognize the great significance of power inequalities. Dahrendorf (1959) has attempted to revise Marx by defining class conflict in terms of power conflicts. He argues that *ownership* of property in itself is not crucial, but rather who controls its use—that is, who has power over whom—is fundamental. Furthermore, he argues that in every imperatively coordinated association, indeed, in every society, there are those with power and those without. In this sense, there is class conflict in socialist countries as well as capitalist ones.

In this chapter we do not assume power is so absolutely dichotomous; we will examine the variations within different aspects of power inequality. The degree to which people are free from others' control and the degree to which they effectively participate in making decisions that affect their lives are two basic aspects of power equality. We will review how these aspects of power have been distributed in America.

This chapter gives special attention to the relationship between power inequality and class and status inequalities. Sociologists generally study how power differences relate to status and class inequality. We will seek to answer questions about *who* has how much power compared to whom.

We will also consider to what extent persons and positions who are ranked high and low in *class* likewise rank high and low in *status*. Finally, we will discuss how class, status, and power all relate to each other. We will describe to what extent the ranking of persons and positions in these three dimensions are consistent. Groups of persons, as well as individuals, are varyingly consistent in class, status, and power. That, too, will receive our attention (Parkin 1971).

In Chapter 2 we discussed the meaning of power. In this book, *power* refers to the probability of persons or groups modifying the behavior of others through coercion, or resisting the efforts of others to modify their behavior (see, for example, Blau 1964, p. 116). By this definition, power necessarily involves coercion, negative sanctions, or punishment. Although these may not be used, the possibility of their use is crucial to the exercise of power. Even the withholding of expected goods or services may be coercive; consider, for example, the form of coercion used in strikes or boycotts. As noted earlier, Weber (1946) made an important distinction between legitimate and nonlegitimate power. Legitimate power, or *authority,* is based on the subordinates' acceptance of the right of the superordinate to command them (Sharp, 1973). The subordinates expect all to obey; they help maintain other's obedience (Blau, 1964). Non-legitimate power is based on force (violent or nonviolent) or the threat of force, which the receivers do not accept as the right of the power wielders to exercise.

As defined here, power is analytically distinguished from other means a person or group can use to modify the conduct of others. Two noncoercive ways should be noted (Kriesberg, 1973): persons and groups may influence others—for example, by appealing to shared values. When those making the appeals have high prestige, they may succeed in modifying behavior. Persons and groups also may induce others to modify their behavior by offering rewards for compliance. For example, persons with higher-class positions may be able to offer monetary rewards that make it worthwhile for persons in lower-class positions to comply. (In some contexts, the capacity to withhold expected material rewards is coercive.) Political systems depend not only on power but also on shared values and exchange of benefits.

Differences in coercive strength are critical to power. Coercive strength depends not only on access and control of the means of violence, but also on the relative size of the groups involved and their relative degree of organization and solidarity.

VARIATIONS IN POWER INEQUALITY

Power varies in its range and distribution and in the mobility of persons in and out of powerful positions. We will consider the range and distribution of two aspects of power: (1) the ability of people to resist efforts to control or modify their conduct and (2) the power of people to make collective decisions. The two, though related, are not simply the opposite of each other; each is separate and each has its own range of conditions. The power to control others is the converse of the inability to resist the others' control. The power to make binding decisions for the entire society or collectivity is opposite to a lack of participation in making such decisions. When considering power in the context of collective decisions, some analysts stress the mobilization of social resources for collective ends: a leader organizes his or her followers so that as a group they get more of what they all want (Parsons, 1969). Others emphasize the conflicting character of such decisions: some people yield more while others gain more out of every decision (Mills, 1956; Dahrendorf, 1959). Such analysts stress that power relations are essentially zero-sum, what one side gains is at the expense of the other side. We shall keep both conceptions in mind.

In this chapter, we will examine power inequality within the political system of the United States. Citizenship rights, governmental policies, the party system, and other elements of the American policy are fundamental areas in which power inequality exists. Nongovernmental and nonpolitical organizations and offices, although they also exercise power, will be considered only briefly.

Range

In discussing the range of power inequality, we focus first on those with the minimal power to resist interference, the crux of civil rights and civil liberties. What is regarded as minimal depends on the standards being used. Standards may be generally shared by all members of a political order, by its elites only, or by the "oppressed masses," or they may be constructs developed by the social analyst. In this book, we will apply conventional contemporary standards, giving particular attention to ones for which comparable indicators are or might become available.

Autonomy. In the United States, as in most contemporary societies, protection of individuals and families from coercion by other persons rests fundamentally on government. The government through its agents inhibits persons from using coercion or threats of coercion to control other persons' property or to force acts of physical compliance or submission.

The officers of the state itself, however, can be tyrannical in imposing obedience and demanding compliance from their "subjects." We must consider both kinds of coercive intrusion below minimal levels of autonomy.

The proportion of the persons in the United States able to resist coercive efforts by others has, with the aid of several levels of government, generally increased over the last two centuries. Although we lack systematic evidence, it is easy to point to patterns in the past that deprived many persons of personal safety, privacy, and autonomy. In the settling of the West, the incoming settlers often lacked the power to resist the coercive intrusions of their fellows. For native Americans, the Indians, collective autonomy was destroyed in many ways. In the South, slavery meant the imposition of almost total power by some humans over others; the state acted as defender of the rights of the slaveholders. In early industrial development, "company towns," where housing and food were available only through the single dominant employer, were established; the autonomy of the individual employee was severely limited, since his economic dependence left him subject to his employer's coercion.

On the other hand, during the predominantly agrarian period of American history, more people lived in more isolated circumstances than they did after industrialization and urbanization. On the farms, there was great familial autonomy. Although buffeted by market forces, farm families were rarely subject to direct coercive control of their behavior.

Adding together what cannot really be summed, the proportion of the American people free from the domination of their fellows has probably increased, and a high level of individual freedom has probably developed. As greater freedom from the interference from others developed, the state itself has become a source of interference in the civil liberties of Americans. This trend has not been consistent, but has varied widely, usually increasing during hot and cold wars and during periods of widespread apprehension among the governing persons. Thus, in early 1950s, a period characterized by "McCarthyism," private citizens and government officials used a variety of coercive means to try to limit the movement and actions and even the thoughts of other citizens (Shils 1956). In recent years, following the revelations associated with "Watergate," we have learned of invasions of privacy of Americans and even harassment of groups regarded by FBI, CIA and other government agencies as extremist.[1] In some cases the coercion even involved violence, as against the Black Panthers. Yet, during this period most persons personally experienced no government coercion.

Collective Decision Making. What constitutes minimal participation in collective decision making is even more difficult to determine than what constitutes minimal power for others' coercive efforts. Being able to vote for or against a political party and its leader is part of minimal participation. To elaborate, voting is significant only to the degree that the voter has clear alternatives and the opportunity to be informed about the alternative candidates and parties. When there is no effective competition among the persons and parties seeking to win an election, casting a vote does not provide meaningful participation.

Although voting may seem a long way from exercising power as defined in terms of coercion, they are related. Political parties struggle to win government offices, and government offices give incumbents the right to exercise coercion. That is an essential quality of government. Such coercion is a legal right; officeholders indeed, may be obligated to use coercion to uphold the law. In addition, political parties exercise coercion over others; they may threaten adversaries with loss of political jobs and the anticipated advantages of political connections. In some places and times and for some people, voting, and voting "right," is done with full recognition of the coercive power of the dominant party in mind. We are not interested here, however, in the motives of individual voters, but rather in voting as a form of minimal participation in choosing who will exercise power. The vote gives people a share in the power, since those who hold or seek office attempt to gain the people's support.

Some competition among persons and parties has always existed in the United States during election campaigns. However, many localities and even regions essentially, for nearly a century, have had what is a one-party system, (Key 1950). Even in the country as a whole, with a two-party system, because both parties seek to appeal to the majority of the electorate, both profess similar goals and even policies (Hamilton 1972).

The most marked change in the electoral process has been the expansion of suffrage. In the early years of the United States, only white adult males could vote and even among them property requirements for voting or holding office were not eliminated until the 1950s (Williams 1960; Chute 1969). After the Civil War, suffrage was formally extended to black males, after World War I to all females. But blacks were, particularly in the South, prevented from voting by a variety of means, including coercion, until the 1960s.

[1] Extremism, in the judgment of the FBI Director J. Edgar Hoover, included Dr. Martin Luther King's leading a nonviolent movement directed at the integration of whites and blacks. (U.S. Senate Select Committee on Intelligence Activities 1976.)

Participation in the political elections can involve more than casting a ballot. Some individuals became candidates for office, some work in electoral campaigns, and others contribute money. Most Americans do little beyond voting; many do not participate even to that extent. Milbrath (1965), on the basis of many studies of political participation, concludes that about one-third of American adults are politically inactive; many are unaware of the political world. He estimates that 60 percent are essentially spectators, watching and voting. Only 1 or 2 percent run for political office. About 4 or 5 percent attend caucus meetings, become active in a political party, or actively work in a campaign. More give money or contact a political leader. About 25 or 30 percent try to convince others to vote in a certain way.

To determine the range of power inequalities both the top of the range as well as the bottom must be examined. How much power do those with the greatest power actually possess? As governmental activities have expanded, the power of persons holding high governmental offices has increased. Federal government leaders, particularly the occupants of the executive office, make decisions affecting military action, trade, taxation, and other policies that, in turn, affect the level and direction of economic activity and social services. This federal expansion should not be exaggerated. Great as the growth in absolute size and staff and expenditures has been during this century, the population and national income have also grown tremendously. Using a constant dollar (corrected for inflation), the size of federal *domestic* expenditures and tax revenues have not increased greatly, relative to the growth of the economy, if unusual expenditures related to military expenses and the depression are excepted (Mosher and Poland 1964; Sharansky 1969).

What has increased is the ability to coordinate many people's actions in a way that was not possible in a more decentralized economy and political order. The increased bureaucratization and size of organizations generally has made more of our actions controllable by those who occupy what C. Wright Mills called the "strategic command posts of the social structure" (1956, p. 4). He used this phrase to refer to the power elite: those who rule the big corporations, run the machinery of the state, and direct the military establishment. A few men, particularly in circumstances they see as crises, make decisions that vitally affect the lives of millions of persons in this country and elsewhere. Although they may take into account what they *think* the general electorate wants, little public discussion or consultation takes place. President Kennedy's handling of the Cuban Missile Crisis of 1962 exemplifies that mode of decision making.

The lower level of the range in power differences within the American political order has moved upward, but it is impossible to calibrate whether the distance between the top and bottom has narrowed or expanded. The formal right to participate in collective decision-making has expanded to include more people. But the magnitude of power concentrated in the highest governmental offices has also increased. This picture will be elaborated when we consider the overall distribution of power in the next section.

Distribution

In discussing power distribution, we will consider autonomy first, then focus on participation in reaching decisions for the collectivity. Our discussion will include all members of the social system, not just those at the extremes.

Autonomy. Previously, we discussed autonomy in terms of the minimal amount of power individuals have. We now focus on how groups, with their divisions and conflicting interests, can organize to protect and control their own activities.

One important basis for people organizing and controlling their own activities is territory. The United States, as a federally organized polity, allows much determination and control at the state or local level. Ideally, the residents of a city, village, or state decide the policies affecting their city, village, or state. Because the United States is a federal system, the local citizens determine policy on more issues than do citizens of more unitary polities, like France. Policies about education, taxation, and crime, for example, vary among the states and localities. Nevertheless, the great expansion in the population of the cities and states has decreased popular control of the decisions made at the local and state level. Social scientists have conducted numerous studies of small towns and cities and of the decision-making process within them (Lynd and Lynd 1929; Hunter 1953; Schermerhorn 1961). Such studies have relevance in the present context because they provide information about changes in the autonomy of the localities.

The development of a national economy has taken some areas of possible decision making away from the local people or local elites and placed them under the control of corporate board members in a few cities (Vidich and Bensman 1958; Miller 1975; Wirt 1976). Although local government expenditures have increased, federal programs increasingly determine policy at the local level. Even when the federal government channels tax money back to the states, the funds are usually designated to support programs originated on the national level.

Partly in response to this decrease in control at the local level, people have been and are now attempting to increase local public participation and decentralize policy-making. "Local control" has long been a tradition in the United States, and new efforts to regain it have been discernible since the 1960s. During the "war on poverty" of the 1960s, many communities made a special effort to obtain the "maximum feasible participation" of the poor in the programs presumably serving them (Clark and Hopkins 1969; Kramer 1969; Marris and Rein 1973). It was believed that this would in itself, give poor people experience that would enable them to begin to move out of poverty. More significantly, it would also help assure programs that would serve the interests of and be accepted by the poor. Though these efforts at gaining popular participation failed to achieve all that was hoped they did contribute to and stimulate actions that continue to influence the provision of human services. Many social service programs now routinely include representatives of the people being served.

191

In addition, people try to protect their autonomy through organizations that take adversary actions. There are organizations to advance the rights of welfare recipients, poor people, rentors, and consumers, to name but a few. These organizations use the courts and the legal system to protect their members' rights; they may also demonstrate, strike, and otherwise act to coerce their members' adversaries.

Collective Decision-Making. Adversary groups and actions are sometimes also vehicles for contributing to decisions for the entire polity. Nongovernmental interest groups lobby the legislative and executive branches of government to influence the enactment of policies and their administration. They work within the political parties to influence the selection of candidates and the party platform.

People organize themselves also in terms of their interests as members of ethnic, religious, and status groups; they frequently organize to promote interests of their class in the labor, capital, and commodity markets; they also form associations to advance particular preferences. Whatever the preference involved, or whatever the interest sought, the organization itself becomes a base for power and members can use its power to further their preferences.

Voluntary associations also give people a way of controlling some aspects of their lives. People can organize leisure-time activities and even work activities, as in cooperatives. In addition, associations provide a basis for participation in collective decision making. The existence of a multitude of such organizations is an important aspect of power equality. DeTocqueville, analyzing the equalitarian character of American democracy in the 1840s, noted the importance of associations and went on to argue that there was a necessary relationship between equality and the principle of association. He wrote:

> Americans of all ages, all conditions, and all dispositions constantly form associations. They have not only commercial and manufacturing companies, in which all take part, but associations of a thousand other kinds, religious, moral, serious, futile, general or restricted, enormous or diminutive . . . . Among democratic nations . . .. all the citizens are independent and feeble . . . none of them can oblige his fellow men to lend him their assistance. They all, therefore, become powerless if they do not learn voluntarily to help one another (1955, Vol. II., 114-115).

More contemporary analysts have argued that voluntary associations and other interest-based groupings are essential to limit the power of the government leaders and power-holders. Without such intervening organizations, the mass of isolated individuals are vulnerable to dictatorial domination (Kornhauser 1959). Societies lacking such associations are "mass societies," susceptible to control by small, powerful elites, some observers argue.

Another way to look at the distribution of power in collective decision-making is to examine the political party system. Aside from voting, most people do not actively participate in the political process (Verba and Nie 1972). Consequently the alternatives offered by the parties is of great significance in giving people the opportunity to express their policy preferences. A two-party system offers different options to voters than a multiparty system. Voting for one of the parties in a two-party system more often results in having voted for the winning party than does voting for one party from among several (although in actuality governing coalitions do form among the many parties). In a multiparty system, however, a voter is more likely to find a party that comes close to expressing this or her personal preferences and interests.

The United States generally has had a national two-party system. But in some regions a single party has dominated, as in the South for many decades after the Civil War. In other areas, third and fourth parties have functioned effectively enough to change electoral outcomes. In New York State, for example, the Liberal and the Conservative parties have sometimes played critical roles in elections. Most strikingly, in 1970 James L. Buckley was elected to the United States Senate on the Conservative ticket, defeating the incumbent Republican senator, Charles E. Goodell, and the Democratic candidate, Richard L. Ottinger.

The manner in which competing parties and candidates formulate the choices and how the people decide to vote also shapes the degree of popular participation in collective decision making. Insofar as parties and candidates articulate policy alternatives and people vote in terms of them, the people are helping to determine policies. However, personal attractiveness of the candidate and the image projected through advertising and the mass media are also important for some of the electorate (Paterson and McClure 1976; Campbell et al. 1960).

Clearly, no single trend toward ever-increasing equality in power is discernible in the United States. The equality of power distribution in some ways has increased, but in many other ways *inequality* has grown. And the distribution of power changes in interesting ways from one short time period to another. In the contemporary period, for example, emphasis seems to have shifted to groups seeking autonomy and freedom *from* others' interference rather than seeking a greater share in making major policy choices.

Mobility

To discuss the mobility of power, we must consider movements of persons in and out of positions of power. The positions people occupy are critical when we consider power. The quality of authority or power is sometimes attributed to an individual as a personality characteristic. Such power, based on great personal attraction, Max Weber termed "charismatic." He thought charismatic power particularly significant in forming social movements and in generating social change. When considering American power inequalities, we have concentrated on the patterns of inequalities largely manifest in positions or offices.

People are elected to political offices for specific terms, making possible, but not assuring, high mobility into and out of elective offices. Incumbents, however, have an advantage in running against challengers, and in many localities the party organization may be sufficiently strong to ensure the reelection of its official candidate. Nagle (1973), in studying the turnover of American senators, representatives, and cabinet members from 1949 to 1969, found that with three changes in the party holding the presidency, cabinet turnover was high. He examined five four-year periods. When the presidency changed parties, 100 percent of the cabinet were newcomers; in other four-year periods, 25 and 50 percent of the cabinet members were newcomers. Turnover in the Senate and House of Representatives, however, was not as great. During each of the same five four-year periods, only 20 to 33 percent of each chamber were newcomers.

Although we lack systematic evidence on the extent to which officeholding is part of a continuing political career, we can make some observations. Even when defeated, political candidates may be appointed to important governmental positions. They move from one elective or appointive office to another. The party represents an organization of power and maintains force by means of actual incumbency, which may be intermittent, or by an incumbency potential sustained by the organization.

We also lack systematic evidence on the intergenerational mobility of government leaders. Stephen Hess, who studied what he called "America's political dynasties," defines dynasty as "a family that has had at least four members, in the same name, elected to federal office" (1966, p. 2). Using this definition, the United States has had twenty-two political dynasties, which have included: Adams, Lee, Roosevelt, Harrison, Taft, Frelinghuysen, Stockton, and Long. He also found that about seven hundred families have provided two or more members of Congress and account for nearly 1,700 of the 10,000 men and women elected since 1774.

This indicates that holding political office is sometimes related to other members of the family holding office, but it is not the prevailing pattern. We lack detailed analysis on the extent to which there is intergenerational mobility in all kinds of political offices. If state and local offices and major appointive offices were included, intergenerational inheritance of political careers would undoubtedly be greater. Persons active in political affairs generally come from politically active families (Hyman 1959), but there is no evidence of any single family or political elite clearly dominating U.S. politics. There is no single small political elite in America. What is more likely is that political leaders are drawn from status or class elites and that these elites are closely integrated. We turn to consider such possibilities in the remainder of this chapter.

POWER AND CLASS INEQUALITIES

The guarantee of political rights and their separation from other aspects of the society has been a major objective of liberal democracies. Each person is considered equal before the law. Laws are to bear equally on every citizen and rank is not supposed to affect the administration of legally determined justice. Every citizen, regardless of wealth, religion, ethnicity, or any other special characteristic should be able to participate equally in voting and holding office. Thus, the political system is formally severed from class and status ranking.

In actuality, of course, class level is correlated with power rank. It is popularly assumed that lower-class people do not have as much power as the well-to-do, but the specific ways in which class position is related to level of power is not as widely recognized. We will consider both autonomy and participation in collective decision making as aspects of power inequality and discuss some of the ways they are related to class inequalities.

Autonomy

A good way to assess variation in autonomy is to examine the operation of the legal system. The state, through the legal system and its agents, is the major protector of the individual's autonomy against the intrusions of others. Our question in this context is the extent to which governmental protection is equally available or depends upon class rank.

In many ways, the poor are less adequately protected than those at middle and higher income levels. The President's Commission on Law Enforcement and Administration of Justice, on the basis of a national survey of crime victimization conducted by the National Opinion Research Center, reported:

> The risks of victimization from forcible rape, robbery, and burglary are clearly concentrated in the lowest income groups and decrease steadily at higher income levels. The picture is somewhat more erratic for the offenses of aggravated assault, larceny of $50 and over, and vehicle theft. Victimization for larceny increases sharply in the highest income group (cited in Schur 1969, p. 26).

This relationship cannot be explained simply in terms of differential policy action, since police conduct seems to vary unpredictably (Wilson 1971). Sometimes, in high-crime low-income neighborhoods, surveillance is heavier than average, verging on what the residents regard as harassment. In other places and times crime in such areas is relatively neglected. In any case, the higher risks are not effectively countered by government policy. The American legal system tends to provide to higher-class persons more autonomy and protection from the incursions of others than it does to lower-class persons. Protection against civil damages often requires the ability to take legal action against the intruder. In civil suits, as in criminal cases, the American legal system is basically an adversary one. Each person is defended by his or her lawyer, who contends against the other side's lawyer. Persons must generally hire lawyers for a fee. Hence, the more money a person has, the more (and often the better) legal services he or she can hire. Some small changes have occurred: The public defender system has expanded a little in recent years; the government provision of a court-appointed lawyer to defend a person against criminal charges has been extended. In the

1960s, Neighborhood Legal Aid Offices were established. These were formed with federal support during the "war on poverty" to help the poor realize what otherwise would be only nominal rights.

Definitions of criminality and the administration of justice affect higher- and lower-class persons differently. One indication of such differential treatment is provided by a consideration of "white-colar" crime. Sutherland defined white-colar crime "as a crime committed by a person of respectability and high social status in the course of his occupation" (1949, p. 9). Sutherland examined the records of the seventy largest manufacturing, mining, and merchantile corporations. He found very widespread criminality. The corporations had frequently been found guilty by the courts or regulatory agencies of restraint of trade, of violating patent, trademark, and copyright laws, of misrepresentation in advertising, of unfair labor practices, and of financial manipulation. Yet, Sutherland points out, the persons violating these laws are not regarded as criminals and rarely suffer personal punishment.

Corporation executives and major owners control great economic resources; therefore, they appear to provide or promise magnificant rewards for society as a whole as well as for individuals. This affects the ways the laws are written and administered. Sutherland argues that one factor in the leniency in implementing laws against white-collar crimes is that the legislators, judges, and administrators both fear and admire the leading businessmen. They fear the loss of financial support and they accord the businessmen high status and deference. Sutherland also noted the relatively unorganized resentment of the public toward such crimes, for which he offers the following explanation: The crimes are diffuse in their effect; the agencies of communication, controlled by business, do not try to explain the complicated white-collar crimes; and the laws governing them are relatively new.

Crimes that are more likely to be committed by low-income persons are subject to harsher laws than are the white-collar crimes mentioned (Rossides 1976). Carlin, Howard, and Messinger (1967), in reviewing the relations between class and justice, found that laws pertaining to rental property favored the landlord, laws pertaining to borrowing money favored the lender. Legal procedures are applied differently to lower-class persons than to higher class persons. Criminal proceedings tend to be used in welfare and family cases involving low-income persons. In many ways, the poor are treated as wards of the state and as incompetent; this may be done on the assumption that special treatment can be provided, but the result is often denial of due process and the lack of procedural safeguards (tenBroek 1966).

The different legal treatment of the rich and poor not only reflects the differences in economic resources people have available to reward and punish others; the laws and their administration also help determine that there be rich and poor and help sustain persons in their relative positions. These legal differences are less pronounced among persons in middle-income levels; the working of the law varies most widely in its treatment of the rich and the poor.

Collective Decision Making

In considering how class position is related to participation in collective decision making, we must recognize that American political parties are generally based on class differences. In the United States, as in other countries, there are a multitude of interests, which are advanced through political parties and which help shape the parties. People's region, life-style preferences, religion, and ethnicity, for example, affect their adherence to political parties and the parties' appeal to them. Yet, it is economic interests generally which have primacy in shaping party policies. Positions on tariffs, taxes, inflation, and employment and legislation relating to corporations, agriculture, and trade unions are the issues that have characterized the differences between the Republican and Democratic parties. Despite the tendency of each to appeal to the majority of the electorate and, hence, to blur their differences, they are generally viewed by the electorate and scholars as different. The Republican party is popularly viewed as the party of big business; the Democratic as the party of the working class (Lipset 1960; Rose 1967).

A fundamental way in which Americans might shape governmental policy toward the economy is by voting and participating in electoral politics. Indeed, reformers hoped and conservatives feared that the expansion of suffrage and mass participation in politics would bring about government action leading to greatly increased economic equality (Marshall 1964). This has not happened to any significant degree, although government policies may have prevented what would otherwise be much greater inequalities. Some of these matters are discussed in other portions of this book. At this point we examine the extent to which class rank is related to rank in the power hierarchy.

A fundamental aspect of citizenship is that it entails political rights: the right of franchise and to hold electoral office (Marshall 1964, p. 71-72). In theory, those rights belong to every citizen, regardless of class level. In practice, they are not exercised equally by persons in all class levels. Low-income persons are much less likely to vote than higher-income persons. For example, as shown in Figure 7.1, in the election of November 1972 only 46 percent of the persons with incomes under $3,000 voted; 79 percent of the persons with incomes of $15,000 and over voted. Milbrath (1963, p. 121) found that income was significantly related to displaying buttons or bumper stickers and to giving money, but less clearly related to working for a political party, attending meetings, and proselytizing in elections.

On the whole, despite the formal rights of participation in collective decision making, much of the citizenry, particularly the lower classes, are not effective participants in collective decision making (Alford and Friedland 1975). Legislators are often not responsive to the general public's views and are more responsive the dominant economic interests. Participation by lower-class persons is particularly low in communities where there is relatively little policy agreement among the classes, suggesting that the political elites mobilize lower-class persons to participate only where major cleavages do not exist. Voting often

197

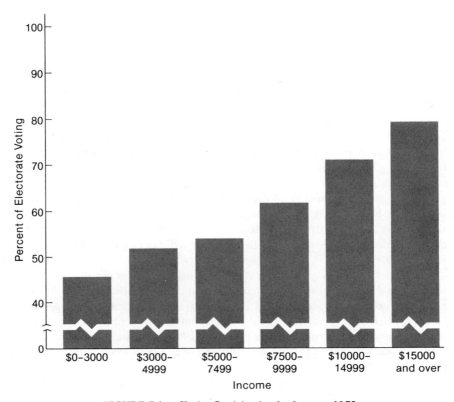

FIGURE 7.1 *Voting Participation by Income, 1972*

Source: U.S. Bureau of the Census, Current Population Reports, Series P-20, No. 253 (Washington, D.C.: Government Printing Office, 1973), Table 11.

seems to be more symbolic than substantive; it appears that electoral politics is not a powerful form of political participation.

Governmental policy is responsive to dominant economic interests partly due to the nature of the fiscal relationship between the state and the economy. Since state revenues depend on taxes, state office holders try to avoid policies which would harm capital accumulation and growth, the fiscal base for taxes. Consequently, since that growth and related fiscal capacity are dependent on private control of investment and production, issues will not be raised which might impinge on such control. Another factor affecting the responsiveness of the government office holders to dominant economic interests are the class origins and occupational careers of office incumbents.

When it comes to holding high offices, the differences among the classes are quite great. We will consider some of the studies done on the class origins of the incumbents of powerful positions and then look at the class level of such persons once embarked on their own careers.

198

TABLE 7.1 Occupational Class Origins of U.S. Senators, 1947-1957 Compared with Labor Force, 1900

Occupational Class	Fathers of U.S. Senators			Labor Force in 1900	Index of Overrepresentation for Total
	Senators Democratic	Senators Republican	All Senators		
Professional	28	19	24	6	4.0
Proprietors and Officials	30	39	35	7	5.0
Farmers	33	31	32	22	1.5
Low-salaried Workers	3	0	2	5	0.4
Industrial Wage Earners	5	7	5	39	0.1
Servants	0	0	0	5	0.0
Farm Laborers	0	0	0	17	0.0
Unknown	0	3	2		0.0
Total Percent	99	99	100		
(N)	(92)	(88)	(180)		

Source: Matthews 1960, adapted from Tables 2 and 3.

Matthews (1960) studied 180 United States senators who held office between 1947 and 1957. He found, as can be seen in Table 7.1, that the senators came largely from upper- and upper middle-class backgrounds. Only 7 percent of the United States senators had fathers who had been salesmen, clerks, industrial wage earners, servants, or farm laborers. Yet, in 1900 two-thirds of the gainfully employed were in those occupations. It is also worth noting that the class origins of Democratic senators do not differ greatly from those of Republican senators. Republicans are only slightly more likely to be children of fathers who were proprietors and officials than Democrats and they are less likely to have fathers who were in the professional class. Matthews (1954) also analyzed the class backgrounds of presidents, vice presidents, and cabinet members from the beginning of the Republic until the mid-1930s. He found that only 4 percent came from working-class or lower-class backgrounds.

Warner and his associates (1963) conducted a study of the social characteristics of the civilian and military leaders of the United States government. In 1959, they collected questionnaires from almost 13,000 executives—over 69 percent of those receiving questionnaires filled them out and returned them. They studied high-ranking men and women (1) in the career civil service, (2) in the foreign service, (3) with political appointments, including members of the cabinet, and (4) in the military, ranging from admirals and generals down to captains in the Navy and colonels in the other services.

Warner and his associates found that civilian federal executives are drawn from working-class as well as business and professional class origins: 21 percent had fathers who were industrial wage earners (17 percent skilled workers); 9 percent had fathers who were white-collar workers (clerks or salespersons); 15 percent had fathers who were business executives (this includes 5 percent foremen and only 5 percent major executives); 20 percent had fathers who were business owners (generally small businesses); 19 percent, in the professions; 15 percent, farmers; 1 percent, in other occupations.

Significantly, the class origin rankings increase with the level of the federal executives (Meier 1975). At the lowest level studied, (General Schedule [GS]-14) 30 percent had fathers who were in professional occupations, were business executives, or owners of medium or large businesses; among those at the highest career civil service levels (GS-16 to GS-18), 45 percent had fathers from those occupations; among those above civil service levels (political appointments), 58 percent had fathers from those occupations.

Class origins also vary among different kinds of executives. Table 7.2 provides information on the class origins of career civil service, foreign service, political, and military executives. It also includes information on business executives, taken from the Warner and Abegglen (1955) study. The information is provided in the form of a ratio, indicating the proportion of persons from each occupational class whose sons became a federal executives or business leaders. (The proportion of fathers of federal executives in a given occupation was

TABLE 7.2   Sources of 1952 Business Leaders[1] and 1959 Federal Executives[2]: Ratio of Proportion of Fathers in Occupational Group to Proportion of Occupational Group in Adult Male Populations

Occupation of Father	Business Leaders	Career Civil Service Executives	Foreign-Service Executives	Political Executives	Military Executives
Unskilled or Semiskilled Laborer	0.16	0.12	0.09	0.06	0.06
Skilled Laborer	0.63	1.27	0.73	0.87	0.80
Owner of Small Business	3.60	2.14	1.71	1.86	1.86
Clerk or Salesman	0.80	0.83	0.58	0.75	0.75
Foreman	1.33	2.50	1.50	2.00	2.50
Minor or Major Business Executive; Owner of Large Business	7.75	4.67	8.00	6.67	7.00
Professional	3.50	4.00	6.25	6.00	4.50
Farm Laborer	0.00	0.00	0.00	0.00	0.00
Farm Tenant or Owner	0.45	0.94	0.75	0.81	0.56
Uniformed Service, etc.	2.00	0.50	1.50	1.00	5.00

Source: Warner et al. (1963); Appendix B, Table 6B.

[1] 1952 business leaders/1920 U.S. adult males = ratios.

[2] 1959 federal executives/1930 U.S. adult males = ratios.

divided by the proportion of all adult males in that occupation in 1930. If the proportion is equal, the ratio is 1.00; insofar as members of a given occupational class contribute disproportionally, the ratio is larger.) Thus, the foreign service executives are disproportionally drawn from the business and professional classes. The military executives are particularly disproportionally drawn from business occupations and uniformed services. On the whole, among these elite groups, the career civil service is most open to sons of fathers who are not from high-ranking occupations.

Janowitz's (1960) study of the military also documents the extent to which the military elite is drawn from the higher class levels. He found that 20 percent of the Army leaders in 1950 had fathers who were in business; 45 percent, in the professions or mangement. Including data on wealth and social status in addition to occupational prestige, he concluded that only 3 percent had upper social class origins, compared to 26 percent in 1910-20. Most came from middle social class origins: 47 percent upper-middle and 45 percent lower-middle, which compared to 66 percent and 8 percent, respectively, in 1910-20.

The extent to which class and power hierarchies are related can also be assessed by examining the lifetime class ranks of persons who occupy powerful positions. Persons holding political office simultaneously hold class positions associated with their other employment or their wealth. They also have class locations and experiences established prior to their political career. Such experiences may make them more sympathetic and more accessible to people in their own class.

Persons holding political office not only have generally higher class origins than nonofficeholders, they currently hold and can anticipate continuing to hold careers of relatively high class standing. Although the rich do not generally hold office, a disproportionate number of government office holders are wealthy. For example, Ralph Nader's Citizens Action Group reported on the net worth of United States Senators in 1976 (Shearer 1976). They sent questionnaires to the United States Senators and made estimates for nineteen who did not respond; they had too little information to estimate the net worth of twenty-two senators. Of the remaining seventy-eight senators, twenty-one, or about 25 percent, were millionaires (23 percent of the Democrats and 31 percent of the Republicans). Only 6 percent had net worths under $50,000.

Freitag (1975) studied the positions all United States cabinet secretaries from 1897 to 1973 held before and after their cabinet appointments. He found that three-fourths of them had interlocks with business, that is, they had been or became corporate directors, officers, or lawyers before or after their cabinet service. Only 12 percent had no interlock and information was unavilable for another 12 percent. He found no clear trends over time nor did he find any clear differences in the interlocks between Democratic and Republican administrations.

President Dwight D. Eisenhower, in his farewell address to the nation in 1961 noted that the "conjunction of an immense Military Establishment and a large arms industry is new to the American experience." He went on to warn: "In the councils of government we must guard against the acquisition of unwarranted influence, whether sought or unsought, by the military-industrial complex" (Melman 1970; Appendix B). Eisenhower's use of the term *military-industrial complex* and his warning about it attracted attention. The speech stimulated inquiries and studies into the relationship between the military establishment and industry.

Studies of the careers of military officers after retiring from military service have yielded equivocal results. Biderman (1964) concluded that although a considerable number of military retirees are employed in the defense industry, their role in the industry and the significance of this career for the military have probably been exaggerated. Other writers (Mills 1956) emphasize the extent to which persons move from high military positions into industrial and political elite positions.

Undoubtedly, the influence of the military in forming collective decisions has grown greatly in the Cold War period (Rose 1967; Mills, 1956). The military ascendancy in decisions relating to foreign policy and defense expenditures has given it considerable influence in the economy. Vast defense expenditures mean that the military and civilian decision makers who formulate so much of the government's policies also exercise control over a vast segment of the economy. Seymour Melman even argues in *Pentagon Capitalism:*

> The government of the United States now includes a self-expanding war machine that uses military power for diverse political operations and is based upon an industrial management that has priority claims to virtually unlimited capital funds from the federal budget. The state-management is economically parasitic, hence exploitive, in its relations to American society at home (1970, p. 34).

He argues that the state-management of the economy has become concentrated within the Department of Defense.

Galbraith (1967) believes that a more general interpenetration of the state and the economy is occurring. He stresses the role of modern large-scale production with its great demands for capital and sophisticated technology which, in turn, results in elaborate organization. The large corporations need to control their markets in order to plan and planning is needed to take advantage of large-scale production. The state is relied upon to regulate the aggregate demand for goods and services and also to stabilize the economy, especially in wages, prices, and employment. The state also is needed to underwrite the expensive technology and provide the educated labor force. In military procurement, space exploration, and atomic energy, the distinction between public and private organization is nearly imperceptible. Even among firms that do not sell most of their output to the government, dependence and the interpenetration of personnel and activities of the large corporations and the state is far advanced.

Thus far we have emphasized the extent to which persons ranking high in class also hold offices ranking high in the power hierarchy. The two hierarchies have other relationships as well. Rank in one hierarchy may provide opportunities to influence or control persons in another hierarchy. Persons with high occupational rank try to induce government officeholders to implement policies that will sustain or improve their class standing. For example, they organize trade associations and lobby for legislation that protects their industry. Or individual companies or owners seek particular benefits for themselves. On the other hand, government leaders may try to induce business owners and executives to conduct their business activities in ways that sustain or improve the power positions of the government leaders. They may, for example, want business to expand activities overseas or not raise prices or wages.

Persons in middle and lower-middle occupational ranks also organize to gain political power, which they use to obtain favorable governmental conduct. For many manual workers and lower white-collar workers, trade unions are the instrument of such power. Trade unions are a means not only for workers to bargain with their employers over working conditions and wages, they are also a means for workers to influence government officeholders to shape laws that support workers rather than employers. Unions do this through mobilizing members and supporters for political campaigns, for educational efforts, and for direct representation in governement.

Persons at the lowest class levels are usually not able to organize and sustain efforts to induce power holders to take actions they desire. If they seek any such influence, they are more likely to use coercion or threats of coercion in the form of demonstrations or riots (Gamson 1975; Hobsbawm 1965). For example, the studies of the ghetto riots of the 1960s indicate that participation was widespread, viewed by blacks as a political means of protest, and indeed did yield political and economic gains (Alford and Friedland 1975; Kriesberg 1973; Betz 1974).

We have seen that there is considerable congruence or consistency in rank between the power and class hierarchies in the United States. People with little power also tend to be poor; the rich tend to also have great relative power. Of course, the congruence is not total. Many individuals of moderate means and middle-class origins and experience may hold, at least for a while, high political office. Poor persons or working-class groups, when organized, may exert influence on specific issues. Very rich persons, on the other hand, usually do not themselves hold important positions in the power hierarchy nor have influence in policy spheres removed from their areas of immediate concern. But in terms of categories or groups of people, the congruence between the two dimensions is great.

The reasons for the congruence are many. First, persons ranking high in one dimension use their resources to gain a high rank in other dimensions. Money can be used to get power and power can be used to get money. Second, persons with low income and low-ranking occupations often develop ways of thinking and acting that are not conducive to holding powerful positions or even to politically participating to the extent of voting: they seem to lack self-confidence, appear passive, and act as if they did not believe they could alter their environment. Third, the rules and structures of the political system and of the economic system on the whole are integrated so that a person's rank in one tends to make him or her fit into a similar rank in the other. Thus, low-income persons generally find it more difficult to participate in collective decision-making than do middle-ranking persons. The choices available are generally structured in terms of the interests of those who are dominant rather than those who are not.

POWER AND STATUS INEQUALITIES

To determine how power and status hierarchies are related, we will discuss how a person's status affects his or her autonomy and participation in collective decision-making.

Autonomy

Who decides which cultural patterns are respected and which are not? Certain aspects of a way of life may not only be denigrated, but declared illegal. Some people argue that certain aspects of the life-style of lower-status persons, for example, seeking excitement and risking physical fights, are conducive to conduct that middle- and upper-status persons regard as delinquent and criminal (Miller, 1958).

Race and ethnic differences in the United States have been closely related to power differences. In nineteenth-century New England, the earlier immigrants—Protestant, Anglo-Saxons—were challenged for political power by the Irish, then by the southern and eastern Europeans. In the Southwest, the Anglos have dominated the Spanish-speaking people who have long resided there, but in more recent decades they too have been challenged, often successfully, by the Chicanos (Burma, 1970).

Race has been a very important basis for differential power. As far as personal autonomy is concerned, blacks have received less protection from the police and other government officials than whites. For example, Wolfgang, Kelly, and Nolde (1972) found that blacks were more likely than whites to be executed after having been convicted and sentenced to death for comparable crimes. It was such evidence that led the Supreme Court to conclude that capital punishment, as it was being administered, was unconstitutional. Bullock (1961) found that whites and blacks are sentenced differently for the same crimes. Blacks received more severe sentences for property crimes but less severe sentences for assault and personal crimes which are usually committed against other blacks.

In the past and to some extent at present, low racial status has been associated with less than equal protection by the state and less than equal civil rights. On the other hand, the legal system has been a major instrument for gaining more equality. The National Association for the Advancement of Colored People (NAACP) and other racially and ethnically based organizations have brought cases to the courts that have resulted in the government's acting to ensure more equality. This legal action has been accompanied and sometimes led by organizations using coercive as well as persuasive means to gain legislation that would enhance power equality.

Gender has also been associated with unequal civil rights. Women in many ways have lacked minimal autonomy, particularly in relationship to their husbands. For example, "the domicile of a married woman automatically follows that of her husband. . . . in the forty-one common-law states, all monies earned by a husband during marriage belong exclusively to him. No monetary value is attached to the wife's domestic services in helping to produce the family income or acquire property" (DeCrow 1974, pp. 167, 169-70).

Collective Decision Making

Status differences sometimes provide an important basis for political differences. Status politics can exist in addition to class politics (Lipset 1960; Gusfield 1963; Lipset and Raab, 1970). Differences in life-style and values sometimes become issues around which people struggle and contend.

For example, the struggle during the 1920s between the "wets" and the "drys"—those opposing and those favoring prohibition of alcoholic beverages—involved people taking a moral stand. Furthermore, these differences were associated with different sets of people: notably the urban Catholics versus the rural Protestants, especially the fundamentalists (Siegfried 1927). Other life-style issues have been the focus of conflict—for example, matters of civil liberties, styles of public education, or race relations and civil rights (Coleman, 1957; Kriesberg, 1973).

Status politics naturally arises out of power struggles among status groups. Ethnic and racial groups organize and press claims for more power. They try to place representatives in high office and to implement policies they favor. Similarly, women compete with men to gain relative power. Such collective efforts and the resulting shaping of political issues help account for the relationship between status rank and power rank. Status groups are a basis for mobilization and the resulting organization can be a source of power. The power that different status groups gain helps raise their existing status rank. High-status individuals and groups use the resources such as deference from others—that high status gives to gain power. Conversely those high in power use coercive strength to garner prestige and honor.

General social status is highly related to power in collective decision making. Most analyses of this topic have focused on the social elite. In Chapter 5 we discussed Baltzell's (1964) and Domhoff's (1967) description of the social elite in America. Domhoff argues that the members of a cohesive social elite attend the same schools, belong to the same social networks, and share the same work and leisure activities. He further argues that this elite, which he calls the upper class, dominate the political process: "the members sit in pivotal government offices, define most major policy issues, shape the policy proposals on issues raised outside their circles, and mold the rules of government" (1971, pp. 105-6).

Status rankings based upon race, ethnicity, or gender are also highly related to power differences. Despite important advances in black participation in collective decision-making, blacks are still significantly underrepresented in national politics. Within recent years, black participation in the electoral process has increased and about equals white participation, certainly when education and occupation levels are equal (Pomper 1975, pp. 120-21).

Women, too, are greatly underrepresented in significant positions within the political system. Until recently, women were even underrepresented in the electoral process: a smaller percentage of the women voted than men (Pomper 1975). The discrepancies are apparent everywhere. Although women make up more than a majority of the electorate, they rarely hold high legislative and executive positions and hold few judgeships (none on the Supreme Court).

High consistency between rank in the power and status hierarchies is perpetuated by a number of mechanisms. Persons ranking high in power and status can use their resources to discriminate against low ranking persons and to deny them access to higher ranks. For example, men with higher status and greater power can use their status and power to exclude women from positions of power and deny them equality of status. On the other hand, those who rank low, insofar as there is consensus about the status hierarchy and insofar as the power differences are regarded as legitimate, may themselves accede to their low rank. They often feel unable to challenge those of higher rank.

CLASS AND STATUS INEQUALITIES

Class and status inequalities mutually sustain each other, aside from their connections with power inequality.

Social status based on life-styles is closely related to class position, since many aspects of a person's life-style depend on his or her economic resources (Kriesberg 1970). Being skilled in a variety of leisure-time activities and maintaining a socially respectable home require a relatively high level of material resources. Conversely, practicing a well-regarded life-style facilitates a person's access to income-generating positions and circles.

Insofar as there are clear status lines, the members of each status group can assist each other to gain and hold the better class positions; high-status members can assist each other to find comparably high-class positions—for example, well paying but undemanding jobs.

Membership in lower-status categories generally is associated with lower-class positions. Thus, blacks generally have lower incomes than whites and women lower incomes than men. In large part difference in income reflects differences in the occupational distribution of blacks and whites and of men and women. Women and blacks are disproportionally represented in the lower-paying occupations. Indeed, the higher the proportion of blacks or of women in an occupation, the lower paid are the whites or the males in that occupation (Hodge and Hodge 1965).

Some efforts have been made to account for these relationships. One explanation emphasizes competition and a split labor market (Hodge and Hodge 1965; Bonacich 1976); another emphasizes segregation and exclusion (Taeuber, Taeuber, and Cain 1966). According to the competition theory, some groups, such as women and blacks, because they lack skills, mobility, savings, or other resources that would allow them some choice of jobs, can bargain less effectively about working conditions than other groups. Therefore they are compelled to work for a lower salary and hence, drive down the wages where they work. The alternate explanation claims that causality works in the opposite direction. It is whites and males, occupying the well-paid, more stable occupations, who discriminate and exclude others from entering the high-paying occupations.[2]

Snyder and Hudis (1976) tested these two explanations by examining the earnings of whites, blacks, males, and females in 1950, 1960, and 1970 in 413 occupations. They related the income of white males in the earlier time to the percentage of black males in each occupation a decade later to see whether or not the number of blacks in a high-paying occupation had decreased a decade later. Their purpose was to test the segregation explanation. They related the percentage of blacks in the earlier period to the income of white males a decade later to test the competition explanation. They could see whether or not a high percentage of blacks in an occupation was related to low wages a decade later. The possible effects of education and hours worked were also taken into account. They conducted the same kind of analysis for women. Snyder and Hudis concluded that black men are systematically excluded from higher paying jobs and from crafts occupations, but women are not. On the other hand, they found some evidence of competition between women and white men at all but the lowest occupational levels. However, their study emphasized the powerful stability in the unequal distribution of blacks and women in high-paid occupations. These findings indicate the importance of historical constraints.

Even within similar occupations, blacks and women generally earn less than whites and males. Some evidence of this may be seen in Tables 5.5 and 7.3.

[2] These arguments have many implications regarding the rationality of discrimination and the possible benefits whites and males derive from the underrepresentation of blacks and females in higher paying occupations. Some analysts have pointed to gains white workers derive from the discrimination against blacks (Becker 1971; Glen 1966; Thurow 1969). Others have argued that white workers also suffer economically because of discrimination against blacks (Reich 1971; Szymanski 1976).

TABLE 7.3 Occupational Distribution and Mean Occupational Earnings by Race, 1975 (Year-round, Full-time, Male Workers)

Occupations	Percent Distribution		Earnings (In Dollars)		Earnings White/Black
	White	Black	White	Black	
Professional, Technical and Similar Workers	17.8	8.6	$18,350	$12,895	.70
Managers and Administrators Except Farm	18.4	5.4	18,241	12,079	.66
Sales Workers	6.6	1.9	16,021	NA	NA
Clerical and Similar Workers	6.3	8.9	12,518	11,743	.94
Craft and Similar Workers	21.3	16.9	13,035	10,927	.84
Operatives	14.7	27.6	11,471	9,495	.83
Laborers, Except Farm	4.3	11.5	9,647	8,031	.83
Service Workers	6.2	16.1	10,619	8,782	.83
Farm Workers (Farmers and Laborers)	4.3	3.2	8,674	4,536	.83
Total	99.9	100.1	$14,388	$ 9,961	.69

Note: NA = Not Available.
Source: Adapted from U.S. Bureau of the Census, Current Population Reports, Series P-60, No. 105; Table 53, 1977.

It might be argued that even within each occupation, women (or blacks) have fewer years experience, work fewer hours, are less trained for the job, and so on. Suter and Miller (1973) analyzed the differences in income of men and women. Taking into account occupational status, education, full-time year-round employment, and lifetime work experience, they found women earned less than men. In fact, considering all these factors, the earnings of women in 1966 was about 39 percent of men's earnings.

Featherman and Hauser (1976) compared the occupational status and earnings of married persons in the experienced civilian labor forces of 1962 and 1973. They took into account family factors, schooling, occupations, and work experience and found that these still did not account for much of the differences in earnings between the husbands and wives. They concluded that, of the earning gap between the husbands and wives, 85 percent in 1962 and 84 percent in 1973 could not be explained by the factors studied; this remainder represents inequality of opportunity or "discrimination."

In Chapter 5 we reviewed changes in the socioeconomic position of women over the last several decades and saw that except for greater participation in the labor force, their position, relative to men, showed little change. An analysis of changes in the socioeconomic position of blacks relative to whites indicates convergences in some areas. The occupational distribution of blacks has become more similar to whites, particularly in the decades between 1940 to 1950 and between 1960 and 1970. Glenn (1974), in reviewing changes in the relative income of blacks and whites since World War II, found that substantial declines in black-white differences occurred only in the second half of the 1960s. Despite these gains, life expectancy of blacks compared to whites did not improve, comparing 1968 to 1960.

Differences in the earnings between men and women and between blacks and whites are in large measure due to discrimination and differential competition. Inequality of opportunity occurs in various ways at several steps in the process of socioeconomic attainment. Discrimination occurs in schooling, in availability of occupations, and in career movement within occupations.[3] This need not be merely the expression of prejudice, although that obviously occurs. It is prejudicial when whites assume a black is inadequately educated or not sufficiently experienced for a better position or males assume that a woman would prefer a job as a typist and lacks competence to do anything else. In addition, informal, unconscious patterns of thought give advantages to those who share status characteristics with those already in the higher class positions. Whites who are dominant in a particular organization, for example, will tend to search for

---

[3]Kluegel (1978) has analyzed the role of job authority as a source of the persistent differences in earnings between white and black males. He found that blacks were much less likely than whites to be in positions of authority, and black men receive a lower income return to authority than do whites. Kluegel estimates that the exclusion of blacks from authority accounts for approximately one-third of the income gap between black and white men.

people like themselves to fill a high position, will trust references from people they know, and will esteem more highly performances like their own. Finally, the very structuring of tasks may be made more congenial to some status characteristics than to others. Jobs are structured so that they may or may not be compatible with other activities that are related to status differences. For example, released time may be allowed for military reserve training, denied for pregnancy or parental responsibilities. Jobs may be organized on the assumption that a "wife" will take on almost total home and parental responsibilities and be mobile at her husband's discretion. Such traditional structures and patterned expectations is what is meant by institutionalized sexism and racism.

CLASS, STATUS, AND POWER INEQUALITIES

We have seen how inequalities in one ranking system tend to be related to inequalities in each of the other two. Now we consider how all three are interrelated, focusing on a particularly significant segment of any social system: the elites.

Several different models of the way in which the class, status, and power elites are integrated have been put forward. Power, class, and status elites may be unified, or one elite may dominate all others, or the elites may contend and compete with each other. In these models, the nonelites, either the populace in general or specific groups, have varying roles in making decisions for the society as a whole.

Relations among the highest ranks in the three dimensions of inequality can be highlighted by focusing on how collective decisions are reached. We ask how the social system acts as a unit, how binding decisions are made for the collectivity, how people act in a unified or coordinated manner. Collective actions are the result of collective decisions, although they may be made by a small group who control a preponderance of resources or most people acting together.

Collective decisions differ in content: they may be about voting procedures, tax policy, going to war, or allocating money for social services. They differ in scope: individuals' conduct may be precisely proscribed or individuals may be left to act within general guidelines or structures, as in choosing fashions within a market system.

One important theory of how collective decisions are made claims that those in the highest ranks of the class hierarchy also dominate the other hierarchies and the overall social system. Thus, Karl Marx argued in the *German Ideology* that under capitalism, "the State is the form in which the individuals of a ruling class assert their common interests" (Tucker 1972, p. 151). The U.S. government, according to this theory, is dominated by those who hold great wealth. They shape the basic policy; the differences among political officeholders are not significant. A contemporary Marxist, Paul M. Sweezy (1962, pp. 131-33), describes how the present-day American ruling class exercises authority.

... its members either directly occupy the key [government] positions. . . , or they finance and thus indirectly control the political parties which are responsible for staffing and managing the routine business of government.

He responds to counter arguments by noting:

Obviously the ruling class has to make concessions and compromises to keep the people, and especially the working class, in a condition of sufficient ignorance and contentment to accept the system as a whole. . . . Capitalists can and do fight among themselves to further individual or group interests, and they differ over the best way of coping with the problems which arise from the class position; but overshadowing all these divisions is their common interest in preserving and strengthening a system which guarantees their wealth and privilege.

Other analysts give much greater significance to the separation of ownership and control (Burnham 1941). Economic considerations are still dominant, but the managerial elite are in control.

Other observers have stressed the status dimension as most significant in overall collective decision making. Thus, Domhoff (1967) and Baltzell (1964), as discussed in Chapter 5, present evidence that a small social elite exists at the national level. Its members provide the country's business and political leaders. Their shared social origins and experiences give coherence and some degree of unity to the power, class, and status elites.

C. Wright Mills (1956) also sees social bonds helping to unify the business, military, and political elites. Common status origins, schools, and social activities help give a common viewpoint to the members of those groups. He argues, however, that the economic elite is of particular importance although the political and military leaders are also significant. He writes:

The American government is not, in any simple way nor as a structural fact, a committee of "the ruling class." It is a network of "committees," and other men from other hierarchies beside the corporate rich sit upon these committees. Of these, the professional politician is the most complicated, but the high military, the warlords of Washington, are the newest (p. 170).

Mills' view of a unified power elite of business, political, and military leaders is related to the idea of "mass society." He sees the top of modern American society as increasingly unified.

The middle levels are a drifting set of stalemated, balancing forces; the middle does not link the bottom with the top. The bottom of this society is increasingly powerless: at the bottom there is emerging a mass society (p. 324).

In a mass society, people are isolated; voluntary associations do not connect people with the centers of power; people lack communities; are dependent on mass communication that does not communicate. People "lose their will for rationally considered decisions and action because they do not possess the instruments for such decision and action" (Mills 1956, p. 324).

Theoretically, it can be argued that the major political officeholders are the dominant power elite, that the leaders of a ruling political party can dominate and control all spheres of activity. Although this may hold true in other societies, it has not been offered as a description of the United States. Some observers, however, have argued that American political officeholders and party leaders exercise considerable autonomy and often make major decisions affecting economic activities and the interests of business leaders. Arnold Rose, rebutting C. Wright Mills, argues:

> The relationship between the economic elite and the political authorities has been a constantly varying one of strong influence, co-operation, division of labor, and conflict, with each influencing the other in changing proportion to some extent and each operating independently of the other to a large extent. Today there is significant political control and limitation of certain activities over the economic elite, and there are also some significant processes by which the economic elite uses its wealth to help elect some political candidates and to influence other political authorities in ways which are not available to the average citizen. Further, neither the economic elite nor the political authorities are monolithic units which act with internal consensus and co-ordinated action with regard to each other (1967, p. 2).

This view is similar to the pluralist idea that power is widely dispersed and that America is ruled by contending groups or interests. Some observers stress the extent to which interest groups block or veto each other and inhibit any collective action (Reisman 1950). The public is also viewed as varying in relative power on different issues. The people may make an issue salient, help pose alternative policies, and choose among contending elites, or they sometimes may be directed by the elites.

The writers mentioned offer evidence to support their descriptions of how decisions affecting the whole society are made. In addition, numerous studies have attempted to systematically assess the validity of the descriptions.

One issue is whether there is an identifiable core of people who can and do direct major collective decisions. Earlier in this chapter, we considered evidence about the extent to which people in elite class, status, and power positions share common backgrounds, exchange roles, and constitute a cohesive social group. We have seen that considerable proportions of the various elite groups do share many common experiences and backgrounds. Yet, a clearly bounded, homogenous, unified group does not occupy the top positions in every hierarchy. It is probably true, however, that many of those who do occupy top positions without the appropriate status and class backgrounds have assimilated the appropriate ways of thinking and acting so that they fit in well enough to work effectively as elite members. What is of particular significance is whether there are relatively independent or autonomous groups or spheres of activity among the leading decision makers.

Hunter (1959) provides some relevant information. In his study of national leaders, he used what is called the "reputational" method. He sought the names of the top leaders in America, as identified by the leaders themselves. Beginning in 1953 with a list of 106 national organizations regarded as potentially influential in national policy development, he and his colleagues polled these associations. Their leaders were asked to nominate other influencial organizations and to name top national leaders. Until 1958, Hunter polled and interviewed persons who were nominated, asking them about each other and for other nominations. "Out of several hundred persons named from all sources, between one hundred and two hundred men consistently were chosen as top leaders. . . . One hundred of these received more votes than all others" (p. 167). Hunter also found that these top leaders generally knew each other; this was less true of the second- and third-level men.

The group of top influentials was heavily weighted with industrial leaders, twenty-three; also included were fifteen United States senators, ten cabinet members, and a variety of other government, labor, business, and professional leaders. Of those who could be identified by political party affiliation, twenty were Democrats and fifty were Republicans (Hunter 1959, p. 199). Individuals often mixed business and government: "seventeen . . . had made a career of politics, thirty-six had never held political office, but forty-six had been in both business and government in their careers" (p. 180). This study does indicate the existence of a national elite and one in which industrial and business leaders are significant. It does not indicate, however, a unity of purpose. Top leaders disagree on many issues, and they are indifferent to or take no active stand on many others.

Another way of studying the extent to which dominance is exercised by a unified power elite or by one group who is on top of a single hierarchy is to examine how particular decisions are made. Many studies of the nature and degree of relations among class, status, and power elites have focused on decision making in the area of foreign policy and military expenditures. Most observers agree that relatively few persons are involved in making decisions in those spheres. Nevertheless, they disagree about how few they are, who they consult or consider in making decisions, and who they are.

In major foreign policy and defense decisions, the top government office holders formally choose the policy to be pursued. But questions can be raised about the class and status interests they share, whom they listen to, and who influences them. One kind of pertinent research has examined the possibility that members of Congress tend to vote for defense appropriations and support a relatively belligerent foreign policy insofar as defense expenditures are relatively high in their home districts. Grey and Gregory (1968) and Russett (1970) have found a weak relationship as hypothesized, but Cobb (1969, 1973) has not. There certainly is not a clear strong relationship. It may be that support for defense expenditures and the belief in their importance is so widely shared in the country that military expenditures in any given district do not significantly effect hawkishness. Perhaps, when there is less consensus about the salience of military defense and a hawkish foreign policy, a stronger relationship between support for such policies and expenditures in home districts will be found.

Other research efforts focus on choices about military procurement. How is the decision made to develop or not to develop a weapon system such as the Polaris nuclear submarine system, the F-111 plane, or the Minuteman missile system? Kurth (1971) examined several decisions about major aerospace procurement. He found that major procurement decisions were timed to keep the major production lines in operation and to aid corporations in financial trouble. Kanter and Thorson (1973) offer alternative and complementary interpretations, but overall, their research supports the contention that the timing of major procurement contracts is not determined by strategic military needs.

Lieberson (1977) examined data on military contracts, corporate size, and federal expenditures over many decades. His findings do not entirely support either the elitist or pluralist positions. They do support the view that there is a military-industrial complex, in that some groups have strong interests in high levels of military spending and are influential in furthering those interests, but the military-industry complex must compete with other similar complexes with special strengths in their spheres.

Assessing the competing characterizations of the congruence of class, status, and power elites also requires taking into account the rest of the population. It is difficult to argue that there is a unified power elite exercising direction of the country independent of the preferences of the masses if those masses share the preferences. Undoubtedly, many of the benefits and values of the dominant persons in the country are shared by most people. In the sphere of military defense policy, it may be argued, as it is by Pilusik: "Our concept is not that American society contains a ruling military-industrial complex, it is more nearly that American society *is* a military-industrial complex (1972, p. 132).

The belief that there is a unified power elite is related to the idea that much of the rest of the society consists of persons who have little autonomy or independent basis for participation in collective decision making. Actually, the American electorate varies considerably by class, ethnicity, region, and other characteristics. Those variations are based upon objective conditions and experiences and therefore cannot be easily manipulated (Hamilton 1972). The diversity of the electorate provides the basis for multiple alliances and hence gives varying opportunities for exercising power to different elite and sub-elite groups.

In the contemporary United States, persons very high in class ranking have considerable control over their own sphere of activity and much influence over decisions in other areas. But many organizations also have considerable autonomy in their own spheres. Furthermore, government offices provide the bases for political leaders to exercise considerable control over many domains of activity, including business, and officeholders are not entirely dependent on business interests for gaining and holding office.

As in every other aspect of equality, an assessment of its degree is best made comparatively. In the next chapter we look at some data comparing power inequality and rank consistency in different countries. Historically, in the United States the large trusts were undoubtedly more dominant around the turn of the century than they now are. During that period, someone allegedly remarked on seeing banker J. P. Morgan's yacht anchored in the Potomac, "I'm glad to see that the government has returned to Washington." That comment expressed a widely shared view of the nature of the integration of class, status, and power in the United States. The power of government has undoubtedly increased. Since World War II, the military has become another focus of power among the dominant groups. At various times in the past, during wars, the military expenditures were an equally large share of the federal budget, but never have they been so high for so long (Lieberson, 1971).

CONCLUSIONS

We have discussed the range, distribution, and mobility of power inequalities, particularly of power as manifested in political or governmental institutions. We considered variations in power inequality in the United States—both power from others for autonomy and the power over or with others to make collective decisions. For the range of autonomy, although we noted a general increase in the proportion of the people with minimal autonomy, we also saw new threats of government interference in civil liberties in recent years. We noted that previously excluded groups have been included in collective decision making, but at the same time, the concentration of political power has also increased. Those holding commanding positions today have more power than ever.

When we considered the distribution of power inequality, we discussed the variety of groups that could have some degree of autonomy over their own affairs. We also discussed the distribution of participation in collective decision making, focusing on the possible roles of groups in influencing policy decisions. The political parties and participation in them are the fundamental vehicles for exercising collective decision-making.

We then examined a number of issues relevant to the relations between power, class, and status inequalities. In considering power and class inequalities, we examined the differences in legal rights by class levels. We also examined the variations among the classes in participation in collective decision making.

Generally, we noted that persons high in class level also had more autonomy and more power in collective decision making. Persons holding positions with great authority are disproportionally recruited from families of high class origins and have had high class levels in their own careers. But there is not, by any means, an indentity of persons in the most significant class and power positions.

When we considered the relationship between power and status we discussed in particular how race and gender were related to differences in power. We noted a tendency for lower status groups to have less autonomy and a generally smaller role in collective decision making.

We also reviewed evidence about the way status and class inequalities sustain each other. We focused again on race and gender as they related to different class levels and found a clear association between lower status and lower-paid jobs. Black men seemed to be excluded from higher-paying occupations and to suffer the effects of a split labor market. Women were at a disadvantage due to their competitive situation. Taking a large number of work-related factors into account, women were still found to earn considerably less than men.

Finally, we examined the relationships among class, status, and power, focusing upon the integration of those occupying the top positions in those hierarchies. We noted the variety of conceptions about the degree and nature of that integration. We saw the considerable amount of commonalities in the personnel occupying those leading positions; much of that is based upon class position. But considerable overrepresentation of persons with high, and shared, status levels serves as a social bond. We also observed that there was probably considerable autonomy in decision making within particular spheres of activity, certainly including the military-industrial complex.

REFERENCES

ALFORD, ROBERT R. and ROGER FRIEDLAND. 1975. "Political Participation and Public Policy." Pp. 429-479 in Alex Inkeles, James Coleman, and Neil Smelser (Eds.), *Annual Review of Sociology*. Palo Alto, Calif.: Annual Reviews.

BALTZELL, E. DIGBY. 1964. *The Protestant Establishment*. New York: Random House.

BECKER, GARY S. 1971. *The Economics of Discrimination*. Chicago: University of Chicago Press.

BETZ, MICHAEL. 1974. "Riots and Welfare: Are They Related?" *Social Problems* 21 (3): 345-355.

BIDERMAN, ALBERT D. 1964. "Sequels to a Military Career: The Retired Military Professional." Pp. 287-336 in Morris Janowitz (Ed.), *The New Military*. New York: John Wiley.

BLAU, PETER M. 1964. *Exchange and Power in Social Life*. New York: John Wiley.

BONACICH, EDNA. 1976. "Advanced Capitalism and Black/White Relations in the United States: A Split Labor Market Interpretation," *American Sociological Review* 41 (February): 34-51.

BULLOCK, HENRY ALLEN. 1961. "Significance of the Racial Factor in the Length of Prison Sentences," *The Journal of Criminal Law, Criminology and Police Science* 52 (November-December):411-417.

BURMA, JOHN H. (Ed.). 1970. *Mexican-Americans in the United States: A Reader.* Cambridge, Mass.: Schenkman.

BURNHAM, JAMES. 1941. *The Managerial Revolution.* New York: John Day.

CAMPBELL, ANGUS, PHILLIP E. CONVERSE, WARREN E. MILLER, and DONALD E. STOKES. 1960. *The American Voter.* New York: John Wiley.

CARLIN, JEROME E., JAN HOWARD, and SHELDON L. MESSINGER. 1967. *Civil Justice and the Poor: Issues for Sociological Research.* New York: Russell Sage Foundation.

CHUTE, MARGARET. 1969. *The First Liberty: A History of the Right to Vote in America, 1619-1850.* New York: E. P. Dutton.

CLARK, KENNETH B., and JEANETTE HOPKINS. 1969. *A Relevant War Against Poverty.* New York: Harper and Row.

COBB, STEPHEN A. 1969. "Defense Spending and Foreign Policy in the House of Representatives," *Journal of Conflict Resolution* 13 (September):358-369.

COBB, STEPHEN. 1973. "The United States Senate and the Impact of Defense Spending Concentrations." Pp. 197-223 in Steven Rosen (Ed.), *Testing the Theory of the Military-Industrial Complex.* Lexington, Mass.: D. C. Heath.

COLEMAN, JAMES. 1957. *Community Conflict.* New York: Free Press.

DAHRENDORF, RALF. 1959. *Class and Class Conflict in Industrial Society.* Stanford, Calif.: Stanford University Press.

DECROW, KAREN. 1974. *Sexist Justice.* New York: Random House.

DE TOCQUEVILLE, ALEXIS. 1955. *Democracy in America, Vols. I. and II.* New York: Vintage Books. (Originally published in 1835 and 1840.)

DOMHOFF, G. WILLIAM. 1967. *Who Rules America?* Englewood Cliffs, N.J.: Prentice-Hall.

DOMHOFF, G. WILLIAM. 1971. *The Higher Circles.* New York: Vintage Books.

FEATHERMAN, DAVID L. and ROBERT M. HAUSER. 1976. "Sexual Inequalities and Socioeconomic Achievement in the U. S., 1962-1973," *American Sociological Review* 41 (June):462-83.

FREITAG, PETER J. 1975. "The Cabinet and Big Business: A Study of Interlocks," *Social Problems* 23 (December):137-152.

GALBRAITH, JOHN KENNETH. 1967. *The New Industrial State.* Boston: Houghton Mifflin.

GAMSON, WILLIAM A. 1975. *The Strategy of Social Protest.* Homewood, Ill.: Dorsey Press.

GLENN, NORVAL D. 1966. "White Gains from Negro Subordination," *Social Problems* 14 (Fall):159-176.

GLENN, NORVAL D. 1974. "Recent Changes in the Social and Economic Conditions of Black Americans." Pp. 447-455 in Joseph Lopreato and Lionel S. Lewis (Eds.), *Social Stratification: A Reader.* New York: Harper and Row.

GREY, CHARLES, and GLEN GREGORY. 1968. "Military Spending and Senate Voting," *Journal of Peace Research* 5(1):44-45.

GUSFIELD, JOSEPH R. 1963. *Symbolic Crusade, Status Politics and the American Temperance Movement.* Urbana, Ill.: University of Illinois Press.

HAMILTON, RICHARD F. 1972. *Class and Politics in the United States.* New York: John Wiley.

HESS, STEPHEN. 1966. *America's Political Dynasties.* Garden City, N.Y.: Doubleday.

HOBSBAUM, E. J. 1965. *Primitive Rebels: Studies in Archaic Forms of Social Movement in the 19th and 20th Centuries.* New York: W. W. Norton. (Originally published in 1959.)

HODGE, ROBERT W., and PATRICIA HODGE. 1965. "Occupational Assimilation as a Competitive Process," *American Journal of Sociology* 71 (November):249-264.

HUNTER, FLOYD. 1953. *Community Power Structure, A Study of Decision-Makers.* Chapel Hill, N.C.: University of North Carolina.

HUNTER, FLOYD. 1959. *Top Leadership, U. S. A.* Chapel Hill, N.C.: University of North Carolina.

HYMAN, HERBERT H. 1959. *Political Socialization.* Glencoe, Ill.: Free Press.

JANOWITZ, MORRIS. 1960. *The Professional Soldier: A Social and Political Portrait.* New York: Free Press.

KANTER, ARNOLD, and STEWARD J. THORSON. 1973. "The Weapons Procurement Process: Choosing Among Competing Theories." Pp. 157-196 in Steven Rosen (Ed.), *Testing the Theory of the Military-Industrial Complex.* Lexington, Mass.: D. C. Heath.

KEY, V. O., Jr. 1950. *Southern Politics in State and Nation.* New York: Knopf.

KLUEGEL, JAMES R. 1978. "The Causes and Cost of Racial Exclusion from Job Authority." *American Sociological Review* 43 (June):285-301.

KORNHAUSER, WILLIAM. 1959. *The Politics of Mass Society.* Glencoe, Ill: Free Press.

KRAMER, RALPH M. 1969. *Participation of the Poor: Case Studies on the War on Poverty.* Englewood Cliffs, N.J.: Prentice-Hall.

KRIESBERG, LOUIS. 1970. *Mothers in Poverty.* Chicago: Aldine.

KRIESBERG, LOUIS. 1973. *The Sociology of Social Conflicts.* Englewood Cliffs, N.J.: Prentice-Hall.

KURTH, JAMES R., 1971. "A Widening Gyre," *Social Policy* 19 (September): 373-404.

LIEBERSON, STANLEY. 1971. "An Empirical Study of Military-Industrial Linkages," *The American Journal of Sociology* 76 (January):562-584.

LIPSET, SEYMOUR MARTIN. 1960. *Political Man.* Garden City, N.Y.: Doubleday.

LIPSET, SEYMOUR MARTIN, and EARL RABB. 1970. *The Politics of Unreason: Right Wing Extremism in America, 1790-1970.* New York: Harper and Row.

LYND, ROBERT S., and HELEN M. LYND. 1929. *Middletown: A Study in American Culture.* New York: Oxford University Press.

MARRIS, PETER, and MARTIN REIN. 1973. *Dilemmas of Social Reform,* 2nd ed. Chicago: Aldine.

MARSHALL, T. H. 1964. *Class, Citizenship and Social Development.* Garden City, N.Y.: Doubleday.

MATTHEWS, DONALD R. 1954. *Social Background of the Political Decision-Makers.* Garden City, N.Y.: Doubleday.

MATTHEWS, DONALD R. 1960. *U. S. Senators and Their World.* Chapel Hill, N.C.: University of North Carolina.

MEIER, KENNETH JOHN. 1975. "Representative Bureaucracy: An Empirical Analysis, *The American Political Science Review* 69 (March):526-542.

MELMAN, SEYMOUR. 1970. *Pentagon Capitalism.* New York: McGraw-Hill.

MILBRATH, LESTER W. 1965. *Political Participation.* Chicago: Rand McNally.

MILLER, DELBERT. 1975. *Leadership and Power in the Bos-Wash Megalopolis.* New York: John Wiley.

MILLER, WALTER B. 1958. "Lower Class Culture as a Generating Milieu of Gang Delinquency," *The Journal of Social Issues* 14 (No. 3):5-19.

MILLS, C. WRIGHT. 1956. *The Power Elite.* New York: Oxford University Press.

MOSHER, FREDERICK C., and ORVILLE F. POLAND. 1964. *The Cost of American Governments: Facts, Trends and Myths.* New York: Dodd, Mead.

NAGLE, JOHN D. 1973. "System and Succession: A Generational Analysis of Elite Turnover in Four Nations." Unpublished paper presented at the annual meeting of the Southern Political Science Association.

PARKIN, FRANK. 1971. *Class Inequality and Political Order.* New York: Praeger.

PARSONS, TALCOTT. 1969. *Politics and Social Structure.* New York: Free Press.

PATTERSON, THOMAS E., and ROBERT D. MC CLURE. 1976. *The Unseeing Eye: The Myth of Television Power in National Elections.* New York: Putnam.

PILUSIK, MARC. 1972. *International Conflict and Social Policy.* Englewood Cliffs, N.J.: Prentice-Hall.

POMPER, GERALD. 1975. *Voters' Choice.* New York: Dodd, Mead.

REICH, MICHAEL. 1971. "The Economics of Racism." Pp. 107-113 in David M. Gordon (Ed.), *Problems in Political Economy.* Lexington, Mass.: Heath.

RIESMAN, DAVID, (in collaboration with Reuel Denny and Nathan Glazer). 1950. *The Lonely Crowd.* New Haven: Yale University Press.

ROSE, ARNOLD M. 1967. *The Power Structure.* New York: Oxford University Press.

ROSSIDES, DANIEL W. 1976. *The American Class System.* Boston: Houghton Mifflin.

RUSSETT, BRUCE. 1970. *What Price Vigilance?* New Haven: Yale University Press.

SCHERMERHORN, RICHARD A. 1961. *Society and Power.* New York: Random House.

SCHUR, EDWIN M. 1969. *Our Criminal Society.* Englewood Cliffs, N.J.: Prentice-Hall.

SHARKANSKY, IRA. 1969. *The Politics of Taxing and Spending.* New York: Bobbs-Merrill.

SHARP, GENE. 1973. *The Politics of Nonviolent Action.* Boston: Porter Sargent, Publisher.

SHEARER, LLOYD. 1976. "The Richest Men in the U. S. Senate," *Parade, Syracuse Herald American,* May 23.

SHILS, EDWARD A. 1956. *The Torment of Secrecy.* Glencoe, Ill.: Free Press.

SIEGFRIED, ANDRE. 1927. *America Comes of Age.* New York: Harcourt, Brace.

SNYDER, DAVID, and PAULA M. HUDIS. 1976. "Occupational Income and the Effects of Minority Competition and Segregation: The Re-analysis and Some New Evidence," *American Sociological Review* 41 (April):209-234.

SUTER, LARRY E., and HERMAN P. MILLER. 1973. "Income Difference Between Men and Career Women," *American Journal of Sociology* 78 (January):962-974.

SUTHERLAND, EDWIN H. 1949. *White Collar Crime.* New York: Dryden.

SWEEZY, PAUL M. 1962. *The Present as History: Essays and Reviews on Capitalism and Socialism.* New York: Monthly Review Press.

SZYMANSKI, ALBERT. 1976. "Racial Discrimination and White Gain," *American Sociological Review* 41 (June): 403-414.

TAEUBER, ALMA F., KARL E. TAEUBER, and GLEN G. CAIN. 1966. "Occupational Assimilation and the Competitive Process: A Reanalysis." *American Journal of Sociology* 72 (November):273-285.

TEN BROEK, JACOBUS, and the Editors of the California Law Review. 1966. *The Law of the Poor.* San Francisco: Chandler.

THUROW, LESTER. 1969. *Poverty and Discrimination.* Washington, D. C.: Brookings Institution.

TUCKER, ROBERT C. 1972. *The Marx-Engels Reader.* New York: W. W. Norton. *(The German Ideology* was written in 1845-46 and published in 1932.)

U. S. Bureau of the Census. 1973. Current Population Reports, Series P-20, No. 253, "Voting and Registration in the Election of November 1973. Washington, D. C.: U. S. Government Printing Office.

U. S. Bureau of the Census. 1977. Current Population Reports, Series P-60, No. 105, "Money Income in 1975 of Families and Persons in the United States." Washington, D. C.: U. S. Government Printing Office.

U. S. Senate Select Committee on Intelligence Activities. 1976. *Intelligence Activities and the Rights of Americans.* Washington, D. C.: U. S. Government Printing Office.

VERBA, SIDNEY, and NORMAN H. NIE. 1972. *Participation in America: Political Democracy and Social Equality.* New York: Harper and Row.

VIDICH, ARTHUR J., and JOSEPH BENSMAN. 1958. *Small Town in Mass Society: Class, Power and Religion in a Rural Community.* Princeton, N.J.: Princeton University Press.

WARNER, W. LLOYD, and JAMES C. ABEGGLEN. 1955. *Occupational Mobility in American Business and Industry, 1928-1952.* Minneapolis: University of Minnesota Press.

WARNER, W. LLOYD, PAUL P. VAN RIPER, NORMAN H. MARTIN, and ORVIL F. COLLINS. 1963. *The American Federal Executive.* New Haven, Conn.: Yale University Press.

WEBER, MAX. 1946. "Class, Status, and Power." Pp. 180-195 in H. J. Gert and C. Wright Mills (Eds.), *From Max Weber.* New York: Oxford University Press. (Originally published in 1921.)

WILLIAMS, CHILTON. 1960. *American Suffrage: From Property to Democracy, 1760-1860.* Princeton, N.J.: Princeton University Press.

WILSON, JAMES Q. 1971. *Varieties of Police Behavior.* New York: Atheneum. (Originally published in 1968.)

WIRT, FREDERICK M. 1976. *Power in the City.* Berkeley, Calif.: University of California Press.

WOLFGANG, MARVIN E., ARLENE KELLY, and HANS C. NOLDE. 1962. "Comparison of the Executed and the Commuted Among Admissions to Death Row," *The Journal of Criminal Law, Criminology and Police Science* 53 (September):301-311.

chapter 8

World Power Variations and Rank Consistency

If liberty is to be the attribute of living men and
not of abstract dummies invested by individualistic
liberalism, then Fascism stands for liberty, and for
the only liberty worth having, the liberty of the State
and of the individual within the State.   *Benito Mussolini*

National states are fundamentally expressions of power and are defined partly in terms of sovereign control over territories we recognize as countries. Therefore it is particularly meaningful, in speaking of the power of individuals or groups, to compare power inequalities among different nation-states. That is the first task of this chapter, but we will also examine the ways in which power, class, and status inequalities within different countries relate to each other.

In the last part of the chapter, we will consider power differences on a global basis. Governments and countries are the fundamental units constituting the world power system, and discussions of balance of power, for example, assume governments to be the basic actors; however, we will also give some attention to nongovernmental, transnational power actors, such as political parties.

COUNTRY COMPARISONS

In comparing relative power within different countries, we want to examine the reality of power inequality, not merely the formal rules describing ideal structures. Generally, it is easier to recognize how reality differs from official doctrine in other societies than to recognize that discrepancy in our own.

Governmental leaders extol their own virtues and the advantages of the political system they lead and represent. They create ideological justifications to interpret and support the political system and educational and propaganda programs inculcate support for the system among the citizens. In the contemporary world, denials of individual rights in the name of the state, as formerly expressed by fascists, are not made. Rather, justifications for political suppression are made in the name of democracy and for the benefit of the people. Leaders within each political system define democracy to fit their system, arguing that other conceptions of democracy are only subterfuges for special interests. Thus, countries that many people in the United States regard as dictatorships are regarded genuinely by their leaders as people's democracies. Leaders in countries governed by the Communist party think of their systems as fundamentally democratic because the state is organized to serve the interests of the masses of the people—the workers and peasants—not the small class of owners of the means of production.

When we compare political inequality in different countries, we cannot avoid ideological controversies, but we will try to be explicit and precise about the words and measures we use and avoid labeling political systems ideologically and contentiously.

We saw in earlier chapters that our understanding about relative rates of intergenerational occupational mobility has altered as new data are collected and research techniques change. In discussing power inequality, we will discover additional difficulties since changes in the ideological climate affect scholarly as well as public views of particular regimes. During the Cold War, for example, some developing countries allied with the United States were viewed by Americans as relatively democratic. With the decline of the Cold War and the growth of politically radical views, beliefs of Americans about political inequality in the Soviet Union and in many developing countries have altered. At the same time, the reality of political inequality in various countries has changed. In the discussion that follows we must be sensitive both to changing realities and to changing perceptions.

Variations in Power Inequality

As we saw in the last chapter, power can be unequally distributed in many ways. It varies in range, distribution, and mobility. There are differences in the level of participation in making collective decisions and in the degree of autonomy or domination over others. Evidence of these differences may be seen in variations of civil liberties, effective suffrage, political party accessibility and in numerous other ways.

These many variations in aspects of power inequality are often grouped together to form typologies of political systems. For example, we speak of regimes as being fascist, dictatorial, communist, totalitarian, liberal democratic, statist, pluralist, authoritarian, and autocratic. Some of these terms imply class or status inequality associated with power inequality. We will try to define different types of political systems solely in terms of power inequality so that we can examine the relations between power, class, and status inequalities as a separate issue.

Types. In considering power inequality, we focus on political inequality and the relations between the government and the people in a society. We describe different types of political systems and variations of each, and we look at measures of those variations that we can use to compare countries of the world.

The typologies proposed by students of political systems help us to understand their variety and suggest criteria by which to characterize political systems. Proposers of the typologies select different principles or dimensions to define and distinguish types of political systems, yet these systems often share similar characteristics and refer to the same specific cases (Eisenstadt 1971; Dahl 1963).

Almond and Powell (1966) focus on the growth and development of political systems and base their typology on the political systems' degree of structural differentiation and cultural secularization. Their typology yields three major systems: primitive systems with only intermittent political structures, traditional systems with differentiated governmental-political structures and modern systems with differentiated political infrastructures, such as political parties, interest groups, and mass communication. Modern systems are further subdivided between mobilized and premobilized systems, in terms of how extensive the secularized political structure is. In a premobilized system, most people "remain for the most part caught up in a web of traditional family and community ties" (p. 284). In mobilized systems, people are urban, literate, and exposed to differentiated economic enterprises. Almond and Powell further divide mobilized modern systems into (1) democratic systems—those with autonomous infrastructures and participant cultures and (2) authoritarian systems, which lack an autonomous infrastructure and the culture mixes patterns in which people are participants and subjects (as to a king).

Finer (1970) uses three dimensions to differentiate types of political systems: (1) the extent to which the mass of people participate in or are excluded from the government process, (2) the extent to which people obey their rulers out of fear or coercion, and (3) the extent to which the rulers reflect the actual and current values of the public or they disregard these for the sake of future values. He uses these dimensions to characterize liberal democracies, quasi-democracies, facade democracies, dynastic regimes, military regimes, and totalitarian regimes.

Blondel (1972) points out three important dimensions of political systems: means, participation, and policy goals. Means range from liberal to authoritarian, varying in the degree to which people (even the opposition groups) are free to discuss issues, to move about, to print news and opinions, and to demonstrate. Participation ranges from democracy to oligarchy, varying with the proportion of the polity making collective decisions. Finally, Blondel states that polities differ in goals, varying from radical to conservative; this is the familiar Left-Right continuum that varies in emphasizing social and economic equality. Using these three dimensions, he characterizes several major kinds of political systems: traditional conservative, liberal democratic, communist, populist, and authoritarian conservative.

These and other typologies of political systems try to encompass several aspects of the governing process. In the discussion of political systems in this book, we are interested primarily in power inequality, which we have discussed in terms of autonomy and participation. Most typologies include these two dimensions, often including references to the content of government policies and then characterizing systems as radical or conservative, Left or Right. Obviously, this is important; it is what political struggles are usually about. We will consider that later when we relate power inequality to class and status differences. But at this point we will concentrate only on variations in power inequality.

If we use the two dimensions of power inequality previously discussed, autonomy and participation, we can construct a two-dimensional space in which political systems can be located. This is done in Figure 8.1, and we have placed a few types of political systems within that space. In the upper left area are a variety of pluralist, or liberal-democratic systems. Systems with more restricted participation in collective decision making and somewhat less autonomy or freedom are authoritarian regimes. Statist regimes are even more restricted in participation and autonomy; they appear in the lower right area of Figure 8.1. We will concentrate on these three types, but two others should also be noted: populist and traditional autocratic. Populist regimes may occur in developing countries where governments seek to mobilize people for economic development and sometimes greater equality. Such regimes are rare and not long-lived; they exist during revolutionary periods when the populace participates directly in policy-making. Finally, in more traditional polities, the rule may be largely oligarchic; only a small segment of the population participate in policy-making, but large areas of social life are left outside governmental domain.

The pluralist, authoritarian, and statist types are the subject of greatest contemporary attention (Eisenstadt 1971) and will be the focus of our discussion. Note in Figure 8.1 that we have not drawn any lines separating these dimensions into categories and thus creating cells; we want to indicate that there are no clear dividing lines along these dimensions and among these types of political systems. No political system is purely statist, authoritarian, or pluralistic; each system blends many elements and has unique features.

Pluralistic, authoritarian, and statist political systems can be understood

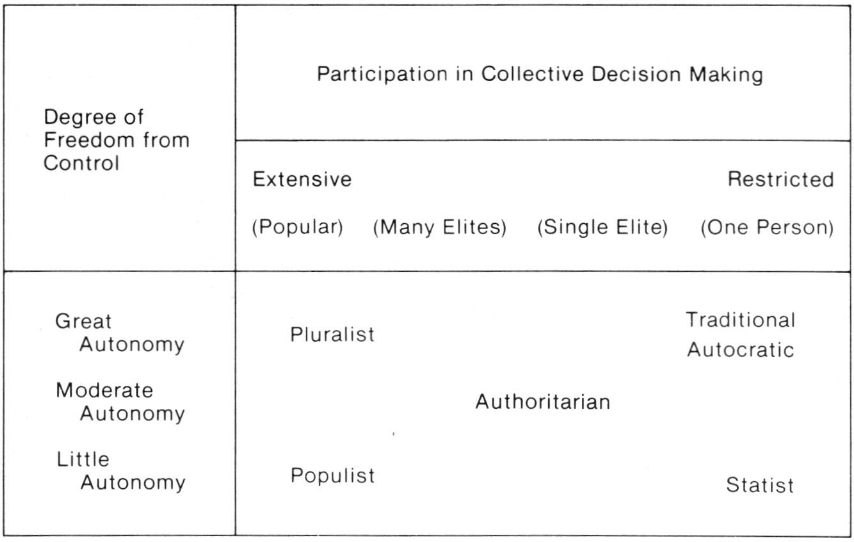

Degree of Freedom from Control	Participation in Collective Decision Making			
	Extensive			Restricted
	(Popular)	(Many Elites)	(Single Elite)	(One Person)
Great Autonomy	Pluralist			Traditional Autocratic
Moderate Autonomy			Authoritarian	
Little Autonomy	Populist			Statist

FIGURE 8.1   *Types of political regimes*

only relative to each other, not in absolute terms. Political systems are generally regarded as pluralistic or liberal democracies if they provide institutionalized opportunities to peacefully compete for political power and do not exclude any significant sector by force. For competition to be effective, civil liberties are essential and therefore are included in the characterization of liberal democracies or pluralist systems.

Statist systems are governed by a single mass party with an explicit, official ideology. The government exercises much domination (as in classical tyranny) and is not limited by laws, although many of its repressive actions are covered by law. The ruling party controls the mass media, the military, and sometimes uses systematic police terror (Kornhauser 1959; Friedrich 1954).

Authoritarian systems do not include autonomous, competing power groups but neither does the ruling government attempt complete domination of the polity. "Authoritarian regimes are political systems with limited, not responsible, political pluralism: without elaborate and guiding ideology . . . without intensive or extensive political mobilization . . . and in which a leader (or small group) exercises power within formally ill-defined limits but actually quite predictable ones" (Linz 1971, p. 522).

Actual political systems do not clearly and fully embody the characteristics of any single type; each is mixed and changes over time. We will briefly describe some political systems or polities in terms of the dimensions of power inequality we have outlined. As we are using the terms, the United States, Great Britain, Canada, France, and Chile (before the overthrow of Allende in 1973) tend to be pluralist. Statist regimes include Nazi Germany and the USSR, Poland and the German Democratic Republic (East Germany) at some period in their histories. Most countries of the world have some kind of authoritarian regime. This includes countries as diverse as Spain, Iran, Jordan, Libya, Kenya, Uganda, Brazil, and Paraguay.

We will first discuss Great Britain as an example of a pluralist society, then discuss a few authoritarian regimes, and finally discuss the Soviet Union as an example of a regime that has been varingly statist. As we examine indicators of power inequality and the relations between class, status, and power, we will consider additional countries.

England holds a unique world historical position. It was the country where many aspects of liberal democracy developed; it was also instrumental in spreading the system in the course of building the British Empire—for example, through settlements in Canada and Australia and through British rule in Jamaica and India. Although England's role helps to account for variations in political equality among the countries in the world, at this point we will consider only power inequality within the contemporary United Kingdom itself.

Within recent decades people in Great Britain had an unusual degree of privacy and personal autonomy. Although lacking a written constitution, the government is constrained by widely shared and firm convictions that civil liberties are to be protected from government intrusion. Those constraints can

be found in the Common Law, statutes of Parliament, and judicial pronouncements (Finer 1970, p. 46). The powers of government are limited both from
intruding on individual and group autonomy and in restricting the opportunities
for participation in making collective decisions.

Freedom of speech and freedom of assembly are widely practiced and
governmentally protected. There is a generally shared consensus that does not
seem to depend upon coercion, and neither the government nor any particular
group uses coercion to intimidate people into obedience. Having that liberty,
people with shared concerns readily form associations to promote their preferences and interests. Voluntary associations are prominent in influencing government policy and themselves carry out actions to realize their members' interests.

Popular participation in collective decision making takes place largely
through the two major political parties—the Labour and the Conservative parties
—and a small third one, the Liberal party. The system is a parliamentary one:
The party that wins a majority of the votes in Parliament forms the government
and the leader of the party heads the government as Prime Minister. Members
of Parliament are elected by a majority vote in each electoral district, but the
district in which they run (or stand, in British parlance) is largely determined
by the political parties. One form of popular participation in collective decision
making is through influencing party policies; this is often done through membership in voluntary associations. The close relationship between the Labour party
and the British trade unions is the most salient example of this. The other form
of mass participation is through the electoral process. Elections are held when
the government does not sustain a Parliamentary majority or upon the Government's choice, as long as it faces the voters within five years of the preceding
election. The elections are conducted without fraud, manipulation, or coercion.
Electoral participation is relatively high (see Table 8.1).

Next, we turn to consider examples of more authoritarian regimes.
Authoritarian systems vary greatly in the extent of popular participation in
collective decision making and in individual and group freedom from control by
others, including government officials. Any attempt to categorize any given
polity leads to controversy. We acknowledge that and proceed to select three
examples. We will briefly describe political inequality in Mexico, Kenya, and
Chile, not as "typical" authoritarian states, but as illustrations of some of the
variety.

Mexico is governed by the Partido Revolucionario Institutional (PRI)
(Scott 1959; Finer 1970). The revolution whose institutionalization the party
represents began in 1910 with the overthrow of President Porfirio Diaz's centralized and extremely authoritarian regime. After a decade of turmoil and
violence, a stable political system gradually emerged. That system is built upon
the dominance of the PRI and a president, who is elected for six years and
cannot be re-elected. Opposition parties sometimes spring into existence at
presidential election times. The only continuously existing opposition party of
significance is the right-wing Partido Accion Nacional (PAN).

TABLE 8.1   Indicators of Political Equality by Country 1965

Country	Indicator			
	Percent Population Voted	**Percent Electorate Voted**	**Electoral Irregularity**	**Press Freedom**
Algeria	–	85.0	1	– 326
Australia	–	95.7	3	253
Bolivia	–	70.0	2	239
Brazil	44.2	–	2	125
Canada	–	83.0	3	272
Chad	–	95.4	–	– 272
Chile	54.1	77.8	3	119
Columbia	–	86.9	2	221
Cuba	–	–	–	– 302
Czechoslovakia	–	99.4	1	– 251
Egypt	–	98.5	1	– 232
France	66.5	80.0	3	192
German Democratic Republic	92.1	99.2	1	– 320
Germany, Federal Republic of	77.6	86.8	3	243
Ghana	–	–	1	34
Greece	–	–	3	137
India	55.8	–	3	98
Indonesia	–	–	3	– 40
Iran	–	66.7	2	– 103
Iraq	–	–	–	– 136
Israel	84.1	79.1	3	175
Italy	89.2	92.9	3	198
Ivory Coast	–	99.6	1	
Jamaica	46.6	72.9	3	216
Japan	72.3	71.1	3	244
Kenya	–	69.3	2	120
Lebanon	–	53.4	3	118
Mexico	49.8	54.1	3	146
Morocco	–	73.0	2	100
Pakistan	–	37.7	3	– 2
Peru	–	87.6	3	276
Poland	–	96.6	1	– 254
Tanzania	–	78.1	2	87
United Kingdom	72.4	77.1	3	237
United States	56.8	58.7	3	272
USSR	97.7	99.9	1	– 308
Yugoslavia	–	90.9	–	8

Source: Prepared from Taylor and Hudson 1971 data.

Popular participation in decision making, insofar as it occurs, is largely through interest groups operating within the PRI. Party membership is grouped into three sections: the agricultural sector, the industrial worker sector, and the

229

"popular" sector. Peasant and farmer associations belong to the first; trade unions, to the second; other occupational and civic associations, to the third. These sectors are represented in regional and municipal committees. The party has a pyramidical structure with the executive committee having firm control over nominations at each level.

Business interests, although not formally included in this party structure, have great informal influence. The participation of workers and peasants in the party and government is currently viewed by some observers as co-optation, in that persons drawn from worker and peasant occupations and organizations do serve in high party and governmental office, but they have little power. Rather, granting the appearance of participation is a way of maintaining popular support (Hansen 1971; Nagle 1977). At times in the past, most notably during the presidency of Cardenas (1934-40), workers and peasants participated to a greater degree.

The nomination for the powerful position of president has become the perogative of the outgoing president. He weighs the balance of forces among the factions in the party and is careful to select a candidate who will be acceptable to all factions. Once the president announces his choice, the party members swiftly come to support that selection. The patronage controlled by the party and the lack of effective opposition make it reasonable to support the party's choice.

The election itself is not a major vehicle for political participation in collective decision making. The campaign gives people an opportunity to express personal grievances and obtain services from the government as the presidential candidate travels about the country to gather support and make himself available for those very services. The elections have sometimes been marked by irregularities favoring the election of PRI candidates, but there is also widespread support for the party and the revolution it represents.

The constitutional prohibition against presidential re-elections produces a relatively high rate of mobility in political office. Nagle (1973) has compared the turnover rate of Mexican cabinet members, senators, and deputies with those in the United States, West Germany, and the Soviet Union. He found the highest turnover rate in the Mexican system.

Civil liberties and freedom from governmental control exist, but within significant limits. Coercion is not extensive, yet violence by the government against student demonstrators in the recent past, for example, has been severe. Although people have the right and the opportunity to meet, discuss, and assert demands, they actually use these opportunities less than do those in pluralistic liberal democracies. When effective opposition begins to appear, the government may resort to repression. Voluntary associations, as noted above, are an important channel for representation within Mexico's one-party system, but participation in voluntary associations is relatively low. For example, Almond and Verba (1963, pp. 302-320) found that over half of the adults in the United States and almost half in Great Britain belonged to voluntary associations; only a quarter of those in Mexico do. A third of the United States adults and 16 percent of the British belonged to more than one voluntary association; only 2 percent of the Mexicans do.[1]

Kenya's political system emerged from a different set of circumstances. Kenya gained its independence from Great Britain in 1963. Unlike the colonies of West Africa, East African Kenya had a large British settlement. In the 1940s a movement, called the Mau Mau, began to seek independence, and after some terrorist attacks in 1952, the British forces mounted a drive to wipe out the movement, killing several thousand Africans. The Kikuyu, the dominant ethnic group of Kenya, were particularly active in the Mau Mau movement. Jomo Kenyatta was convicted of leading the movement and jailed; after independence he became President of Kenya and remained so until his death in 1978. Kenyatta, unlike many other leaders of new nations did not come into power as the leader of an organization he had forged. He had been in prison from 1953 to 1961, the years in which the political parties had formed. His role had been one almost above parties, negotiating among factions.

The dominant party is the Kenya African National Party (KANJ). The party has been subject to considerable splits, as well as unions with other parties. Popular electoral participation has been high, about 85 percent of the electorate voting in the general elections of 1963 (Bienen 1974, p. 90). But participation has fallen greatly and become low. There is some irregularity in the electoral processes. Much of the effective power and control that exists is exercised through the civil service.

In general, power is fragmented and the autonomy and independence of persons and groups in part derives from that fragmentation. "A great deal of political life still goes on outside the reach of central rulers. Nor can a ruling personal clique extend its client system in such a way that power flows from the top to all the nooks and crannies. . . . Despite the rhetoric of need for social mobilization and economic development, there is no evidence that Kenya's rulers think they can yield total power" (Bienen 1974, p. 117-118). Voluntary associations, such as the trade unions, have some autonomy. There is general support for the regime and widespread coercion is not depended upon by the rulers. But coercion and intimidation is sometimes exercised against challenging individuals and groups. This marks the limits to civil liberties.

Brazil has a history of several different kinds of political regimes (Horowitz 1964; Lewis 1975). Vargas dominated Brazilian politics as a quasi populist dictator from 1930 to 1945. Relatively free democratic elections were held for two decades, although fraud was not unusual and the electorate was limited. The governments pursued policies that were populist in appeal; there was high inflation and considerable economic growth. In 1964, the military seized control of the government and imposed a strong dictatorship and a severe economic

---

[1] In the surveys from which these data were drawn, national samples were used in the United States and Great Britain; only residents in cities of 10,000 or more population were interviewed in Mexico. A sample of the entire country would yield even smaller proportions in voluntary associations.

austerity program. The military leaders have since increased their control over the political system.

In 1965, the ruling military group dissolved all political parties, then gave legal recognition only to those sponsored by the 120 federal deputies and 20 senators. As a result, a two-party system emerged: the Renovating National Alliance (ARENA), a progovernment party, and the Brazilian Democratic Movement (MDB), an antigovernment coalition. The military instituted indirect election of the president through the congress. Free elections do not exist, since opposition candidates are harassed by the government. The MDB boycotted the 1966 gubernatorial and presidential elections. In the contest for congressional seats, about 20 percent of the electorate failed to vote, 20 percent turned in blank ballots to protest the election, and about 25 percent voted for the opposition (Lewis 1975, pp. 156-57).

Voluntary associations are under severe government control: the trade union leadership has been purged; student organizations are regulated and prohibited from political activity. Still, despite repressive measures, some agitation against the government persists. Personal and group autonomy exist in some nonpolitical spheres, but collective decision making is subverted through widespread reliance on coercion. Police use torture and urban guerrillas use terrorism.

The authoritarian systems of Mexico, Kenya, and Brazil, briefly described, differ considerably in political inequality. They also differ in the relationship between power and class and status inequalities, as we shall see later. In all, however, private spheres of activity and some autonomous activity exist. In statist regimes, such autonomy is less. We will briefly describe the Soviet Union as an example of such a regime.

The Bolshevik Revolution of 1917 led to a great transformation of Russia. The remnants of feudalism and the newly emerging capitalist aspects of the society were largely destroyed. In their place a state-planned and directed economy has been created. The basic mechanism through which collective decisions are made is the Communist Party of the Soviet Union (CPSU).

As explained in Pravda, ". . . only the Communist party, comprising the most conscious and active people from the working class, the peasantry and the intelligentsia, only the party, exerting effectual influence on all forms of public activity and on the work of state and mass organizations, is capable of correctly utilizing all forces and opportunities to strengthen and develop a socialist society and to advance it to communism" (Pomelov 1967).[2]

---

[2] The words socialist and communist, to characterize societies, are used differently by Soviet and American writers. In the United States and in most non-Communist countries, communist refers to countries that are governed by Communist parties. Socialist refers to countries that are governed by socialist, social democratic, or labor parties or that are characterized by a highly developed social welfare state. In the USSR and in other countries governed by a Communist party, communist refers to a yet-to-be-realized society that fulfills the Marxist-Leninist expectations of a society in which each person gives what she or he can and receives what he or she needs. Socialist refers to societies in which capitalism has been overthrown and efforts are being made to bring the society to communism. The so-called social-democratic countries of Western Europe are regarded as capitalist countries along with all others not led by Communist parties.

Power inequality, even in and through the CPSU, has varied. During most of Stalin's administration, he was able to exercise one-man domination of the party and the state. That domination was associated with and partly depended on extensive coercion (Medvedev 1972). The secret police, forced-labor camps, and purges imposed positive loyalty to Stalin. That regime has been categorized as totalitarian. Since Stalin's death in 1953, the Soviet Union has become much less totalitarian and presently might be more accurately called bureaucratic authoritarian or bureaucratic elitist (Lane 1976).

The present locus of power in the Soviet Union is the collective leadership of the Politburo of the CPSU (Lane 1971a). The members of the Politburo work as a colleagual group and make decisions that are generally binding for the party and the government. Formally, the Central Committee (a larger body than the Politburo) has authority extending over the Politburo. Khrushchev, when out-voted in the Politburo in 1957, went to the Central Committee to sustain himself in office. But in 1964 he was voted out of office by the Politburo and, lacking support in the Central Committee, was toppled. On the whole, the Politburo has had very low levels of mobility, compared to the leading offices in the United States, West Germany, or Mexico (Nagle 1973). Personnel turnover in the Central Committee is not, however, equally low.

The CPSU does not have total domination of the society. People have interests based on their occupations, industrial sphere, ethnicity, and area of residence, and they seek to promote their particular concerns. The meshing and coordination of these interests occurs through government ministeries but ultimately in the Politburo. Although coercion exists, decisions depend on the workings of rewards and persuasion within a bureaucratic setting.

The Soviet people are urged and sometimes required to actively support the policies and directives of the party and the government. Participation in making those policies is through recruitment into leadership positions and through informal influence. There are no competitive elections nor open lobbying by interest groups. Interest groups participate in decision making through presenting information and informally making their case to government and party officials (McLennan 1975).

Of particular importance within the Soviet political system is the role of the official creed of Marxism-Leninism. This, as authoritatively interpreted by the leadership, provides a means for evaluating and, hence, controlling nearly all aspects of social life. Associational and intellectual activity are conducted within the confines of this creed. Some underground opposition does exist, but it is limited to a few people. Although the massive terrorism of Stalin's dictatorship has been ended, considerable reliance on coercion remains. Nevertheless, widespread popular support for the government and the policies it pursues probably exists (Barghoorn 1965).

Although we have considered a wide variety of systems of power inequality, we have omitted other kinds of political regimes. We have not discussed traditional autocratic regimes that make limited efforts at mobilizing all the people to participate in the governmental process, for example, Saudi

Arabia, Haiti, or Iran. We have not considered regimes that make few demands upon the populace and provide few services to them. We have not examined newly revolutionary regimes seeking to involve the masses in the transformation of the society, but without totalitarian control, as was happening in Chile before the military takeover of power in 1973. Only a few ways in which various elements of power inequality fit together in specific polities have been illustrated. The configuration of political inequalities in each country is unique.

Dimensions. We can think of many dimensions of power inequality and compare those dimensions among several countries, disregarding the context within each country. We will look at indicators of political inequality in different countries so we can more readily test different explanations of those inequalities. The data are largely from 1965, because information for that year is readily available on computer tape, and many investigators have used it in testing explanations of varying inequality. We will review these studies later, and it will be useful to be familiar with the data.

We will consider four indicators of political equality: (1) proportion of the population voting in the previous election, (2) proportion of the electorate voting, (3) competitiveness of electoral procedures, and (4) freedom of the press. The first indicator refers to the proportion of the total population aged twenty years or over who voted in the most recent elections of the national assembly, parliament, or congress, or of a national executive. The second indicator refers to the proportion of eligible and registered adults who voted in the most recent national elections. A small proportion of the population voting presumably indicates lack of participation in collective decision-making, but voting rates must be viewed in conjunction with the openness of the election. A 100-percent turnout for a single party may indicate a totalitarian insistence on involvement and support. A low turnout and rigged elections may indicate an authoritarian or traditional autocratic regime.

We can assign each country an electoral irregularity score. Taylor and Hudson (1971) used parliamentary journals, news indexes, and country sources to develop such a score. They classified each country as having elections that (1) were rigged, (2) had substantial irregularities, or (3) were competitive or reasonably free. To be classified as having free elections a country must have "an independent judiciary; an honest, non-partisan machinery for running the election; a developed party system; and a general acceptance of the 'rules of the game' which place limits on the struggle for power" (Taylor and Hudson 1970, p. 115).

The Press Freedom Index was created by the School of Journalism, University of Missouri, to "measure the independence of a nation's broadcasting and press system and its ability to criticize its own local and national governments. The index is comprised of the judgments of panels of native and foreign newsmen on 23 aspects of the press (e.g., extent of legal controls, licensing, government ownership, criteria and censorship). . . . The index, which consists of averages of the judges' scores, has a range from -4.00 for less freedom to +4.00 for more" (Taylor and Hudson 1970, pp. 116-117).

The value for each indicator for selected countries is presented in Table 8.1. These indicators, of course, are not independent of each other. The proportion of the adult population and the proportion of the electorate voting are highly related (the correlation is .765) for all the countries for which the data exists (N = 47). But the discrepancy is also revealing. In some countries the number of people who are eligible is restricted. For example, in Chile only persons who are over the age of 21 and pass a literacy test can vote. This accounts for about 80 percent of the adult population (McLennan 1975, p. 152).

Press freedom and electoral regularity are highly related to each other among the countries for which we have data (correlation = .795 among the 73 countries with data). This reflects, in part, the scoring of countries governed by the Communist party as not having free elections and not having a free press. The Communist countries also partly account for the negative relationship between electoral participation and both press freedom and electoral competitiveness. Participation by the population in elections in countries governed by the Communist party is very close to 100 percent. This reflects their totalitarian insistence on active participation in support of the ruling party and government.

The data in Table 8.1 also reveal some interesting variations. Even among polities led by the Communist party, the degree of freedom of the press differs, as assessed by the judges. Thus, among the Communist countries in the table, the German Democratic Republic had a score of -320 while Czechoslovakia had a score of -251. Among countries with a competitive electoral system, there is a large range in Press Freedom Index scores given by the judges. Thus, Peru scores 276 and Canada and the United States scored 272, while Pakistan received a score of -2 and Indonesia, -40.

Each of these indicators has serious limitations and political leaders would not agree about their validity. But if we keep in mind what they measure, we will find them useful for particular purposes. Better measures of popular participation in collective decision making in many of these areas would be desirable, but they would be difficult to develop. For example, much participation in collective decision making takes place outside the electoral process through pressure groups and informal influence within and among political party factions. But it is difficult to assess and measure in any comparable way varying degrees of popular participation through these mechanisms.

Measures of personal and group autonomy present additional problems. It is difficult to assess logically degrees of group or even individual autonomy when the demands for it within different polities vary greatly. For example, some polities are ethnically homogeneous, others have several ethnic minorities of substantial size, still other countries are divided between a majority and a few small minority groups. Language or cultural tolerance for groups in those different circumstances would have different meanings. Measures of personal safety from governmental intrusion may be conceptually clearer, but data on political arrests and official repression are obviously difficult to attain. Measures of civil rights actually adhered to and the freedom of movement within a country as well as the freedom to leave would also be desirable.

Freedom House, an American organization working in the area of democratic institutions, assesses the level of civil and political rights in the countries of the world. Raymond D. Gastil (1976), who directs the assessment, uses a seven-point scale to rate the relative freedom of countries. He describes the political rights scores as follows:

> States ranking (1) for political rights have an operative electoral system in which the elected have a near monopoly on political power. . . . A state in rank (2) has an operating system with partial deficiencies such as outside control . . . high illiteracy making elections less meaningful, or restrictions on civil rights . . . that impede a fair presentation of issues in campaigns. States in ranks (3) and (4) generally have elections, but the electorate is restricted (as in South Africa), the political parties are restricted (as in Mexico), or those elected have limited powers. . . . States in rank (5) have a variety of mixes of freedom and tyranny. They may have only one party, but considerable dispute within the party; or no elections and yet persisting political parties (as in Mexico). Elections may be closely controlled; or the resulting parliament restricted as in Indonesia, . . . Spain, and Paraguay; or the present ruler may have been elected in the recent past, although most democratic forms have subsequently been annulled or restricted as in Uruguay, the Philippines, or South Korea.

> Nations at ranks (6) and (7) for political rights are dictatorships. Yet at level (6) there are political ways to expression through controlled voting as in Jordan and Yugoslavia, among varied groups, as in Nigeria or Bolivia. A state may be ruled (6) because of an assumed consensus from tradition, as in Iran. . . . At rank (7) are found states in which an individual or group has used force to set itself up as a tyrant. Governments such as that in Albania or Uganda monopolize all political power, and ruthlessly use it to maintain that power (pp. 12, 14).

The meaning of the civil rights ranking is described as follows:

> At rank (1) there is a free press and rule of law, and few persons walk in fear of expressing their opinions, while at rank (2) . . . violence or lack of adequate news media or occasional censorship are found. At rank (3) these latter factors are more prominant; for example, in Turkey or Portugal violence and suppression has been sufficient at times to silence an important range of opinion. States at rank (4) are characterized by the assumption that certain ideas cannot be expressed in public, by the occasional jailing of political opponents for their views, and by the frequent use of security forces to suppress dissidence. . . . At level (5) we expect to find struggling news media: Reporters are regularly faced with censorship or even jail. In spite of fear, argument and political organization go on, and churches maintain their right to criticize, as in Chile, Paraguay, and Rhodesia . . . people are often jailed for political reasons. . . . States

TABLE 8.2 Political Rights and Civil Rights Rank Scores for Selected Countries

Country	Political Rights	Civil Rights
Algeria	7	6
Australia	1	1
Bolivia	6	5
Brazil	4	5
Canada	1	1
Chad	7	6
Chile	7	5
Colombia	2	3
Cuba	7	7
Czechoslovakia	7	6
Egypt	6	4
France	1	2
German Democratic Republic	7	7
Germany, Federal Republic of	1	1
Ghana	7	5
Greece	2	2
India	2	5
Indonesia	5	5
Iran	6	6
Iraq	7	7
Israel	2	3
Italy	1	2
Ivory Coast	6	5
Jamaica	1	2
Japan	2	1
Kenya	5	5
Lebanon	4	4
Mexico	4	3
Morocco	5	5
Pakistan	5	5
Peru	6	4
Poland	6	6
Tanzania	6	6
USSR	7	6
United Kingdom	1	1
United States	1	1
Yugoslavia	6	6

Source: Gastil 1976, p. 15.

ranked (6) in civil rights do not have independent judicial systems nor an independent press . . . at level (6) there is still some open talk, especially among close groups of acquaintances or with foreigners, and carefully disguised underground as well as foreign, literature may exist, as do traditional blocking institutions (such as the religious establishment in Libya). In level (7) states we hear little of opposition, for opposition voices are simply not raised (p. 14).

Table 8.2 presents the political and civil rights scores for selected countries. The political rights score is similar to the electoral irregularity score in Table 8.1. Some discrepancies are due to changes within the countries between 1965 and 1975, for example, Chile. Interestingly, among all the countries in the world, more score relatively high on denial of civil rights than on denial of political rights, for example, thirty countries score 7 on political rights and twenty score 7 on civil rights. These scores, it should be recalled, would be rejected as ideological and wrong by the leaders of many of the countries described.

Power inequality has many dimensions and aspects. No single measure can capture them all. We have considered how some aspects are related to others in statist, authoritarian, and pluralist regimes and also discussed how a large number of countries are scored on a few indicators of political inequality. Next we consider how power inequalities relate to class and status inequalities.

Power and Class Inequalities

Being powerless—that is, not being able to participate in making decisions affecting the entire polity or lacking control over one's personal or group life—is a deprivation. But it might be compensated for by other benefits: by relative economic well-being, by relatively high status ranking, or by other ways, such as glory or power for the collectivity with which one identifies. People may feel that sacrificing individual power is worth these other gains. Often, however, those who are relatively powerless are also relatively low in class and status ranks and benefit little from the assumed power of the polity as a whole. In this section we look at some of the ways power inequality is actually related to class and status inequality in different countries.

The relations between power and class inequalities provide a basis for comparing countries in terms of the Right-Left, reactionary-progressive, or conservative-liberal distinctions. Such designations may refer only to the class origins and standing of the government officeholder or to the whole range of policies pursued by the government. In the first case, officeholders who administer and control the state may be largely persons of upper-class background and experience or they may be representative of the society as a whole. In the second case, what is pertinent is whose class interests are served by the state: do the rules, programs, and policies advance the interests of the industrial skilled workers, the farmers, or the owners and managers of the large corporations?

In this chapter we examine the extent to which places in the class structure are related to ranks in the power hierarchy and we consider the class nature of the political process and the roles occupied by persons of different class strata. We focus on power inequality in making collective decisions.

Pluralist polities. We examine pluralist regimes within industrially developed market economies. In the *Communist Manifesto* of 1848, Marx and Engels (1932) asserted what they believed to be the relations between class and power in capitalist countries: "The executive of the modern state is but a committee for managing the common affairs of the whole bourgeoisie." That assertion is not only a description of the close relationship between the controllers of the state and the owners of the means of production, but an assertion of the dominance of one by the other.

Before proceeding to the evidence, we should note that the state and the government are not the same thing. As Miliband (1969, p. 49) writes, "It is not very surprising that government and state should often appear as synonymous, for it is the government which speaks on the state's behalf." The state consists not only of the government, but also of the bureaucracy of the state and of regulatory agencies, central banks, and other such elements. The state also includes the military and paramilitary elements as well as the judiciary. We need to see how each and all of these elements are related to class ranking.

The control over the government is certainly important in understanding control over the state, even if it is not the same thing. Industrially developed, capitalist societies generally have governments that are chosen through free, competitive elections. The governments are formed by the leadership of political parties. The parties' policies and the class character of the parties' support, then, are critical in the formation of governments.

The political parties in such countries vary in the degree to which they are based upon class. Parties can appeal to people for support in terms of status issues such as ethnicity. They can also appeal for and garner support on the basis of issues that are not stratified, for example, those related to regional differences within a country. Many studies have been made of the electoral support for different parties in countries of the world (Lipset and Rokkan, 1967).

Alford (1963) compared the degree of class voting in four Anglo-American countries: Australia, Canada, Great Britain, and the United States. He found a much higher degree of correspondence between class strata and support for the "Left" party in Great Britain and Australia than in the United States or Canada. In both Great Britain and Australia there are Labour parties, closely tied to the trade union movement. In the United States, it is true, the Democratic party is popularly seen as representing the interests of the workers and the Republican party is generally viewed as representing the interests of the rich and of the business people (Bailey 1959). But both parties make broad appeals on many nonclass issues. This is even more true in the case of Canada.

Throughout the world working-class voters generally tend to support left-wing parties (Lipset 1960). Parties which favor more equalitarian economic and welfare policies are usually designated as Left and those which oppose such policies as Right. In some countries, the parties of the Left are socialist in the sense that they favor at least comprehensive welfare programs and some state ownership of industry. In many countries of Western Europe, such parties have won elections and formed socialist governments that have remained in power for many years; Sweden, for example, had a socialist government for forty-four years, until it was defeated in the 1976 elections.

The formation of a government by a socialist or labor party often results in persons with working-class background and experience entering into the highest government offices. This may be seen, for example, by comparing the class origins of cabinet members in British Labour governments and Conservative governments. When the Labour party came to power after World War II, it included no aristocrats (unlike preceding governments), and twelve out of twenty members were of the working class. When the Conservatives returned to power in 1951, five of the sixteen cabinet members were aristocrats; none were of the working class (Guttsman 1965, p. 78). As shown in the previous chapter, differences in social origins between Republican and Democratic government officeholders in the United States are very small compared to the more class-based parties of Great Britain. The existence of the Labour party in Great Britain also helps account for the less disproportionate representation of legislators from professional backgrounds in the United Kingdom compared to the United States (see Table 8.3).

Even with working class representation in the top governmental positions, other elite positions of the state can, and usually do, continue to be occupied by upper-middle and upper class persons. This is the case for the higher civil servants, the military, and the judiciary elites. Miliband writes, ". . . in terms of social origin, education, and class situations, the men who have manned *all* command positions in the state system have largely, and in many cases overwhelmingly, been drawn from the world of business and property, or from the professional middle class" (1969, p. 66).[3]

The sphere of influence exercised by different classes is also significant if we are to understand class and power relations. Business leaders need not administer the state to have commanding control. Generally, the control of the managers and dominant owners of large corporations over vast economic resources gives them access to the highest levels of government; even heads of socialist or leftist governments seek to maintain the confidence of the business leaders. Added weight is given to maintaining that confidence because of the international character of modern business.

The business leaders in one country can mobilize support from colleagues abroad, particularly through the major international banks, the multinational corporations, and through international organizations such as the World Bank and the International Monetary Fund. This is particularly telling in countries with significant foreign investments. Workers, through the trade unions, generally do not have the resources to be as influential. They also lack unity,

[3]Meier (1975) has compared the representativeness of the high levels of civil service in the United States, United Kingdom, Denmark, France, Turkey, and India. The civil service in the United States is most representative of the country as a whole, the United Kingdom next. India and Turkey have the least representative higher civil servants.

TABLE 8.3   Class Background and Sex of Legislators in Selected Countries (in Percent)

Country	Class Background					Women	Year of Information
	Professional	Business Managers	Other White-Collar	Farmers	Manual Workers		
Canada	56	25	6	12	–	1	1963
Chile	51	30	9	5	5	6	1969
Columbia	66	20	10	–	–	6	1970
Egypt	14	12	13	18	32	1	1969
Finland	15	16	34	21	8	17	1970
France	26	30	26	6	3	2	1968
Germany, West	21	21	22	11	6		1961
Ghana	30	19	30	8	2	1	1969
India	27	11	32	27	1	6	1969
Italy	28	20	37	1	10	3	1968
Lebanon	45	38	15	–	–	NA	1968
Poland	6	5	54	15	17	14	1969
Turkey	41	23	24	7	–	1	1965
USSR	–	6	44	19	27	31	1965
United Kingdom	23	23	34	7	8	4	1970
United States	51	22	11	10	1	3	1968
Yugoslavia	2	53	37	1	1	13	1969

Source: Blondel 1973, Appendix C, pp. 160-162.

being divided ideologically between Christian, communist, and socialist ideologies in many countries. Nevertheless, in societies with pluralist political systems, no one elite, not even the business elite, is dominant. Hewitt (1974) studied a wide variety of issues acted upon by British governments since the end of World War II. He did not find that the decisions coincided with the positions of any single interest group.

Authoritarian polities. When considering whether class inequalities are highly related to power inequalities in authoritarian countries, particularly industrially developing ones, it is important to keep in mind that many developing economies, as discussed in Chapter 4, are dependent on the advanced industrial countries. Business leaders of the dependent or peripheral country are often closely connected with business leaders from the dominant countries. Dependency often involves ties between the business leaders from the dominant country with the political leaders of the economically dependent country. The state can and often does play a critical role either in facilitating or working against external involvements; it may be more or less economically nationalist.

In some states those who rule are closely related to the economically dominant group and the incumbents of government offices are drawn from the same stratum as the economic elite (see Table 8.3). These are generally conservative regimes. Other states may be more open to a variety of class interests, following a more centrist policy and being more open to participation from many classes. Socialist or Leftist states may try to exclude private business elites from participating in decision making and seek support from worker and peasant organizations. These different kinds of states can be governed by particular elite groups, such as the military, political leaders drawn from a closely knit ideological party, or pragmatic political bosses.

A social revolution or a struggle for national liberation may seem to sweep away the previous ruling class and replace it with new leaders drawn from previously unrepresented classes: often the poor workers or peasants. Yet, in most cases, the changes are less sweeping or less enduring than they appear at first. For example, the Mexican Revolution of 1910 did greatly weaken the dominance of the great landowners and the church, business, and government. It opened opportunities for leaders of armies, sometimes coming from peasant backgrounds. But as the revolution has become institutionalized, the persons holding high government positions have tended to be from middle class and upper class backgrounds and often are themselves rich.

Nagle (1977, pp. 170-173) examined the primary occupations of Mexican deputies, senators, governors, and cabinet members in the six presidential administrations since 1940. He found that in the politically powerful positions of governor and minister, representation of workers and employees has decreased, but in the more purely symbolic positions of deputies and senators, the representation of workers and other employees has increased slightly. Military representation has decreased in all positions. Nagle concludes that effective political control has been increasingly monopolized by the upper social strata while individuals have been increasingly co-opted from the wage-working classes to help legitimatize the regime.

On the whole, "Mexico's present-day upper class is not so monolithic as it was in prerevolutionary days when social, economic, and political power resided in a single group" (Scott 1959, pp. 84-85). The business elite and the political elite overlap, but they do not coincide, and they do not coincide more fully because of the changes wrought by the revolution. The political power of the old ruling group was broken and even the source of some of their wealth—the land—was taken away. But they were able to use their resources in the newly developing economic activities: banking, commerce, and industry. So they created an autonomous base. Yet, the political leaders could not, even if they wanted to, simply enter into a complete identification with the new business elite. They are dependent on organized and aroused workers, peasants, and lower middle class groups. "Politically ineffectual the Mexican masses may be, but they are sufficiently aware and overwhelmingly numerous enough to preclude any hope of success in a complete sell-out of their interests to the commercial-industrial-banking economic power-elite" (Scott 1959, p. 86).

As previously noted, some Mexican interest groups, especially the workers and peasants, are directly represented within the ruling party, the PRI. Business organizations and interests exert their considerable influences on government decision making by (1) their representation on government boards and commissions that affect their interests, (2) their petitioning about proposed legislation, and (3) their informal consultation with government agencies that submit proposed legislation to interested groups (Lewis 1975, p. 230). Big business dominates in these consultations and in the industrial and commercial associations as they have been established by the government.

Statist polities. In a statist system, the regime would dominate the economic organization. The control of the economy is a manifestation and a reinforcement of the centralization of decision making and the reduction of nonelite autonomy. When governmental leaders have direct control over economic activities, the opportunities for resistance to control in other spheres of life is reduced. This is magnified if the state also owns the means of production. In reality, these elements of the economy are combined in different ways. Yugoslavia does not have private ownership nor central planning, but is ruled through a single party, mobilizing support for the state. In Nazi Germany, private ownership continued and government direction and control of the economy, though considerable, was not total.

What is the relationship between economic classes and leading political positions in statist countries? Statist regimes have ruling parties and prevailing ideologies that vary in class alliances. The political leaders of Nazi Germany and Fascist Italy had close relations with leaders in private industry. Trade unions were instruments of the regimes, not independent representatives of workers. Although often anticapitalist in their propaganda, the Nazis in many ways carried the processes of business concentrations and organization to their logical fulfillment. Brady wrote in 1943 that Germany business leaders "face the prospect of being able to expand their private economic empires, by the aid, advice, and consent of the new German-dominated totalitarian system which they expect shortly to extend" (p. 54).

The class relations of regimes led by the Communist party are quite different. For example, the Bolsheviks' coming to power in Russia in 1917 meant the destruction of large-scale private businesses. According to Marx, the basic class distinction is between the owners of the means of production and the propertyless wage workers. Official Communist party interpretations of the Soviet social structure, then, contend that antagonistic classes no longer exist in the Soviet Union. If we consider class differences only in terms of income differences or of occupational position, however, classes do exist in the USSR and other countries ruled by the Community party.

To what extent are occupational rank and political power positions associated in the USSR? Working class representation within the political elite is relatively high. As shown in Table 8.3, members of the Supreme Soviet, the government legislature, in 1965 included 27 percent manual workers and 19 percent collective farmers. The proportion of workers and farmers is even slightly larger in regional, local, village, and town Soviets (Lane 1971a, Table 15). Among members of the Communist party in 1968, 39 percent were manual workers and 16 percent were collective farm peasants (Lane 1971b, p. 121). The party elite, however, increasingly is being drawn from nonmanual strata. Even as recently as 1952, 53 percent of the members of the Central Committee were factory workers; only 22 percent were professionals. Members of the Soviet Central Committee, however, hold leadership positions in the government and party bureaucracies and increasingly are trained for engineering and other professional tasks. By 1971, 26 percent of the members of the Central Committee were factory workers, 4 percent were agricultural workers, 17 percent were technicians, 37 percent were professionals, and the remainder were office workers, managers, and military and police officers (Nagle 1977, Table 21). Nevertheless, the members of the Central Committee are still predominantly of worker and peasant parental origins.

Another way of assessing the relationship between class and power ranks is to consider the relations among persons occupying high governmental and industrial positions. Soviet leaders deny that there are differences of interests among occupational groups. It follows that they deny that there are alliances among some of them constituting a military-industrial complex. One commentator wrote in *Krasnaya Zvezda*, the official newspaper of the Soviet Defense Ministry:

> The CPSU [Communist Party of the Soviet Union] coordinates and directs the efforts of Soviet society aimed at strengthening the economic and defensive might of the USSR. This is the indisputable fact that is being distorted by the bourgeouis ideologists, who are now proclaiming the existence in our country of some kind of self-contained "military-industrial complex" and alleging that there are differences between the Soviet military leaders and government leaders. What exists in the Soviet Union is

the monolithic social, political, and ideological unity of society and the complete identity and inseparability of the interests of the people and the interests of the state (Cited in Aspaturian 1972, p. 2).

Nevertheless, varying weight seems to be given to policy alternatives by different elements within the Soviet leadership and these differing policy emphases appear related to differences in occupational position. Thus, the relative importance assigned to heavy industry investment or consumer goods, to industry or agriculture, to military defense or nonmilitary uses are matters of contention. There is evidence that the military establishment, leaders in the heavy industry sphere, and conservative Communist party leaders are mutually supportive and cooperative in pursuing common interests. There is no large-scale interchange of personnel among these spheres, but members of the military bureaucracy and defense-industrial bureaucracy work together within subgroups (Aspaturian 1972).

On the whole, class origins of leading political figures differ considerably between capitalist and communist countries (Stack 1976). About 44 percent of the members of parliament came from the manual class in the German Democratic Republic (Blondel 1973; Bruckner 1974); 31 percent of the Romanian (Blondel 1973) and about 23 percent of the Czechoslovakian parliamentarians are from manual backgrounds (Busek and Spulber 1957; Krejci 1972). Legislators in totalitarian polities, however, do not exercise independent power, as do those in pluralist polities.

In summary, the world picture shows manual workers are generally underrepresented in high political offices; the higher the office, the more underrepresented they tend to be. Nevertheless, among the countries of the world there is considerable variation in their relative representation both in the life-time careers of the persons and their parental origins. The degree to which the governmental and the economic elites are unified, coincide, or have independent spheres of activity also varies considerably.

Power and Status Inequalities

Finally, we examine how status levels relate to power inequalities and make some observations about the extent to which class differences are also related to power and status inequalities. Status rankings by way of life, by lineage, by sex, and by race and ethnicity are pervasive in the world.[4] We will

---

[4] Sex differences are elaborated in every culture and the inferior status of women is generally reenforced by subordination. That subordination is embedded within religious and legal institutions. In many religions, women are excluded from direct participation in sacred ceremonies or leadership of them. In marriage and in control of property, they are often limited in rights and regarded simply as dependents of their husbands. This dependency is reinforced by moral and religious doctrine. For example, in the Christian New Testament (Timothy 2:11,12), Paul said, "Let the women learn in silence with all subjection, but I suffer not a woman to teach, nor to ursurp authority over a man, but to be in silence." Confucious, whose thought was very influential in traditional China, stressed that a woman was born to obedience. Her duty was to follow three rules: "In childhood and early youth she obeys her father; when she is married she obeys her husband; in widowhood she obeys her son" (Mace and Mace 1959, p. 67). The Laws of Manu of the Hindu religion assert the same rules (Mace and Mace, 1959, p. 70).

examine similarities and variations in the way power inequalities are related to such status differences within countries with pluralist, authoritarian, and totalitarian political systems.

Pluralist polities. Great Britain, although it has a pluralist democratic form of government, is also a constitutional monarchy. The power of hereditary position holders (the monarch and lords) has certainly declined, but remnants remain. The House of Lords can delay all but money bills for a year. What is noteworthy in the present context is that some political power is attached to lineage, to ascribed status.

More generally, an upper-status stratum persists in England, determined by birth and marked by a way of life acquired at private schools and within the confines of the social life of that level. Members of the stratum, simply as members, are likely to have opportunities for political power, at least through informal influence.

Power inequalities are also associated with other kinds of status inequalities in England. For example, women struggled mightily for many years, beginning before the turn of the century, to gain the right to vote. Only in 1918 did women over the age of thirty win suffrage and not until 1928 did women gain equal voting rights with men and to this day only a very small fraction, about 4 percent, of the members of Parliament are women (see Table 8.3). The proportion in the Labour party has been slightly greater than in the Conservative Party, although at present, the leader of the Conservative party is a woman, Margaret Thatcher. More significant representation of women exists in local government; they account for almost a quarter of the members in some local councils and up to 12 percent in the country as a whole (Sullerot 1971, pp. 222-223).

Authoritarian polities. In many authoritarian countries, ethnic differences are a significant basis of status inequality. Often this is related to the country's having been a colony with the dominating political elite's having come from the imperial power's homeland; sometimes these elites intermarried; sometimes they allied themselves with one ethnic group against another. Now, many newly independent states have dominion over territory that coincides with former colonial boundaries and encompasses several ethnic groups, tribes, or peoples. The groups frequently share only a rudimentary collective identity and the absence of a sense of common nationhood can aggravate the tensions and discontent arising from status, power, and class inequalities. Whatever ethnic or racial divisions exist in a country can be the basis for political domination, although a multiplicity of ethnic groups or a relative balance in the size and class standing of various ethnic groups can moderate the political domination by one over the others.

In Kenya the largest ethnic group is the Kikuyu and it is generally viewed as having a dominant political role. The ruling party, the KANU, is Kikuyu-dominated and the Kikuyu are disproportionally represented in the civil service and other elites. The degree of overrepresentation, however, is not great, as indicated in Table 8.4. There are allegations and some evidence that the Kikuyu

TABLE 8.4 Kenyan Population and Elites by Ethnicity

Ethnic Group	Percent of Population (Percent)	Civil Servants (Percent)	Elected or Appointed Representatives (Percent)	Nongovernmental Professionals (Percent)
Kikuyu	20	29	17	27
Luo	14	23	12	26
Luhya	13	20	13	25
Kamba, Wakamba	12	9	6	5
Maru	7	1	4	2
Kisii	5	1	5	–
Embu	4	–	3	1
Kipsigis	3	2	3	1
Nandi	2	2	1	–
Others (less than 3 percent)	16	11	31	11
Not Stated	–	2	5	2
Totals	96	100	100	100

Source: Based on Tables 11-11 and 11-14 from "The African Elite," by Gordon M. Wilson, in *The Transformation of East Africa: Studies in Political Anthropology*, edited by Stanley Diamond and Fred G. Burke, © 1966 by the Program of Eastern African Studies, Maxwell Graduate School of Citizenship and Public Affairs, Syracuse University, Basic Books, Inc., Publishers, New York.

have benefited more than other ethnic groups in the Africanization policy, which meant the displacement by Kenyans of Europeans and Asians from government, business, and agricultural land (Bienan 1974).

The major ethnic or racial differences in Mexico and Brazil are the result of colonial experiences. Spaniards, Portuguese, and other Europeans settled in each territory and had children with the American Indians. In addition, Africans were brought to Brazil as slaves, which led to children of mixed racial parentage. In Mexico, prior to the 1910 Revolution the *criollos* were white, powerful, and wealthy; the Indians and *Mestizos* (those of mixed European and Indian parentage) were poor, dark-skinned, and excluded from governance (Finer 1970, p. 115). The revolution ended the dominating rule of the *criollos*. Although class rank and skin color tend to be associated in contemporary Mexico, the relationship is not an exclusionary one and does not extend to holding political office or having political influence. Moreover, culture is a more important distinction among persons than skin color. Those who speak Spanish and wear some "Western" clothes are *Mestizos* (or *Ladinos*) and are not Indians; hence, Indians can become *Mestizos* (Stavenhagen 1968). In Brazil, the rejection of ethnic or racial discrimination or prejudice is a widely supported policy. Hence, even if there is a correlation between skin color and class standing, race in itself is not a basis of power or of powerlessness.

Statist polities. The possibilities for status differences to be related to power differences would seem to be great in statist systems. The official ideologies can promote, even insist, that governmental or public power be restricted by ethnicity. Thus, the Nazis included racism as part of their official ideology and excluded many groups on racial grounds from participating in the governance of Germany. Conversely, statist regimes may have ideologies that emphasize equality, as does the Soviet Union and other countries led by the Communist party.

In the Soviet Union, nationalities are granted the right to maintain cultural identity, within the context of adherence to Marxism-Leninism. The Russian people, however, are the preponderant nationality within the USSR. In 1970, 53 percent of the Soviet population were of Russian nationality. They tend to be overrepresented among the top leadership of the Communist party. As can be seen in Table 8.5, Russians constituted 65 percent of the Politburo Presidium and CPSU Secretariat between 1919-35 and 79 percent in the 1936-63 period (Lane 1971b, Tables 12 and 14). Most of the other nationalities are very small and are generally underrepresented; however, because they are so small, their representation sometimes appears to be a disproportionate share.

The Soviet government, from its beginning, has made attempts to emancipate women from male domination. Education and occupational opportunities have been greatly equalized (see Tables 6.4 and 6.5). In 1967, women accounted for 52 percent of all professional employees in the Soviet Union; this included 72 percent of the doctors (Lane 1971b, p. 88). Women participate in the political processes to a much greater extent in the USSR than in other countries,

TABLE 8.5   Ethnic Composition of USSR Population and Ethnic
Composition of Politburo-Presidium and CPSU
Secretariat (in Percent)

Nationality	Soviet Population 1959	Membership of Politburo-Presidium and CPSE Secretariat	
		1919-35	1939-63
Russians	54.6	65	79
Ukranians	17.8	0	10
White Russians	3.8	0	2
Uzbeks	2.9	0	2
Tatars	2.4	0	0
Kazakhs	1.7	0	0
Azerbaydzhanies	1.4	0	0
Armenians	1.3	3	2
Georgians	1.3	6	3
Lithuanians	1.1	0	0
Jews	1.1	18	2
Moldavians	1.1	0	0
Others	9.5	8	2
Totals	100.0%	100%	100%
(N)	208.82 million	(34)	(58)

Source: Adapted from Lane 1971b, Tables 12, p. 92, and 14, p. 98.

yet their participation is less than equal and decreases still more at the higher political ranks: 43 percent of the governmental deputies are women, but only 28 percent of the Supreme Soviet are women. About 20 percent of the party members at the 1966 Party Congress were women, but less than 3 percent of the Party's Central Committee and no members of the Politburo are women (Lane 1971b, pp. 89-90). Given the centralized character of the Soviet political system, representation at all except the highest levels indicates that power equality is more symbolic than actual.

In the People's Republic of China, too, the Communist party and the government have made considerable effort to bring about equality between men and women. Women had endured extreme subordination to men, but significant progress has been made since the revolution toward women's emancipation. Although the patriarchal system no longer exists, traditional sex-role differences remain; wives take care of the children, do the cleaning, cooking, and laundry. Women are often employed outside the home, but some discrimination in pay and in holding higher supervisory positions remains. Women are active in the political system, but their participation, although relatively high, is not equal to men's, again, especially at the highest levels. Women constitute 22 percent of the 2,885 deputies in the National People's Congress; 20 percent of the 219 members of the Presidium; and 7 percent of the 42 in the State Council (Hong 1976, p. 550).

249

250 Variations in Inequality

Summary

In reviewing several aspects of power inequality within countries we discussed, in particular, three major kinds of political systems—pluralist, authoritarian, and statist—representing different combinations of autonomy and participation. We noted the ways people participate in collective decision making in these various systems; representation within parties, choosing between parties, through voluntary associations that are closely related to the parties or the government, and through informal influence. We also examined the extent to which persons of different class and status ranks had access through these means to powerful persons and positions. Despite some variations, we found similar patterns of congruence among class, status, and power hierarchies.

GLOBAL POWER INEQUALITIES

If we view the world as a power system, countries are fundamental units constituting such a system. Countries are defined on the basis of territory under the control of governments claiming sole legitimacy to the use of violence. Governments usually recognize each other's claims; that is, their sovereignty. The organized means of violence at the command of governments is an important part of the global power system. Noncountry units, intergovernmental structures, and nongovernmental organizations also help make up the global power system. These include political and social movements with members and supporters in many countries and revolutionary and terrorist movements which function across national boundaries. Although these kinds of actors play a lesser role than do countries and governments in the global power system, they make significant contributions, and we include them in this discussion.

Inequality Among Countries

At the conclusion of World War II, the prevailing image was that of a world dominated by the victorious allies, especially the United States, England, France, and the Soviet Union. Then the Cold War and the bipolar world arose. Power was divided between the United States and its allies and the USSR and its allies. Indeed, at its height, every country in the world was called upon to choose sides. Since then, the division of power has become considerably less bipolar. The Third World, those countries that are still developing industrially and whose governments seek not to be aligned with either bloc, emerged. In many ways, too, the growth of issues that divide countries according to their level of industrial development has reduced the Cold War, or east-west confrontation. In addition, the solidarity of each camp in the Cold War has lessened greatly, notably with the break between China and the USSR and the growing autonomy of Europe.

Power inequalities among countries are generally viewed in terms of military strength and political alliances. At present two superpowers dominate: the United States and the Soviet Union. American power extends almost globally; Soviet power is less extensive. In addition, several other countries, such as Great Britain, France, and China, have great military strength and often political alliances as well, which gives them dominance over restricted territories.

The superpowers have not sought to dominate each other directly. They compete to dominate nonaligned countries or they use violence against small allies of the other side, as in the Korean and Vietnam wars. Power is used to maintain the alliances and thus may sometimes be used against allies or countries that may appear to be leaving the bloc of friendly countries. Thus, the Soviet Union intervened in Hungary in 1956 and Czechoslovakia in 1968 in order to maintain friendly regimes.

The world has many "weak" states (Singer 1972). Militarily and politically they are dependent on the great powers. Sometimes when that dependence has been based largely on coercion and when it serves the apparent interests of the dominating power, a new elite in the dependent country seizes power and looks to the enemy of the previously dominating power for support, as did Castro's regime in Cuba and Nasser's in Egypt.

The works of Singer (1972) and Travis (1975) make it possible to sketch the scope and intensity of both military and political dependence. Travis studied nine states: the United Kingdom, France, the Soviet Union, the United States, South Africa, Italy, Belgium, Germany, and Japan. He constructed eight measures of the *scope* of military dependence for each state. The measures include: the number of countries the state has major defense responsibilities for by treaty obligation, the number of countries in which the state has a major group of military advisors, and the number of countries to whom the state gives aid in amounts that exceed 1 percent of the dependent country's military budget. On every indicator, the United States has the greatest scope of military dependence. The Soviet Union, United Kingdom, and France have 60 percent, 40 percent, and 35 percent as many dependents as the United States. Belgium and South Africa have only 5 percent as many dependents as the United States; Italy and Germany have dependents only on a single variable, that is, military sales.

The *intensity* of military dependence was also measured by eight indicators, which included the operational forces of a power in the dependent country as a percentage of the dependent country's total forces, the average aid to the dependent country that exceeded 1 percent of the dependent country's military budget, and the average percentage of jet planes the power supplies of all jets the dependent country buys. The Soviet Union has the highest rank in the intensity of military dependence, followed by the United States, then the United Kingdom and France.

Measuring the *scope* of political dependence, Travis (1975) constructed five indicators, including number of major interventions between 1947 and 1972 and number of members of associations sponsored by the power. The United States has by far the greatest scope of political dependence, followed by the United Kingdom, France, and the Soviet Union. The *intensity* of political dependence was also measured by five indicators, some of which required estimates. Among the indicators were: estimated strength of the power's control or direction of the political, military, or ideological associations it sponsors and the average operational personnel and advisors relative to the number of personnel in the dependent country. The Soviet Union ranks highest in the intensity of political dependence, followed by France, the United States, South Africa, Belgium, and the United Kingdom.

Clearly, the United States ranks highest in overall political and military dominance; the Soviet Union has more intense domination over a smaller range of countries. France and the United Kingdom each exercise a great deal of power within their own spheres, which are mostly outgrowths of their former colonial empires.

These dominant-dependent relations between countries are between some people in each pair of countries. They involve relations among government and party leaders, among military personnel, and among suppliers of arms and government officials. Others in each country may be opposed to or indifferent to many of these ties. Involvement in such relations strengthens the position of some groups in each country relative to other groups. In the dependent country those tied most directly to the dominant power have their internal position strengthened by the availability of coercive support. On the other hand, their legitimacy is subject to withdrawal by domestic opponents who can charge that they are too beholden to foreign masters. In either instance, such ties to foreign powers are likely to increase power inequality within the dependent country. The availability of external coercive force and domestic opposition to such alien strength may foster power inequalities. Thus, regimes in Eastern Europe whose power is partly dependent upon the Soviet armed might can afford to be and in some ways must be domestically more coercive and totalitarian than they might otherwise be. The same holds true in many Latin American countries dependent upon United States power (Petras and Tomich 1977).

Countries form a global power system in ways other than military and political dominance rankings. To a significant degree, governments relate to each other within the arenas of international organizations, especially the United Nations. They also relate to each other through organizations which themselves become entities: the Organization of Petroleum Exporting Countries (OPEC) or the European Economic Community (EEC). Within the United Nations, the former dominance of the United States has decreased greatly as the membership of the organization has expanded. Most new members are former colonies and are economically underdeveloped. Their numbers, within the structure of the United Nations, have given them power they would not have had without it.

OPEC is another organization that has given countries who were relatively weak additional military and political power.

Transcountry Inequalities

Governments and countries are not the only units of global power inequalities. Political parties and movements based on ideologies make claims and function transnationally. Communist parties all over the world, in some ways, act as an international unit. In the past, they were wholly dominated by the Communist party of the Soviet Union, but Soviet dominance has been splintered in several ways and greatly reduced. Nevertheless, some of the organizational strength of the Communist parties of the world is based on shared ideology that makes claims on all parties who accept it. Social Democratic parties from different countries also meet to share ideas and these party ties have sometimes served as channels for common efforts on a transnational basis.

Other transnational movements and organizations are based on ethnicity, race, and religion. Such groups raise funds for arms, send members to join armed struggles, help commit terrorist acts, and help mobilize political support from accessible regimes. Thus, military support and aid has been mobilized among persons of Irish descent in many countries to support combatants in Northern Ireland. Jews in many parts of the world contribute to sustain and increase the military and political power of the State of Israel. Arabs in several countries lend support to chosen factions in other countries to promote their preferred policies.

This discussion should suggest the ambiguity in determining the units in any system of power inequality. People fight to determine what shall be defined as the units. Was Algeria a part of France prior to independence in 1962? Many people in the French mainland and in the territory of Algeria thought so. Others disagreed. People may call a struggle a civil war or a war of independence. One side may regard the government as a dependent instrument of another government; the other side may not. Such disagreements, and the ambiguous reality they reflect, should make problematic any analysis of power inequality within a single country as if the country were a completely independent and autonomous unit.

CONCLUSIONS

We have reviewed political systems in a few countries from the vast diversity of present and past systems of power inequality. Everywhere we have noted limits to political equality. The Freedom House survey of political and civil rights summarized their findings to report that in 1975, 45 percent of the people of the world (33 percent of the nations) were not free; 35 percent of the people (40 percent of the nations) were partly free, and 20 percent of the people (27 percent of the nations) were free.

Over the last century, however, the world has been undergoing a fundamental democratization (Mannheim 1940; Janowitz 1974). Polities throughout the world have extended basic citizenship rights to categories of people previously excluded: those without property, the illiterate, women, and various ethnic and racial groups. Claims of people for the right to participate in making collective decisions and for civil rights are generally acknowledged as proper (if regretably denied due to an emergency). In addition, national autonomy has gained general acceptance as a legitimate aspiration and has actually increased somewhat with the dissolution of colonial empires. Many people in many countries have considerable autonomy as individuals. In some countries civil rights have increased, but the expansion of the central governments' authority has enabled ruling groups to decrease personal autonomy in other countries.

We also examined variations in the relations among power, class, and status ranks. In every country we saw strong ties between class levels and power positions. In capitalist countries this has generally meant close relations between persons with power and those with wealth or upper-class positions. In countries with governments led by the Community party, persons of working-class background play a greater role than in other systems, but the incumbents of high managerial and professional positions have relatively great influence in governmental decision making, as they do in capitalist countries. Privately held wealth, however, is not a class base for political influence.

Status differences are also related to power inequality. Family background and lineage still play a role in governmental influence in countries with an aristocracy. Ethnicity often is associated with power differences, but the extent of the differences varies greatly. Sex differences are associated with power inequalities throughout the world; but the degree of inequality between men and women in their political and citizenship roles varies greatly.

In Chapters 9 and 10, we examine consequences of the inequalities described thus far and concentrate on those that have implications for persistence and change in the degree of inequality.

REFERENCES

ALFORD, ROBERT A. 1963. *Party and Society*. Chicago: Rand McNally.
ALMOND, GABRIEL A., and SIDNEY VERBA. 1963. *The Civil Culture*. Princeton, N.J.: Princeton University Press.
ALMOND, GABRIEL A., and G. BINGHAM POWELL, JR. 1966. *Comparative Politics: A Developmental Approach*. Boston: Little, Brown.
ASPATURIAN, VERNON V. 1972. "The Soviet Military-Industrial Complex— Does it Exist?" *Journal of International Affairs* 26 (1):1-28.
BAILEY, STEPHEN K. 1959. *The Condition of Our National Political Parties*. New York: An Occasional Paper of the Fund for the Republic.

BARGHOORN, FREDERICK C. 1965. "Soviet Russia: Orthodoxy and Adaptiveness." Pp. 450-511 in Lucian W. Pye and Sidney Verba (Eds.), *Political Culture and Political Development*. Princeton, N.J.: Princeton University Press.

BIENEN, HENRY. 1974. *Kenya: The Politics of Participation and Control*. Princeton, N.J.: Princeton University Press.

BLONDEL, JEAN. 1972. *Comparing Political Systems*. New York: Praeger.

BLONDEL, JEAN. 1973. *Comparative Legislatures*. Englewood Cliffs, N.J.: Prentice-Hall.

BRADY, ROBERT A. 1943. *Business as a System of Power*. New York: Columbia University Press.

BRUCKNER, ALFRED, et al. 1974. *Introducing the GDR*. Dresden: Volkerfreundschaft.

BUSEK, VRATISLAW, and NICOLAS SPULBER. 1957. *Czechoslovakia*. New York: Praeger.

DAHL, ROBERT A. 1963. *Modern Political Analysis*. Englewood Cliffs, N.J.: Prentice-Hall.

EISENSTADT, S. N. (Ed.). 1971. *Political Sociology: A Reader*. New York: Basic Books.

FIECHTER. GEORGES-ANDRE. 1975. *Brazil Since 1964: Modernization Under a Military Regime*, New York: John Wiley. Translated from the French by A. Braley. (Originally published in 1972.)

FINER, SAMUEL E. 1970. *Comparative Government*. London: Allen Lane, the Penguin Press.

FRIEDRICH, CARL. 1954. *Totalitarianism*. Cambridge, Mass.: Harvard University Press.

GASTIL, RAYMOND D. 1976. "The Comparative Survey of Freedom—VI," *Freedom in Issue* (January-February):11-20.

GUTTSMAN, W. L. 1965. *The British Political Elite*. London: MacGibbon and Kee.

HANSON, ROGER D. 1971. *The Politics of Mexican Development*. Baltimore: Johns Hopkins Press.

HEWITT, CHRISTOPHER J. 1974. "Elites and the Distribution of Power in British Society." Pp. 45-64 in Philip Stanworth and Anthony Giddens (Eds.), *Elites and Power in British Society*. Cambridge, England: Cambridge University Press.

HONG, LAWRENCE K. 1976. "The Role of Women in the People's Republic of China: Legacy and Change," *Social Problems* 23 (June):545-557.

HOROWITZ, IRVING LOUIS. 1964. *Revolution in Brazil*. New York: E. P. Dutton.

JANOWITZ, MORRIS. 1974. "Toward a Redefinition of Military Strategy in International Relations," *World Politics* 26 (July):473-508.

KORNHAUSER, WILLIAM. 1959. *The Politics of Mass Society*. Glencoe, Ill.: Free Press.

KREJCI, JAROSLAW. 1972. *Social Change and Stratification in Post War Czechoslovakia*. New York: Columbia University Press.

LANE, DAVID. 1971a. *Politics and Society in the USSR*. New York: Random House.

LANE, DAVID, 1971b. *The End of Inequality? Stratification Under State Socialism*. Middlesex, England: Penguin Books.

LANE, DAVID. 1976. *The Socialist Industrial State*. Boulder, Colo.: Westview Press.

LEWIS, PAUL H. 1975. *The Governments of Argentina, Brazil, and Mexico.* New York: Crowell.

LINZ, JUAN. 1971. "An Authoritarian Regime: Spain." In S. N. Eisenstadt (Ed.), *Political Sociology: A Reader.* New York: Basic Books.

LIPSET, SEYMOUR MARTIN. 1960. *Political Man.* New York: Doubleday.

LIPSET, SEYMOUR M., and STEIN ROKKAN (Eds.). 1967. *Party Systems and Voter Alignments: Cross-National Perspectives.* New York: Free Press.

MC LENNAN, BARBARA N. 1975. *Comparative Political Systems.* North Scituate, Mass.: Duxbury Press.

MANNHEIM, KARL. 1940. *Man and Society in an Age of Reconstruction.* New York: Harcourt Brace.

MACE, DAVID, and VERA MACE. 1959. *Marriage East and West.* Garden City, N.Y.: Doubleday.

MARX, KARL, and FRIEDERICH ENGLES. 1932. "Manifesto of the Communist Party." Pp. 320-343 in Max Eastman (Ed.), *Capital, The Communist Manifesto and Other Writings.* New York: Modern Library. (Originally published in 1848.)

MEDVEDEV, ROY A. 1972. *Let History Judge: The Origins and Consequences of Stalinism.* New York: Knopf.

MEIER, KENNETH JOHN. 1975. "Representative Bureaucracy: An Empirical Analysis," *The American Political Science Review* 69 (March):526-542.

MILIBAND, RALPH. 1969. *The State in Capitalist Society.* New York: Basic Books.

NAGLE, JOHN D. 1973. "Systems and Succession: A Generational Analysis of Elite Turnover in Four Nations." Unpublished paper presented at the annual meeting of the Southern Political Science Association.

NAGLE, JOHN D. 1977. *Systems and Succession: The Social Basis of Political Elite Recruitment.* Austin, Tex.: University of Texas Press.

PETRAS, JAMES, and DALE TOMICH. 1977. "Images and Realities of Violence: The United States and Latin America." Paper presented at the Annual American Sociological Association Meetings, Chicago, Ill.

POMELOV, I. 1967. "The Communist Party in a Socialist Society," *Pravda* (February 20). Pp. 90-93 in Paul Hollander (Ed.), *American and Soviet Society: A Reader in Comparative Sociology and Perception.* Englewood Cliffs, N.J.: Prentice-Hall.

SCOTT, ROBERT E. 1959. *Mexican Government in Transition.* Urbana, Ill.: University of Illinois Press.

SINGER, MARSHALL R. 1972. *Weak States in a World of Power.* New York: Free Press.

STACK, STEVEN. 1976. *Inequality in Industrial Society: Income Distribution in Capitalist and Socialist Nations.* Unpublished Ph.D. dissertation, University of Connecticut.

STAVENHAGEN, RUDOLFO. 1968. "Classes, Colonialism, and Acculturation." Pp. 31-63 in Joseph A. Kahl (Ed.), *Comparative Perspectives on Stratification.* Boston: Little, Brown.

SULLEROT, EVELYNE. 1971. *Women, Society and Change.* New York: McGraw-Hill. (Translated from the French by M. S. Archer.)

TAYLOR, CHARLES LEWIS, and MICHAEL C. HUDSON. 1971. *World Handbook of Political and Social Indicators II Section I: Aggregate Data; Section II; Annual Event Data.* Ann Arbor, Mich.: Inter-University Consortium for Political Research.

TRAVIS, TOM. 1975. "Toward a Comparative Study of Imperialism." Paper presented at the Sixteenth Annual Convention of the International Studies Association, Washington, D.C.

PART III

Consequences and Explanations

chapter 9

Consequences
for
Individuals

I will tell you the truth. When I am among you people,
I am not the man I am. I am the man you
think I am. A fool!   *A Compesino in Del Rio, Texas,*
quoted in Steiner, 1961.

The inequalities we have been describing have consequences for individuals. People delight in others' deference, cringe at others' power over them. They fall ill and die prematurely because of poverty, or engage in entertaining, frivolous activity because they have the leisure and money to do so. In this chapter we examine individual and family reactions or adaptations to their place in the class, status, and power systems. We ask what kinds of behavior and ideas are related to being ranked high or low and then consider their implications. But first we must raise and discuss a few underlying issues.

ISSUES

Understanding three interrelated issues will help us analyze the consequences for individuals of their ranking. First, because class, status, and power rankings tend to be highly correlated, how can we examine the extent to which each or all of them together affects how people act, feel, and think? Second, because people often are higher in one hierarchy than in others, their rank is not consistent. Such inconsistency may have its own effects. Third, people may act and feel as they do in a given stratum because they have been socialized to do so or because they respond to their circumstances. This issue concerns the extent to which the rich, the poor, ethnic groups, or the political elites have subcultures. Each of these issues must be considered in greater detail.

Class, Status, and Power Combined

As we have already noted, persons ranking high in one dimension of inequality are likely to rank high in other dimensions. People tend to have similar ranks in various dimensions. Furthermore, people are regarded and regard themselves in terms of all their rankings. To some extent, rankings are added together or averaged to assess where persons stand. This argues for constructing summary indices of ranking, taking into account several kinds of inequality.

Studies of social class, of social status, and of socioeconomic rank have used a variety of composite indices. Some of these indices—for example, those developed by Warner and Hollingshead—were discussed in Chapter 5. It is sufficient for our purposes here to note only a few such indices. For a study of psychiatric disorders and social stratification in New Haven, Connecticut, Myers and Roberts (1959) developed an Index of Social Position (ISP). This index combined residential, occupational, and educational scales; the three scales were weighted differently in constructing the index; they also used a two-factor index: occupation and education. Ellis, Lane, and Olesen (1963) proposed an Index of Class Position based on occupation and class self-identification. These various indices tend to emphasize social status and the likely existence of groups who distinguish themselves from each other and have distinctive ways of life. Efforts have been made to assess the extent to which such indices or single measures are most highly related to various style of life attributes. For example, Haer (1957) found that the Warner Index of Status Characteristics was highly related to many behavioral and attitudinal variables. Landecker (1960) tried to discern if there were any clear boundaries between different strata, using four ranking systems: income, occupational, educational, and ethnic-racial. He found only one apparent boundary, setting off an elite from the rest of the population. This elite stratum has members who have completed college, have high professional or executive occupations, and whose income is among the highest 7 percent of all income receivers. Otherwise, he found no boundaries and a continuous ranking system.

Despite the apparent advantages of adding together several rankings to construct a summary social-position ranking, disadvantages abound (Kriesberg 1963; Jackson and Curtis 1968). One difficulty is particularly significant. If more than one dimension or aspect of ranking are combined, it is difficult to know which accounts for those attitudes and behavior found to be related to rank. Income and prestige are related to each other, and each affects the way people think and behave. If we combine them in an index and the index is related to certain attitudes and conduct, we cannot assess whether that association is the result, for example, of differential opportunities made available simply by having more or less money or of different tastes acquired through social interaction with persons in one rather than another stratum. Being able to make such distinctions is important. If we know what it is about a ranking that affects conduct and thought, we can better predict what will change those behaviors and attitudes. It would also have relevance for policy issues, if one wanted to alter particular patterns related to social rank.

Another important reason for keeping dimensions of inequality separate is that not all dimensions have the same effects on many patterns of thought and conduct. For example, occupational prestige and income are positively correlated with job satisfaction. But years of education are negatively correlated with job satisfaction, taking into account occupational prestige and income. Without taking into account any other variables, job satisfaction is highest for the least well educated, declines among those with more years of schooling, and then is somewhat higher again for those who completed college (Campbell, Converse, and Rodgers 1976, p. 300).

One other difficulty arises with simply summing scores on several dimensions of rank. The scores may not be additive in their consequences. To illustrate, an artist living in poverty may be regarded by others as having low rank, despite high creativity, education, and social origin. The artist might attach little importance to the poverty and be incensed at the low regard others show him because of it. Rank inconsistency can have its own peculiar effects. We will discuss that in the next section.

The decision to use an index of several rankings or single indicators of each dimension cannot be settled for all purposes. What is used should depend on the application. If one wants to predict the social participation of persons with each other in a community, a combined index is probably best. If one wants to assess the determinants of particular rank-related patterns of conduct, a variety of indicators is best. In any case, simply constructing an index and distributing the resulting scores into different strata does not, in itself, demonstrate that clear boundaries rather than a continuous ranking exist between social strata. The extent to which clearly bounded social strata exist is an empirical question. We examine pertinent evidence in this chapter and the following one.

Rank Consistency

Sociologists have noted that people interact with each other in terms of their expectations about which rankings go together. As Hughes (1944) observed, in addition to the characteristics essential to fulfilling a position, a set of associated characteristics tend to develop. Writing in America in 1944, Hughes discussed the expected and accepted characteristics associated with being a physician. He observed that a white, male, Protestant physician of old American stock would be acceptable to almost any kind of patient; physicians with other characteristics would be less acceptable to at least some category of patients. Some people may even feel uncomfortable with persons who do not hold the expected set of characteristics, simply because they are expected. Most persons will try to act toward others in terms of those characteristics of theirs that confer high rank. But others tend to select people's low ranks in acting toward them (Galtung 1964). The result may be discomfort, then, for persons who rank high in some systems and low in others. The argument may be made that being high in some rank dimension does not compensate for being low in another; it aggravates the dissatisfaction of being low. It is even more galling to be treated as lowly when, by some standards, one has a claim to be treated as superior. Being ranked high in some dimensions also means having resources that should make it easier to alter the low ranking in other dimensions. As long as that alteration has not been made, the low rank is particularly irritating.

In a study that provoked a great deal of discussion and research, Lenski (1954) argued that people who had inconsistent rankings tend to be dissatisfied with the existing social order, want to change, and act to do so. He considered support for Democratic party candidates to be an indicator of efforts to reform or change the society. Rank inconsistency was measured between occupational, educational, ethnic-racial, and income dimensions. He found that persons with greater inconsistency (or low status crystallization, as he termed it) were more likely to support the Democratic party than were persons of consistent rank. Many other researchers, however, have not been able to replicate his findings.

Some sociologists argue that not all kinds of inconsistency are the same; different patterns of rank inconsistency or incongruence have different consequences. Thus, persons who ranked high on ascribed dimensions (such as ethnicity) or dimensions that could be considered investments (such as education) but low on achieved or reward dimensions (occupational status or income) can be called underrewarded. They will feel disappointed and angry (Jackson 1962; Geschwender 1967). On the other hand, persons who are ranked low on ascribed or investment dimensions and high on achieved or reward dimensions would feel successful and contented, perhaps even guilty.[2] Geschwender (1968) studied unrest among male, manual workers and found that underrewarded inconsistents did tend to exhibit symptoms of individual unrest.

It is also argued that people feel dissatisfied in relation to the number of areas in which they are ranked low and all their rankings added together or averaged. This is an additive model of the effects of rank inconsistency rather than one in which the different rankings are presumed to interact in their effects. On the whole, the many studies done in this area suggest that the additive model better explains variations in the effect being studied than does the interactive model (Treiman 1966; Lauman and Segal 1971; Laslett 1971; Goffman 1957; Hornung 1972; Olsen and Tully 1972; Kriesberg 1973). Furthermore, there are severe methodological difficulties in disentangling the interactive explanation from the additive one (Blalock 1967a; 1967b).[3]

There may be particular responses to different patterns of rank incongruence, and we should be sensitive to those possibilities as we study reactions to inequalities. But we should not expect all kinds of incongruence to have the same effects or to have very great effects, compared to the additive impact of rank standings. Being ranked low in every dimension is generally more oppressive than being low in only some of them.

Cultures and Situations

The third major issue underlying analyses of the consequences of inequality pertains to the relative role of cultures or situations. Perhaps classes, status groups, or power strata have their own subculture so that when growing up, children are socialized to learn the ways of thinking and acting appropriate for

[2] If inconsistency has opposing effects, depending upon the pattern of inconsistency, then no overall "inconsistency effect" may be discernible. This is one of the methodological problems with this concept. It is necessary to be specific about which effect is hypothesized from each specific kind of inconsistency.

[3] The methodological difficulty arises from the identification problem. In examining any of the effects of two independent variables upon the dependent variable, the results could arise from many different combinations of independent variable effects. There are many different additive and interactive models that might produce the observed results (Kriesberg, 1973, pp. 72-74).

their station in life. This idea has gained most attention in recent years in relation to the poor and the alleged culture of poverty they share (Lewis 1959, 1966). On the other hand, people in a given stratum may be the way they are because they are responding to their circumstances; it may be that anyone in the same circumstances would respond the same way (Kriesberg 1970; Valentine 1968; Leacock 1971).

Let us examine these possibilities in more detail. Oscar Lewis, on the basis of his anthropological field work in Mexico and the United States and his reading of social science studies and novels, inferred that there is a culture of poverty. As he wrote in the introduction to his study of five families, "One can speak of the culture of the poor, for it has its own modalities and distinctive social and psychological consequences for its members. It seems to me the culture of poverty cuts across regional, rural-urban, and even national boundaries" (1959, p. 16). He was impressed by the similarities in family structure, the nature of kinship ties, the quality of husband-wife and parent-child relations, time orientation, spending patterns, value systems, and the sense of community found in lower-class settlements in London, Puerto Rico, Mexico City slums, Mexican villages, and among lower-class Negroes in the United States.

Using the term *culture* to summarize and account for these alleged similarities carries several implications. Cultures are passed from generation to generation through social experience along family lines. They are designs for living, and their values, norms of conduct, and patterns of behavior tend to be integrated (Lewis 1966, p. 19).

On the other hand, the situational approach emphasizes the extent to which the poor and the nonpoor hold the same values and goals. "Attention to the existential conditions in which the poor live points to the possibility that what may appear to be profound and deep-seated differences in orientations are only accommodations to particular circumstances" (Kriesberg 1970, p. 9).

The cultural and situational approaches differ in several regards (Kriesberg 1970). First, the approaches vary in how distinctively they view the poor and the nonpoor and their stress on the similarities between the poor and the nonpoor. This raises a general and very important point. In comparing strata, members of one are more likely than another to hold certain beliefs or act in particular ways; but even if the difference is statistically significant, the overlap between the two strata can be considerable. For example, poor people are less likely to recommend or prefer that their children go to college than are persons with higher income. But most people in every income category want their children to go to college; only the proportions differ. We generally emphasize the differences, which can result in stereotyping and the presumption that within a group where a smaller proportion want a particular end, none do. In making any comparisons among strata, we must guard against such exaggeration.

Cultural and situational approaches also differ in their views of the relationship between values and conduct. We often presume, when we see two categories of people acting differently, that members of each category are acting as they do because they want to; they are acting on their values and norms; they are conforming to their culture. We must recognize the possibility that they do not differ in values and norms, but rather that one group is constrained by circumstances from acting on the values and norms. Thus, people in two groups may share the desire for regular employment, but people in one group will lack the physical strength or technical skill for the available jobs (Liebow 1969).

The third way in which cultural and situational approaches differ is in the importance given to intergenerational learning and to contemporary influence. In the cultural approach, patterns of marital relations and child-rearing, for example, are assumed to be acquired from one's parents, then maintained. In a situational approach, attention is given to the current circumstances that account for people's conduct. Thus, if there is a higher incidence of single-parent families among blacks than whites, a cultural explanation might stress the presumed history and culture pertaining to marital instability, even going back to slavery. A situational approach would emphasize the current conditions that discourage or make it difficult to maintain a two-parent family.

Finally, cultural and situational approaches vary in their emphasis on various ways people are influenced. Thus, observers using a cultural approach stress social sources of influence, subjective orientations, and learning through the efforts of others. They emphasize how people in the same stratum associate with each other and influence each other. Those taking a situational approach give greater attention to the effects of nonsocial factors, to objective circumstances, and to the way people accommodate to or respond to others. Writers emphasizing a situational approach stress how people respond to their circumstances, including the physical and social environment, for example, whether persons in other ranks treat them oppressively or deferentially.

The preceding discussion should help us interpret the findings that we will now review. Although the cultural and situational approaches have been illustrated, particularly as they involve the differences between the poor and nonpoor, the discussion is relevant for the differences among any strata. Some of the same issues, for example, are relevant for explaining differences between men and women, and among racial and ethnic categories (Chafe 1972; L. A. Kriesberg 1973; Freeman 1975). As we consider the differences in values, norms, and patterns of conduct among various social ranks, we will compare the alternative explanations for the differences.

CONDUCT AND THOUGHT

Sociologists and other social scientists have conducted innumerable studies reporting differences in values, norms, feelings, and patterns of behavior related to differences in class, status, and power. There hardly seems to be any type of conduct or way of thinking that is not related to a person's rank. Public opinion polls show variations in nearly every aspect of life among persons of different income, education, and occupation. In this review, we will concentrate on demographic and health differences, variations in child rearing, family life, community involvement, and general life style.

Demographic and Health Differences

In this section we review evidence about differences by rank in death rates, illness incidence, use of medical services, and fertility rates.

Death rates. As stated in Chapter 2 in Max Weber's terminology, a class exists "when (1) a number of people have in common a specific causal component of their life chances," insofar as this is represented by economic interests under market conditions (Weber 1946, p. 181). The most literal meaning of *life chances* is the probability of staying alive, of life expectancy.

Not surprisingly, persons with higher incomes tend to live longer than persons with lower incomes. But the degree to which class variations are related to differentials in mortality rates varies. Antonovsky (1967) reviewed over thirty studies of class differentials in life expectancy and mortality rates. Prior to the rapid expansion of world population beginning in the mid-seventeenth century, birth and death rates were high and balanced; conceivably during that period differentials among strata were not very large. But with the improvements in housing, water supply, sanitation, and nutrition and, much later, in medical care, differentials became great. Antonovsky cites a study made in 1839 in a suburb of London: The average age of death of gentlemen, professional men, and their families was 45 years; tradesmen and their families died, on the average, at age 26; and mechanics, servants, laborers and their families died at age 16. With increased life expectancy, class differentials have declined. In the Netherlands, where mortality rates are among the lowest in the world, the difference between the occupational group with the highest and lowest mortality rates is very small, barely reaching statistical significance (DeWolff and Meerdink 1954). In the United States, life expectancy is relatively long, yet some class differences remain. They persist between the lowest class and all other classes; there is little differential among the classes above the lowest (Antonovsky 1967).

Ethnic and racial status differences are also often related to differences in life expectancy and death rates. For example, in the United States in 1973, whites had an average life expectancy of 72.2 years; Negroes and others, 65.9 years. The difference in life expectancy was even greater in the past. In 1920, the life expectancy of whites was 54.9; for Negroes and others it was only 45.3 (U.S. Bureau of the Census, *Statistical Abstract* 1976, Table No. 82). An important component of life expectancy is survival at infancy and survival of mothers bearing children. As can be seen in Table 9.1, whites and nonwhites differ markedly in infant death rates and maternal death rates. These differences, too, were even greater in the recent past.

Health. The mortality differences related to social rankings suggest that exposure to death risks and/or the utilization of good medical care are still

TABLE 9.1   Infant and Maternal Death Rates by Race 1940 to 1973

Years	Infant Deaths[1]		Maternal Deaths[2]	
	White	Negro and Other	White	Negro and Other
1940	43.2	73.8	319.0	773.5
1950	26.8	44.5	61.1	221.6
1960	22.9	43.2	37.1	97.9
1970	17.8	30.9	14.4	55.9
1973	15.8	26.2	10.7	34.6

[1] Deaths per 1,000 live births of infants under one year old.

[2] Deaths of mothers per 1,000,000 live births from deliveries and complications of pregnancy, childbirth, and the puerperium.

Source: U. S. Bureau of the Census, *Statistical Abstract* 1976, Table 88, p. 63.

unequal, but decreasingly so. To what extent do classes differ in exposure to risk and use of medical services? How well do the cultural and situational approaches account for the differences?

High class ranking is inversely related to illnesses and accidents and their consequent disabilities. That is, people with higher incomes are less likely to be ill and disabled than are those with lower incomes. This relationship is most marked for severe disabilities and for persons in families with incomes less than $3,000 (in 1968) compared to those in higher income levels (see Table 9.2). The incidence of acute, short-run illnesses are not as closely related.

The relationship between chronic illness or disability and low income is a two-way one (Lerner 1975). On one hand, poverty creates conditions that increase the chances of illness and disabling accidents. Nutrition is often inade-

TABLE 9.2   Days of Disability per Person per Year by Type of Disability and Family Income, United States 1968

Family Income	Restricted Activity	Bed Disability
Less than $ 3,000	25.4	10.2
$ 3,000-$ 4,999	17.5	7.1
5,000- 6,999	14.3	6.1
7,000- 9,000	13.9	6.2
10,000- 14,999	12.8	5.3
15,000 or more	11.0	5.1

Source: U. S. National Center for Health Statistics, "Disability Days, United States 1968," *Vital and Health Statistics: Data From the National Health Survey*, Series 10, No. 67 (Washington, D. C.: U. S. Government Printing Office, January 1972), p. 7. Based on household interviews of the civilian noninstitutional population and adjusted to the age and sex distribution of the total civilian noninstitutional population of the United States, 1968.

269

quate among the poor.[4] Employment in occupations that threaten health and safety are greater among the poor. Housing conditions are worse and, therefore, are more likely to be the source of infectious and other illnesses (Wilner et al. 1962). In the other direction, persons who are themselves ill or disabled or who have ill or disabled family members tend to have reduced earning capacity and increased costs. Thus, illness and disability result in low income and poverty. This, in turn, makes further deterioration of health more likely.

Communicable diseases are a less important cause of illness, impairment, and death in the United States now than they once were and still are in many countries of the world. Typhoid fever, tuberculosis, smallpox, and typhus are such illnesses. Higher class families often have been able to avoid such diseases and the conditions inducing them. Where communicable diseases are major sources of illness, differentials in health by class rankings are greater than where they have been largely eradicated.

— What are the cultural and situational explanations for the relationship between ranking and health? One cultural argument is that low-ranking persons tend to have lower self-regard than higher-ranking persons. This would be particularly true of persons low in status. Low-ranking persons also tend to feel less competent to deal with their environment, more fatalistic; this is particularly true of those who are relatively powerless. Another cultural explanation for social differences in health would be that such feelings inhibit people from taking action that would prevent or cure poor health. They would make less effort to protect and care for the body; they would be less likely to feel that their health deserves attention or that it can be protected. They would be less likely to care about nutrition and to avoid accidents (Koos 1954; Rainwater 1968).

More specific cultural explanations can be offered. The emphasis on "machismo," masculinity defined in terms of physical toughness, risk-taking, and bravery in the face of physical danger, is greater among working-class men than middle-class men (Miller 1958). It also varies by ethnic and national cultures. This, too, would increase the rate of accidents, disability, and death. Another kind of cultural explanation would stress the lack of knowledge that low-ranking persons have, as compared to higher-ranking persons, about health care.

On the other hand, situational explanations emphasize the externally compelling character of work place, housing, and nutritional conditions. People

---

[4] For example, the mean caloric intake of white persons aged one through seventy-four with income below the poverty line in the United States in 1971-72 was 1,846. Among whites above the low income level the mean caloric intake was 2,000. Among blacks below the low income level the mean caloric intake was 1,681, and among blacks above the low income level, 1,905. For further details see the U.S. Bureau of the Census, *Statistical Abstract* 1976, Table No. 149. Note that these figures refer to the actual caloric intakes, based upon a national survey. They are not based, as were the figures presented in Chapter 4 and Table 4.3, upon the nutrients available for consumption. Those figures, based upon production estimates and ignoring all loss or waste, are obviously greater.

generally do not want to be exposed to unhealthful pollutants and to accidents in their work. But lower-paying and lower-prestige jobs tend to be less safe in these regards. People generally do not want to live in dangerously crowded housing or suffer malnutrition. But low income increases exposure to those conditions.

The evidence supports a situational explanation if we consider the overall patterns and trends in rank inequalities and health. The persistence of the most significant gap in health conditions between the lowest strata and all others and the diminution of differences among all other strata suggest that when minimal resources are available, they are used to avoid illness, disability, and death. The great shift in causes of death from communicable to degenerative illnesses accounted for the great leveling in death rates among different social ranks. That shift was due to changes in public health conditions: external conditions rather than cultural choices of particular population groups. This does not preclude the possibility, indeed the great likelihood, that among particular status or class groups, some cultural variations also have some effect on dietary patterns or occupational choices, which, in turn affect the risks of particular diseases or kinds of accidents.

The other factor that affects illness, disability, and death is the utilization of medical and dental services. Indicators of utilization include rates of visits to hospitals, physicians, and dentists. Class differences in hospital usage have declined greatly (Kriesberg 1963). In the 1930s, persons of lower socioeconomic rankings were much less likely than others to be admitted to hospitals. By the early 1950s, differences in such utilization no longer existed by income levels. Most recently, usage rates are greater for low-income persons than higher-income persons, presumably reflecting the greater incidence of medical conditions requiring hospital treatment. Changes in the patterns of physician usage are similar, although usage is not more frequent among lower-income persons. This is attributable to the greater utilization of physicians for less acute conditions and for preventive care by higher-income persons (McKinlay 1975).

Difference in utilization by dentists for professional service are greater by class rankings than are hospital or physician usage. The differences have declined considerably since the 1930s but have not disappeared (Kriesberg, 1963; U.S. Department of Health, Education, and Welfare 1975).

To account for the changes in the relationship between class and utilization of professional services, we will briefly compare the cultural and situational explanations. The major cause for the decline in class differences in the use of hospitals and physicians seems to be the increased availability of such care, particularly through the expansion of health insurance plans. It is not likely that there ever were great differences in valuing or desiring health among persons of different social rank. Differences in beliefs about the effectiveness of medical care and about the ability to maintain one's health may have existed and perhaps remnants of such differences remain. But the increased utilization and effectiveness of medical care would reduce the differences in such beliefs. Such cultural variations may account for some underutilization of medical services and probably help account for the different rates in obtaining dental services. In the case of dental utilization, class differences in the value of maintaining one's own teeth and believing that it is possible to do so appear to occur (Kriesberg and Treiman 1960). On the whole, however, situational differences in the access to dental care are much greater than in access to medical care. Insurance plans much less frequently provide for dental services. Even in the case of medical care, important situational variations also help account for the remaining differences in utilization by class, taking into account differential need. Thus, Rushing (1975) has found that lower-income areas of the country have many fewer physicians for each 100,000 persons than do higher-income areas.

Of course, the quality of care varies with class, aside from rates of utilization of professional services. This, in part, reflects the time and specialized skills that can be paid for by persons with adequate amounts of money. It also is affected by the social distance between elitist professionals and working-class patients (Waitzkin and Waterman 1974). Status stereotypes and prejudices as well as differences in language skills and styles interfere with full communication, for example, between physicians and working-class patients. Inadequate communication reduces the effectiveness of medical care.

Fertility. Families of lower class and status rankings have generally higher fertility rates and larger families than families of higher status and class levels. This is true whether ranking is measured by family income, mother's education, father's occupational status, or similar measures.[5] The differences by social and class levels, however, have been decreasing (Rindfuss and Sweet 1977). In the United States this convergence has resulted in part from an increase in the birth rates for women of higher status and class, at least among those of child-bearing age between 1920 and 1950 (Matras 1973). This is a result of increased marriage rates among higher ranking women. In Western countries, class level and birth rates are generally inversely related, and differences among the classes have been decreasing.

The pattern is not universal. In Arabic Islam, no discernible pattern between occupational status and birth rates is found. For example, a study by El-Badrey, cited by Goode (1963, p. 116), reported that the highest birth rates in Egypt were among persons in religious occupations, followed closely by teachers and merchants. The lowest rates were among the technical occupations; skilled and unskilled workers and other white collar occupations were in between. Indeed, in agricultural areas in the Western countries or regions, prior

---

[5] The issue is complex if we consider income. For example, poverty measures often take into account number of children in the family, and family income includes the wife's employment, which is related to number of children. If we relate fertility to husband's income, we do not find an inverse relationship (Rindfuss and Sweet 1977). Recent fertility refers to number of children under 3 years of age. But this lack of relationship may simply reflect the timing of births in relation to the husband's earnings.

to the decline in fertility in the 1870s and 1880s, fertility rates were positively related to status (Wrong 1958). This was true in the American south, Australia, and probably rural French Canada as late as 1941. It is true of agricultural areas in underdeveloped areas.

In general, it appears that normative standards provide guidelines about how many children are desirable. These standards are probably consonant with the circumstances in which people are living. Class and status differences generally reflect differences in the ability to realize those norms. Thus, in countries or regions or among cultural groups that prefer large families, high-status people, at least in the past, have tended to have more children than lower-ranking persons because the lower-ranking persons lack the resources to support as many children as they might want. On the other hand, to control fertility also requires resources. Knowledge about contraceptive techniques is not equally available to all ranks, and certainly access to the physician-controlled means of birth control has not been equally available. In recent years, equality of access to contraceptive means has increased in the United States. This is in large part responsible for the converging of class differentials in birth rates among married women.

Early Socialization

The ways in which people raise their children is fraught with implications for the lives of the children and their futures as adults. To what extent do people in different class, status, and power levels differ in their child-training methods and goals? A very extensive sociological literature provides answers to that question. It is not possible to review all or even most of the pertinent literature in this area, but we will consider some of the evidence about three topics: child-rearing practices, socialization values, and educationally relevant training.

Child-rearing practices. Many studies have been made of differences in toilet-training, feeding, and disciplining infants and children. Some of this work had been stimulated by psychoanalytic theory and by Freud's theories that infant and early childhood experiences have profound and long-lasting effects upon the personality. Studies have often focused on class and status differences in the permissiveness or rigidity with which children are trained to control urinating or the extent to which they are fed on a fixed schedule rather than whenever they are hungry.

Bronfenbrenner reviewed the extensive literature on childhood socialization practices as related to class and status. He found that the studies revealed a clear trend:

> From about 1930 till the end of World War II, working-class mothers were uniformly more permissive than those of the middle class. They were more likely to breast feed, to follow a self-demand schedule, to wean the

child later both from breast and bottle, and to begin and complete both bowel and bladder training at a later age. After World War II, however, there has been a definite reversal in direction; now it is the middle-class mother who is the more permissive in each of the above areas (1958, p. 424).

The studies reviewed by Bronfenbrenner also revealed that middle-class mothers were

Consistently more permissive toward the child's expressed needs and wishes. The generalization applies in such diverse areas as oral behavior, toilet accidents, dependency, sex, aggressiveness, and freedom of movement outside the home.

Though more tolerant of expressed impulses and desires, the middle-class parent, throughout the period covered by this survey, has higher expectations for the child. The middle-class youngster is expected to learn to take care of himself earlier, to accept more responsibilities about the home, and—above all—to progress further in school.

In matters of discipline, working-class parents are consistently more likely to employ physical punishment, while middle-class families rely more on reasoning, isolation, appeals to guilt, and other methods involving the threat of loss of love (1958, p. 424).

Although class and status ranks may differ consistently in child rearing practices, the differences are often small. We should not think that because the proportion of parents in the working class are more or less likely than parents of the middle class to engage in any particular pattern of conduct that they are completely different. For example, consider the tendency of working-class parents to use more physical punishment than middle-class parents. Melvin Kohn (1969) did a careful study of 339 mothers from white middle-class and working-class families who had a fifth-grade child in a Washington, D.C., school. To specify under what conditions what kinds of punishment might be used, the mothers were asked about eight specific situations and whether their fifth-grade child was involved in them.

Reports of the child's engaging in the activities generally do not differ by class. Furthermore, most mothers in both classes reported that they generally ignored the children's actions. When the child persists in the behavior, there is a slight tendency for working-class mothers to report the use of physical punishment. The behavior of the mothers in each of the eight circumstances and for sons and daughters were compared. In only three of the sixteen comparisons are the differences statistically significant: when sons persist in wild play, when sons fight with brothers or sisters, and when daughters fight with other children. The largest difference among all these comparisons is that 43 percent of the working-class mothers report using physical punishment when sons persist in fights with brothers or sisters, compared to 17 percent of the middle class mothers. In most comparisons the differences are much smaller, are nonexistent, or are even reversed. Erlanger (1974), drawing upon several studies and national survey data, concludes that the relationship between class levels and the use of physical punishment is very weak.

Socialization values. Kohn was interested in examining how parents reacted to different kinds of conduct so that he could assess to what extent their reactions were consistent with the different values of middle-class and working parents. He found in the Washington Survey, in a national United States survey, and in a similar study in Turin, Italy, that higher-class parents value self-direction more than lower-class parents do; they also put less value on conformity to externally imposed standards. Again, the differences are generally in this direction for a large number of survey questions, but the differences are not large, sometimes are nonexistent, and may even be in the other direction. Kohn argues that the value differences are reflective of the different occupational circumstances of middle-class and working-class persons. The conformist values and orientation of the lower ranks is a product of the limited education and constricted job conditions to which they are subject. Men of higher-class ranks have the opportunity to be self-directed at work and they want that away from work as well (Wright and Wright 1976).

Working conditions are one aspect of persons' current circumstances that help account for class differences in values and conduct related to child-rearing. Other current circumstances may also be relevant. Lower-class persons tend to live in crowded conditions and have few resources to handle or control children in ways that do not require conformity and obedience. On the other hand, it might be argued that these different classes have their own subcultures, that the values and patterns of conduct are transmitted from one generation to the next.

In a study of persons living in and around public housing projects in Syracuse, New York, an effort was made to untangle these possibilities. Kriesberg (1970) compared husbandless and married mothers in poverty and not in poverty. The mothers were asked about their values and beliefs about child-rearing and about their conduct in relationship to a particular child. They were also asked about their own families of origin and their parents' values and practices. For example, the mothers were asked how much they agreed that a boy should obey his parents without talking back. As can be seen in Table 9.3, poor mothers are likely to value obedience more than nonpoor mothers. Among married mothers, having lower socioeconomic origins does not significantly affect that value; their current circumstances seem more important. Among the husbandless mothers, their socioeconomic origins have an affect in addition to current circumstances. Without the presence of a husband, mothers of high socioeconomic origin do not particularly tend to value children's obedience. There is an interaction effect between the current circumstances and their social origins. These and other findings indicate that current circumstances are more important in explaining class differences in child-rearing patterns than are subcultural factors. Nevertheless, intergenerational influences do exist, particularly among husbandless mothers.

Educational preparation. Extensive research has also been done on values, beliefs, and practices relevant to education. Of obvious relevance are parental preferences about the extent of their children's formal education. It is well known that parents of lower-class rankings do not aspire to as many years of schooling for their children as do parents of higher-class rankings. Persons of lower-class rank, however, may aspire to more years of education for their children *relative* to *their* educational level than do higher-class, better educated parents. On the whole, formal education is highly valued by everyone in this society.

In Chapter 5 we saw the important role schooling plays in intergenerational occupational mobility and noted the moderately high correlation between educational attainment and parental class and educational levels. Many sub-cultural and situational factors may account for the linkage between parental class and educational levels and the educational attainments of the children. It should be pointed out that a gap between aspirations and attainment is much more likely to be found among lower than higher socioeconomic strata (Kriesberg 1963). The failure of lower-class children to attain the educational levels to which they aspire may be due to the cultural deprivation they experience at home and/or the situational constraints they face.

There is evidence that educational aspirations and attainment are affected by parental values and beliefs about education (Sewell and Shah 1968). There is also abundant evidence that parental activities provide an environment that affects the children's school attainments and achievements. The quality of parental language, parental academic guidance, and intellectuality in the home are related to achievement test scores (Bloom, 1963, pp. 124-125). Having parents who are involved in their schooling and having a quiet room for study, reference books, and similar resources are inversely related to a child's dropping out of school (Evariff 1957; Bertran 1962). Years of school attainment are positively related to high grades and academic achievement.

Many of these conditions are related to class and status levels. Some are situational conditions associated with material resources and they also may reflect patterns of living that are intergenerationally transmitted. Evidence of intergenerational transmission of values about education, however, is not strong. In the Syracuse study of fatherless families, parental aspirations regarding children's education was found to be only slightly correlated with father's socioeconomic rank (the correlation was .13). Furthermore, situational pressures may lead persons to higher aspirations for their children, perhaps in a compensatory fashion. Thus, in the same study, husbandless mothers were found to have higher educational aspirations for their children than married mothers (Kriesberg 1970, pp. 225-261). This may also be involved in the finding that blacks have higher educational aspirations than whites when class levels are held constant (Jencks et al. 1973, pp. 141-143).

Jencks and his associates (1973) conducted an extensive review of the literature and reanalysis of many large studies to assess the relationship between

TABLE 9.3   Percent Who Agree Very Much that Boy Should
Obey without Talking Back by Father's
Occupational Socioeconomic Rank by Income,
and by Marital Status

Father's Socioeconomic Rank	Married Mothers		Husbandless Mothers	
	Poor	Not Poor	Poor	Not Poor
Low	77.8	57.5	75.8	65.5
	(36)	(134)	(33)	(29)
Not Low	70.6	52.5	50.0	26.9
	(17)	(118)	(22)	(26)

Source: Kriesberg 1970, Table 8.1, p. 208.

family origins, educational attainment, and income. They found that the correlation between a white child's educational attainment and his father's occupational status is about .50. Combining parental occupation and income probably raises the correlation to about .55. They further conclude that this correlation has been stable throughout the first half of the twentieth century.

Jencks and his associates (1973, pp. 138-141) estimate the factors that account for that correlation. They estimate that less than 10 percent of the effect of parental economic status is explained by the fact that economically advantaged children have what they call superior IQ genotypes (genetic transmission of intelligence). Another 20 to 25 percent of the effect is attributed to the fact that economically advantaged parents provide environments that favor the development of cognitive skills valued by schools. They attribute about 10 or 15 percent of the difference to money itself. This leaves about half of the gap unexplained. They consider a variety of possible explanations and conclude that cultural attitudes, values, and taste for schooling play a very large role. Furthermore, even if middle-class students do not enjoy school, they evidently assume they must stay in school a long time. Such social expectations are part of their circumstances. These estimates of relative importance should be considered suggestive only and the isolation of genetic contribution particularly doubtful. The magnitude of each factor's contribution varies with historical periods and the variation in each of the factors at a given period.

Family Life

The most intimate aspects of life are shaped by class and status rankings, even sexual relations between men and women and the many aspects of husband-wife roles. People are more likely to marry others of similar class standing than persons of very different classes. This partly reflects the tendency of people to marry those who live nearby and people live in areas that are differentiated by class (Peach 1974).

Marriage age varies directly with class (Bogue 1969, pp. 638-646): that is, working-class men and women marry at a younger age than those in higher ranks. Such marriage patterns are related to educational attainments and to occupational choices. In earlier periods, when marriage was more often arranged by families, those from noble and well-to-do rural families married relatively early because they did not have to support themselves or prepare for a profession. Among the poorer families or where there was little free land, marriage tended to be later (Goode 1963, p. 41).

Within the family, husbands and wives can divide and share the tasks of managing the household in many different ways. In the actual performance of household activities—cleaning, washing, shopping, preparing food, caring for children, and so on—husbands and wives can share all the tasks, take turns performing them, or divide them up. Sex-role segregation tends to be greater in working-class than in middle-class families (Blood and Wolfe 1960; Komarovsky 1962). Yet when it comes to family decision making, men in higher-class positions tend to have relatively more power than men at lower-class levels, a particularly interesting finding considering the greater prevalence of traditional views about male dominance among working-class husbands. Middle-class husbands may be ideologically more equilitarian, but they have greater bargaining power relative to their wives than do working-class husbands. Wives in the working class are more apt to earn money more nearly comparable to their husbands' earnings than are wives of middle-class husbands, hence, their relative bargaining power is greater, which seems particularly important in determining husband-wife decision making power (Goode 1963, p. 373).

Divorce and separation are inversely related to income and other class and status measures (Udry 1966, 1967).[6] Thus, the lower the male's income and occupation, the more likely are they to divorce and separate, despite the publicity surrounding the divorces of the rich and famous. Several reasons for this can be given (Goode 1963). Lower income and lower status impose strains on a family, strains that are less acute as class levels rise. The inadequacy of material resources provides a basis for quarrels and for a sense of failure; family members are vulnerable to additional distress with every added crisis. In addition, the wife of a lower-income husband can earn money more equal to her husband's earnings; consequently, the wife of a low-earning husband has less to lose by a divorce. A husband earning little also is likely to have an occupation that makes it easier for him to disappear without sustaining great loss; those in professional, business, or upper-management occupations have more to lose. Kinship systems also bind people differently in different class and status levels.

---

[6]Education, too, is inversely related to marital instability, but that relationship is largely due to other correlates of education. Thus, the effects of a wife's education upon marital instability is greatly reduced when age at marriage is taken into account (Bumpass and Sweet 1972).

A lower-ranking woman, anticipating marital disruption and given the greater sex-role segregation, tends to maintain closer relations with her mother and other women relatives. She has a source of support in time of trouble and an option to a distressful marriage. On the other hand, in upper status and class ranks, extended kinship ties help keep controls over all members so that each conforms to family and class codes; this has long included the rule not to divorce (Hollingshead and Redlich 1958).

Despite this reasoning, recent evidence indicates that high education among white women is associated with a relatively high incidence of marital disruption (Udry 1966). The relationship between years of formal education and divorce is becoming curvilinear. Furthermore, Campbell, Converse, and Rodgers (1976) have found that more educated persons are less likely to be completely satisfied with their marriage than are men and women completing only grade school or some high school. They reason that satisfaction depends partly on aspirations and more highly educated persons are more likely to have higher aspirations.

Goode (1962) examined data on divorce rates throughout the world. In general he found more marital instability within the lower strata than the upper. Whether the greater marital instability is exhibited in divorce proceedings or not depends on how easy or inexpensive a divorce is. Where divorce is difficult and costly, it is primarily an upper-class "privilege."

An important aspect of family life are relations to kin beyond the nuclear family. Related to this is the role neighbors and friends play in social life. The research about such interpersonal relations indicates that kin play a more important role in social life among working-class persons than among middle-class families (Kriesberg and Bellin 1965; Cohen and Hodges 1963). Working-class persons entertain at home, largely with their relatives rather than work associates or other friends. These findings hold true even when changes in residence and moves to suburban developments increase the physical distance from parents and siblings. This was found in an English study where working-class families earning income comparable to white-collar workers were interviewed (Goldthorpe et al. 1967). Neighbors, too, play a more important role in the social life of working-class than middle-class families. Soviet studies also indicate that persons of higher social standing are much more likely to spend leisure time with work associates rather than relatives, compared to persons of low social standing (Lipset and Dobson 1973, p. 139).

Cohen and Hodges (1963) report the results of a comprehensive study of social class on the San Francisco peninsula; respondents were asked several questions about their social life. They compared four strata; the upper-middle, lower-middle, upper-lower, and lower-lower. Lower-lower stratum persons visited relatives most often (averaging 4 visits a month) while upper middle stratum made such visits least often (averaging 2 visits a month). The lower the stratum the more likely were the respondents to mention relatives among their

TABLE 9.4   Category of People Entertained at Home by Class Level

People Have to House Most Often[1]	Class Level			
	Upper-Middle	Lower-Middle	Upper-Lower	Lower-Lower
Neighbors	10.6	6.9	13.4	14.6
Relatives	15.9	20.8	41.2	58.5
Friends (Work)	21.2	29.1	10.1	4.9
Friends (Elsewhere)	52.2	43.1	35.3	21.9
Totals (Percent)	99.9	99.9	100.0	99.9
(N)	(113)	(72)	(119)	(41)

[1] The question was, "Who are the people you have over to your home (for parties or night-time visits) *most* frequently or often (check one): (a) neighbors; (b) relatives; (c) friends from work; (d) friends you have met elsewhere?"

Source: Cohen and Hodges 1963; based upon Table 2, p. 310.

closest friends. Entertaining at home was most usually with relatives among the lower-lower stratum and with friends not from work among the upper-middle (see Table 9.4). Of course, persons at each stratum interact with relatives, neighbors, and friends from work and elsewhere. And many lower-lower persons most frequently entertain friends not associated with employment and many upper-middle persons most frequently have relatives visit them at home. But, in general, lower-ranking persons have more restricted social networks—indeed, are more likely to have no close friends, compared to higher-ranking persons (Kahl 1957, p. 138).

Several factors help account for the varying patterns of social interaction among the different class and status ranks. Physical mobility of middle-class persons in the professions and managerial occupations disrupts ties with relatives and makes frequent visiting difficult. The greater sex-role segregation among low-income families may tend to exclude friends from work as *family* friends. Work activities for many persons are not challenging; this is most marked for operatives and service workers, but is also relatively true for clerical and sales jobs (Campbell, Converse, and Rodgers 1976, p. 301).[7] Furthermore, the lower-lower class work is often of short duration. Friendships derived from employment are not likely for persons whose work is not central to their life.

Community Life

The varying patterns of social relations among persons in different class and status levels is related to how they differ in their use of leisure time and involvement in organized groups. Local and national studies have all documented

[7] Analysis of the 1976 NORC General Social Survey reveals that skilled manual workers are as likely as professional and technical workers to be very satisfied with their work (57 percent compared to 55 percent). Clerical workers are less likely to be very satisfied (51 percent are), but more likely than operatives (46 percent) or laborers (35 percent). Farmers are most likely to be very satisfied (73 percent).

a very high relationship between class or status and participation in voluntary organizations. Persons with higher incomes, more years of education, more prestigeful jobs (particularly business and professional ones) are likely to belong and be active in voluntary organizations (Wright and Hyman 1958). Persons in unskilled occupations with low income generally do not join organizations. Cohen and Hodges reason that persons in the lower-lower stratum have difficulty in envisaging events relatively remote from their immediate concrete experiences, do not feel that their participation will make any important difference in how things turn out, and seek the attainment of their goals and the satisfaction of social interaction "through a network of particularistic, highly personal relationships" (1963, p. 316).

Many situational constraints, however, may account for the relationship between class and involvement in voluntary associations. Such participation requires resources of money, social skills, and some control over one's own time. Involvement is more likely if there are rewards from others for participation and the experience of success in it. Even the values and beliefs that are relevant to participation may be the result of the current circumstances, rather than intergenerationally transmitted. In the Syracuse study of social mobility and public housing, respondents were asked about their parents' involvement in voluntary associations. Among the married mothers there was no relationship between their own participation in voluntary organizations and either their mothers' or their fathers' involvement. Among the husbandless mothers, there was a small relationship (correlation was .18) between their involvement and their mothers' (Kriesberg and Bellin 1965, p. 252). No relationship between the socioeconomic level of the family of origin and participation in voluntary associations was found. These findings do not indicate that intergenerational, subcultural processes significantly contribute to explaining the relationship between class and involvement in voluntary associations.

There certainly are wide differences in the use of leisure time by social class. These differences are sometimes caricatured by depictions of highbrows, lowbrows, and middlebrows in relationship to high culture (Lynes 1949) or highbrow, upper middlebrow, lower middlebrow, and lowbrow in terms of sex and marriage patterns (Simon and Gagnon 1969). The nature and extent of the differences in the use of leisure time have been documented in many studies (Clarke 1956; Hollingshead 1949; Warner and Lunt 1941; Hodges 1964). Persons in high class and status levels, more than persons in other levels, attend concerts, plays, and special lectures, read more frequently and read "serious" books and magazines. Lower-ranking persons are likely to spend time in taverns and watching television. Participating and attending sports activities also varies by social class: "the higher an American's social class position, the likelier he is to be a sports 'doer' than a sports 'viewer' " (Hodges 1964, p. 166).

In the Soviet Union, too, research indicates that persons of higher occupational status are more likely to have libraries of over one hundred books, to read, and to have a piano or accordian; they are less likely to have a television set than are persons in low-skilled white-collar and manual occupations (Lipset and Dobson 1973, pp. 140-141).

Many of these differences are probably significantly affected simply by differences in income and the opportunities that money makes possible and its absence makes impossible. To some extent, too, the conditions of employment affect particular uses of leisure time. Many workers seek to escape the routine and monotony of their jobs, to get away from it all (Blum 1953). In matters of taste, however, there is some evidence of intergenerational transmission of patterns of conduct. For example, in the Syracuse social mobility and public housing study, the authors found that going to concerts, plays, and museums was related to current income almong married mothers and to the socioeconomic rank of their fathers (Kriesberg and Bellin 1965, p. 228). Among busbandless mothers, however, there was no relationship between those activities and current income or the status of their family or origin; probably the circumstances of being without a husband had an overwhelming effect on engaging in such activities. In the case of reading books, the level of socioeconomic origins is associated moderately with reading among husbandless mothers and only slightly among married mothers (Kriesberg and Bellin 1965, p. 232).[8]

Subjective States and Social Conduct

People can react in many different ways to their ranking in an evaluative hierarchy. People who are regarded as low may come to think of themselves as unworthy and of little account, or they may reject and rebel against the ranking system, or they may withdraw from the ranking system. Persons toward the top may feel self-confident and have high self-regard or they may keep striving for even greater status. What does the evidence show about the variety of possible ways in which people react to their rank? We will study mental illness, happiness, self-esteem, and interpersonal conduct as related to class and status rankings.

Inkeles (1960) examined results in several countries from surveys that asked about people's satisfaction and happiness. No matter how the question was asked, persons of lower class or status ranking were less likely to say they were happy than were persons of higher ranks. Cantril (1965) undertook a systematic comparative study of human concerns in many countries of the world. To make the results comparable from country to country, he used a self-anchoring ladder. That is, respondents were asked to imagine the best possible life and then the worst. Then they were shown a picture of a ladder with steps from zero to ten and the interviewer said:

> Here is a picture of a ladder. Suppose we say that the top of the ladder
> represents the best possible life for you and the bottom represents the

---

[8] Socioeconomic status of the family of origin was dichotomized in terms of the father's occupational status. Using the index developed by Otis Dudly Duncan, low was an index of 18 or less and high was 19 or more. The degree of association was measured by Kendall Tau C, measuring the ranks correlation in between socioeconomic origins and books read. Among the husbandless mothers, the correlation was .20 and among the married mothers only .12.

TABLE 9.5 Personal Self-Ratings by Socioeconomic Level and Country

Country	Socioeconomic Level	Personal Ratings				
		High (Steps 7-10)	Middle (Steps 4-6)	Low (Steps 0-3)	%	Totals (N)
Brazil	High	51	43	6	100	(205)
	Middle	22	48	30	100	(1443)
	Low	15	43	47	100	(1091)
Cuba	High	56	38	6	100	(272)
	Middle	49	42	9	100	(441)
	Low	43	46	11	100	(769)
Dominican	High	13	52	35	100	(190)
Republic	Middle	NI	NI	NI	–	–
	Low	1	9	90	100	(2226)
India	High	15	66	19	100	NI
	Middle	5	56	40	100	NI
	Low	2	40	58	100	NI
Israel	High	54	43	3	100	NI
	Middle	30	55	15	100	NI
	Low	13	44	43	100	NI
Nigeria	High	41	53	6	100	102
	Middle	NI	NI	NI	–	–
	Low	21	49	30	100	2748
Panama	High	32	57	11	100	(370)
	Middle	NI	NI	NI	–	NI
	Low	13	54	33	100	(964)
Philippines	High	48	45	7	100	(301)
	Middle	18	62	20	100	(560)
	Low	9	53	38	100	(527)
United States	High	63	32	5	100	(825)
	Middle	50	43	7	100	(915)
	Low	40	50	10	100	(827)
West Germany	High	40	55	5	100	(40)
	Middle	22	68	10	100	(281)
	Low	24	52	24	100	(157)
Yugoslavia	High	30	56	16	100	NI
	Middle	27	59	14	100	NI
	Low	19	57	24	100	NI

Note: NI indicates information was not included for these categories.

Source: Cantril 1965, Appendix D, Tables 21, 22, 23 and Appendix B.

worst possible life for you. Where on the ladder do you feel you personally stand at the present time? Step number   (p. 23).

The respondents were also asked to evaluate their position five years ago and five years into the future. We will discuss only the findings about the present.

As can be seen in Table 9.5, in every country, persons of higher socioeconomic levels tend to regard themselves as higher on the ladder, closer to the best possible life for them. The range is sometimes very large; for example, in Brazil, 51 percent of the respondents of high socioeconomic level placed themselves high on the ladder, but only 15 percent of the persons low in socioeconomic level did so; of the high socioeconomic persons, only 6 percent placed themselves at the low end of the ladder, while 47 percent of the low-ranking persons placed themselves there.

Table 9.5 also indicates very marked differences among the countries. In some countries (e.g., the Dominican Republic and India) few persons place themselves high on the ladder. In some countries (e.g., the United States and Cuba) few persons locate themselves at the bottom of the ladder. The average rating varies considerably among the countries studied: a sample of Israelis living in Kibbutzim had the highest average score, 7.0, followed by the United States with 6.6, and Cuba with 6.4. At the other end, the Dominican Republic had an average score of 1.6 and India, 3.7 (Cantril 1965, Table 9:1).[9]

Persons in relatively low class status and power ranks, then, tend to be dissatisfied with their conditions. They can cope with this dissatisfaction, unhappiness, and distress in a variety of ways. They may hold themselves responsible for their conditions, blame themselves, and sink into despair. Or they may strive diligently to improve their lot. People may tend to blame others, individually or collectively. They may struggle along, trying to make the best of the circumstances without denegrating themselves. Or they may organize with others similarly situated to try to alter their shared circumstances; we will consider that possibility in the next chapter. In this chapter we review the evidence about mental illness and the impairment of mental functioning that might be related to relatively low ranks in class, status, and power.

Although many studies have related socioeconomic rank and mental disorders, interpreting findings in this area is difficult. If lower-ranking persons suffer higher incidences of mental disorder, is that because they face harsher circumstances, which provoke mental breakdowns? Or, do people who are mentally impaired become low ranking? Or, do higher-ranking persons protect their friends and relatives who are having psychiatric difficulties from being institutionalized or otherwise treated in ways that are recorded? Are persons generally less tolerant of the ways in which lower-ranking persons behave? Do

---

[9]The average rating for two other countries are reported, although information comparable to that presented in Table 9.5 was not available. The average rating in Egypt was 5.5, following Cuba, and in Poland it was 4.4, just above India (Cantril 1965, Table 9:1). The correlation between a country's socioeconomic level and these average ratings is high: .67 (Cantril 1965, p. 194). The ladder ratings are relatively low, given the level of socioeconomic level in the Dominican Republic and Poland, and relatively high in Cuba and Egypt. In addition to the general socioeconomic level, perhaps the involvement with one's country as a whole and its political conditions affect personal feelings of satisfaction.

they consequently tend to label such behavior as deviant and mentally disturbed? We cannot completely untangle all these possibilities, but relevant studies give us some help.

One of the early large-scale studies relating mental illness to socioeconomic levels was done by Faris and Dunham (1939). During a 12-year period they studied over 30,000 persons who had been admitted to hospitals in Chicago for treatment of mental disorder. They related the type of mental disorder to the patients' area of residence and concluded that psychosis was associated with poverty. This was particularly marked in the case of schizophrenia. Such findings, however, are subject to other interpretations: perhaps psychotics drift into slum and poor neighborhoods or perhaps the actual incidence of mental illness is higher in more well-to-do neighborhoods but mentally ill persons from those areas are not hospitalized.

Later studies have sought to resolve such questions. Hollingshead and Redlich (1958) studied psychiatric patients in the New Haven, Connecticut, area receiving care from private psychiatrists and patients who were institutionalized. They found that schizophrenia and manic-depressive illnesses were more prevalent at lower socioeconomic levels than at higher levels. They also found that treatment varied by class level. Lower-class persons are more likely to be treated by residents and interns and to be given shock therapy; patients of higher socioeconomic levels are more likely to be treated by psychiatrists using psycho-analysis and psychotherapy.

The next step was an intensive study of the population at large, including untreated persons who might be mentally ill. An interdisciplinary group attempted this in a study of an area of Manhattan, New York. Srole et al. (1962) called the area Midtown; they interviewed a sample of the people in Midtown and used the data to assess the degree of mental impairment. They found a very strong direct relationship between socioeconomic level (SES) and mental well-being. For example, they differentiated twelve SES levels based upon occupation, education, income, and household rent. Severe impairment is particularly great in the lowest stratum; this was also found in the Hollingshead and Redlich (1958) study. Parental SES also was found to be highly related to the respondents' mental health. For example, considering three parental SES levels, impairment was found among 10 percent of those from the highest levels, 17 percent from the middle level, and 20 percent from the lower level (Srole et al. 1962, Table 12-2).

Living conditions associated with different class levels impose diverse strains and provide different kinds of support. Variations in ways of coping with such problems and tolerance for the coping effects also tend to penalize persons in lower-class levels.

Persons in lower ascribed status levels should also be expected to have higher mental illness rates. Many studies relate gender to mental illness, as measured by self-reported symptoms, admissions to mental hospitals, and treatment by private physicians. The results are not completely consistent and clear. Gove and Tudor (1973) surveyed these studies and concluded that women are more likely to be mentally ill, no matter how measured, than men. The difference seems most marked for neuroses. Dohrenwend and Dohrenwend (1976) reviewed studies done in the United States and Europe. They concluded that among females there are relatively high rates of neurosis and manic-depressive psychosis, both of which share a depressive symptomatology. On the other hand, among males rates are relatively high in personality disorders with a possible common denominator of irresponsible and antisocial behavior. There is not a simple relationship between sex roles and overall stress related to the status of men and women, which is then reflected in rates of mental impairments. The ways of handling stress are certainly channeled by other aspects of sex role differentiation. What is tolerated and what is deemed to require treatment or institutionalization also varies by sex. Since a greater range of behavior is regarded as appropriate for men, women commit more behaviors that are regarded as "ill" or unacceptable (Chesler 1972, p. 39).

Race in America is another basis of ascribed status inequality and could result in different rates of mental impairment. Pettigrew (1964), reviewing the studies of mental illness rates among blacks and whites, concludes that psychoses rates for blacks are higher than the rates for whites, especially for schizophrenia and some organic psychoses. The difference for neuroses is lower and rates of conditions like character disorders may be higher among whites than among blacks.

Persons ranked low in status may escape some of the possible psychological harm of their placement in a variety of ways. Insofar as they do not agree with the rating given them by the status system and share with the high-ranking persons the relative evaluations, they protect their self-esteem. Psychological well-being depends greatly on interpersonal and intimate support; this can be acquired within small groups and families at any rank level. Perhaps even more crucial in the context of understanding stratification is what persons perceive as the reasons for their placement in the status and class system. If the person's status is ascribed, it is not a matter of personal responsibility; she or he need not blame herself or himself. If opportunities are closed through discrimination, failures may be easier to accept and may cause less damage to one's self-esteem than if opportunities are viewed as open and yet one is not successful.

Evidence supporting this reasoning was found by Parker and Kleiner (1966) in their study of blacks in Philadelphia. They interviewed a large community sample and a representative sample diagnosed as mentally ill. Respondents were asked how often they thought success actually resulted from working hard, saving money, and being ambitious. The mentally ill were somewhat more likely to reply "very often" than were the respondents in the community sample (p. 51). It seems that the mentally ill blacks are somewhat more likely than other Philadelphia blacks to think that the path to goal achievement is open; hence, they experience more stress at their failure to attain their goals.

Finally, we will consider one other consequence of social ranking: modes of interaction. We focus upon the ways in which lower-ranking persons interact with their "superiors." Jo Freeman (1973) has characterized some of the similar accommodating manners of blacks and women: feigning ignorance, indicating deference by voice tone and flattery, and carefully studying how the dominant group is susceptible to influence.

Pieces of systematic evidence indicate accommodating behavior by low-ranking persons in the presence of higher-ranking persons. For example, on juries, women and persons in lower-prestige occupations participate less and are less likely to be elected foreman (Strodtbeck and Mann 1956; Strodtbeck, James and Hawkins 1958). Whites initiate more interactions than blacks in biracial work groups; blacks talk more to whites than to blacks (Katz, Goldston and Benjamin 1958). Archibald (1976) notes a few other patterns in interactions across class, status, and power lines: persons of different ranks tend to avoid each other; when persons of different ranks do interact, they tend to do so in a narrow, role-specific manner rather than in a personal manner; an element of hostility underlies much interaction between unequals.

As in discussing other consequences of class, status, and power levels, such patterns of interaction between unequals can have alternative explanations. One possibility is that differences in subcultures and socialization account for the patterns of interaction among unequals. It may be that lower-ranking persons expect and believe that higher-ranking persons indeed are superior in knowledge and therefore that properly they should initiate action and be influential; moreover, higher-ranking persons expect lower-ranking persons to be less able to act and think correctly (Berger, Cohen, Zelditch 1972). It might also be argued that threat and coercion account for the patterns of conduct (Archibald 1976). Those in high positions feel somewhat endangered by those in lower positions because "the former's privileges depend upon the continued deference and acquiescence of lows. . . . Many of the 'underprivileged' realize that greater equality is in their best interest. . . . That those of low position would be threatened by those higher than themselves is also obvious" (Archibald 1976, pp. 821-822). A variety of evidence indicates that threat does exist in interaction among unequals and helps contribute to the previously noted patterns of interaction. This contribution may be particularly great in formal settings, particularly work-related ones, but it is not absent in informal status structures.

CONCLUSIONS

In this chapter we reviewed theories and research about the consequences of class, status, and power ranking on the way people think and act. Rather than try to summarize the many findings, we will discuss their implications. We consider three general questions: Are there major differences in life styles of diverse strata and what determines whatever differences there are? What are the implications of these differences in life styles for the allocation of persons within class, status, and power hierarchies and for the maintenance and change of those hierarchies? What are the implications of these variations for the persistence and change of the hierarchies?

Different Life Styles and Their Determinants

There has been much controversy over the reality of strata. Observers disagree about the extent to which different strata have distinctive life styles and to what extent those differences are situationally determined or culturally transmitted.

One division in particular among class levels has been the subject of discussion: that between the working class and the middle class. A major controversy here has been about the "embourgeoisement" of the working class (Zweig 1960; Hamilton 1964; Goldthorpe et al. 1969; Massey 1975). The argument for this thesis is that with the general affluence and increasing income of the working class, its members are adopting more and more of the life styles of the bourgeoisie, the middle class. The general emphasis upon consumption and leisure-time activities and the increased earnings of manual workers tend to diminish and eventually erase the dividing line between working class and middle class.

The evidence noted earlier in this chapter does show varying degrees of distinctiveness between manual and white-collar workers over time and in different spheres of social life. But the evidence does not demonstrate that the differences in life style between working-class and middle-class members has completely disappeared, even in advanced industrial societies. This might be taken as evidence for the argument that strata differences are perpetuated by intergenerationally transmitted subcultures rather than contemporary circumstances. It should be noted, however, that even when manual workers earn incomes comparable to lower white-collar workers, their life circumstances still differ in significant ways. Many manual jobs, even when remunerated as highly as white-collar jobs, have lower social standing and are sometimes even a basis for embarrassment. The work itself is often more boring and mind-numbing and also less secure. Furthermore, even if remuneration on an hourly basis is comparable, lifetime earnings and opportunities for career advancement are usually lower. There is some evidence, as noted in the studies of Kohn (1969), Blum (1953), Hamilton (1967), Goldthorpe et al. (1967) and Glenn and Alston (1968), of differences in values and conduct between working-class and middle-class persons.

Another possibility is that clerical workers are becoming proletarianized and share more characteristics with manual workers than other white-collar workers (Hamilton 1966; Gorz 1973). There is evidence that this is true for friendship choices (Lauman 1973), intergenerational mobility, and residence patterns (Vanneman 1977).

One issue about the embourgeoisement idea is the extent to which a distinct line can be drawn between the working class and the middle class. Vanneman and Pampel (1977) ingenuously tested this. They compared the way that status as a continuous dimension and that class as a dichotomy affect a variety of attitudes and behaviors. They categorized people according to their occupation: first as being either in manual or in white-collar occupations, then according to the Socio-economic Index of their occupations. Vanneman and Pampel found that life satisfactions and organizational memberships were better explained by the continuous status rating than the class dichotomy. On the other hand, areas that are more clearly societal—for example, confidence in national institutions—show stronger class relationships than occupational prestige relationships. The class differences, then, have particular relevance for collective reactions to inequality, the topic for the next chapter.

Racial, ethnic, and other status categories might also be expected to have different life styles attached to them, particularly insofar as membership is ascribed and considerable social segregation exists. Nevertheless, variations in life style among different ethnic and racial groups in the United States are largely attributable to class differences. When class characteristics are held constant, ethnic and racial differences in life style characteristics are reduced considerably or vanish.

We have considered two sets of factors that might account for variations in feelings, conduct, and thought among persons in different class, status, and power ranks: cultural and situational. We have seen some evidence for each set of factors. However, variations in life styles among different class, status, and power strata seem to be in large measure accounted for in terms of the circumstances of the members. Subcultural explanations are most likely to be significant when we seek to account for life styles of relatively isolated communities and for groups with ascribed membership. Cultural processes are probably also particularly pertinent for aspects of the way of life that are relatively independent of material resources or observable consequences. In other words, if we wanted to account for different views of the nature of God, material circumstances are less likely to be important than if we wanted to account for variations in taking extended vacations (Kriesberg 1963, 1970).

There appears to be considerable consensus in this society, and probably in most societies, about what is important and valuable. Indeed, people agree to a considerable extent in most societies about the importance of many aspects of life, particularly personal economic well-being (Cantril 1965). The shared values within a society are an incentive for those who rank low to try to improve their position in the hierarchies. The agreement that places them low, then, is a spur to try to alter their placement. This brings us to the next set of implications.

Implications for the Allocation of Persons

Whatever the bases for the variations in the way people think, feel, and act, the variations have implications for their own and their children's placement in class, status, and power rankings. Some of the differences among social strata that we have discussed do not have known consequences for the way people are located within such hierarchies. Although much work has been done on child-rearing and child-training, it is not clear that early or late weaning, for example, has particular implications for social mobility; we will discuss, only broadly, how variations in life styles may affect the allocation of persons.

Many of the ways people accommodate to their circumstances probably help keep them there. The adaptations that people make are often responses to difficult problems; they do not abolish the problem. Thus, if low-ranking persons "play dumb" in order to protect themselves and to fend off their "superiors," they are not improving their chances of advancing in the hierarchy dominated by those "superiors." Low-ranking persons may also adapt by apathetic withdrawal and by loss of confidence; again, these adaptations inhibit effective advancement within the existing hierarchical structure. The mutual expectations that unequals develop help sustain both sides in their roles. If teachers expect middle-class children to do well in school and complete many years of formal education but do not expect the same of working-class children, the children are likely to share the expectations of the teacher and this becomes an added pressure upon them.

Studies of impoverished workers indicate how survival techniques used under adverse circumstances make escape from those circumstances more difficult. For example, if employment is sporadic and pay is very low, there are advantages for an extended family or group of persons to provide aid to the member who is in trouble (Davis 1946); after all, someone else's turn will undoubtedly come soon. The security that is denied in the job market can be partially gained in the social network of family and friends. But this means that individual success cannot be used for personal advancement outside that network. Inducement for personel investment and long-range planning is reduced, and sometimes even the inducement to strive beyond a minimal effort is reduced.

Some of the ways that persons at different rank levels adapt and the ways of life that they develop help to alter the allocation of persons. The dominant groups are generally skilled in   activities that are valued by society and regarded as important. That may be one reason why they are dominant. Or the dominant group may be able to make what they do well the important activities of the society. In any case, they have a vested interest in maintaining the primacy of those activities and training their children in them. If opportunities for new kinds of activities emerge, however, many of them may be less adept at the new undertakings than persons from surviving subdominant ranks. Thus, various aristocracies have been overtaken by emerging merchant and industrial classes.

This discussion brings us to a consideration of how patterns of thought and conduct associated with different strata may affect class, status, and power hierarchies. We turn to that next.

Implications for Persistence and Change of Hierarchies

How people in different ranks generally feel, think, and act tends to stabilize and destabilize the hierarchies we have been discussing. Aside from who is placed where, the very ordering of locations is affected by the way people adapt to their stations in life. Some of these connections will be suggested; systematic evidence is sparse.

We first consider those connections that tend to stabilize the inequalities. These connections are among the high-ranking strata and the low-ranking strata. Persons in higher status, power, and class strata are disproportionally likely to have a sense of confidence and the trained skills appropriate to their positions. This helps sustain the hierarchy. Persons in elite positions are also likely to be relatively solidary and cohesive, both because of their relatively fewer members and their resources for keeping in close communication. On the other hand, lower-ranking persons, by personally trying to cope with their circumstances and to do the best they can, cater to the high-ranking persons and thus help to sustain the inequality.

In some ways, however, the connections between ranks and ways of living tend to destabilize the system of inequality. It is possible, and has happened in the past, that members of high-ranking strata become corrupt, self-indulgent, and indolent. Living in an isolated social order in which their relative standing with each other becomes paramount, they lose touch with the requirements of the changing external social and material environment. The fall of the French and Russian aristocracies in revolutionary upheavals illustrates a possible consequence of such developments. Furthermore, the low-ranking persons may contribute to the transformation of the stratification system by increasing passivity and withdrawal; this isolates the dominant strata and lessens the effective functioning of the social system as a whole. If low-ranking persons feel deprived, even the alternative of revolt and the turmoil it entails may come to seem attractive. If they are desperate enough, low-ranking persons find that the high-ranking persons have smaller and smaller claims to make effectively and, therefore, control them less.

At this point, we are beginning to discuss how people in different strata think and act as groups to sustain or to change the system of stratification. Certainly many changes, particularly radical and rapid ones, are brought about by the actions of organized groups. People do deliberately organize to change and to maintain systems of inequality. These matters are the subject of the next chapter.

REFERENCES

ANTONOVSKY, AARON. 1967. "Social Class, Life Expectancy and Overall Mortality," *Milbank Memorial Fund Quarterly* 45 (April):31-73.

ARCHIBALD, W. PETER. 1976. "Face-to-Face: The Alienating Effects of Class, Status and Power Divisions,"*American Sociological Review* 41 (October): 819-837.

BERGER, JOSEPH, BERNARD P. COHEN, and MORRIS ZELDITCH. 1972. "Status Characteristics and Social Interaction," *American Sociological Review* 37 (June):241-255.

BERTRAN, ALVIN L. 1962. "School Attendance and Attainment: Function and Dysfunction of School and Family Systems," *Social Forces* 40 (March):228-253.

BLALOCK, HUBERT M., JR. 1967a. "Status Inconsistency, Social Mobility, Status Integration and Structural Effects," *American Sociological Review* 32 (October):790-801.

BLALOCK, HUBERT M., JR. 1967b. "Status Inconsistency and Interaction: Some Alternative Models," *American Journal of Sociology* 73 (November): 305-315.

BLOOD, ROBERT O. and DONALD M. WOLFE. 1960. *Husbands and Wives.* Glencoe, Ill.: Free Press.

BLOOM, BENJAMIN S. 1963. *Stability and Change in Human Characteristics.* New York: John Wiley.

BLUM, FRED H. 1953. *Toward a Democratic Work Process.* New York: Harper.

BOGUE, DONALD J. 1969. *Principles of Demography.* New York: John Wiley.

BRONFENBRENNER, URIE. 1958. "Socialization and Social Class Through Time and Space." Pp. 400-425 in E. E. Maccoby, T. M. Newcomb, and F. L. Hartley (Eds.), *Readings in Social Psychology.* New York: Holt.

BUMPASS, LARRY L. and JAMES A. SWEET. 1972. "Differentials in Marital Instability." *American Sociological Review* 37 (December):754-766.

CAMPBELL, ANGUS, PHILIP E. CONVERSE, and WILLARD L. RODGERS. 1976. *The Quality of American Life.* New York: Russell Sage Foundation.

CANTRIL, HADLEY. 1965. *The Pattern of Human Concerns.* New Brunswick, N.J.: Rutgers University Press.

CHAFE, WILLIAM H. 1972. *The American Woman: Her Changing Social, Economic, and Political Role, 1920-1970.* New York: Oxford University Press.

CHESLER, PHYLLIS. 1972. *Women and Madness.* Garden City, N.Y.: Doubleday.

CLARKE, ALFRED C. 1956. "The Use of Leisure and Its Relation to Levels of Occupational Prestige," *American Sociological Review* 21 (June):301-307.

COHEN, ALBERT K., and HAROLD M. HODGES. 1963. "Characteristics of the Lower-Blue-Collar Class," *Social Problems* 10 (Spring):303-334.

DAVIS, ALLISON. 1946. "Motivations of the Underprivileged Worker." Pp. 84-106 in William F. Whyte (Ed.), *Industry and Society.* New York: McGraw-Hill.

DE WOLFF, P., and J. MEERDINK. 1954. "Mortality Rates in Amsterdam According to Profession," *Proceedings of the World Population Conference, 1954, Vol. 1.* New York: United Nations (E/Conf. 13/413).

DOHRENWEND, BRUCE P., and BARBARA SNELL DOHRENWEND. 1976. "Sex Differences and Psychiatric Disorders," *American Journal of Sociology* 81 (May):1447-1454.

ELLIS, ROBERT A., W. CLAYTON LANE, and VIRGINIA OLESEN. 1963. "The Index of Class Position: An Improved Intercommunity Measure of Stratification," *American Sociological Review* 28 (April):271-277.

ERLANGER, HOWARD S. 1974. "Social Class and Corporal Punishment in Childrearing: A Reassessment," *American Sociological Review* 39 (February):68-85.

EVARIFF, WILLIAM. 1957. "How 'Different' Are Our Dropouts?" *Bulletin of the National Association of Secondary-School Principals* 41 (February): 212-218.

FARIS, ROBERT E. L., and H. WARREN DUNHAM. 1939. *Mental Disorders in Urban Areas*, Chicago: University of Chicago Press.

FREEMAN, JO. 1973. "The Building of the Gilded Cage." Pp. 166-185 in Jerome H. Skolnick and Elliott Currie (Eds.), *Crisis in American Institutions*, 2nd Ed. Boston: Little, Brown.

FREEMAN, JO (Ed.). 1975. *Women: A Feminist Perspective*. Palo Alto, Calif.: Mayfield.

GALTUNG, JOHAN. 1964. "A Structural Theory of Aggression," *Journal of Peace Research* 2:95-119.

GESCHWENDER, JAMES A. 1967. "Continuities in Theories of Status Consistency and Cognitive Dissonance," *Social Forces* 46 (December):160-171.

GESCHWENDER, JAMES A. 1968. "Status Inconsistency, Social Isolation, and Individual Unrest," *Social Forces* 46 (June):477-483.

GLENN, NORVAL D. and JON P. ALSTON. 1968. "Cultural Distance Among Occupational Categories," *American Sociological Review* 33 (June):365-382.

GOFFMAN, IRWIN W. 1957. "Status Consistency and Preference for Change in Power Distribution," *American Sociological Review* 22 (June):275-281.

GOLDTHORPE, JOHN H., DAVID LOCKWOOD, FRANK BECHHOFER, and JENNIFER PLATT. 1969. "The Affluent Worker and the Thesis of Embourgeoisement: Some Preliminary Findings," *Sociology* 1 (January):11-31.

GOODE, WILLIAM J. 1962. "Marital Satisfaction and Instability: A Cross-Cultural Class Analysis of Divorce Rates," *International Social Science Journal* 14 (No. 3), 507-526.

GOODE, WILLIAM J. 1963. *World Revolution and Family Patterns*, New York: Free Press.

GORZ, ANDRE. 1973. *Socialism and Revolution*. Garden City, N.Y.: Anchor Press. (Translated by Norman Denny.)

GOVE, WALTER R., and JEANNETTE F. TUDOR. 1973. "Adult Sex Roles and Mental Illness," *American Journal of Sociology* 78 (January):812-835.

HAER, JOHN L. 1957. "Predictive Utility of Five Indices of Social Stratification," *American Sociological Review* 22 (October):541-546.

HAMILTON, RICHARD F. 1964. "The Behavior and Values of Skilled Workers." Pp. 42-57 in Arthur B. Shostack and William Gombeg (Eds.), *Blue Collar World*. Englewood Cliffs, N.J.: Prentice-Hall.

HAMILTON, RICHARD F. 1966. "The Marginal Middle Class: A Reconsideration," *American Sociological Review* 31 (April):192-200.

HAMILTON, RICHARD F. 1967. *Affluence and the French Worker*. Princeton, N.J.: Princeton University Press.

HEISS, JEROLD, and SUSAN OWENS. 1972. "Self-Evaluations of Blacks and Whites," *American Journal of Sociology* 78 (September):360-370.

HODGES, HAROLD M., JR. 1964. *Social Stratification*. Cambridge, Mass.: Schenkman.

HOLLINGSHEAD, AUGUST B. 1949. *Elmtown's Youth*. New York: John Wiley.

HOLLINGSHEAD, AUGUST B., and E. C. REDLICH. 1958. *Social Class and Mental Illness*. New York: John Wiley.

HORNUNG, CARLTON ALBERT. 1972. *Status Consistency: A Method of Measurement and Empirical Examination*. Unpublished Ph.D. Dissertation, Department of Sociology, Syracuse University.

HUGHES, EVERETT C. 1944. "Dilemmas and Contradictions of Status," *American Journal of Sociology* 50 (March):353-359.

INKELES, ALEX. 1960. "Industrial Man: The Relation of Status to Experience, Perception, and Value," *The American Journal of Sociology* 66 (July): 1-31.

JACKSON, ELTON F. 1962. "Status Consistency and Symptoms of Stress," *American Sociological Review* 27 (August):469-480.

JACKSON, ELTON F. and RICHARD F. CURTIS. 1968. "Conceptualization and Measurement in the Study of Social Stratification." Pp. 112-149 in Hubert M. Blalock and Ann B. Blalock (Eds.), *Methodology in Social Research*. New York: McGraw-Hill.

JENCKS, CHRISTOPHER, MARSHALL SMITH, HENRY ACLAND, MARY JO BANE, DAVID COHEN, HERBERT GINTIS, BARBARA HEYNS, and STEPHAN MICHELSON. 1973. *Inequality: A Reassessment of the Effect of Family and Schooling in America*. New York: Harper and Row.

KAHL, JOSEPH A. 1957. *The American Class Structure*. New York: Holt, Rinehart and Winston.

KATZ, IRWIN, J. GOLDSTON and L. BENJAMIN. 1958. "Behavior and Productivity in Bi-Racial Work Groups," *Human Relations* 11:123-141.

KOHN, MELVIN L. 1969. *Class and Conformity: A Study in Values*, Homewood, Ill.: Dorsey Press.

KOMAROVSKY, MIRRA. 1962. *Blue-Collar Marriage*. New York: Random House.

KOOS, EARL L. 1954. *The Health of Regionville*. New York: Columbia University Press.

KRIESBERG, LOIS ABLIN. 1963. "Dilemmas and Contradictions of Married Educated Women." Unpublished paper.

KRIESBERG, LOUIS, and BEATRICE TREIMAN. 1960. "Socio-Economic Status and the Utilization of Dentists' Services," *Journal of the American College of Dentists* 27 (September):147-165.

KRIESBERG, LOUIS. 1963. "The Relationship Between Socio-Economic Rank and Behavior," *Social Problems* 10 (Spring):334-353.

KRIESBERG, LOUIS, and SEYMOUR S. BELLIN. 1965. "Fatherless Families and Housing: A Study of Dependency." Publication. Syracuse, N.Y.: Syracuse University Youth Development Center.

KRIESBERG, LOUIS. 1970. *Mothers in Poverty*. Chicago: Aldine.

KRIESBERG, LOUIS. 1973. *The Sociology of Social Conflicts*. Englewood Cliffs, N.J.: Prentice-Hall.

LANDECKER, WERNER S. 1960. "The Structure-Continuum Controversy," *American Sociological Review* 25 (December):868-877.

LASLETT, BARBARA. 1971. "Mobility and Work Satisfaction: A Discussion of the Use and Interpretation of Mobility Models," *American Journal of Sociology* 77 (July):19-35.

LAUMANN, EDWARD O. and DAVID R. SEGAL. 1971. "Status Inconsistency and Ethnoreligious Group Membership as Determinants and Social Participation and Political Attitudes," *American Journal of Sociology* 77 (July): 36-61.

LAUMANN, EDWARD O. 1973. *Bonds of Pluralism: The Form and Substance of Urban Social Networks*. New York: John Wiley.

LEACOCK, ELEANOR BURKE (Ed.). 1971. *The Culture of Poverty: A Critique*. New York: Simon and Schuster.

LENSKI, GERHARD E. 1954. "Status Crystallization: A Non-Vertical Dimension of Social Status," *American Sociological Review* 19 (August):405-413.

LERNER, MONROE. 1975. "Social Differences in Physical Health." Pp. 80-134 in John Kols and Irving Kenneth Zola (Eds.), *Poverty and Health: A Sociological Analysis*, Rev. Ed. Cambridge, Mass.: Harvard University Press.

LEWIS, OSCAR. 1959. *Five Families*. New York: Basic Books.

LEWIS, OSCAR. 1966. "The Culture of Poverty," *Scientific American* 215 (October):19-25.

LIEBOW, ELLIOT. 1969. *Tally's Corner: A Study of Negro Streetcorner Men*. Boston: Little, Brown.

LIPSET, SEYMOUR MARTIN, and RICHARD B. DOBSON. 1973. "Social Stratification and Sociology in the Soviet Union," *Survey* 88 (No. 3, Summer):114-185.

LYNES, RUSSEL. 1949. "Highbrow, Lowbrow, Middlebrow," *Harpers* 145 (February):175-180.

MC KINLAY, JOHN B. 1975. "The Help-Seeking Behavior of the Poor." Pp. 224-273 in John Kosa and Irving Kenneth Zola (Eds.), *Poverty and Health: A Sociological Analysis*. Cambridge, Mass.: Harvard University Press.

MASSEY, GARTH. 1975. "Studying Social Class: The Case of Embourgeoisment and the Culture of Poverty." *Social Problems* 22 (June):595-608.

MATRAS, JUDAH. 1973. *Populations and Societies*. Englewood Cliffs, N.J.: Prentice-Hall.

MILLER, WALTER B. 1958. "Lower Class Culture as a Generating Milieu of Gang Delinquency," *Journal of Social Issues* 14 (No. 3):5-19.

MYERS, JEROME K., and BERTRAM H. ROBERTS. 1959. *Family and Class Dynamics in Mental Illness*. New York: John Wiley.

OLSEN, MARVIN E., and JUDY CORDER TULLY. 1972. "Socio-Economic-Ethnic Status Inconsistency and Preference for Political Change," *American Sociological Review* 37 (October):560-574.

PARKER, SEYMOUR and ROBERT J. KLEINER. 1966. *Mental Illness in the Urban Negro Community*, New York: Free Press.

PEACH, CERI. 1974. "Homogamy, Propinquity and Segregation: A Re-Evaluation," *American Sociological Review* 39 (October):636-641.

PETTIGREW, THOMAS F. 1964. *A Profile of the Negro American*. Princeton, N.J.: D. Van Nostrand.

RAINWATER, LEE. 1968. "The Lower Class: Health, Illness, and Medical Institutions." Pp. 259-278 in Irwin Deutscher and Elizabeth J. Thompson (Eds.), *Among the People*. New York: Basic Books.

RINDFUSS, RONALD R., and JAMES A. SWEET. 1977. *Postwar Fertility Trends and Differentials in the United States*. New York: Academic Press.

RUSHING, WILLIAM A. 1975. *Community, Physicians, and Inequality*. Lexington, Mass.: Lexington Books.

SEWELL, WILLIAM H. and VIMAL P. SHAH. 1968. "Some Social Determinants of Educational Aspiration," *The American Journal of Sociology* 73 (March):559-572.

SIMON, WILLIAM and JOHN GAGNON. 1969. "How Fashionable Is Your Sex Life?" *McCall's* 94 (October):58-59.

STEINER, STAN. 1969. *La Raza.* New York: Harper and Row.

STRODTBECK, F. L., and R. D. MANN. 1956. "Sex Role Differentiation in Jury Deliberations," *Sociometry* 19 (March):3-11.

STRODTBECK, F. L., R. M. JAMES, and C. HAWKINS. 1958. "Social Status in Jury Deliberations." Pp. 379-388 in E. E. Maccoby, T. M. Newcomb, and E. L. Hartley (Eds.), *Readings in Social Psychology*, 3rd Ed. New York: Holt.

TREIMAN, DONALD J. 1966. "Status Discrepancy and Prejudice," *The American Journal of Sociology* 71 (May):651-664.

UDRY, J. RICHARD. 1966. "Marital Instability by Race, Sex, Education, and Occupation Using 1960 Census Data," *American Journal of Sociology* 72 (September):203-209.

UDRY, J. RICHARD. 1967. "Marital Instability by Race and Income Based Upon 1960 Census Data," *American Journal of Sociology* 72 (May):673-674.

United States Bureau of the Census. 1976. *Statistical Abstract of the United States: 1971* (96th Edition). Washington, D.C.: Government Printing Office.

United States Department of Health, Education and Welfare, Public Health Service. 1975. *Health United States, 1975*, Publication No. (ERA) 76-1232, National Center for Health Statistics, Rockville, Maryland.

VALENTINE, CHARLES. 1968. *Culture and Poverty: Critique and Counter Proposals.* Chicago: University of Chicago Press.

VANNEMAN, REEVE. 1977. "The Occupational Composition of American Classes: Results from Cluster Analysis," *American Journal of Sociology* 82 (January):783-807.

VANNEMAN, REEVE, and FRED C. PAMPEL. 1977. "The American Perception of Class and Status," *American Sociological Review* 42 (June):422-437.

WAITZKIN, HOWARD B., and BARBARA WATERMAN. 1974. *The Exploitation of Illness in Capitalist Society.* Indianapolis: Bobbs-Merrill.

WARNER, W. LLOYD, and PAUL S. LUNT. 1941. *The Social Life of a Modern Community.* New Haven, Conn.: Yale University Press.

WEBER, MAX. 1946. "Class, Status, and Power." Pp. 180-195 in H. H. Gerth and C. Wright Mills (Eds.), *From Max Weber.* New York: Oxford University Press. (Originally published in 1921.)

WILNER, DANIEL M., ROSABELLE PRICE WALKLEY, THOMAS C. PINKERTON, and MATHEW TAYBACK. 1962. *The Housing Environment and Family Life.* Baltimore: Johns Hopkins Press.

WRIGHT, CHARLES R., and HERBERT H. HYMAN. 1958. "Voluntary Association Memberships of American Adults: Evidence From National Sample Surveys," *American Sociological Review* 23 (June):284-300.

WRIGHT, JAMES D., and SONIA R. WRIGHT. 1976. "Social Class and Parental Values for Children: A Partial Replication and Extension of the Kohn Thesis," *American Sociological Review* 41 (June):527-537.

WRONG, DENNIS H. 1958. "Trends in Class Fertility in Western Nations," *The Canadian Journal of Economics and Political Science* 24 (May):216-229.

ZWEIG, FERDINAND. 1960. *The Worker in an Affluent Society.* London: Heinemann.

chapter 10

Conflict: A Collective Reaction

Oh freedom, oh freedom
Oh freedom over me,
And before I'd be a slave,
I'll be buried in my grave,
And go home to my Lord and be free.   *Negro Spiritual*

Inequalities have consequences for members of large categories and they react collectively: classes revolt; ethnic groups seek to separate themselves from their oppressors; parties excluded from governance struggle for control. This chapter focuses on reactions that become social conflicts, particularly group efforts to reduce, increase, or maintain the existing inequalities. The outcomes of such struggles help shape the stratification system.

Chapter 9 examined individual responses to inequality. In a sense, the convergence of such individual efforts constitutes collective reactions. People develop collective solutions to shared problems, including the problem of being located in a given stratum. Collective reactions, then, can be adaptations to shared circumstances, they can be cooperative efforts with those in other strata. Or, they can be symbiotic or exchange relations between groups in different strata. Collective reactions can also include other-worldly, religious movements, seeking withdrawal from earthly trials and deprivations. Conflict is one kind of collective reaction.

A conflict is a relationship in which two or more parties (or their spokespersons) think they have incompatible objectives (Kriesberg 1973). The means used in conducting a struggle are open. Conflict is usually thought of as involving coercion, typically violent coercion or threats of violence. If coercion or threats of coercion are not involved, or are highly regulated, conflict, although less obvious, is still present, even in collective bargaining, election contests, or judicial proceedings. This chapter gives the greatest attention to conflicts that are *not* highly regulated, partly because they indicate efforts at major changes in the system of inequality and partly because relatively regulated conflicts, such as the political participation and legal experiences of different ranks, have already been discussed.

We should also note that a conflict is a social relationship. Two or more adversaries must regard each other as having incompatible goals. A struggle does not arise simply from the demands of an oppressed stratum. It depends upon the response to those demands and to the other strata's own demands.

TYPES OF CONFLICTS

We will consider struggles relating to class, status, and power inequalities and examine different stages of struggles. As mentioned earlier in this book, Marx viewed class conflict as the fundamental human conflict and the basic

298

source of social change. He analyzed the underlying objective difference of interests between the capitalist class and the wage-earning proletariat. He foresaw emerging class consciousness by the workers, trade-union struggles growing to political struggles, and finally the overthrowing of the capitalist class and the establishment of communism.

Dahrendorf (1959) has argued that power conflicts are primary and he even defined class conflicts in those terms. There are certainly conflicts that are essentially struggles between elites, factions, parties and other groups whose only difference is unequal power. The European revolutions of the nineteenth century for political rights and participation in governance are instances of this. Contemporary revolutions, military seizures of power, and social movements struggling for political rights are additional examples.

Finally, some conflicts are primarily based on status inequalities. Oppressed nationalities or racial groups revolt; they try to secede from the larger country of which they are a part. Or, they may try to gain power for their own ethnic group, replacing the previously dominating ethnic group from the ruling positions it had occupied. National liberation movements and ethnically based civil wars are examples of these phenomena. There are also struggles between males and females, between aristocrats and plebians, and between groups who differ in some aspects of their life styles.

In actuality, class, status, and power conflicts are usually intertwined. Ethnic ranking, wealth inequalities, and relative access to powerful positions tend to coincide. Persons relatively low in one dimension tend to be low in the others. One grievance aggravates the others. The superimposition of lines of cleavage tends to intensify conflict (Dahrendorf 1959; Kriesberg 1973). Thus, in the Mexican Revolution of 1910, the landless peasants lacked political power and had low status as Indians and mestizos; they struggled vigorously against the ruling criollo, the landlord class that controlled the government.

Sometimes, lines of cleavage are not superimposed, but instead crosscut each other. Thus, people who are deprived in ethnic status may still have a moderate income; an ethnic group with relatively average income may be politically powerful. Insofar as such inconsistencies prevail, each group will have different allies and different adversaries in each struggle about a particular inequality. This mitigates against the clear recognition of a conflict and lessens the intensity of the struggle. The way a conflict emerges and its intensity is affected by other factors and even the relationship with cross-cutting ties is more complex than the direct relationship as stated (Kriesberg 1973).

Conflicts also differ in the means used to resolve them. Coercion may or may not be employed: if coercion is used, it may be violent or nonviolent. Conflicts differ in the extent to which the adversary parties commit their resources or the extent to which there is widespread involvement. They differ in the nature of their outcomes or sought-for outcomes, in whether there is little reform or a major restructuring of the stratification system. These variations are best considered in the context of examining the stages of social conflicts.

Struggles go through several stages, and we should be clear about which conflict stage we are discussing. We can distinguish, at least analytically, four stages linked with several processes: (1) the latent or objective conflict relationship, aside from the participants' awareness of the conflict; (2) the adversaries emerging awareness that they are in conflict; (3) the actual pursuit of the incompatible objectives, the on-going struggle itself; (4) the ending of the fight, at least temporarily, and the resultant outcome. We discuss the basis and emergence of conflict in this chapter, and later, in the context of conflict theorists' explanations, we will consider factors that affect the outcomes of struggles. The course of particular struggles as they escalate and deescalate, as different means are used, or as they terminate are all treated at greater length elsewhere (Kriesberg 1973).

OBJECTIVE CONFLICT

Even aside from the participants' awareness of incompatible objectives, we can analytically discern conditions that underlie a conflict. Inequality is a fundamental basis for conflict. If a hierarchy or a ranking of strata exists, persons within such systems will want to be located in higher rather than lower strata. They agree about which way is up; they agree about the standards being applied. Conflicts based upon class, status, or power inequalities are generally *consensual conflicts*. Conflicts also arise over disagreement about what is desirable. One adversary may believe that its religion, political ideology, or other particular ways of thinking and acting are the correct ways and, moreover, should be adhered to by nonbelievers. Even if the nonbelievers do not accept those beliefs, the adversary party may seek to impose them. That is a *dissensual conflict*. Although, in any actual struggle, consensual and dissensual elements are mixed, we will attend largely to the consensual components, since they usually predominate in struggles over status, power, and class position.

In order for a latent consensual conflict based on rank differences to exist, the parties must not only want greater status, material resources, or power, they must also believe that those qualities are scarce and that one side can gain only at the expense of the other side. This need not be the actual case. All groups in a given social system might increase their material resources by expanding the total amount of resources available within the social system, either at the expense of outsiders or by increasing the production of what they desire. But the *relative* standing of one group is always dependent on the other groups. If there are two classes in the social system, an increase in the *relative* share of one class must be at the expense of the other class.

Status and power differences are generally viewed as relative. Having power usually means having power over others; hence, those others have less power. Changes in relative power in making collective decisions are, therefore, conflicting. The discussion of minimal power—in the form of personal or group autonomy—might be viewed as something that could be increased without taking away power from anyone else. Groups exercising much power over others may or may not have that conception. Similarly, status is generally viewed in relative fashion. To defer to others is to put oneself down. Yet, acknowledging minimal status to others is certainly possible without diminishing one's own status.

Prevailing views about scarcity and the ways of increasing power, status, and material resources within a social system are crucial in determining whether or not inequality constitutes a latent conflict relationship. The assumption of objective conflict relationships is also related to which conception of class, status, and power differences we are considering.

Karl Marx's conception of classes illustrates the assumption that an objective conflict can exist, aside from the participants' awareness of that underlying conflict. Thus, the exploitation of the proletariat by the capitalist class is an objective conflict between those two classes, even if the proletariat are not aware of their exploitation. As far as Marx was concerned, workers have a "false consciousness" if they are not aware of their real class interests, as analyzed in Marx's theory.

The idea of latent or objective conflict is theoretically troublesome. How do we measure or even observe that which is only latent and which is not thought about or acted upon by members of the different strata? As theoretical constructs, these ideas may or may not be useful. They are useful if they help us think about and explain what we wish to understand. They must also be testable, which requires depending upon indirect measures. We determine the probable consequences if these ideas were correct, then examine to what extent those consequences actually occur. Insofar as they do, we assume the constructs are correct and useful.

In order to test ideas about latent conflict, then, we must consider how conflicts emerge into awareness and how incompatible goals are pursued. We must also consider if the way that this happens is related to the constructs of objective conflict. Does assuming that there are objective conditions underlying social conflicts help to predict their occurrence and course of development?

EMERGENCE INTO AWARENESS

An essential component of a social conflict is that two or more parties *think* they have incompatible goals. For groups to develop that belief, three elements must be present. First, there must be contending parties, categories of people who think of themselves as a collective unit. Second, the members of those groups, or their spokespersons must feel aggrieved; they must feel sufficiently dissatisfied with their circumstances to want to alter them. Third, these potential contenders must formulate goals that they recognize as incompatible with those of another group.

Collective Identity

For a category of people to become a collectivity, they must share a common identity. They must believe they have a common fate, face common circumstances, and share a common history. Their collective identity may be symbolized by special names based on class, status, and power.

To what extent members of a particular stratum are aware of themselves as a collectivity has been the subject of much discussion and research. Class consciousness has been extensively studied, particularly class identification and awareness of the class structure. We will also review the research on status and power consciousness and the correlates of such perceptions.

Class consciousness. The assertion that the United States is a middle-class country has often been made. In the past, one kind of evidence for this has been the responses people have made to questions about their class identity. The Gallup polls found 88 percent of the respondents in a 1939 survey saying they were middle class; Cantril, using 1941 data, found 87 percent of the people saying they were middle class (Centers 1949, pp. 30-31). But in such surveys, respondents were given the choice of *only* upper, middle, or lower class. When Richard Centers conducted a national survey in 1945, he used the following wording to question people: "If you were asked to use one of these four names for your social class, which would you say you belonged in: the middle class, lower class, working class or upper class?" (Centers 1949). With that wording, 52 percent of the people said working class, 36 percent said middle class, 4 percent said upper class, and 5 percent said lower class; 3 percent said they did not know (Centers 1949, p. 79). Clearly, people identify themselves as working class—not as lower class. Studies using comparably worded questions have gotten similar results. The National Opinion Research Center (NORC) uses the identical wording in its national surveys. The results in the 1974 General Survey were: 47 percent of the respondents said working class, 46 percent said middle class, 4 percent said lower class, and 3 percent said upper class. In 1976, the results were: 46 percent, 48 percent, 4 percent, and 2 percent, respectively (less than 1 percent said they did not know). Perhaps there is a slight trend toward a larger proportion of the American people identifying themselves as middle class.

The overall division between working-class and middle-class identification is similar throughout the world. In 1948, Buchanan and Cantril (1953) coordinated surveys in nine countries: Australia, Britain, France, West Germany, Italy, Mexico, Netherlands, Norway, and the United States. Respondents in each country were asked to say if they belonged to the middle class, working class, or upper class. The proportion replying working class varied from 60 percent in Britain and the Netherlands to 41 percent in Germany and 42 percent in Italy; in the United States, 51 percent said working class.

Class consciousness involves more than identifying oneself with a given class. It includes awareness of a class structure and perceptions of class relations and their bases. Class consciousness also refers to ideas about the interests shared

302

by members of the same class. From such elements of class consciousness, a class may become solidary and act in a struggle against other classes. In Marx's terms, the class in itself (*Klasse an sich*) becomes a class for itself (*Klasse für sich*) (Marx 1963). At this point in our examination of class consciousness, we can review the work about perceptions of classes: their number and the criteria used to define them.

When people are asked how many classes there are or what they are, about 20 percent of the people cannot answer. They lack a clear image of the class structure in their society. Willener (1957, p. 161), found the same to be true in French Switzerland; Popitz et al. (1961, p. 233) found the same thing in their study of the industrial Ruhr area of Germany. Studies in the United States also indicate that a substantial proportion of the people say they do not know how many classes there are in the country as a whole (Haer 1957). In Australia and in Puerto Rico, a larger proportion of the people have an image of the class structure in their country (Oeser and Hammond 1954; Davies and Encel 1965; Tumin and Feldman 1961).

If people are aware of classes, they also have an idea about the criteria or dimensions they use to distinguish classes and how many classes there are. People may distinguish classes in terms of occupation, income, attitudes about class interests, or aspects of their style of life.

In the national survey conducted by Centers (1949, pp. 89-91), respondents were asked whether or not persons in diverse occupations belonged in the class that they had chosen. Then the respondents were asked which other thing was most important in determining a person's class: family, money, education, or beliefs. After occupation, Centers found that 47 percent of the population thought beliefs were the most important characteristic to know about someone to determine class membership. Education was mentioned by 29 percent, family by 20 percent, and money by 17 percent of the population.

Results from other studies have yielded different findings, varying with the wording of the question and perhaps with the time and place in which the study was conducted. Such variations indicate, too, that there is not a very high consensus about the conception of class or that people have multiple criteria in mind which they combine to categorize people. Survey questions do not readily capture such configurations.

Kahl and Davis (1955), in a study of men in the Boston area, used open-ended questions with many probes in order to assess respondents' views of social classes.[1] They concluded that 61 percent of the people used income and/or

---

[1] An open-ended question is one in which alternative answers are not included in the question and presented to the respondent. The respondent, instead, can answer in any way he or she wants. Probes are follow-up questions. In this case, the question asked was: "There has been a lot of talk recently about social classes in the United States. I wonder what you think about this? What social classes do you think there are in this part of the country?" The series of probes included: "Which social class do you think you are in? What puts you in that class?"

the style of life it bought as the main criterion of differentiation; 8 percent mentioned a specific occupational level as the main criterion, 9 percent mentioned morale, and 16 percent insisted that there was no single criterion. Manis and Meltzer (1954), studied a highly industrialized community (Paterson, New Jersey) and asked a sample of male textile workers what criteria they used in deciding who belongs to which class. Money or wealth was mentioned by 68 percent of the men, occupation by 21 percent, culture or style of life by 18 percent, and education by 14 percent.

The findings from Runciman's (1966, pp. 158-159) study in England and Wales indicate that the distinction between manual and nonmanual occupations is the most important criterion people use when they talk about middle and working classes. Being "ordinary people" is also mentioned in reference to the working class and being "rich" or having a "middle-class style of life" are mentioned in reference to the middle class. A study in Melbourne, Australia (Oeser and Hammond 1954, pp. 283-284), gave respondents a closed list of factors from which to choose. In this study 36 percent of the respondents selected education as the most important determinant; 26 percent selected income; 19 percent, family background; and 18 percent, occupation.

Class, as popularly used, clearly refers to a person's economic or market position. But equally clearly, it has strong connotations of social status, as indicated by style of life and occupational prestige.

Class consciousness also implies a conception of the overall class structure. Marx and other theorists, emphasizing the importance of conflict in social life, argue that the class structure is essentially dichotomous. A conflict comes down to two sides. It is "them against us." How many classes people actually think there are has been investigated. For example, Manis and Meltzer (1954) in their study of Paterson, New Jersey, found that 43 percent of the respondents thought there were two classes in their community; 42 percent thought there were three. But in the nation as a whole, only 25 percent thought there were two, 38 percent thought there were three, and 24 percent did not know (in the community, 4 percent did not know). In general, studies in the United States and in other countries have found that people are more likely to report three classes than two (Kahl and Davis 1955; Tumin and Feldman 1961; Mayntz 1958; Svalastoga 1959). The basic dichotomous view of them versus us would appear to be generally modified by the view that there are those on top, those on the bottom, and some in the middle (Lopreato and Hazelrigg 1972, pp. 136-142).

A fundamental issue, theoretically and practically, is the extent to which class identity and organization transcends national identity. The events around the outbreak of World War I are illuminating. Socialist parties in many countries were joined together in an international association (the Second International). In 1912, they drafted a resolution opposing the participation of the working class in any war. For them, a war could only mean "shooting one another for the sake of the capitalists' profits, for the sake of the ambitious of dynasties, for the accomplishment of the aims of secret diplomatic treaties" (cited in Wilson 1955, p. 446). But in August 1914, the Social Democratic members of the German Reichstag voted for war credits, and the socialists in France and Russia supported their governments in the war. Lenin, in exile, and a few others continued to oppose the war and called for international solidarity of the working class.

The extent to which people throughout the world have class identities that transcend any nation has not been extensively studied. Buchanan and Cantril (1953), however, did include some relevant questions in surveys conducted in nine countries. A sample of persons in each country were asked which class they would say they belonged to: middle class, working class, or upper class. Then they were asked if they felt they had anything in common with their own class of people abroad and then if they felt anything in common with people of their own nation who are not in their own class. If the respondents answered *yes* or *no* to both questions, they were asked with which they would say they had most in common. The results are presented in Table 10.1.

A substantial proportion of the populations studied feel they have something in common with members of their own class abroad. However, an even greater percentage feel they have something in common with persons from their own country who do not belong to the same class. Moreover, if forced to choose which they have more in common with, the proportion choosing persons of their own country exceeds the proportion choosing persons of their own class but not of their own country. Some countries show interesting variations. Australia seems to have particularly broad class identities, but it also has a high proportion of people who feel they have something in common with their countrymen. The United States is relatively low in breadth of class identity, but high in national identity.

What is also interesting is that people of the middle class are *more* likely to feel they have something in common with their class members in other countries than those who say they belong to the working class. By that measure of class consciousness, the working class is less likely to feel international class solidarity than are persons in the middle class. Middle-class persons are also more likely than those who identify themselves as working class to feel they have something in common with persons of their own country but of a different class. Indeed it seems from these surveys that middle-class persons are more likely to identify with a wider range of persons than are working-class persons. Buchanan and Cantril (1953, p. 22) believe that low wealth, and social status and particularly lack of education discourage sentiments of commonality both at home and abroad.

Correlates of class consciousness. Discussions of the factors that affect class consciousness have been extensive and considerable relevant research has been done. Much of the work on the determinants or correlates of class consciousness has focused on the characteristics of individuals. Most frequently,

TABLE 10.1   National and Class Identities by Country

Country	Percent Feeling Something in Common		Percent Feeling More in Common	
	With Own Class Abroad	With Countrymen Not of Own Class	With Class Abroad	With Countrymen Not of Own Class
Australia	67	78	6	51
Britain	58	67	7	34
France	43	63	12	34
Germany	30	64	5	20
Italy	41	50	9	24
Mexico	40	56	NA	NA
Netherlands	61	56	9	24
Norway	41	64	7	22
United States	42	77	7	32

Source: Adapted from Buchanan and Cantril 1953, Table 2, p. 18.

studies have related a person's "objective" class position with his or her "subjective" position. The research demonstrates that self-identification by class is
highly related to income, education, and occupation (Centers 1949; Buchanan
and Cantril 1953; Murphy and Morris 1961).

Table 10.2 presents the results from a national survey conducted in 1976,
in which respondents were asked which social class they thought they belonged
in: lower, working, middle, or upper. There is a moderate relationship with
income: the higher family income is, the more likely are people to identify with
the middle class. But class identification is not fully determined by income.
Even at the lowest income level, almost half of the respondents say they belong
to the middle or upper class. Perhaps some of these persons were previously
wealthy or had high-prestige occupations and are now retired; perhaps they are
students who expect to enter high-prestige occupations. Some of these persons
may also think of social class in terms of friendship circles or morality of life
styles.

Class identification by sex and occupational prestige is shown in Table
10.3. In the first column, the proportion of men identifying with the working
or lower class is presented according to the prestige rating of their own occupation. There is a very strong relationship between the man's occupational prestige
and his identification with the middle or upper class. Among women, too, there
is a strong relationship between their occupational prestige and class identification; however, at the highest prestige levels, women are more likely than men to
regard themselves as belonging to the working or lower class. Perhaps this
reflects the fact that they tend to have lower prestige and lower-paying
positions, within the broad categories being compared. It may also result from
the use of the spouse's occupation to help determine class identification. The
last two columns suggest that the husband's occupational prestige is more highly
related to class identification than is the wife's.

Hodge and Treiman (1968) analyzed a 1964 national survey conducted by
the National Opinion Research Center (NORC) to assess which objective characteristics were most highly related to class identification. They found that
occupation was more highly correlated with class identification than either
income or education; the partial correlation between class identification and
occupation, holding constant income and education, was .24, almost twice as
large as the partial correlations of either income or education, holding
occupation and the other variable constant. Each characteristic, however,
contributes to class identification: the multiple correlation of all three variables
with class identification is .44.

Class identification, clearly, is not completely determined by "objective"
conditions as measured by occupational position, income, and education. Hodge
and Treiman (1968) argue that one reason for the relationship between objective
class rank and class self-identification not being higher is that the several
measures of objective class position are not highly correlated with each other.
Consequently, persons may be high in one class characteristic, but not in

TABLE 10.2 Class Identification by Family Income

Annual Family Income[1]	Class Identification				Totals	
	Lower	Working	Middle	Upper	(%)	(N)
$ 3,999 or Less	10.8	44.8	42.4	2.0	100.0	(203)
4,000-$ 6,999	10.2	49.1	39.4	1.4	100.1	(216)
7,000- 9,999	3.3	48.9	37.2	0.6	100.0	(180)
10,000- 14,999	2.6	58.6	37.5	1.3	100.0	(309)
15,000- 19,999	0.5	42.9	56.6	0.0	100.0	(205)
20,000- 24,999	0.8	36.2	61.4	1.6	100.0	(127)
25,000 and Over	0.7	22.4	72.8	4.1	100.0	(147)

[1] Respondents were asked about all sources of income in 1975, before taxes.

Source: Based on data from the NORC 1976 General Social Survey.

TABLE 10.3   Percent Identifying as Working Class or Lower Class by Sex and Occupational Prestige

Occupational Prestige	Males (Own Occupation)	Females (Own Occupation)	Males (Spouse's Occupation)	Females (Spouse's Occupation)
10-19	76.1 (67)*	76.0 (75)	65.5 (29)	74.4 (39)
20-29	67.2 (73)	67.7 (136)	56.5 (62)	75.6 (78)
30-39	60.9 (169)	54.1 (183)	54.4 (92)	53.1 (147)
40-49	55.6 (169)	39.1 (189)	45.7 (28)	55.8 (64)
50-59	21.5 (93)	30.0 (40)	17.9 (28)	23.4 (64)
60 and Higher	14.1 (57)	32.4 (71)	26.1 (46)	15.9 (44)

*Number upon which percentage is based.

Source: Based data from the NORC 1976 General Social Survey.

another. No one characteristic is therefore highly determining of class identification. In addition, they point out that people have social relations with person of different classes. Such social relations modify the impact of their own class position.

Intergenerational mobility is another reason that current class circumstances do not completely predict class identification. Downwardly mobile people tend to cling to their higher class origins by continuing to regard themselves, for example, as middle-class (Wilensky and Edwards 1959). On the other hand, upwardly mobile people may not shed the class identification of their family of origin. For example, having grown up in a working-class family, a person continues to hold that self-identification, even if she or he has entered a professional or clerical occupation. It is even possible for people to identify with the class that they aspire to enter. A small amount of upward mobility may then induce someone to regard himself or herself as middle-class or upper-class, although the current objective circumstances might not be consistent with that self-designation.

On the whole, there is a relationship between class origins and class identification. For example, Hamilton (1966) found that almost half of the clerical and sales workers in a 1956 national survey regarded themselves as members of the working class, these persons generally reported coming from working-class families; while those who regarded themselves as middle class usually did not have working-class origins. Similarly, men in manual occupations whose fathers were also in manual occupations are more likely to regard themselves as working class than are manual workers whose fathers were in white-collar occupations.

Class consciousness or one of its components, class identification, is affected by the quality of work and the social context in which persons earn a living. Work may be more or less alienating, monotonous, and degrading; both manual work and clerical work vary considerably in these regards. Furthermore, if workers are concentrated together in large numbers they have a greater opportunity to share perspectives and develop a sense of solidarity, just as in those circumstances they may well suffer from a more impersonal and perhaps arbitrary control (Marx and Engels 1932; Vanneman and Pampel 1977). Membership in organizations representing class or occupational interests increase class consciousness. For example, trade union membership is associated with working-class consciousness and militancy (Leggett 1964).

The perception of social conditions and, hence, their impact on class consciousness in part depends upon the prevailing ways of thinking within a whole society. In the United States, few leaders urge class consciousness; indeed, there is a widespread pride in the absence of class consciousness. The lack of class antagonisms is viewed as important in maintaining a cohesive society on a vast scale. What is more widely shared in the United States is job consciousness or wage consciousness: that is, despite some sense of separation between workers and employers, that relationship is also seen to involve a partnership (Manis and Meltzer 1963; Commons et al. 1936).

In Europe, political parties are more sharply organized around class differences and they make efforts to arouse class consciousness rather than dampen it (Hamilton 1966). The availability of particular ideologies—for example, Marxism and socialism—also help make it likely that people who are alienated from their work, or suffer unemployment and job insecurity, will become militantly conscious of class (Zeitlin 1970).

In the developing countries of the world, ideologies based on Marxism are particularly appealing. The analysis of capitalism, class conflict, and the rise of socialism presented by Marxist parties appeals for several reasons (Watnick 1952; Shils 1960). Such ideologies hold up the prospect of rapid industrial development; they explain the failure of development in terms of the exploitive actions of the advanced capitalist countries and corporations, and they are consistent with struggles against colonial powers. The existence of Marxist parties increases the likelihood of class consciousness.

Thus far, we have considered class identification and class consciousness only in terms of class conditions. But real people do not separate class considerations from status and power considerations. The popular conception of class, as we have seen, has large elements of status and probably some notions of power inequality built into it. We should expect, then, that status and power conditions affect people's class consciousness. We will consider status and power identification separately and then see how they interact with class consciousness.

Status and power consciousness. Status differences necessarily entail awareness. People in a status hierarchy evaluate each other and group consciousness emerges readily from interactions based upon such evaluations. The group differences and self-identification are re-enforced by segregation—self-imposed and imposed by others. As we have noted, such status differences may be based on ethnicity, lineage, race, or occupation. The community studies by Warner and his colleagues and by others indicate that people in small towns and even in cities tend to regard certain sets of people as being "better" than others—as having the proper behavior and background (Warner and Lunt 1941; Warner et al. 1949; Hollingshead 1949). At the national level there is even evidence of a sense of shared status among persons constituting a social elite (Domhoff 1967). The rest of the society is not differentiated into a single set of ranked status groups with group consciousness. Rather, a variety of status groups, each with a sense of identity, cross-cut each other. For example, many ethnic groups have self-identities that include members throughout the American society and usually transcend it to include persons of the same ethnic groups in other countries. Members of many occupations form status communities (Bensman 1972). Professional persons extend their sense of identity widely and even have networks of personal relations throughout the occupational community. This sense of occupational identification is related to job consciousness rather than class consciousness.

Persons with more power and those with less power also form self-identifying groups. This group formation is most marked among the elites. Persons occupying high positions in the government (military or civilian) tend to view themselves as an identifiable group, separate from those out of power. Other persons recognize the power-holders as a group, either as antagonists, rivals, or patrons. Interactions based upon mutual awareness of such power differences reinforces the solidarity of the elite groups. Power differences throughout the social system are not as readily or clearly recognized and thus do not provide as firm a basis for collective identity. Power elites may develop constituencies. Political parties are the basic mechanism for such constituency grouping and these form important bases for identification.

People at all rank levels have some conceptions of the way in which power is distributed in the society and these conceptions vary by social strata. Analyzing interviews with respondents in a Michigan industrial community, Form and Rytina (1969) found that the rich and middle-income strata were most likely to think that a political pluralistic model of power best describes the American power system. Poor persons and blacks were more likely than the other strata to think that an elitist or economic model best describes how power is distributed in America.

Class, status, and power consciousness. The argument has been made that the very multiplicity of dimensions of inequality and the lack of crystallization in the United States has reduced class solidarity (Wilensky 1966). Racial differences and differences in national origins, for example, have weakened working class cohesion. In this view America is a pluralist society and Marxian predictions are invalid (Rosenberg 1953; Hodge and Treiman 1968).

A Marxist explanation for class consciousness gives primacy to the economic position of people, particularly their situation in the labor market and their ownership of the means of production. An explanation in terms of people's interests has also been put forward, sometimes as a modified Marxist approach. According to this view, class awareness and identification develop from general socio-economic prestige and income. Jackman and Jackman (1973) argue that these dimensions tend to be sufficiently correlated to affect strongly class consciousness. They re-analyzed the survey data previously used by Hodge and Treiman (1968) and, performing different modes of analysis, they arrived at different interpretations. Jackman and Jackman used path analysis to assess the additional contribution various circumstances make to accounting for class identification. They concluded that the status of friends and neighbors, when added to the respondents' education, income, and occupational prestige, did not contribute in any significant way to accounting for class identification.[2] They also found that ownership of capital, in the form of owning any stocks, bonds, or real estate, does not help explain class identification.

Race has a strong effect. Leggett (1964) and Purcell (1953) have found

[2] The income, education, and occupational prestige of respondents have a multiple correlation of .419 with class identification. When having a high status neighbors or friends is added, it raises the multiple correlation only to .430. High status contacts do help interpret the effects of objective socioeconomic standing; they are an intervening variable linking objective rank with subjective identification (Jackman and Jackman 1973, p. 574).

that blacks tend to be more class-conscious than whites. Jackman and Jackman analyzed several national surveys that included questions about class identification and concluded that "the low prestige accruing from ascriptive ethnic status is of such overwhelming salience to blacks that any additional prestige they may gain from more universalistic, achieved criteria such as education, occupational attainment, and income has at best a negligible impact on their self-location in the socio-economic structure" (Jackman and Jackman 1973, p. 579). On the whole, they conclude that neither the pluralist nor the unmodified Marxism explanation accounts for the patterns of class identification in contemporary United States. Rather, the interest-group approach best seems to fit the data.

Class, as the word is popularly used, has social-status connotations; hence, both class and status characteristics affect self-identification. Nevertheless, these characteristics are so closely associated with each other that awareness of belonging to one group as opposed to other groups and interests is likely. People whose ranks in class and status are consistent tend to make class identifications that are in agreement with their objective conditions more than do persons whose rankings are less consistent (Landecker 1963).

In some societies at one period or another class divisions may predominate. In others, power or status inequalities may be the fundamental bases for cleavage, identification, and organization. The way these dimensions do or do not coincide also has important implications for the collective identities that are formed.

Sense of Grievance

For a social conflict to exist, the adversaries must not only have a sense of identity, they must also feel they have a grievance—that is, they must believe that their conditions are unsatisfactory and can be improved. Group members must regard their circumstances as unjust or unfair; they must believe that a social remedy can be found for their plight. Unhappiness is not a grievance in this sense. For example, people unhappy about their mortality or the deaths of loved ones do not have a grievance, unless they believe that others are denying them adequate access to food or medical services.

Students of social conflict often emphasize the grievance of protest groups as the main component of struggles. But struggles also develop from the grievances of persons in relatively privileged groups who believe they should have a *larger* share of the privileges they already possess. In either case, there is a standard by which they judge their circumstances to be wrong. One set of factors for the emergence of a conflict is developments or characteristics within a stratum. We will examine these factors before discussing other determinants of the emergence of conflicts.

Three kinds of characteristics of potentially antagonistic groups may be determinants of a sense of grievance: absolute deprivation, rank disequilibrium, and changing expectations (Kriesberg 1973). An explanation in terms of absolute deprivation argues that people generally recognize who has more and who has less within any system of inequality. Those who have the lowest status, least power, and least material resources know it and feel most deprived. Some writers assume that certain inherent qualities of humans provide standards by which an observer could assess the basis for a grievance. Marx assumed humans were so constituted that certain conditions were objectively contrary to their human nature or species being. For example, work that entails being unfamiliar with the total process of producing the object worked upon and that requires repetitive movement of a very circumscribed kind is inherently alienating. Dahrendorf (1959) and Blau (1964) also assume that persons inherently dislike being subject to another person's power. Subordination may be accepted because of coercion or even acknowledged as legitimate. The benefits of being subordinate may make the cost of enduring subjection to another's power satisfactory, but it is recognized as a cost.

Even without assuming any inherent human standard by which to measure deprivation, there usually is enough agreement within a given social system that having lower class, status, or power ranking in that system is worse than having higher ranking. To the degree and extent people are ranked low, they are likely to feel aggrieved, as discussed in Chapter 9.

There are several reasons why the more areas in which groups are deprived, the greater will be their sense of grievance. The homogeneity of ranking facilitates interaction. In addition, conflict lines will be superimposed and not cross-cutting; consequently, antagonism will not be muted (Kriesberg 1970, pp. 68-69). There is certainly abundant evidence that low-ranking persons, along any dimension, are more likely to be dissatisfied and to be intensely dissatisfied than are high-ranking persons. For example, Inkeles (1960) reviewed data about feelings of satisfaction, variously measured, from many societies; he found that persons of lower occupational or income levels tended to be less happy and more dissatisfied with life than higher-ranking persons. Studies of occupations and of communities report this finding in unvarying form (Friedmann and Havighurst 1954; Blauner 1964; Bradburn and Caplovitz 1965). Personal satisfaction, nevertheless, is strongly affected by other factors—family relations, personal health, and friendships.

A sense of grievance may also arise from rank disequilibrium—that is, persons ranked low on one dimension will feel especially aggrieved if they have a higher ranking on another dimension. Instead of feeling compensated for their low ranking, they may feel unfairly treated because they deserve more in terms of their relatively higher standing on another dimension. We discussed evidence bearing on this idea in Chapter 9. What makes the idea particularly relevant in the present context is that a sense of grievance does not depend merely on a feeling of dissatisfaction. One must also feel that the social conditions causing the distress can be corrected and one's effort could help the correction. If someone ranks relatively high on some dimensions, he or she has social resources that can be applied to correct the grievances. This may be why marginal persons often become leaders of protest and of efforts to redress grievances (Shibutani and Kwan 1965).

The third often-noted stratum characteristic related to a sense of grievance is a changing relationship between expectations and attainments. Revolutions do not always occur when conditions are at their worst; they often erupt after some improvement in social conditions (Davies 1962; Gurr 1970; Feierabend, Feierabend, and Nesvold 1969). Expectations are based partly on experience; if conditions are improving, people come to expect continuing betterment. A worsening of conditions or even a slowdown in the rate of improvement can be experienced as particularly grievous. The difference between actual attainments and expectations creates a gap that could be the source of revolution or protest. For example, Davies (1962) traces the general improvement in conditions in Russia and the emancipation of the serfs from 1861 until 1905, when hundreds of protesting workers were killed, and the Russian army and navy were disastrously defeated by the Japanese. Following the revolt of 1905, social and economic conditions deteriorated with only brief partial recoveries followed by the disasters of the war with Germany. Revolutions began in Russia in February 1917.

Some ways in which gaps between attainment and expectations arise are depicted in Figure 10.1. Gaps can arise from a marked deterioration of previously stable conditions: from a worsening of a society's relative international position, from a war, or from natural disasters affecting, for example, food production. A gap can also arise from a rise in expectations based not upon

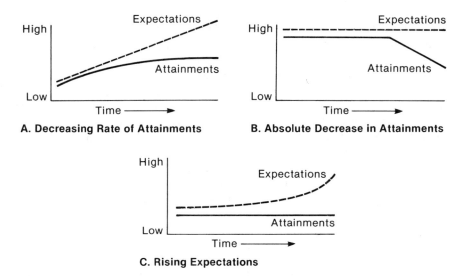

A. Decreasing Rate of Attainments

B. Absolute Decrease in Attainments

C. Rising Expectations

FIGURE 10.1   *Types of changes in the relationship between attainments and expectations*
Source: Adapted from Kriesberg 1973, Figure 3.1

experience with their own conditions but awareness of conditions elsewhere. Knowing how well off other societies or groups of people are can raise expectations by demonstrating what is possible.

A sense of grievance arises not simply from characteristics of the stratum members. Awareness or acknowledgement of a grievance also is affected by the relations between the potential antagonists and the social environment in which they interact. Two aspects of the relations between possible adversaries are particularly important: the degree of integration and their relative power. Integration refers to the amount of interaction between the parties, including both conflicting and nonconflicting relations. If most interaction is cooperative interaction and little is conflicting, the conflicting aspects will tend to be ignored and a struggle will not emerge (Morris and Jeffries 1968). Of course, greater interaction provides greater opportunity and bases for disagreements and fights. Many such disagreements may be ignored and grievances allowed to accumulate so that once a conflict does become manifest, it may be particularly intense. The frequency and intensity of struggles are not simply a function of the degree and nature of the integration between the parties. Each of these aspects of the relationship affects the sense of grievance and the emergence of conflicts (Kriesberg 1973, pp. 89-92).

Great power inequality may enable the dominant group to surpress the less dominant one. Consequently, a deprived group may not even acknowledge its grievance if redress seems unattainable. On the other hand, the dominant group may raise its own expectations and demand more because its demands seem readily attainable at the expense of the weaker party.

The sense of grievance depends on the legitimacy accorded existing inequality. To what extent do people feel that the class, status, or power inequalities are fair and just? Views of the inequalities presented by the higher-ranking persons are often the prevailing views. Insofar as lower-ranking people accept the meaning of inequality as so presented, they will not develop oppositional views, feel aggrieved, and formulate goals to alter the stratification system (Parkin 1971). One formulation of the prevailing meaning of the system of stratification is that it is an achieving society (Offe 1976). According to this model, social status is distributed equitably in line with performance. Parsons (1970) believes that equality and inequality are legitimated by the necessity of motivating performance and also by equality of opportunity. But not all people accept the interpretations of inequality that are used to justify them. We will next examine how goals to change the system of inequality develop.

Goals

The third component essential for the emergence of a conflict is the formulation of incompatible goals. This means constructing goals whose attainment would mean diminishing a grievance at the expense of an adversary. What is critical here is that an aggrieved party sees an outcome that would reduce its sense of unfairness and that outcome must be seen as attainable (Kriesberg 1973). A deprived group might have cause to complain, but if its members believe they lack the resources to alter and correct their conditions, they will not formulate a goal that will bring them into conflict with an adversary. This is why the most destitute and disadvantaged do not rebel and why groups who have gained some improvement in their conditions may rebel. This is also why persons whose rankings are inconsistent may be active in leading struggles. The belief in the ability to attain desired goals may also rest on the availability of resources from third parties. Having allies outside of the system may provide the base, sometimes literally so, for mounting an attack upon an adversary. Foreign assistance may not "cause" a revolution, but it can be critical in making its success seem possible (Gross 1966).

The ability of people to mobilize themselves for collective action is a critical component of social protest or any other conflict action (Tilly 1975; Oberschall 1973; Kriesberg 1973). The group must have the resources, organizational skills, finances, and time to be able to mobilize. An important part of a group's ability to mobilize is their preexisting network of social relations: people are often drawn into supporting one side or another in a struggle by the social ties they already have with people who are already involved in the struggle.

Variations in goals. The changes sought by members of strata seeking to improve their conditions vary greatly. Their goals have great consequences for the means used in a struggle, for the likelihood of attaining the objective, and hence, for the resulting degree of inequality. The goals may be to restructure the system of relations—that is, to change the rules of the game—or they may be more reformist, simply to modify the inequalities within the prevailing system of stratification (Baumgartner, Burns, and DeVille 1978).

A system of inequality may be fundamentally restructured in several ways. One possibility is to break up the system: a group leaves or is forced from the social system in which it had low status. Thus, the dominating group may expel low-ranking categories, or such groups may succeed in establishing their own social system. Such goals are the most likely choice for those attempting to alleviate ascribed status differences related to ethnicity and race. To such groups, establishing a separate national state may seem possible, although it is not an option open to other kinds of social strata. An example of such a separatist movement is the Jewish support for Zionism in Tsarist Russia. The expulsion of "Asians" by the government of Uganda and, in the early years of this century, the massacre of Armenians in Turkey exemplify the dominant group's pursuit of goals that radically alter the status system.

Ranking systems may be radically altered in other ways. Often these involve fundamentally reducing the inequality while keeping the people within the social system. Thus, peoples' standards may change; certain differences in culture or ethnicity may no longer be evaluated negatively. The consensus underlying the status hierarchy is lost. This may happen when pluralist ideas become dominant or when groups no longer agree about how race or ethnicity should be ranked. For example, the assertion that "black is beautiful" is a rejection of a status ranking in which blacks are inferior.

The destruction of rank differences among class and power strata is also conceivable. Certain kinds of class differences may be abolished, as when manorial estates are broken up and the land appropriated by the peasants after a revolution. Power inequalities may also be radically transformed, as when previously powerless groups are enfranchised and become able to participate in making collective decisions or when minimal civil liberties are accorded all members of a polity.

A goal of radical restructuring need not be a fundamental reduction of inequality; it may also be to create or restore an extreme degree of inequality. Thus, the creation of a totalitarian system or a newly racist one may impose profound inequality not previously existing.

Reformist goals are more common. They can take the form of preserving inequality among positions while changing the groups that occupy those positions. This is most typically found in the case of power inequalities. Groups who have been excluded from power replace those previously holding power but the degree of inequality remains unchanged. This can occur through an electoral process or by the seizure of power through a military coup.

Reform is generally understood to mean a modification in the degree of inequality. Usually, reformers aim at reducing inequality, but sometimes their goal may be to increase it. Thus, the changes argued by Communist party leaders in Eastern Europe over the years have often centered on appropriate differences in wages for different occupational strata. Various interest groups have argued for and against greater inequality. Members within a given stratum or social rank may differ about the goals which they think the group should pursue. For example, in the United States some groups within the women's movement seek greater equality between men and women by trying to have women compete more equally within the existing rank system. Other groups struggle to restructure a social system that they regard as too hierarchical and based too exclusively on masculine values rather than on more wide-ranging human values (Bernard 1978; Carden 1978).

Factors affecting the goals. The goals that members of a stratum formulate and pursue are shaped by the characteristics of that stratum, the relations members have with other strata, and the social environment within which the conflicting strata exist. Most research has focused on strata characteristics, and we will consider that factor first.

The nature of the stratum members' grievance is the most frequently noted characteristic of a stratum affecting its goals. The degree and content of the grievance should affect the radicalness of the goals and the form of change sought, and evidence supports those suppositions. For example, Dunlop (1951) has found that during periods of severe economic depression groups within the American labor movement were more likely to voice relatively radical aims; during periods of improved working conditions trade unions with reformist goals expanded in membership. Studies of blacks in the United States in the 1960s show that those with higher education and income tended to be conventional militants; those who were more uniformly deprived were more likely to support black separatist objectives (Marx 1969, p. 47, 117).

The idea that greater deprivation results in efforts for fundamental changes can also be assessed by studying the bases of support for radical organizations or political parties. For example, we might examine support for the Communist party, although the relevance of findings about sources of Communist party support, is questionable. The Communist party is not simply a party of radical change or of the Left, in the sense of advocating the most extreme equalitarian policies. Arthur Koestler once observed that Communism is not Left, it is East. At least in the past, support for the Communist party could mean to some extent support for the Soviet Union or opposition to its adversaries. Furthermore, in many contemporary societies the Communist party is splintered; some parties are more radical than the Communist party loyal to the Soviet Union. Nevertheless, in most European political spheres the Communist party in its propaganda and program stands for greater equality in the distribution of material benefits than do the other major political parties. Korpi (1971) studied party preferences among manual workers in Western Europe and concluded that a model assuming that voters act rationally in terms of their material self-interest is consistent with the evidence about support for the Communist party—that is, the workers who are materially worse off are most likely to support the Commjnist party.

The content of the goals is affected by the nature of the grievance. Members of a stratum who feel deprived because of their ethnicity are more likely to consider separatist goals than are members of a stratum who feel materially deprived. A grievance arising from a decline from relatively high rank is likely to have different consequences than one arising from a halted gradual improvement from low rank. For example, if a dominant ethnic group's generally high political and material position is lessened through the successful competitive efforts of new ethnic groups, the previously dominant group is relatively prone to support conservative, even reactionary, organizations. After studying right-wing extremism in the United States since 1790, Lipset and Raab conclude:

> Right-wing extremist movements in America have all risen against the background of economic and social changes which have resulted in the displacement of some population groups from former positions of dominance. . . .Behind the Know-Nothings were the technological advances which began to corrode the hegemomy of the skilled craftsmen in the cities with unskilled labor, at the same time that it foreshadowed the movement back to the cities. . . .In the 1950s of McCarthy, the displacement was on a national scale as America's corporate position in the world seemed to slip badly. And the Birch Society, perhaps the last backlash gasp of economic royalism, began to reflect a new displacement, that of white dominance. George Wallace flourished on that displacement (1970, p. 485).

Persons who feel they are being displaced tend to give primary attachment to their past position. Certain styles of life, religious habits, or other customs then symbolize their lost group status.

In the modern world, the state is generally seen as the agent to redress grievances. Issues are politicized. People in each class, status, and power stratum tend to support government action that will improve their relative position (Centers 1949). In the 1976 National Opinion Research Center General Survey, for example, respondents were asked whether they thought too little, about the right amount, or too much was being spent on welfare. Of the persons in families with less than $4,000 annual income, 26 percent said too little and 47 percent too much; among those in families with incomes of $25,000 or more, only 8 percent thought too little money was being spent on welfare and 72 percent thought too much was being spent.

Form and Rytina (1969) studied the perceptions and preferences about national political power of people in one industrial community. They listed twelve interest groups and asked respondents which one they thought *should* have the most influence in Washington. Rich respondents were relatively likely to say big business; 39 percent did so, compared to only 8 percent of the respondents as a whole. The respondents were most likely to volunteer that *all* groups *should* be equal. Further questions showed that most interviewees thought that the big business and rich groups actually had the most power.

In addition to the basis of the grievance, the leaders of a stratum influence the form of the goals and the degree to which they are radical. Leaders play a critical role in formulating programs and ideologies that set forth the members' objectives. Of course, the followers decide which programs make the most sense, given their grievances and their general way of thinking. But they choose from among the programs proferred by leaders appealing to them. Leaders face many dilemmas in formulating objectives. Long-range objectives that stress fundamental changes seem to offer more, but immediate attainment of such objectives is less likely. Leaders can urge coherent and doctrinally pure programs, and, hence, tend to gather a narrow range of followers, or they can appeal to a diverse coalition and formulate vague or nonideological objectives. To gain support, leaders must combine diverse appeals to formulate an attractive program.

In the history of the American trade union movement we can see many efforts that foundered. Leaders and small groups sought major structural changes but failed to create large viable organizations. The American Federation of Labor, under the leadership of Samuel Gompers, developed a program that set some long-term goals but also sought immediately attainable goals. The combination of many specific objectives and the lack of any overarching ideology was an appealing construction of objectives (Perlman 1928).

In addition to characteristics of the stratum members themselves, the nature of the relations among the strata fundamentally shape the goals. One side's goals help determine the other side's goals. Goals develop through interaction. If one group believes that the other attaches very great importance to a particular point and is thus unlikely to yield, it may decide that to insist on that point is not worthwhile. Immediate goals tend to be chosen from the array of possible goals, giving consideration to what the adversary is likely to yield.

Strata relations shape the nature of the conflicting goals. An excellent examination of the way class relations mold the formulation of conflicting goals is provided by Paige (1975) in his analysis of export agriculture in the underdeveloped world. He found that in each type of agricultural organization certain kinds of conflicting goals tended to emerge. Paige analyzed the types of agricultural organization (discussed in Chapter 4) in terms of the relations between two major classes: the cultivators and the noncultivators. Each class, he argued, derived their income from one of two sources. The cultivators either earn their income from the land, selling the agricultural products they raise, or they are paid wages. The noncultivators either derive their income from the land, earning their income by owning the agricultural product, or they derive their income from owning the capital used in agricultural production. By combining these different sources of income for cultivators and noncultivators, Paige constructs four major categories or types of agricultural organization, as depicted in Figure 10.2. In one type, both cultivators and noncultivators draw their income from the land. This category includes the commercial hacienda

Noncultivators' Income Sources	Cultivators' Income Sources	
	Land	Wages
Land	COMMERCIAL HACIENDA (coffee, cotton)	SHARECROPPING (cotton, grains) MIGRATORY LABOR (coffee, grapes)
Capital	SMALL HOLDING (coffee, cocoa, cotton, tobacco, fruits and nuts, grains)	PLANTATION (rubber, tea, sugar)

FIGURE 10.2   *Typical forms of agricultural organization and sources of income of cultivators and noncultivators*

Source: Paige 1975: Adopted from Figure 1.1 and Table 2.1

system in which laborers living on the landlord's land are paid in some combination of wages and usage rights; included, too, are systems in which owners of tiny subsistance holdings are employed as laborers on nearby estates. The noncultivating class in this category is dependent on its control of the land to gain rent, labor, taxes, or profits from the peasants. In this agricultural organization, conflict focuses on property rights and peasant efforts to gain control over the land in an agrarian revolt.

In the plantation category, the noncultivating class draws its income principally from industrial and financial capital; the cultivating class, from wages. This category includes sugar plantations that are corporately owned and industrialized; it includes individually owned and poorly mechanized rubber estates. Both cultivator and noncultivator classes tend to be well organized and the focus of conflict is on the distribution of income from property, not control of the property itself. The workers' objectives are typically reformist.

The category in which cultivators earn wages and noncultivators receive their income from the land consists of two major subcategories: the migratory labor estate and the sharecropped estate. In the migratory labor estate, individually owned enterprises, lacking power-driven machinery, are worked by seasonal migratory wage laborers. This includes the coffee systems of Central America and the sheep ranches in Chile. Paige found that revolutionary nationalist movements were likely to occur in migratory estate systems in colonial areas, as in Angola, for example.

The sharecropping system "is most common in annual crops which require minimal processing, and most of these crops could be efficiently produced by small holders. This system is most common in the rice economy of South and Southeast Asia and in the cotton economy of the Middle East" (Paige 1975, p. 369). Typically, the landlords are indigenous to the land and therefore, unlike the migratory labor estate systems, sharecropping usually divided the land-owning class and the cultivating class. The collective reaction is more likely to take the form of a struggle for revolutionary socialism rather than revolutionary nationalism.

The family small holding is a system of individually owned enterprises worked by the owner and his family. The cultivating class is dependent on the land, but the upper class is dependent on commercial capital; they are the middlemen. The cultivators' political organizations are generally weak and dependent on outside political parties (Paige 1975, pp. 45-47). Conflict is most likely to take the form of economic warfare over control of the commodity market. The typical movement goals are reformist. Within the context of an industrial economy, some agrarian movements appear relatively radical (Lipset 1950).

One of the important contributions Paige makes to our understanding of collective reactions to inequality is to demonstrate how certain structural class conditions tend to produce particular kinds of social movements and conflicts. Furthermore, several specific conditions combine to produce a particular collective reaction. Thus, migratory workers may feel aggrieved, but they usually lack the resources for organizing to seek redress. But if migratory workers are thrown back to village subsistence holdings when the harvest season is over, the traditional tribal or peasant leadership could provide the resources needed for organization. Whether or not the traditional village authorities join with the members of their village who have labored as migratory workers on the estates depends on their own economic circumstances. They are willing to join the migratory workers "only when their own economic base of support is being eroded by the same estate system that is exploiting the poor laborers" (Paige 1975, p. 361). This has occurred in Vietnam and Angola.

In addition to the characteristics of the strata and the relations between the conflicting strata, the environment of the strata help shape the goals. The strata members are part of a general and widespread socio-political system, hence they are likely to share ways of thinking. For example, in the contemporary world issues are frequently viewed as matters of polities. Problems often are thought to require political means of settlemnt and the solutions must involve governmental action. In addition, in any given historical period, particular ideologies are likely to be widely known and significant in shaping the way people think of their goals. Thus, Marxism is a widely known and influential political ideology; the ideas associated with liberal democracy are also widespread and help shape the formulation of particular objectives.

Finally, the degree to which the conflict process is regulated and institutionalized affects the nature of the conflicting goals. If conflict between two strata is highly regulated and institutionalized, then each adversary accepts the legitimacy of the other. The goals, then, are more likely to be reformist than radical. This may be seen in the development of collective bargaining between labor and management.

CONCLUSIONS

In this chapter we have examined collective reactions to inequality, particularly the bases and emergence of conflicts between different strata. We discussed objective conflict and the underlying conditions for the emergence of a conflict. Conflicts are often based on consensus: both sides agree about what is desirable; they disagree only about the allocation or distribution of what is desirable.

For a conflict between different strata to emerge, more is needed than the existence of a latent conflict. The adversary strata must have some collective identity. This awareness of group membership and the sense of shared fate reflects social reality. As the several studies of class consciousness indicated, there is a high relationship between personal class identification and objective class position.

The other major component in the emergence of a conflict is that members of at least one of the adversary strata believe they are exploited or otherwise have a grievance. The members of a stratum must believe they *should* have more of what they desire, that it is possible to have more, and that another group is blocking the attainment of what they desire. Such beliefs are often related to expectations based on past experience. Being ranked low is inherently deprivational and, therefore, a likely grievance. But the belief that those conditions can be rectified is critical. Having been in better circumstances recently makes improvement credible.

The third element in the emergence of a conflict is the formulation of goals. The goals can vary in several ways: we considered the dimension of reformism and radicalism. Many factors can shape the goals: we considered characteristics of each stratum, the relations between the conflicting strata, and the strata's social environment.

We have not discussed in this chapter the actual course of struggles and their outcomes. Obviously, this is a complex topic with an extensive literature, including studies of particular revolutions and military seizures of power and social movements (Lipset 1950; Trotsky 1934; Gott 1971; Leggett 1973). Although we will not try to review this subject, we will mention some pertinent considerations.

Struggles vary greatly in the way in which they are pursued. There may be more or less recourse to violence, ranging from isolated terrorist actions to large-scale social revolutions with popular participation. There may be more or less resort to nonviolent means of protest and action, including demonstrations, strikes, and other forms of noncooperation (Gamson 1975; Sharp 1973). Even noncoercive means are used to a greater or lesser extent, as in appeals to shared values and reasoning in terms of the antagonists' own interests. Noncoercive means include concessions or contingent rewards; one side may offer such inducements to its antagonists in order to gain their acquiescence. This may be done particularly to discourage coalitions.

The means used depend on many characteristics of the members of a stratum, including their previous experience with different conflict modes (Kriesberg 1973). The relations between the contending strata are also important, particularly their relative power, integration, and responsiveness to each other. Finally, the wider social environment is important; the possible intervention of third parties affects the choice of means as does the overall institutionalization of the conflict.

The result of social conflicts have profound effects upon the stratification system (Moore 1966). The revolutions in China, Russia, Cuba, and Mexico radically reduced at least some aspects of inequality. The military coups in Chile and Brazil and the 1936-39 civil war in Spain halted movements toward greater equality. In other cases, radical changes in stratification systems were introduced by the intervention in one society by military forces from another, as in Japan, Poland, and East Germany after World War II. One or another stratum within a society often seeks and finds support from allies abroad: others of the same ethnic group, political persuasion, or class level (Eckstein 1964).

This discussion provides a basis for looking at sequential changes in stratification systems. One can study the changes and persistence of inequalities as a series of events in the on-going flow of history, but on the whole, we do not try to do that here. Rather, we are looking at general processes that are needed to understand and account for such historical sequences. We will now go on to examine several major kinds of explanations of inequality, including conflict theories. That examination will help provide a more systematic approach to understanding how social conflicts account for variations in inequality.

REFERENCES

BAUMGARTNER, TOM, TOM R. BURNS, and PHILIPPE DEVILLE. 1978. "Clinflict Resolution and Conflict Development." Pp. 105-142 in Louis Kriesberg (Ed.), *Research in Social Movements, Conflict, and Change,* Vol. 1. Greenwich, Conn.: JAI Press.

BENSMAN, JOSEPH. 1972. "Status Communities in an Urban Society: The Musical Community." Pp. 92-107 in Holger R. Stub (Ed.), *Status Communities in Modern Society.* Hinsdale, Ill.: Dryden Press.

BERNARD, JESSE. 1978. "Models for the Relationship Between the World of Women and the World of Men." Pp. 291-340 in Louis Kriesberg (Ed.), *Research in Social Movements, Conflict and Change,* Vol. 1. Greenwich, Conn.: JAI Press.

BLAU, PETER M. 1964. *Exchange and Power in Social Life.* New York: John Wiley.

BLAUNER, ROBERT. 1964. *Alienation and Freedom: The Factory Worker and His Industry.* Chicago: University of Chicago Press.

BRADBURN, NORMAN M., and DAVID CAPLOVITZ. 1965. *Reports on Happiness.* Chicago: Aldine.

BUCHANAN, WILLIAM, and HADLEY CANTRIL. 1953. *How Nations See Each Other.* Urbana, Ill.: University of Illinois Press.

CARDEN, MAREN LOCKWOOD. 1978. "The Proliferation of a Social Movement." Pp. 179-196 in Louis Kriesberg (Ed.), *Research in Social Movements, Conflict, and Change.* Greenwich, Conn.: JAI Press.

CENTERS, RICHARD. 1949. *The Psychology of Social Classes.* Princeton, N.J.: Princeton University Press.

COMMONS, JOHN R., DAVID J. SAPOSS, HELEN L. SUMMER, E. B. MITTLEMAN, and H. E. HOAGLAND. 1936. *History of Labour in the United States,* Vol. 1. New York: Macmillan.

DAHRENDORF, RALF. 1959. *Class and Class Conflict in Industrial Society.* Stanford, Calif.: Stanford University Press.

DAVIES, A. F., and S. ENCEL. 1965. "Class and Status." In A. F. Davies and S. Encel (Eds.), *Australian Society.* Melbourne: F. W. Cheshire.

DAVIES, JAMES C. 1962. "Toward a Theory of Revolution," *American Sociological Review* 27 (February):5-19.

DOMHOFF G. WILLIAM. 1967. *"Who Rules America?"* Englewood Cliffs, N.J.: Prentice-Hall.

DUNLOP, JOHN T. 1951. "The Development of Labor Organization." Pp. 48-
56 in Joseph Shister (Ed.), *Labor Economics and Industrial Relations.*
Chicago: J. B. Lippincott.

ECKSTEIN, HARRY (Ed.). 1964. *Internal War.* New York: Free Press.

FEIERABEND, IVO K., and ROSALIND L. FEIERABEND and BETTY A.
NESVOLD. 1969. "Social Change and Political Violence: Cross-National
Patterns." Pp. 632-687 in Hugh Davis Graham and Ted Robert Gurr
(Eds.), *Violence in America.* New York: Bantam Books.

FORM, WILLIAM H., and JOAN RYTINA. 1969. "Ideological Beliefs on the
Distribution of Power in the United States," *American Sociological Review* 34 (February):19-31.

FRIEDMANN, EUGENE A., and ROBERT J. HAVIGHURST. 1954. *The
Meaning of Work and Retirement.* Chicago: University of Chicago Press.

GAMSON, WILLIAM A. 1975. *The Strategy of Social Protest.* Homewood, Ill.:
Dorsey Press.

GOTT, RICHARD. 1971. *Guerilla Movements in Latin America.* Garden City,
N.Y.: Doubleday.

GROSS, FELIKS. 1966, *World Politics and Tension Areas.* New York: New
York University Press.

GURR, TED ROBERT. 1970. *Why Men Rebel.* Princeton, N.J.: Princeton University Press.

HAER, JOHN L. 1957. "An Emprical Study of Social Class Awareness," *Social
Forces* 36 (December):117-121.

HAMILTON, RICHARD F. 1966. "The Marginal Middle Class: A Reconsideration," *American Sociological Review* 31 (April): 192-199.

HODGE, ROBERT W., and DONALD J. TREIMAN. 1968. "Class Identification in the United States," *American Journal of Sociology* 73 (March):
535-547.

HOLLINGSHEAD, AUGUST. 1949. *Elmtown's Youth.* New York: John Wiley.

INKELES, ALEX. 1960. "Industrial Man: The Relation of Status to Experience,
Perception, and Value," *The American Journal of Sociology* 66 (July):
1-31.

JACKMAN, MARY R., and ROBERT W. JACKMAN. 1973. "An Interpretation
of the Relation Between Objective and Subjective Social Status," *American Sociological Review* 38 (October):569-582.

KAHL, JOSEPH, and JAMES DAVIS. 1955. "A Comparison of Indexes and
Socio-Economic Status," *American Sociological Review* 20 (June):317-
325.

KORPI, WALTER. 1971. "Working Class Communism in Western Europe:
Rational Nonrational," *American Sociological Review* 36 (December):
971-984.

KRIESBERG, LOUIS. 1973. *The Sociology of Social Conflicts.* Englewood
Cliffs, N.J.: Prentice-Hall.

LANDECKER, WERNER S. 1963. "Class Crystallization and Class Consciousness," *American Sociological Review* 28 (April):219-229.

LEGGETT, JOHN C. 1964. "Economic Insecurity and Working-Class Consciousness," *American Sociological Review* 29 (April):226-234.

LEGGETT, JOHN C. 1973. *Taking State Power.* New York: Harper and Row.

LIPSET, SEYMOUR MARTIN. 1950. *Agrarian Socialism.* Berkeley and Los
Angeles: University of California Press.

LIPSET, SEYMOUR MARTIN. 1959. *Political Man.* Garden City, N.Y.: Doubleday.

LIPSET, SEYMOUR MARTIN, and EARL RAAB. 1970. *The Politics of Unreason: Right Wing Extremism in America, 1790-1970.* New York: Harper and Row.

LOPREATO, JOSEPH, and LAWRENCE E. HAZELRIGG. 1972. *Class, Conflict and Mobility.* San Francisco: Chandler.

MANIS, JEROME G., and BERNARD N. MELTZER. 1954. "Attitudes of Textile Workers to Class Structure," *American Journal of Sociology* 60 (July): 30-35.

MANIS, JEROME G., and BERNARD N. MELTZER. 1963. "Some Correlates of Class Consciousness Among Textile Workers," *American Journal of Sociology* 60 (September):177-184.

MARX, GARY T. 1969. *Protest and Prejudice.* New York: Harper and Row.

MARX, KARL. 1963. *The Poverty of Philosophy.* New York: International Publishers. (Originally published in 1847.)

MARX, KARL and FRIEDERICH ENGELS. 1932. "Manifesto of the Communist Party." Pp. 320-343 in Max Eastman (Ed.), *Capital, The Communist Manifesto and Other Writings.* New York: Modern Library. (Originally published in 1848.)

MAYNTZ, RENATE. 1958. *Soziale Schichtung and Sozialer Wandel in einer Industriegemeinde.* Stuttgart: Ferdinand Enke.

MOORE, BARRINGTON. 1966. *Social Origins of Dictatorship and Democracy.* Boston: Beacon Press.

MORRIS, RICHARD T., and VINCENT JEFFRIES. 1968. "Violence Next Door," *Social Forces* 46 (March):342-358.

MURPHY, RAYMOND J., and RICHARD T. MORRIS. 1961. "Occupational Situs, Subjective Class Identification, and Political Affiliation," *American Sociological Review* 26 (June):383-392.

OBERSCHALL, ANTHONY. 1973. *Social Conflict and Social Movements.* Englewood Cliffs, N.J.: Prentice-Hall.

OESER, O. A., and S. B. HAMMOND. 1954. *Social Structure and Personality in a City.* London: Routledge and Kegan Paul.

OFFE, CLAUS. 1976. *Industry and Inequality.* London: Arnold. Translated by J. Wickham. (Originally published in 1970.)

PAIGE, JEFFREY M. 1975. *Agrarian Revolution.* New York: Free Press.

PARKIN, FRANK. 1971. *Class Inequality and Political Order.* New York: Praeger.

PARSONS, TALCOTT. 1970. "Equality and Inequality in Modern Society, or Social Stratification Revisited." Pp. 13-72 in Edward O. Lauman (Ed.), *Social Stratification.* Indianapolis: Bobbs-Merrill.

PERLMAN, SELIG. 1928. *A Theory of the Labor Movement.* New York: Augustus M. Kelley.

POPITZ, HEINRICH, HANS P. BAHRDT, ERNST A. JURES, and HANNO KESTING. 1961. *Das Gesellschaftsbild des Arbeiters*, 2nd Ed. Tubingen: J. C. B. Mohr.

PURCELL, THEODORE V. 1953. *The Worker Speaks His Mind on Company and Union.* Cambridge: Harvard University Press.

ROSENBERG, MORRIS. 1953. "Perceptual Obstacles to Class Consciousness," *Social Forces* 32 (October):22-27.

RUNCIMAN, W. G. 1966. *Relative Deprivation and Social Justice.* Berkeley and Los Angeles: University of California Press.

SHARP, GENE. 1973. *The Politics of Nonviolent Action.* Boston: Porter Sargent.

SHIBUTANI, TAMOTSU, and KIAN KWAN. 1965. *Ethnic Stratification*. New York: Macmillan.

SHILS, EDWARD. 1960. "The Intellectuals in the Political Development of the New States," *World Politics* 12 (April):329-368.

SVALASTOGA, KAARE. 1959. *Prestige, Class and Mobility*. Copenhagen: Cyldendal.

TILLY, CHARLES. 1975. "Revolutions and Collective Violence." Pp. 483-555 in F. I. Greenstein and N. W. Polsby (Eds.), *Handbook of Political Science*, Vol. 3. Reading, Mass.: Addison-Wesley.

TROTSKY, LEON. 1934. *The History of the Russian Revolution*. London: Victor Gollanca. (Originally published in 1930.)

TUMIN, MELVIN M. with ARNOLD FELDMAN. 1961. *Social Class and Social Change in Puerto Rico*. Princeton, N.J.: Princeton University Press.

VANNEMAN, REEVE and FRED C. PAMPEL. 1977. "The American Perception of Class and Status," *American Sociological Review* 42 (June):422-437.

WARNER, W. LLOYD, and PAUL S. LUNT. 1941. *The Social Life of a Modern Community*. New Haven, Conn.: Yale University Press.

WARNER, W. LLOYD, with the collaboration of W. C. BAILEY, A. COOPER, W. EATON, A. B. HOLLINGSHEAD, C. MCGUIRE, M. MEEKER, B. NEUGARTEN, J. ROSENSTEIN, E. Z. VOGT, JR., and D. WRAY. 1949. *Democracy in Jonesville*. New York: Harper.

WATNICK, MORRIS. 1952. "The Appeal of Communism to the Underdeveloped Peoples." Pp. 152-172 in Bert F. Hoselitz (Ed.), *The Progress of Underdeveloped Areas*. Chicago: University of Chicago Press.

WILENSKY, HAROLD L. 1966. "Class, Class Consciousness, and American Workers." Pp. 12-44 in William Haber (Ed.), *Labor in a Changing America*. New York: Basic Books.

WILENSKY, HAROLD L., and HUGH EDWARDS. 1959. "The Skidder: Ideological Adjustments of Downwardly Mobile Workers," *American Sociological Review* 24 (April):215-231.

WILLENER, ALFRED. 1957. *Images de la société et classes sociales*. Bern.

WILSON, EDMUND. 1955. *To the Finland Station*. Garden City, N.Y.: Doubleday. (Originally published in 1940.)

ZEITLIN, MAURICE. 1970. *Revolutionary Politics and the Cuban Working Class*. New York: Harper and Row. (Originally published in 1967.)

chapter 11

Theoretical
Explanations

"What is the answer?" the dying Gerturde Stein asked.
Hearing no reply, she said,
"In that case, what is the question?"

This chapter examines several distinctive and fundamental kinds of explanations for social inequality. They provide answers to a variety of questions and yet, to test their validity, we need to compare how each explanation answers the same question. We need to be clear about the questions the theorists set for themselves, because writers argue past each other if they try to answer different questions.

QUESTIONS AND ANSWERS

Questions

Some questions pertain to universal aspects of social inequality. For example, the question might be posed: Why is social inequality found in every society? Or, the question may be: Why do particular kinds of inequality seem to be found everywhere? Why are occupations related to healing illness consistently ranked higher in prestige than those related to growing food?

Cast in such general and universal terms, these questions are susceptible to innumerable alternative answers which cannot be tested. Any other universal factor can be said to be the reason for the universal phenomenon being explained. Thus, such questions might be answered by saying, "That's human nature," or "Every social system requires it." Such answers cannot be refuted as long as the phenomenon actually is universal.[1]

An adequate question must ask about the variability of a phenomenon (Abrahamson 1972). Of the many kinds of questions about variations in inequality that might be posed, we distinguish three sets: First, questions might be asked about the content or form of inequality. We might ask, why do certain occupations or ethnic groups have higher relative status in one country than in another? Second, questions might be asked about the allocation or rank attainment processes. Thus, we could ask why persons of different races differ in the proportions in which they occupy powerful offices. We have been most interested in this book in a third set of questions: those pertaining to variations in the degree of equality.

---

[1] No theory can be proven true absolutely because at any later time, some evidence that will refute it can appear. A theory may be consistent with all known evidence and seem to be true, but another theory may also be consistent with all the known evidence. Our awareness of alternative and equally well supported theories must weaken our conviction of the validity of any single theory. For this reason, it is wise to consider the full range of possible explanations and seek to refute them all, hoping that only one will survive the test.

Answers

Theories vary in the emphasis they place on different factors in accounting for social inequality. This chapter will discuss major theoretical approaches and representative writers in each orientation.

Before considering theories that refer to social factors, we should consider the possible role of biological, genetic, and idiosyncratic factors. In recent years there has been a revival of attention to the biological components in human behavior. Since other species have ranking or pecking orders, it might seem that stratification is inherent in the biological nature of humans (Tiger and Fox 1971). But, of course, there are an immense number of species with different behaviors and almost any point can be made if species are selected as evidence for a particular point.

Mazur (1973) compared ranking in small established groups among species ordered in a biologically pertinent manner. He compared primates in terms of their increasing similarity to humans: tree shrews, lemurs, squirrel monkeys, baboons and macaques, gorillas, and chimpanzees. Mazur listed several characteristics of human ranking behavior in small groups. Although the evidence is scanty, he inferred that humans share a few similarities in ranking behavior with closely related species. Thus, he suggests that humans share ranking gestures that are subtle rather than overt with chimpanzees and gorillas, but not with other species. Chimpanzees and gorillas, but not other species, are tolerant of group members of different rank and usually are not combative. High-ranked members perform services and control activities among humans, baboons, gorillas, and chimpanzees, but probably not among other species.

Even if evidence were to accumulate to indicate that humans share some ranking characteristics with closely related species, this would refer only to face-to-face interaction within small groups. As Mazur points out, we have not observed large-scale stratification in nonhuman species. Although analogous to face-to-face behavior, there is no biological justification for explaining macro-social stratification by analogy. There is no basis for generalizing from the face-to-face level to the macro-societal.

Other kinds of nonsocial explanations stress human variability in aggressiveness, dominance need, intellectual prowess, or other capacities that might account for differences in ranking. Since variations in those capacities presumably are similarly distributed within any human population, variations in ranking between different populations could not be explained by such factors. If intelligence within every population, for example, is distributed in a bell-shaped curve, with most people having average intelligence, then differences in intelligence could not account for differences in the distribution of material goods among different populations. It might be argued that different populations have different distributions of intelligence, or dominance, or some other characteristic relevant for social inequality. Thus, males or whites might be argued to have more aggressiveness or dominance behavior than women or nonwhites. But this would not account for variations in the relative rankings by

331

sex or race in different societies. Perhaps, however, genetic or biological differences do combine in particular ways with social factors to produce variations that cause sex and race inequalities in different societies. We will consider such possibilities in the context of social explanations later in this chapter and the next.

Five theoretical approaches will be discussed; each emphasizes different sets of factors. No major theorist denies the relevance of all the factors we discuss; each differs in which factors he or she stresses and how he or she relates the factors to each other and to inequality. Two approaches are varieties of the functionalist perspective. One emphasizes values and norms and also the integration of the functional subsystems of the society. The other emphasizes the necessity for the social system to motivate people to do what needs to be done and specifically the relationship between functional importance of positions and scarcity of personnel to fill the positions.

Two other approaches see the social system as persons and groups contending with each other. In one, coercive factors are emphasized; coercion is seen as accounting for power differences and those power differences are considered basic to other forms of inequality. In the other, economic classes, differentiated on the basis of their relationship to the modes of production, struggle with each other.

Finally, some theorists emphasize the demographic and technological factors. They give less weight to values or to actors' intentions or strivings than do the other theorists.

These theories are general orientations aimed at accounting for universal characteristics of inequality. They are not formulated as a set of interrelated, testable propositions about variations in equality. In order to highlight the differences among the theoretical approaches, we will give greatest attention to how the theories differ, rather than to how much they have in common. We will also propose specific hypotheses that are consistent with the general orientations. In the next two chapters, we will relate the data we have been examining to those hypotheses. We can then see how the different orientations might be combined to give a full explanation of variations of different aspects of inequality.

FUNCTIONAL THEORIES

A major approach to sociological analysis is functionalism. Sometimes functionalism is conceived to mean relating parts of a society to the whole and one part to another. So broadly conceived, it is virtually synonymous with sociological analysis (Davis 1959). However, as we shall see, the way particular functionalists try to account for inequalities is more specific and differs from the ways in which nonfunctionalists try to account for inequalities, which is helpful because for a theory to be useful, it must assert that some factors or aspects are more significant than others in answering a given question.

Values and Functional Integration

One idea usually stressed by functionalists is the high degree of inter-dependence among the parts of a social system. The subsystems or components of any social system are highly integrated; for example, family, religion, and the economy are mutually consistent and supportive. The high degree of integration among the components of the society helps perpetuate the system as it is.

Functional analysts also generally stress the importance of value and normative consensus. Agreed-upon rules are essential for the persistence of the social system. A social system such as a society also has an integrated cultural system. This cultural system includes evaluative standards.

Functionalists also emphasize the society or the social system as a whole. Component parts have meaning and significance as parts of a whole, not inde-pendent of it. In this sense the whole is more than the sum of the parts. The integration of the parts and the emphasis on the entire social system makes it possible to think of the system as having needs or requirements. That is, the social system, if it is to survive as such, must have certain requirements met. We can then argue that a given pattern of activity or peculiar form of institu-tional organization is the way it is in order to maintain the social system. If the needs of the social system were not met, then the system as a whole would cease to exist.

Parsons. In this section of the chapter, we will consider the ways in which one major functional theorist, Talcott Parsons, seeks to explain social inequality. Parsons stresses the integration of the societal system and the importance of consensus. He has applied this to social stratification in articles written in 1940, 1953 and 1970. In general, Parsons has argued that the shared values and norms of a society provide the basis for evaluation. Since some people will more com-pletely fulfill the normative demands of the culture, they will be more highly esteemed. That is inherent in having evaluative standards.

Writing in 1940, Parsons argues that moral evaluations of individuals are the central criteria of ranking. He seeks to explain social stratification defined as the differential ranking of persons, assuming that status is the primary dimen-sion of inequality. For example, in the United States, status is accorded for achievement, particularly in the economy and achievement then determines other characteristics that are evaluated. He discusses wealth and income as *symbols* of achievement, going on to say that those symbols sometimes gain enough independence for the possessor of wealth to claim status apart from achievement and even to have such status recognized. In short, moral standards generally determine status. Parsons also analyzes how the stratification system is closely related to other systems. For example, he discusses occupational status in relation to sex roles in the family. He notes that a clear separation of sex roles serves to keep husbands and wives from competing occupationally and thus avoids invidious comparisons that might be disruptive of the family.

In his 1953 article, Parsons more sharply distinguishes the valuational aspect of stratification from its other aspects. Nevertheless, he still asserts that the analysis of stratification should focus on the common value aspects that provide the evaluative basis for ranking. He regards power as indicating the discrepancy between the actual state of affairs and what they would be if only valuational aspects were determining stratification. This is a recognition that stratification is not completely shaped by values, but also by power differences.

Writing in 1970, Parsons still emphasizes status, but largely in terms of occupational prestige. He assumes that inequality is inevitable if the adaptive requirements of society are to be met on the grounds developed by Davis and Moore (1945) and discussed in the section on motivation and functional contribution. The legitimation of inequality is of greater interest to him. How much inequality of what kind, he asks, is justified on the basis of which values? Institutionalization of stratification provides the legitimation of equality and inequality. Parsons believes that modern societies place a high value on equality, and therefore, inequality needs to be justified. It is legitimated by arguing the necessity of motivating people to strive for and to fill competently functionally important tasks. Equality of opportunity is stressed as consistent with this belief and itself becomes a justification for inequality.

Critiques. Because criticisms of this, as of other theories, help clarify what the theory is asserting, they should be examined. What might otherwise appear common sense becomes problematic and testable. The criticisms of Parson's eforts at explaining inequality and variations in it, constitute a critique of functional explanations in general.

One criticism is based upon the apparent policy implications of the theory. Functionalism is sometimes charged with justifying the status quo, whatever it may be. Presumably, things are the way they are because they fit together and express shared understandings and the needs of the system as a whole. This charge is refuted by functionalists, who argue that they do recognize dysfunctions. They also acknowledge that some arrangements may not be functional for the system as a whole, but only for some segment of it (Merton 1949, p. 34). Functional theorists also argue that they recognize that many functional equivalents or substitutes are possible. Merton (1949, p. 35) states that a major theorem of functional analysis is that the same function may be diversely fulfilled by alternative items.

Critics argue that social systems do not have needs or even requirements, that only particular persons and groups of persons do. Critics also argue that assertions of functional requirements cannot be tested when functional requirements are simply posited and any given pattern may be said to contribute to some functional requirement.

Several methodological problems have also been raised. Functional theorists do not specify how much consensus is needed for a social system to survive nor are they clear about the measures of values and norms, independent of how people conduct themselves. Yet, we need ways of assessing values and norms, aside from actions, if we are to determine whether they direct conduct or whether they follow conduct. For example, is the presence of mass higher education in the United States an indicator of the value we place on equal opportunity? Is that value then to be used to explain the pattern of mass higher education? That would be circular reasoning. Perhaps the reason we have mass education at the college and university level is that such institutions proliferated early in American history because each of the many denominations in the United States wanted to train ministers in its own schools. Once established, these schools grew and competed with each other, promoting as a way of increasing their market, the doctrine of opening up opportunities for everyone.

Similarly, it may be argued that particular roles are viewed as functionally important, not because they actually are so, but because the incumbents of certain roles are able to create conditions that make what they are doing seem important. Perrow (1972, p. 200) illustrates this possibility with the hypothetical example of a peaceful agricultural people who bestow honors upon those who promise rain and solve disputes. Suddenly they are threatened by a newly arrived tribe. After a protracted struggle, they succeed in defending their land from the intruders. The warriors are honored, but peace now threatens the high rank of the warriors. The warriors seek out another possible adversary. Triumphing again, they continue to seek out enemies and garner more rewards from their people. Perrow speculates that a visiting functionalist might then conclude that warriors have high prestige and should dominate because it is functional that they do so since the people have a hostile environment and their lands are challenged.

Nevertheless, it is important to try to find evidence that will make it possible to refute this and other explanations of inequality. To do so, we must overcome the methodological problems as well as we can. We will examine some of the available evidence in the next chapter. In this chapter, we examine major alternative explanations and specify them so that they might be tested. Thus, we will point out what factors functionalists regard as particularly significant and hypothesize how they might vary and thereby help account for the variations in inequality.

Hypotheses. According to the Parsonian orientation, variations in values and in integration should be related to variations in inequality. First, we discuss how the content of the values shared by members of a society is expected to be related to the degree of inequality. For example, Parsons (1951, pp. 58-67) has distinguished five pattern variables. These are polarities; an actor must choose a side for a situation to have meaning for him or her. They constitute dilemmas in every situation. He maintains that these five pattern variables constitute a system. Among them are the following two dichotomies: universalism-particularism and ascription-achievement. In the first, the actor has a dilemma between treating objects in a situation in accordance with a general norm covering all objects in that class or in terms of the object's relationship to the actor or the actor's collectivity. In other words, does he or she treat someone universally, in terms of generalized standards, or preferentially, in terms of their relationship to the actor (for example, same ethnicity, sex, or age). In the case of the ascription-achievement pattern variable, the dilemma is between treating an object for what it is in itself or for what it does. In other words, is priority given to a person's innate qualities or attributes, or to his or her actual or expected performances?

Parsons regards the United States as a society that emphasizes universalism and achievement. We might expect that in such societies mobility would be greater than in ascriptive societies and that status differences would be less salient than in societies that tend to be particularistic. To test such hypotheses, we should compare countries that differ in ascriptive and universalistic orientations and compare their stratification systems. Presumably, too, changes in time in these value orientations would be followed by changes in mobility and status inequalities.

Lipset (1967) has argued that cultures differ in whether they emphasize equality or elitism. This choice of emphasis would be reflected in differences in the actual degree of inequality. Parsons does not regard this choice as at the same level as the pattern variables, but he recognizes this value dimension as very important. Indeed, the value of equalitarianism is an important part of the idea of modernism. Modernism is a set of ideas related to industrialization, urbanization, and education. As the ideas of modernism diffuse in the world, an emphasis upon equality also spreads. Parsons sees some contemporary societies as more modern than others. To test this assertion, we might compare different societies that are considered "modern" in ideas and valuation of equality and see if they are actually more equalitarian than are less modern societies.

Functional theory also explains variations in inequality in terms of the relative importance of different functional requirements. Thus, in particular societies or particular historical periods, one functional requirement may be more important than another. For example, adaptive requirements may be especially important not only because of the values of a given society, but because of environmental challenges. If so, those roles making a relatively large contribution to meeting the adaptive requirements of a society will be most highly regarded. Testing these ideas requires further specification and a more exact determination of what operations would indicate contributions to adaptive requirements.

Functional explanations of variations in inequality also stress the requirements of other institutions or subsystems within the society. Thus, the nature of the kinship system is expected to have consequences for occupational mobility. For example, societies or periods with extended and solidary kinship systems would be expected to have less intergenerational occupational mobility than societies characterized by isolated nuclear families. Family systems are also expected to be related to the relative status of women. Sex-based status inequalities are to be explained, then, in terms of both cultural values and consistency with the functional requirements of the family and occupational systems.

Motivation and Functional Contribution

Davis and Moore. Still other elements of functional theory can be emphasized to account for various aspects of inequality. In 1945 Davis and Moore formulated a set of questions and answers that have been very influential and controversial. They sought to explain the universality of inequality and some of the similarities and variations in rewards associated with different positions. Their concern was with the rewards associated with positions and not with the persons or the allocation of persons into positions.

They reasoned that people had to be induced to do what society needed done and people had to be motivated to fulfill the required role activities by extrinsic rewards. They thought that the interaction of two factors determines the relative ranking of positions: differential functional importance and differential scarcity of personnel. Thus, positions with the greatest importance for the society and requiring the greatest training or talent would be most highly rewarded. A society does not need to reward positions in direct proportion to their functional importance. It must also base the rewards on how difficult the position is to fill. Davis and Moore reason that all positions require some skill or capacity for performance, and these are acquired by talent or training. If the talents required for a position are widely possessed and the training is easy, the rewards need not be great.

Davis and Moore explain differences in stratification systems by variations in functional importance and scarcity of personnel. For example, the importance of religion varies in different societies depending on the general level of popular education and of economic production that provides a surplus of goods beyond subsistence needs; the highest general position awarded a priest occurred in the medieval type of social order. External conditions such as relations with other societies and size of the population also affect the magnitude of inequality. For example, Davis and Moore assert that a small population limits the degree of functional specialization in a society; hence, it limits the magnitude of inequality.

Critiques. The Davis and Moore paper was criticized at length by Tumin (1953), and a series of scholarly critiques and rejoinders has followed and continues to the present (Davis 1949, 1953; Wrong 1959; Abrahamson 1978). The criticisms are ideological, methodological, and substantive.

To some critics, what Davis and Moore wrote seems inordinately conservative and appears to suggest an invisible hand working to insure that the right person is in the right position. Critics allege that Davis and Moore's explanation justifies the existing degree of inequality. Davis and Moore have countered by arguing that they are not discussing how people actually are allocated into positions; they in fact acknowledge that many social forces affect the placement of persons into positions. Furthermore, they note that the degree of inequality in rewards may be greater than is functionally necessary. Again, other forces that artificially increase or decrease the rewards associated with a given position may be operative; for example, incumbents of an occupation may restrict the number of persons who are allowed to receive the training necessary for the position.

These acknowledgements raise methodological issues. Testing the theory is difficult if the theory does not indicate how one can determine how much inequality is necessary nor acknowledge that many other unspecified factors actually determine the magnitude of inequality. Methodological criticism of the Davis and Moore formulation has often focused on the difficulty in measuring functional importance. To assess functional importance on the basis of the rewards accorded various positions obviously leads to circular reasoning. Davis and Moore agree that ascertaining functional importance is difficult, but argue that difficulty in measurement does not make a concept useless. In the next chapter, when we examine evidence to test the several theories, we will note how functional importance has been operationally measured.

Several substantive criticisms also have been made of the Davis and Moore formulation. Tumin (1953) for example, argued that people could be and were motivated by many considerations other than external rewards. For example, performing the activities of many positions is intrinsically gratifying; other jobs are unsatisfying and presumably need additional external rewards to attract willing entrants. It might also be argued that there is generally an abundance of persons capable of filling even "difficult" positions, that most jobs can be filled by almost anyone who is given an opportunity to learn them. In addition, preparation or training for a position should not be assumed to be a sacrifice that needs to be compensated for by later rewards; training is often pleasurable, having its own rewards and involving no greater sacrifice than entering an easy or low position that requires little training. Much of the argument about the functional explanations of inequality involves hypothetical possibilities. We will try to apply the theoretical explanations to actual inequality variations.

Hypotheses. Because explanations for a universal pattern are difficult to test, we do need to consider how the Davis and Moore formulation could account for variations in inequality. One variation is the relative prestige and material rewards attached to positions in different societies. Depending on the stage of internal development, on external conditions, or on general cultural values, one or another societal function may be especially important. Consequently, positions meeting those functional requirements would have greater rewards. For example, some societies may be preoccupied with the sacred and the religious; hence, relative high prestige and material rewards would be associated with priestly roles.

Variations in the range and in the distribution of prestige and material rewards are related to the degree of specialization in the society. Davis and Moore reason that since specialization is greater in larger societies, the magnitude of inequality would be greater than in small societies. Certain kinds of relations with other societies also affect internal inequality. For example, Davis and

Moore suggest that the free movement of ideas tends to have an equalitarian effect.

Variations in the rate of mobility are also affected by the stage of cultural development. Davis and Moore suggest that as the cultural heritage grows, so does specialization, which in turn contributes to the enhancement of mobility. The content of the cultural values also affects mobility, thus they suggest that an emphasis upon sacred matters places a brake on social mobility.

The functionalist explanations of inequality, as exemplified by Parsons and by Davis and Moore have much in common, but they differ in their emphases. In trying to assess them against empirical variations, we will want to keep in mind both the shared ideas of functionalists and the variations.

CONFLICT AND MATERIAL CONDITIONS

Conflict explanations are often contrasted with functionalist theories. In general, conflict theorists account for the patterns of inequality in terms of contending groups. Groups of people struggle with each other for dominance, wealth, and prestige. The outcome is the result of such efforts and is not determined by the needs of the larger social system of which the contending groups are members. Values and norms reflect the victor's interests. In this approach, ideas are often viewed as instruments of control, not as a source of change.

There are many conflict approaches. We will note a few varieties and then discuss two particular formulations: those of Marx, Engels, and contemporary Marxists, who emphasize material or economic conditions, and those of non-Marxists, who emphasize coercion. Conflict theorists differ in which groups they consider to be the primary adversaries. For example, Marxists generally consider classes based upon economic relationships as primary. Other conflict theorists give great weight to status groups and the struggles, for example, between ethnic groups (Gumplowicz 1899; Wilson 1973). Finally, some conflict theorists regard power differences based upon coercion as primary (Dahrendorf 1959; Collins 1975).

Other theorists also seek to explain variations in inequality by reference to the interacting efforts of groups and of individuals. But they do not emphasize the coercive quality of the contentions. Rather, they see groups, or more likely individuals, competing with each other and carrying out exchanges with each other. Economists are an important group of social theorists who take this approach (Becker 1957; Gordon 1972; Chiswick 1974). Some aspects of economists' explanations of income inequalities are similar to the functionalist as well as conflict approaches, but economists work from their own intellectual tradition and with their own methods. We should, nevertheless, consider the kinds of explanations they offer and note their possible contributions to answering the questions raised in this book.

The dominant economic view is that of neoclassical marginal productivity theory (Brown 1977; Bibb and Form 1977). According to this theory, under hypothetical perfect competition, each factor of production would be paid its marginal product. Thus, workers are paid according to their productivity, wages ae equal to the value of output attributable to the last worker hired, and they are set by supply and demand forces in the market place. Earned income distribution, then, reflects the varying abilities and hence marginal productivity of the workers. The distribution of nonearned income also reflects the marginal productivity of the other factors of production. Economists recognize the need to modify the assumptions of perfect competition, but they appear to believe the outcomes are not greatly changed.

Since many aspects of this model are indeterminant and, in any case, it does not seem to fit the actual distribution of income, some economists have sought to elaborate marginal productivity theory (Thurow 1970). One version is the human capital approach which argues that the marginal productivity of workers depends on their enhanced capacity to produce; human capital is indicated by schooling, on-the-job training, work experience and even motivation. Groups of people who have less of these resources, perhaps as a result of discrimination, would earn less than persons with more resources and hence earnings would be unequal. This approach has some similarity to functional explanations, characterizing sacrifices people make for training as investments for future reward.[2]

Evidence inconsistent with the human capital approach has helped stimulate a revision of economic explanations of inequality. Thurow (1975), for example, argues that a job competition model is superior to a wage competition model. According to this model, two distributions are important: the distribution of jobs and the distribution of people in relationship to access to the jobs. A person's productivity depends on her or his job, and getting the opportunity to learn the tasks of the job is critical, but those skills are acquired on the job. In effect, workers "line up" to be selected by an employer in order to get the opportunity to learn how to do the jobs that are available. The distribution of jobs and the productivity associated with the jobs determine the distribution of earnings. This approach has some similarities with the conflict approach which views control of access to jobs as critical in shaping earning distributions.

Although these and related economic explanations of income and wage distribution are often ingenious and contribute to our understanding of class inequality, we will not examine them in this book. An examination would require familiarity with micro- and macro-economic theory, which this book

[2] Simpson (1956) proposed to modify the Davis–Moore formulation by abandoning the concept of functional necessity, since it is value-laden, unmeasurable, and assumes the functionality of activities that is simply not supportable. He suggests a straightforward supply-and-demand model. Demand for position holders is affected by cultural values, technology, and the power endowed on their holders to reward themselves. This modification makes the explanation no longer a functional one. It becomes a blend of orthodox economic theory and conflict theory.

cannot provide and does not assume. Furthermore, these economic theories are more restricted than our concern in seeking to understand class inequality (Brown 1977). Economists' theories generally apply to market economies, but we seek explanations of nonmarket economies as well. More fundamentally, economists generally take social structure and even the class and status structure as givens within which the market functions. We are concerned here with the bases of those very structures. Nevertheless, economists' theories help provide ideas about the linkages between the social structure and wages, as we saw in the discussion of the split labor market in Chapter 7. Some economists reject the basic ideas of the dominant view and draw on the Marxist tradition to account for income inequalities.

Marxists and Radicals

The basic ideas of Marx and Engels were set forth in Chapter 2. Marx and Engels emphasized that material conditions underlay human thought and, in particular, that the means of production constitute the basis for the social organization of production or for the mode of production. They did not argue that the superstructure of ideas was completely determined by these material conditions, but were so only in the "last instance." Class relations are fundamental in explaining changes in and persistence of patterns of inequality. Classes are based on people's relationship to the means of production and classes exist objectively; but in order to be agents of change or maintenance of those stratification systems, members sharing the same class position must become aware of their shared interests. The approach of Marx and Engels is also dialectical.[3] They argued that contradictions underlie all social processes, and social change comes from the working out of contradictions.

Critiques and responses. Marx and Engels, writing in the nineteenth century, were trying to account for the effects of capitalist system they saw about them in the context of its rise and expansion. Using their theoretical approach to further the revolutions they wished would eventuate, they predicted future developments of capitalism and its ultimate supercession; they also speculated about the nature of the communist alternative. Their analyses and predictions have been subjected to continuing and extensive critiques. The criticisms have been met by many elaborations and modifications, or reiterations, of Marxism. The ideas of Marx and Engels refer to a particular historical period; contemporary Marxists believe the basic approach is correct but must be adapted to the present historical circumstances. We draw upon the writings of radical economists and radical sociologists; they generally have taken Marx and Engels' work and applied it to the present circumstances.

---

[3] Dialectic refers to the conception that a given condition, often referred to as "thesis," creates its own opposition or "antithesis." The result of the struggle between these opposing forces is a new condition, a "synthesis," that then creates a new opposition. Consequently, change is constant and each social system bears the seeds of its own destruction.

Many critics of Marxism have argued that the developments in advanced capitalist societies refute Marxism (Aron 1968; Avineri 1968). They point out that the working class in advanced industrial societies has not overthrown the bourgeoisie. The first revolution led by the Communist party occurred in Russia, a relatively underdeveloped capitalist society. Later, relatively autonomous revolutions occurred in agrarian societies. When communism has come to industrialized capitalist societies, it has come about by external imposition rather than as a result of an internal revolution. Within advanced capitalist societies, the plight of the working class has not worsened; indeed, their standard of living has risen greatly from the times of early industrialization.

The developments in countries led by the Communist party is the basis for other criticisms. The end of private ownership of the means of production, it is argued, has not ended the exploitation of man by man. Class differences in material conditions between types of workers persist. The elites live in a grand style and ensure that their children share in their privileges (Djilas 1957).

Contemporary Marxists and radicals counter these criticisms in several ways (Baran and Sweezy 1966). For one, they argue capitalism cannot be understood within the confines of a single country. Capitalism is a world system; the workings of the capitalist economy link and transcend the countries that make up the world system (Wallerstein 1974; Lenin 1939; Zeitlin 1972). In that view, capitalists in the advanced countries particularly exploit the workers in the less developed or dependent countries, employing them on plantations and in mines, producing for a foreign market. Workers in the third world, in the neo-colonial countries, and in the peripheral countries are exploited. Communist revolutions are likely to occur in those countries. Meanwhile, in the more advanced countries, the workers may derive benefits from the exploitation of workers in the dependent countries. Imperialist wars and the preparation for such wars provide a way to avoid the crises of capitalism and unemployment, which would otherwise occur.

Some Marxist and radical theoreticians also argue that capitalists follow policies that avoid the development of proletarian class consciousness and revolt. For example, Gintis (cited in Gordon 1972, p. 63) argues that economic growth provides to workers the promise of a better future for their children. Workers can earn an increasing amount of money, even under capitalism. As Mandel (1968, p. 145) writes:

> In fact, it is not the absolute level of wages that matters to capital. The latter prefers, certainly, that wages should be as low as possible in its own enterprises—but it wants at the same time to see wages as high as possible paid in competing enterprises or by the employers of its customers! What matters to capital is the possibility of extracting more surplus labour, more unpaid labour, more surplus value, more profit from its workers. The growth in the productivity of labour, which makes possible the growth of relative surplus value, implies the possibility of a slow rise in real wages. . . on condition that the equivalent of these increased real wages is produced

in an ever shorter period of time, i.e., that wages rise less quickly than productivity. . .

The rise in real wages does not follow *automatically* from the rise in the productivity of labour. The latter only creates the *possibility* of such a rise, within the capitalist framework, provided profit is not threatened. For this potential increase to become actual, two interlinked conditions are needed: a favorable evolution of relations of strength in the labour market. . .and effective organization. . .of the wage workers which enables them to abolish competition among themselves and so to take advantage of these "favourable market conditions" (author's emphasis).

Employers find it in their interest to create a highly stratified labor market. They emphasize slight differences in the employment conditions, which pit workers against each other as they strive to gain a little status or material improvement compared to their fellow workers. Employers also foster separate labor markets through discrimination by race, sex, and age. They create special kinds of jobs for blacks, women, and teenagers, which force them to compete against each other and for poorer jobs. Such low-paid workers are potential threats to the more privileged workers.

Some Marxists and radicals present evidence and argue that conditions under capitalism, in effect, are consistent with what Marx and Engels predicted. For example, Mills (1951) analyzes the degradation of white-collar workers and their virtual proletarianization. Braverman (1974) has tried to demonstrate that working conditions for nearly all workers have been degraded in many ways. Workers are compelled to perform increasingly specialized tasks and less and less meaningful work, even when their titles are upgraded. Braverman believes that it is possible that a similar process occurs in the Soviet Union, but there it is imitative of the forms developed in capitalist societies, rather than inherent in a socialist industrialized society.

On the issue of inequalities within socialist countries three kinds of rebuttals are made by Marxists (Lane 1976). The first is made by those living in the Soviet Union and countries following its Communist party. They have developed Marxism-Leninism to excuse or explain away inequalities, providing justifications for the status quo (Ossowski 1963). Class differences are defined as nonantagonistic, and income, power, and status differences are justified as transitional stages of the dictatorship of the proletariat while the conditions for true communism are being built. In addition, special conditions arise from the fact that the Communist party came into power in Russia and did not spread to encompass the entire capitalist system. Thus, Stalin (1947, p. 632) pointed out that Engels predicted the state would wither away when no class is held in subjection by another class. But, Stalin explained, capitalist encirclement endangered a socialist country and the socialist state is essential for the defense of the socialist land from foreign attack. "The bourgeois states and their organs send spies, assassins and wreckers into our country and are waiting for a favorable opportunity to attack it by armed force." He went on to say that differences in material rewards are important inducements for speedy development, particularly during the transition period when the old bourgeois ways have not been eradicated and the new Soviet person not yet created. After all, communism has not been attained; the Soviet Union is a socialist country building toward communism.

Many Marxists in the West and also, in different ways, Chinese and Yugoslav Marxists are critical of the social organization of the Soviet Union. No comprehensive Marxist explanation of the Soviet social structure exists (Lane 1976, p. 29). But anti-Soviet Marxists provide many significant criticisms and explanations of state socialism as it developed in the Soviet Union. One view characterizes Soviet society as bureaucratic state capitalism (Marcuse 1958). The state dominates, by centralized authoritarian control, the productive processes in order to maintain and enhance its privileged position rather than to further the interests of the working class. Cliff (1964) argues that industrialization and collectivization of agriculture in a backward country led to the formation of state capitalism. The state acts like capitalists in drawing off surplus value from what the workers produce.

Mao and Chinese Maoist theorists view the Soviet Union under Stalin as a socialist society; but they argue that it has degenerated since then. They regard the revolutionary transformation of society to be a very long process. The post-Stalin leaders of the Communist Party of the Soviet Union (CPSU) followed "revisionist policies" by promoting a market system and the capitalistic principle of profit. They failed to maintain the dictatorship of the proletariat and fell back into a form of capitalism (Lane 1976, pp. 31-34).

A third group of Marxists takes up a position between the Soviet Marxist-Leninists and the critics of bureaucratic state capitalism. Trotsky (1958), as a leader of the Bolshevik revolution, justified it; however, he criticized Soviet society as it developed under Stalin. Mandel (1968) has elaborated Trotsky's analysis of the Soviet society as comprising a workers' state and a transitional economy. Mandel does not think that the Soviet Union displays the fundamental aspects of a capitalist economy. The Soviet system is in transition between capitalism and socialism. He is critical of the bureaucracy, which stands apart from the working class and the party rank and file. But the extensive inequality and bureaucratic privilege is a product of Russia's capitalist past and environment rather than inherent in the Soviet system.

Hypotheses. Given the variety of Marxist and radical accounts, we can choose among alternative Marxist hypotheses to explain existing inequalities in both Communist and non-Communist countries. We present only a few, likely to be shared by many Marxists and radicals.

First, countries with large segments of their economy dependent upon foreign capital will be more unequal in material conditions than less dependent countries. Furthermore, political inequality will be greater in dependent countries because external forces will militarily prop up regimes that assist the foreign investors, even against the popular will. According to Marxist and radical theory, economic changes generally precede and underlie changes in power relations. [4] The primacy of the mode of production means that the class relations are the basis of power relations, at least, in capitalist societies.

Sex and ethnic inequalities will be greater in capitalist than in socialist countries, given the interests of the employers to divide the workers and induce them to compete against each other rather than become conscious of themselves as a class with common interests. Sex inequalities would also be related to differences in the contributions men and women make to material production (Mitchell 1973).

Conflict and Coercion

Non-Marxists also account for degrees of inequality in terms of contending groups, stressing coercion and power differences rather than economic relations and class differences. As in the case of Marxism, there are diverse non-Marxist conflict approaches. For example, Dahrendorf (1959) defines classes in terms of having or not having power; his interest is to account for variations in class *conflict*. Lenski (1966) studies societies on an evolutionary scale, from hunting and gathering to advanced industrial societies. He compared what he called conservative and radical (or functional and conflict) explanations of inequality, concluding that power factors greatly affect inequality. We will examine Lenski's findings in Chapter 12 when we assess the evidence testing alternative explanations. In presenting a conflict-and-coercion approach to explain inequality, we draw particularly on the work of Collins (1975) for he synthesizes and elaborates the thought of other conflict theorists in an explicit and comprehensive manner.

Collins. Wealth and income distribution are not determined by identical factors, but organization of power is critical for both, argues Collins. The distribution of wealth depends on the total amount of wealth available in the society and on the way power is organized in that society. "As a general principle, wealth is based on power, both as it directly operates to appropriate goods and services, and as it indirectly operates to limit access to markets" (Collins 1975, p. 438). When the state controls economic distribution, then the distribution of property and income is expected to be highly correlated with the distribution of political power. "If the state does not more or less completely control the economy. . .but merely confines itself to upholding the system of property, the variables affecting income and those affecting property will differ. We may expect, in general, that the extent of the political participation in such a state will primarily affect the distribution of property rather than the distribution of income" (Collins 1975, p. 439). The distribution of wealth and income

---

[4] In practice, Marxist governing parties use state power to create what they regard as the material conditions necessary for a communist society.

within a market system depends on the ability of organizations to dominate the market, since organizations struggle to subject others to the conditions of the market and protect themselves from it. Within organizations, it is largely income that is distributed—individuals and groups struggle for power within organizations and that power in great measure determines their income.

Collins argues that the overall political structure of a society also sets the conditions for social mobility, determining the kinds of positions that exist and the total amount of movement. Mobility is affected by changes in the opportunity structure, by expansion or contraction of positions at different rankings. Expansion of positions at the higher levels, for example, depends on the outcome of a struggle between incumbents of those levels trying to restrict expansion and persons below trying to create additional positions for themselves at the higher level. Economic development, according to this view, is the result of groups creating markets that provide opportunities to expand positions for manufacturers, administrators, professionals, and so forth. The rate of "structural mobility" or "forced mobility" is indicative of the "concentration of resources among contending groups for limiting or expanding desirable positions" (Collins 1975, p. 449).

The question of allocation of particular persons within a given structure is a separate issue. Who moves into previously existing high-ranking positions is primarily determined by how well a possible entrant fits with the people who are already successful. Does the person have the right manners and right background, as defined by those who occupy the higher positions? If so, the person will be admitted. This view is similar to the popular idea that it is not *what* you know, but *who* you know that counts.

This discussion of the factors determining the distribution of class positions and determining mobility rates emphasizes power, particularly the organization of power in the political system. The question that then arises is, what determines political power? Collins begins his answer with the assertion that the state consists of the people who have the guns and who claim a monopoly of their use. In studying political power, then, it is necessary to study the ways in which violence is organized.

The magnitude of inequality in power is limited by the resources available in a society. "The greater the surplus of goods produced per worker in primary production beyond what is necessary to stay alive, the greater the potential for political organization and political inequality" (Collins 1975, p. 355). The greater the economic surplus, the more can be taken by a few to dominate others.

One major determinant of power inequality is the way in which the means of violence are organized. Violence and the threat of violence depend on the weapons available and the number of people who have access to them. Andrzejewski (1954) argues that the higher the proportion of the population in the armed forces, the greater the equality; a small military force can be an instrument of domination over an unarmed citizenry. Among the several propositions Collins proposes about organized violence, the following are particularly pertinent here:

> The greater the *economic surplus*, the greater the potential size of armies proportional to the population.
>
> The organization of armies is determined by the expense of weapons, and whether they are wielded individually or by a group. [e.g.] The more reliance on *expensive, individually operated weapons*, the more fighting is monopolized by an aristocracy of independent Knights, and the greater the stratification of the society; [and] the more reliance on *expensive weapons operated by a group*, the more an army takes the form of a central common hierarchy and a subordinate group of common soldiers (1975, p. 357).

Violence, unless exercised by large groups and coalitions of groups, however, is not an effective determinant of power. One individual cannot coerce and dominate a society; allies are needed, and orders must be carried out by loyal supporters. Therefore, if we are to understand how variations in power inequality are determined, we must understand organizations: how they are united and how they can mobilize resources.

Group strength depends upon the solidarity and cohesiveness of the members, and it is systems of belief and ritual that bind people together and provide a basis for legitimacy for those exercising power. Building on the work of Weber and Durkheim, Collins proposes that the "ideals of loyalty and morality reflect the social unit to which the individual must orient for his physical safety and support" (1975, pp. 369-370).

Group strength for particular goals depends on the group's commitment to their attainment. Purposes that are held with conviction will be pursued at the risk of greater cost than ones that are regarded as unimportant. Goals are sometimes ideological and are often embedded within an ideological context. Collins argues that "the intensity of commitment to an ideology depends on the social density of interaction and the level of physical threat" (1975, p. 379). As members of a group are in greater contact with each other and are threatened by violence, the greater is their commitment to the group and its symbols.

Finally, we should note the importance of a group's mobilization of resources. Insofar as members of a group can control material and social resources, the greater will be the group's political influence on behalf of its interests (Collins 1975, p. 385).

The conflict approach to explaining inequalities in class and power can also be used to explain status differences. Several observers have accounted for race and ethnic differences in status ranking largely in terms of differences in power (Wilson 1973; Mason 1971; Cox 1948; Blumer 1958). Existing power differences are explainable partly in terms of the way in which contact was first established and who dominated whom.

A few writers have explained even status differences based on gender in terms of a conflict approach (Millett 1970; Brownmiller 1975; Collins 1975). A distinguishing and significant idea in a conflict explanation of sexual status inequality is male coercion of females. The peculiarity of gender as a basis for status inequality is that humans have strong drives for sexual gratification and men and women are sexually attractive to each other. Since men, on the average, can physically overpower women, men as a group can and often do establish structures in which women become sexual property.

According to Collins (1975, pp. 237-254) variations in the pattern of sexual stratification is the result of the forms of social organization affecting the use of force and affecting the market position of men and women. Thus, in most preindustrial societies, the basic social unit is the fortified household. The state does not monopolize the use of force and the owner of a farm or workshop makes it the place of his home and his family helps in the work. Male sexual dominance is maximized in this form of social organization. In the industrialized, affluent market economies, the state has the monopoly of violence. Nevertheless, some male violence is available and in classes where it is greater, women are more puritanical. Women are not economically equal to men in the market, but a number of different things can be bargained in the market: social status, personal compatibility, deference, emotional support, as well as sexual attractiveness and income resources. On the whole, status inequalities by gender in an industrial society are not as great as in the fortified household society.

Critiques.[5] As in the other approaches, there are difficulties in defining and measuring basic concepts. Power and coercion are actually difficult to access because people do accede to commands they think are proper or, at any rate, legitimately given and accession not due to fear cannot be called coercion. There is also a risk of circularity in measuring some of the relationships between power, class and status. Can we assess the coercive strength any group has while ignoring the material resources it may have with which to reward compliance? Given the close relationship between class, status, and power, it may not be possible to confirm or disconfirm the idea that power differences shape inequalities in wealth and income, rather than the other way around.

Substantively, the relative neglect of normative and value factors has been criticized. Primacy is given to power in too deterministic a manner. Thus, van den Berghe (1963) criticizes Dahrendorf's simple reversal of the Marxian chain of causation asserting economic factors to be derived from unequal authority but he does not demonstrate such priority. Furthermore, as noted in the beginning of Chapter 7, some theorists do not regard power inequality as necessarily leading to conflict. Parsons (1969) reasons that persons in authority

---

[5] Some people might find aspects of this kind of conflict approach uncomfortable. They might feel that an emphasis on violence underlying inequalities to be overly cynical. There is also often a tone of pessimism that troubles some people; thus, in Dahrendorf's view, power inequality is inherent in associations; hence, conflict and struggle are inevitable. Marxism is relatively optimistic because it assumes major improvements in the social conditions of humans are possible—for example, by ending private ownership of the means of production.

act to mobilize resources of the entire social system for the benefit of the collectivity as a whole.

More specific substantive criticism can be made of the detailed propositions. For example, Collins makes a sharp distinction between economies controlled by the state and those that are not. But state direction of the economy varies in its degree. For example, centrally planned economies as in Poland allow significant market forces to operate; in Yugoslavia (without private ownership of the means of production) there is considerable individual and group autonomy in the market; France has considerable government direction; even in the United States, the government shapes the market by acting on the tax structure and interest rates, by making direct purchases, and in many other ways. Furthermore, state power can be used to impliment a variety of income distribution policies. As we saw in Chapter 4, at different times in Soviet history wage differences have increased and decreased depending upon the government policies. We will consider other criticisms as we proceed with the testing of the approaches in the next chapter.

Hypotheses. Collins offers many specific propositions about variations in class, status, and power inequality. Other propositions are implicitly or explicitly presented in the works of C. Wright Mills (1956), Dahrendorf (1959), and Andrzejewski (1954). Many of these proportions refer to large-scale changes in historical perspective but can also be applied to comparisons among contemporary societies. For example, according to the conflict approach, we expect that societies where most segments of the population are involved in interest-group activity would tend to be more equal in income distribution than societies where few participate in societal governance. Where there are greater concentrations of wealth and monopolization of industry, we would expect greater income inequality. Collins proposes that greater concentration of state power results in increased wealth and income inequalities. During periods of war, we expect state power to become more concentrated; hence, class inequalities should increase. Andrzejewski (1954) hypothesizes, however, that when participation in the armed forces is larger, inequality is less.

TECHNOLOGY AND POPULATION

Finally, we should consider factors that can affect equality regardless of the contending intentions of actors or the shared understandings of a functionally integrated system. An ecological approach (Duncan and Schnore 1959; Hawley 1950) emphasizes objective conditions aside from subjective meanings, emphasizing factors such as technology, population, organization, and environment. Certainly the theorists we have been considering—Marx, Collins, Parsons, and Davis and Moore—all regard these factors as important. Conflict theorists generally give considerable importance to technology as the underlying basis of stratification. Nevertheless, technology and population may be considered to affect inequalities even more directly. This discussion will also help us better understand the meaning of inequality, both conceptually and operationally.

Population

Population size and demographic characteristics such as age distribution and differential birth affect equality in a variety of ways. As we noted earlier, Davis and Moore believe that population size limits the extent of specialization, and therefore the extent of inequality, larger societies tending to be more unequal in the range of status and material regards. But one problem that occurs when discussing population size is determining the boundaries of the population. When we study isolated, self-sufficient communities or peoples, the population size is relatively clear, but when we consider social systems such as "feudalism" or "capitalism," the population boundaries are not clear. At present, the existence of a world system makes the boundaries of a society or a population quite problematic.

The age distribution of a population has intriguing possible effects on the calculation of income inequalities. Income is largely earned and earnings are related to the life cycle. Since earnings rise with age after entering the labor market, and then level off and decline greatly after retirement, Paglin (1975) argues, we can expect to have more persons with low income as the population includes more and more elderly persons. If such elderly persons have enough money to maintain independent households and we study the distribution of income of families and unrelated individuals or of households, increased life expectancy can be said statistically to increase the proportion with low income.

One other way in which demographic factors directly affect equality is through the variation in birth rates among different ranks in a stratification system. The changes of intergenerational upward mobility would be affected by the birth rates of the higher ranks compared to the lower. If there were no generational changes in the proportion of positions at each level, but the occupants of the higher ranking positions did not have enough children to reproduce themselves, then some upward mobility would be necessary. As we discussed in Chapter 9, birth rates do vary somewhat by class and status levels. In some periods, birth rates were greater among the highest ranks; we can assume that this would have tended to curtail upward mobility and might have created some downward mobility. In the contemporary United States, differences in birth rates by social ranks are slight; but rates are higher among lower ranks, and this contributes to upward mobility.

Technology

The theorists we have discussed all accord importance to the role of technology in shaping stratification patterns. Marx believed that the technology of production was the primary determinant of the social organization of production that in turn shaped the way in which classes are formed. Collins regards the technology of the means of violence as an important determinant of the political structure, and hence, of the class structure. In addition, the technology of the means of production significantly affects the economic surplus available in a society; the size of the surplus, according to such writers as Collins and Lenski, establishes opportunities for inequality. These analysts all introduce a wide variety of additional factors that in interaction with technology help shape the patterns of stratification.

Within the study of economic development and comparative studies, some observers have stressed the direct effects of industrialization on the social structure (Kerr et al. 1964; Bauer et al. 1956; Inkeles and Smith, 1974). They have argued that the logic of industrialization tends to make societies similar in class and political structure. They see societies becoming pluralistic, with the state regulating competition and conflict among a multiplicity of interest groups. As industrialization develops societies become more homogenized in the sense that the gap between the top and the bottom decreases and the relative size of the middle strata expands. This is seen as a result of the changing occupational structure and the expansion in the number of higher-level positions, requiring high standards of education and commanding relatively high rewards. Furthermore, the state pursues policies that increase social and class equality. The logic of industrialization will result in statist or authoritarian societies encouraging a more pluralistic system in order to gain the consent of the labor force and foster the initiative needed to make the modern economy function effectively. Consistency between class, status, and power rankings will also increase; achievement rather than ascription will be emphasized. Related to all of this, industrialization will result in relatively high social mobility, with an emphasis on *occupational* achievement. The educational system will play an increasingly critical role in the allocative process. We will consider critiques of this approach along with a review of relevant empirical studies in the next chapter (Goldthorpe 1969).

CONCLUSIONS

In this chapter, several major approaches to explaining variations in inequality have been presented. Each orientation should at least seem plausible. After all, many persons have worked with these approaches over many years, convinced of their validity. They are likely to have found some good reasons to sustain their convictions. Becoming familiar with a variety of approaches has several advantages: First, if one possible explanation is inadequate to account for a given set of data, other possible explanations can be tried. Furthermore, since scientific theories cannot be proven false, refuting alternative theories serves to strengthen our faith in the nonrefuted theory. Finally, ideas that at first seem obvious become more controversial, therefore more interesting, when equally plausible opposing ideas are argued.

For the reasons given above, this chapter has stressed the differences and the uniqueness of the several approaches. The distinctive elements of functional and conflict theories and even some varieties of each have been emphasized with the hope that this makes each theory clearer than it would otherwise be. Often an idea becomes clear only when contrasted with another idea.

The theorists, however, often try to broaden their theories by including some elements of the thinking of others, and, to some extent, they must synthesize the work of all their predecessors. Certainly, we, as students of the subject, might seek to synthesize different theories. After we have reviewed pertinent empirical research, we will be in a better position to do so. In trying to synthesize and combine particular propositions from several different theories, however, we should be careful not to rip ideas out of a general theoretical context. Certain aspects of functional theory cannot be combined with elements of conflict theory. For example, the idea that a whole *system* has needs does not combine with the idea that basically each group in a social system has its own interests and groups struggle with each other to serve their own interests.

The theories discussed in this chapter are abstract and are at a high level of generality but they offer comprehensive ways of understanding the many aspects of inequality. Also relevant to understanding the continuities and discontinuities in stratification are the ideas in Chapter 9, about individual accommodations and reactions to the patterns of inequality, and in Chapter 10, regarding collective reactions. Now we can usefully integrate those ideas with the more abstract theories examined in this chapter. In Chapters 12 and 13, we will apply the theories to the variations in inequality presented in Chapters 3 through 8. As we see how well the different theories explain the variations described, we also will test the theories.

REFERENCES

ABRAHAMSON, MARK. 1972. "On the Structural-Functional Theory of Development." Pp. 63-72 in Manfred Stanley (Ed.) *Social Development.* New York: Basic Books.

ABRAHAMSON, MARK. 1973. "Functionalism and the Functional Theory of Stratification: An Empirical Assessment," *American Journal of Sociology* 78 (March):1236-1246.

ABRAHAMSON, MARK. 1978. *Functionalism.* Englewood Cliffs, N.J.: Prentice-Hall.

ANDRZEJEWSKI, STANISLAW. 1954. *Military Organization and Society.* London: Routledge and Kegan Paul.

ARON, RAYMOND. 1968. *Main Currents in Sociological Thought,* I. Translated by R. Howard and H. Weaver. Garden City, N.Y.: Doubleday. (Originally published in 1965).

AVINERI, S. 1968. *The Social and Political Thought of Karl Marx.* Cambridge: Cambridge University Press.

BARAN, PAUL, and PAUL SWEEZY. 1966. *Monopoly Capital.* New York: Monthly Review Press.

BAUER, RAYMOND A., ALEX INKELES, and CLYDE KLUCKHOHN. 1965. *How the Soviet System Works.* Cambridge, Mass.: Harvard University Press.

BECKER, GARY S. 1957. *The Economics of Discrimination.* Chicago: University of Chicago Press.

BIBB, ROBERT and WILLIAM H. FORM. 1977. "The Effects of Industrial, Occupational, and Sex Stratification on Wages in Blue-Collar Markets," *Social Forces* 55 (June):974-996.

BLUMER, HERBERT. 1958. "Race Prejudice as a Sense of Group Position," *Pacific Sociological Review* 1 (Spring):3-7.

BRAVERMAN, HARRY. 1974. *Labor and Monopoly Capital.* New York: Monthly Review Press.

BROWN, HENRY PHELPS. 1977. *The Inequality of Pay.* Berkeley: University of California Press.

BROWNMILLER, SUSAN. 1975. *Against Our Will: Men, Women and Rape.* New York: Simon and Schuster.

CHISWICK, BARRY R. 1974. *Income Inequality: Regional Analyses within a Human Capital Framework.* New York: National Bureau of Economic Research.

CLIFF, TONY. 1964. *Russia: A Marxist Analysis.* London: Socialist Review Publishing Co.

COLLINS, RANDALL. 1975. *Conflict Sociology.* New York: Academic Press.

COX, OLIVER CROMWELL. 1948. *Caste, Class, and Race.* Garden City, N.Y.: Doubleday.

DAHRENDORF, RALF. 1959. *Class and Class Conflict in Industrial Society.* Stanford, Calif.: Stanford University Press.

DAVIS, KINGSLEY. 1949. *Human Society,* New York: Macmillan.

DAVIS, KINGSLEY. 1953. "Reply to Tumin," *American Sociological Review* 18 (August):394-397.

DAVIS, KINGSLEY. 1959. "The Myth of Functional Analysis," *American Sociological Review* 24 (December):759-772.

DAVIS, KINGSLEY, and WILBERT E. MOORE. 1945. "Some Principles of Stratification," *American Sociological Review* 10 (April):242-249.

DJILAS, MILOVAN. 1957. *The New Class.* New York: Praeger.

DUNCAN, OTIS DUDLEY, and LEO F. SCHNORE. 1959. "Cultural, Behavioral, and Ecological Perspectives in the Study of Social Organization," *American Journal of Sociology* 65 (September):132-146.

DURKHEIM, EMILE. 1951. *Suicide.* Translated by J. A. Spaulding and G. Simpson. Glencoe, Ill.: Free Press. (Originally published in 1897.)

GOLDTHORPE, JOHN H. 1969. "Social Stratification in Industrial Society." Pp. 452-465 in Celia S. Heller (ed.), *Structured Social Inequality.* New York: Macmillan. (Originally published in 1964 in *Sociological Review.*)

GORDON, DAVID M. 1972. *Theories of Poverty and Underemployment.* Lexington, Mass.: D. C. Heath.

GUMPLOWICZ, LUDWIG. 1899. *The Outlines of Sociology.* Translated by F. W. Moore. Philadelphia: American Academy of Poliical and Social Science.

HAWLEY, AMOS. 1950. *Human Ecology.* New York: Ronald Press.

INKELES, ALEX, and DAVID H. SMITH. 1974. *Becoming Modern.* Cambridge, Mass.: Harvard University Press.

KERR, C., J. Y. DUNLOP, F. HARBISON, and C. A. MYERS. 1964. *Industrialism and Industrial Man.* New York: Oxford University Press. (Originally published in 1960.)

KINDERT, PETER H., and JEFFREY WILLIAMSON. 1976. "Three Centuries of American Inequality." Pp. 69-123 in Paul Uselding (ed.). *Research in Economic History.* Greenwich, Conn.: JAI Press.

LANE, DAVID. 1976. *The Socialist Industrial State.* Boulder, Colo.: Westview Press.

LENIN, V. I. 1939. *Imperialism: The Highest Stage of Capitalism.* New York: International Publishers. (Originally published in 1917.)

LENSKI, GERHARD E. 1966. *Power and Privilege.* New York: McGraw-Hill.

LIPSET, SEYMOUR MARTIN. 1967. *The First New Nation.* Garden City, N.Y.: Doubleday. (Originally published in 1963.)

MANDEL, ERNEST. 1968. *Marxist Economic Theory.* Translated by B. Pearce. New York: Monthly Review Press.

MARCUSE, HERBERT. 1958. *Soviet Marxism: A Critical Analysis.* London: Routledge and Kegan Paul.

MASON, PHILIP. 1971. *Patterns of Dominance.* London: Oxford University Press.

MAZUR, ALLAN. 1973. "A Cross-Species Comparison of Status in Small Established Groups," *American Sociological Review* 38 (October):513-530.

MERTON, ROBERT K. 1949. *Social Theory and Social Structure.* New York: Free Press.

MILLETT, KATE. 1970. *Sexual Politics.* Garden City, N.Y.: Doubleday.

MILLS, C. WRIGHT. 1951. *White Collar.* New York: Oxford University Press.

MILLS, C. WRIGHT. 1956. *The Power Elite.* New York: Oxford University Press.

MITCHELL, JULIET. 1973. *Woman's Estate.* New York: Vintage Books. (Originally published in 1971.)

OSSOWSKI, STANISLAW. 1963. *Class Structure and Social Consciousness.* New York: Free Press.

PAGLIN, MORTON. 1975. "The Measurement and Trend of Inequality: A Basic Revision," *American Economic Review* 65 (September):598-609.

PARSONS, TALCOTT. 1940. "An Analytical Approach to the Theory of Social Stratification," *American Journal of Sociology* 45 (May):841-862.

PARSONS, TALCOTT. 1951. *The Social System.* New York: Free Press.

PARSONS, TALCOTT. 1953. "A Revised Analytical Approach to the Theory of Social Stratification." Pp. 92-128 in R. Bendix and S. M. Lipset (eds.), *Class, Status and Power.* New York: Free Press.

PARSONS, TALCOTT. 1969. *Politics and Social Structure.* New York: Free Press.

PARSONS, TALCOTT. 1970. "Equality and Inequality in Modern Society, or Social Stratification Revisited." Pp. 13-72 in Edward O. Lauman (ed.) *Social Stratification.* Indianapolis: Bobbs-Merrill.

PERROW, CHARLES. 1972. *Complex Organization: A Critical Essay.* Glenview, Ill.: Scott, Foresman.

SIMPSON, RICHARD L. 1956. "A Modification of the Functional Theory of Social Stratification," *Social Forces* 35 (December):132-137.

STALIN, JOSEPH. 1947. *Problems of Leninism.* Moscow: Foreign Languages Publishing House.

THUROW, LESTER C. 1970. *Investment in Human Capital.* Los Angeles: Wadsworth.

THUROW, LESTER C. 1975. *Generating Inequality.* New York: Basic Books.

TIGER, L. and R. FOX. 1971. *The Imperial Animal.* New York: Holt, Rinehart and Winston.

TROTSKY, LEON. 1943. *The New Course.* Translated by Max Shachtman. New York: New International Publishing Co.

TROTSKY, LEON. 1958. *The Revolution Betrayed: The Soviet Union, What It Is and Where Is It Going.* New York: Pioneer Publishers. (Originally written in 1936.)

TUMIN, MELVIN M. 1953. "Some Principles of Stratification: A Critical Analysis," *American Sociological Review* 18 (August):387-394.

VAN DEN BERGHE, PIERRE L. 1963. "Dialectic and Functionalism: Toward a Theoretical Synthesis," *American Sociological Review* 28 (October): 695-705.

WALLERSTEIN, IMMANUEL. 1974. *The Modern World-System.* New York: Academic Press.

WILSON, WILLIAM J. 1973. *Power, Racism, and Privilege.* New York: Macmillan.

WRONG, DENNIS H. 1959. "The Functional Theory of Stratification: Some Neglected Considerations," *American Sociological Review* 24 (December): 772-782.

ZEITLIN, IRVING M. 1972. *Capitalism and Imperialism.* Chicago: Markham.

chapter 12

Explaining Class Variations

Whatever phenomenon varies in any manner,
whenever another phenomenon
varies in some particular manner,
is either of a cause or an effect
of that phenomenon, or is connected with it
through some fact of causation.   *John Stuart Mill*

This chapter is devoted to two interrelated tasks: first, to explain the variations in class inequality already presented and second, to test the alternative explanations set forth in the preceding chapter. In recent years many studies have sought to account for variations in class inequality and to test the functionalist and other theories. We will draw upon these studies and other relevant material.

In this chapter we examine variations in the distribution of material resources, especially wealth and income. We discuss variations in the distribution of material resources, especially the proportion below a minimal standard of living. We analyze data on: (1) societies ranging from preliterate hunting and gathering bands to large industrialized countries, (2) recent decades in United States history, (3) comparisons among contemporary countries, and (4) industrialized countries that have and do not have centrally planned economies.

SOCIETIES IN EVOLUTIONARY PERSPECTIVE

We begin by considering the major types of societies, ordered in their presumed evolutionary sequence. In describing these societies and the inequalities to be found in them, discussion is not restricted to class inequalities, but will also cover power and status inequalities.

Types of Society

For perhaps two or three million years, humans lived in small groups, subsisting on the fruit, nuts, and other food they could gather and on the animals they could hunt. Anthropologists have observed small, isolated bands who have lived this way until recently: the Sirono of Eastern Bolivia have been studied by Holmberg (1950) and the Andamanese of the Andaman Islands by Radcliff-Brown (1948).

Perhaps little more than 10,000 years ago, people in the Middle East began to live in settlements and gather and store wild grain (Harris 1975). Domestication of animals and grains followed. Plant cultivation was simple at first, cultivators used only digging sticks. With the advent of metallurgy, this *simple horticultural* economy was followed by an *advanced horticultural* system, with metal hoes and more diversified plants; these made larger and more dense populations possible. The Incas of Peru, the Mayans of Yucatan, and the Yoruba of Nigeria had empires and advanced horticultural economies prior to contact with Europeans.

Five to six thousand years ago, in the fertile valleys of the Middle East, the *agrarian* system developed, relying on the plow and the use of animal power to work the plow. More extensive crops and greater production of food made it possible to support large, densely settled populations. Agrarian societies include ancient Egypt, medieval Europe, and China and India for most of their history.

Our knowledge of these societies is based on the archeological record, historical accounts, and the observations of contemporary peoples. These data are, of course, limited. We cannot know to what extent contemporary horticultural societies are like ones that existed 10,000 years ago. We have no direct knowledge about the language, family patterns, or class structures of societies of 10,000 years ago, despite the great skill and ingenuity of archeologists. In comparing hunting and gathering societies, simple and advanced horticultural societies, agrarian societies, and industrial societies, then, we cannot assume we are noting evolutionary patterns of social organization. Nevertheless, it will be useful to think about the variations in inequality of material resources among societies that vary so greatly.

Lenski (1966) has made an extensive survey of this range of societies in order to compare conflict and functionalist explanations of inequality and to synthesize these explanations in the light of the findings. We will use his descriptions of the patterns of inequality in these societies as variations that the theories we have reviewed should be able to explain. Afterwards, we will consider Lenski's own synthesis.

The basic pattern of relations between types of societies and inequality is presented in Figure 12.1. Hunting and gathering societies generally have very equal distribution of material goods. For example, Radcliff-Brown (1948) reports that the Andaman Islanders own their land communally, although they own the produce of the land privately. However, there are customs that compensate for some of the inequality that would result from such private ownership. For example, people who have food are expected to share it with people who do not. Inequality in other areas is lessened by the custom of exchanging presents and honoring persons who are generous.

Prestige, however, is generally unequally distributed in hunting and gathering societies. In the case of the Andaman Islanders, honor is accorded older persons, persons with supernatural powers, and persons with valued personal qualities such as "skill in hunting and warfare, generosity and kindness, and freedom from bad temper" (Lenski 1966, p. 105). Although honor is more unequally distributed than goods, it is more equally distributed than in other types of societies (Lenski 1966).

Power inequalities are generally highly related to prestige differences in such societies. Power is based on personal qualities rather than office, which tends to limit the degree of inequality, particularly since extreme political domination is not possible because there is no group specializing in the use of violence. The headman in such societies must depend on his influence. For example, Holmberg (1950), in describing the Sirino of Bolivia, reports that there

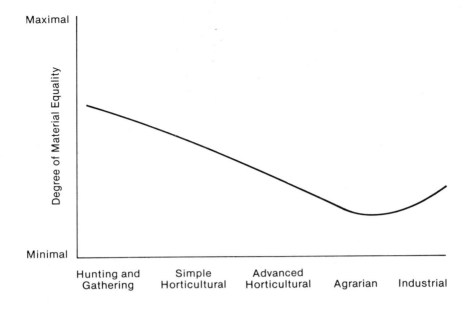

Maximal

Degree of Material Equality

Minimal

| Hunting and Gathering | Simple Horticultural | Advanced Horticultural | Agrarian | Industrial |

Cross-National
Comparisons

FIGURE 12.1 *Material inequality by type of society*

Source: Adapted from Lenski 1966, Figure 1, p. 437.

is no obligation to obey a chief, his authority rests on his personal qualities as a leader.

Intergenerational mobility generally is very high since the inequalities that exist are largely based on personal qualities, which are difficult to transmit. In these societies no positions can be passed on by inheritance. Intragenerational mobility also tends to be relatively high since personal qualities change and many are linked to the life cycle.

Social inequality is generally much greater in advanced horticultural societies than in simple horticultural societies. In some advanced horticultural societies of Africa, leading individuals are regarded as virtual gods. There is much greater institutionization of office, hence, inheritance of positions.

Social inequality is most marked in agrarian societies. Lenski (1966, pp. 210-219) describes the political histories of nearly all agrarian states as a series of intrigues and struggles for control of the state. These struggles were to gain the power, prestige, and material benefits that control of the state provided. For example, toward the end of the fourteenth century, English kings had incomes that on the average were forty times greater than that of the richest member of the nobility. The Persian emperor, Xerxes, is believed to have had an annual income in gold that would be worth $35 million; Suleiman the Magnificent of Turkey, $421 million; Aurangseb of India, $270 million (in 1966 dollars). Some of this income was spent on maintaining the government, but much of the vast wealth that rulers amassed was personal, for under the proprietary theory of the state, the land and business of the realm were regarded as belonging to the sovereign, to the king.

Material resources were certainly distributed very unequally in agrarian societies. Lenski (1966, p. 228), reviewing studies of England in the seventeenth century, China in the late nineteenth century, and other countries concludes *"the governing classes of agrarian societies probably received at least a quarter of the national income of most agrarian states, and . . . the governing class and ruler together usually received not less than half.* In some instances their combined income may have approached two-thirds of the total" (author's emphasis). Thus, in the agrarian societies, such as Imperial China or preindustrial England and France, the top 1 or 2 percent of the population received about half of the total income of the country.

Considering these societies in an evolutionary sequence, we can see an evolutionary movement toward greater inequality. With industrialization, however, that movement is reversed. This is charted in Figure 12.1. Less inequality exists within mature industrial societies than in agrarian societies. Political power is less concentrated in industrial societies than in agrarian societies. In many industrial societies people have extensive citizenship rights entailing civil rights and a voice in collective decision making. Even in statist and authoritarian political systems in industrial societies, the political elite pursues policies that in some ways are designed to benefit the masses. Material resources are also more equally distributed in mature industrial societies than in agrarian societies. This can be seen by comparing the figures regarding income inequality and wealth inequality reported in Chapters 3 and 4 with those cited in the preceding paragraph. For example, in the United States, the top 5 percent of the families received 17 percent of the aggregate money income in 1975 (Table 3.6).

Variations in inequality among the types of societies described could be accounted for in a variety of ways. Each of the theorists we have examined could, and to some extent does, explain the variations. In the following brief application of the theories, I wish to stress the distinctive thrust of each, and of course I will be over-simplifying. The reader can utilize the fuller description of the theories in the preceding chapter and in the theorists' own writing to provide a more comprehensive explanation.

Value and Functional Integration

Parsons (1966, 1971) stresses the evolutionary development of societies. One of the fundamental aspects of evolutionary social change is increasing social differentiation.

The hunting and gathering societies, small and preliterate, are relatively undifferentiated. Similarities in roles and contributions result in similarities in reward. With the development of more differentiated societies, with written languages and urban centers, specialists in what is valued by the society emerge and receive a greater proportion of the rewards available. Increased specialization increases the range of positions and their inequality. The elites, however, are still largely undifferentiated: religious, political, military, even fashion leaders are unified.

With even greater differentiation, as in modern societies, elites, too, begin to become separated (Keller 1963), and political leaders are no longer also fashion and religious leaders. This high degree of specialization now leads to increasing equality: a greater proportion of the people are needed to fill functionally important tasks. New values emerge along with this change. Religious differences among groups of people who live within the same society lead to pluralistic values and tolerance of diversity. In addition, the development of the idea of personal salvation produces a sense of individual worth. Values about achievement and universalism fostered capitalism and in turn were furthered by the new economic order. According to Parsons, these values support the modern emphasis on equality and help account for the reversal in the evolutionary trend toward increasing inequality.

Motivation and Functional Contribution

Davis and Moore (1945) suggest several variations in types of society that could be applied to explain the patterns of inequality noted above. Small societies that are limited in functional specialization are limited also in the magnitude of inequality; hunting and gathering societies are very small social units and societies have generally increased in scale from hunting and gathering groups to agrarian empires and countries. They also suggest that as the cultural heritage grows, increased specialization becomes necessary. These and similar propositions might account for the evolutionary increase in inequality, but not for the reversal of that trend. In discussing the increasing functional importance of technical knowledge, however, they suggest that the very specialization of the social structure circumscribes the concentration of prestige, rewards, and power in the hands of a government or priesthood of engineers or social scientists. Specialization, they say, becomes self-limiting in producing inequality. In an industrial society a higher proportion of people have the relatively high minimal skills needed to function, and this closes the gap between the masses and an elite. They claim, for example, that the highest ranking of the priesthood occurs in medieval societies where the surplus is large enough to support an organized priesthood, but the populace is illiterate and therefore highly credulous.

Marxists

Marx and Engels begin the *Communist Manifesto* of 1848 with the assertion that "the history of all hitherto existing society is the history of class struggles" (1932, p. 321). In later years, Engels explained that this referred to written history. In the prehistory of society, primeval communities existed with common ownership of land. But with the dissolution of primitive communistic societies, differentiation into antagonistic classes began. Marxists give considerable attention to the economic surplus and how some people acquire it (see Chapter 2). Ownership of property is critical in this regard. Class struggles have taken place throughout history, but Marx and Engels assert that the epoch of capitalism is distinctive in that it has simplified the class antagonisms: two great classes, the bourgeoisie and the proletariat, directly face each other. Previously there was a more complicated gradation of social rank. This classical Marxist view fits the change from the relative equalitarian hunting and gathering societies to the increased inequality of horticultural and agrarian societies. But it does not fit the movement toward greater equality in mature industrial societies—at least not if the unit within which we consider inequality is a single country. But if we shift to the world economy as the system which we examine, the fit is better (Chirot 1977). We will look into this explanation later when we examine cross-national data.

Conflict and Coercion

Conflict theorists, such as Collins (1975), also attribute importance to the increase in surplus, but they emphasize the use of coercion to seize and amass the surplus. The development of technologies of violence is critical in accounting for the numbers of persons who can be coerced and whose surplus can be drawn off by those with power. The extent of an empire depends on the nature of its armies and their ability to move quickly to suppress rebellion. The shift to greater equality with industrialization is explained by the increased proportion of the people who are mobilized. The movement of people to the cities and the organization of work in the factories and offices leads to new concentrations of political resources and to mass politics (Collins 1975, p. 424).

Each of these theorists can provide a plausible explanation for the pattern of inequality described above. Some may seem to fit better than others, but we need much more detailed analyses of the variations among this wide variety of societies to test the explanations. In Lenski's comprehensive analysis of societal types on an evolutionary scale, he compares the functionalist and conflict approaches and synthesizes some components of both. He concludes that the level of technology has a "threshold effect"; that is, an advance in technology causes or makes possible an advance in political organization. It is the distribution of power that primarily determines the distribution of privilege or material resources, which, in turn, largely determines the status inequalities.

Lenski believes the evidence indicates that additional factors affect inequality: constitutionalism, ideology, personal characteristics of the leaders, birth control methods, and the military participation ratio. Constitutionalism refers to the growth of the rule of law and right rather than a political regime's reliance on naked force. Ideologies about equality have their greatest impact in more advanced societies. Personal qualities of leaders seem particularly important in advanced societies when constitutionalism is not very high. The availability of effective birth control methods also affects inequality because without it population tends to increase to the limits of the economy, excluding what is diverted by the elite; this leaves the rest of the people as an expendable class. The military participation ratio refers to the proportion of the adult male population involved in military activities: the higher the proportion, the greater the equality. In general, Lenski attributes a pivotal role to power and the state in explaining the patterns of class and status inequalities.

Lenski applies his theory to account for the rise in equality associated with the emergence of industrial societies. He argues that technological changes have done more than make available a larger surplus. The increased complexity of technology has meant that those in authority know less and less of what those beneath them are doing. Subordinates must be given discretion, which results in their gaining power, status, and material rewards. The rapidity of the advances in productivity has also made possible increases in equality, since greater productivity makes it easier for the elites to grant concessions without an absolute loss to themselves. The development of effective birth control methods has reduced the intensity of the competitive pressures among the laboring classes. In addition, the spread of literacy, the expansion of knowledge requiring skilled workers, and the development of political democracy in industrial societies have all contributed to increased equality. But Lenski argues that the rise and spread of the new democratic ideology is more important than these other factors. This ideology asserts that the state belongs to the people. Consequently, the disadvantaged classes can mobilize in an idealistic cause that also serves their own interests. The governing groups, under this ideology, must be the servants of the people.

AMERICAN SOCIETY IN HISTORICAL PERSPECTIVE

In Chapter 3, we examined the trends in American class inequality over the last several decades. We noted a general decline in the proportion of people in poverty, defined in contemporary standards, from the 1930s to the present. Periods when the proportion of the population in poverty increased, notably in the early 1930s, were followed by periods of relative stability. We also noted both changes and consistencies in the distribution of personal income, wages, and wealth; inequality increased from 1820 to 1860, decreased until the mid-1890s, then increased again until 1929. Inequality lessened in the 1930s and 1940s and has remained little changed since then.

Values and Functional Integration

An explanation of these patterns of class inequality in American history in terms of values and functional integration can take a few forms. To begin, we can consider changes in values relevant to class inequality and see if those changes precede changes in class inequalities, but no systematic investigation has been made. On the whole, Parsons stresses the continuity in values in American culture, and he and Lipset point out that if we read descriptions of American culture and society of the 1830s, such as those by deTocqueville, we have no difficulty recognizing the great similarities in values and patterns of conduct (Lipset 1963, pp. 125-138). Although such descriptions may be useful in substantiating the great persistence of the patterns of inequality, they do not contribute to our understanding of those changes that have occurred. It can also be argued that the high valuation placed upon equalitarianism in modern societies affects the United States as well and that the international expansion of the idea of social rights has contributed to the decline in the proportion of the American population in poverty. But the specific variations in the rate of poverty do not seem to match variations in the values concerning social welfare and social rights.

Nor do changes in functional imperatives and in functional integration seem to account for the changes in the pattern of inequality. Indeed, the evidence may even be contrary. One of the major elements in the decline in the proportion in poverty and some of the decline in income distribution inequality has been the increase in families with two wage earners. In more and more families, the wife and the husband both earn the wages that constitute the family income. Parsons has pointed out that a wife's employment outside the home does not fit well with the functional requirements of the family; hence, it is constrained, particularly in the nuclear family. Yet, this constraint, if indeed it is a constraint, has not prevented the expansion of female participation in the labor force.

Motivation and Functional Contribution

A few researchers have tried to directly test the ideas of Davis and Moore. We will review their studies before trying to apply Davis and Moore's theoretical formulation to the general patterns of inequality in recent American history.

Abrahamson (1973) tested the hypothesis that during war the rewards of positions directly bearing on the war will increase relative to other positions. To test the hypothesis, he compared four positions involving military matters with four civilian positions of equivalent occupational prestige: corporal in the regular army with a machine operator in a factory, captain in the regular army with instructor in the public schools, and diplomat in the foreign service with a college professor. He examined relative changes in salaries in three war periods, 1939-43, 1947-51, and 1963-67, and three nonwar periods, 1943-47, 1951-55, and 1959-63. He was able to find data to compare the three pairs of occupations for several of these time periods. In nearly all instances, the changes in relative income were consistent with the hypothesis. Vanfossen and Rhodes (1974), in their critique of Abrahamson's paper, argue that conflict theory could also explain the findings. They go on to assert that other kinds of income differences are not explained by the functional theory; for example, during wartime the income of privates increased at a much higher rate than that of officers, particularly generals. The results do not definitively test Davis and Moore's formulation.

Broom and Cushing (1977) examined the largest American corporations in order to test the Davis and Moore functionalist theory in a different way. They reasoned that, according to the theory, the compensation (reward) of the chief executive officers would be related to the responsibility of the position, measured by the assets of the company. They found moderate support for this hypothesis. However, alternative explanations were not considered. They also tested the hypothesis that compensation for the chief executive officer would vary with the company performance, in accord with Davis and Moore's formulation of functional theory. The findings did not indicate such a relationship.

The results of these and similar studies are equivocal. We still lack a comprehensive assessment of the Davis and Moore formulation as compared to alternative theories. What we have are several efforts to test the theory by looking at particular sets of data, collected for that purpose. Given the nature of the concept in the theory, especially the idea of functional importance, measures of key concepts can always be faulted. We will look at other special studies of the Davis and Moore formulation when we discuss occupational prestige. We now try to apply the Davis and Moore version of functionalism to the patterns of class inequality in the United States.

Since Davis and Moore discuss rewards made to positions, rather than to persons, we should apply their explanation to the inequalities in pay for different occupations rather than to inequalities in income for families or individuals. As discussed in Chapter 3, between 1820 and 1860, there was a great increase in the differential pay of unskilled and skilled workers (Lindert and Williamson, 1976). Income gaps narrowed during the Civil War, then returned to prewar levels by about 1873. Pay differentials converged until about 1896, then they widened greatly. Between 1929 and 1950, pay differentials again converged slightly. Since then, there has been a slight drift toward greater inequality.

The urbanization and emerging industrialization of the United States prior to the Civil War might have lead to increased functional importance of skilled workers and that rapid change might have required extra inducements for persons to undergo the necessary training. Although this is plausible, it is not consistent with the actual leveling in the rate of pay inequalities from the Civil War to just before the turn of the century and the convergence in pay rates from 1929 to 1951. Neither the general movements of relative pay rates nor the more specific relative change of specific occupations seem to be well accounted for by the Davis and Moore formulations.

Marxist

Much of the attention of Marxists is directed to the general level of economic development in capitalist societies and the recurrent crises. A fundamental contradiction of capitalism, according to Marxists, is that more is produced than can be consumed (Dobb 1958). This occurs because the producers do not receive income equivalent to what they produce. Rather, the owners of land and capital take profits, appropriating part of the value of the workers' productions; that difference is surplus value.[1] Increasing capital accumulation (and increasing worker productivity) means ever-increasing surpluses and therefore ever-increasing crises. This has been staved off only by external events. Baran and Sweezy (1966), for example, see war as a major external development, but they also credit the development of steam and the railroads and then of the automobile as innovations that absorbed much investment capital. In the periods between such external developments they saw economic stagnation and high unemployment. Plausible as this may seem regarding the general level of economic development, it does not fit well with the patterns of income inequality observed in the United States. Although unemployment was extremly high during the depression of the 1930s, income inequality declined somewhat rather than increasing.

Some post-Marxists argue that the capitalist economy must be considered as a single world entity and that we cannot, therefore, understand inequality within a part of the total economic system. As Rubinson (1976) phrases it, we cannot explain the relative equality of income in the suburbs aside from the suburbs' relationship to the cities they surround, since the overall metropolitan area may have high inequality. We should look then at changes in the role of the United States within the world capitalist system.

Rubinson argues that in dominant countries within the world economy, class inequalities will be less than in dependent countries. Dominant countries are ones that have strong state control, that economically penetrate other countries, and that have a large enough internal market to be relatively independent of external trade. In such dominant countries, the class structure is more equal because a small elite oriented to external trade does not limit a large and diversified domestic manufacturing class. Furthermore, in dominant countries a more diversified and expanded occupational structure emerges and workers have greater bargaining power. The shifts in income inequality we have previously noted correspond, according to Rubinson, with changes in the relative dominating position of the United States. The United States became the dominant country in the world system in the 1930s and its relative position

---

[1] Some radical economists use a slightly different definition of surplus. Weisskopf (1972), for example, writes that the surplus is the excess of potential total production over socially essential production. What is critical here is the idea of socially essential production as the minimum amount of production required to maintain the population at a standard of living necessary for its survival. He also regards the absorption of surplus as the critical problem in capitalist society.

leveled off in the mid-1950s. Rubinson does not, however, refer to earlier changes in class inequality. The increasing inequality between 1820 and 1860 might be explained by the growing dependency at that time, but that explanation does not fit the increasing inequality of the period from 1896 to 1929.

Explanations of income inequality have largely focused on the persistence and incidence of poverty. Baran and Sweezy (1966, p. 286) write: "At the root of capitalist poverty one always finds unemployment and underemployment—what Marx called the industrial reserve army—which directly deprive their victims of income and undermine the security and bargaining power of those with whom the unemployed compete for scarce jobs." This may account for the general persistence of poverty, but not for the variations and incidence as we have described them.

A variety of economists and sociologists have sought to account for the incidence, variation, and persistence of poverty in the United States in greater detail. In doing so, some of them have utilized elements of Marxism and share with that tradition an emphasis on the characteristics of the capitalist economic system as being crucial in explaining the persistence of poverty. These explanations often refer to social and political forces such as discrimination and the welfare system. In Chapter 7, we discussed how the split labor market and discrimination may produce the low wages and high unemployment and underemployment of nonwhites and of women. Those ideas are relevant here, and since these explanations have high admixtures of conflict and coercive factors, we will examine them as we discuss conflict explanations of income inequalities in the United States.

Conflict and Coercion

Conflict theorists stress relative power in controlling the state as critical in determining income shares. The increasing inequality around the turn of the century and until the Great Depression marked the period of dominance of American political life by the robber barons and major capitalists. The decreasing inequality in the 1930s and 1940s might be explained by the increased coercive strength of lower-income persons. It is true that the 1930s saw the great increase in trade union organization and a new-found influential role in the Democratic Party's New Deal. Research indicates that unionized workers earn higher wages than nonunionized workers (Levinson 1951; James and James 1964). But the differences vary considerably depending on the periods studied. Lewis (1963, p. 194) concluded that in the early 1930s, unionism may have raised the relative wages of union workers by more than 23 percent. But during the inflation following World War II, unionism had little effect. More recently, it may have raised the relative wages of union labor by about 7 to 11 percent. Trade union activity can also affect income equality by influencing the redistribution policies of the government. Hicks, Friedland, and Johnson (1978) studied the impact of business and labor organizations on the extent to which government expenditures and revenues redistributed income to poor families. They compared forty eight American states around 1960 and found that large business corporations negatively affect governmental redistribution while labor unions positively affect it.

Political power may also account for the improvement of the relative earnings of farmers during the 1930s and early 1940s. The increase in their relative earnings contributed to income equality gains. Market forces undoubtedly also played a role in changes in farmers' relative earnings.

The increase in the military participation ratio in World War II would also help account for the decrease in inequality during the early 1940s. Another interpretation would place less emphasis on coercion and more on relative bargaining power. In the forties the demand for all kinds of labor, and especially for lower-paid workers, increased; in the fifties the competition for unskilled and semiskilled workers of the war years abated (Miller 1966, pp. 102-103).

The perpetuation and variation in poverty, according to this approach, is not explicable simply in terms of the economic system. Rather, the social and welfare policies pursued by the government (federal, state, and local) largely determine how many people are supported and at what level. This in turn may be a function of prevailing ideologies. The emphasis on "self-reliance" and on each person obtaining income only from the capital he or she owns or the wages he or she earns is consistent with the interests and values of the dominant groups in the society and this works against welfare support above the poverty level (Tussing 1975). But the coercive strength of the poor is also relevant to the level of support they receive and, hence, helps determine their share of the national income.

Piven and Cloward (1971) have studied the development of welfare programs in the United States and have found that relief arrangements are expanded or begun when there are outbreaks of civil disorder produced by mass unemployment. Relief measures are contracted or abolished when political stability is restored, whether or not there has been an economic recovery. When there is political stability, the minimal welfare provisions serve to ensure that people will be willing to work at minimal wages. As can be seen in Tables 3.1 and 3.2, the proportion in poverty declined during World War II and after the Great Depression, but remained relatively stable until the small decline during the 1960s. The 1960s, it should be recalled, was a period of civil disorders. Relief rolls did expand and various social policies were introduced to reduce poverty. Of course, the social protest was often related to the civil rights and black liberation movements and to other struggles for social equality; however, economic equality was part of the demands.

Income and wage inequalities are also related to the emergence of dual economies. One kind of dual economy depends on the differences in productivity of different industries. It might be argued that in industries where technological or other developments have made possible more efficient production, owners and workers in those industries will receive higher returns than in relatively backward industries. Some evidence supports this. But it is also possible that persons working in industries that do not show the same increases in productivity will increase in relative cost. It will be necessary to pay workers in those industries the going wage rates or they will compete to work in the more productive industries. Service industries, for example, have not increased in productivity as compared to the electronics industry. Consequently, what we pay for services (such as haircuts) has increased greatly compared to what we pay for many kinds of manufactured goods (such as radios). It appears that the maintenance of dual economies requires additional factors. If there are forces that prevent everyone from competing to enter the industries with high productivity, inequalities are more likely to be sustained. Such forces may include the relative isolation of segments of the population in rural areas with poor farmland or exhausted mining resources, for example (Tussing 1975). Such forces may also include the organizational strength of different groups to control competition. If some groups can exclude others from competing in highly productive industries, they can garner a larger share of the benefits of the more efficient production.[2]

The second basis for a dual economy is restrictions on the labor force. As we discussed in Chapter 7, discrimination and a split labor market produce inequality and even poverty. Thus, it may be that nonwhites and women are excluded from higher-paying jobs, allegedly because they lack the abilities and experiences necessary to fulfill the tasks of the occupational position. Their opportunities may also be restricted because of prior discrimination.

The evidence about the incidence of poverty is consistent with the idea that there are dual economies within which blacks, women, isolated rural residents, and weakly organized persons in relatively inefficient industries seek employment. Low incomes and poverty are the consequence of such dual economies (Tussing 1975; Gordon 1972). Shifts in the distribution of income and in poverty are also a result of changes in occupational distribution and in labor force participation. This is related to the dual economies and also to technological and demographic changes, to which we turn next.

Technological and Population Factors

All the theorists in one way or another recognize technological and demographic factors as being significant in accounting for class inequalities. This is particularly true of the Marxists and the conflict theorists and also true of traditional market explanations by economists. In the United States, the decrease in inequality and poverty during the war years would be in significant measure accounted for by the movement of workers out of inefficient and low-

---

[2] Groups in the less efficient industries may also organize and restrict the number of entrants in their occupations in order to force higher payments for their goods or services. Trade unions and professional associations have sometimes been able to accomplish this for some occupations, e.g., physicians.

paying rural occupations into the urban industries. The labor shortage of World War II also suddenly opened employment opportunities for blacks and for women. They became qualified when jobs were unfilled. Some of the creeping decline in poverty and decrease in inequality is accounted for by the increase in the number of earners in a family, since the increase in women's participation in the labor force contributed greatly to family income, particularly of low-income families.

Concluding Observation

It is difficult to explain definitively by any one theory a change, or a period of stability, in income levels or in the proportion of people in poverty. The change, or lack of change, may be produced by the interaction of several contradictory forces. It appears that wealth tends to concentrate and income inequalities increase unless there are contrary processes, since persons with higher income and wealth use those resources to gain even greater resources. One important contrary force is organized effort by lower income groups to demand, sometimes through persuasive and sometimes through coercive means, a greater share in the national income. Such contrary forces may balance each other and no overall changes in the distribution of income occur.

CROSS-NATIONAL COMPARISONS

The growth of comparable data about many countries, as presented in Chapter 4, makes possible cross-national studies of inequality. Several researchers in recent years have related characteristics of a country to several indicators of class inequality (Cutright 1967; Paukert 1973; Rubinson 1976). We will review these findings and see how they fit the different theoretical approaches we are comparing.

We begin by considering the findings about the relationship between class inequality and economic development. Many of the cross-national studies have focused on this relationship and theorists have sought to account for it. It is a central matter for theorists who emphasize technological factors. They reason that advanced economies require skilled workers, which necessitates a high level of rewards for the people as a whole. Therefore, equality is expected to be greater among more economically developed countries than less developed ones.

The expectation that economic development and industrialization are associated with increasing equality might seem to be contrary to Lenski's idea that larger material surpluses make possible greater inequality. But we have seen that he argues that this trend is reversed with industrialization. When we compare contemporary countries, we are comparing societies with varying mixtures of agrarian and industrial systems of production. As shown in Figure

12.1, we are now considering only a segment of the range of societies discussed earlier.

Before examining the evidence about the magnitude and nature of the relationship, we must note the ways in which the variables are measured.

Economic development is frequently measured by GNP per capita, but this indicator is not available for societies with centrally planned economies. Another frequently used indicator is energy consumption per capita; these two indicators are highly correlated with each other. A third indicator that is also sometimes used is the proportion of the labor force in nonagricultural employment.

Until recently, inequality was assessed by calculating the degree to which income is distributed unequally among the major sectors of the economy, called sectoral income inequality (Cutright 1967; Jackman 1974). More recent studies have been able to use data on the distribution of personal, pretax, family, or household income (Paukert 1973; Chase-Dunn 1975; Rubinson 1976). As discussed in Chapter 4, another kind of measure might be used to assess the standing of countries in terms of the proportion of the population who have more than a minimal standard of living. One might use life expectancy, infant survival rates, or calories consumed per capita. In all these measurements physiological constraints set maximum human levels. Higher life expectancies, lower infant mortality rates, and higher calorie consumption per capita mean that more people have a minimal standard of living.[3]

In Figure 12.2, we have plotted the relationship between Personal Income Inequality and GNP per capita for the countries listed in Table 4.5. The information is taken from the Gini Ratios presented in Table 4.5 and the GNP per capita data in Table 4.2. From inspection, there seems to be a tendency for equaliy to increase along with increases in GNP per capita.

One issue in assessing such a relationship is whether it is a linear or nonlinear relationship (Goldthorpe 1969; Jackman 1975). Does equality increase at the same rate as the indicator of economic development or does equality tend to increase at a decreasing rate at higher economic levels? Figure 12.3 depicts a linear and a curvillinear relationship.

Jackman (1974, 1975) tried to assess whether the relationship between development and equality was or was not linear. He used energy consumption per capita as the indicator of economic development and carried out a regression analysis with sectoral income inequality. He also carried out a regression analysis using the logarithmic of energy consumption per capita.[4] He found that the

---

[3] Average life expectancy and the other measurements are affected by other factors than the proportion of the population below a poverty level, but they do indicate the general standard of living and the extent to which people lack minimal life-sustaining conditions.

[4] A regression analysis tells us how much the regressed-on variable increases with a given increase in another variable. Regression analysis can only test for linear relationships. In order to test for a nonlinear relationship, a variable must be transformed. Logging a variable is one way to transform it. This transformation has the effect of reducing the magnitude of

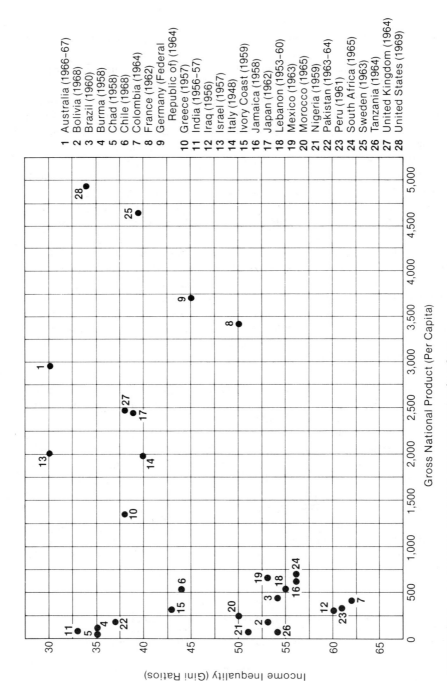

FIGURE 12.2 *Income inequality by per capita gross national products*

Source: Tables 4.2 and 4.5.

1   Australia (1966–67)
2   Bolivia (1968)
3   Brazil (1960)
4   Burma (1958)
5   Chad (1958)
6   Chile (1968)
7   Colombia (1964)
8   France (1962)
9   Germany (Federal
        Republic of) (1964)
10 Greece (1957)
11 India (1956–57)
12 Iraq (1956)
13 Israel (1957)
14 Italy (1948)
15 Ivory Coast (1959)
16 Jamaica (1958)
17 Japan (1962)
18 Lebanon (1953–60)
19 Mexico (1963)
20 Morocco (1965)
21 Nigeria (1959)
22 Pakistan (1963–64)
23 Peru (1961)
24 South Africa (1965)
25 Sweden (1963)
26 Tanzania (1964)
27 United Kingdom (1964)
28 United States (1969)

Gross National Product (Per Capita)

Income Inequality (Gini Ratios)

logarithmic of energy consumption fit the pattern of inequality better than energy consumption not logged. He concluded therefore that the relationship is not linear. Rubinson (1976) also concluded that a log transformation gave a better fit using personal income data. Looking again at Figure 12.3, a curved line does seem to come closer to all the countries than a straight line.

Inspection of Figure 12.2 reveals a rather weak relationship between development and inequality. The magnitude of the relationship varies with the indicators used. For example, per capita energy consumption (logged) is correlated –.68 with the sectoral income inequality and –.70 with infant mortality, but only –.18 with personal income inequality (Kriesberg 1976; Rubinson 1976). These data refer to societies with market economies; the number of countries varies among those different tests from 35 to 47. Economic development is strongly related to widely shared minimal living standards and to sectoral income equality, but only slightly related to personal income equality.

Now we turn to each of the theoretical orientations we have been examining to see how well the factors they regard as important are related to cross-national variations of inequality. We also discuss how each approach would interpret the relationship between economic development and class equality.

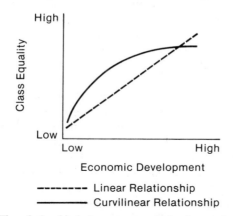

FIGURE 12.3   *The relationship between economic development and class equality*

increases in the variable; that is, the interval between each unit becomes smaller at higher values of the variable. This squeezing together of numbers would straighten out a relationship if it were curvilinear. A simplified depiction is presented below:

	6
4	5
	4
3	3
2	2
1	1
Linear Scale	Logarithmic Scale

Values and Functional Integration

A possible explanation of the relationship between economic development and equality can be offered in terms of values. The reasoning is that along with the spread of the technologies of industrialization, the values that generated it and sustain it also were diffused. In other words, the ideas of modernization spread out from the advanced industrial societies and as a result of that diffusion of new values, other societies which develop economically also become more equal. Parson's (1970) ideas about the value of equalitarianism as part of modernism would be consistent with this interpretation. To test this idea we would need information about the diffusion of "modern" ideas and diffusion of the values and beliefs of Western Europe. Testing a cultural explanation of societal variations in equality would require having information about the earlier and present value systems of those different societies. Unfortunately, we do not have any systematic data on the value systems of different societies.

Looking at Figure 12.2, we can account for the location of each country by ad hoc explanations. For example, Australia (1) is relatively equal, as is Israel (13), especially given their level of economic development. Australia has developed a particular emphasis upon worker solidarity and sharing (Lipset 1968). Israel, as a Labor-Zionist society embattled for its survival, values equal sacrifice. France (8) is relatively unequal, given its level of economic development, as a result of a tradition of particularism and ascription that is maintained by the elites (Lipset 1968). But such characterizations are difficult to apply without systematic, comparable data.

Wilensky (1975) examined the relationship between the welfare ideologies of political elites and the proportion of GNP spent on social security programs. He examined the ideological stance of the ruling parties or dominant coalitions between 1950 and 1965 in twenty-two countries. Ideological stance was measured in terms of six issues, including provisions for social welfare, redistribution of wealth, economic planning, and equality of opportunity. He found *no* significant relationship between elite ideology and social welfare effort. The general level of economic development, he argues, is the root cause of welfare-state development and the proportion of the population over age 65 is the most important proximate cause of social welfare effort (and it is related to economic level).

One proxy for value systems in different societies might be the prevalence of different religions. The religious ideas people hold do include values and norms. Islam, stressing submission, individualism, and status differences (especially by sex), would be expected to contribute to inequality; but the Koran also specifies egalitarian rules in some matters. Furthermore, Islamic values and norms vary among different sects and communities, and adherence to religious values and norms can be considerable. Kriesberg (1976) examined the relationship between the proportion of Muslims in a country with several indicators of inequality. Although the percentage of Muslims was not related to

374

sectoral income inequality and only slightly to personal income inequality, it was moderately and significantly related to infant mortality rates. That Muslim values or norms foster practices that result in infant mortality is consistent with the finding that the relationship persists even when holding constant the level of economic development. The percentage of Catholics also is related to personal income inequality, but not to infant mortality, and the linkage between Catholicism and inequality is not evident. These findings suggest that value differences possibly play an independent role in affecting class inequalities. This may be the case for aspects of inequality associated with the particular values under consideration. Thus, infant mortality rates might be especially affected by the relative status of women which reflect Islamic ideas. On the whole, however, major religions are not accurate indicators of value differences; each religion embraces a variety of values, and certainly a variety of actual practices.

Ideas derived from the requirements for functional integration could also explain the correlation between economic development and equality. Thus, it might be argued that to make a modern economy work, nearly all members of that society must have high levels of literacy and the material resources needed to be efficient and skilled workers. The generally high standards of living in the developed societies, even among the lower-ranking persons, would be consistent with that. It is also true that there is a very high relationship between the level of education of the population and the level of economic development. We need information on a sequential basis, however, in order to assess the direction of the relationship. It may be that the increase in material resources associated with economic development is fought for and seized by groups depending on their relative strength. We will consider that interpretation later when we review the conflict and coercion approach.

Motivation and Functional Contribution

The Davis and Moore formulation of functionalism suggests a few additional variables that might account for the variation in inequality among the countries of the world. Larger populations could be more differentiated than smaller ones; therefore, inequality might be expected to be greater in larger countries. Earlier (1976) I tested this possibility. It turns out that population is moderately and *negatively* related to personal income inequality and to sectoral income inequality. Population size is moderately related to infant mortality rates. The percentage of the population living in large cities might also be expected to be related to differentiation and inequality. The results are not consistent with the theory: the relationships are negative and for some dimensions of inequality strongly so. Finally, I also tried to construct a variable to measure the scarcity of trained personnel for functionally important roles. I took the percentage of the male labor force engaged in professional and technical occupations and divided it by the percentage of the population over

25 years of age who had completed four or more years of higher education. As the ratio increases, inequality should increase, particularly income inequality. The results, however, reveal no relationship in the hypothesized direction for either personal or sectoral income inequality. Only for infant mortality is there a relationship in the hypothesized direction that is moderate and statistically significant.

Given the earlier findings about the relationship between economic development and equality, we need to consider the possibility that the findings noted above are spurious[5] or that other findings are obscured by the variations in economic development. If we combine the functional variables and the economic development variables into a single test, we can see which variables continue to be related to inequality and which do not. The method used was a multiple regression.[6] The economic development variables continue to have the same relationships with the measures of inequality that they had without taking into account these functional variables. The size of population, however, now does have a moderate positive relationship with inequality as the theory would predict, taking into account the proportion of the male labor force engaged in manufacturing and mining. The other functional variables are not affected. On the whole, these variables do not contribute to accounting for the variation in class inequality among the contemporary countries for which there is comparable information.

Marxists

The level of economic development, whether thought of in terms of the technology of production or of material surplus, should be an important determinant of class inequalities. One interpretation of classical Marxism is that within capitalist societies increasing economic development leads to concentration of wealth and increasing inequality. We have noted previously how contemporary Marxists and non-Marxists explain the failure of advanced industrial capitalist societies to have become ever more unequal in the distribution of wealth. One major consideration, employed by both Marxists and non-Marxists, is that each country is part of a world economy. The degree of inequality within a country depends on the position of that country within the world economy.

Countries that are economically dependent tend to have internal

[5] Two variables are spuriously related to each other when there is no causal relationship between them and they vary together because they both are related to a third variable. For example, suppose years of education is positively related to opposing federal full employment policies. That relationship would be spurious if we found that each was related to income and within each income level the relationship did not hold.

[6] As noted in Footnote 3, regression analysis tells us how much one variable increases with a given increase in another variable. A *multiple* regression can tell us how much the dependent variable increases with changes in two or more independent variables, considered simultaneously. The multiple regression also indicates how much one variable is related to the variable regressed on when all other variables are held constant.

inequality for many reasons. First, we shall consider debt or investment dependence. The greater the per capita profits earned by foreign investors, the greater the penetration of the country by foreign capital investment and the greater the dependence. Another measure of debt dependency is the amount of foreign loans made to the government calculated on a per capita basis. Chase-Dunn (1975) reasons that such dependency induces inequality because the ruling groups are able to resist redistribution because they are backed up by support from the dominant investing countries. He found there was a moderate (but not quite statistically significant)[7] relationship between debt dependence and invest-ment dependence with personal inequality, as he hypothesized. My own (1976) analysis yielded similar results.

Jackman (1975) constructed a trade composition index that measured the proportion of manufactured goods to raw materials in impors and in exports as an indicator of trade dependency. He concluded that trade dependency increases sectoral income inequality. It is striking when different researchers, using some-what different measures and indices, arrive at similar results. That gives strong support to the validity of the finding.

Rubinson (1976) examined still other aspects of the relative position of a country in the world economy. He argued that countries are not dominated insofar as the state is strong and is therefore able to regulate the economic activity of its population. In addition, domination is avoided insofar as a small proportion of the total economic production within the country is based on external trade. Rubinson found that state power and lack of dependence on foreign trade each contributed to personal income equality. These factors were more highly related to personal income equality than was economic develop-ment, as measured by energy consumption per capita. Elsewhere (1976) I reasoned that if investment *debts* indicate dependence, then investment *earnings* relative to GNP indicate dominance. I found that investment earnings were strongly and negatively related to inequality, as the world-economy theorists would predict.

In addition, I also analyzed the impact of dependency on infant mortality rates as an indicator of the attainment of minimal living standards. A high rate of foreign trade relative to gross national product turns out to be negatively related to infant mortality. This suggests that, for most countries, involvement in the world economy *contributes* to achieving minimal living standards. These results help explain the findings reported at the beginning of this section: per capita energy consumption is highly related to low rates of infant mortality but only slightly related to personal income equality. These results are more

---

[7]Relationships between two variables differ in magnitude and in statistical significance. For example, a correlation can range from 0 to 1; a correlation of .8 is high and .2 low. The higher the correlation the greater the degree to which one variable varies with the other. Statistical significance refers to the probability of a given event or relationship occurring by chance. For example, a probability of .001 is very low; one in a thousand. Statistical signifi-cance is affected by size of sample and other matters.

consistent with non-Marxist than Marxist explanations of economic development and of inequality.

Conflict and Coercion

According to certain aspects of conflict theory, economic development and larger surpluses can produce conditions that increase equality since an absolute increase in the size of a society's output expands the amount that can be distributed. If there is more to divide, an elite group can increase its absolute amount of material resources without increasing its relative share. The pie has grown larger for everyone. Furthermore, the increase in the absolute amount of material resources available to lower-ranking persons gives them access to other skills and resources, which in turn provide the basis for demanding even more. Rising segments of a society can and do demand citizenship rights and use those rights to struggle for more equal social and economic rights.

More specifically, conflict theorists expect that the degree of class inequality within a country is strongly affected by the nature of the group that controls the state. Jackman (1975) conducted a detailed analysis of the possible impact of several political factors on class inequality. He used two indicators of class inequality. One measured sectoral income inequality, the other was a social welfare index made up of four components: live births per thousand births, per capita caloric consumption, per capita protein consumption, and number of physicians per million inhabitants. Jackman analyzed sixty countries, excluding those with centrally planned economies.

Jackman hypothesized that political equality would contribute to class equality. He constructed an Index of Democratic Performance, which consisted of four components: percent of the adult population voting, the competitiveness of the party-voting system, freedom of elections, and freedom of the press. He found that democratic performance was not related to class equality, if one held constant the level of economic development (measured by energy consumption per capita). He found, however, that political stability did contribute to class equality.

Rubinson and Quinlan (1977) replicated this study using personal income data. Information about personal income inequality is superior to information about intersectoral income inequality used by Jackman, but it is available for fewer countries. Rubinson and Quinlan found that democracy was associated with personal income equality, even holding constant the level of economic development.

Jackman also investigated the reasonable possibility that the direction of political action would have some impact on class equality. He examined the effects of the non-Communist leftist political parties and of labor unions. He found some relationship between the strength of the socialist parties and the development of social insurance programs, but no relationship to either sectoral income inequality nor to the Social Welfare Index. Trade union strength was found to have some effect on both sectoral income inequality and the social welfare index. Interestingly, he found that neither the size of government expenditures nor the size of public expenditures was related to these measures of inequality, when economic development was held constant. Civilian government expenditures per capita do have an impact on sectoral income inequality and seem to account for the relationship between economic development and sectoral income inequality. "This suggests that governments of wealthier countries allocate more expenditures to meet social needs. This, in turn, affects the equality of the distribution of income" (Jackman 1975, p. 201).

Hewitt (1977) conducted an extensive cross-national study of several indicators of class inequality: share of personal income received by the highest 5 percent of the population, share received by the highest 20 percent, and the redistributive effect of the government budget. He found that political democracy itself was not related to these measures of inequality when he controlled for economic development. The length of a country's social democratic experience, however, is correlated with class equality by these measures, even holding economic development constant. Hewitt also examined educational opportunity (access to higher education by persons from ranks below middle-class). Socialist experience turns out to be inversely related with educational opportunity. This is consistent with Lipset's (1963, pp. 259-261) argument that socialist countries stress equality of outcome; they are less concerned with achievement. On the whole, these findings support the argument that the direction of government policy does affect class equality.

Another factor emphasized by some conflict theorists is participation in the armed forces of a society. As noted earlier, Andrzejewski (1954) argued that a high ratio of military participation would result in relative equality. This has been tested by a few researchers (Cutright 1967; Kriesberg 1976; Garnier and Hazelrigg 1977). Cutright divided his analysis of non-Communist countries into three categories according to the countries' economic level. He found evidence contrary to the hypothesis among the countries with a high GNP per capita and evidence consistent with it among the countries at the middle level. Cutright used intersectoral income inequality as his measure of inequality. Kriesberg (1976) found that the military participation ratio was strongly and positively related to personal income equality and sectoral income equality, taking into account economic development through a regression analysis. The military participation ratio, however, did not affect the proportion attaining minimal living standards as measured by infant mortality rates, once economic development was taken into account. Garnier and Hazelrigg (1977) made a detailed analysis of the relationship between military participation ratio and personal income inequality and also found that a high ratio contributed markedly to income equality, even taking into account a variety of other factors.

Concluding Observation

The recent cross-national studies suffer from a severe lack of accurate data. The indicators for many concepts are often very indirect and it is extremely difficult to obtain comparable data from different countries. Furthermore, a correlation between two variables does not, in itself, reveal the causal connection. In some cases, it is true, information about presumed independent factors pertains to years prior to the years for the dependent variables, and this helps interpret the causal direction, but does not resolve all difficulties. Nevertheless, some findings have clearly emerged and they help test the different theoretical approaches. Economic development does tend to be associated with greater material equality although the correct interpretation of that relationship has not been resolved since different theorists give different meanings to that finding. Clearly, too, the relative position of a country in the world economy and its economic relations with other countries strongly affects internal equality. Other factors, including cultural values, government policy, and the extent of military participation, also have impact upon class inequality.

COMPARISONS BETWEEN COMMAND AND MARKET ECONOMIES

The cross-national studies, as we have discussed them, generally have not included Communist countries. Given the important differences between market economies and command or centrally planned economies, some kinds of data cannot be compared: their meaning would be too disparate. In addition, many kinds of data are not available from countries with governments controlled by Communist parties. In Chapter 4 we described the similarities and differences between and among centrally planned and market economies. Now let us see how the theoretical approaches we have been comparing explain these variations.

Values and Functional Integration

In contrast to the ideal of communist equality, one can emphasize the similarities in inequalities between Communist and non-Communist countries. Parsons (1951, pp. 159-160), for example, writes, "Marxist ideology, including Lenin's own statements, did radically deny that any competence above that of ordinary 'worker' was a legitimate basis for differential valuation. But what has happened in fact is that, with the developing industrialization of the Soviet Union, both facilities and rewards have become markedly differentiated, including monetary reward." The functional requirements of providing differential facilities and rewards in relationship to competence and responsibility make for similarity in rewards when the degree of differentiation is similar. This is the same kind of argument that Davis and Moore make.

Nevertheless, variations are found among Communist countries and between Communist and non-Communist countries. One factor responsible for these variations might be the differences in cultural values among these societies. We lack systematic information about the values of these societies, other than that the governing elites adhere to different ideologies. The Communist party generally does uphold the value of equality of reward and the providing of material resources in terms of people's needs. Inequalities in reward are generally justified as temporarily needed under the prevailing circumstances, but the degree of inequality considered appropriate or necessary varies considerably. The Communist party of the People's Republic of China, under the leadership of Mao, favored a relatively radical equalitarianism and, by many reports, the reward system in China has been relatively equal in distributing material resources (Bettelheim 1974; Goldwasser and Dowty 1975; Committee of Concerned Asian Scholars 1972; Leys 1977).

Giving weight to such ideological factors, however, is similar to the kind of analysis that conflict theorists might make. The ideologies reflect the interests of the groups holding governmental power. They are not the long-standing, traditional patterns developed within each culture.

Motivation and Functional Importance

One of the differences between the Communist and non-Communist countries of Europe is that white-collar workers tend to earn more relative to manual workers in Western European countries than in the Eastern European countries. The Soviet Union and the countries under its influence have long stressed the primary importance of industrialization and of concentrating on developing heavy industry. Functional theorists could argue that this reflects the special functional importance to the skills needed for production in heavy industry. As a result, the rewards given to industrial workers would be relatively high. Because such workers are otherwise not highly paid, raising their wages tends to decrease inequality. Again, it is peculiar to regard the emphasis on the development of heavy industry as a matter of functional importance. Rather, the emphasis is a matter of governmental and leadership policy, and, within a centrally planned economy, those in authority can decide what is important and allocate rewards accordingly. In this sense, functional explanations fit the circumstances of centrally planned economies very well (Ossowski 1963). In such economies, a central agency is acting, presumably thoughtfully, for the benefit of the system as a whole. But this very consciousness on the part of a group acting in the name of the society could equally well be viewed as consistent with conflict approach. The group, using the coercive strength of the state which it controls, pursues policies that express its interests. For example, different factions within the Soviet Union's leadership struggle to control the state. The factions may disagree about the relative emphasis to be placed on heavy industry versus consumer items or they may disagree about emphasizing the power of the central leaders versus regional interests (Skilling and Griffiths

1971; Cocks 1976). For a further example, leaders in post-Mao China are shifting towards increased benefits for professionals and managers. This may reflect their aggrandizement rather than a shift in ideology or even simply a pragmatic decision to increase material incentives in order to better discipline workers and improve productivity.

Marxists

A fundamental difference in the degree of class inequality between Communist and non-Communist countries is the variation in ownership of wealth. Abolishing private ownership of the means of production decreases inequality in that regard. However, we must remember that Communist countries themselves vary in what may be privately owned, and we must also bear in mind, as discussed earlier, that *control* of the means of production can be concentrated in ways other than ownership. The restrictions on private ownership of wealth, in any case, do reduce inequalities in income. The very highest incomes in capitalist countries are derived from wealth, not simply from wages and salaries. These factors, which accord with traditional Marxist ideas, help account for greater class equality in Communist countries compared to non-Communist countries. We have less information, however, about the degree to which members of the governing elite have effective discretionary or personal control over extensive material resources.

Data on relative wages of different occupational strata are more accessible than data on family income inequalities. As we saw in Chapter 4, wages in Eastern European countries tend to be somewhat more equal, compared to Western European countries. We also have seen that inequalities in the Soviet Union have varied, increasing during the 1930s and decreasing after the mid-1950s. The argument might be made that the Soviet Union and the other countries led by the Communist party are part of the world economy (Rubinson 1976). Their relative autonomy and ability not to be dependent, due to the strength of their states, might account for their greater equality. This might hold true if they are compared to dependent countries, but it does not account for their relative equality compared to the dominant countries in the world economy.

Yugoslavia presents an interesting test case. Private ownership of the large-scale means of production does not exist, nor does great private wealth. Nevertheless, wage differentials are more similar to those of Western European countries than to those of other countries governed by the Communist party. It is not ownership, then, and probably not even ideology that accounts for this result. Yugoslavia in many ways has a functioning market system rather than a command economy. Firms, although collectively owned, compete in the market, and it is this competition that presumably produces the prevailing wage structure.

Conflict and Coercion

The determining factor, according to many conflict theorists, should be who controls the state. To what extent do different classes control the states of Eastern and Western Europe? In Chapter 6 we reviewed the evidence about the extent to which members of the legislatures of various countries were drawn from working-class backgrounds. Persons of working-class origin are more likely to be members of the legislative bodies of the Communist governments than of other governments. Among the Communist party governments, East Germany has a particularly high proportion of legislative members who have been manual workers—44 percent—and Yugoslavia, a particularly low proportion—1 percent (Blondel 1974). These variations are consistent with variations in wage inequalities.

Another element of conflict theory significantly accounting for variations in income inequality is the military participation ratio. We noted that higher military participation ratios among non-Communist countries were associated with less inequality. Cutright (1967), however, had reasoned that among relatively economically developed countries increased military expenditures would instead drain off funds that would otherwise be devoted to economic progress and to the reduction of inequality. He found, as we noted earlier, that among the economically developed countries the military participation ratio was related to intersectoral income inequality. He did a similar analysis of eight Eastern European Communist countries and found that the military participation ratio was related positively and strongly to intersectoral income inequality. Perhaps the size of the military forces is related to the repressive strength of the state and the repressiveness can maintain greater inequalities than would otherwise be the case, even in Communist countries.

Cutright also found that the level of economic development was strongly and inversely related to intersectoral income inequality. In other words, more economically developed Communist countries, like non-Communist countries generally, tend to have more equal income distributions.

Concluding Observations

Some of the forces that affect income equality among non-Communist countries also affect class inequalities among Communist countries and between Communist and non-Communist countries; the level of economic development is one such factor. In general, political ideologies and governmental policies, as shaped by whose interests are represented in the government, play important roles in determining income distribution. In many Western European countries, social democratic parties, during their many years of rule, have pursued socialist policies. Yet, as we have seen in Chapter 4, this has not resulted in notably different income inequalities from other advanced industrial Western countries.

It is true, however, that the social democrats have pursued policies that stressed equality of opportunity more than equality of outcome (Parkin, 1971). Their policies have been directed particularly to the establishment of social welfare programs and the attainment of substantial minimal standards for everyone. In that they have been relatively successful, the proportion of the population living in poverty in countries with long-ruling social democratic governments is very small and is smaller than in other countries that are equally or even more economically developed (Chandler 1969).

In addition to these forces, wage and income equality is strongly affected by the degree of state control of the economy. Relatively greater equality is attainable when private ownership of wealth is restricted. Furthermore, insofar as labor, commodity, and investment markets are directly regulated, with the objective being substantial equality, then inequality does not drift to the level that other factors would otherwise force it to.

REFERENCES

ABRAHAMSON, MARK. 1973. "Functionalism and the Functional Theory of Stratification: An Empirical Assessment," *American Journal of Sociology* 78 (March):1236-1246.

ANDRZEJEWSKI, STANISLAW. 1954. *Military Organization and Society.* London: Routledge and Kegan Paul.

BARAN, PAUL, and PAUL SWEEZY. 1966. *Monopoly Capital.* New York: Monthly Review Press.

BETTELHEIM, CHARLES. 1974. *Cultural Revolution and Industrial Organization in China.* New York: Monthly Review Press.

BLONDEL, JEAN. 1974. *Comparative Legislatures.* Englewood Cliffs: Prentice-Hall.

BROOM, LEONARD, and ROBERT G. CUSHING. 1977. "A Modest Test of an Immodest Theory: The Functional Theory of Stratification," *American Sociological Review* 42 (February):157-169.

CHANDLER, JOHN H. 1969. "Perspectives on Poverty, 5: An International Comparison," *Monthly Labor Review* 92 (2):55-62.

CHASE-DUNN, CHRISTOPHER. 1975. "The Effects of International Economic Dependence on Development and Inequality: A Cross-National Study," *American Sociological Review* 40 (December):720-738.

CHIROT, DANIEL. 1977. *Social Change in the Twentieth Century.* New York: Harcourt Brace Jovanovich.

COCKS, PAUL. 1976. "The Policy Process and Bureaucratic Politics." Pp. 156-178 in P. Cocks, R. V. Daniels, and N. W. Heer (eds.), *The Dynamics of Soviet Politics.* Cambridge, Mass.: Harvard University Press.

COLLINS, RANDALL. 1975. *Conflict Sociology.* New York: Academic Press.

COMMITTEE OF CONCERNED ASIAN SCHOLARS. 1972. *China! Inside the People's Republic.* New York: Bantam.

CUTRIGHT, PHILLIPS. 1967. "Inequality: A Cross-National Analysis," *American Sociological Review* 32 (August):562-578.

DAVIS, KINGSLEY, and WILBERT E. MOORE. 1945. "Some Principles of Stratification," *American Sociological Review* 10 (April):242-249.

DOBB, MAURICE. 1958. *Capitalism Yesterday and Today.* London: Lawrence and Wishart.

GARNIER, MAURICE A., and LARRY HAZELRIGG. 1977. "Military Organization and Distributional Inequality: An Examiniation of Andreski's Thesis," *Journal of Political and Military Sociology* 5 (Spring):17-33.

GOLDTHORPE, JOHN H. 1969. "Social Stratification in Industrial Society." Pp. 452-465 in Celia S. Heller (ed.), *Structured Social Inequality.* New York: Macmillan. (Originally published in 1964 in the *Sociological Review.*)

GOLDWASSER, JANET, and STUART DOWTY. 1975. *Huan-Ying: Workers' China.* New York: Monthly Review Press.

GORDON, DAVID M. 1972. *Theories of Poverty and Underemployment.* Lexington, Mass.: D. C. Heath.

HARRIS, MARVIN. 1975. *Culture, People, Nature: An Introduction to General Anthropology*, 2nd ed. New York: Crowell.

HEWITT, CHRISTOPHER. 1977. "The Effect of Political Democracy and Social Democracy on Equality in Industrial Societies: A Cross-National Comparison," *American Sociological Review* 42 (June):450-464.

HICKS, ALEXANDER, ROGER FRIEDLAND, and EDWIN JOHNSON. 1978. "Class Power and State Power: The Case of Large Business Corporations, Labor Unions and Governmental Redistribution in the American States," *American Sociological Review* 43 (June):302-315.

HOLMBERG, ALLAN. 1950. *Nomads on the Long Bow: The Sirino of Eastern Bolivia.* Smithsonian Institution, Institute of Social Anthropology, Publication No. 10.

JACKMAN, ROBERT W. 1974. "Political Democracy and Social Equality: A Comparative Analysis," *American Sociological Review* 39 (February):29-45.

JACKMAN, ROBERT W. 1975. *Politics and Social Equality: A Comparative Analysis.* New York: John Wiley.

JAMES, RALPH and ESTELLE JAMES. 1964. "Hoffa's Impact on Teamster Wages," *Industrial Relations* 4 (October): 60-76.

KELLER, SUZANNE. 1963. *Beyond the Ruling Class.* New York: Random House.

KRIESBERG, LOUIS. 1976. "Alternative Explanations of Class Inequalities," Department of Sociology, Syracuse University. Unpublished paper.

LAMPMAN, ROBERT J. 1971. *Ends and Means of Reducing Income Poverty.* Chicago: Markham.

LENSKI, GERHARD E. 1966. *Power and Privilege.* New York: McGraw-Hill.

LEVINSON, HAROLD M. 1951. "Unionism, Wage Trends, and Income Distribution, 1914-1947," *Michigan Business Studies*, 10, No. 1. Ann Arbor: Bureau of Business Research, Graduate School of Business, University of Michigan.

LEWIS, H. GREGG. 1963. *Unionism and Relative Wages in the United States.* Chicago: University of Chicago Press.

LEYS, SIMON. 1977. *Chinese Shadows.* New York: Penguin.

LINDERT, PETER H., and JEFFREY WILLIAMSON. 1976. "Three Centuries of American Inequality." Pp. 69-123 in Paul Uselding (ed.), *Research in Economic History.* Greenwich, Conn.: JAI Press.

LIPSET, SEYMOUR MARTIN. 1963. *The First New Nation: The United States in Historical and Comparative Perspective.* Garden City, N.Y.: Doubleday.

LIPSET, SEYMOUR MARTIN. 1968. *Revolution and Counterrevolution: Change and Persistence in Social Structures.* New York: Basic Books.

MARX, KARL, and FRIEDERICH ENGELS. 1932. "Manifesto of the Communist Party." Pp. 320-355 in Max Eastman (ed.), *Capital, the Communist Manifesto and Other Writings.* New York: Modern Library. (Originally published in 1848.)

MILLER, HERMAN P. 1966. *Income Distribution in the United States.* Washington, D.C.: Government Printing Office.

OSSOWSKI, STANISLAW. 1963. *Class Structure and Social Consciousness.* New York: Free Press.

PARKIN, FRANK. 1971. *Class Inequality and Political Order.* New York: Praeger.

PARSONS, TALCOTT. 1951. *The Social System.* New York: Free Press of Glencoe.

PARSONS, TALCOTT. 1966. *Societies: Evolutionary and Comparative Perspectives.* Englewood Cliffs, N.J.: Prentice-Hall.

PARSONS, TALCOTT. 1970. "Equality and Inequality in Modern Society, or Social Stratification Revisited." Pp. 13-72 in Edward O. Lauman (ed.), *Social Stratification.* Indianapolis: Bobbs-Merrill.

PARSONS, TALCOTT. 1971. *The System of Modern Societies.* Englewood Cliffs, N.J.: Prentice-Hall.

PAUKERT, FELIX. 1973. "Income Distribution at the Different Levels of Development: A Survey of Evidence," *International Labor Review,* 108 (August-September):97-125.

PIVEN, FRANCES FOX, and RICHARD A. CLOWARD. 1971. *Regulating the Poor.* New York: Vintage Books.

RADCLIFF-BROWN, A. F. 1948. *The Andaman Islanders.* Glencoe, Ill.: Free Press. (Originally published in 1922.)

RUBINSON, RICHARD. 1976. "The World Economy and the Distribution of Income within States: A Cross-National Study," *American Sociological Review* 41 (August):638-659.

RUBINSON, RICHARD, and DAN QUINLAN. 1977. "Democracy and Social Inequality: A Re-analysis," *American Sociological Review* 42 (August): 611-623.

SKILLING, H. GORDON, and FRANKLYN GRIFFITH (eds.) 1971. *Interest Groups in Soviet Politics.* Princeton, N.J.: Princeton University Press.

STIGLER, GEORGE. 1970. "Director's Law of Public Income Redistribution," *Journal of Law and Economics* 13 (April):1-10.

TUSSING, A. DALE. 1975. *Poverty in a Dual Economy.* New York: St. Martin's Press.

VANFOSSEN, BETH E., and ROBERT I. RHODES. 1974. "A Critique of Abrahamson's Assessment," *American Journal of Sociology* 80 (November):727-732.

WEISSKOPF, THOMAS E. 1972. "The Problem of Surplus Absorption in a Capitalist Society." Pp. 364-374 in R. C. Edwards, M. Reich and T. E. Weisskopf (eds.), *The Capitalist System.* Englewood Cliffs, N.J.: Prentice-Hall.

WILENSKY, HAROLD L. 1975. *The Welfare State and Equality: Structural and Ideological Roots of Public Expenditures.* Berkeley: University of California Press.

chapter 13

Explaining Status and Power Variations

The principle of equality,
which makes men independent of each other,
gives them a habit and a taste for following in their private actions
no other guide than their own will.
This complete independence, which they constantly enjoy
in regard to their equals
and in the intercourse of private life,
tends to make them look upon all authority
with a jealous eye and speedily suggests to them
the notion and the love
of political freedom.   *Alexis de Tocqueville*

In this chapter we continue to test several theoretical explanations of social inequalities, now by applying them to variations in status and power inequalities. In the concluding section we will assess the theories in the light of these applications.

STATUS INEQUALITIES

In earlier chapters, we considered a variety of status inequalities. We described inequalities based on family lineage and ways of life and those based on sex and race. We studied occupational prestige differences and intergenerational occupational mobility. We even discussed global status inequalities, considering countries as units. In this chapter, we will try to account for variations.

We will not try to account for global *status* ranking, just as we did not try to account for *class* inequalities on a global basis. The world system is taken as a setting within which we try to account for inequalities. We will not try to apply the theories to status inequalities based on family lineage, race, or ways of life. Three topics will be examined in this chapter. Two have direct applicability for the theorists and have been central to sociological studies of stratification for many years: occupational prestige and intergenerational occupational mobility. The third, status inequality based upon sex, has not been as systematically examined in terms of stratification, but it is increasingly being so considered.

Occupational Prestige

We have described several aspects of occupational prestige that we might now explain: the occupational prestige hierarchy in the United States; changes in the hierarchy and its great stability; changes in the distribution of occupations by prestige; similarities in occupational prestige hierarchies throughout the world; and variation in the prestige hierarchy among countries of the world. We will try to apply the theories under consideration to one segment of these findings: the similarities and differences among contemporary societies in their occupational prestige hierarchies.

Values and functional integration. When Inkeles and Rossi (1956) reported the similarities in occupational prestige hierarchies among industrial societies, they concluded that this suggested a relatively invariable prestige hierarchy associated with the industrial system. Additional studies and later comparisons found similarities in nonindustrial societies as well (Hodge, Treiman, and Rossi 1966; Wood and Weinstein 1966). This suggests universal functional requirements of large social systems; but, as we discussed earlier, we cannot test explanations for universals. Perhaps similarities among all societies are due to universal functional requirements of all societies, but such similarities could also result from inherent human characteristics, or commonalities of power structures, or some universally shared values. Our best approach is to consider *variations* in the prestige hierarchies.

According to the value and functional integration approach, some variations in prestige hierarchies among the countries of the world could be expected. For example, Parsons (1953) characterized the USSR as a society in which goal direction of the system is a paramount value; consequently, the standard of evaluation would give the highest regard to contributions to it. In the United States, instrumental achievement and goal attainment are central values; consequently, we expect that occupations pertaining to setting goals (for example, political leadership positions), would be less highly regarded. But this is not the case. Rossi and Inkeles (1957) found that, among Soviet citizens who had been taken from the USSR by the Germans in World War II and who did not return, party leaders and persons in managerial positions were reported *not* to be highly respected. Sarapata and Wesolowski (1961) found in their study of Warsaw residents that a minister in the national government is regarded relatively *lower* than a cabinet member is regarded in the United States.

The official glorification of manual work in Communist countries may account for the higher prestige of manual workers compared to white-collar workers. Thus, in the Soviet and Warsaw samples, the occupation of accountant appears to be relatively lower in prestige than it is in the United States. The analysis presented earlier about wage differences between white-collar and manual workers would again be applicable. Treiman (1977) argues that the relatively higher prestige of manual workers follows from their relatively higher wages, not the other way around. The limits to which ideology can affect occupational prestige hierarchies is indicated by Israeli data that shows that despite the labor Zionist emphasis upon working with one's hands, especially in agricultural labor, occupations in Israel have prestige rankings very similar to those in the United States (Lissak 1970). Even being a member of a Kibbutz (collective farm) does not carry high prestige among Israelis.

Motivation and functional importance. Differences in cultural values and variations therefore in what is functionally important, are also posited by Davis and Moore. Culturally unique emphases, however, are difficult to compare transculturally (Haller and Lewis 1966). We usually compare occupations that are similar enough in different societies to be comparable. Nevertheless, some differences, even for similar occupations, appear to exist among cultures. For example, the importance of religion probably varies considerably among societies. As noted in Chapter 6, the Buddhist priest in Japan appears to have lower prestige than a minister or priest has in the United States, Great Britain, or New Zealand. In the Warsaw sample, too, a priest seems to have relatively lower prestige than a priest in the United States (see Table 2.4 and 6.1).

Davis and Moore argue that prestige, like material rewards, is attached to positions according to their functional importance and the scarcity of personnel with the requisite training and talent for the positions. A few researchers have tried to test this idea, but the difficulty in assessing functional importance has hampered their work. In the previous chapter we saw that one way researchers measure functional importance is to compare periods in which the functional importance of certain positions would generally be regarded as different: for example, military positions during war and peace (Abrahamson 1973). Another way is to ask a sample of respondents to rate occupations on the dimensions of prestige, material reward, functional importance, and skill, then to see how well these several rankings correlate with each other. Lewis and Lopreato (1963) did this and found that rankings of occupational skills were highly related to the rankings of the occupations' prestige and reward. Functional importance was only moderately related and, when skill rankings were taken into account, the correlations were greatly reduced. The functional importance and prestige rankings were correlated 0.57 with each other; functional importance and reward were correlated 0.45. When skill is used as a control variable, the correlations drop to 0.37 and 0.19, respectively. *Imputed* functional importance does not seem to be a factor in prestige rankings in the small, special samples studied.[1]

Another way of assessing the possible relationship between these several dimensions of occupational rankings is to examine the relationships at the individual rather than the aggregate level. This shows whether or not persons who think a given occupation requires relatively high skill are also likely to think that that occupation has high prestige. I did this, using data from a national survey (Kriesberg 1962). Respondents were asked to rate the prestige of dentists and several other occupations. They were also asked to give their perceptions of the importance of dentists' work, their perception of the scarcity of persons with the requisite skills, and their perception of many other characteristics of the occupational role and of the incumbents of that role. It turns out that the many views of the dentists' occupational role were not markedly related to the prestige accorded it. The one relationship that showed strongly was that between

[1] They conducted the study in high schools in Amherst, Massachusetts, and Las Vegas, Nevada (N = 185). In another paper, Lewis and Lopreato (1963) compared the prestige ratings of educational occupations and gambling occupations. They found that gambling occupations tended to have a higher prestige rating in Las Vegas, Nevada, than in Amherst, Massachusetts, a "college town." Educational occupations had a slightly higher prestige rating in Las Vegas than in Amherst, contrary to what might be expected according to the Davis and Moore formulation. But the students in Las Vegas gave two gambling occupations about the same rating as did the Amherst students. The Las Vegas students saw two others as having higher prestige. The higher prestige occupations required more skill and had other associations that raised their status; the Amherst students simply did not know enough about the occupations to make the distinction. Lewis and Lopreato concluded that, overall, the national prestige rankings were so persuasive that community variations had little impact.

the prestige rating of dentists and of other professional occupations relative to the nonprofessional occupations surveyed. Apparently, respondents locate a given occupation within general categories and rate it according to their understanding of the relative ranking of those categories. People's perceptions of an occupation's prestige probably influence their beliefs about other occupational characteristics rather than vice versa. Prestige ranking is socially visible since deference must be shown if it is to exist. We learn and are taught which roles are to be treated with deference and which with disdain.

These findings help explain the way occupational prestige hierarchies change and are sustained (Offe 1976). People learn the prestige hierarchy from their experience with deference and from what they are taught. The rankings do not reflect general values nor perceptions of the importance of the role or the skills necessary for filling it. Wood and Weinstein's (1966) analysis of occupational evaluations in Uruguay is consistent with this interpretation. They found that persons who had more experience with industrial occupations tended to accord them more prestige. This ranking was made independently of more abstract values.

Marxists. Explanations for prestige ranking of occupations is of less interest to Marxists than to functionalist theorists. Nevertheless, they do offer an explanation for prestige rankings; the prevailing ideas of any period are those of the ruling class and prestige rankings are part of those prevailing ideas. Some of the variations we have seen between capitalist countries and those governed by the Communist party might be seen as consistent with this argument. In addition, the implication from the empirical studies described above that prestige rankings are learned would indicate that whoever controls the educational system can strongly affect the prestige hierarchy. However, the great similarities among the countries we have been comparing indicate that imposition of prestige ratings by a ruling class is not readily and effectively done.

Conflict and Coercion. Rather than positing a single ruling class, the conflict-and-coercion approach gives more credence to struggle among various groups, including occupational ones. They compete and fight about prestige as well as material rewards. How much prestige an occupational group has, then, is largely determined by its strength and by how well the members organize to establish a monopoly of skills and restrict entrance to the occupation. Thus, members of occupations strive to control educational and licensing requirements. Professions, for example, largely succeed in themselves setting the standards of admission and practice. They are able to use the power of the state to enforce the licensing regulations, which they largely write. Trade unions as well as professional associations strive to gain control over their working conditions. Members of occupations try to change the name of their occupation—*undertaker* becomes *funeral director*—or they increase the educational requirements so as to label their occupations "professions" and raise their prestige (Hughes 1960; Vollmer and Mills 1966). Seen this way, education is not so much a means of acquiring the knowledge and skills necessary for doing a job as it is a way of including certain kinds of people and excluding others (Collins 1971; Berg 1971; Squires 1977).

Organizational strength can even be used by members of an occupation to exclude persons with particular ascribed statuses. This becomes a way of restricting competition and improving the monopoly position of the members of an occupation. Excluding persons with low ascribed status characteristics may also serve to raise the prestige of an occupation. These factors may be illustrated by the success of the American medical profession in gaining control of supervising childbirth and, further, in excluding women from the practice of medicine. In 1910, about 50 percent of all babies were delivered by midwives. Obstetricians mounted a campaign that resulted in state after state outlawing midwifery. Midwives were attacked as incompetent, but they were not given training to become more skilled in order to remain an independent occupation, as they are in Europe. Instead, they were forced out of competition. Interestingly, a 1912 study indicated that most American doctors were less competent than the midwives in child delivery (Ehrenreich and English 1973; Kobrin 1966).

To test the applicability of this approach for explaining variations in occupational prestige, we need data on the organizational strength and relative power of a variety of occupational groups in different countries. For example, we would need to know whether physicians are particularly powerful in the United States and to what extent European professors have more relative power and control over their activities than American professors. Although we lack such data on a systematic basis, some evidence indicates that American professors have relatively less power, for example, than university administrators and that their counterparts in other countries have relatively more (Kaplan 1961; Kriesberg 1973, p. 235).

Concluding Observation. Sufficient evidence is lacking to definitively test the theoretical approaches we have been considering. The differences in occupational prestige hierarchies among the countries of the world might be best related to the ability of different occupational groups to construct monopolies of skills and to use their organizational strength to claim prerequisites and perquisites that carry connotations of honor and therefore receive deference. Simple coercion, however, is not enough. We have seen that in East European communist countries, leading political and managerial positions are not so highly regarded. Presumably, the power must be regarded as legitimate. While partly a matter of socialization, legitimacy also depends on shared values and identity. Legitimation may also require that an equitable exchange exist; that is, people must regard the goods and services they receive from members of an occupation as a reasonably fair exchange for the deference and payment they give. The sense of equity is based then on shared understandings and past expectations, and not simply on the coercive strength of the contending groups.

Treiman (1977) has conducted detailed comparative analyses of occupational prestige. In his analyses he sought to test alternative explanations for the great similarities in occupational prestige ranking in the countries of the world and also for the variations. The evidence is inconsistent, he contended, with the idea that the prestige ordering of occupations is determined by idiosyncratic cultural values. He concluded that it was also inconsistent with the idea that the Western pattern of occupational evaluation was diffused throughout the world. He also found that the evidence did not support the explanation that prestige orderings are similar because the Western system of organizing production spread throughout the world and brought with it a similar hierarchy of occupations in terms of power.

Treiman offered his own theory, which, in some ways, synthesizes some elements from the approaches we have been examining. His theory consists of four propositions: First, "specialization of tasks is efficient and therefore a division of labor develops in all social systems large enough to support specialists" (1977, p. 7); and furthermore, since all societies face similar "functional imperatives", similar tasks exist in each society. In addition, the social roles developed to meet those tasks are dependent on each other, creating organizational imperatives. The second proposition is, "specialization of functions into distinct occupational roles inherently gives rise to differential control over scarce and valued resources" (pp. 12-13). Since occupations differ with respect to knowledge and skill, economic control, and authority, they have differential power. Third, power gives those who possess it the opportunity, almost invariably used, to acquire special privileges. This comes about through supply-and-demand market forces and through the ability of groups in superior positions to maximize their own advantage. Finally, since power and privilege are highly valued everywhere, powerful and privileged positions are highly regarded.

Treiman finds that this theory is consistent with the available evidence about the similarities and the few variations in occupational prestige in the countries of the world. Thus, he applies his theory to explain the tendency for clerical occupations to have lower prestige and manual occupations to have higher prestige in Eastern European countries than in the world as a whole. He argues, convincingly, that the higher prestige of manual workers follows from their relatively privileged position, their higher wages. He explains societal differences in the prestige of particular occupations in terms of their differential power or privilege.

Intergenerational Occupational Mobility

We saw in Chapters 5 and 6 that the data about changes over time or among different societies are limited. And because the original data are not strictly comparable, comparisons over time or space are difficult. Moreover, there are grave methodological problems in constructing comparable measures of mobility. As we discussed in Chapters 5 and 6, many attempts to solve these problems have been made, but no solution covers every problem and no single measure of mobility can summarize all aspects of intergenerational occupational mobility.

In this section, we use two summary measures of intergenerational mobility between major occupational strata in order to assess explanations for variations in mobility among contemporary countries. As described in Chapter 6, Hazelrigg and Garnier (1976) constructed comparable ratios of intergenerational occupational mobility for seventeen countries. Their ratios are based on a threefold division of occupations: nonmanual, manual, and farm.

The ratios constructed by Hazelrigg and Garnier do not measure observed mobility. Observed mobility is important and is what people experience most directly, but the extent of such mobility is largely determined by the differences in occupational structure between the two generations studied. Observed mobility is also partly due to people *exchanging* positions. We cannot compare mobility among different countries aside from the effects of changing occupational structures without developing ratios or indicators that control for those changes. That is, observed mobility consists of structural or forced mobility plus exchange mobility; to assess exchange mobility, structural mobility must be held constant.

The Hazelrigg and Garnier ratios measure exchange mobility. In one ratio, they adjusted the size of the occupational categories in the destination of sons' generation so that their size would be the same as in the origin or fathers' generation. This holds constant the structural effects of the change in occupational distribution. We call this an intrasocietal exchange ratio. This ratio does not take into account that the occupational structures in the origin generation differ among societies, but the relative size of different occupational categories in the origin generation also affects mobility rates. To hold this factor constant, Hazelrigg and Garnier constructed a ratio adjusting the size of the occupational categories so that they would be the same for *all* countries. This, called the transsocietal exchange ratio, makes it possible to compare exchange mobility in different countries, holding constant their different occupational structures.

The ratios for seventeen countries, presented in Table 6.4, vary considerably. Before trying to apply the theories to account for these variations, we will review Hazelrigg and Garnier's analysis of the relationship between these ratios of intergenerational occupational mobility and economic development or industrialization. As in explanations of class inequalities, the level of economic development has often been asserted to be related to mobility (Lipset and Zetterberg 1966; Treiman 1970).

To measure economic development, Hazelrigg and Garnier used energy consumption per capita, averaged over a twenty-five year period immediately prior to the year when the national survey of occupational mobility was conducted. The energy consumption variable was logarithmically transformed.[2] Hazelrigg and Garnier found a very high relationship between energy consump-

___

[2] See Footnote 3 in Chapter 12.

tion and the intersocietal measure of intergenerational mobility (a correlation of 0.75). This is similar to the finding of Cutright (1968), who used a different method to summarize and compare intergenerational occupational mobility. But when Hazelrigg and Garnier examined the relationship between exchange mobility, using the transsocietal measure, they found no relationship between it and energy consumption. Their study indicates that the level of economic development is related to cross-national differences in occupational distribution, but it does not otherwise affect intergenerational occupational mobility. Now we turn to the theorists we have been considering and discuss what explanation they can offer for the variations and relationships we have noted.

Values and functional integration. The relationship between economic development and the intrasocietal exchange mobility measure might be used to support the idea that values promoting mobility (universalism and achievement, for example) are tied to economic development and produce high rates of mobility. But the lack of relationship between economic development and exchange mobility measured transsocietally argues against this interpretation. Economic development is related to mobility due to its relationship to the occupational distribution (Hazelrigg and Garnier 1976).

However, cultural values, varying among the societies studied, may still account in part for the variations in transsocietally measured exchange mobility. We lack sufficient systematic information about the cultural patterns of different societies to test this hypothesis. A visual inspection of Table 6.4, however, does not appear to support this explanation. It is difficult to conceive of the cultural values relevant to mobility and shared by low-ranking countries as being different from the values shared by the high-ranking countrues.

Another idea is suggested by the values and functional integration approach. Since the several institutions in a society tend to form a mutually determining system, the nature of the family and kinship system might be expected to be related to intergenerational occupational mobility rates. Parsons (1943) has reasoned that while any family system tends to inhibit completely free circulation, open mobility is particularly limited when extended families and kinship systems with arranged marriages are prevalent. The United States, with its isolated nuclear family and open marriage arrangements, would be consistent with relatively high mobility circulation. Again, we lack systematic data to test this idea. An indirect test is possible using birth rates as a crude indicator of family size. We should expect, according to this approach, that higher birth rates would be negatively related to circulation rates. Actually, we find no relationship (-0.066) with intrasocietal exchange mobility and a moderate *positive* relationship (0.453) with transsocietally measured circulation (Kriesberg, 1978). Later, we will consider another possible interpretation of this finding.

Motivation and functional importance. The Davis and Moore formulation regarding inequality of ranking, in itself, does not offer any explanations of variations in intergenerational mobility. They suggest, however, that societies with secular emphases and societies at later stages of cultural development would tend to have greater mobility. The general explanation they make of the variations in circulation rates is similar to the analysis we presented in the preceding paragraphs (Davis 1949). Davis (1962) has argued that open mobility enhances economic development. Mobility presumably means selection by talent rather than by birth and has a beneficial influence on maintaining economic growth. That, of course, is considering how mobility affects economic development, not the other way around. In any case, there would be an association. As we have seen, the association is with exchange mobility insofar as it is affected by occupational distribution. If we hold occupational distribution constant, the level of economic development is not associated with exchange mobility.

Marxists. Mobility rates are of particular interest for Marxists because mobility may have implications for the development of solidarity within the working class. Nevertheless, Marxists do not offer a systematic accounting of the determinants of exchange mobility. We can utilize the Marxist approach ourselves to interpret the findings we have presented. The evidence that the level of industrialization affects exchange mobility strongly and does so by its relationship with occupational distribution is consistent with the Marxist emphasis on technology and the material conditions of production. It is also consistent with its emphases on objective conditions affecting human conduct.

The Marxist approach might also lead us to expect important differences in mobility between economies with and without private ownership of the means of production. The evidence does not indicate, however, any clear difference in mobility rates between the countries of Eastern Europe with governments led by the Communist party and non-communist countries (Dobson 1977). It may be argued that almost no one owns the means of production in any advanced industrial country. The only significant ownership of the means of production in terms of a country's population is ownership of farming land. Perhaps widespread small-farm ownership enhances occupational inheritance. We will test that idea after we consider related hypotheses derived from a conflict approach.

Conflict and coercion. The organized efforts of occupational and status groups to protect and extend themselves could also explain variations in occupational mobility. Thus, in societies significantly divided by ethnic, racial, or other ascribed characteristics, caste-like differences would impede mobility. The dominant group can use language and cultural differences to maintain incumbency in higher occupations for its own members and to deny entrance to the subdominant groups. Again, we lack systematic evidence to characterize societies in those terms and relate that variable to rates of occupational mobility.[3]

---

[3] An indirect test of this is possible using a measure of ethnolinguistic fractionalization (Taylor and Hudson 1972). The number of people in various groups differing in language or ethnicity are calculated as a proportion of a country's total population. According to the conflict-and-coercion approach, we expect that ethnolinguistic fractionalization would be negatively related to circulation rates. Consistent with that hypothesis, it is moderately negatively related to intersocietal exchange mobility (-0.446) but is not related to transsocietally measured circulation (0.103).

A related possibility is that countries that have clear ways of life associated with classes and occupational strata would have reduced exchange mobility. Perhaps societies with continuing aristocracies tend in that direction. Again, we lack systematic relevant data, but a visual inspection of the data in Table 6.4 suggests that this idea might be supported if systematic evidence were gathered.

The conflict-and-coercion approach also suggests that differences in occupational and class organization or corporativeness would contribute greatly to inhibit exchange mobility. To test this ideal, information about the ability of professional and other nonmanual occupations to deny entrance to would-be entrants is needed. This argument is similar to the Marxist contention that the extent of ownership of the means of production is crucial in determining circulation rates. The conflict-and-coercion approach makes a more general argument. What is crucial is the ability of any group to control entrance to any set of roles. In the case of intergenerational mobility, the families' ability to pass on their occupational position to their children is critical. Considering fathers and sons (as these studies do), we expect circulation rates to be lower when the labor force is self-employed and a father can pass on the farm or business to his son. Similarly, we expect that if agricultural land is equally distributed, circulation rates will tend to be lower than if land is unequally distributed. This turns out to be the case. The higher the proportion of men employed by others, the higher the intrasocietal exchange mobility (0.737) but the relationship does not hold for transsocietal exchange mobility (-0.127) (Kriesberg 1978).

Sociologists taking the conflict-and-coercion approach would also argue that insofar as people have equal resources to enter every occupational stratum, circulation rates will be higher. Therefore, we expect that in countries with less income inequality and less inequality of agricultural land distribution, circulation rates would tend to be higher. This tends to be the case (Kriesberg 1978). Personal income inequality is negatively related to both intersocietal exchange mobility (-0.620) and to transsocietal exchange mobility (-0.395). Land inequality is not related to intersocietal exchange mobility, but it is negatively correlated with transsocietal circulation rates (-0.540) as hypothesized. The number of cases is small, however, and the findings in regard to transsocietal exchange rates are not statistically significant.

Concluding observations. In addition to the factors previously noted, we should recognize that differential birth rates also affect intergenerational mobility (Blau 1977). If lower-ranking families have high birth rates and higher-ranking families have low birth rates, upward mobility will be greater than if birth rates were the same in different ranks.

To test this idea, we can use a country's birthrate as an indicator of differential birth rates among major class strata, reasoning that among contemporary countries, low birth rates indicate that agricultural and manual strata birth rates have become similar to those of nonmanual workers. It turns out that high birth rates are moderately related to transsocietal intergenerational mobility rates, as hypothesized (Kriesberg 1978).

Much of the research about intergenerational occupational mobility has been concerned with discovering how much exists, which has turned out to be a very complex and difficult matter to assess. Nevertheless, we have some evidence about the factors affecting rates of mobility. If we consider *observed* intergenerational occupational mobility, the rates are significantly affected by changes in occupational distribution between generations. Exchange mobility, measured intrasocietally, tends to be greater in more economically developed countries, apparently partly because less developed countries have larger proportions of their populations self-employed and therefore able to pass on their occupational position to their children. Exchange mobility, measured transsocietally, seems to be related to equal birth rates among occupational strata and inversely related to class inequality.

Gender as a Status Difference

Differences between men and women, as we have seen, are often categorized, evaluated, and ranked. Direct measures of the status ranking of men and women are not accessible, because the differences between men and women are so fundamental and the bonds between them so intimate and complex that they cannot be reduced to a hierarchy. Yet, ranking does exist. For analytical purposes, we will focus on indirect measures of status. In Chapters 5 through 8, we have seen the many different ways in which women have less power and material resources than men. In this section, we apply the theories we have been considering to explain variations in women's participation in the occupational and educational systems. We give particular attention to variations among the countries of the world. Historical changes in the United States and other indicators of women's status will be supplementary to this major application.

We begin by relating women's participation in the occupational system to industrialization and economic development. We do this for two reasons. First, we have seen that in the grand sweep of human history the transformations of human life have been associated with changes in the basic ways of organizing material production. This is aside from the issue of whether the modes of production shape ways of thought or, conversely, changes in ways of thinking shape the organization of production. Second, all the theorists we have been considering accord great importance to the transformation of the world associated with industrialization and urbanization.

Boulding (1969) conducted a comprehensive cross-national study of industrialization and the participation of women in society. She found that energy consumption per capita was somewhat related to participation of women in the nonagricultural labor force. The correlation, based upon data from 82 countries, was 0.235. The relationship was even greater between energy consumption and the percent of all white-collar workers who are women (0.396; 59 countries). But economic development does not produce more participation by women in all spheres of the occupational system. Boserup (1970) has argued that industrialization has driven many women who had been independent entrepreneurs out of the market place. Manufactured goods and large-scale marketing forced women out and the responsible production and distribution positions of the large-scale enterprises were taken over by men. Boulding (1969, p. 45) found, as a matter of fact, that economic development was slightly negatively related to the percentage of females independently employed. The correlation was –0.157 (59 countries) between energy consumption per capita and independent employment; the correlation with the percentage of the population living in urban areas was more strongly negative: –0.277 (63 countries).

Boulding conducted a similar analysis of women's participation in the educational system. She found substantial relationships between economic development and the proportion of women enrolled in secondary schools. For example, the correlation in 1960 was 0.505 (86 countries) between energy consumption per capita and female enrollment in secondary schools. A variety of interpretations or explanations of these findings can be made. One possibility is that the logic of industrialization and the occupational differentiation that accompanies it require more extensive female participation in the nonhousehold economy. Education is necessary for participation and necessary for the functioning of an urban, industrial society. The relationships we have seen, however, are not very strong. Even if this interpretation is valid, many other factors certainly affect the degree of equality accorded women. We had best consider these additional factors and the relationship between industrialization and women's participation in the society as we consider the major theoretical approaches under review.

Values and functional integration. According to this approach, the degree of equality of participation of women in the employment and educational system varies with the society's cultural patterns and the role of women in other institutional systems. We will consider a few dimensions of value differences among the countries of the world and see how they relate to women's equality of participation.

An important institution and bearer of cultural patterns is religion. Boulding (1969, pp. 143-144) coded religions on a localism scale, ranging from localist animist religions to the centralized bureaucracies of Islam and Byzantium. She hypothesized that the most localist religions will be associated with greater freedom for women. She categorized the religions in the countries of Asia and Africa in these terms: (1) low localism (Moslem, Catholic, Orthodox); (2) medium localism (Protestant, Jewish, Moslem when with strong minority religions); and (3) high localism (Animist, Hindu, Buddhist). In a series of analyses of African and Asian countries, Boulding found that localism of the traditional religion was associated with more equal participation of women in the occupational and educational systems, even holding constant level of economic development.

The differences between men and women have been elaborated in every culture. A widespread "traditional" women's role constrained the autonomous individuality of women. Their lives were circumscribed and restricted. Boulding, using ethnographic reports and other data, categorized the countries of Asia and Africa in terms of the degree of women's individuated role about 1900. She constructed an eight-item scale, then divided the countries into three ranked categories of individuated women's roles. Among the items were the age of marriage, freedom of marriage choice, property rights, inheritance rights, divorce rights, range of movement from hearth, degree of money handling, and freedom to be a trader.[4] Boulding found that the traditional women's role was highly and negatively related to participation in contemporary societies. This was true even holding constant the traditional religion and the economic development level.

Boulding's analysis also indicated that, controlling for cultural factors, economic development continues to be related to women's participation in the employment and educational systems of the countries of Asia and Africa. The role of cultural factors seems to have an additional important impact on the status of women. Although such factors may not account for the changes in the participation of women over short historical periods—during the 1930s, 1940s, and 1950s in the United States, for example—they do account for some of the lack of change and the variations among different countries of the world.

Motivation and functional importance. Davis and Moore (1945), in their paper on stratification, did not discuss variations in the relative ranking of women. Since the differences between men and women are generally ascribed rather than achieved, the issue of motivation is different than when seeking to account for variations in the prestige and rewards associated with different positions. The ascription refers to unchangeable characteristics attributed to persons, thus considerations other than motivation must be introduced to account for the varying ascribed allocation of men and women. Davis (1949) has argued that the division of labor by sex is related primarily to the differences in the reproductive roles of females and males.[5] Women are generally assigned those tasks associated with the household. He writes, "social efficiency is served by ascribing to women such occupations as will not interfere with child-bearing" (1949, p. 101). This may help account for some of the similarities in the sexual

---

[4] For example, age at marriage was coded as low in individuation if the common, expected, or average age at marriage was 14 years or younger; middle if 15 to 17 years of age; and high if 17 years or older. Marriage choice was coded as low in individuation if the woman had practically no say in whether or not she must give consent; middle if women has some say about the choice; and high if couples primarily decide themselves.

[5] Marwell (1975) has elaborated a related functional explanation of ascription by sex. He reasons that: (1) family units have performed several societal functions: reproduction, material nourishment and emotional support of family members; (2) a division of labor in performing tasks is efficient; (3) if many of the tasks can be ascriptively attached to males and females, training will be efficient and every family unit will have a wide variety of skills available in it. However, this reasoning does not explain why the different ascribed characteristics are ranked so that males have higher status than women. Marwell himself notes that new historical conditions (for example, extensive literature literacy and formal education in modern societies) may make ascription no longer functional.

division of labor, but not necessarily the status ranking. Combined with other factors, it might even help to explain variations in the division of labor. Which occupations will and will not interfere with child-bearing depends on the technology of production and the social organization of child-bearing and rearing. We will discuss these matters next, when we consider the Marxists' explanations for variations in women's equality.

Marxists. Contemporary Marxists draw upon the analysis by Engels (1942) in *The Origin of the Family, Private Property, and State.* The analysis is set in an evolutionary context, showing how private property originated and how it undermined the equalitarian tribal order. Before property, men and women worked and shared equally within households; families as such did not exist. The emergence of property rights over resources with productive potential, privately held by men, created the unequal family. Women, children, and propertyless men became dependent on those with productive property such as domesticated animals. Women came to work for their husbands rather than society.

There is some evidence that in small hunting and gathering bands, men and women are relatively equal (Boulding 1976). In pre-agricultural and simple horticultural societies, women often produce the major proportion of the caloric input for the household. Hunting by men may have produced a special treat, but the roots, berries, and other food gathered by the women provided the staples. Sanday (1974) has found that women's status was equal to men's insofar as their production of food was about the same as men's.

The development of the class system, greater surpluses, and greater inequality in agrarian societies also led to increased inequality between men and women. Sacks (1974) suggests that a contributing factor was the split between the public and domestic spheres. Men were pressed into public service and involvement in the public sphere by the actions of the ruling class. Women were increasingly restricted to the private and domestic sphere. Boulding (1976) titled her historical survey of women *The Underside of History* to emphasize the separate and domestic structures within which women have lived.

Why does industrialization seem to mark a change in the direction of sexual equality? Part of the answer, according to this approach, may be that with industrialization most men no longer own the means of production. They have become individual wage earners. Industrialization, moreover, removed women's productive activities from the domestic household as home production lost out to factory production. Women are equally propertyless and can be equally productive as wage earners. But there is still considerable inequality between men and women. As we discussed in Chapter 11, some Marxists suggest that such inequality results at least in part from the capitalists' actions, which divide the working class, pitting different segments against each other. Were this so, then in non-Capitalist, industrialized societies, the participation of women would equal that of men. In fact, the data reported in Chapters 6 and 8 indicate greater equality in countries governed by the Communist party than in other economically developed countries. We will consider an alternative explanation for this finding in the next section. We should also note that even in Communist countries, the equality of participation is at the lower and middle ranks of the occupational system. Women are underrepresented at the highest administrative levels in industry and government.

Conflict and coercion. This approach claims that the state plays a critical role in determining sexual equality as it shapes other forms of equality. As discussed in Chapter 11, the coercive strength of men, according Collins (1975), is moderated by the development of the state with its monopoly of legitimate violence. The extent to which the state can and does ensure that physical coercion is not used to dominate other humans is related to equality of the sexes. We lack systematic evidence on this variable, but another dimension of the political system may pertain to the relative equality of women. Among contemporary countries, states differ in their degree of corporate mobilization. That is, some regimes seek to unify and integrate society members and emphasize collective objectives. Such regimes might be particularly likely to enhance equality of women because of ideological egalitarianism and because the regime seeks to incorporate all citizens into the national mainstream and to transform them into agents of the state. Weiss and Ramirez with Tracey (1975) analyze the relationship between indicators of corporate state construction and female participation in the labor force. They used data from almost fifty contemporary countries and found a moderate positive relationship, which remained even when the level of economic development was controlled.

Recent changes in the relative status of women and their participation in American society can also be explained partly in terms of the women's movement. Women have organized and used their collective strength to try to gain equality. Although they have increased their participation in the labor force significantly over the last decade, many other indicators of equality of participation have remained little changed. This may reflect the relative strength of men as an adversary group. It may also reflect the relevance of some of the other factors we have discussed in conjunction with the other theoretical approaches.

Concluding observation. Explanations of the relative status of women must draw on aspects of all the theoretical approaches we have discussed. The evidence does not permit us to decide that one or another approach is primary or fundamental. Perhaps, in this case, all are closely intertwined. The case of the !Kung is illustrative. The !Kung are a hunting and gathering people who are gradually becoming agricultural. As a hunting and gathering group, men and women had similar status and shared equally in most activities. Population was stable and fertility was low. Children of all ages and of both sexes played together, since they were too few in number for sex and age groups to emerge. But with agricultural settlements, nutrition improved and so did fertility. When women bore children more frequently, they were more tied to childbearing and child-rearing activities. Food production and household tasks became more separated by sex. With more children in denser settlements, age and sex groups emerged. Consequently, sex role differentiation became elaborated and socialization into sex roles increased. As a result of these interconnected changes, the status of women among the !Kung declined.

POWER INEQUALITIES

As we have seen in Chapters 7 and 8, assessing degrees of equality in power is fraught with problems. No metric exists to assess the distribution of power in a society or even the proportion of people who have certain minimal civil rights. Yet, we can, or at least we do, make comparisons about relative power equality. In this section we look at some of the systematic evidence about factors affecting relative power equality, concentrating on cross-national comparisons.

We begin by relating measures of power inequality to level of economic development, because economic surplus has been found relevant to other dimensions of inequality and because all the theories in one way or another regard economic development, industrialization, modernization, and related changes as significant conditions affecting inequality.

Jackman (1975) examined the relationship between a measure of democratic performance and energy consumption per capita (logged). The measure of democratic performance consists of four components: (1) the proportion of the voting-age population that voted; (2) the competitiveness of the political party system (five categories); (3) electoral irregularity; and (4) freedom of the press. He found a moderate relationship between energy consumption (logged) and democratic performance; the correlation was .566 for the 60 countries studied (countries governed by the Communist party were not included).

In Figure 13.1, we have presented the findings graphically. We used the countries listed in Table 4.5 for which Jackman was able to prepare democratic performance scores. Jackman's analysis included many other countries not listed in Table 4.5, and the pattern is the same for the larger set of countries. *Among* countries with relatively high energy consumption per capita, democratic performance is also relatively high (with the exception of South Africa), but it is not correlated with energy consumption. *Among* countries with relatively low energy consumption, democratic performance scores vary greatly and are slightly correlated with the level of energy consumption. Overall, the relationship is curvilinear, as indicated by the line in Figure 13.1.

It should be noted that any cross-sectional analysis is limited to the historical period to which the data pertain. If a similar cross-sectional study were undertaken in the 1930s, the results would be somewhat different. During the 1930s, many countries with relatively developed economies had nondemocratic regimes—Fascist Italy, Nazi Germany, and other statist regimes of Central and Eastern Europe.

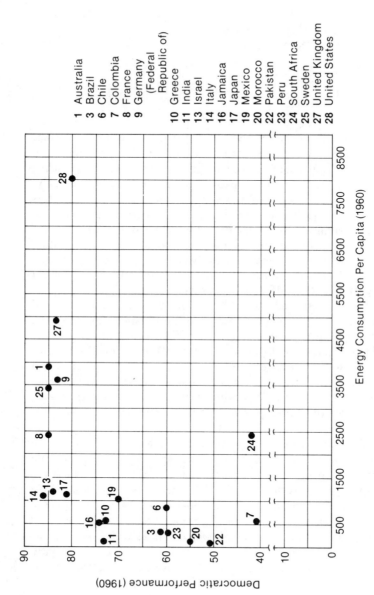

FIGURE 13.1 *Economic Development and Democratic Performance*

Note: Information about democratic performance not available for countries 2, 4, 5, 12, 15, 18, 21, and 26.

Source: Jackman 1975, Table D; and Table 4.2 from this book.

404

Functionalism

In explaining inequalities in power, we will not discuss different functionalist approaches. In the previous applications it was useful to distinguish an emphasis on values and functional interaction from an emphasis on motivation and functional importance. This distinction, however, has not been developed by functionalists for power inequality. We will consider the writings of Parsons, Davis, Moore, and others employing a functional orientation as a single approach.

These theorists argue that power inequality is functional for a society; it is needed to coordinate activities and to settle disputes. Functionalists also recognize that power is inherently unequal but believe that people can be content with such inequality. Thus, people may be satisfied with the workings of a government; "so long as it satisfies the expectations of the people, it may remain in power. The people may, in fact, conceive an absolute regime as the best instrument for achieving their ends" (Davis 1949, p. 498).

Which group has particular power within a society depends on the importance of the function the group serves. Thus, the military will have more power during times of war when they are more important functionally (Davis and Moore 1945).

Explanations of the general level of power inequality at the societal level should be affected by society's value system, according to this approach. Again, it is possible that Western values about democracy and political liberty diffused with the spread of industrialization; this would account for the relationship between energy consumption and democratic performance, as reported by Jackman. Modernism includes an emphasis on equality and the idea of citizenship and citizen rights.

Lipset (1967a) examines the relationship between the value systems and the stability of democratic political systems in the United States, Great Britain, Canada, Australia, France, and Germany. All are relatively industrialized, have related religious traditions, and have capitalist or mixed economies. To compare their values systems, he uses three of Parsons' pattern variables: ascription-achievement, particularism-universalism, and diffuseness-specificity. He adds a new one: elitism-equalitarianism. In comparing the United States, Canada, Great Britain, and Australia, Lipset regards Great Britain to be most elitist, ascriptive, particularistic, and diffuse. He regards the United States to be least ascriptive, particularistic, and diffuse. He thinks Australia is most equalitarian in values; otherwise, Canada and Australia fall between the United States and Great Britain. He notes that many characteristics of the political system of these countries are related to their value systems. For example, the relative strength of populist movements in the United States and Australia reflects their equalitarianism. Lipset notes, "though civil liberties will be stronger in elitist democracies than in equalitarian ones, the latter may be regarded as more 'democratic' in the sense that the electorate has more access to or power over the elite" (1967a, pp. 308-309).

405

Because of certain characteristics of their value systems, France and Germany have been less stable as democracies than Great Britain, the United States, Canada and Australia. France, for example, has cleavages resulting from the fact that ascriptive-particularistic values were never eliminated, despite the Franch Revolution. The values continue in such key institutions as the church and in commerce and industry. French small businessmen emphasize the maintenance of family fortune and status, expect particularistic loyalty from their employees, and have attempted to deny representation rights to trade unions. On the other hand, the French workers have supported the revolutionary values of achievement, equalitarianism, and universalism. Value cleavages also exist in Germany, but they are the obverse in some ways of those in France. Ascriptive and particularist values were maintained by the aristocracy and elites, particularly in the political sphere. In many ways achievement and universalism, but not equalitarianism, were encouraged in the economic order.

In trying to explain the differences in the emergence of democratic governments in developing countries, Lipset (1967b, p. 196-212) and many other political sociologists have emphasized the importance of social mobilization, noting the varying rates at which diverse groups are integrated into the modernizing sector of the society. Lipset suggests that the predominant political cleavage characteristic of many developing nations is the division between modernizing and traditionalist elements. In some ways this supercedes the Left-Right conflict based on stratification to be found in older polities. The cleavage accounts for the apparent anomoly of elite groups sometimes following leftist policies. To some degree they see socialism and communism as associated with the "ideology of independence, rapid economic development, social modernization, and ultimate equality" (1967b, p. 201).

Marxists

Traditional Marxism leads us to expect industrialization to play a fundamental role in shaping the political system. But the relationship between the means of production and the political order is not simple and direct. Thus, the transition to socialism and communism should be a crucial division. Our assessment of this approach depends on the aspects of the political order we examine.

Cutright (1963) studied political development, measured in terms of stable, institutionalized, and differentiated governments. He included countries governed by Communist parties. Cutright found a very strong relationship between his measure of political development and levels of urbanization, education, employment outside of agriculture, and especially of communication (telephones, newsprint consumption, domestic mail, and newspaper readers, all per capita). Given their levels of socioeconomic development, the political development of communist countries was only a little lower than one would expect. If we used a definition of political development that gave great weight to contending political parties or to competitive expressions of political views, the results would be quite different.

Marxists would assert that there is a clear relationship between the means of production and the political system, if we take into account the way in which technology is socially organized. Marxists, however, often define political democracy quite differently than non-Marxists. They regard formal political rights and apparently competitive parties as trivial compared to the domination of the political system by the ruling class in capitalist countries. Given the definitions of political equality we have been using in this book, however, we conclude that polities controlled by Communist parties are much less politically equalitarian than countries with similar technologies of production. The power of the state and the differential power of groups that control the state is crucial.

According to Marxist theory, the class structure of a society underlies the political structure. Rubinson and Quinlan (1977) tested this possibility, conducting a cross-national, cross-sectional analysis similar to that of Jackman (1975) and Cutright (1967). As mentioned in the last chapter, Jackman and Cutright tested the possible effect of democratization and government policy on class inequality. Rubinson and Quinlan reversed the relationship and examined the possible effects of class inequality on democratization. They used the proportion of personal income received by the third quintile (the middle 40 to 60 percent of the population) as the indicator of the relative strength of the middle class and the Gini index to measure income inequality. They found that the relative size of the middle class is positively related and the Gini index negatively related to democratization. They conclude that a class structure with great economic power of middle-income groups helps explain intercountry variations in democratization.

Rubinson and Quinlan also tested the idea that if different branches of the government are independent rather than dominated by a single branch or by an extragovernmental agency, democratization is higher. They found evidence consistent with this hypothesis. The conflict-and-coercion approach provides an explanation for these findings and is also consistent with the next set of arguments and findings.

The Marxist view of the world economic system suggests that within economically dependent countries class rankings tend to be relatively unequal. Indeed, this inequality may contribute to the relationship we have noted between economic development and democratic performance. In economically dependent countries, the class inequalities are created and sustained by the relationship with the dominant or core countries. Governments in the dependent countries tend to pursue policies that are consistent with the policies of the dominant country despite domestic opposition. Consequently, government leaders are likely to have reasons to be repressive domestically, and they may even feel freer to be repressive because they believe that they will be given external assistance. Petras and Tomich (1977) develop this argument for Latin America in explaining the overthrowing of Allende in Chile. This idea also has empirical support in the finding of Midlarsky and Tanter (1967) that revolutionary attempts are more often made in those Latin American countries with more foreign investment.

Conflict and coercion. A conflict-and-coercion approach to the explanation of power differences risks tautology. Since power differences are based on coercion, it is circular to explain power differences in terms of coercion. This circularity is avoided if we explain power inequalities in one sphere in terms of social conflicts or of coercion within other spheres or systems. This may be done in several ways.

The technology of violence might be expected to account for differences in societal power inequality. Thus, if the technology is relatively costly and privately exercised, power differences tend to be great (Collins 1975). The power of knights and feudal lords exemplifies such circumstances, but among contemporary countries, the technology of violence does not differ greatly. Extremely costly, collectively administered means of violence exist in every country; the governments of every state have great coercive strength relative to the mass of citizenry. Perhaps this helps account for the similarities in the limited participation in collective decision-making by the population as a whole.

Given the highly developed technologies of violence, variations in the general level of social organizational skills can help account for differences in political power. Thus, in industrializing or modernizing countries, the military organizations may have special relative strength. Military leaders are trained to administer and coordinate activities; moreover, they have control over resources not available to many others in the society. In relatively economically developed countries with older autonomous governments, more groups of persons have resources and skills that give them strength relative to the military. Hence, military domination is more likely in emerging and economically developing countries, and power is less equally divided than in countries not so dominated by the military (Janowitz 1964; Horowitz 1972).

External conflicts also contribute to the centralization of power by the government in office. This occurs partly as a consequence of a government's limiting, if not repressing, dissent. Wars not only increase domestic power inequalities, they tend to shift resources to the military leadership. Thus, with the added resources they control, the military leadership can garner even more power. Even without a shooting war, protracted external hostilities strengthen the relative power of the military and of the governmental officeholders. This may be illustrated by the emergence of a military-industrial-political complex or of power elites (Mills 1956; Rosen 1973).

The conflict-and-coercion approach helps explain the radical transformations in stratification that occasionally occur. Fundamental changes in the political order, as in the class order, most often result from revolutions or external imposition. The expansion of citizenship rights has been spurred by revolutionary efforts and by violent and nonviolent coercive efforts by disenfranchised groups. Social protest movements have been successful in gaining external imposition. The expansion of citizenship rights has been spurred by nonviolent coercion works as well as violent coercion (Gamson 1975). Increases in power inequalities have also been brought about by coercion, as in counter-revolutions and coups.

CONCLUSIONS

In applying the different theoretical approaches to variations in inequalities, the global system of inequalities has generally been taken as given and as contributing to our understanding of inequalities within societies. A comprehensive explanation of inequalities would include attention to the determinants of the patterns of global inequalities, but such an effort is beyond the scope of this book. It would require attention to the world economy and to relations among socialist and nonsocialist countries. It would also call for examining the way in which governments try to control certain commodities in the world market—as, for example, the Organization of Petroleum Exporting Countries (OPEC) tries to control oil. We would also consider changes in values and ideologies as they spread throughout the world and weigh to what extent a world civilization is developing. Finally, the power inequalities resulting from coercive efforts at the global level must be taken into account, since wars and nonviolent struggles among governments and between governments and groups that seek to establish themselves as governments are important factors in the transformation of the global stratification system.

We have not attempted to succinctly synthesize the theories previously presented in explaining all the variations for two main reasons. First, and fundamentally, we lack the evidence to do so. The data and the analyses have not been carried to the point where many ideas can be clearly refuted. Second, I do not want to impose a comprehensive synthesis because I think the readers should work with alternative approaches as long as the evidence is consistent with each. I hope the presentation in this and the preceding chapters will encourage readers to think about a variety of inequalities and apply the various theories to explain them. This will suggest kinds of evidence to seek out to assess the competing explanations. An understanding of the theories and an explanation of the variations that is subjectively convincing will arise from one's own active application of the theories.

In this concluding section, nevertheless, I offer some observations about assessing the theories and about comprehensive explanations of variations in inequality.

Assessing the Theories

The theories we have been examining each seem to have some special usefulness and some limitations. Because each has been developed to provide answers to particular questions, their relative explanatory power varies with the questions being answered: what dimension of inequality, over what range of time, and among which units are the variations to be explained? For example, if we compare time periods in which there have been no value changes, we cannot expect value differences to account for changes in inequality. With this in mind, let us consider the validity and usefulness of the different theoretical approaches.

409

Technological factors certainly are important in accounting for large-scale variations in class inequality. On the scale of world history and among the countries of the world, differences in economic development and material surplus are related to inequalities of power and class. But the meaning of that relationship is not self-evident. Thus, a particular technology does not dictate a particular form or level of inequality. The relationship may be interpreted in terms of functionalist, Marxist, or conflict approaches.

The functionalist approach is particularly useful for explaining the persistence of inequality. When values are shared within a system, that consensus helps sustain existing patterns of stratification. Moreover, insofar as different elements of a system are integrated, changes in inequality are impeded. Since status is based on standards of evaluation, value patterns would be particularly relevant for understanding changes and variations in status inequality.

The functionalist approach, as developed thus far, is less useful in accounting for abrupt changes or for changes on other than an evolutionary scale. Power differences that are not rooted in legitimacy are also not readily explained in functionalist terms.

The Marxist attention to the world economy is a useful context for understanding contemporary and historical changes and variations in class and power inequalities. The Marxist concern with objective, material conditions is a powerful tool in accounting for change, but the response to those conditions varies with factors only partially explicable in terms of Marxism as presently developed. Marxism is useful in providing an account of the inequalities in capitalist societies. But this is also a limitation since, as the approach is currently applied, it does not help to explain inequalities in contemporary noncapitalist countries.

The conflict-and-coercion approach is particularly helpful in understanding the transformations, as well as the persistence, of stratification systems. Conflict among groups helps explain relative control over material resources and variations in deference, as well as power differences. The risk in explaining inequalities in terms of coercion and conflict is that differences in strength are inferred from differences in outcome and that would produce tautological explanations. Of course, each theoretical approach is subject to the same risk. But the emphasis in this book on alternative explanations is one way to reduce the risks of circular reasoning.

Explaining Inequality

No one approach, narrowly applied, explains all the variations in inequality we have described. To account for the persistence and change in the patterns of inequality discussed here, we need to develop a more comprehensive theory than those already presented. We need to specify the conditions under which various combinations of the several theories apply. To fully account for any particular variation in inequality, we could not apply the theoretical approaches narrowly.

Advocates of each of these approaches, themselves, when trying to explain a particular aspect of inequality, tend to broaden the approach and include factors and considerations central in other approaches.

Thus, suppose we want to explain variations in class inequalities among contemporary countries. We find in several approaches elements that significantly contribute to our explanation: the relations of dominance and dependency among the countries; the absolute level of economic development and material surplus; the relative organizational strength of different occupations; and the exchange or bargaining position different occupations and groups have in the market.

To account for the differences in status inequalities as measured by occupational prestige, we must give considerable attention to the relative organizational strength of different occupational groups to construct monopolies and control requisites of position. But we must also recognize the importance of exchange benefits available to persons in different occupations and the expectations and standards people have regarding different occupations.

Power inequalities vary with the general level of economic development, but many other factors contribute greatly to explain variations in participation in collective decision-making. The content of values and the degree of value integration contribute to our understanding. After all, legitimacy rests on norms and what is perceived as legitimate also rests on expectations. Related to such expectations is the actual balance of exchange struck between persons with varying political strength. Relative organizational strength and control of the means of violence also fundamentally affect the degree of political inequality.

We should note that the theoretical approaches examined do not extensively treat the role of exchange and complementary relations among different groups. But a full understanding of inequality must consider the way people exchange material resources, deference, and control. Differentiation and specialization of activities are the bases for inequality (Eisenstadt 1971) and exchange processes are one way in which differentiation produces inequality. Persons carrying out one set of activities can trade the benefits they receive for the services and products others produce. Such exchanges of rewards differ from coercion; they are not the same as satisfying functional needs for the collectivity as a whole. We need to consider how persons in different roles trade deference as well as material resources with each other. An imbalance in the exchange gives one party power over the other (Blau 1964). Thus, if one party is dependent on the other for something it wants, the other can command obedience and deference as compensation.

Power, status, and class inequalities affect each other. People use the resources in one ranking system to better their position in another. High rank in one system is a resource that can be traded, in relations with other persons, to increase ranking in another hierarchy. This further complicates attempts to account for the variations in inequality with any single approach.

Which theoretical approach we think most correct influences what we think is possible about reducing or increasing different aspects of inequality and therefore what policies we pursue to bring about the changes we seek. We consider such matters in Chapter 14.

REFERENCES

ABRAHAMSON, MARK. 1973. "Functionalism and the Functional Theory of Stratification: An Empirical Assessment," *American Journal of Sociology* 78 (March):1236-1246.
BERG, IVAR. 1971. *Education and Jobs: The Great Training Robbery.* Boston: Beacon Press.
BLAU, PETER M. 1964. *Exchange and Power in Social Life.* New York: John Wiley.
BLAU, PETER M. 1977. *Inequality and Heterogeneity.* New York: Free Press.
BOSERUP, ESTER. 1970. *Woman's Role in Economic Development.* London: George Allen and Unwin.
BOULDING, ELISE MARIE BIORN-HANSEN. 1969. "The Effects of Industrialization on the Participation of Women in Society." Unpublished Ph.D. Dissertation, University of Michigan, Ann Arbor, Michigan.
BOULDING, ELISE. 1976. *The Underside of History: A View of Women Through Time.* Boulder, Colo.: Westview Press.
COLLINS, RANDALL. 1971. "Functional and Conflict Theories of Educational Stratification," *American Sociological Review* 36 (December):1002-1019.
COLLINS, RANDALL. 1975. *Conflict Sociology.* New York: Academic Press.
CUTRIGHT, PHILLIPS. 1963. "National Political Development." Pp. 569-582 in N. W. Polsby, R. A. Dentler, and P. A. Smith (eds.), *Politics and Social Life.* Boston: Houghton Mifflin.
CUTRIGHT, PHILLIPS. 1967. "Inequality: A Cross-National Analysis," *American Sociological Review* 32 (August):562-578.
CUTRIGHT, PHILLIPS. 1968. "Occupational Inheritance: A Cross-National Analysis," *American Journal of Sociology* 73 (January):400-416.
DAVIS, KINGSLEY. 1949. *Human Society.* New York: Macmillan.
DAVIS, KINGSLEY. 1962. "The Role of Class Mobility in Economic Development," *Population Review* 6 (July):67-73.
DAVIS, KINGSLEY, and WILBERT E. MOORE. 1945. "Some Principles of Stratification," *American Sociological Review* (April):242-249.
DOBSON, RICHARD B. 1977. "Mobility and Stratification in the Soviet Union." Pp. 297-329 in A. Inkeles, J. Coleman, and N. Smelser (eds.), *Annual Review of Sociology,* Vol. 3. Palo Alto, Calif.: Annual Reviews Inc.
EHRENREICH, BARBARA, and DEIDRE ENGLISH. 1973. *Witches, Midwives, and Nurses: A History of Women Healers.* Old Westbury, N.Y.: Feminist Press.
EISENSTADT, S. N. 1971. *Social Differentiation and Stratification.* Glenview, Ill.: Scott, Foresman.
ENGELS, FRIEDERICH. 1942. *The Origin of the Family, Private Property, and the State.* New York: International Publishers. (Originally published in 1884.)
GAMSON, WILLIAM A. 1975. *The Strategy of Social Protest.* Homewood, Ill.: Dorsey Press.

HALLER, ARCHIBALD O., and DAVID M. LEWIS. 1966. "The Hypothesis of Intersocietal Similarity in Occupational Prestige Hierarchies," *American Journal of Sociology* 72 (September):210-216.

HAZELRIGG, LAWRENCE E., and MAURICE A. GARNIER. 1976. "Occupational Mobility in Industrial Societies: A Comparative Analysis of Differential Access to Occupational Ranks in Seventeen Countries," *American Sociological Review* 41 (June):498-511.

HODGE, ROBERT W., DONALD J. TREIMAN, and PETER H. ROSSI. 1966. "A Comparative Study of Occupational Prestige." Pp. 309-321 in Reinhard Bendix and Seymour Martin Lipset (eds.), *Class, Status, and Power,* 2nd ed. New York: Free Press.

HOROWITZ, IRVING LOUIS. 1972. *Foundations of Political Sociology.* New York: Harper & Row.

HUGHES, EVERETT C. 1960. "The Professions in Society," *The Canadian Journal of Economics and Political Science* 26 (February):54-61.

INKELES, ALEX, and PETER H. ROSSI. 1956. "National Comparisons of Occupational Prestige," *American Journal of Sociology* 61 (January): 329-339.

JACKMAN, ROBERT W. 1975. *Politics and Social Equality: A Comparative Analysis.* New York: John Wiley.

JANOWITZ, MORRIS. 1964. *The Military in the Political Development of New Nations.* Chicago: University of Chicago Press.

KAPLAN, NORMAN. 1961. "Research Administration and the Administrator: U.S.S.R. and U.S.," *Administrative Science Quarterly* 6 (June):51-72.

KOBRIN, FRANCES E. 1966. "The American Midwife Controversy: A Crisis of Professionalization," *Bulletin of the History of Medicine* 40 (July-August):350-363.

KRIESBERG, LOUIS. 1962. "The Bases of Occupational Prestige," *American Sociological Review* 27 (April):236-244.

KRIESBERG, LOUIS. 1973. *The Sociology of Social Conflicts.* Englewood Cliffs, N.J.: Prentice-Hall.

KRIESBERG, LOUIS. 1978. "Comparing Explanations of Variations in Occupational Mobility in Industrial Societies." Unpublished paper.

LEWIS, LIONEL S., and JOSEPH LOPREATO. 1963. "Functional Importance and Prestige of Occupations," *Pacific Sociological Review* 6 (Fall):55-59.

LIPSET, SEYMOUR MARTIN. 1967a. *The First New Nation.* Garden City, N.Y.: Anchor Books.

LIPSET, SEYMOUR MARTIN. 1967b. *Revolution and Counterrevolution: Changes and Persistence in Social Structures.* New York: Basic Books.

LIPSET, SEYMOUR MARTIN, and HANS ZETTERBERG. 1966. "A Theory of Social Mobility." Pp. 561-573 in R. Bendix and S. M. Lipset (eds.), *Class, Status, and Power,* 2nd ed., New York: Free Press.

LISSAK, MOSHE. 1970. "Patterns of Change in Ideology and Class Structure in Israel." Pp. 141-161 in S. N. Eisenstadt, R. Bar Yosef, and C. Adler (eds.), *Integration and Development in Israel.* Jerusalem: Israel Universities Press.

MARWELL, GERALD. 1975. "Why Ascription? Parts of a More or Less Formal Theory of the Functions and Dysfunctions of Sex Roles," *American Sociological Review* 40 (August):445-455.

MIDLARSKY, MANUS, and RAYMOND TANTER. 1967. "Toward a Theory of Political Instability in Latin America," *Journal of Peace Research* (3):209-226.

MILLS, C. WRIGHT. 1956. *The Power Elite.* New York: Oxford University Press.

OFFE, CLAUS. 1976. *Industry and Inequality.* London: Arnold. Translated by J. Wickham. (Originally published in 1970.)

PARSONS, TALCOTT. 1943. "The Kinship System of the Contemporary United States," *American Anthropologist* 45:22-28. Reprinted in T. Parsons, *Essays in Sociological Theory.* Glencoe, Ill.: Free Press, 1949.

PARSONS, TALCOTT. 1953. "A Revised Analytical Approach to the Theory of Social Stratification." Pp. 92-128 in R. Bendix and S. M. Lipset (eds.), *Class, Status, and Power.* Glencoe, Ill.: Free Press.

PETRAS, JAMES, and DALE TOMICH. 1977. "Images and Realities of Violence: The United States and Latin America." Paper presented at the Annual American Sociological Association Meetings, Chicago, Illinois.

ROSEN, STEVEN (ed.) 1973. *Testing the Theory of the Military-Industrial Complex.* Lexington, Mass.: Heath.

ROSSI, PETER H., and ALEX INKELES. 1957. "Multidimensional Ratings of Occupations," *Sociometry* 20 (September):234-251.

RUBINSON, RICHARD, and DAN QUINLAN. 1977. "Democracy and Social Inequality: A Reanalysis," *American Sociological Review* 42 (August): 611-623.

SACKS, KAREN. 1974. "Engels Revisited: Women, the Organization of Production, and Private Property." Pp. 207-222 in M. Z. Rosaldo and L. Lampere (eds.), *Women, Culture, and Society.* Stanford, Calif.: Stanford University Press.

SANDY, PEGGY R. 1974. "Female Status in the Public Domain." Pp. 189-206 in M. Z. Rosaldo and L. Lamphere (eds.), *Women, Culture and Society.* Stanford, Calif.: Stanford University Press.

SARAPATA, ADAM, and WLEDZIMIERZ WESOLOWSKI. 1961. "The Evaluation of Occupations by Warsaw Inhabitants," *American Journal of Sociology* 66 (May):581-591.

SQUIRES, GREGORY D. 1977. "Education, Jobs, and Inequality: Functional and Conflict Models of Social Stratification in the United States," *Social Problems* 24 (April):436-450.

TAYLOR, CHARLES L., and MICHAEL C. HUDSON. 1972. *World Handbook of Political and Social Indicators*, 2nd ed. New Haven, Conn.: Yale University Press.

TREIMAN, DONALD J. 1970. "Industrialization and Social Stratification." Pp. 207-234 in Edward O. Laumann (ed.), *Social Stratification: Research and Theory for the 1970s.* Indianapolis: Bobbs-Merrill.

TREIMAN, DONALD J. 1977. *Occupational Prestige in Comparative Perspective.* New York: Academic Press.

VOLLMER, HOWARD M., and DONALD L. MILLS (eds.). 1966. *Professionalization.* Englewood Cliffs, N.J.: Prentice-Hall.

WEISS, JANE A., and FRANCISCO O. RAMIREZ with TERRY TRACY. 1975. "Female Participation in the Occupational System: A Comparative Institutional Analysis." Unpublished paper.

WOOD, JAMES R., and EUGENE A. WEINSTEIN. 1966. "Industrialization, Values, and Occupational Evaluation in Uruguay," *The American Journal of Sociology* 72 (July):47-57.

ZIMMER, TROY A. 1975. "Sexism in Higher Education: A Cross-National Analysis," *Pacific Sociological Review* 18 (January):59-67.

chapter 14

Possibilities of More Equality

I have a dream that one day this nation will rise up
and live out the true meaning of its creed:
"We hold these truths to be self-evident:
that all men are created equal."

I have a dream that one day on the red hills of Georgia
the sons of former slaves and the sons of former slaveowners
will be able to sit down together
at the table of brotherhood.

I have a dream. . . . *Martin Luther King, Jr.*

Some men see things as they are
and say why. I dream things that never were
and say why not.   *Robert F. Kennedy*

Throughout this book we have investigated types and variations of inequality. We have found that a society may be relatively equal in one dimension, but not another, and societies vary in inequality in each dimension. Therefore, it is conceivable that the degree of inequality in a given dimension can be modified. In this chapter, we consider programs which have been employed to reduce inequality, particularly in the United States; we examine possible programs and the probable limits on the reduction of inequality; and finally, look at trends and future prospects for increasing and decreasing inequality. These matters all are intertwined with moral questions, discussed in Chapter 1, and with understandings about the causes of inequality, considered in Chapters 11-13.

PAST PROGRAMS TO REDUCE INEQUALITY

Throughout the world, groups have struggled to reduce inequalities they regarded as unjust. We examined such efforts in Chapter 10. Now we focus on specific programs, generally government-sponsored or administrated, aimed at reducing some aspects of inequality. Many government programs not intended to either increase or decrease inequality nevertheless do affect inequality, and we must make at least passing reference to such programs. We concentrate on programs in societies with market economies and especially in the United States.

Class Inequality

The United States government and governments in other non-Communist countries pursue policies that affect inequality of outcome or are intended to do so. We examine inequalities in the distribution of income and wealth and also in the proportion of people who have more than minimal material resources.

Three sets of programs are considered: those pertaining to income transfers, those entailing the provision of services, and those impacting on class inequalities. We should keep in mind that governmental programs generally are intended to serve many purposes and reduction of inequality is not a primary one. Taxes, for example, are levied to raise money to support government activities. Even Federal income taxes, with rates that increase as income rises, are not primarily viewed as a means of redistributing income (Blum and Kalven, 1963). We will examine taxes only as they do relate to income transfers.

Income transfers. In the United States, as in other capitalist countries, the government is involved in many programs that take money from one set of people and give it to another. The social welfare programs are probably the most obvious examples. Some people refer to public assistance as welfare. Public assistance, however, is only a portion of the social welfare system, which consists of all the programs intended to maintain and protect income. Included are federally aided *public assistance* in the form of Aid to Families with Dependent Children (AFDC) and Supplementary Security Income (SSI), for the aged, blind, and disabled. In addition, unemployment compensation, workmen's compensation, the Old-Age, Survivors', and Disability Insurance (OASDI) program (social security and medicare) are part of the welfare system. These are called social *insurance* programs (Lynn 1977).

Welfare programs were developed as formal ways to provide for persons who fall victim to disability or illness and for their dependents. Widows and their dependent children, categorized as deserving of assistance, are supported through the welfare system (Matza 1966). Diverse principles underlie the establishment of such programs. One is the belief that everyone deserves minimal living conditions. Another is that insurance should be provided, since misfortune can strike anyone. The programs also ensure that people (especially children) will later be able to contribute to society or they compensate people for what they have already contributed to society.

Danziger and Plotnick (1977) examined the distribution of income before and after each transfer payment by the federal government. They used detailed household data from two surveys, one conducted in 1965 and one in 1975. Inequality was measured by the Gini ratio, computed from forty three income classes. The pretransfer income Gini in 1965 was 0.441 and in 1975 it was 0.476; inequality had increased by about 8 percent. The posttransfer income was a little more equally distributed: the 1965 Gini was 0.392 and in 1975 it was 0.408; an increase of 4 percent. Clearly, government cash transfers have helped lessen income inequality, and they helped somewhat more in 1975 than in 1965.

The programs considered thus far are all direct and explicit cash transfers. Other programs implicitly transfer income. When provisions of the federal income tax allow people to deduct certain kinds of expenses from their taxable income, it is a kind of income transfer, since the tax burden is carried by others who do not have such deductions. Such implicit transfers written into the tax laws are called tax expenditures. In the fiscal year 1971, deductions of medical expenses cost the federal government $1,900 million in lost tax revenues (Tussing 1975). Other items and sizes of tax expenditures in 1971, in millions of dollars, are listed below:

Deductibility of interest on home mortgages for owner-occupied homes	$2,400
Deductibility of property taxes for owner-occupied homes	$2,700

Exclusion for employee
pensions $3,650

Additional exemption,
retirement income credit,
and exclusion of OAS-
DHI income for the
aged $3,250

Deductibility by individ-
uals of charitable
contributions $3,200

These estimates were prepared by the Tax Analysis Staff of the U.S. Treasury (cited in Tussing 1975, p. 63).

The welfare program also provides subsidies to particular groups through special programs: farm price support programs and low-income housing subsidies, for example. Other programs, which are discussed later, attempt to affect market conditions in ways that will protect people's income and help insure a decent standard of living.

In general, benefits in the United States and in Europe offset the regressive effects of taxes to reduce income inequality for the lowest income households, but the benefits have little effect on other income groups. Clearly, some of the decrease in the proportion of the population who are living in poverty has been brought about by various transfer payments. Such programs reduce the rate of poverty, defined in terms of minimal standards.

Provision of services. In addition to income transfers, government programs offer many services, including medical care, recreation, and schooling. When these services are made available to persons regardless of income, they may not have any redistributive effect. Higher-income people can and do utilize universally available services more effectively than lower-income persons (Stigler 1970). For example, Hansen and Weisbrod (1969), studying higher public education in California, concluded that higher-income families were more likely to send their children to colleges and universities than lower-income families. Moreover, the level of schooling and, consequently, the amount of subsidy per student also varied by family income. Thus, the subsidy for students attending a junior college, a state college, and a university were $1,050, $3,810, and $4,890, respectively. Pechman (1970), however, points out that if one takes into account what higher income groups pay out in taxes, they pay for the benefits they receive.

Wilensky (1975) argues that these studies ignore how social background affects *quality* of education and that this is the most important regressive effect of higher education. This can be seen even in California, which has the world's largest mass higher-education system. California has three tiers of higher education: two-year community colleges, state colleges and universities, and the University of California campuses. The costs of educating students is lowest in community colleges, greatest at the University of California campuses. Recruitment and self-selection by social background produces student bodies of different class backgrounds in each of the tiers. The community colleges train people for jobs as bank clerks, X-ray technicians, engineering aides, and other semi-technical occupations. Graduates of the state colleges and universities enter middle-class positions in teaching, commerce, and industry. The University of California campuses channel their graduates into professions and higher executive positions.

Provision of medical care and social services is more likely to be redistributive than provision of educational services. In this country, as in most others, educational opportunities are allocated on apparent merit or ability rather than on need or simple equality. The provision of social services related to health and welfare are more egalitarian in distribution. During the 1960s, the programs providing assistance in kind greatly increased. For example, after urging by President Kennedy and President Johnson, Congress enacted food stamp legislation in 1964. Benefit outlays for food stamps were $36 million in 1965, $251 million in 1969, and $2,865 million in 1974. Medical benefits rose from $296 million in 1965 to $5,883 million in 1974 (Plotnick and Skidmore 1975, Table 6.9).

The multiplicity and complexity of these many income transfer programs and social services makes an assessment of their consequences very difficult. Furthermore, the extent to which these programs are redistributive depends on their financing. Thus, if the taxes that are collected and that pay for the programs are regressive, then the redistributive effects of the programs may be canceled out, even if lower-income persons benefit disproportionally. Furthermore, the effects may be different for different segments of the population.

Since many of the welfare programs are directed particularly at the poor, we would expect that, at least for them, the programs would be somewhat egalitarian in outcome. This seems to be the case (Wilensky 1975). Lampman (1971) analyzed the redistributive effects of all kinds of transfers. He used family expenditure data and very broad definitions of income transfers, including cash and noncash and public and private transfers. Lampman calculated that in 1967 transfers totaled $132 billion. He further calculated how much went to families that were poor prior to the transfers; they received $49.2 billion, half in the form of public assistance and social insurance. They paid out $10.7 billion in taxes, so their net gain was $36.5 billion. The nonpoor contributed $121.3 in taxes and other transfers and received $83.8 billion. He estimates that all the taxes and benefits combined raised the proportion of income the poor receive from 3 percent of predistribution income to 9 percent of predistribution income.

Reynolds and Smolensky (1977) examined the overall distribution of income as effected by all public expenditures, taking into account all government revenues. They included government expenditures on education and highway as well as social security and other welfare programs. They also took into account state and local sales taxes, social security contributions, and federal income taxes. They calculated Gini ratios for income distribution before and after taking into account government benefits and burdens. It must be understood that such calculations are based on many contestable assumptions about allocating taxes and benefits. Although they made a variety of different assumptions, we will discuss only what they consider the standard assumptions, made by most analysts. Reynolds and Smolensky made their calculations for 1950, 1961, and 1970. For 1970, they estimate the initial income distribution to have a Gini ratio of 0.446; after taking into account government taxes and expenditures, the Gini ratio is 0.339. In other words, government fiscal activities on the whole are somewhat redistributive.

Interestingly, Reynolds and Smolensky found that between 1950 and 1970 the initial income distributions became more unequal. Inequality in the final distribution of income, however, did not increase; rather, it decreased slghtly. This was not due to any greater progressivity in taxes. Indeed, taxes became somewhat more regressive during the period. It was the rise in government transfer payments that preserved or slightly increased equality of the final income distribution (Haveman 1977).

Other programs. A wide variety of programs are directed at the economy itself and at the wage structure in ways which affect income distribution. For example, the federal government legislates a minimum wage standard, partly intended to ensure that persons working full time receive at least a minimum standard of living. But because wages are not related to number of dependents, a person can work full time, receive a minimum wage, and still not have a minimally adequate income for his or her family. Moreover, not all jobs are covered by minimum wage standards. Such legislation, nevertheless, serves as a ceiling for public assistance benefits (Pivan and Cloward 1971).

Many federal government policies regarding interest rates, deficit spending, corporate taxes, and public service employment affect unemployment, inflation, and the rate of growth of the economy. Unemployment obviously increases the incidence of poverty and affects the general income distribution. High rates of inflation can also affect the incidence of poverty and income distribution, because inflation hurts people with fixed income more than others.

None of the programs or policies we have considered thus far have substantial impact upon inequalities of wealth. Yet wealth inequalities are an important generator of income inequalities as well as of power and status inequalities. Inheritance taxes do not appreciably alter inequalities of wealth. In some countries, particularly where there have been substantial land reforms and where industries have been nationalized, government policies have modified wealth inequalities.

Equality of Opportunity

One of the great goals of liberal societies has been to improve the equality of opportunity. Even in social democratic countries, the emphasis has been not to substantially reduce inequality in the distribution of income and wealth so much as to provide everyone with a basic minimum standard of living and an equal chance to move up (Parkin 1971).

In the United States, the major thrust of the war on poverty, launched in 1964, was to create more equal opportunities. Programs to directly transfer money or to otherwise directly equalize outcomes were not part of the initial policies (Haveman 1977). Rather, a variety of programs were aimed at improving opportunities for the poor to help themselves. Training to give poor persons needed work skills was to be achieved through the Job Corps, the Neighborhood Youth Corps, and the Manpower Development and Training Act. To improve the education of the children of the poor, another set of programs was begun: Head Start, Upward Bound, and Teacher Corps. Head Start, for example, was intended to give preschool children educationally relevant experiences, which they presumably did not get in their homes. They would then not begin school at a disadvantage. The effects of poor nutrition and of illness, which interfered with education and with getting and holding jobs, were to be countered by establishing emergency food aid and school lunch programs and by neighborhood health centers and Medicaid.

Many of these programs were premised on the theories we have previously discussed. A culture of poverty was thought to exist; the poor were culturally deprived, and this was thought to impede moving out of poverty. Improving the skills and attitudes of low-income people would increase their human capital, and they would be employable and earn more in the competitive labor market.

These programs were only moderately successful in reducing the incidence of poverty, but they probably helped lessen status and power inequalities. Together with the expectations raised by the war on poverty, they did help bring about the expansion of large public assistance and social insurance income transfers. These transfers, not originally planned as part of the war on poverty, expanded during the 1960s and significantly lowered the incidence of poverty (Plotnick and Skidmore 1975; Haveman 1977). The war on poverty, with all its problems, stimulated demand for greater income transfers and benefits in kind. The stigma of public assistance was lessened. Government officials became more aware of low-income persons and more sensitive to their needs. As the status and power of women, minorities, and poor people improved, their demands for greater income transfers were heeded more than they would otherwise have been. This is consistent with the ideas of the conflict-and-coercion approach to explaining inequality.

Education is often viewed as a fundamental mechanism of opportunity. Equal access to schools of equal quality, therefore, is an important component of equal opportunity. This is true whether persons are rich or poor, male or female, members of dominant groups or minorities. Because most schools are supported by taxes, governments determine, to a great extent, educational opportunities. Some programs initiated during the war on poverty attempted to increase equality of the educational experience for low-income persons. Some were designed to teach basic cognitive skills, some to teach specific job skills, and some to increase the number of years spent in schools. In some of these areas there was improvement; in others there was little or none. Furthermore, the improvements have done little to alleviate poverty (Levin 1977).

The expansion of schools and of colleges and universities has also been viewed as a way to provide more equal opportunity. In other countries that have tried to equalize opportunities, the expansion of universities has been an important effort. Yet this does not in itself produce equality of opportunity; it can create a credential inflation. The expansion of higher education can simply result in the requirement of more schooling by employers. If everyone has a high school diploma, that credential becomes less valuable as a screening device. When more and more people have a college degree, that credential has less competitive value. In addition, qualitative differences (or presumed qualitative differences) can continue to channel people of higher and lower class backgrounds differentially. This is what we would expect from the arguments of the social conflict theorists.

Status Inequality

Status depends on agreed-upon value standards and hence might seem un-susceptible to government policies. But we have noted that efforts by socialist and communist governments to influence occupational prestige have had some success. Perhaps prestige is altered not by propaganda and educational campaigns, but by actual changes in conditions of work; increased pay, for example, may increase a position's prestige. Treiman (1977) so argues on the basis of his comparative analysis.

Within the United States, extensive direct campaigns to improve the relative status of racial minorities and of women have not been waged. But in recent years, court decisions and legislation have placed the weight of the law and the authority of the government against discrimination. These policies implicitly assert the status equality of Americans, regardless of race or sex.

These policies have come about in part through the demands and persuasive efforts of minority group members and women. The pressures for improvement of status and recognition of equality have altered the language; it is now the blacks and the women themselves who help determine how they are to be regarded and referred to as well as how they are to be treated.

The reduction in social discrimination against blacks, in public accommo-dations and in schools, has been most marked in the Southern states. Attitudinal changes indicating greater status equality have occurred relatively quickly in the South.

Earlier in this book we used differences in occupational distribution and income as indicators of possible discrimination and, therefore, of low status. On the basis of such indicators, the relative status of blacks has been slowly improv-ing. Significantly, Farley (1977) has found that the differences between blacks and whites in education, occupation, and income declined not only in the relatively prosperous 1960s, but also in the not-so-prosperous 1970s. This suggests that reductions in racial prejudice, more liberal government policies, and demands of blacks have been a palpable force. In addition, the increasing urbanization of blacks and the consequences of advances made in earlier generations also help account for the continuing improvement.

Although women's participation in the labor force has increased steadily, remarkably little change is seen in the occupational distribution or in income differences between men and women.

Power Inequality

Interestingly, some government policies in recent years have been directed at increasing power equality. Administrative, judicial, and legislative actions have increased the power of those with little political strength. Thus, civil rights and voting rights legislation have helped enfranchise blacks in the South; the Supreme Court decision requiring regular revision of congressional districts to reflect population changes has helped give equal representation to all persons, regardless of where they live. In addition, the war on poverty included a mandate to see the maximum feasible participation of the local poor, particularly in community action programs (Moynihan 1969). Actual participation of low-income persons varied; it was low in Chicago and greater in New York, Detroit, and Syracuse (Clark and Hopkins 1969; Kramer 1969; Greenstone and Peterson 1973). In general, such local efforts to encourage participation strengthened the political resources of the poor and of blacks and helped spur participation in many spheres of governmental action.

In addition, the collective reactions of blacks and other minorities to their low status have taken the form of striving for political power. Civil rights groups conducted voter registration drives, and campaigns for legislation that would give them access to political power; these very efforts increased the organizational base for individuals and groups seeking political office. Women's organizations have taken similar action.

Not all government actions have aimed at reducing power inequalities. As discussed in Chapter 7, particularly during the mid-1950s and again in the late 1960s and early 1970s, some agencies of the government invaded citizens' privacy in an attempt to interfere with and repress protest organizations.

Interplay and Determinants of Programs

Some government programs reinforce each other to lessen inequality. For example, efforts to increase employment opportunities which reduce income inequality, would also tend to reduce discrimination and thus contribute to lessening status inequality. Low income or low status groups can use, and have used, their increased power to garner more favorable tax and benefit policies. The struggle of women and minorities for equal rights has become institutionalized with legally sanctioned procedures for advancing equality.

On the other hand, programs that decrease one aspect of inequality sometimes tend to increase another. For example, government efforts to reduce class inequalities may require greater centralization of power in the hands of government officials.

Governmental programs to assure citizens minimal living standards are a universal modern phenomena. With industrialization and urbanization has come the welfare state. It emerged earlier in some countries—Germany, for one—than in others, such as the United States, and it has expanded at different rates. On the whole, however, researchers have found a strong, positive relationship between the level of economic development and the extent of welfare programs (Cutright 1965; Wilensky and Lebeaux 1958; Aaron 1967). Furthermore, considerable similarity in policies is found among the relatively developed countries, despite differences in political ideology (Wilensky 1975). This holds true even when we compare countries that have market economies with countries that have centrally planned economies (Pryor 1968). The relationship between economic development and welfare expenditures probably helps to account for the relationship between economic development and class equality.

Wilensky (1975) has pointed out an important additional variable affecting the extent of welfare programs: the proportion of old people in the population. This is important since many programs of the welfare state are designed to provide security and benefits for the elderly. Elderly persons tend to form a large and politically influential proportion of the population in economically developed countries, which helps explain the relationship between economic development and social welfare programs.

Among the economically developed countries, welfare expenditures vary widely. The United States spends much less of its national income on welfare than, for example, Austria, West Germany, Belgium, Netherlands, France, Sweden, Italy, and Czechoslovakia. In 1966 the United States spent 7.9 percent of its GNP for social security programs: Austria, West Germany, and Belgium spent 21 percent, 19.6 percent and 18.5 percent, respectively. Among the twenty two countries for which comparable data were gathered, only Japan spent, at 6.2 percent, less (Wilensky 1975, Table 2).

Many factors account for this range of spending and for the relatively low expenditures in the United States. Wilensky argues that welfare-state programs tend to be more extensive in countries with centralized governments, with a strongly organized working class, with modest rates of intergenerational occupational and educational mobility, and where the private welfare system is not highly developed and the middle strata do not regard their tax burdens as grossly unfair compared to the rich.

In America specifically, involvement with the Cold War has also probably depressed the allocation of funds for welfare programs. Wars that entail large-scale mobilization have an equalitarian effect, as previously noted. However, heavy military expenditures compete with social welfare programs for funding and, in the absence of total mobilization, inhibit the growth of welfare programs and benefits (Wilensky 1975).

PROGRAMS FOR GREATER EQUALITY

What policies could bring about greater class, status, or power equality? We will consider answers to that question and point out some of the problems in implementing them.

Class Inequality

Some people, using the motivation and functional importance approach, express concern that if class inequality is reduced, the incentive for work would be reduced. They argue that current class differences are needed to motivate people to work. But there certainly are reasons to doubt that the existing degree of inequality is needed to produce adequate incentives. For example, Thurow (1976) has pointed out that the inequality among all persons in the United States is much greater than the inequality among those who earn money. Presumably, the inequality among working persons is incentive enough for them to do what they are doing. If the income inequality of the total population, then, were about the same as that of the working force, we would have much more equality and no change in the incentives for the labor force.

Overall inequality in the distribution of income could be reduced by more extensive transfer payments and publicly provided services (Miller and Roby 1970). One obstacle to this in the United States is a widely shared belief that people who receive transfer payments or services should be "deserving." Such moral evaluations tend to limit transfer arrangements, since people often disagree about who is worthy enough to receive aid. Moral evaluations are less salient when transfer payments are indirect, as they are for groups such as home owners, ship builders, tobacco farmers, and petroleum producers. But, insofar as the competition for government benefits is based on a variety of grounds from incentive to national security and protection of particular industries, such transfers will not effectively decrease inequality.

Income equality can also be increased by reducing earning inequalities, but this is particularly difficult for the government to effect within a relatively open labor market. Programs that significantly increase the supply of persons for high-paying positions and reduce the availability of persons for low-paying positions can be developed. For example, public funds might be made available to increase the training of persons for the higher-paying professions. Discrimination against applicants for higher-paying jobs might be reduced. Earnings from low-paying positions could be raised if employment rates were high. These programs would reduce competition for low-paying jobs.

Wealth inequality is another matter. It is much greater than income inequality and it generates many other kinds of inequality. Some people contend that wealth inequality is necessary for the functioning of the economy. One argument is that amassing personal wealth is an incentive for work. This is doubtful, given the fact that most people work very hard and have little wealth beyond what they spend on consumables, yet many people with great wealth do not work hard. Another argument is that extensive private ownership of the means of production is necessary to assure on-going investments. That is, persons must amass large fortunes so as to provide the necessary capital for investment. However, in our present state of capitalism, investment funds can be raised by corporations largely from internal sources.

The opportunity to amass wealth and the right to pass it on to others through inheritance is often argued as inherent to the nature of property. Actually, just which rights are included in the ownership of property is always socially determined. The use of property is circumscribed in many ways in every society. Its appreciation in value could be regarded as a social product, which the community therefore has a claim on. The extent of ownership is always in contention. How far, for example, does ownership of land extend into the space above and how far into the ground below?[1]

It is possible that the concentration of wealth in the United States could be greatly reduced without adversely affecting the functioning of our economy, but to do so would surely transform the society radically. It is difficult to see how this could be done within the current procedures of our society. Inheritance taxes might be greatly increased, but they are largely avoidable by the wealthy. Those European social-democratic countries that have tried to reduce wealth inequalities by raising inheritance taxes have not found them very effective.

Reduction of wealth inequalities is not a popular demand. Few seem to begrudge the rich their wealth. Dissatisfaction with one's own circumstances is a greater motivation for protest and change. Indeed, the existence of rich persons seems to offer many people in the United States a promise that they or their children might someday also become rich.

The reduction of the proportion of people in poverty has been the subject of special concern in recent years. Many proposals to reform the social welfare programs in the United States have been put forth and debated. Some are intended to reduce waste, confusion, and numerous undesired side effects of current welfare programs. Some could effectively end income poverty in the United States: poor families could simply be given enough money to bring their income up to the minimal level. They would not pay taxes on income received below that level.

Recent public discussion has included proposals for child allowances,

---

[1] In some countries (for example, Mexico) private ownership does not extend below the soil. Thus, oil discovered at subsoil levels belongs to the country as a whole. In the United States, space at a certain height above the ground is not privately owned and at an even higher level is not under the jurisdiction of any government.

universal income supplement, negative income tax, the family assistance plan, and work-benefit and income support plans (Kriesberg 1970; Marmor 1971). Child allowances give a family a set amount of money (perhaps $50.00 a month for each preschool child). As a way of reducing poverty, this would not be very efficient, since money would be given to nonpoor and poor alike. But if it were coupled with the ending of income tax deductions for dependents, it would involve a significant income transfer. It could also be seen as recognition that rearing children is productive labor and hence status-enhancing for mothers.

The President's Commission on Income Maintenance, appointed by President Johnson in 1968, proposed a universal income supplement (UIS) plan. Under this system the federal government would provide a fixed benefit for each adult ($750) and child ($450) and reduce benefits by 50 cents for each dollar earned. This would be a universal program; it would provide incentive to earn money, but at the proposed rate it would leave a family below the poverty line if the family had no earnings.

The negative income tax was originally proposed by economist Milton Friedman, and several variations of it have been proposed by many persons, including presidential candidate George McGovern. Under this plan the concept of income tax would be extended so that when income falls below a certain level, the tax becomes negative. The federal government would transfer payments to bring the family income up to a minimal level. From that level up to another fixed level (for example, the poverty line), families would be taxed on their earnings. One such plan was described in *The Yale Law Journal* (1969). According to this plan, the federal government would set a basic income supplement of $3,200 for a family of four. If the family had no earnings, it would receive the $3,200. A matter of concern in all these plans is to provide an incentive for earning wages. If earned income is heavily taxed, the cost of the program is reduced but the incentive to earn money or to change to a higher-paying job is also reduced. In this model, a 50 percent tax was proposed. That is, a family earning $1,000 would keep $500 and receive an additional $3,200 from the government (the government would receive $500 in taxes). A family earning $6,400 would receive no transfer payment and would keep all $6,400 income after taxes. This program would be administered through the Internal Revenue Service.

The Family Assistance Plan (FAP) was proposed by the Nixon Administration in 1969; Congress rejected it in 1972 (Marmor and Rein 1973). The FAP was a variation of the negative income tax plan, but benefits were set at a low level and it was to be available only to families with children. It set the guarantee level at $1,500 per year for a family of four—a figure that was 45 percent of the official poverty level. A difficult problem in setting any levels of benefit to be provided by the federal government is that cost of living and wage rates vary among the states, as do the current state levels of support. Thus eight states paid benefits below FAPs proposed federal minimum.

The FAP, like many other welfare proposals, stresses negative sanctions as well as positive incentives. Recipients must accept "suitable" work or training or face deductions from their grant. Actually, considerable evidence indicates that people work without such negative sanctions. Having some secure income provides a base, which is an incentive to earn additional income (Kriesberg 1970). Experiments with graduated work-incentive programs, conducted by Mathematica, Inc., and by the Institute for Research on Poverty at the University of Wisconsin, indicate that income transfers reduce the labor supply slightly among wives and hardly at all among males (Marmor and Rein 1973; Pechman and Timpane 1975; Watts and Rees 1977).

In 1977, President Carter sent a message to Congress proposing an overhaul of the welfare system (*New York Times*, 7 August 1977). Central to this plan were two kinds of benefits that, again, were variations on a negative income tax (see Figure 14.1). One, called income support, is for the aged, blind, or disabled and for single parents of children under 14 years. A family of four, eligible for full support and with no other income, would receive $4,200 a year. Earned income would be taxed at 50 percent and federal payments would be phased out entirely when the family earns $8,000 in outside income.

The other major benefit would be the work-benefit program. This is for two-parent families, single people, childless couples, and single parents with no children under 14 years. In these families, someone is expected to work full time. For a family of four, the basic federal payment would be $2,300. The family could earn up to $3,800 in outside income without paying taxes on the earnings. Above that level and up to earnings of $8,400, the outside income would be taxed at 50 percent.

These two programs are designed to provide minimal support and incentives for employment. This is consistent with two social goals that the public generally seem to regard as contradictory: to provide for the deserving needy and to push all who can to work. As already noted, the evidence does not indicate that there is actually any contradiction for most poor people (Goodwin 1972). Political support for welfare reform, nevertheless, is dependent upon balancing these concerns. The proposed welfare proposal goes further and includes an effort to secure jobs for the principal wage earner in low-income families with children; this is an important element in a comprehensive program to meet the needs of poor people.

As a way to reform public assistance programs a negative income tax system has several advantages: It would be less costly to administer and be easier to modify than the many public assistance and social insurance programs currently in existence. Built-in work incentives can be included easily; people can begin to draw benefits and to stop drawing them more easily than at present. However, difficulties exist in gaining political support and politicians and government officials find it easier to increase services and payments in kind rather than directly transfer money. Nevertheless, coupled with a major tax reform, a negative income tax would reduce inequality a little and could virtually end poverty.

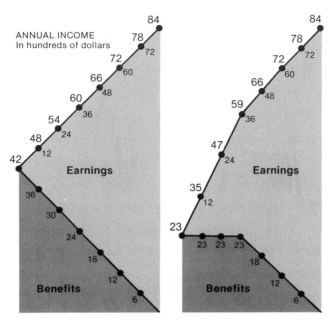

INCOME SUPPORT[1]   **WORK BENEFIT[2]**

FIGURE 14.1   *Proposed income benefit programs*

[1] For aged, blind or disabled, and for single parents of children under 14. (Single parents with children aged 7 to 14 will be required to accept part-time work and, if appropriate day care is available, full-time work.) A family of four eligible for full income support would receive a basic Federal benefit of $4,200 a year. Benefits would be reduced 50 cents for each $1 in outside income earned, with the Federal payments phased out entirely if the family earns $8,400 in outside income.

[2] For two-parent families, single people, childless couples, and single parents with no children under 15, all of whom are expected to work full time. A family of four in this category would receive a basic Federal benefit of $2,300. The family could earn up to $3,800 in outside income without benefits being reduced. From $3,800 up to $8,400 earned in outside income, the Federal benefit would be reduced by 50 cents for each $1 earned.

Source: The White House, cited in *The New York Times,* 7 Aug. 1977.

Poverty, defined in terms of a minimal income level, can be abolished. The United States Government estimated that in 1973 the amount of money needed to bring all the families and individuals who are below the official poverty line up to that line was $11,975 million dollars (United States Bureau of Census 1976). That is 2.8 percent of the federal, state, and local revenues and less than 1 percent of the GNP in 1973. If the problem of poverty were met comprehensively, many people could actually earn more of the income they need. Taxes paid on earnings and the decreased need for social services and subsidies would eventually reduce the costs to the nonpoor segments of the population.

Status Inequality

The possibilities of reducing inequality of ascribed status would seem to be particularly limited since the very idea of ascribed status implies that people in a society regard those status rankings as fixed at birth. But status inequality based upon ascribed characteristics such as race, ethnicity, or sex is not securely based in the American value system (Myrdal 1944; Williams 1951). The Declaration of Independence proclaims that we are all created equal, with certain "inherent and inalienable rights, that among these are life, liberty, and the pursuit of happiness." This provides a basis for claiming equality of respect. Nevertheless, ethnicity and race have been used to rank people and low-ranking persons are discriminated against in ways that reduce their power and class levels. Their lack of political power and low income can then, in turn, become the bases for according them low status. Consequently, policies that create more equality in power and class can also decrease status inequality. Differences in life style may persist but not all differences need be hierarchical; they can be acknowledged without being ranked.

Status inequality based on sex has special peculiarities because of the critical role played by sex differences in the family and the pivotal role of the family in relation to other societal institutions. Essential equality of status between men and women probably requires fundamental alteration in many other institutions. For example, child-rearing and housekeeping tasks and responsibility would have to be shared or else made external to the family. Within the occupational system, jobs would have to be restructured to assure that persons with familial responsibilities could remain employable. Only then could careers be pursued by men and women without the subsidy provided by a "wife," someone who maintains a household, assists in the spouse's career activities, and is emotionally supportive.

Yet we can make some progress toward greater status equality between men and women without such radical transformations, perhaps by providing or expanding services that make possible the same set of options for women as for men. For example, the establishment of day-care centers for children could enable women to take regular jobs. Antidiscrimination and affirmative action programs, although limited in attaining their objectives, can have some impact.[2]

Greater equality in the status accorded different occupations could come

[2] As noted, increased equality in one area may lessen it in another. Thus, the greater participation of women in the labor force in the past has acted to decrease poverty and income inequality, because women worked to supplement a husband's earnings. More recently, women married to higher-income husbands have entered the labor force in increasing numbers. They do so with generally higher education and assume jobs with higher earnings than women in the past. This, in turn, will tend to increase family income inequality.

about through several changes, some related to changes in the occupational incumbents. Because the status of the occupational incumbents reflects on the status of the position, as occupations are less segregated by sex and race, some of the prestige differential of the occupations would be reduced. In general, increased equality in wages and working conditions lead to increased equality in prestige. However, the consistency and stability of occupational prestige ratings, which we described earlier, indicates that there are considerable limits to how far occupational status equality will go.

Power Equality

In the United States, there are no extensive popular efforts or even extensive discussions about lessening power inequalities. But various groups want to increase their power in specific areas. Those efforts and the possibilities they suggest might counter the inherent tendencies of persons with greater power to use what they have to gain more.

Individuals' minimal power, the rights of individuals for autonomy, could be increased throughout the world, and even in the United States. Restrictions on governmental intervention into essentially private spheres has varied over time, reflecting, in part, collective opinion and judicial and legislative interpretations of public opinion and tradition. Civil rights can be strengthened by legislative safeguards and further buttressed by establishing offices to help protect citizens. The institution of an ombudsman's office is one such device; persons holding such offices respond to citizens' complaints against government agencies.

Variations in autonomy also greatly depend upon the resources persons have to protect themselves. As individuals and as groups, then, increased class and status equality will produce greater equality in minimal power. In addition, organizations devoted to the protection of human and civil rights can be an important support. Since governments themselves are a threat to, as well as protector of, civil rights, transnational organizations to protect the rights of persons are particularly important. Amnesty International, for example, monitors and publicizes instances of governmental repression and has assisted individuals in gaining liberty from prison and torture in many countries of the world. The expansion and proliferation of transnational groups based upon ethnicity, religion, and occupation can also serve to protect individual liberties in each country.

Participation in collective decision making could become more equalitarian in the immediate spheres of social life. The American tradition of local control in many areas of life has been strengthened as previously excluded groups are included. This is illustrated by the workings of schools and government agencies. In one important sphere, however, popular participation is relatively limited, at least compared to some other countries. That is in the work sphere. The possibilities of greater worker control over the conditions of employment and participation in the governance of the factories and offices are considerable and are only beginning to be realized (Hunnius et al. 1973).

Participation in collective decision making beyond the local community is hindered by the increasing scope, apparent complexity, and technical nature of the issues. Yet even here, some gains are possible. The use of nonviolent action to argue a point of view has given groups who had not been included in decision making a greater voice. We see this in issues relating to abortion, environmental pollution, defense expenditures, and integration, to name a few.

The general increase in the level of education makes technical decisions more understandable to more people than in previous generations (Inglehart 1978). The proliferation of adversary interest groups, with their respective experts, can also illuminate issues. Conflicting information could be presented in ways that would facilitate wider participation in making collective decisions. For example, citizen advisory boards could be established for many governmental agencies. The growth of the consumer movement and of groups concerned with conservation and pollution have provided new grounds for citizen representation on advisory boards for agencies at various government levels.

The expansion of technology and its increasing impact on society has augmented the relative power of those scientists and engineers working most closely with each new innovation. Yet scientists often disagree among themselves about the implications of an innovation and hence about decisions regarding its use, as they have about nuclear power. Disputes among experts may seem to make it even more difficult for the public to participate in making crucial decisions affecting their lives. One way to help the layperson make informed judgments is to create science courts. Within an adversary setting, experts would take different sides of a controversial technical issue, directly confronting each other before a panel who would ensure that the disagreeing experts focus their discussion on the same matters of fact.

Decisions about science and technology also involve value choices and the people themselves are the best judge of the values they wish to advance. What they need to know, as accurately as possible, are the likely consequences of alternative developments.

The concentration of power in making decisions affecting the country as a whole can be self-generating. This can be countered by increased strength of, and popular participation in, political parties. One vehicle for this might be greater bonds between local political party units and those at the national level, which would provide additional channels for information and control to flow from the ranks to the leaders. The development of voluntary associations expressing the interests of the relatively less powerful would also serve as an instrument of power equalization.

The expansion of the national government's activities and responsibilities and the increased complexity and interrelatedness of those activities does tend to lessen popular participation in collective decision-making while it increases the interests of people to be involved in those decisions. The growth of governmental activities tends to put more power into the hands of those in high office. A basic handicap to increased power equality derives from the great power of those in high office.

The proposals discussed have generally been limited to domestic programs and forces. Yet, the findings reported in this book demonstrate how inextricably intertwined internal inequality is with external relations. Thus, if the United States government is able to develop less militarily hostile relations abroad and even reduce reliance on violence and threats of violence, domestic political equality will have an opportunity to increase. More political equality will mean more effective influence by the poorer classes and hence will foster class equality. It is true that income equality has increased during major wars, apparently as a consequence of the massive societal mobilization which major wars have produced. But, a major war increasingly risks nuclear devastation, and living with the threat of war while conducting intense international conflict does not foster class equality.

This discussion of possible ways to increase equality is based on my synthesis of the theoretical explanations of inequality examined in the previous chapters and on my beliefs about the social, economic, and political conditions in this country and the world. I have drawn particularly on the conflict approach and have assumed that grievances regarding inequality are not widespread; people are not pressing for fundamental changes, except perhaps for members of some status categories. Consequently, the proposals discussed have been essentially reformist and dependent on small changes resulting from political pressures.

If the reader gives greater weight to a Marxist approach the suggestions for ways to reduce inequality would be different. One would then stress the need to alter the distribution of wealth in a fundamental fashion if changes in other dimensions and aspects of inequality are to be made. Depending on one's reading of the present conditions and pressures for changing the distribution of class, status, or power, more or less radical transformations might be proposed. If, however, the reader gives particular weight to a functionalist perspective, proposals might emphasize education and changes in values; the possibilities of making major or even many minor alterations would seem more circumscribed and less susceptible to manipulation than those I described.

TRENDS

Aside from the possibilities outlined above, we can reflect on what seems to be happening and what might continue to happen. The dual trends of increasing equality in some areas and decreasing inequality in others should be noted. They are a consequence of a wide variety of social forces. The theories we have been considering posit some forces as being more significant than others.

Although I will not attempt to systematically relate the trends to the theories we have studied, their relevance is implicit.

Increasing Pluralism

Consensus about status in American society has declined in recent years. Within occupations, the prestige hierarchy of positions and locations is less clear as people take a greater variety of values into consideration in choosing and changing positions. A greater variety of life styles are recognized as legitimate than heretofore. Even the primacy of material rewards seems to have declined, particularly within the younger generations. Obviously it is still very important, but the consensus about its significance has declined (Inglehart 1978).

We also see a decline in the consensus about status ranking of race, ethnic, and sex differences. People regarded as having low status are increasingly likely to reject that evaluation. Differences in ways of thinking and acting are increasingly viewed as valid and as unrelated to status. In general, agreement about the essential human equality of persons of different races is increasingly evident. This trend is likely to continue, given the evidence about the relationship between education and age with such agreement: it is more evident among the young and more educated (Stember 1961). Throughout the world we see signs of increasing claims for ethnic autonomy, even as national states often seek greater national authority (Boulding 1979).

Increasing Importance of Education

Several observers, most notably Daniel Bell (1973), have argued that the role of education or knowledge is of growing importance in social life. One implication of this trend is that schooling and credentials become increasingly significant in occupational mobility. Insofar as education is equally available, it increases intergenerational occupational exchange mobility. There may well be more equality of opportunity on an intergenerational basis. Formal schooling, insofar as it entails acquiring credentials for different positions, however, can impede mobility within a lifetime. Expansion of educational opportunities at mid-career stages is one way to overcome that difficulty, but it also reinforces the propriety of requiring credentials.

If formal training were a requirement for taking positions and the training were competitive, with equal opportunity for everyone, then the possibility of a meritocracy would be created (Young 1961). We would be ruled by people who were placed in high positions on the basis of their "merits." This would give them more authority than persons in high-ranking positions already possess. It might also reduce the availability of capable persons to work for and with groups that are in lower-ranking positions. The disparities in resources, prestige, and authority between people would increase.

Countervailing forces, referred to in the previous discussion of increasing pluralism, mitigate against that development. I think it is more likely that the increasing importance of education will provide the basis for yet another ranking system, as indicated by attention to experts. The growing significance of knowledge and of schooling adds to the proliferation of elites and offers a new basis for ranking people. The proliferation reduces the consensus about status and the consensus underlying authority.

Environmental and Social Constraints

America, like most Western countries, has had its systems of inequality shaped during a period of world history marked by a high rate of increasing productivity and surplus. We may be entering a period where the costs of growth will become greater and greater; hence, the rate of growth will be smaller. Much of the growth in surplus has depended on low-cost energy; as fuel becomes more expensive, so too will many other primary resources. A slowing down in the rate of increase in the surplus or possibly a stabilization of per capita surplus would place a great strain on the stratification system. It would lessen the tolerance people have of the existing inequalities. With increasing surpluses, persons at each rank level could improve their absolute position—which is some compensation for not changing their relative position—but such improvement may become less and less likely.

Aside from such constraints, as basic material needs are satisfied, the goods and services people consume are more dependent on relative position. As Hirsch (1977) points out, one needs *relatively* more than others to enjoy many kinds of goods and services. If nearly everyone can afford a townhouse and a country house, the pleasure of exclusiveness is lessened. Generally increasing levels of income and wealth spoil their advantages for each one of us.

All the above trends may exacerbate class conflict and conflict between status groups. Antagonisms that were muted by expansion become increasingly salient and intensive and people who lack power will be forced into impoverishment. Another possibility is an increased pluralism, as discussed earlier. People will differentiate themselves in more and more ways as they determine what they want to spend their time, energy, and money for. Perhaps, too, enthrallment with growth and bigness will decrease and small will be seen as beautiful (Schumacher 1975). Another possibility is a greater collectively determined allocations of goods and services; equalitarianism would come to be seen as a way of morally sharing what is available. But this could enhance the power of the state, perhaps leading to intensified struggles for control of the government and the state. The direction we move in depends in part on the direction of the fourth and final trend.

World Integration

The world has become a single system which affects inequality in many ways. We have seen how the existence of a world market helps produce and maintain the inequalities within each country. Global power differences and the associated conflicts between governments enhance the concentration of power within countries and raise the relative position of the military elites. At the same time, the diffusion of ideas and knowledge increasingly creates a shared world civilization with a shared basis for status rankings. Changes at the world level, then, impact on inequality within every unit making up the world. Although it is obviously extremely difficult to assess how world conditions will tend to change, I will present some likely possibilities.

On the one hand, the world seems to be becoming increasingly integrated. Trade and communications bind people together more closely than ever. Moreover, organizations connect people directly, bypassing to some extent the authority of the state. Transnational organizations are growing in number, size, and significance, most notably multinational corporations. Trade union, professional, and international nongovernmental organizations unrelated to occupations are also expanding (Skjelsbaek 1972). In many spheres of activity, such nongovernmental transnational organizations are becoming alternative social structures. A growing autonomy of such organizations would herald the coming of a global society integrated across many dimensions and not divided essentially into sovereign states (Lakey 1973; Mitrany 1966; Kriesberg 1972).

On the other hand, states are assuming increasing responsibility for their citizens. Popular demands for social services, security, and economic development throughout the world thrust obligations on governments. National government leaders promise extensive benefits. As a consequence, government authority is growing, and states are becoming more autonomous and the boundaries among them increasingly closed.

The trends toward increased world integration and the trend toward greater governmental autonomy are in many ways contradictory. The opposition between these movements is the source of one kind of crisis. Governments assume more and more responsibility but have less and less ability to manage the affairs which they seek to control.

This crisis is exacerbated by the nature of the world stratification system. Power differences at the world level are immense and dominated by two countries: the United States and the Soviet Union. Their governments, locked in continuing conflict, encourage different aspects of these contradictory trends. On the one hand, the United States government promotes world integration and views many of the efforts at increased governmental control as antagonistic to its interests. Yet it promotes nationalist concerns in order to thwart international communism as a unified world movement. On the other hand, the Soviet government tends to support governments that throw up barriers to integration within what they regard as the world capitalist system, but it counters nationalist efforts which become obstacles to the spread of its ideological views. These diverse trends have mixed implications for reducing inequality at the world level and within countries.

Many governments in the developing nations try to assume more and more control over the natural resources within their countries so as to reduce their dependency on dominant countries or foreign corporations based in them. Sometimes they are aided by an adversary of the dominant power, as when the Soviet Union aids Cuba. If a government of a dependent country is able to control investment and trade, it could act to reduce internal inequalities, but it could also increase them if it were so inclined. Such governmental power may also be used to command higher prices for the commodities produced domestically. The success of the OPEC nations may be difficult to duplicate with other commodities, but increased governmental power among the developing countries would make comparable efforts more likely and assure at least partial success. This would aggravate the difficulties in increasing the rate of productivity and growth of surplus in other countries, poor as well as rich ones. These developments would also tend to strengthen further the role of governments. An enlarged government role often means more centralization of decision making, particularly if the growth of state power coincides with adversary relations with other states.

Some counter trends warrant mentioning. An increase in material surplus and in the standard of living in developing countries will make possible an increased role for their citizens in collective decision making; they will strengthen the chances for increased civil rights and autonomy for citizens. Greater affluence and efficiency in production in the developing countries will also enlarge the market for products and services from the United States and other developed countries, thus enlarging the material resources available for distribution within them.

CONCLUSIONS

The diverse and contradictory trends noted give us reason to believe that we have alternatives that can mold and lessen our patterns of inequality. The future will blend the trends we have described and fashion something new. Quite probably, the growing power of the state will be modified by the contrary trends. To what extent one trend dominates another depends partly on your, my, and other people's preferences and actions. Gans foresees a clash between the trend toward political and economic centralization and rising expectations for more autonomy, democracy, and a higher standard of private and public living. He expects "that as more people are directly affected by the restriction of economic and political opportunities, and as they become better educated and politically more sophisticated, a politically significant number will eventually become aware of and act on the conflict between their expectations and the structural tendencies of post-industrial society" (1973, p. 239).

On the whole, lessening class inequality, particularly a lessening of the proportion of the people living below contemporary minimal standards, seems likely. Movements toward greater status equality also seems underway in the United States and in most of the world. A lessening of power inequalities at the societal level, however, seems much more problematic. The struggle for greater equality creates its own problems, particularly as humanity's success confronts us with social and material constraints.

We need to know the extent of inequalities and understand the forces behind them if we are to effectively alter or maintain them as we wish. We need to comprehend the benefits and disadvantages of different kinds and degrees of inequality to wisely change the stratification system. We need to know much more, yet we will never have all the information and insight we would like to have. Meanwhile, we must act on the basis of what we know: whatever we do or fail to do does matter.

REFERENCES

AARON, HENRY J. 1967. "Social Security: International Comparisons." Pp. 13-48 in Otto Eckstein (ed.), *Studies in the Economics of Income Maintenance.* Washington, D.C.: Brookings Institution.

BELL, DANIEL. 1973. *The Coming of Post-Industrial Society.* New York: Basic Books.

BLUM, WALTER J., and HARRY KALVEN, JR. 1963. *The Uneasy Case for Progressive Taxation.* Chicago: University of Chicago Press. (Originally published in 1953.)

BOULDING, ELISE. 1979. "Ethnic Separation and World Development." In Louis Kriesberg (ed.) *Research in Social Movements, Conflicts, and Change* Vol. 2. Greenwich, Conn.: JAI Press.

CLARK, KENNETH B., and JEANETTE HOPKINS. 1969. *A Relevant War Against Poverty.* New York: Harper & Row.

CUTRIGHT, PHILLIPS. 1965. "Political Structure, Economic Development, and National Security Programs," *The American Journal of Sociology* 70 (March):537-550.

DANZINGER, SHELDON, and ROBERT PLOTNICK. 1977. "Demographic Change, Government Transfers, and the Distribution of Income," *Monthly Labor Review* 100 (April):7-11.

FARLEY, REYNOLDS. 1977. "Trends in Racial Inequalities: Have the Gains of the 1960s Disappeared in the 1970s?" *American Sociological Review* 42 (April):189-209.

GANS, HERBERT J. 1973. *More Equality.* New York: Random House.

GOODWIN, LEONARD. 1972. *Do the Poor Want to Work? A Social-Psychological Study of Work Orientations.* Washington, D.C.: Brookings Institution.

GREENSTONE, J. DAVID, and PAUL E. PETERSON. 1973. *Race and Authority in Urban Politics: Community Participation and the War on Poverty.* New York: Russell Sage Foundation.

HANSEN, W. LEE, and BURTON A. WEISBROD. 1969. "The Distribution of Costs and Direct Benefits of Public Higher Education: The Case of California," *Journal of Human Resources* 4 (Spring):176-191.

HAVEMAN, ROBERT H. 1977. "Introduction: Poverty and Social Policy in the 1960s and 1970s—An Overview and Some Speculations." Pp. 1-19 in Robert H. Haveman (ed.), *A Decade of Federal Antipoverty Programs.* New York: Academic Press.

HIRSCH, FRED. 1977. *Social Limits to Growth.* Cambridge, Mass.: Harvard University Press.

HUNNIUS, GERRY, G. DAVID GARSON, and JOHN CASE (eds.). 1973. *Workers Control: A Reader on Labor and Social Change.* New York: Vintage Books.

INGLEHART, RONALD. 1978. *The Silent Revolution: Changing Values and Political Styles Among Western Publics.* Princeton, N.J.: Princeton University Press.

KRAMER, RALPH M. 1969. *Participation of the Poor: Case Studies on the War on Poverty.* Englewood Cliffs, N.J.: Prentice-Hall.

KRIESBERG, LOUIS. 1970. *Mothers in Poverty.* Chicago: Aldine.

KRIESBERG LOUIS. 1972. "International Nongovernmental Organizations and Transnational Integration," *International Associations* 42 (11):520-525.

LAKEY, GEORGE. 1973. *Strategy for a Living Revolution.* San Francisco: W. H. Freeman.

LAMPMAN, ROBERT J. 1971. *Ends and Means of Reducing Poverty.* Chicago: Markham.

LEVIN, HENRY M. 1977. "A Decade of Policy Developments in Improving Education and Training for Low-Income Populations." Pp. 123-188 in Robert Haveman (ed.), *A Decade of Federal Antipoverty Programs.* New York: Academic Press.

LYNN, LAURENCE E., JR. 1977. "A Decade of Policy Development in the Income-Maintenance System." Pp. 55-117 in Robert H. Haveman (ed.), *A Decade of Federal Antipoverty Programs.* New York: Academic Press.

MARMOR, THEODORE R. (ed.). 1971. *Poverty Policy: A Compendium of Cash Transfer Proposals.* Chicago: Aldine-Atherton.

MARMOR, THEODORE R., and MARTIN REIN. 1973. "Reforming 'The Welfare Mess': The Fate of the Family Assistance Plan, 1969-1972." Pp. 3-28 in Allan P. Sindler (ed.), *Policy and Politics in America.* Boston: Little, Brown.

MATZA, DAVID. 1966. "The Disreputable Poor." Pp. 289-302 in R. Bendix and S. M. Lipset (eds.), *Class, Status, and Power.* New York: Free Press.

MILLER, S. M., and PAMELA ROBY. 1970. *The Future of Inequality.* New York: Basic Books.

MITRANY, DAVID. 1966. *A Working Peace System.* Chicago: Quadrangle. (Originally published in 1943.)

MOYNIHAN, DANIEL P. 1969. *Maximum Feasible Misunderstanding: Community Action in the War on Poverty.* New York: Free Press.

MYRDAL, GUNNAR. 1944. *An American Dilemma.* New York: Harper.

PARKIN, FRANK. 1971. *Class Inequality and Political Order.* New York: Praeger.

PECHMAN, JOSEPH A. 1970. "The Distributional Effects of Public Higher Education in California," *The Journal of Human Resources* 5 (Summer): 361-370.

PECHMAN, JOSEPH A. and P. MICHAEL TIMPANE (eds.). 1975. *Work Incentives and Income Guarantees: The New Jersey Negative Income Tax Experiment.* Washington, D.C.: Brookings Institution.

PIVEN, FRANCES FOX, and RICHARD A. CLOWARD. 1971. *Regulating the Poor*. New York: Vintage Books.

PLOTNICK, ROBERT, and FELICITY SKIDMORE. 1975. *Progress Against Poverty*. New York: Academic Press.

PRYOR, FREDERICK L. 1968. *Public Expenditures in Communist and Capitalist Nations*. Homewood, Ill.: Irwin.

REYNOLDS, MORGAN, and EUGENE SMOLENSKY. 1977. *Public Expenditures, Taxes, and the Distribution of Income: The United States, 1950, 1961, 1970*. New York: Academic Press.

SCHUMACHER, E. F. 1975. *Small is Beautiful*. New York: Harper & Row. (Originally published in 1973.)

SKJELSBAEK, KJELL. 1972. "The Growth of International Nongovernmental Organization in the Twentieth Century." Pp. 70-92 in Robert O. Kechane and Joseph S. Nye (eds.), *Transnational Relations and World Politics*. Cambridge, Mass.: Harvard University Press.

STEMBER, CHARLES HERBERT. 1961. *Education and Attitude Change: The Effect of Schooling on Prejudice Against Minority Groups*. New York: Institute of Human Relations Press.

STIGLER, GEORGE. 1970. "Director's Law of Public Income Redistribution," *Journal of Law and Economics* 13 (April):1-10.

THUROW, LESTER. 1976. "The Pursuit of Equity," *Dissent* 23 (Summer): 253-259.

TREIMAN, DONALD J. 1977. *Occupational Prestige in Comparative Perspective*. New York: Academic Press.

TUSSING, A. DALE. 1975. *Poverty in a Dual Economy*. New York: St. Martin's.

U.S. Bureau of the Census. 1976. *Statistical Abstract of the United States: 1976*, 96th edition, Washington, D.C.: Government Printing Office.

WATTS, HAROLD W. and ALBERT REES (eds.). 1977. *The New Jersey Income Maintenance Experiment*. Vol. 2. *Labor-Supply Responses*. New York: Academic Press.

WILENSKY, HAROLD L. 1975. *The Welfare State and Equality: Structural and Ideological Roots of Public Expenditures*. Berkeley: University of California Press.

WILENSKY, HAROLD L., and C. N. LEBEAUX. 1958. *Industrial Society and Social Welfare*. New York: Russell Sage Foundation.

WILLIAMS, ROBIN M., JR. 1951. *American Society*. New York: Knopf.

YALE LAW JOURNAL. 1969. "A Model Negative Income Tax Statute," *The Yale Law Journal* 78:269-288.

YOUNG, MICHAEL. 1961. *The Rise of the Meritocracy: 1870-2033*. Baltimore: Penguin. (Originally published in 1958.)

Author Index

Verba, S., 43, 48, 192, 221, 230, 254
Vernon, R., 109, 117
Vidich, A. J., 191, 221
Vogt, E. Z., Jr., 151, 328
Vollmer, H. M., 391, 414

Wagatsuma, H., 173, 183
Waitzkin, H. B., 272, 296
Walkley, R. P., 296
Wallace, S. E., 138, 151
Wallerstein, I., 101, 117, 342, 355
Warner, W. L., 25, 49, 76, 81, 139-141, 151,
    200, 221, 281, 296, 311, 328
Waterman, B., 272, 296
Watnick, M., 311, 328
Watts, H. W., 428, 440
Weber, M., 169, 184, 186, 221, 296
Weinberg, N., 114, 117
Weinstein, E. A., 389, 391, 414
Weisbrod, B. A., 418, 438
Weiss, G., 49, 66, 67, 70, 80
Weiss, J. A., 402, 414
Weisskopf, T. E., 366N, 386
Wesolowski, W., 155-157, 184, 389, 414
Wilensky, H. L., 310, 312, 328, 386, 418,
    419, 424-425
Wiley, N. F., 26, 49
Willener, A., 303, 328
Williams, C., 189, 221
Williams, R. M., 430

Williamson, J., 58-59, 79, 354, 365, 385
Williamson, N. E., 174, 184
Wilner, D. M., 296
Wilson, K., 305, 328
Wilson, J. Q., 195, 221
Wilson, W. J., 339, 347, 355
Windmuller, J. P., 113, 117
Wirt, F. M., 191, 221
Wolfe, D. M., 278, 292
Wolfgang, M. E., 205, 221
Wood, J. R., 389, 391, 414
Woodward, C. V., 173, 184
Wray, D., 151, 328
Wright, C. R., 281, 296
Wright, J. D., 296
Wright, S. R., 296
Wrong, D. H., 273, 296, 337, 355

Yanowitch, M., 117
Yauger D., 183
Young, L., 154, 184
Young, M., 7, 17, 434

Zeitlin, M., 72, 73, 81, 311, 328, 342, 355
Zelditch, M., 287, 292
Zetterberg, H., 394, 413
Zimmer, T. A., 414
Zweig, F., 288, 296

Subject Index